Sustainable Graphic Design

Tools, Systems, and Strategies
for Innovative Print Design

Wendy Jedlička, CPP

with

> *Paul Andre, Dr. Paul J. Beckmann, Sharell Benson, Arlene Birt,*
> *Robert Callif, Don Carli, Jeremy Faludi, Terry Gips, Fred Haberman,*
> *Dan Halsey, Jessica Jones, Curt McNamara, Jacquelyn Ottman,*
> *Dr. Pamela Smith, Dion Zuess*

> *Biomimicry Guild, Carbonless Promise, Chlorine Free Products*
> *Association, Environmental Paper Network, Eureka Recycling,*
> *Package Design Magazine, Printing Industry of Minnesota,*
> *Promotional Product Solutions, Sustainable Green Printing*
> *Partnership,[SM] Sustainable Packaging Coalition[SM]*

Additional contributions by:
> *Amelia McNamara, John Moes, Tom Nelson, Holly Robbins,*
> *Sharon Sudman*

Foreword by:
> *Marc Alt*

WILEY

John Wiley & Sons, Inc.

D1219198

This book is printed on acid-free paper.♾

Copyright © 2010 by John Wiley & Sons, Inc.
All rights reserved

Published by John Wiley & Sons, Inc., Hoboken, New Jersey

Published simultaneously in Canada

No part of this publication may be reproduced, stored in a retrieval system, or transmitted in any form or by any means, electronic, mechanical, photocopying, recording, scanning, or otherwise, except as permitted under Section 107 or 108 of the 1976 United States Copyright Act, without either the prior written permission of the Publisher, or authorization through payment of the appropriate per-copy fee to the Copyright Clearance Center, 222 Rosewood Drive, Danvers, MA 01923, (978) 750-8400, fax (978) 646–8600, or on the web at www.copyright.com. Requests to the Publisher for permission should be addressed to the Permissions Department, John Wiley & Sons, Inc., 111 River Street, Hoboken, NJ 07030, (201) 748-6011, fax (201) 748-6008, or online at *www.wiley.com/go/permissions.*

Limit of Liability/Disclaimer of Warranty: While the publisher and the author have used their best efforts in preparing this book, they make no representations or warranties with respect to the accuracy or completeness of the contents of this book and specifically disclaim any implied warranties of merchantability or fitness for a particular purpose. No warranty may be created or extended by sales representatives or written sales materials. The advice and strategies contained herein may not be suitable for your situation. You should consult with a professional where appropriate. Neither the publisher nor the author shall be liable for any loss of profit or any other commercial damages, including but not limited to special, incidental, consequential, or other damages.

For general information about our other products and services, please contact our Customer Care Department within the United States at (800) 762-2974, outside the United States at (317) 572-3993 or fax (317) 572-4002.

Wiley also publishes its books in a variety of electronic formats. Some content that appears in print may not be available in electronic books. For more information about Wiley products, visit our Web site at www.wiley.com.

Library of Congress Cataloging-in-Publication Data:

Jedlicka, Wendy, 1959–
  Sustainable graphic design : tools, systems and strategies for innovative print design / Wendy Jedlicka.
     p. cm.
  Includes bibliographical references and index.
  ISBN 978-0-470-24670-2 (pbk.)
  1. Graphic arts—Social aspects.   2. Commercial art—Social aspects.   3. Sustainable design.   I. Title.
  NC997.J37   2009
  741.6—dc22   2009017330

Printed in the United States of America

10 9 8 7 6 5 4 3 2 1

Environmental Benefits Statement

This book is printed with soy-based inks on presses with VOC levels that are lower than the standard for the printing industry. The paper, Rolland Enviro 100, is manufactured by Cascades Fine Papers Group and is made from 100 percent post-consumer, de-inked fiber, without chlorine. According to the manufacturer, the use of every ton of Rolland Enviro100 Book paper, switched from virgin paper, helps the environment in the following ways:

Mature trees saved	Waterborne waste not created	Waterflow saved	Atmospheric emissions eliminated	Solid wastes reduced	Natural gas saved by using biogas
17	6.9 lbs.	10,196 gals.	2,098 lbs.	1,081 lbs.	2,478 cubic feet

Contents

Contents

Hello Neighbor!

8 WAYS
TO FEEL GOOD
FROM
THE FEEL-GOOD PHARMACY

elephant PHARM

Hello Neighbor!

ELE...
GRA...
AUGU...

10.30am Ribbon...

3.00pm Meet...

Lots of fun...
• Great **raffle** prizes...
...ons of free samples and...
...Adina, Body Coffee, Lip...
...dic Naturals, & Strau...

...E ELEPHANT PHARM...
...L OF FEEL-GOOD P...
for first 100 custom...

...8 South California...
...(Trader Joe's) in W...

THE FEEL-GOOD PHARMACY

Str...
...a

Mak...
new...

Go na...

Ma...
s...

Fe...

Str...
yo...

Get

Ex...
ch...

⑧
⑦
⑥
⑤
④
③
②

$3
...
...
...

8 WAYS
TO FEEL GOOD
FROM
ELEPHANT PHARM

elephant PHARM

Foreword

A paradox of sustainability is that there is an underlying, commonsense simplicity beneath what appears on the surface to be a very complex discipline. One of the key points that the authors of *Sustainable Graphic Design* have made in their years of educating, evangelizing, and writing about sustainability, and one that is reinforced gently but persistently in this book, is that "Sustainability isn't hard; it's just not simple."

It is an interesting challenge to write the opening remarks and observations for a book that may be looked at in a few decades as quaint and outdated, a relic of an earlier age. I should take a step back and mention that many proponents of sustainability feel that their purpose and mission is in essence to make themselves obsolete. Their basic calling is to reveal missing or forgotten connections between cause and effect, between decisions and consequences.

Where we find ourselves today is the result of millions of these disconnects, accrued steadily over time, consciously or unconsciously, as our population and its ever-expanding need grows at a pace that outstrips traditional or balanced ways of doing things. Exactly when, why, or how our society lost that balance and began outrunning the carrying capacity of the planet is the subject of endless debate. One thing we can all agree on, however, is the need for immediate solutions.

Designers like to claim privilege of being in a unique position to change things. I don't disagree with this opinion, but I think it needs an update. A new generation of designers has realized that in order to deliver on this promise, the profession needs to move beyond its traditional calling and embody a new set of universal principles that address the *consequences* of design.

It is said that design decisions account for an average of 80 percent of the life cycle impacts of a product or service. Understanding the importance of this math and building the discipline and leadership to equip current and future generations of designers with the knowledge, direction, and inspiration to take responsibility is the challenge of this decade.

This book is filled with inspiration, ideas, and actionable advice from an extraordinary group of sustainability leaders. It will give designers at any stage in their careers frameworks for rethinking and assessing their daily design activity. It gives dimension to complex ideas and brings a sometimes-daunting topic to life in a way that is understandable and approachable. It provides a solid foundation in the underlying principles of design for sustainability that are a fundamental discipline of our time. I'm optimistic about a future in which there will be no need for a book entitled *Sustainable Graphic Design*. Until that day, this volume is an essential guidebook, a road map to an achievable future where all design is well considered, and where sustainability is systemic.

Marc Alt
Co-Chair, AIGA Center for Sustainable Design

Sustainability isn't all just "feel good"—but sometimes that's just what the doctor ordered. Celery Design created this promotional door hanger for Elephant Pharmacy. These cards with wellness tips and fun activities (like finger-Pilates using the natural latex band) are made from 100 percent post-consumer-waste fiber and are chop-cut to minimize trim waste.

Introduction

Wendy Jedlička, CPP
o2 International Network for Sustainable Design

You must be the change you wish to see in the world.

—*Mahatma Gandhi*

"One day, son, this will all be yours."
Photo: W. Jedlička, 1996

In theory, picking an eco-material is better than a non-eco one. Lists filled with materials and vendors can be found in an ever-growing field of "green" books and on "green" supplier Web sites. But these are only simple indexes of companies that offer materials, goods, or services with some level of green/eco/sustainability as part of their point of difference. Many of these companies are third-party certified and are willing to back up their environmental marketing claims; many are not.

ix

If one doesn't know why a material is eco, how to apply its use correctly, or even if the material or process actually *is* eco, it is possible to create a piece with environmental and economic impacts far worse than where the project started.

In addition to applying eco-materials properly, clients are looking to their designers to help them meet new, more restrictive legislation; new initiatives from their own clients (e.g., Walmart's scorecard); and a whole host of hot-button issues. These are problems much bigger than picking a recycled paper and calling it good; they require a careful look at the system of the design, not just a substrate or two.

In approaching problems the same way they always have, many companies seem to think they have done their part if they can just locate what could be referred to as the "happy list" of magically green materials. They then pick something off the menu for their project and check "get eco" off their to-do list. Any eco-practitioners worth their salt who receive a request for such a list will ask if the inquirer understands systems thinking concepts or if the company has a training program in place to help the people using the list figure out what actually will *be* eco for their applications. Today more often than not, the answer is still "No, we don't do any of that; we just want the list."

One thing that never fails to get eco-practitioners to smile is when very earnest people say, "We want to see pictures of your really cutting-edge eco-examples." Apparently, they believe that if they could just look at an eco-example, they'd be able to copy it, as they've done for any other "fad." But the reality is, sustainability isn't a "fad" or even a "movement," it's a long-term paradigm shift.

To understand sustainable design, you must tell an honest story, leverage audience triggers for the greater good, understand the economic impacts of design choices, and know how all of that fits in a verifiably sustainable context. Without that depth of background, we're just painting another pretty picture and calling it "green."

How to Use This Book

One of the author's requirements for doing this book was that the question of sustainable design related to print and graphics needed to be approached in a completely new way, not only looking at systems thinking in general terms, but looking deeply into the very soul of design and its stakeholders. In addition, rather than the outpouring of a single voice, the book needed to be a collection of many voices. This chorus of voices allows people new to sustainable design to experience the broad range of contributions the pioneers of sustainability and today's eco-practitioners draw from. Readers find they can hit the ground running, as they race to catch up with the overwhelming flow of sustainability information coming out daily.

This book is designed to help people clearly see the big picture, what all that means for design, how all the various groups that serve industry connect and interact—all in a sustainability context.

For those in academia, this book is representative of the core approach of Minneapolis College of Art and Design's (MCAD) Sustainable Design Certificate Program (*mcad.edu/sustainable*). Most of the key contributors to this book are Sustainable Design Certificate faculty, who welcome the opportunity to open a dialogue about higher education's roll and responsibility in reshaping industry. Taking a holistic approach, MCAD's Sustainable Design Certificate students are taught how to think in sustainability terms, and are empowered to become fellow agents for positive change.

Just as one should not pick from a "happy list" of eco-materials and consider the job done, this book is not a complete one-size-fits-all tome. It is a comprehensive guide to sustainability approaches applied to design and business employed by today's sustainability leaders and eco-practitioners using graphics and print as the industry where examples are drawn from, the ideas expressed in this book though, are the fundamentals of applied systems thinking and can be applied to any effort. The goal of this book is to show the reader not only sustainability ideas but the logic behind them.

This book is meant to be used as a portal to works by the original content providers as it takes the reader through the design process, touching on inputs that make up what design is really about. By seeing how those works fit together into the bigger picture, and how they flow together and overlap, identifying quality resources that will address specific needs becomes much easier.

To get an even more detailed picture, it is suggested that readers expand their library to include Wiley's companion book to this work, *Packaging Sustainability: Tools, Systems and Strategies for Innovative Package Design www.packagingsustainability.info*. Putting sustainable design into practice is an integral part of today's global competitive market. Written by practitioners from the wide variety of fields that make up the packaging industry, *Packaging Sustainability* is a comprehensive, single source of actionable information that enables everyone involved in the design and development process to make smart, informed decisions, opening new possibilities for creating truly innovative solutions.

Sustainable design options today are growing faster than any one person can keep up with. It is highly recommended that design professionals subscribe to one or more of the information update services mentioned throughout this book. In collecting cases and examples for this book, it became apparent we would not be able to fit in all of the great work from both past and current production cycles. This in no way is a comment on the value of the work not included. This book is not a portfolio collection of the most eco-works ever produced. Examples and cases were selected from companies that are creating solutions of interest for their category and that were willing to offer readers a deeper look at their processes and design logic.

Some of the examples showcased in this book are very good; some are just a solid step in the right direction. But in all cases, the companies contributing were willing to talk about the issues they weighed to arrive at their solution. We are still in the early stages of this paradigm shift, and many people are shy about helping to train their competition. Eco-leaders, though, have recognized that the greatest benefits come when ideas and efforts, successes as well as failures, are shared openly. They've found that the louder you are, the greater the rewards, and the stronger your market position—leaving competitors scrambling for the me-too slot—which itself creates a positive ripple effect throughout the whole industry.

The Making of This Book

Wiley is committed to continuous reevaluation of its environmental impacts and partnering with stakeholders to help achieve ever-improving performance. The paper for the pages of this book is Rolland Enviro100 Print, manufactured by Cascades Fine Papers Group. It's made from 100 percent post-consumer fiber and processed chlorine free. Cascades' Rolland Enviro100 is a Chlorine Free Products Association endorsed product.

According to Cascades, for every ton of Rolland Enviro100 Book paper used instead of traditionally processed virgin pulp source paper, the environment is served in these ways:

— 17 mature trees saved

— 6.9 pounds. waterborne waste generation avoided

— 10,196 gallons waterflow saved

— 2,098 pounds atmospheric emissions eliminated

— 1,081 pounds solid waste reduced

— 2,478 cubic feet natural gas use eliminated by using biogas

Giving Thanks

This book features the work and ideas of many current eco-practitioners. But we all stand on the shoulders of giants—those who walked tirelessly forward in spite of the obstacles set before them. Today we are empowered to make their dreams a reality.

We offer this work as a tribute to the example they set and whose work we are building on. For making our work possible, we would like to extend our deepest gratitude to:

R. Buckminster Fuller, Victor Papanak, David Orr, Sim Van der Ryn, Fritjof Capra, E. F. Schumacher, Karl-Henrik Robèrt, Janine Benyus, Paul Hawken, Hunter Lovins, Amory Lovins, John Thackara, J. I. and Robert Rodale, and of course Rachel Carson.

Contributing Authors

Wendy Jedlička, CPP
Contributing Editor / Creative Contributor

An IoPP Certified Packaging Professional, Jedlička is president of Jedlička Design Ltd. (*www.jedlicka .com*), with over 20 years of packaging and print experience, coupled with 11 years as a retail industry insider. As a design and business strategy vendor, she has served clients such as 3M, Target, Hormel, Anchor Hocking, and Toro. Jedlička writes the regular feature "Sustainability Update" for *Package Design Magazine*; is the contributing editor for two books by Wiley, and is regularly tapped to speak on eco-packaging and print design as well as a variety of sustainable design and business issues.

As part of her professional outreach efforts, Jedlička is the United States co-coordinator for the o2 International Network for Sustainable Design (*www.o2.org*) as well as Upper Midwest chapter chair (*www.o2umw.org*). Working to change minds in higher education, Jedlička is program development team member and faculty for the ground-breaking Sustainable Design Certificate Program at Minneapolis College of Art and Design (MCAD) (mcad.edu/sustainable).

Attracted to packaging since beginning to learn origami at age eight, Jedlička started her formal art training through the Minneapolis Society of Fine Arts experimental youth art program, continuing through high school at Parsons School of Design and the Art Students League of New York. She completed her bachelor's degree in graphic and industrial design at the University of Bridgeport and her master's degree in international management with a certificate in marketing at the University of St. Thomas.

Paul Andre

Designer and creative team leader at the Minnesota Pollution Control Agency, Andre has worked for many years doing intensive, multimedia outreach campaigns on topics ranging from backyard garbage burning to global climate change. More recently, he has helped develop large-scale, citizen-focused green events that attempt to inspire eco-minded behavior and consumption changes.

Dr. Paul J. Beckmann

Paul J. Beckmann, Ph.D. (*beckm002@umn.edu*) is a curious polymath. He holds degrees in physics (BA), biophysical sciences (MS), and cognitive and biological psychology (Ph.D). He has experience in such diverse projects as implantable medical device development, machine vision and robotics, reading by people with visual impairment, color formation in microwavable foods, office lighting design to minimize fatigue and maximize legibility, information flow from fast food restaurant menu board systems to customers, simulation of the information processing in the human eye, design and implementation of emergency communications systems for state and local agencies, and photoelectric photometry of variable stars. His current research explores the mental maps created and used by people with visual impairment as they navigate large office buildings. In addition, he has recently established a laboratory to investigate visual signaling of affordances by common graspable objects.

Trained in awareness, native skills, and tracking at Tom Brown's school in New Jersey, Beckmann found a focus for his connection to the natural environment and brings that perspective to much of his current work. He has taught at a number of universities in Minnesota, including courses in sensation and perception; physiological psychology; human–machine interaction; alcohol, drugs, and behavior; research methods; cognition; and learning and memory.

Sharell Benson

Sharell Benson (*www.sharellbenson.com*) is an independent packaging contractor specializing in green marketing, research and project management. She has been in the packaging business for more than 20 years and has expertise in color management, folding cartons, corrugated, pressure-sensitive labels, and paper recycling. Benson holds a master's degree from the University of Minnesota.

Arlene Birt

Arlene Birt (*www.arlenebirt.com*) is a visual storyteller at Haberman & Associates, Modern Storytellers for

Media + Marketing, a public relations and marketing agency dedicated to telling the stories of pioneers who change the way business is done or make the world a better place. She created *Background Stories,* her master's thesis, while studying in the Netherlands on a Fulbright grant. Birt is also faculty for MCAD's Sustainable Design Certificate Program and a member of the o2 International Network for Sustainable Design.

Robert Callif

Robert Callif is vice president, and second-generation owner, at BCM INKS USA, Inc., and was featured on CBS's "Eye on America" for their eco-forward ink solution, Eekoflex. Calif has been a speaker within the flexographic industry for AICC, ACCCSA, and FPPA, and has written articles about inks for *Corrugated Today* and other magazines. Callif is a graduate of University of Florida with a bachelor's degree in finance.

Don Carli

Don Carli is senior research fellow with the non-profit Institute for Sustainable Communication and chairperson of SustainCommWorld.com and Principal of Nima Hunter Inc., a consultancy founded in 1986 that offers strategic planning, market research, technology assessment, and marketing advisory services to clients on a worldwide basis. He is also an Alfred P. Sloan Foundation Industry Studies Research Affiliate scholar as well as professor in the Advertising, Design and Graphic Arts Department at the City University of New York City College of Technology.

Jeremy Faludi

Jeremy Faludi (*www.faludidesign.com*) is a product designer and researcher specializing in eco-design. He has consulted for Rocky Mountain Institute, Janine Benyus, Chorus Motors, ExBiblio, Lawrence Berkeley National Labs, and others. He was a finalist in the 2007 California Cleantech Open competition and is a juror for Dell's ReGeneration contest on green computing. A bicycle he helped design appeared in the Cooper-Hewitt National Design Museum's exhibit Design for the Other 90%.

In addition to his design work, Faludi is a contributing editor to worldchanging.com and is one of the many authors of *Worldchanging: A User's Guide for the 21st Century*. His articles have appeared in *GreenBiz, Package Design Magazine*, Samsung's *DigitALL* magazine, and the Secretariat of the Commonwealth of Nations' newsletter *Commonwealth Today*. He also speaks at conferences, schools, and businesses around the world. Faludi is active in the o2 International Network for Sustainable Design, serving the o2 Bay Area and Cascadia groups. He is also on the faculty for MCAD's Sustainable Design Certificate Program and is a lecturer in the product design program at Stanford University.

Terry Gips

Terry Gips is a widely published ecologist, agricultural economist, sustainability consultant, certified independent Natural Step Framework Instructor, speaker, author (*Breaking the Pesticide Habit* and *The Humane Consumer and Producer Guide*), and member of the faculty for MCAD's Sustainable Design Certificate Program. Gips, president of Sustainability Associates, works with business, government, and organizations to save money, improve performance, and become socially and environmentally responsible. (*www.sustainabilityassoc.com*)

Previously, Gips served as Aveda Corporation's director of ecological affairs and sustainability, Cargill grain merchant and assistant to the chief economist, a congressional and White House aide, Wall Street brokerage assistant, and cofounder and director of the Cooperative Extension Sacramento Community Garden Program.

Gips volunteers as the cofounder and president of the Alliance for Sustainability (*www.afors.org*). As a founding board member of Ceres (*www.ceres.org*), he helped develop the Ceres Principles for Corporate Environmental Responsibility. He completed his MS in agricultural and applied economics at UC Davis and an MBA at the Yale School of Management.

Fred Haberman

As the cofounder and CEO of Haberman & Associates (*www.modernstorytellers.com*), Fred Haberman specializes in brand and cause-related storytelling. He has counseled hundreds of companies on how to create emotional connections between their brands and their customers to generate brand awareness, sales, and positive change.

Dan Halsey
Contributing Author/Photography Contributor

Daniel Halsey (*www.Halsey1.com*) is a certified permaculture designer, graphic designer, and food photographer. He lives with his wife, Ginny, in South Woods of Spring Lake, Minnesota, a 25-acre wetland with an edible forest garden installed by the Twin Cities Perma-culture Collaborative. He is working on a degree in temperate-climate polyculture design at the University of Minnesota, and is faculty member for MCAD's Sustainable Design Certificate Program. His articles have appeared in *Package Design Magazine*.

Jessica Jones

Jessica Jones spent her childhood in the deserts of Phoenix, Arizona, and the forests of the Black Hills, South Dakota, and credits much of her creativity to these landscapes. The inviting forms, shapes, and colors of these natural places have inspired her design style and continue to influence her work at the Biomimicry Guild. Jones graduated from the University of Montana, Missoula, with a bachelor's in recreation management, an option in nature-based tourism, and minors in media arts and nonprofit administration. While an intern for both the Biomimicry Institute and the Montana Natural History Center, Jones designed interpretive exhibits and other marketing materials. Before joining the Biomimicry Guild, she was an interpretive naturalist for Custer State Park in South Dakota, where she developed and presented natural history programs to visitors of all ages. She is also a member of the National Association for Interpretation. Jones thinks interpretation, information design, and being well versed in many disciplines, especially biology, are valuable studies for graphic designers. For a current example of Jones's work, download the "Guild's Complete Product and Services Reference," available at www.biomimicryguild.com/guild_services_complete.html.

Curt McNamara, P.E.

Curt McNamara, P.E. (*c.mcnamara@ieee.org*), is a practicing designer with 20 years' experience in commercial and industrial markets. He is an R. Buckminster Fuller scholar and authored the entry on Fuller in the UNESCO *Encyclopedia of Life Support Systems*, and his articles have appeared in *Package Design Magazine*. An active Institute of Electrical and Electronic Engineers member, McNamara received the IEEE Millennium Medal in 2000 for his ongoing work in education. McNamara is a board member and serves as the engineering liaison for the o2-USA/Upper Midwest chapter of the o2 International Network for Sustainable Design. McNamara is also a faculty and program development team member for MCAD's Sustainable Design Certificate Program, as well as an Engineering Instructor for the Biomimicry Institute's Two Year Certificate Program.

Jacquelyn Ottman

Since 1989, Jacquelyn Ottman has been helping businesses find competitive advantage through green marketing and eco-innovation. President and founder of J. Ottman Consulting, Inc., she advised clients such as IBM, Interface, DuPont, and the US EPA's Energy Star® label. A popular speaker at industry conferences around the world, Ottman authored *Green Marketing: Opportunity for Innovation* (second edition), described by the American Marketing Association as the "definitive work on the subject." For seven years, she chaired the special Edison Awards for Environmental Achievement jury. Her firm is the principal organizer of Design:Green, a pioneering eco-design educational initiative endorsed by the Industrial Designers Society of America. (*www.designgreen.org*)

A graduate of Smith College, Ottman also attended the NYU Graduate School of Business. She holds a certificate from the Creative Education Foundation in facilitating the Osborn Parnes Creative Problem Solving Process. Ottman is also a faculty member for MCAD's Sustainable Design Certificate Program and a longtime member of the o2 International Network for Sustainable Design.

Dr. Pamela Smith

Pamela J. Smith, PhD, is a faculty member in the Department of Applied Economics at the University of Minnesota. Her specializations include international economics and econometrics (statistics). (*www.apec.umn.edu/Pamela_Smith.html*). Smith is also a faculty member for MCAD's Sustainable Design Certificate Program, and her articles have appeared in *Package Design Magazine*.

Dion Zuess

With over a decade of design experience in eco-design and visual communications, Dion Zuess is a green advocate who believes designers have a unique opportunity to integrate talent, communication strategies, and social responsibility. Her studio, ecoLingo, is dedicated to green design, blending design ecology, style, and sustainability. The award-winning studio (*ww.ecolingo.com*) is an approved member of Green America's Green Business Network as well as a member of 1% for the Planet, Design Can Change, the Designers Accord, and the o2 International Network for Sustainable Design.

Her work has been published in a variety of publications, including *Package Design Magazine*, and she is frequently invited to be a guest speaker, guest teacher, mentor, portfolio reviewer, writer, and consultant. In 2006, Zuess received an American Graphic Design Award for excellence in communication from Graphic Design: USA. In 2007, she was nominated as a candidate for a Communications Design Award as part of the prestigious Smithsonian Cooper-Hewitt National Design Museum's National Design Awards program. Zuess is also a faculty member for MCAD's Sustainable Design Certificate Program.

Contributing Groups

Biomimicry Guild

Since 1998, the Biomimicry Guild has been helping companies and communities find, vet, understand, and emulate life's time-tested strategies. An ecosystem of individuals and organizations spread all over the world, the Guild brings together the expertise needed to help projects succeed. By emulating 3.8 billion years of well-adapted technology, the Guild helps innovators realize the shared goal of designing sustainable products and processes that create conditions conducive to all life. In addition to workshops, research reports, biological consulting, and field excursions, the Biomimicry Guild has a wide range of experienced speakers available to organizations to learn about the potential of Biomimicry and the methods of implementing Biomimicry ideas. (*www.biomimicryguild.com*)

Carbonless Promise

It is the belief at Carbonless Promise that carbon is the currency of the future. It represents both a new asset class and a new risk paradigm that all organizations will need to manage. CP Holdings LLC (dba Carbonless Promise), founded in 2007, works with corporations, institutions, governmental units, and other organizations to help them identify and manage their greenhouse gas risks and opportunities. CP delivers expertise and tools that enable organizations to quantify and create a management plan that minimizes their carbon liabilities and optimizes their carbon assets. CP Holdings is headquartered in Stillwater, Minnesota, with field offices across the United States.

Eric Jackson, cofounder of CP Holdings LLC, has been working in international agriculture and energy markets since the early 1980s and leads the group's GHG Management practice. (*www.carbonlesspromise.com*)

Chlorine Free Products Association

The Chlorine Free Products Association (CFPA) is an independent not-for-profit accreditation and standard-setting organization. The primary purpose of the association is to promote Total Chlorine Free policies, programs, and technologies throughout the world. Its mission is to provide market awareness by providing facts, drawing direct comparisons, and highlight process advantages for Totally Chlorine Free (TCF) and Processed Chlorine Free (PCF) products. (*www.chlorinefreeproducts.org*)

Environmental Paper Network

Environmental Paper Network is a diverse group of over 100 nonprofit social and environmental organizations joined together to achieve the Common Vision for the Transformation of the Pulp and Paper Industry. The EPN provides information, tools, events, and strategic collaboration to advance a more socially and environmentally responsible paper industry. (*www.environmentalpaper.org*)

Eureka Recycling

Eureka Recycling is one of the largest nonprofit recyclers in the United States and an industry leader demonstrating the best waste reduction and recycling practices not only for the Twin Cities metro area but for the nation. For over 15 years, Eureka Recycling has been St. Paul's nonprofit recycler. Under a long-term contract with the city, Eureka Recycling provides recycling services to St. Paul's homes and apartments. In addition, Eureka Recycling is a leader in waste reduction education and advocacy. (*www.EurekaRecycling.org*)

Package Design Magazine

Package Design Magazine delivers the news and information professionals need to stay on top of the latest innovations and technology driving industry. Sustainability is driving changes in industry to protect the earth and find efficient solutions. In addition to its monthly feature column, "Sustainability Update," *Package Design*'s year-end issue is devoted to the latest sustainable materials, initiatives, processes, and advances affecting the packaging industry. (*www.packagedesignmag.com*)

Printing Industry of Minnesota (PIM)

PIM is the trade association for one of the largest industries in Minnesota. The mission of PIM is to be a leading resource for the printing and graphic communications industry in the areas of advocacy, education, safety and environmental information to enhance the strength and profitability of its members. PIM is one of the driving groups behind the evolution of (and currently manages) the groundbreaking Great Printer Environmental Initiative certification program, a collaborative project undertaken initially by the Council of Great Lake Governors, the Environmental Defense Fund, and the Printing Industries of America. (*www.pimn.org*)

Promotional Product Solutions

Promotional Product Solutions (PPS) was the first distributor in the promotional products industry of the United States to provide custom-tailored, high-quality Socially Responsible Promotions.® PPS is a Green America (formerly Co-op America) approved Green Business and is a member of 1 percent for the Planet. Jocelyn Azada, chief executive of PPS, is an entrepreneur with a background in theological ethics and socially responsible investing and a passion for increasing environmental and social awareness. Azada spearheads social responsibility, environmental, and diversity initiatives at PPS, and uses proprietary supplier evaluations of environmental, labor, and diversity practices to ensure that the company's product sources are ethically and environmentally sound.

Sustainable Green Printing Partnership^{SM}

Launched in 2008, the Sustainable Green Printing Partnership^{SM} (SGP Partnership program) provides a pathway for printing facilities to begin their sustainability journey. The mission of the SGP is to encourage and promote participation in the worldwide movement to reduce environmental impact and increase social responsibility of the print and graphic communications industry through sustainably green printing practices. (*www.sgppartnership.org*)

Sustainable Packaging Coalition^{SM}

The Sustainable Packaging Coalition^{SM} (SPC) is an industry working group dedicated to creating and implementing sustainable packaging systems.

Through informed design practice, supply chain collaboration, education, and innovation, the coalition strives to transform packaging into a system that encourages an economically prosperous and sustainable flow of materials, creating lasting value for present and future generations. (*www.SustainablePackaging.org*)

The Sustainable Packaging Coalition is a project of GreenBlue,[SM] a nonprofit, 501(c)3 tax-exempt institute committed to sustainability by design. (*www.GreenBlue.org*)

Creative Contributors

Amelia McNamara
Illustration

Amelia McNamara is a student at Macalester College in St. Paul, Minnesota. Beginning her professional education at the University of Cincinnati's College of Design, Architecture, Art, and Planning, she continues to be passionately interested in graphic and lighting design. Today she balances her left and right brains with a double major in English and mathematics at Macalester. (*www.linkedin.com/in/ameliamcnamara*)

Dan Halsey's Product Photography Team

ALEX CARROLL

Carroll is pursuing his interest in advertising photography and commercialized portraiture, and continues to explore everything there is to know about photography.

ANGIE REED

Reed is a musician, artist, and photographer originally from Grand Rapids, Minnesota. She is currently finishing her bachelor of science degree in digital photography.

JESSICA SCHMIDT

Schmidt has studied photography for over a decade and is now pursuing her passion in advertising and commercial photography.

Tom Nelson
Additional Photography

Tom Nelson (*www.tnphoto.com*) earned his bachelor's degree in political science from Macalester College in St. Paul, Minnesota. An Upper Midwest native, Nelson has traveled extensively around the world, adding to an already impressive catalog of both captured and created photographic art. Nelson is a board member and serves as the photo industry liaison for o2-USA/Upper Midwest.

Sharon Sudman
Book Design

Sharon Sudman (*www.ImageSpigot.com*) has been working in graphics and packaging for over 30 years. Her award-winning work has been part of our daily lives. Currently principal of her own firm, Image Spigot, she works with commercial clients as well as nonprofit groups. Her passion is in advocacy work for peace, justice, and sustainability. She is also active with a variety of groups working to effect meaningful change.

Additional Contributions

Holly Robbins

Holly Robbins is currently a creative manager for Target Corporation. She is a graduate of the design program at the University of Wisconsin-Stout. She also studied graphic design and art metals in Hildesheim, Germany, at the Fachhochschule Hildesheim/Holzminden. In 1994, Robbins, with partner John Moes, founded Studio Flux, a boutique design firm focused on ecologically sustainable design and quality, award-winning work. Her work has appeared in *Print, American Corporate Identity*, American Graphic Design Awards, *How*, and AIGA shows, including two AIGA national Greening of Design and five AIGA/Minnesota Green Leaf awards.

Robbins has written articles and lectured on the subject of eco-design and helped develop guidelines for designing more sustainably, including the Green-Blue SPC Design Guidelines for Sustainable Packaging and AIGA Green Leaf award criteria. She also is a representative to the Sustainable Packaging Coalition on behalf of Target and contributes to themightyodo.com, a collaborative of creatives seeking to reconnect people to nature though design. Robbins is also a program development team member and faculty for Minneapolis College of Art and Design's Sustainable Design Certificate Program.

John Moes

John Moes is a graphic designer and art director specializing in eco-graphic design. He is also a founding member of Organic Design Operatives (ODO), a collaborative of like-minded creatives seeking to reconnect people with nature via design. His clients include Target Corporation and Ecoenvelopes. In 1994, Moes, along with partner Holly Robbins, cofounded Studio Flux, one of the first eco-minded graphic design firms. He has written articles on sustainable design, contributed to the AIGA Green Leaf award criteria, and created the ODO Eco-Design Toolkit specifically aimed at graphic designers. (*www.themightyodo.com*)

Moes was educated in the design program at the University of Wisconsin-Stout. He also worked an extended stint at the well-known multidisciplinary firm Design Guys, where he designed a vast array of high-visibility projects for Target, Virgin, Neenah Paper, and Apple. Over the years, he has received many honors for his work, including recognition from AIGA, Communication Arts, Print, How and IDSA. His work for Target was honored by the Smithsonian Cooper-Hewitt National Design Museum 2003 National Design Awards and 365 AIGA Annual Design Competition: Gold Certificate of Excellence. Moes is most proud of his awards for eco-minded design, which include two AIGA national Greening of Design awards and five AIGA/Minnesota Green Leaf awards. Beyond graphic design, Moes has an appreciation for the amazing design model of nature, organic architecture, and designing and building just about anything.

① Making the Business Case

Wendy Jedlička, CPP
Minneapolis College of Art and Design
Sustainable Design Certificate Program

With additional contributions from:
Don Carli, Mark Randall
Ceres, Sustainable Is Good

You must be the change you wish to see in the world.

—*Mahatma Gandhi*

Today, business and government attitudes are changing around the world. New, more aggressive laws are being written in all major global markets, and businesses are looking to free themselves from the insecurity of petroleum as their only energy (and/or product material) option. In addition, the economy and all the issues surrounding deregulated markets are now forcing companies in all industries to find new ways of doing business. As markets flail around trying to reset, the need for transparency, a key element in sustainable business practice, is becoming part of the strategy of recovery.

Photo: W. Jedlička, 2009

1

After standing alone for years on the moral high ground, eco-practitioners are finally seeing the shift from *if* companies should get into that green thing to *how* and *how soon* sustainability practices can be incorporated into business operations.

Using the language of change, businesses are asking what natural capital is and how it is spent. What economic lessons can be drawn from nature? How do market forces shape the way we live, work, and even play? How can we nurture the green thumb on the invisible hand? Today's eco-leaders understand the interplay between producer and consumer, governments and people, stockholders and stakeholders, humans and the environment, and how all of these things interconnect and direct what and how we create.

Consumption and Renewal

The concept of birth, life, death is linear. It has a beginning, a middle, and an end. We view the things we surround ourselves with as having the same linear quality. Things are made, we use them, and then we toss them away. But the reality is, there is no "away." All things we make have a life after we use them, as garbage (landfill or incineration) or feeder stock for new objects (recycling or reuse reclamation). Objects are reborn (recycled or reclaimed) and put back into the system again, becoming part of a circular pattern of consumption that imitates nature: making, using, and remaking without limit. Imagine an upwardly spiraling system where we not only refresh what we take and use but we restore what we have previously destroyed through linear consumption. To get to this level, we need to start reexamining not just how we do what we do but why we do it.

Choices, Choices, Choices

Examples of human impact on the environment abound in both recent and ancient history. The best-known one is the fate of the Easter Islanders. This group, it has been suggested, drove themselves to extinction by their own excesses and lack of planning. As we consider the choices we make each day, think about what must have been going through the mind of the Easter Islander who cut down the last tree, leaving his people no way to build, repair, or heat their homes; build or repair boats to fish (their main food source); or even get off the island. With a simple strike of his ax, he sealed his people's collective fate.

In our lifetime, we may not be faced with this dilemma, but every choice we make each day adds or subtracts from the resources available to us tomorrow. Bad choices are accumulating like a death by a thousand cuts. Our salvation will come in much the same way: by regular people making everyday choices.

One of the most powerful ways we can have an impact is by what and how we choose to consume. What we buy reveals a lot about how we frame our own impacts. A great example is buying a perfect red apple rather than one that is blemished but just as sweet and free of chemicals needed to attain that perfection.

Nature's Path really understands its customers' drive for more than just a breakfast cereal. For their

This seemingly small redesign—"Same net weight, 10% less box"—by Nature's Path resulted in significant energy, water, and wood resource savings. In addition to resource savings, Nature's Path uses the box's "billboard" to communicate with its audience about eco-issues, using text and graphics to both inform the mind and entertain the eye.

Same net weight,
10% less box.

Global
Sustainability

USDA
ORGANIC

product Heritage Flakes they use organic grains, but they also support sustainable farming practices and biodiversity efforts.

Not only does the box illustrate an attractive product plus key into potential buyers looking for more healthful choices and good taste, it seals the deal by talking about packaging-reduction efforts. "Same net weight, 10% less box" is featured on the front. Finally, someone has addressed a nagging thorn in the consumer's side since boxed cereal was first marketed over 100 years ago: how to fill the box without leaving such a huge space at the top.

On the product's side panel, Nature's Path continues the discussion of packaging reduction by citing annual water savings (700,000 gallons), energy savings (500,000 kilowatts), and paperboard savings (about 1,300 trees). These are serious and significant impacts that come from a 10 percent reduction in box size. Now, along with information detailing nutrition and sustainable production practices, consumers can make an educated decision about the food they eat and the impact of that choice. By connecting with consumers on a deeper level, Nature's Path has armed them with the information needed to know they do have a choice—and to recognize that what instinctively seemed wrong was indeed very wrong.

As we look at the decisions we make with regard to design, in order to achieve more than simply making things less bad, we have to provide ways for users/ viewers to participate in the pursuit of good.

Like Nature's Path, we need to consider all of our design choices as part of a greater contract with society. As producers of goods, a group of resource consumers whose design choices are compounded by the millions of units produced, we are charged with nothing less than the health and safety of our fellow beings. Nowhere was this contract more brutally illustrated than in the case of the Tylenol murders in the early 1980s, which showed how easily our distribution system can be compromised and how seemingly benign design choices could lead to harm.

At the time, Johnson & Johnson, the maker of Tylenol, was distributing the product using common and completely legal techniques for this product category. To its credit, Johnson & Johnson responded quickly and decisively. It not only pulled all of the company's products immediately from the store shelves but became very active in the development of tamper-evident packaging—the norm across the pharmaceutical industry today.[1]

As designers, we're charged with nothing less than the health and safety of our fellow beings.

Underconsumption

It's odd to think of not consuming enough, but this in fact is a very real problem. Malnutrition is a form of underconsumption (not having access to enough nourishment); so is lack of education (not taking in or being allowed access to knowledge). Lack of research and the foresight it enables also is a type of underconsumption (not consuming enough time to make sure the effort, project, or piece will be smart in the long run).

There are also systematic imbalances caused by underconsumption in nature. The standard mode of forest management for the past century has included the aggressive suppression of natural fires. By doing so, too much underbrush is allowed to build up. When this accumulated brush catches fire, what would have been taken care of by nature's renewal system quickly becomes a devastating catastrophe resulting in complete destruction. More progressive forest managers have found that working within nature's plan allows their areas to remain healthier, more diverse, and better able to recover after disturbances.

On the industry side, underconsumption of recycled goods has kept market viability for these goods out of balance with virgin goods. With few exceptions, recycled goods can be cheaper to produce than virgin goods, enjoying lower energy inputs, less processing needed, and so on. And yet, due to "low demand" in some categories, the price for a recycled option might be higher than its virgin equivalent.

As we begin to examine products and behavior with an eye to restore what we've been taking out of natural systems, rather than create unstable monocultures for our convenience, balance becomes key. We must look at things as a system and find ways of working to maintain all elements in harmony. To do this, we need to not rush to find *the* solution—one that is convenient for us but completely ignores long-term impacts.

Overconsumption

Writer Dave Tilford tackled the idea of consumption in a 2000 Sierra Club article, "Sustainable Consumption: Why Consumption Matters":

Our cars, houses, hamburgers, televisions, sneakers, newspapers and thousands upon thousands of other consumer items come to us via chains of production that stretch around the globe. Along the length of this chain we pull raw materials from the Earth in numbers that are too big even to conceptualize. Tremendous volumes of natural resources are displaced and ecosystems disrupted in the uncounted extraction processes that fuel modern human existence. Constructing highways or buildings, mining for gold, drilling for oil, harvesting crops and forest products all involve reshaping natural landscapes. Some of our activities involve minor changes to the landscape. Sometimes entire mountains are moved.[2]

An ecological footprint is defined as the amount of productive land area required to sustain one human being. As most of our planet's surface is either under water or inhospitable, there are only 1.9 hectares (about four football fields) of productive area to support each person today (grow food, supply materials, clean our waste, and so on). That might sound like a lot, but our collective ecological footprint is already 2.3 hectares. This means that, given the needs of today's human population, we already need 1.5 Earths to live sustainably. But this assumes all resources are divided equally. Those with the largest footprint—the biggest consumers of global resources—are U.S. citizens, who require 9.57 hectares *each* to meet their demands. If everyone in the world consumed at that rate, *5 Earths* would be needed to sustain the population. People in Bangladesh, in contrast, need just 0.5 hectares; for people in China today, the footprint is 1.36 hectares.[3]

What will China's footprint look like in just a few decades? As China continues to prosper and grow, what will happen when its new population of 1.5 billion citizens demand *their* fair share of the pie? If the rest of the world continues to use the United States as the benchmark for success, we would need 25 Earths to meet that level of consumption. Something has to change. (Want to make it personal? Calculate your own footprint: *www.footprintnetwork.org.*)

Part of why the U.S. footprint is so large has to do with trade access to more than the country's balance of natural capital. Much of this natural capital comes from countries that have some resources but not much else from which to earn cash. Due to corruption, or desperation, many of those countries are selling off their resources quickly, regardless of the long-term consequences. With such unbridled access fueling its success, North America (and the United States in particular) hasn't yet become deeply concerned about the need to use resources efficiently. After six months, 99 percent of the resources to make the things we use is converted to waste—disposed of as finished goods, but mostly as process waste.[4]

How did the United States get into this position? After World War II, the chairman of President Eisenhower's Council of Economic Advisors stated that the American economy's ultimate goal was to produce more consumer goods. In 1955, retail analyst Victor Lebow summed up this strategy that would become the norm for the American economic system:

> Our enormously productive economy . . . demands that we make consumption our way of life, that we convert the buying and use of goods into rituals, that we seek our spiritual satisfaction, our ego satisfaction, in consumption. . . .

We need things consumed, burned-up, replaced and discarded at an ever accelerating rate.[5]

This mid-twentieth-century view is in sharp contrast to how resources and goods were viewed in preindustrial times, when moving goods around or even making them in the first place was a really big deal. In those days, people in the Old World thought hard about resource use. What they had around them was pretty much all there would be, so they had to figure out how to make it work. In contrast, the New World was perceived as nothing but space, filled with endless vistas of trees (and a few indigenous people). Because of this seemingly limitless abundance, the New World was detached from the realities of resource management. The idea that resources are limitless and easily obtained still lingers today compounded by the high level of resources demanded to meet consumption demands led by the West, and the United States in particular. Dave Tilford notes in his article "Sustainable Consumption: Why Consumption Matters,"

"Since 1950 alone, the world's people have consumed more goods and services than the combined total of all humans who ever walked the planet before us."[6]

As the new sustainability paradigm works its way into daily practice, companies are making the terms *right-sizing, supply chain optimization, energy reduction,* and others part of their language. In

December 2008, computer maker Dell announced changes to its packaging that will save more than $8 million (and 20 million pounds of material) over the next four years. This latest expansion of its green-packaging program is targeting reductions for desktop and laptop packaging worldwide.

It should be noted, that though it's not a steadfast rule; it is becoming more and more common for companies undergoing sustainability-driven change (including its associated change drivers such as overhead reduction, risk reduction, and so on), to start to look for opportunities both for the thing being targeted for change, as well as all associated objects and systems. In the case of packaging, for instance, this would include looking hard at print (inserts, manuals, promotional items), transport and logistics, and warehousing—as well as the package itself. As companies, and even consumers, reposition themselves both for the new paradigm, as well as to better weather the storms of financial uncertainty, the idea of "consuming well" rather than simply more, is becoming the mantra for a better and more sustainable economy.

Understanding Consumption

If all developing countries consumed as the West does, we would need several Earths to satisfy that "need." The concept of spending every dime ever made—like using resources until they're gone—must change, or we as a species have no hope of survival.

Civilizations have understood the concept of capital (money) for thousands of years. How much we have and how quickly we earn it has come to be the indicator of successful effort. But with the idea of long-term change in mind, we need to reexamine why and how we consume, look for ways to move in a more restorative direction, and also look for new ways to measure our success.

Each year since 1995, San Francisco-based think tank Redefining Progress has been using a tool they created, Genuine Progress Indicator (GPI), to measure how well Americans (or any country) are doing both economically and socially. This GPI paints a very different picture of American society than mainstream indicators such as gross domestic product (GDP), or gross national product (GNP). Over the years, a variety of conferences sponsored by various groups, have brought together interested parties with the ultimate aim of coming up with a globally applicable index of "gross national happiness (GNH)," and "genuine progress index" (GPI). It is the intent of the groups supporting these indicators that these metrics supersede the current global economic indicators, GNP and GDP, with the more realistic indicators to include things like: income distribution, quality of life, education, value of household and volunteer work, crime, resource depletion, environmental damage, military spending, and so on.[7]

Tillford highlighted some of the problems with our current economic metrics:

> In 1998, more than $100 billion was spent in the United States dealing with water, air, and noise pollution—and considered growth by the nation's GDP. That same year, criminal activity added $28 billion to the GDP through replacement of stolen goods, purchase of home security systems, increased prison building, and other necessary responses.

> By the curious standard of the GDP . . . the happiest event is an earthquake or a hurricane. The most desirable habitat is a multibillion-dollar Superfund site. . . . It is as if a business

kept a balance sheet by merely adding up all "transactions," without distinguishing between income and expenses, or between assets and liabilities.[8]

The originator of the GDP (and GNP) measure, Simon Kuznets, acknowledges these indicators were not a measure of well-being but only economic activity. Expanding on this idea in her booklet "Economic Vitality in a Transition to Sustainability," economist Neva Goodwin notes: "Qualitative improvement of goods as services determines material well-being as much or more than physical quantity of output (especially in the more developed economies)." Goodwin goes on to point out:

> It is not inherent in market systems that they will orient towards social goals. It is a half-truth that market capitalism is the best economic system yet invented. The other half of the truth is that, when markets are allowed to work as though they were self-contained systems, operating within a vacuum, they become increasingly self-destructive, because they degrade the social and environmental contexts in which they exist, and upon which they are entirely dependent.[9]

These ideas have huge implications for print, product, and packaging, the backbone of today's free market system. Too many of the things humans create today have remained market viable simply because they have not had to carry their true weight—their true costs for resource impacts, transportation impacts (greenhouse gas loads, plus fuel extraction and refinement), human health and its economic impacts, and so on.

For industries that exist on the sheer volume of units produced, how will producers survive when people start to ask such fundamental questions as: Can we each be happy without having more and more stuff? Can we create more economic activity without creating stuff (service-based versus manufacturing-based economy)? Can the activities we value happen without having stuff at all? Is stuff really the problem, or is it just the way we perceive and produce stuff? And, if we're in the business of making and selling stuff, how can we key into new ways of thinking to help drive true innovation, especially when "satisfaction" is a moving target? (Want to know more? Watch Free Range Studio's *Story of Stuff* at *www.storyofstuff.com*.)

Change will come not by just thinking outside the box but by throwing the box out the window and looking at the space it leaves behind. Was the box or effort needed, will we miss it or some part of it? Was it done well? What impacts did it make? Was making it an investment in our future? Did it add to natural capital (resources each nation naturally possesses), or was it simply a drawdown of our account? Is it possible to "create more good," as systems thinking pioneer William McDonough is often heard to ask?

With perhaps a few exceptions, no one wakes up in the morning calculating how to trash the planet. Instead, our daily lives are a series of choices, each minuscule in its individual impact. But when multiplied billions of times, day after day and year after year, the impact is enormous.

So far, what we've been doing is "successful" because of—or in spite of—our choices. The funny part about being successful, though, is that it can turn you into a one-trick pony, creating a huge disincentive to change. Capital investment in one production system or reliance on one material type or resource flow, as is common practice, locks a firm into a narrow operating model. Though the rewards are great when the timing is right, there's no guarantee it can go on forever—that is, be sustainable in the original sense of the word. But in the general scheme of evolution, the species that can adapt quickly are the ones that survive.

In its report *Sustainable Consumption Facts and Trends: From a Business Perspective,* the World Council for Sustainable Development looked at these consumption trends:[10]

1. Global drivers of consumption

   Global consumption levels and patterns are driven by a variety of factors. Rapid global population growth is one of the most obvious. With world populations expected to grow to 9 billion by 2050, all sectors will be growing. Of particular concern will be sharp raises in middle-class levels of consumption in developing countries patterned on the Western style of "consumerism."

2. Global consumption patterns and impacts

   Global consumption has put unsustainable and increasing stress on Earth's ecosystems. In only the past 50 years, human kind has degraded 60 percent of Earth's ecosystem services. The consumption of natural resources (energy and materials) is expected to rise to 170 percent of the planet's biocapacity by 2040, even though human well-being does not require high levels of consumption.

3. The role of the consumer

   Consumer attitudes and behaviors are becoming increasingly focused on environmental, social, and economic issues, with some market sectors becoming more and more willing to act on those concerns. However, "willingness" to act does not always translate into change. A variety of "barrier" factors include: availability, affordability, convenience, product performance, conflicting priorities, skepticism, and force of habit.

4. The role of business in mainstreaming sustainable consumption

   Business approaches to sustainable consumption can be grouped into these broad categories:

   — *Innovation.* Business processes for any effort are beginning to incorporate ideas to maximize societal value and minimize environmental cost.

   — *Choice influencing.* Through the use of value-based marketing, companies are leveraging techniques to encourage and empower consumers to help shift markets in a more sustainable direction.

   — *Choice editing.* "Unsustainable" products and services are finding it difficult to remain in the market as consumer groups and other players focus attention on their impacts.

5. The challenge ahead and options for change

   To help drive real and far-reaching change, consumers need to be well informed, provided with healthful choices, and encouraged to embrace a fundamental shift in the way they approach their daily lives. Businesses, governments, and stakeholders need to continue (or open) dialogs about how to best position opportunities for change for the long-term benefit of all.

Your product in its natural environment.

Nearly All New Products Fail

The old ways of coming up with this week's brilliant ideas and then churning them out by the gazillion despite the consequences still works great. Or does it? Store shelves, or any audience-demanding media, are bulging with "brilliance," each competitor fighting with its neighbor to be the lucky one to connect. With the markets brimming with choice and competition, there is a generally accepted industry rule of thumb that nearly 70 to 90 percent of all new products fail. Why?

The simplest answer is that the whole social environment is changing. Or maybe the old products aren't as good as they could be. In addition, audiences are becoming better educated. From required information printed on pieces/products, to information provided by advocacy groups, to instant information access through the Internet, the days of dumping "whatever" out there (at least in the developed world) are over. Finally, there are simply more of us, not only to distribute to, but to compete with. As the days of the one-trick pony draw rapidly to a close, not only must the things we make do everything they promise, but they must offer more to cut through the noise of the competition.

Nothing exemplifies this concept of offering more better than sustainable products. These products are produced to not only meet a need; depending on the item, they are also: healthier, more energy efficient (saves run-time dollars), more resource efficient (meaning more selling units possible per resource unit), and have minimal impact on the waste stream compared to their less conscientious competition. In other words, these products are in general better for both the end user and society at large.

Why Aren't All Products Already Sustainable?

Manufacturers, their creative service vendors, and potential end users all play a part in trashing our planet, and fear is one of the key factors why change is slow to arrive: Potential end users fear that unfamiliar products aren't as good (or what they're used to) coupled with fear of wasting their ever-stretched dollar; manufacturers fear that potential end users won't accept the new product; and the manufacturer's creatives fear being fired (losing the account) for stepping too far outside the norm.

Yet innovation is about embracing fear and using it to your advantage. Fear is good, and a powerful motivator. In the PricewaterhouseCoopers LLP 2002 Sustainability Survey Report, respondents acknowledged the fear that failure to adopt green business practices would have an adverse effect on consumer perception and thus negatively impact their market share.

In its 2007 Cause Evolution & Environmental Survey, Cone LLC (coneinc.com), a strategy and communications agency, found that, of the people responding:[11]

— 93 percent believe companies have a responsibility to help preserve the environment.

— 91 percent have a more positive image of a company when it is environmentally responsible.

— 85 percent would consider switching to another company's products or services because of a company's negative corporate responsibility practices.

One fear industries have is that if they do not adopt sustainable business practices, they will be legislated into action anyway—and not in a way advantageous to the industries. Farsighted industries recognize this and stay ahead of this curve to be best positioned for the inevitable.

What Does Change Look Like?

If change is inevitable, what will it look like? What is *sustainability*? To answer that in a design context, let's step back and look at the bigger picture in a systems context.

The world is a very complicated place, so it's no surprise that each industry is, too. Add to that the business of implementing sustainability, which will require us to reexamine the way we do everything, covering a great mix of industries and disciplines. Naturally, everyone will want their voices heard and their bottom lines respected. Defining just what is sustainable is such an important question that the Sustainable Packaging Coalition (SPC) has made nailing down the answer for packaging their top-most priority.

The SPC looked to create a set of goals, not mandated rules. Its general idea was that if you define the solution, the problems will take care of themselves. The SPC criteria for a sustainable package are applicable to *any* effort, have eight clearly defined points, but really only ask these simple questions:

— Does it make us or the planet sick? Don't do it!

— Can we use renewable resources—energy as well as materials—and then use them again without going back to virgin sources?

— Are we doing it efficiently, considering all true costs (supply chain "eco-ness" [going past simple environmental regulation compliance], materials use, loop participation, social impacts, etc.)?

What Is Sustainability?

Goals and ideas used to define what a sustainable package or product might look like do not supply a full definition of what sustainability is. So again we ask: What exactly is sustainability?

The simplest answer is one that's been kicking around for some time; it was formalized in 1987 by the United Nations' World Commission on Environment and Development (the Brundtland Commission):

Sustainable Development is development that meets the needs of the present without compromising the ability of future generations to meet their own needs.[12]

This most basic idea has been at the core of human society since settled communities began. Ideas like "Don't eat your seed corn" and "Do unto others as you'd have others do unto you," that form the core of sustainability thinking, are concepts that have been overlooked in our collective push to the future. Let us discuss each of these ideas.

"Don't eat your seed corn." In today's environment, this phrase means do not use up what you need to keep the system going. With that in mind, one can quickly pull an example from sustainable forestry practices. Traditional clear-cutting is a very efficient and low-cost way to harvest wood. This method treats wood like annually tilled wheat rather than what it really is, the slow-growing cornerstone of a region's survival system. Sustainable forestry practices using planting, growing, and harvesting methods that mimic nature, though, have allowed for healthful and profitable ecosystems for generations.

"Do unto others as you'd have others do unto you." This idea is perfectly illustrated by the new directives companies are giving their suppliers. In addition to establishing the Walmart scorecard that sets new benchmarks for packaging[13] and has made the entire packaging industry review what it's doing, Walmart also announced plans to measure the energy use and emissions of the entire supply chain for seven product categories, looking for ways to increase energy efficiency.[14] Eventually this initiative is expected to include other products (if not all) carried by the company. It would be no surprise then that other big-box retailers as well as consumer goods producers (CPGs) have begun implementing similar benchmarks for their vendors.

Put simply, companies are demanding of their suppliers the same criteria for ethics and foresight that consumers and legislators are demanding of them. Rather than simply accepting whatever a company feels like selling, retailers (and other commercial buyers) are now saying to their suppliers, "Do unto us as others would have us do unto them."

What Sustainability *Is Not*

Sustainability is not a tax on production. It is the end to hidden subsidies and the beginning of assigning true costs. The best illustration in current terms is producer- (or user-) pays policies. Here, those people who use and benefit from a thing or service pay the full load for it—from the impacts of collecting the raw materials all the way through processing at end of life.

Dave Tilford explains:

> Over 2,500 economists, including eight Nobel Prize winners, support the notion of market-based mechanisms for environmental solutions—like carbon taxes and emission auctions, where polluters pay for the right to emit, develop, or use nature's services. In addition, though many economists are hesitant to question our current measurements of economic growth, a small but active number believe only a true cost accounting of economic activities will give us an accurate figure of the state of the economy.

> These true cost economists note that, as the GDP climbed 3.9 percent in 1998, the cost to taxpay-

ers from loss of wetlands and their economic services (like water filtration) climbed 3.7 percent. From 1973 to 1993, the GDP rose by 55 percent, while real wages dropped by 3.4 percent nationally. The emerging field of "ecological economics" is beginning to question these accounting incongruities.[15]

One can easily ask: Is paying the full cost of creating, using, and disposing of a product a tax or just the end of the free ride? What could be more fair than saying "If you want it, you must pay?"

Sustainability is also not specifically a barrier to trade in the classic sense. Setting standards for health, whether applied to the product itself (e.g., banning lead paint in toys) or to issues affecting our collective health (e.g., wood certified as not having been harvested from rain forests or old-growth forests), sets the stage for eliminating poorly conceived or manufactured goods and serves our collective long-term best interests. Insisting trading partners not create goods in a way (or with materials) that have been outlawed at home is hardly an unreasonable request. Companies able to meet these standards find new audiences and markets are open to them, while companies wishing only to dump whatever wherever are being forced to rethink this shortsighted strategy.

Tearing Down the Tower of Babble

Sustainability is quickly becoming the common language for business. Unlike the never-ending stream of business fads that get chief executives excited but leave middle management cringing, now management, marketing, design, engineering, production, procurement, and logistics can all sit down at the conference table and at least begin on the same page. Although each discipline still has its own language and motivations, the conflicting babble that was the norm of conference rooms everywhere is becoming united in some sort of vision, with shared goals and ethics.

Coming now from a similar place of understanding, marketers understand that they must have a clear and verifiable reason for demanding certain design criteria. Designers now know that if they want to specify a given decorative material or technique, the impacts of that choice must have sound reasons— simply being "pretty" or "different" isn't enough. Along these same lines, purchasing agents understand that if their design colleagues keep telling them to ask vendors to avoid certain materials, that guidance must be heeded, no matter how attractive "other stuff" that's "cheaper" may sound.

Another advantage of using sustainability as part of a company's core ethics has been to increase employee satisfaction, thus reducing turnover. Everyone wants to feel good about the work they do.

We are seeing the very beginning of one of the most amazing times since the dawn of the industrial revolution. Today, we have the opportunity to completely remake everything we do but to get it right this time rather than just stumble into solutions. From the biggest buildings and entire communities to a simple brochure—every new project is an opportunity for innovation. Every innovation is an opportunity for increasing market share or adding to natural capital (putting back natural resources we've blasted through). Every change we make in the market and in how we manage resources is an opportunity to redefine the way we will live over the next 100 years and beyond. Sustainability is hope, it's exciting, and it's a complete paradigm shift. There has never been a better time to create real, lasting, and positive change.

Even the longest journey starts with one small step. As consumers and lawmakers push for solutions, all eyes are turning to designers for answers. The time for a leisurely stroll has past; now it's time to hit the ground running.

Today we have the opportunity to completely remake everything we do, but to get it right this time, rather than just stumbling into solutions.

The Next Great Era of Design

In the western world, at the dawn of the Industrial Revolution, production was the domain of the craftsman. Ordinary objects were artful, durable, and meant to be respected for their function and value as a needed object. Everything was hard to come by, and once a thing outlived its primary function, new uses were found for its parts. Nothing was wasted. As mass-produced goods started to come on the scene, much of the decoration added by craftsman was reproduced in the factory-made product to let consumers know that even though the thing wasn't handmade, it still had value. This era was the age of Industrial Arts.

As the pace of life accelerated, we entered the era of streamlined design, form follows function—

Bauhaus, prairie style, mission style, mod, pop, futuristic—smooth elegant lines, bold shapes, fun, playful, sleek, streamlined. All of these ideas made up the palette of choices in the new age of Industrial design.

But something happened as life raced through the 1900s. As the century screamed to a close, form and function became slaves to price and quantity. Quality, aesthetics, fit, and finish—all were abandoned to hit that ever-lower price. But that wasn't all that was abandoned. Integrity, fair play, stewardship—these ideals got tossed by the wayside, too, as companies leveraged loopholes and backdoor subsidies found in lax environmental regulations, inhumane worker laws, and artificially cheap energy that was openly subsidized or did not carry its full environmental and health impact costs. Poverty became ever more entrenched for most, even as living standards improved for many, while whole ecosystems were collapsing and there was nowhere to go but down.

Thankfully, that's not the end of the story. Today we're watching the dawn of a new era. In September 2007, a sustainableday.com blog entry noted:

> The IDSA [Industrial Designers Society of America] has come full circle to openly embrace sustainable design since once supposedly banning environmental design legend Victor Papanek from the society for speaking up against the damage that the industrial design profession has done.

> . . . In this age of mass production when everything must be planned and designed, design has become the most powerful tool with which man shapes his tools and environments (and, by extension, society and himself). This demands

high social and moral responsibility from the designer.

As we merged into the new era and the us-versus-them ideas from the green-versus-mainstream days started to find new direction, a flurry of articles came out titled "Green Is Dead." If you paid the slightest bit of attention, though, it was obvious they were out to shock, nothing more. Once you read the articles, you would discover that green as a late twentieth-century "movement" was not dead per se but was finally maturing from a rabble of unshaven idealism to real and actionable strategies for sustainable living and business. A place to actually be rather than a place to simply dream about. In the early days, the image of the radical green proponent made selling the concepts of sustainability nearly impossible for working designers committed to "green" in practice. Afraid to seem too "alternative," too "out there," and too far from the norm, designers continued to produce products they knew were not forward-thinking simply for fear of losing market share.

Today, the concepts of sustainability—not "green-ness" alone—are being integrated into business models and product strategies across the board. Rather than being legislated into action, businesses—not limited to the fringe faithful, but big corporations—are actively looking at their total impact and opportunities (*triple bottom line*) as triggers for increased competitive advantage, creative levers, and profitability, and, of course, as a tool to increase positive consumer perception and market share.

The time was right for change. Green was being perceived as exclusive rather than inclusive, "only for the true believers," which limited the further integration of its actionable principles.

If green were dead, as the articles claimed, then its legacy is not only living on but thriving—and moving closer to the reality green originally had hoped for. Not through calls for the immediate dismantling of capitalism but through thousands of actions taken every day, by regular people, who recognize opportunities to make positive incremental changes. These changes are made for a variety of reasons—some ethical, some legislated, and some profit driven—but all with an eye on sustaining a positive advantage.

As with any maturing system, there will come a day when we won't have to talk about sustainability. Not because it's dead but because it's simply just another part of good business. Governments, companies, designers, and consumers are waking up to embrace new products, services, and ideas that deliver on the promises they make. Things that aren't just all surface beauty or brief functionality but truly innovative and useful. And, most important, they were created with all stakeholders in mind, including ones not born yet.

So though it's not "official," and even the idea of naming a design era is a western-centric one, it is not too soon to say that the early twenty-first century marks the next great era of design: sustainability.

How to Avoid Change

"Those of us who have spent years working towards sustainable prosperity, trying to move investors and corporate leaders to take action to address major environmental and social threats, have often felt like Sisyphus of Greek mythology—destined to spend our lives rolling a huge boulder uphill. Today, it is possible to survey our progress and feel that we have reached a point where that boulder is not going to roll back down the hill," Mindy S. Lubber, president of Ceres, notes.[16]

For change agents steeling themselves up for the long haul, pulling those resistant to change into the new era will be a task with us for some time. Entrenched interests hate change. Ending slavery, women's suffrage, and universal equal rights were all "crazy" ideas that reactionaries swore would doom civil society if they became law. Yet society prospered, becoming better by being able to benefit fully from the talents and contributions of all citizens. With tongue planted firmly in cheek, in a January 2008 sustainableisgood.com piece titled "7Rs of Anti-Sustainability," author Dennis Salazar asks reactionaries and laggards alike to consider these helpful tips as they look for ways to resist shifting to a world that benefits more than the select few:

1. Refuse to consider thoughts and opinions other than your own. If you are right and everyone else is wrong, why bother?

2. Remain glued to the status quo. After all, if what you have been doing works, why take a chance on changing anything?

3. Reject any idea that even remotely sounds like compromise even though sometimes that is the best way to accomplish progress.

4. Resist any new technology unless it is absolutely perfect and supports your position. "See, I told you it wouldn't work" can be so satisfying.

5. Ridicule anyone who appears to be profiting from their work in sustainability, especially if their margin appears to exceed your own.

6. Repel anyone seeking knowledge or help. Everyone knowing as much as you do cannot be a good thing.

7. Resign yourself to the fact that the environmental problem is too large to be fixed. Seek new goals that are easier to achieve!

It's the Other Guy's Problem

One of the things heard over and over from those slow to embrace change is "We're not changing until the other guys does, or he'll have an unfair advantage." In their defense, this is absolutely true. As long as the full cost of impacts for the things we make and the way we make them are not managed by enforceable law, someone is going to cash in on that hidden subsidy. To the other guy, however, *you* are the "other guy" expected to make the first move.

The problem, of course, is that if everyone is waiting for the other guy to act, no one will. Keeping the whole system stagnant often makes the

---

For the first time in the brand's history, Burt's Bees has released a comprehensive Corporate Social Responsibility (CSR) Report, *"The Greater Good Social and Environmental Progress Report: 2008 and Before,"* documenting the brand's commitment to sustainable business practices. After many years of pioneering sustainable practices and leading the Natural Personal Care industry, Burt's Bees intends to rigorously measure its progress and has set ambitious, quantitative goals to better assess its achievements and understand its challenges.

Even the materials chosen for the report convey their values. The company chose 100 percent post-consumer recycled, FSC (Forest Stewardship Council) Certified stock and vegetable-based inks and printed only a limited quantity to minimize paper, and instead drove traffic to a flip-through pdf on its Web-site, www.burtsbees.com. They also diagram the resources saved by the choice of paper to help put these efforts into perspective.

Today.

Following our North Star, the business model we call The Greater Good™, calls for a deep commitment to our consumers and the world we share. It's a pledge to operate our company with the highest level of social and environmental responsibility, and to share what we learn. The Greater Good™ means working to create a world where we all have the information and tools we need to make meaningful, ethical choices for ourselves, our families, and the world around us.

We believe that business is among the most powerful forces on earth. But if business is to be a meaningful, positive force, then we're not talking about business as usual. Exactly the opposite. We want Burt's Bees to enhance the traditional business model. Our reasoning is simple. A model that puts shareholders ahead of stakeholders is one that puts the outcomes of the few ahead of the many...

Many of these people have a personal relationship with our brand...

sense and common good. We use natural ingredients because these are the time-tested ones. Our "kitchen chemistry" approach means minimal processes that maximize purity. Our packaging is made of materials that are post-consumer recycled (PCR) whenever possible, recyclable, and designed to minimize waste. And we don't believe animals were put on this earth to be tested on.

> "Offering a natural product wrapped in environmentally sensitive packaging is only part of the story."

Our vision is a commitment to sharing ingredients responsibly...

Our Vision:
We will be the #1 natural personal care business in the world, adored by consumers, desired by our customers and working in harmony with our environment.

Today our goal is to be a fully sustainable business. But what do those words mean to us?

Last year our business increased by 25 percent, while our energy consumption dropped by 3 percent...

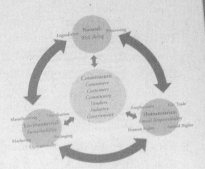

The GREATER GOOD™ Business Model
Operating our company with the highest level of social responsibility.

THE GREATER GOOD™
Social and Environmental
Progress Report
2008 & Before

"Goodness is the only investment that never fails."
Henry David Thoreau

BURT'S BEES

Burt's Bees, Inc.
633 Davis Drive
Suite 600
Morrisville, NC 27560

www.burtsbees.com

Thanks for your time and interest in our Social and Environmental Progress Report. If you would like to share your thoughts, suggestions, and/or questions please let us hear from you at CSR@burtsbees.com.

Printed using vegetable-based inks

consequences much worse than if everyone had just done their bit to begin with. In game theory, the idea of waiting for the other guy is part of "The Prisoner's Dilemma."

Two prisoners are arrested for the same crime. Put in separate cells, unable to get their stories in line, the guards try to coax each to implicate the other. If neither goes along with the guards, they will both receive a sentence of just 1 year. If one accepts the deal and the other keeps quiet, then the squealer goes free while the quiet one gets 10 years. But if they both implicate the other, they each get 5 years.

If one prisoner wants to attempt to get out of responsibility and get off scot-free, he will try and put all the blame on the other guy, even though he risks the other guy doing the same. Even if each conspirator assumes the other would crack, they would still be better off implicating the other, as they would get only 5 years each rather than perhaps get 10 years alone for keeping quiet. A rational person acting in her own self-interest would always betray her fellow prisoner. Yet that puts both in jail for 5 years, when, in theory, they could have had only a year each if they had both just kept quiet. In other words, if they had taken a chance and done the hard thing rather than try to stick it to the other guy, the outcome would have been better for the two as a community.

In a September 2007 *Economist* article, "Playing Games with the Planet," the author argues that the pessimistic among us would assume that the international response to climate change (and so sustainability in general) will go the way of the prisoner's dilemma. Noting that rational leaders will always neglect the problem, on the grounds that others will either solve it, allowing their country to become a free-rider, or let it fester, making it a doomed cause anyway, the author concludes the world would be condemned to a slow roasting even though global impacts could be averted if everyone simply cooperated and took on a share of the load no matter what.[17]

The article goes on to cite a study by Michael Liebreich of New Energy Finance, a research firm. Liebreich draws on game theory to reach the opposite conclusion. The game in general changes dramatically, Liebreich points out, if players know they can play more than once. With this expanded option, players have an incentive to cooperate with their opponent to maintain good favor in later rounds.

Liebreich's paper in turn cites a study by Robert Axelrod and William Hamilton, which highlights three elements for successful repeat play:

1. Players begin the game cooperating.

2. They should deter transgressions by punishing the offender in the next round.

3. Rather than hold grudges, players should cooperate with misbehaving players again after imposing an appropriate punishment.[18]

With this new insight into game play and its possible implications for negotiating action on sustainability issues, the *Economist* article notes:

> Mr. Liebreich believes that all this holds lessons for the world's climate negotiators. Treaties on climate change, after all, are not one-offs. Indeed, the United Nations is even now trying to get its members to negotiate a successor to its existing treaty, the Kyoto Protocol, which expires

in 2012. Many fear that the effort will collapse unless the laggards can be persuaded to join in. But the paper argues that rational countries will not be deterred by free-riders. They will continue to curb their emissions, while devising sanctions for those who do not.

Due to the complexities involved in sustainability in general and all the details that would need to be covered to mandate specific change, establishing basic codes of ethics is becoming part of the total strategy for holding players accountable for their actions—even if specific laws do not yet exist. Codes of ethics give both players and governing bodies tools by which to judge transgressors as well as a means to prod those who would try to get a free ride. Covering more turf than any one law, codes of ethics help pull all of the intricate and scattered threads into one more manageable guide., Codes of ethics, beyond the basics (the Sarbanes-Oxley Act in the U.S., for example, also known as the Public Company Accounting Reform and Investor Protection Act of 2002, was enacted as a reaction to a number of major corporate and accounting scandals [Enron, WorldCom]), have become essential tools for farsighted companies, especially privately held companies not usually held to new transparency regulations, to get ahead of legislative action, allowing them more time to better manage inevitable change. They also provide benchmarks for improvement to maintain and increase forward progress and to promote (and maintain) positive consumer (or investor) perception. Codes of ethics help companies show a variety of efforts (environmental, fair trade, community involvement), in a tangible way: "We're not there yet, and we have a way to go, but these are our goals, and this is what we've done so far."

Taking Responsibility and Thriving

Codes of ethics for design have a long history., The Code of Hammurabi, the first written code of law in human history, was established by the sixth Babylonian king, Hammurabi (ca. 1760 BCE). The laws are numbered 1 to 282 and are inscribed in cuneiform script on an eight-foot stela.[19] Numbers 229 to 233 assign stiff penalties for compromising production integrity. Personal guarantees meant much more than today's platitudes:

> If a builder build a house for some one, and does not construct it properly, and the house which he built fall in and kill its owner, then that builder shall be put to death.

Imagine what products would be like if these laws were applied today. Perhaps we would be less far along in terms of progress, or maybe we would have evolved our society in a much more thoughtful way. Doing things more thoughtfully is the idea behind the precautionary principle.

The Precautionary Principle

Long-used aphorisms such as "An ounce of prevention is worth a pound of cure," "Better safe than sorry," and "Do no harm"—the latter still in the Hippocratic Oath for doctors—are accepted as part of humankind's collective "common sense" and the core of the precautionary principle, a moral and political principle set.

Though there are many definitions of the precautionary principle in use to justify all sorts of preemptive action strategies, at a 1998 meeting of scientists, lawyers, policy makers, and environmentalists at Wingspread, headquarters of the Johnson Foundation (a philanthropic effort founded by Herbert Fisk Johnson, Jr. the third generation leader of S.C. Johnson & Son, Inc.), the precautionary principle was summarized this way:

> When an activity raises threats of harm to human health or the environment, precautionary measures should be taken even if some cause and effect relationships are not fully established scientifically. In this context the proponent of an activity, rather than the public, should bear the burden of proof. The process of applying the precautionary principle must be open, informed and democratic and must include potentially affected parties. It must also involve an examination of the full range of alternatives, including no action. .[20]

This idea is most often applied to impacts on human and environmental health—highly complicated systems with very unpredictable interactions. Release of radiation or toxins, massive deforestation, reduction in biodiversity or wholesale ecosystem collapse, and use of ozone-depleting fluorocarbons causing global adverse impacts all imply:

> . . . a willingness to take action in advance of scientific proof [or] evidence of the need for the proposed action on the grounds that further delay will prove ultimately most costly to society and nature, and, in the longer term, selfish and unfair to future generations.[21]

The core of this concept embraces people's ethical responsibility to maintain the health of natural systems and acknowledges the fallibility of humankind. In the absence of perfect understanding, an ounce of prevention (or forethought) is worth a pound of cure.

In 1982, the United Nations' General Assembly adopted the World Charter for Nature, the first international endorsement of the precautionary principle.[22]

World Charter for Nature

Reaffirming the fundamental purposes of the United Nations, in particular the maintenance of international peace and security, the development of friendly relations among nations and the achievement of international cooperation in solving international problems of an economic, social, cultural, technical, intellectual or humanitarian character,

Aware that:

(a) Mankind is a part of nature and life depends on the uninterrupted functioning of natural systems which ensure the supply of energy and nutrients,

(b) Civilization is rooted in nature, which has shaped human culture and influenced all artistic and scientific achievement, and living in harmony with nature gives man the best opportunities for the development of his creativity, and for rest and recreation,

Convinced that:

(a) Every form of life is unique, warranting respect regardless of its worth to man, and, to accord other organisms such recognition, man must be guided by a moral code of action,

(b) Man can alter nature and exhaust natural resources by his action or its consequences and, therefore, must fully recognize the urgency of maintaining the stability and quality of nature and of conserving natural resources,

Persuaded that:

(a) Lasting benefits from nature depend upon the maintenance of essential ecological processes and life-support systems, and upon the diversity of life forms, which are jeopardized through excessive exploitation and habitat destruction by man,

(b) The degradation of natural systems owing to excessive consumption and misuse of natural resources, as well as to failure to establish an appropriate economic order among peoples and among States, leads to the breakdown of the economic, social and political framework of civilization,

(c) Competition for scarce resources creates conflicts, whereas the conservation of nature and natural resources contributes to justice and the maintenance of peace and cannot be achieved until mankind learns to live in peace and to forsake war and armaments,

— Reaffirming that man must acquire the knowledge to maintain and enhance his ability to use natural resources in a manner that ensures the preservation of the species and ecosystems for the benefit of present and future generations,

— Firmly convinced of the need for appropriate measures, at the national and international, individual and collective, and private and public levels, to protect nature and promote international co-operation in this field,

— Adopts, to these ends, the present World Charter for Nature, which proclaims the following principles of conservation by which all human conduct affecting nature is to be guided and judged.

General Principles

1. Nature shall be respected and its essential processes shall not be impaired.

2. The genetic viability on the earth shall not be compromised; the population levels of all life forms, wild and domesticated, must be at least sufficient for their survival, and to this end necessary habitats shall be safeguarded.

3. All areas of the earth, both land and sea, shall be subject to these principles of conservation; special protection shall be given to unique areas, to representative samples of all the different types of ecosystems, and to the habitats of rare or endangered species.

4. Ecosystems and organisms, as well as the land, marine, and atmospheric resources that are utilized by man, shall be managed to achieve and maintain optimum sustainable productivity, but not in such a way as to endanger the integrity of those other ecosystems or species with which they coexist.

5. Nature shall be secured against degradation caused by warfare or other hostile activities.

Over the years, the precautionary principle has been at the heart of codes of ethics of many groups as well as government's environmental policies, especially in the European Union (EU). On the corporate side, adoption of the precautionary principle can be seen in the 2006 Chemicals Strategy for The Body Shop International, a UK-based cosmetics and personal care products company.[23]

In government, the European Commission's new regulatory system for chemicals, REACH (*r*egistration, *e*valuation and *a*uthorization of *ch*emicals) explicitly cites these principles as a basis for decision making whenever the scientific data are insufficient. Virtually unknown in the United States for years since its introduction in 2003 (formally adopted 2007), it is now gaining ground. In December 2001, the *New York Times Magazine* listed the principle as one of the most influential ideas of the year, citing the intellectual, ethical, and policy framework the Science and Environmental Health Network (SEHN) had developed around the principle as an example.[24]

In 2003, the city of San Francisco passed a precautionary principle purchasing ordinance, with Berkeley following suit in 2006.[25] Encompassing everything from cleaning supplies to computers, this ordinance requires the city to weigh the environmental and health costs of its annual purchases.

Items in the ordinance not only touch on solid sustainability principles and put them into practice but implement far-reaching ideas, such as accounting for true costs (the cost of all impacts along a supply chain, not just direct impacts of a single good or service).[26]

Hannover Principles

As complex as the planet itself, sustainability cannot be approached in a one-size-fits-all way. Different industries have different opportunities as well as unique obstacles. Ultimately, it's not important how we get there, as long as we're all moving in the same direction—and doing it sooner rather than later.

Like the precautionary principle, the Hannover Principles[27] were created to provide a guide for designers, planners, governmental officials, and all involved in setting design priorities for humanity, nature, and technology. Commissioned by the city of Hannover, Germany, as the general principles of sustainability for the 2000 World's Fair, and first drafted by William McDonough and Michael Braungart, the Hannover Principles, along with the Earth Charter and Blue Planet 2020 plan, are intended to serve as the basic tools for the development and improvement of humankind and as part of a commitment to once again live as part of the earth.

The principles ask us to:

1. Insist on the right of humanity and nature to coexist in a healthy, supportive, diverse, and sustainable condition.

2. Recognize interdependence. The elements of human design interact with and depend upon the natural world, with broad and diverse implications at every scale. Expand design considerations to recognize even distant effects.

3. Respect relationships between spirit and matter. Consider all aspects of human settlement including community, dwelling, industry, and trade in terms of existing and evolving

connections between spiritual and material consciousness.

4. Accept responsibility for the consequences of design decisions upon human well-being, the viability of natural systems, and their right to coexist.

5. Create safe objects of long-term value. Do not burden future generations with requirements for the maintenance of vigilant administration of potential danger due to the careless creation of products, processes, or standards.

6. Eliminate the concept of waste. Evaluate and optimize the full life cycle of products and processes to approach the state of natural systems, in which there is no waste.

7. Rely on natural energy flows. Human designs should, like the living world, derive their creative force from perpetual solar income. Incorporate the energy efficiently and safely for responsible use.

8. Understand the limitations of design. No human creation lasts forever, and design does not solve all problems. Those who create and plan should practice humility in the face of nature. Treat nature as a model and mentor, not an inconvenience to be evaded or controlled.

9. Seek constant improvement by the sharing of knowledge. Encourage direct and open communication among colleagues, patrons, manufacturers, and users to link long-term sustainable consideration with ethical responsibility, and reestablish the integral relationship between natural processes and human activity.

Kyosei

During most of the Edo Period (1603–1867), Japan closed itself off to the world, suffering no invasions but also forgoing outside trade. Due to this self-imposed isolation, old skills as well as new ideas for resource management for this island nation became of the utmost importance. Nothing was to be wasted, and everything must have purpose.[28] Over the years, *Kyosei*, the idea of living and working together for the common good, has been applied to a variety of subjects from biology to business. More recently, it has become synonymous with corporate responsibility, ethical decision making, stakeholder involvement, and user and producer responsibility. A specific code of ethics, called the *shuchu kiyaku*, has direct roots in Confucian writings.[29]

Originating in China, Confucian writings were highly influential in the evolution of ethical codes and principles in Japan. The following is a short list of some highlights of Confucian philosophy:

— Reciprocity should be practiced throughout one's life. In short, treat others the way you would like to be treated.

— Virtue, not profit, should be the goal of the superior person.

— There should be a balance between self-interest and altruism.

— We do not exist in isolation; we are part of a larger and more complex family (literally and figuratively) where harmony can be achieved by acting appropriately with one another.

Caux Round Table

The Caux Round Table (CRT) is an international network of principled business leaders working to promote moral capitalism, where sustainable and socially responsible prosperity can become the foundation for a fair, free, and transparent global society. The CRT was founded in 1986 by Frederick Phillips, former president of Philips Electronics, and Olivier Giscard d'Estaing, founding Dean and Director General of INSEAD business school, as a means of reducing escalating trade tensions. At the urging of Ryuzaburo Kaku, then chairman of Canon, Inc., the CRT began focusing attention on global corporate responsibility in reducing social and economic threats to world peace and stability.[30]

Formally launched in 1994 and presented at the UN World Summit on Social Development in 1995, the CRT Principles for Business articulate a comprehensive set of ethical norms for businesses operating internationally or across multiple cultures. The principles emerged from a series of dialogues catalyzed by the Caux Round Table during the late 1980s and early 1990s. They are the product of collaboration among executives from Europe, Japan, and the United States, and were fashioned in part from a document called the Minnesota Principles. The principles have been published in 12 languages, reprinted in numerous textbooks and articles, and utilized in business school curricula worldwide. They are recognized by many as the most comprehensive statement of responsible business practice ever formulated by business leaders for business leaders.

The Caux Round Table believes that the world business community should play an important role in improving economic and social conditions. Through an extensive and collaborative process in 1994, business leaders developed the CRT Principles for Business to embody the aspiration of principled business leadership. As a statement of aspirations, the principles aim to express a world standard against which business behavior can be measured. The CRT has sought to begin a process that identifies shared values, reconciles differing values, and thereby develops a shared perspective on business behavior acceptable to and honored by all.

These principles are rooted in two basic ethical ideals: *kyosei* and human dignity. As mentioned, the Japanese concept of *kyosei* means living and working together for the common good, enabling cooperation and mutual prosperity to coexist with healthy and fair competition. Human dignity refers to the sacredness or value of each person as an end, not simply as a means to the fulfillment of others' purposes.

An excerpt from the Caux Round Table Principles for Business follows. (The full document is available at *www.cauxroundtable.org*.)

Excerpt from the Caux Round Table Principles for Business

Principle 1.
The Responsibilities of Businesses Beyond Shareholders Toward Stakeholders

The value of a business to society is the wealth and employment it creates and the marketable products and services it provides to consumers at a reasonable price commensurate with quality. To create such value, a business must maintain its own economic health and viability, but survival is not a sufficient goal. Businesses have a role to play in improving the lives of all their customers, employees, and shareholders by sharing with them the wealth they have created. Suppliers and competitors as well should expect businesses to honor their obligations in a spirit of honesty and fairness. As responsible citizens of the local, national, regional and global communities in which they operate, businesses share a part in shaping the future of those communities.

Principle 2.
The Economic and Social Impact of Business Toward Innovation, Justice, and World Community

Businesses established in foreign countries to develop, produce, or sell should also contribute to the social advancement of those countries by creating productive employment and helping to raise the purchasing power of their citizens. Businesses also should contribute to human rights, education, welfare, and vitalization of the countries in which they operate.

Businesses should contribute to economic and social development not only in the countries in which they operate, but also in the world community at large, through effective and prudent use of resources, free and fair competition, and emphasis upon innovation in technology, production methods, marketing, and communications.

Principle 3.
Business Behavior
Beyond the Letter of Law Toward a Spirit of Trust

While accepting the legitimacy of trade secrets, businesses should recognize that sincerity, candor, truthfulness, the keeping of promises, and transparency contribute not only to their own credibility and stability but also to the smoothness and efficiency of business transactions, particularly on the international level.

Principle 4.
Respect for Rules

To avoid trade frictions and to promote freer trade, equal conditions for competition, and fair and equitable treatment for all participants, businesses should respect international and domestic rules. In addition, they should recognize that some behavior, although legal, may still have adverse consequences.

Principle 5.
Support for Multilateral Trade

Businesses should support the multilateral trade systems of the GATT/World Trade Organization and similar international agreements. They should cooperate in efforts to promote the progressive and judicious liberalization of trade and to relax those domestic measures that unreasonably hinder global commerce, while giving due respect to national policy objectives.

Principle 6.
Respect for the Environment

A business should protect and, where possible, improve the environment, promote sustainable development, and prevent the wasteful use of natural resources.

Principle 7.
Avoidance of Illicit Operations

A business should not participate in or condone bribery, money laundering, or other corrupt practices: Indeed, it should seek cooperation with others to eliminate them. It should not trade in arms or other materials used for terrorist activities, drug traffic or other organized crime.

In industry, Canon first announced its *kyosei* corporate philosophy in 1988. Its environmental initiatives include a global recycling program for ink cartridges and certification under their International Organization for Standardization (ISO) 14001 Certification Initiative. Canon's corporate Web site presents its position:[31]

> The world is undergoing a major transformation from a "throwaway" to a "recycling" society. Not satisfied with the progress made to date, Canon is making progressive efforts for the next generation, including the creation of a total cyclical system unifying the development, manufacturing and sales functions, while supplying products that are increasingly friendly to the environment. Canon will continue its quest to become a truly global corporation by fulfilling its environmental responsibilities.

"Canon is a company devoted to the environment and sustainability. As an organization, we are guided by the corporate philosophy of Kyosei—all people, regardless of race, religion, or culture, harmoniously living and working together into the future," said Joe Adachi, president and chief executive officer, Canon USA, Inc. "With this philosophy at our core and adhering to high-performance standards, such as the ISO standards, we are continuously improving our environmental assurance and performance in all business activities to have the least impact on our environment and burden for future generations."

Triple Bottom Line

Everyone has heard the complaint "We'd like to go eco but are afraid our customers won't buy it," or the flat-out "Green doesn't sell." That might have been true once, but it is not anymore.

Sociologist Paul Ray reported in his groundbreaking study of consumer attitudes, *The Cultural Creatives: How 50 Million People Are Changing the World,* that about a quarter of U.S. adults fit into a segment he tagged "cultural creatives." Their readiness to act on personal ethics as a purchase decision-making tool and their willingness to speak out about product impacts as well are becoming hot-button issues in today's boardrooms. Those practices are spilling into and influencing society in general, and forward-thinking businesses are keen to get ahead of the wave.

Cultural creatives consider themselves strongly aware of global warming, rain forest destruction, overpopulation, and exploitation of people in poorer countries. They want to see more positive

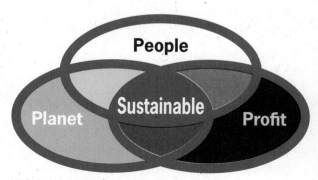

Visualizing the Triple Bottom Line.

action on these problems and are more than willing and able to buy and invest according to their values—sustainability values. It's these values, and the devastating effect a tarnished image has on brand equity, that is causing the greatest concern for brand owners. Businesses, take note: Consumer activism works—and not for your convenience.

In Europe, consumers responding to rate increases for trash removal staged a revolt. Rather than tote home packaging that would need to be disposed of on their dime, they repacked purchased items in reusable containers from home, leaving the original packages piled at the end of the checkout line for the store to deal with.

This quiet revolution was an example of attitude changes that led to the creation of producer responsibility laws there. But rather than simply rolling over and absorbing the new costs, or blindly pushing the problem down the distribution chain, firms started selling their waste to the expanding recycling industry as a valuable resource—turning a disposal liability into a profit center. In addition, companies paid more attention to reducing packaging and product needs overall, increasing per-unit profitability.

In the best of all worlds, according to general sustainability models, goods would be produced and consumed locally. In the real world, that's not how it works. We live in a global economy, and not all communities are able to produce all of the goods they need. But the fact that we're transporting goods outside the reach of our own laws doesn't mean that manufacturers can, or should want to, produce things and waste with reckless abandon. Even the most conservative study will show there are sound bottom-line arguments to be made for achieving

Everything we do makes a statement on how we feel about the environment on some level. What are your products saying about you?

profitability and positive image goals through basic sustainable business practices.

The Price Behind the Sticker

Beyond the general view of landfills bursting at the seams, ills related to print and packaging abound. Consider forests laid bare by clear-cutting to produce pieces that are used only once before being tossed in the bin. Marine animals, starved to death by plastic bags filling their bellies wash up on what were once pristine shores, their corpses rotting amid soda bottles and tampon applicators. Not all award-winning design is viewed in a gallery.

It's estimated that winning back an audience costs as much as five times more than it did to attract it in the first place. Even if the actual figure is a fraction of that, it makes good economic sense to take great care with the image being conveyed to audiences, past, present, and future.

Everything we purchase, produce, deliver, and sell makes a statement regarding how we feel about the environment and ultimately the consumers served on some level, What is your work saying about you?

In a September 1999 *Economist* article, the author notes:[32]

Companies with an eye on their "triple bottom line"—economic, environmental and social sustainability—outperformed their less fastidious peers on the stock market, according to a new index from Dow Jones and Sustainable Asset Management.

This triple bottom line is known by many names: TBL; 3BL; People, Planet, Profit (the 3Ps); and Ecology, Economy, Equity (the 3Es). All describe the idea of the major forces of our world that must be served to achieve sustainable balance, given our current market models. John Elkington has been attributed with coining the phrase "triple bottom line" in 1994, with an expansion in his 1998 book, *Cannibals with Forks: The Triple Bottom Line of 21st Century Business.*[33] The concept, as well as its companion, the triple top line (effects to a company's top-line financial performance because preventive measures require less capital investment and reduce the cost of capital), requires that a company's responsibility be to stakeholders (all people involved in or impacted by a venture) rather than shareholders (only those who profit from the venture). According to stakeholder theory, rather than the business of a business being to maximize shareholder (owner) profit, ventures should be looking to benefit all concerned—workers, management, shareholders, and the communities and firms on the supply chain. Triple-bottom-line ideas go much further than those that deal with purely environmental impacts.

After the 2007 ratification of the International Council for Local Environmental Initiatives (ICLEI), triple-bottom-line criteria for urban and community accounting became the dominant framework for public sector full-cost (true-cost) accounting. Then additional UN standards were developed to focus on natural capital and human capital needs to assist in assigning values for triple-bottom-line accounting and ecological footprint reporting.

"People + Planet + Profit" is one of the most common triple-bottom-line heuristics to describe the complex interactions of sustainability and business demands. It doesn't matter how eco a business is, if it's not profitable, it cannot sustain its efforts or its positive impacts in that market sector.

In the equation, *People (human capital)* refers to equitable and beneficial business practices: how a company treats its workers, the community, and the region in which it operates. A triple-bottom-line venture tries to benefit the many groups it interacts with and impacts, and works to not exploit or endanger them. The "people" section here would see "upstreaming" of a portion of profit from the marketing of finished goods back to the original producer of raw materials. Fair trade, too, is a core part of this section. A triple-bottom-line venture would never knowingly use child labor, would pay fair salaries to its workers, would maintain a safe work environment and tolerable working hours, and would not otherwise exploit a community or its labor force. Such a venture often participates in giving back to the community through healthcare and educational efforts. Quantifying the "people" portion of the triple bottom line is a relatively new effort, as it is extremely subjective. The Global Reporting Initiative (GRI) has developed guidelines to enable corporations and nongovernmental organizations to report on the social impact of a business.

Planet (natural capital) refers to a venture's environmental practices. A triple-bottom-line venture embraces the core concepts from the precautionary principle "Do no harm." "Natural capital" is a term closely identified with the Natural Capitalism economic model outlined by Paul Hawken, Amory Lovins, and Hunter Lovins in their 1999 book, *Natural Capitalism: Creating the Next Industrial Revolution* (*www.natcap.org*). A triple-bottom-line venture looks to minimize its ecological footprint by carefully managing its consumption of energy and materials inputs, reducing manufacturing waste, and ensuring that waste is not toxic before disposing of it not just in a legal manner but with an eye on long-term impacts. Ethical cradle-to-grave planning is the minimum framework for triple-bottom-line manufacturing businesses. Life cycle assessment of all components to determine true environmental impact and costs is key. This assessment includes looking at impacts from the growth or mining of raw materials, to manufacture, to distribution, to eventual disposal by the end user. Companies going one step further consider a Cradle to Cradle™ approach, looking at the same cradle-to-grave impacts but also considering remanufacture and material afterlife opportunities and impacts.

In today's materials-handling model, the cost of disposing of nondegradable or toxic products is borne by the communities the things finally end up in. In a triple-bottom-line scenario, any venture that produces and markets a product would be responsible for it all the way through to final disposal. As the full costs for impacts are borne by the company ultimately profiting by the venture, triple-bottom-line companies would avoid ecologically destructive practices (example: overfishing or unchecked use of nonrenewable resources). Paying close attention to environmental sustainability is more profitable for a business in the long run, as costs for clean-up or restitution would be paid in inflated dollars, with impact costs far exceeding profits from taking actions with only the short term in sight. Arguments that it costs more to be environmentally sound are usually disproved when time, depth, breadth, and ripple-through of impacts are permitted to be fully accounted for. The first question one must always ask when countering the cost questions is: Is the long-term health of the company what's important, or just the next quarter? Reporting metrics for sustainability are becoming more standardized internationally and are more tangible than metrics for social impacts. Respected reporting institutes and registries include the Global Reporting Initiative (GRI) (*www.globalreporting.org*), Ceres (*www.ceres.org*), Institute 4 Sustainability (*www.4sustainability.org*), and others.

Profit (*monetary capital*) is the goal shared by all businesses, regardless of their ethics. Within a sustainability framework, the idea of profit needs to be seen as the economic benefit enjoyed by all stakeholders, not just the company's stockholders. It's the idea that only a healthy company, earning ethically derived profits, is truly a contributing member of the community and society at large. A company operating at a loss or burdened with huge liabilities even if its base operations make money not only earns no income for its owners but has no resources to help support anything else (tax dollars, corporate giving, wages, etc.). The company is, in essence, a drain on resources, both economic and environmental. *Which side of the bottom line are you standing on?*

Blended Value Proposition

In addition to the triple bottom line and triple top line, readers should be aware of the blended value proposition (BVP). In an article introducing BVP, Joel

Makower, contributing editor for GreenBiz.com, and author of the book *Strategies for the Green Economy*, notes:[34]

> Before you glaze over about yet another sustainability-minded catchphrase, consider that this brave new term is being bandied about in the nation's top business schools—or, at least, those with sustainability programs. It's been a featured topic in mainstream business and investing publications, and has been uttered by the venerable John Elkington, who coined "triple bottom line" in the first place.

> The BVP concept is embedded in the growing world of social enterprise and social entrepreneurs—the moniker given to nonprofit businesses that David Bornstein, author of *How to Change the World*, describes as entrepreneurs with the "determination, savvy, and ethical fiber to advance an idea for social change in society on a large scale." The notion of social enterprise, which has gained traction in the U.K., also is being seen by China's government as a means of meeting the needs of its communities and providing training, employment, education, and other benefits to its citizens.

The idea of the BVP is a different from triple-bottom- or top-line approaches. Here, instead of measuring a discrete economic, environmental, and social accounting lines on a company's balance sheet, Jed Emerson, the father of BVP, began to consider a single "blended" figure. He says, "We've lost sight of the reason we create companies and make investments: to make our lives better—the manifestation of the human drive toward value."[35]

Emerson, originally a social worker, was interested in why some nonprofits were far more effective than others. It was through his investigation into this topic work that he developed the methodologies for SROI (social return on investment). Being able to quantify SROI became the key that foundations were looking for to aid in investing their endowments, enabling them to better identify companies that did not undermine the very social problems the foundations were trying to solve. After BVP proved itself as an investment tool, it became a way of assessing corporate value in general.

In his article, Makower goes on to say:

> Unlike socially responsible investing, which is laden with "good" and "bad" companies, BVP does not strive to be so virtuous. It acknowledges, for example, that there's value in creating economic wealth, so long as it is balanced with creating other forms of value. That idea alone could blunt the skeptics.

> BVP has a long and arduous path ahead, but don't count it out quite yet. Those frustrated with the slow growth of "triple bottom line" thinking in the corporate world would be wise to tune in to the BVP conversation taking shape. It's bound to be instructive—no matter where it all ends up.

Transparency and Honesty

Companies at the forefront of sustainability today have a history of commitment to their message. They continuously address their impacts as part of their operating strategy. The idea that it's cheaper to nip problems in the bud as opportunities and technologies arise rather than deal with huge calamities later is a key element in making long-term sustainability sustainable.

For those new to sustainability, the simple plan of action should be to use the opportunity for creating trust (and foster brand loyalty) by actually being trustworthy. Although no one can address all issues overnight, everyone can make a genuine pledge to do what they can now while they continue to address the rest as technology and economics allow, and as opportunity arises.

Ceres

Pledging to do what they can now and taking verifiable steps to show progress toward a more sustainable future are the member companies of Ceres. Ceres (pronounced "series") is a network of investors, environmental organizations, and public interest groups working to address sustainability challenges.[36]

Mission: Integrating sustainability into capital markets for the health of the planet and its people.

In 1989, Ceres introduced a bold vision, where business and capital markets promoted the well-being of society as well as the protection of the earth's systems and resources. Ceres brought together investors, environmental groups, and other stakeholders to encourage companies and markets to incorporate environmental and social challenges into everyday business. By leveraging the collective power of investors and other key stakeholders, Ceres has achieved dramatic results over the years.

Ceres launched the Global Reporting Initiative, now the de facto international standard used by over 1,200 companies for corporate reporting on environmental, social, and economic performance.

Ceres member Nike became the first global apparel firm to disclose the names and locations of its contract factories worldwide in 2005. Ceres member Dell Computer agreed in 2006 to support national legislation to require electronic product recycling and "take-back" programs, and Ceres member Bank of America announced a $20 billion initiative in 2007 to support the growth of environmentally sustainable business activity to address global climate change.

Over the years, Ceres has brought together Wall Street and corporate leaders along with the United Nations to address growing financial risks and opportunities posed by climate change. These groundbreaking meetings have produced plans seeking stronger analysis, disclosure, and action from companies, investors, and regulators on climate change.

Ceres publishes cutting-edge research reports to help investors better understand the implications of global warming. Among the reports are *2008 Investor Summit on Climate Risk Final Report*; *Managing the Risks and Opportunities of Climate Change: A Practical Toolkit for Investors*; *Mutual Funds and Climate Change: Opposition to Climate Change Begins to Thaw*; *Investor Progress on Climate*

Risks; and *Opportunities, Corporate Governance and Climate Change: The Banking Sector.*

Ceres Principles

In the fall of 1989, Ceres announced the creation of the Ceres Principles, a 10-point code of corporate environmental conduct to be publicly endorsed by companies as an environmental mission statement. Embedded in the code was the mandate to report periodically on environmental management structures and results. In 1993, following lengthy negotiations, Sunoco became the first Fortune 500 company to endorse the Ceres Principles. As sustainability ideas matured and gathered more support, numerous other firms have adopted their own equivalent environmental principles.

By adopting the Ceres Principles or similar code, companies not only formalize their dedication to environmental awareness and accountability but also actively commit to an ongoing process of improvement, dialogue, and comprehensive public reporting. Jeffrey Swartz, president and chief executive officer (CEO) of The Timberland Company, a Ceres member firm, explains in its 2006 Corporate Social Responsibility (CSR) Report:

> Publishing a statement of accountability is necessary, but not sufficient. If we write a report and fail to initiate a conversation, we have missed an opportunity. And if our report represents our only venue for engagement, then we have failed. An engaged community—a convening of stakeholders committed to environmental stewardship, community strength, global human dignity, and the quality of life for our workers and those citizens with whom we are privileged to serve—is my intent. Our process of reporting is not "us" to "you." This report is a forum for you. React, respond, challenge, commit. I commit back to you that we will listen and act.

Overview of Ceres Principles

Protection of the Biosphere

We will reduce and make continual progress toward eliminating the release of any substance that may cause environmental damage to the air, water, or the earth or its inhabitants. We will safeguard all habitats affected by our operations and will protect open spaces and wilderness, while preserving biodiversity.

Sustainable Use of Natural Resources

We will make sustainable use of renewable natural resources, such as water, soils, and forests. We will conserve nonrenewable natural resources through efficient use and careful planning.

Reduction and Disposal of Wastes

We will reduce and where possible eliminate waste through source reduction and recycling. All waste will be handled and disposed of through safe and responsible methods.

Energy Conservation

We will conserve energy and improve the energy efficiency of our internal operations and of the goods and services we sell. We will make every effort to use environmentally safe and sustainable energy sources.

Risk Reduction

We will strive to minimize the environmental, health and safety risks to our employees and the communities in which we operate through safe technologies, facilities, and operating procedures, and by being prepared for emergencies.

Safe Products and Services

We will reduce and where possible eliminate the use, manufacture, or sale of products and services that cause environmental damage or health or safety hazards. We will inform our customers of the environmental impacts of our products or services and try to correct unsafe use.

Environmental Restoration

We will promptly and responsibly correct conditions we have caused that endanger health, safety or the environment. To the extent feasible, we will redress injuries we have caused to persons or damage we have caused to the environment and will restore the environment.

Informing the Public

We will inform in a timely manner everyone who may be affected by conditions caused by our company that might endanger health, safety, or the environment. We will regularly seek advice and counsel through dialogue with persons in communities near our facilities. We will not take any action against employees for reporting dangerous incidents or conditions to management or to appropriate authorities.

Management Commitment

We will implement these Principles and sustain a process that ensures that the Board of Directors and Chief Executive Officer are fully informed about pertinent environmental issues and are fully responsible for environmental policy. In selecting our Board of Directors, we will consider demonstrated environmental commitment as a factor.

Audits and Reports

We will conduct an annual self-evaluation of our progress in implementing these Principles. We will support the timely creation of generally accepted environmental audit procedures. We will annually complete the Ceres Report, which will be made available to the public.

For the full content of the Ceres Principles, go to: *www.ceres.org.*

Designers Accord

One of the ways designers can make a huge step toward a more open and sustainable society is by taking ownership of their responsibilities. Most impacts happen not beginning in manufacture but on the drawing board, where the ideas that get produced were put into motion in the first place. Enter the Designers Accord.

The Designers Accord is not an industry representative body or a third-party certification standard. As noted in an October 2008 *Fast Company* article, it is "an agreement to reroute design, manufacturing, and even the economy toward a livable ecological

future." The article quotes founder Valerie Casey, "Our goal isn't to create a thing. It's to re-create our mind-set."[37]

Made up of over 100,000 members of the creative community, the Designers Accord is a global coalition of designers, educators, researchers, engineers, and corporate leaders who pledge to reduce their organizations' carbon footprints, raise social and environmental impact with every client and every product, and collaborate with one another. The last item, to collaborate, is a concept that may be totally new to some designers outside the sustainability community. At one time, protecting "secrets" was considered the only way to gain advantage; today, transparency and openness are becoming the new benchmarks by which investors and potential clients judge a well-run business. Additionally, as people search for answers, companies willing to share their knowledge are finding new clients looking for project partners rather than just service vendors.

The Designers Accord Web site (*www.designersaccord.org*) notes:

> Adopting the Designers Accord provides access to a community of peers that shares methodologies, resources, and experiences around environmental and social issues in design. . . . The vision of The Designers Accord is to integrate the principles of sustainable design into all practice and production. Our mission is to catalyze innovation throughout the creative community by collectively building our intelligence around sustainability.

Endorsed by AIGA (American Institute of Graphic Arts), Cumulus, the IDSA (Industrial Designers Society of America), and the o2 International Network for Sustainable Design, the Designers Accord asks participants to "invert the traditional model of competition, and encourages sharing best practices so all can innovate more efficiently."

The accord asks all adopters, supporters, and endorsers to follow a basic code of conduct:

> Do no harm; Communicate and collaborate; Keep learning, keep teaching; Instigate meaningful change; Make theory action.

A company without eco-ethics itself cannot produce a truly eco-product. As companies look for ways of initiating change, the guidelines of the Designers Accord provide a simple framework. Firms may already be following many of the framework's requirements, such as educating their teams (provide education allowances) and sharing information with clients (create value added). Other requirements are a bit more work, but when firms get a handle on their carbon footprint, for example, they can look deeper at other expenses, such as energy use, materials, travel, and work flows (person hours)—all cash outflows that impact their bottom line.

In a typical 12-step program, they say that the first step is admitting you have a problem. As firms find ways to negotiate change, the first step is to embrace change and be an active part of it. The Designers Accord is a great first step.

Promotional Product Solutions (PPS) was one of the promotional-product industry's early providers of socially responsible promotion options. In 2008, it joined Ceres to improve disclosure and help advance the company's environmental and social responsibility goals. PPS is one of more than 70 companies in the Ceres company network, which includes nearly 30 Fortune 500 corporations.

Sustainability Means Business

In addition to statistics tracking performance showing superior performance by Dow Jones and Sustainable Asset Management, in October 2007, Innovest Strategic Value Advisors released the Carbon Beta and Equity Performance study. The study evaluates the relationship among climate change, companies' ability to manage the associated risks and opportunities, and their financial performance. Innovest notes this is the first study to take this approach, and it lays the foundation for further research and investment products. According to this review of 1,500 companies, there is a strong, positive, and growing correlation between industrial companies' sustainability in general and climate change in particular, and their competitiveness and financial performance.[38]

Historically, though many have understood the need for embracing larger sustainability issues, tangible action has been slow. Innovest suggests there have been a number of reasons for this, some of which include:

> Investment professionals have long believed that company resources devoted to environmental issues are either wasteful or actually injurious to their competitive and financial performance and therefore to both the performance of the companies themselves and investor returns.

> Until recently, there has been a dearth of robust, credible research evidence and analytical tools linking companies' environmental performance directly with their financial performance.

Innovest points out that since there is now growing and incontrovertible evidence that superior overall environmental performance can in fact improve profitability as well as reduce risk levels, there is little doubt that there is now sufficient motivation to get companies to address their impacts as part of their long-term strategic plans.

As background for the study, Innovest states:

> Few environmental issues pose as real, significant, and widespread a financial threat to investors as climate change. International policy responses aimed at cutting greenhouse gas emissions, together with the direct physical impacts of climate change will require investors and money managers to take a much closer look at how their portfolios might be affected by company "carbon" risks and opportunities.

In their report, Innovest asks investors and other fiduciaries to assess their portfolios for carbon risk for a variety of reasons.

> There is increasing evidence showing that superior performance in managing climate risk is a useful proxy for superior, more strategic corporate management, and therefore for superior financial performance and shareholder value creation.

> In the longer term, the outperformance potential will become even greater as the capital markets become more fully sensitized to the financial and competitive consequences of environmental and climate change considerations.

These ideas have already started to work into the decision-making process of those in industry. The Walmart scorecard that has set new benchmarks for packaging is only one criteria set in one part of its operation. Today, as more and more verifiable data and tools to handle them become available, we're seeing a variety of new initiatives, from carbon footprint metrics to verified resource and supply chain integrity. All are being implemented to help companies better—and more quickly—identify partners willing and able to help them reach their own sustainability goals.

"How companies perform on environmental, social, and strategic governance issues is having a rapidly growing impact on their competitiveness, profitability, and share price performance," said Dr. Matthew Kiernan, founder and CEO of Innovest, in a February 2, 2005, article from SRI World Group.[39] In the bigger picture, one of the attractive things about adopting sustainability practices as part of a company's larger strategic plan is risk management. It is no surprise, then, that some of the first companies to invest serious time and effort in understanding and using sustainability criteria for long-term business strategies were insurance companies and insurance underwriters. As sustainability practices mature and develop, providing tangible historical data to reflect on, this question is bound to come up: Were the companies that resisted change the ones that could only operate with the help of hidden subsidies funded by the well-being of future generations? Companies should now be asking themselves: How much more, in inflated future dollars, will it cost us to change if we wait?

Design and Sustainability

In December 2007, *Packaging Digest* and the Sustainable Packaging Coalition (SPC) released the results of a joint survey looking at the state of sustainability and packaging and to use as a benchmark of current attitudes and practices. The survey showed that "sustainability is a hot button for the industry, and its impact is likely to grow in the coming years."[40] Though this survey came out of the packaging industry, packaging is not an isolated component of commerce. Concerns or regulation changes that apply to packaging will, or already are, impacting product and print producers.

The *Packaging Digest*/SPC survey was drawn from the SPC membership as well as subscribers to *Packaging Digest* and *Converting* magazines. The respondents represented a cross-section of today's packaging industry, with the biggest share coming from CPGs, followed by materials manufacturers, converters, machinery manufacturers, packaging services, and retailers.

Looking at the survey data, 73 percent reported that their companies have increased emphasis on packaging sustainability over the year leading up to the survey. This is no surprise, given the timing of policy changes by the world's biggest retailer, Walmart, to focus on sustainability in general and packaging in particular in this time frame and the full adoption of the EU Directive on Packaging and Packaging Waste. The data also indicate that while awareness surges, packaging businesses (and print efforts in general) have been slow to incorporate sustainable business practices, particularly in the United States, where sustainability directives are not as deeply and federally mandated as they are in other countries.

In their article announcing the survey, editorial director John Kalkowski comments on the difficult position packaging firms find themselves in:

> Pressure is mounting on the industry to act now . . . sustainability is reaching new levels of awareness across the industry, especially among companies with more than 1,000 employees and those with formal, written sustainability policies,

where 46 percent of respondents rated themselves as "very familiar." Still, only 21 percent of all respondents claimed they were very familiar with the issues of sustainability in packaging. Nearly 40 percent said they were "somewhat familiar," while 10 percent said they were not familiar at all.

Change in general seems to be a big issue, with about a third of the *Packaging Digest*/SPC survey respondents expressing concerns about the rise in current raw materials prices as well as how to implement sustainability practices using their existing infrastructure. Moving to sustainability sparks concerns similar to those triggered by change due to purely economic factors. In capital- and process-intensive industries, these concerns are understandable. But resistance to change due to fear should not be considered a viable option. As *The Economist* article discussing implementing sustainability practices and the prisoner's dilemma points out, the world will be condemned to a slow roasting, even though global impacts could be averted if everyone simply cooperated and took on a share of the load in the first place.[41]

In his talk at the 2006 Sustainable Packaging Forum, Tyler Elm, then sustainability director for Walmart, noted that the move toward a more sustainable business model for the company was initiated as a defensive strategy—to reduce operations costs, liabilities, and exposure. Walmart is, after all, a very large target. But as management dug deeper into what sustainable business practice really meant, they discovered instead of a defensive tool, it was a powerful offensive strategy. Risk and exposure were reduced or eliminated as they dealt with issues before they became problems or additional costs. And systems or operations that were costs under

the old way of doing things were now generating income.

Walmart's online Environmental Overview states:

> Ecologically responsible business practices result in significant gains for our customers, associates, and shareholders. For example, by inventing trucks that get twice the mileage of our current vehicles, we will radically reduce emissions and fossil fuel, but we'll also save millions of dollars at the pump.[42]

Here we can see that rather than simply demanding the lowest cost at any price strictly from the goods it sells, Walmart is looking to leverage a variety of opportunities within its own organization to maintain the price structure customers expect while still serving the need to maintain a viable profit structure.

In a February 7, 2008, Reuters article, "Walmart to Pay More for 'Greener' Goods," author Nichola Groom details Walmart's policy changes. To incorporate sustainability in both operations and product offerings, and to meet aggressive impact reduction and efficiency goals, Walmart is openly saying it is willing to pay more, if need be, for products that last longer, hurt the environment less, and better address stakeholder issues not reflected in previous pricing structures. According to the article, Walmart management feels that adding sustainability to the mix does not absolutely need to result in automatic increases in end retail prices. It quotes Walmart's senior vice president of sustainability, Matt Kistler:

> Bad quality products create waste, and so having tighter standards on the social side, on the environmental side, and on the quality side will

reduce waste. . . . We are looking at a very small amount of dollars, and the savings in the supply chain that we are finding because of sustainability in some cases will more than offset the incremental costs of what we are paying for a better quality item.

In 2004, Walmart launched a company-wide, long-term initiative "to unlock" its "potential." Leaders from nearly every part of Walmart formed entrepreneurial teams focusing on areas such as packaging, real estate, energy, raw materials, and electronics waste. These teams partnered with environmental consultants, nonprofit organizations, and other groups to help examine Walmart's business practices "through the lens of restoration and sustainability."

Kistler goes on to reflect:

What we are learning about our footprint on the environment is both shocking and inspiring. Despite our excellence in efficiency, commerce creates a lot of waste. Fortunately, we've identified plenty of opportunities that, if captured, can transform our entire industry. Because we're experimenting in many areas, we expect to make mistakes along the way.

Walmart has established three aggressive goals for its sustainability efforts:

1. To be supplied 100 percent by renewable energy
2. To create zero waste
3. To sell products that sustain our resources and environment

In the service of its sustainability efforts, Walmart acknowledges:

What gets measured gets managed. Our teams are developing sets of common sense metrics that hold us accountable for the goals we're setting. We will share these metrics on this Web site once they are established.

It would be fairly easy to dismiss sustainability efforts as only the turf of Walmart-size giants. In any discussion, such companies are the elephant in the room that simply cannot be ignored—plus a little action on their part has huge ripple-through impacts. But consumer advocacy groups are happy to point out that cost and environmental impact savings are accessible to the individual as well as the corporate giant. And it is in fact the actions and ethics of the individual that help drive corporate-level change.

After all, corporations are simply collections of individuals acting as a group. The journey begins with us asking ourselves "How will history judge us?" Once we understand what drives individual choices, we can use that knowledge to empower individuals to make good decisions. With all eyes turning to industry professionals for answers, we have the opportunity to completely remake everything we do—but get it right this time.

Footprint of Print and Digital Media Supply Chains

Don Carli
The Institute for Sustainable Communication

Print has profoundly changed the world since the days of Johannes Gutenberg, but now due to the prodigious volumes of energy and materials consumed and mountains of waste produced, the printing industry is challenged to profoundly change itself. Current patterns of print and digital media production and consumption are unsustainable and must be reconfigured if we are to enjoy the essential services and benefits they provide to business, government and society.

Most of us think about the flows of energy and materials associated with print and digital media the way fish think about water; it just "is." This is despite the fact that large organizations typically spend between 5 and 35 percent of every dollar spent (exclusive of labor) on paper and printing. To put the amount of energy involved in context, according to the Energy Information Administration (EIA), the U.S. papermaking industry used 75 billion kilowatt hours of energy in 2006—second only to the petroleum industry.[43]

It is unlikely that print can or will be fully replaced by digital media, as many resource-reduction proponents seem to think. Packaging is still a major use of print that cannot be replaced, and digital media, though not tangible, consumes prodigious amounts of electricity. In 2006, the EIA reports that data centers and servers in the United States used over 60 billion kilowatt hours of electricity.

Print as we know it must be reinvented so that it can be used to package knowledge and goods for human consumption in ways that also address the challenges of sustainability, energy security, and climate change. The reinvention of print and digital media will require a new "greening."

In order for it to succeed, this new greening of print cannot be based on the "Greening 1.0" moral-ethical imperatives urged by environmentalists or on purely emotional appeals. The "Greening 2.0" of print and digital media must be based on a conceptual framework called "sustainability" that is being used to redefine the way business is done by Fortune 1000 companies—one that balances economics, the ecology, and social equity using emotional appeals grounded in a triple-bottom-line business case.

Sustainability, energy security, and climate change are challenging issues that compel every business, every government, and every individual to rethink the ways in which energy is used and waste is managed. This section will raise more questions than it answers, but that is primarily because the printing industry has not yet responded to many of the urgent questions that exist.

Sustainability, energy security, and climate change are also becoming mainstream corporate governance priorities among the largest corporations in the world. Supply chain sustainability is now the focus of a growing number of companies that are also dependent on print for the packaging, promotion and advertising of their products. In response to initiatives from organizations such as the Carbon Disclosure Project, The Carbon Trust and the Climate Group, corporate and publishing giants like Walmart, Procter & Gamble, Time Incorporated and NewsCorp are beginning to press their supply chains to reduce their carbon footprints and reconfigure their products and services to measure, manage, report, verify and continuously improve their triple-bottom-line performance.

In response, printers and their suppliers will need to rethink what they say about being "green." Because papermaking and other print-related processes are among the largest industrial uses of energy in the world, print supply chains will need to reconfigure the flows of energy, materials, and waste associated

Corporate and publishing giants are beginning to press their supply chains to reduce their carbon footprints and reconfigure their products and services to measure, manage, report, verify, and continuously improve their triple-bottom-line performance.

with printing if they want to win the business of such Fortune 1000 clients.

Addressing the new green priorities of business will require that printing companies and their suppliers look beyond cost, productivity, and print quality. They will also have to reach beyond superficial measures undertaken to green up the image of a company in a hurry. Companies that fail to understand and address issues of climate change, energy security, and sustainability in measurable and material ways are more than likely to be shunned.

A key question is whether investor, consumer and print buyer priorities will demand the greening of print supply chains in ways that exceed the ability of the graphic arts industry to respond in a timely and effective manner. To a great extent, the answer to this question will depend on printers receiving clear and unambiguous market signals from print buyers that sustainability, energy security, and climate change are priorities in their vendor selection criteria and purchasing decisions. An

example of such a signal is aligning the reward and recognition buyers and suppliers with innovation and the achievement of triple-bottom-line benefits. It will also depend on graphic arts firms sending clear signals to their suppliers that they require more and better standards-based information about the environmental aspects and impacts associated with the goods and services that they buy. An example would be requiring ISO 14040-based life-cycle analysis of all input raw materials to the printing process.

For most printers, being green used to mean complying with the law and "doing the right thing" for the planet, whether it was good for business or not. However, the new meaning of green is as much about doing the right things for business as it is about doing the right things for the planet. The greatest challenge that the printing industry faces is shaking off outmoded ways of thinking about environmental or green issues and developing new ways to identify, analyze, and act on information relevant to sustainability and climate change.

According to Professor Kenneth Macro Jr. of Cal-Poly's Graphic Communication program:[44]

> It seems that many if not most of the printers that I talk to are unfamiliar with the concept of sustainability, and they seem to hope that this preoccupation with climate change and things green will blow over. This is no time to be thinking like an ostrich. Instead of putting our heads in the sand we need to be putting our heads together to take action and ensure that our industry is sustainable and that print is seen as a responsible medium.

While historically, being green referred to environmental regulatory compliance, the new green is about beyond compliance sustainability that seeks to continually improve the environmental, social, and economic performance of a business, product, or service. Green products historically have been expected to cost more and to have lackluster performance, but the promise of the new green was perhaps best described by Walmart CEO Lee Scott. At a meeting of the Walmart Sustainable Value Networks in March 2007, Scott said: "A working family shouldn't have to choose between a product that they can afford and a sustainable product."[45] The new green being championed by companies like Walmart, GE, Timberland, Bank of America, Unilever, Starbucks, and others creates and delivers value for money and is designed to do a better job of satisfying the primary needs sought. Greener printing must do the same.

The new meaning of green is as much about doing the right things for business as it is about doing the right things for the planet.

The new wave of green sweeping over business is the crescendo of a movement that has been under way for over a decade, and there is little evidence that it will subside. According to John Grant, author of the "Green Marketing Manifesto," the new interest in green is not likely to fade because it is so strongly linked to a climate change agenda that is scientific.[46] Grant maintains that on top of climate change, there is a related set of issues:

[W]ater shortages (not just from low rainfall, but because we have seriously depleted the underground aquifers), seas holding only 10 percent of the edible fish stocks they did 100 years ago, soil erosion, storms, spreading diseases. Add war, economic turmoil, food shortages, water shortages and social disintegration and you can see why some call the impending (climate) crisis a global Somalia.

According to Michael Longhurst, member of the UN Environmental Program advertising advisory committee and senior vice president of business development at McCann-Erickson:

Sustainability is not "green marketing." It is not energy saving. It is not a social program. It is all of these things and more. Sustainability is a collective term for everything to do with responsibility for the world in which we live. It is an economic, social and environmental issue. It is about consuming differently and consuming efficiently. It also means sharing between the rich and poor, and protecting the global environment, while not jeopardising the needs of future generations.

The goal of sustainable consumption was adopted at the Rio Earth Summit in 1992, and in Johannesburg in 2002 the world will meet to assess what has been achieved. Sustainability is an issue for governments, for industry, for companies and ultimately for consumers.[47]

There has been a sea change in the degree to which sustainability, climate change, energy security, and corporate social responsibility are on the lips and on the minds of consumers, Fortune 500 CEOs, institutional investors, judges, and politicians. Three-time Pulitzer Prize–winning *New York Times* columnist and author Tom Friedman recently described conservation and energy efficiency as a national security imperative and rebuffed criticisms that environmentalism is a concern of the "girlie man," calling it "the most tough-minded, geo-strategic, pro-growth and patriotic thing we can do."[48]

Proactively addressing the challenges of climate change and sustainability will position companies to meet the growing demand for greener products and sustainable supply chain partners. Failure to identify and reduce the greenhouse gas, energy, and resource footprint of business operations and supply chain may put businesses at risk.

Sustainability is not "green marketing." It is not energy saving. It is not a social program. It is all of these things and more.

Michael Longhurst
Senior vice president of business
development at McCann-Erickson

The sustainability of print will depend on how printing companies and their suppliers respond to these questions:

— Can your company quantify and communicate how the print-related products and services that it offers are economically, environmentally, and socially preferable to nonprint alternatives?

— Is your company prepared to provide buyers with a life cycle greenhouse gas inventory or footprint analysis of your operations and of the goods and services that you sell to them?

— Is your company prepared for significant spikes in the price of energy or of materials that depend on the affordable and available petro-chemicals and fossil fuels?

— Is your company prepared to address the likelihood of state and or federal legislation to cap and trade greenhouse gas emissions?

— Is your company prepared to take advantage of a Green Employment Tax Swap (GETS) in which a tax on carbon dioxide is used to rebate federal payroll taxes?

— Is your company prepared to pay a premium on insurance and/or loans for failing to implement a comprehensive ISO 9000/14001/26000 quality/environmental/social responsibility management system?

— Is your company prepared to tell a prospective high-potential employee about how your company's dedication to sustainable business practices will improve his or her quality of life and career opportunities?

To address these questions, it is important to understand some of the powerful forces that have been at play in recent years. Among the major factors redefining what it means to be green are profound shifts taking place in the attitudes and behaviors of investors, consumers, and business leaders with regard to sustainability in general as well as energy security and climate change in particular.

Major corporations are reexamining the standards of conduct and measures of performance that determine how they do business. Demand and action frameworks for sustainable supply chain management and procurement are arising from individual companies, such as Walmart, and from industry groups, such as the Sustainable Packaging Coalition, the Sustainable Advertising Partnership, and the Sustainable Green Printing Partnership and from organizations such as the Institute for Supply Management and the Supply Chain Council. As a result, the world's largest corporations are scrutinizing the corporate social responsibility performance of their operational practices and supply chain business practices—including what they print, how they print and how print-related products and services are valued.

> **The world's largest corporations are scrutinizing the corporate social responsibility performance of their operational practices and supply chain business practices—including what they print, how they print and how print-related products and services are valued.**

For many companies in sectors such as pharmaceuticals and automobiles, the greening of their supply chain practices began a decade ago with a focus on their tier-one suppliers. Despite the fact that printing can represent 20 percent or more of every dollar spent by most corporations, it is not typically considered a tier-one supply chain function. As a result, printing has come under scrutiny only recently, now that the lean-and-green sustainability initiatives directed at tier-one supply chain purchases are beginning to yield diminishing returns. While there is heightened interest in familiar topics such as the use of postconsumer recycled content, two new topics are the carbon footprint associated with printing and print-related logistics as well as fiber source's chain of custody associated with paper.

While debates about the relative merits of various forest certifications, such as the third-party certifier Forest Stewardship Council, the forest industry's own Sustainable Forestry Initiative, and the chain-of-custody group Forest and Chain-of-Custody Certification have been making headlines in the trade press of late, climate change, energy security, corporate social responsibility, and carbon disclosure are the issues of greatest significance in the business press. Business leaders from major companies are feeling growing pressure from investors, markets, and regulators to address the challenges of sustainability and the impacts of climate change. For example, the Carbon Disclosure Project[49] has called on over 2,500 of the world's largest companies to voluntarily report on the greenhouse gasses emitted by their operational and supply chain activities.

Some may see voluntary reporting of greenhouse gas emissions as a burden or a risk. Yet others see the process of conducting greenhouse gas inventories and transforming business processes to reduce their carbon intensity as providing them with critical expertise and experience for what is likely to be a dramatically different regulatory environment in the next three to five years. The majority of

Fortune 500 companies publish voluntary corporate social responsibility reports in accordance with the guidelines established by the Global Reporting Initiative.[50] Few printing companies do so.

Starting in 2007, and continuing in 2009, the United States Congress is considering several bills that would establish caps on greenhouse gas emissions and then allow businesses to trade credits in order to stay below those limits. In addition, the governors of five western states recently agreed that they would coordinate efforts to set caps for greenhouse gas emissions from their region and create a market-based, carbon-trading program.[51]

In March 2007, a group of 50 major U.S. investors with over $4 trillion under management asked the U.S. Congress to enact tough federal legislation to curb carbon emissions and dramatically change national energy policies. They called for the United States to "achieve sizable, sensible long-term reductions of greenhouse gas emissions" and recommended three policy initiatives:

1. Realignment of energy policy to foster the development of clean technologies

2. Directions from the Securities & Exchange Commission specifying what companies should disclose to investors on climate change in their financial reporting

3. A mandatory market-based solution to regulating greenhouse gas emissions, such as what has come to be known as cap-and-trade.[52]

In addition to investor pressure for greenhouse gas reporting, consumer attitudes toward climate change and the environment have also changed. A nationwide poll conducted by Knowledge Networks[53] asked American consumers how much they have heard about "the problem of global warming or climate change due to the buildup of greenhouse gases." In response, 72 percent said a great deal or some (22 and 50 percent, respectively), up from 63 percent a year earlier, when 15 percent said a great deal and 48 percent some. Those who said "not very much" or "not at all" dropped from 38 percent to 28 percent. Of the respondents, 75 percent embrace the idea that global warming is a problem that requires action. Perhaps most interesting, when asked to "suppose there were a survey of scientists that found that an overwhelming majority have concluded that global warming is occurring and poses a significant threat," the percentage saying that they would favor taking high-cost steps increased sharply, from 34 percent to 56 percent.

As evidence of this change, there are an estimated 63 million adults in North America who are currently considered "LOHAS" consumers.[54] LOHAS stands for *l*ifestyles of *h*ealth *a*nd *s*ustainability and describes a $226.8 billion U.S. marketplace for goods and services focused on health, the environment, social justice, personal development, and sustainable living. One of the factors that caused Walmart to see sustainability as a game-changing business growth strategy was the overwhelming and unexpected response of consumers to an organic cotton yoga outfit.[55] The other was the inspiring response of Walmart employees to Hurricane Katrina.

As businesses wrestle with these issues, they are finding that climate change, energy security, and the intensifying focus on sustainable business practices can have a significant impact on how they do business; on whom they buy their equipment, energy, and materials from; on their ability to attract and retain talented and motivated employees; on which markets they have permission to operate in;

and on which customers they are valued by. As the world reaches consensus on understanding climate change and the importance of striving for sustainability in the supply chains of business, companies are increasingly looking at how to manage sustainability's triple bottom lines,[56] navigate a carbon-neutral[57] path, and position themselves for success is an increasingly complex and carbon-constrained world.

Addressing the issues at the nexus of commercial opportunity and sustainability presents the graphic communication industry with new opportunities.

For a myriad of reasons, a growing number of large corporations, publishers, and government agencies are under pressure to manage the sustainability and climate change impacts of the supply chain practices. As a result, major corporations are rewriting their vendor qualification scorecards, putting new environmental management and greenhouse gas emissions information requests in their requests for information and new sustainability reporting and verification provisions in their requests for proposals.

Increasingly, printing companies can expect to be asked:

— How do you measure, manage, and report on your company's environmental performance and its carbon footprint?

— Does your company have a dedicated director of sustainability and a published sustainability policy as well as a formal environmental management system that tracks energy and materials use, greenhouse gas emissions, and waste?

— How much time does your senior management spend guiding your company's sustainability policy and its sustainability performance strategy?

— How is your senior management recognized and rewarded for achieving your company's sustainability performance objectives?

— Does your company document the environmental life cycle impacts, energy use, and greenhouse gas emissions associated with the products and services that you manufacture and purchase?

— What is your company doing to develop continuous improvement strategies addressing climate change and sustainability in its supply chain practices?

Since 1987, the Social Value Network has been a forward advocate of the triple-bottom-line ideals. Approaching their twentieth anniversary, the organization wanted to further raise awareness of their work as well as boost membership to meet new market opportunities. SVN's creative team, design firm BBMG, interviewed 20 pioneering business leaders to see how they turned their values into action and what it would take to transform business in the twenty-first century, creating the commemorative booklet "20 Ideas that Changed the Way the World Does Business." In addition, BBMG's overhaul of SVN's visual presence, coupled with key marketing efforts, resulted in annual membership levels increasing, and sold-out conferences. The pieces shown here were printed by an FSC-certified printer using renewable energy, contain FSC-certified 50% PCW paper, and are printed with vegetable-based inks.

20

ideas *that changed*
the way the world
does business

world changing ideas
innovation in action

SOCIAL VENTURE NETWORK

Social Venture Network Fall 2007 Conference
October 11 - 14 La Jolla, California

SOCIAL VENTURE NETWORK

Get involved

Join the leading network of socially responsible business leaders and social entrepreneurs. Attend an event, apply for membership, or visit us online at svn.org.

Social Venture Network
P.O. Box 29221
San Francisco, CA 94129-0221
415.561.6501

The world depends on print to a far greater extent than is commonly understood, and yet print is not sustainable. This is not a time for the graphic arts to rest on its laurels and wait for buyers and specifiers of print to change their priorities. It is a time, instead, for graphic arts print service providers to redefine themselves and work together to identify, analyze, and act on making print sustainable and addressing the challenges presented by global warming in timely and innovative ways.

Addressing the issues at the nexus of commercial opportunity and sustainability presents the graphic communication industry with new opportunities to reinvent the ways in which the industry packages knowledge and goods for human consumption. There is opportunity to create new fortunes and a sustainable future for print. Our common future will depend largely on our ability to communicate and collaborate as well as on our ability to design, produce, and distribute knowledge and goods in ways that manage their life cycle costs, measure their triple-bottom-line impacts, and create significant quality of life benefits.

The Psychology of Graphics

Dr. Paul J. Beckmann
Research Associate, University of Minnesota,
Department of Psychology

A picture is worth a thousand words.

—Old adage

Sustainability is a system and a journey but not a tangible thing. How do we know when we've arrived? Many definitions are out there, but all of them are confronted with trying to relate a large collection of small things (e.g., consumer items) to a gigantic and complex web of interrelated, dynamically changing, and evolving systems (collectively, the Earth's ecosystems).

Just when it seems you're "doing the right thing," like driving a hybrid car, you find out that metals used in the batteries are mined and processed in very eco-unfriendly ways.[1] Most consumer items have complex and multifaceted interactions with our world's ecosystems, as human processes create, deliver, and market these goods. Products also have a life after use that is finally receiving much-needed attention.[2] How can graphic arts help communicate the complex web of relationships of a product to the world that gave it birth and must deal with it after it dies? Even more, how can graphic arts help communicate the complex web of relationships that will bring home how each of us impacts our planet?

We can start by asking: What is a graphical design? In this chapter, a graphical design will be viewed as a messenger that communicates information to a viewer/audience. The design can be considered successful if most viewers receive the intended message (e.g., of quantities, their relationships, and the changes in both over time).

In this book's companion work, *Packaging Sustainability*, Dr. Elise L. Amel, an industrial-organizational psychologist, and Dr. Christie Manning, a cognitive and biological psychologist, look at the mechanisms of human behavior that center around choice. The idea is that, as over 70 percent of all purchase decisions are made in the store, if you do not understand how people make decisions in a product's natural environment, you cannot make an effective package. If your package doesn't do *all* it needs to do—protect, inform, *and* sell—you will have wasted not only the resources that went in to making the package but also the resources that went into making the product inside it.

As we look now at print design, of which packaging is also a part, we will look deeper still at the things that trigger choice mechanisms as well as how graphics act as a critical partner in conveying

information for any application. This chapter is about the principles of experimental psychology that might be useful in developing and evaluating the graphical communication of sustainability. These principles can act as a design or test framework to determine if the work:

— Delivers the intended message to the audience.

— Delivers the message in a way that is fast and effortless for the audience to decode.

— Is correctly interpreted by people across generational and cultural boundaries.

— Is correctly interpreted by people with visual and/or cognitive impairments.

— Distinguishes itself visually from other similar messages.

By focusing on the message, designer and client are encouraged to sharpen their thinking early in the process. Candidate works can be compared in a straightforward way once the message is clearly understood. A map is helpful only if you know where you are to begin with.

Communication through Graphics

The primary purpose of a graphical design is the communication of a message to its viewer. An effective design requires a number of steps, including:

— Determining the message you want the graphic to communicate to the viewer.

— Encoding of a message (selection of elements that, when assembled, will be interpreted correctly by the viewer).

— Proper presentation of the message (size, location on package or display, etc.) to attract and hold attention.

— Interpretation of the message by the viewer. (This interpretation process goes on in the viewer's head and is very difficult to measure directly.)

— Action based on the message received by the viewer. (This is what is most often measured.)

A message goes through a sequence of steps from the sender (printed object) to the receiver (audience). Graphic designers encode the message, as they understand it, into a piece to meet the need of communicating the desired message. The graphic is picked up from the environment by the sensory system of the viewer (may include special limitations, e.g., color blindness). Finally, the viewer interprets the received graphic, based on past personal experience and cultural context. The two messages at the beginning and the end of the chain should match.

Determining the Message

Suppose we wanted to convey this message: This product uses very little water during manufacture. This message, while sounding very simple at first, is not specific enough. Do we want to communicate how much water is used in absolute terms (15.3 liters per product unit), relative terms (half of that consumed by the most popular competing product), the flow of water out of and into the ecosystem during its manufacture, or what exactly? Also, what

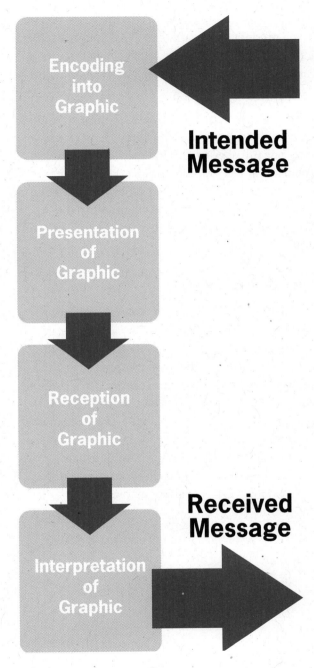

Intended Message

Encoding into Graphic

Presentation of Graphic

Reception of Graphic

Received Message

Interpretation of Graphic

A message is transformed into a graphic and presented in a context. The viewer extracts a message—the intended one, it is hoped—by interpreting that graphic in that context.

does it mean to "use water"? Does the water end up in the product, in the atmosphere as steam, back into a natural water source but at a higher temperature, or just dumped wherever, contaminating the area's drinking water?

Designer and client need to address these questions early to avoid problems later. If the client wants to send one message to the audience and the designer creates a perfect graphic to convey another message, the designer has wasted all resources used to create the work as well as the client's time and money, and may even threaten the client's hard-won brand equity.

Encoding the Message

The next step is encoding the intended specific message within a design. A graphical design can be static—one that does not change over time—or dynamic. A printed label is an example of a static design; a Web animation is an example of a dynamic design. What palette do we have to use in a static graphical design? A place to start is to consider what the human visual system *can* decode as the message of the graphic. In this way, the graphic artist does not use a technique to encode a message that the viewer's visual system cannot extract from the graphic.

The visual system can decode information from these aspects of a static environment:

— Shape

— Intensity (contrast)

— Color

— Size

— Distance

A person can visually extract information about absolute quantities from each of these source types. However, a person's vision is much better at determining relative estimates—for example, if one part of the environment is lighter or darker than another. The exception to this pattern is the extraction of information from absolute shape, a highly developed visual skill.

Use of dynamic designs for a graphic add:

— Additional distance cues.

— Movement (velocity and direction).

These static and dynamic sensitivities are the dimensions that graphic designers must use as their palette if the message is to be accurately decoded by a viewer. The visual system has limited abilities to extract information along each of these dimensions, however. It cannot, for example, look up at the sky and tell if a particular star has planets circling around it, and it may not be able to tell the difference between each of the millions of colors that a modern computer display claims to be able to generate. To make things even more complicated, our visual abilities change depending on the rest of the visual environment. For this reason, it is important that specific works be tested in their target environments, not just standing alone by themselves. There is no handbook or manual that will allow a designer to determine what can and cannot be seen in every circumstance. Specific designs require specific evaluations.

To help its client Ocean Conservancy communicate its efforts, BBMG felt it was important to not only feature the client but to go further by helping to get people to see the oceans as an urgent conservation issue that's relevant to our daily lives.

Once we know what the audience's visual system can detect in the environment, we can use those dimensions to form graphical elements that carry meaning. What concepts can be signaled within a collection of graphical elements? Here are some possibilities:

— Absolute quantities (often using text or numbers)

— Closeness or relatedness

— Hierarchy/priority

— Sequences

— Transformations (input/output relationships)

— Relative size/importance

— Association

— Movement

— Interaction

The last concept type is important to the type of message that sustainability is often concerned with communicating (i.e., the impact the production and presence of a product has on the ecosystem through its interactions). These interactions are often very difficult to understand and require graphical explanations to allow the viewer to build the correct mental model.[3]

Influence of Visual Context

How and where a graphic appears—its visual context—influences its interpretation. Seeing the standardized man on wheelchair as handicapped icon in the context of a parking space leads to the interpretation that the space is reserved for those with special-needs parking privileges. However, seeing the same symbol on a restroom sign does not lead to the same "reserved for" conceptual interpretation but an "accommodation available" interpretation due to the different context. The visual "messages" people get when they see a snake appear in their bed versus in a zoo are totally different.

Interpretation of the Message

Once the context for interpretation is set by the circumstances of its presentation, the viewer must interpret it and what message it may contain. There is no "fixed" message for any graphical element. *Context* guides the user to select one of a set of assumptions based on past experiences within that same context. It is very difficult for many people to accept how much past experience determines the most basic of interpretations. A classic example is that published by the anthropologist Colin Turnbull in 1961.[4] In the 1950s and 1960s, Turnbull studied the Pygmy culture in the dense forests of what is now Zaire. In one incident, an intelligent, well-adjusted member of a tribe interpreted the "image" of a water buffalo viewed from a distance as insects viewed from a much closer perspective. It turns out that the man had lived in such dense jungle his entire life that he had never experienced visual images of objects getting smaller as he went farther away (even though objects stay the same physical size). For this reason, he was unable to correctly interpret what his eyes were sending him and instead "saw" the objects as small, odd insects.

Using their personal collection of assumptions, viewers make a "best guess" about the message contained within the graphic. Ignoring how strong this influence might be can result in inconsistent interpretations of a design. This is a central and important point to consider in the creation and evaluation of graphical designs as message bearers. While your design will not likely be viewed by a Pygmy from Zaire, it will be viewed by individuals from different cultures and different generations. Membership in particular cultures (or subcultures, e.g., the vocal and active LOHAS demographic [Lifestyles of Health and Sustainability]) drives interpretation of elements in the audience's environment in particular ways. (In some respects, these interpretations largely define what the culture is.) Likewise, experiences common to individuals within a particular generation—for example, those who lived through eras, such as the 1930s depression, World War II, or the Vietnam War—result in interpretations that differ from those of other generational groups.

Acting on the Interpretation

The interpretation of the environment goes on inside a person's head and is unavailable to a designer for use in the evaluation of the graphic. Actions by the viewer, however, are important to measure for two reasons.

1. The actions viewers take can be thought of as a "window" onto their interpretation of the message.

2. We are ultimately interested in changing the audience's behavior (i.e., purchasing and use actions).

Example: How can a particular graphical design be evaluated? In their 1991 study on how the method of encoding information affected the accuracy of comparison judgments, Legge, Gu and Luebker investigated observers' ability to perceive the mean and variability of collections of values.[5]

To illustrate their approach, they show two distributions of values rendered in three different ways. In A, the values are rendered as lists of numbers; B shows values as stars at a particular height above the bottom of the box, with the bottom representing zero and the top representing 100; C shows values as levels of gray between zero (black) and 100 (white).

The participants in the study were asked to decide if the values on the left in box A had a higher or lower average than the values on the right. They were also asked to make the same decision about the relative size of the variability of the values in lists of the other boxes. In brief, the study's results support the idea that humans are better at making these sorts of comparisons (average and variability) when the values are rendered as in B than in A (worst) or C (second best). In other words, people are able to manage and judge visual information better than pure quantitative information.

Using this and similar techniques, studies in vision science have compared the efficiency of the visual system in accessing information encoded in different ways.[6]

Finally, some displays are designed to convey the relationship between two or more concepts. These are direct renderings of, for example, the relationships of relative sequence in time, relative position or sequence in space, importance, cause-effect, and direction of influence. The resulting designs are often referred to as maps and typically contain conceptual icons as well as special symbols of relationship connecting these icons.

Combinations can be fairly simple, however. The example of an icon rendered to ask campers not to build fires is actually a combination of two icons: a campfire and slashed circle indicating

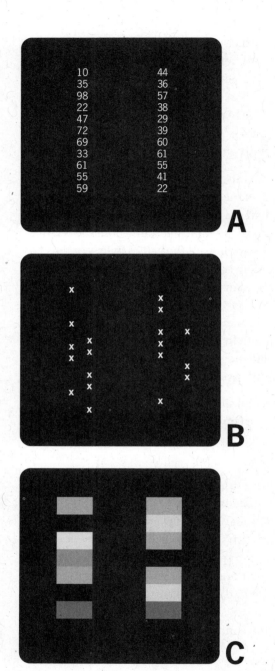

Legge, Gu, and Luebker looked at an observers' ability to perceive the mean and variability of collections of values.
Source: Redrawn from G. E. Legge, Y. Gu, and A. Luebker, "Efficiency of Graphical Perception," Perception & Psychophysics 46 (1991): 365–374.

The relationship communicated between icon elements through who's-on-top graphical ordering.

"no." Notice that the icon falls apart, or is at least greatly weakened, if you place the campfire on top of the slashed circle. This is a good indication that there is a relationship communicated between these two icons through the who's-on-top graphical ordering.

Icons and Graphemes

Works created by a graphic designer can be considered a collection of graphical elements, each of which is known as a grapheme. For a design to be a "good" design, it is critical that the audience can tell the difference between each element and other possible graphemes in that location. It is also important that the elements can be found and interpreted quickly and that the correct "message" is extracted. Detection, discrimination, and reaction time tasks can be used to objectively evaluate candidate graphemes and grapheme arrangements on these dimensions.

Elements of an Icon

— *Shape:* Leaf, tree, sun, ocean, endangered animals, rain forest elements

— *Color:* Green

— *Movement elements:* Circular arrows (recycling, circle of life, etc.)

Graphemes that communicate concepts usually are called icons. Typical icons would be the commonly occurring symbols for male and female restrooms as well as the red "slashed circle" used to communicate "not" for whatever it overlays.

Concepts in Visual Perception

A number of principles apply to the quantitative evaluation of graphical elements. These principles come primarily from the fields known as cognitive psychology and perceptual psychology. (See the notes to this chapter for specific sources.)

Sensation versus Perception

In the field of sensory psychology, a distinction is made between sensations and perceptions. A sensation is an uninterpreted package of information received from a sense organ—for example, the information from the retina of one eye. A perception is an interpretation of that sensation that is based on previous visual experience, and context influences this interpretation.

Many people are surprised to learn that many interpretations are possible from most of the sensations we receive from the environment.

In the next figure, the interpretation of A generates sensations that typically would be interpreted as two overlapping disks that look like B when moved apart. This, however, is not the only possible interpretation. These sensations could also be generated by one "whole" disk and one that had a chunk cut out of it, laid side by side C. The reason that people perceive the sensations as B instead of C is that B is more likely based on our experience. We

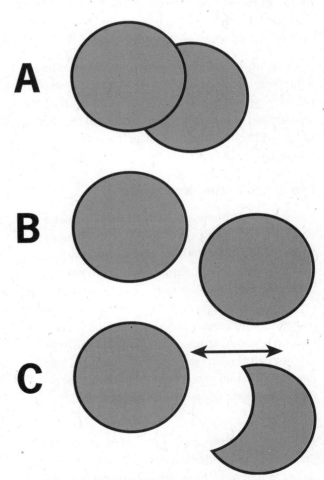

A perception is an interpretation of a sensation that is based on previous visual experience and context influencing that interpretation.

just don't encounter many disks with pieces cut out of them, much less ones that are cut out just right to fit next to another disk of the same size.

Visual illusions are very closely associated with this idea of interpretation through experience. People develop what might be called a "visual vocabulary" based on what their eyes have received in the past when a particular situation has been true "out there." Illusions are misinterpretations of sensations that occur because we are trying to align what we are "seeing" to what we "know."

Interpretation is a key element in understanding what people gain from a graphical image. One of the primary roles of graphic artists is forming an image, a collection of sensations, that likely will be interpreted as the intended "message" they desire to convey.

Dealing with the "Real World"

There is a big difference between most research done in a laboratory and the situations encountered in everyday life. Laboratory studies usually eliminate any "extraneous" information from being presented and focus on a very small aspect of visual capability. This poses a problem for curious graphic designers who are not afraid to go to the library and look up research articles (perhaps with the help of a research librarian). How can what has been uncovered about visual perception in research laboratories be applied to day-in, day-out graphical applications?

The examples given might lead to the assumption that these capabilities have been useful only since the advent of housing, artificial illumination, the printed word, and video technology. Nothing could be further from the truth. The ability to deal with

changing illumination when moving from the grassland pastures to the forest, the ability to pick out a cougar from the tan grass partially blocking your view of it, and performance on countless other visual tasks heavily influenced the chances of early humans surviving and reproducing. We are the beneficiaries of all those countless successes at dealing with the natural world. It's fortunate that we have been developed technology compatible with these hard-won abilities, for the abilities take many thousands of years to develop and change.

The Information Is in the Differences: Contrast

The whole visual system is set up to process differences between one part of the visual environment and another. The difference between two parts of the visual scene is called contrast. Once contrast is established, other processes come into play that attempt to put different pieces of the scene together as belonging to one object "out there"; then the shape of the object is analyzed and identified.

Contrast can be present in the scene in many different forms. Brightness (luminance or value) comes from a difference in lightness between one part of the scene and another. An example would be the contrast between a letter and its background. If a black letter is printed on a white background, the contrast is very high. If a black letter is printed on a gray background, the contrast is lower. If a black letter is printed on a black background, the contrast is zero.

Differences in color can establish contrast. Blue graphics on a green background would have high color contrast but may have no brightness contrast, especially if the values for these colors are very similar. The visual system can use the color contrast to segment the graphic from the background and identify the shape—a stream from the forest background, for example.

Motion can also establish contrast, as can texture. Being aware of contrast is an important aspect of graphical design. If there is not good contrast, the viewer either will not be able to identify the graphic at all or, at best, will be slower in identification performance. How many times has a client complained that an image didn't "pop"? When competing in a "noisy" environment, "pop" can mean the difference between success and fizzle.

Caring Only about What's Important: Adaptation

Visual information about the world arrives at the eye with large variations over many dimensions. It's the same world, but the color or intensity of illumination, for example, can drastically change the amount and spectrum of light reaching the eye. How can the visual system deal with these changes and still tell something about the actual object in the environment? The answer is through the process of *adaptation*.

The basic idea of adaptation is that the visual system makes its best guess about the level and color of the illumination of the scene and then factors that information out. What is left is what the person really wants: information about the contents of the scene, not what the light is like.

Illumination engineers and theatrical lighting designers are naturally interested in the characteristics of light. Often, though, they design the lighting system based on aesthetic or "building code" criteria, having lost sight of the purpose of their illumination, which is to provide patterns of light at the audience's eye that allow the visual system to perform the task at hand. There are abundant examples of office spaces with uneven or glare-producing lighting that work against the visual tasks undertaken in these spaces. Inattention to the needs of the workplace means greater job dissatisfaction, higher stress levels, higher sick leave needs, and higher turnover. Careful consideration of workplace needs, which includes taking advantage of natural lighting, leads to healthier and more productive staff as well as much lower energy costs.

BRIGHTNESS ADAPTATION

Two principal types of visual adaptation are luminance and color adaptation. The visual system works over a surprisingly wide range of intensity of light received by the eye. The eye receives 1,000 times more light from a white piece of paper in direct noontime sunlight than the same paper in typical living room lighting.[7] If you are trying to read black type on that piece of paper, the amount of illumination isn't important to making out the letters. It's the difference, or contrast, between the light received from the white paper and the black type. (See the section titled "The Information Is in the Differences: Contrast.") Adaptation takes out much of the effect of changing illumination levels, letting the rest of the visual system operate on a much narrower range of input when trying to make out letters.

One demonstration of the operation of adaptation in the interpretation of the darkness/lightness of a surface is called simultaneous contrast. In a classic art school exercise, the viewer is presented with two squares. The central squares on both the left and right part of the figure have equal value; however, one appears much darker than the other.

One way to think about how this happens is that perception uses the much larger surrounding background to estimate how bright the illumination

Interpretation of the darkness/lightness of a surface is called simultaneous contrast.

of both it and the central square might be. Using that estimate, the lightness or darkness of the material making up the central square is estimated. Because the illumination is estimated to be much higher in the case of the light background, the central square's surface is perceived as darker than in the other case.

COLOR ADAPTATION: PIGMENT AND ILLUMINATION

An important distinction in perception, especially color perception, is between some part of the environment and the light your eye receives from that part of the environment. The color of an object provides information about the material at its surface; the color of the object is only part of the story. The light your eye receives also has to do with the illumination falling on the environment.

However, our visual system takes care of most of the effects of changes in illumination through adapta-

tion. Since the visual system is most interested in differences between one part of the scene and another, and since a scene usually is illuminated with the same color light, the visual system "reverses" the shift in the light reaching our eyes due to changes in illumination. It does this by estimating, essentially, what light a "white" surface would send to the eye. Knowing this, it can make a good guess about the color of the other surfaces in the environment.

Color adaptation is similar to luminance adaptation. The amount of light of various colors in the light illuminating a scene is different when, for example, you move from the outdoor, naturally lighted environment to an interior environment lighted with fluorescent bulbs. The light falling on objects on the forest floor in summer contains much more green light than light falling on the same objects late in autumn, when the leaves have fallen. The visual system adapts to these changes in illumination color, removing most of their effects on the light reaching the eyes. This natural ability leaves the rest of the visual system with input that is fairly consistent from one illumination setting to another.

Taking the World Apart: Segmentation

The world is made up of many individual objects, and many objects have multiple parts. The ability to take apart the scene into its constituent elements so that each part can be identified separately is called segmentation. Being able to tell where x ends and y begins is important in many tasks involving x and y.

Segmentation allows vision to identify the multiple pieces of a scene and to process them independently for identification. The tree trunk in the foreground of the picture and the individual plants on the forest floor are "segmented" from each other and the other elements of the scene. This segmentation allows the object identification processes of vision to work on them individually.

Camouflage results when an arrangement of color and/or lightness makes it difficult to segment out the camouflaged object from the rest of the scene. Camouflage can be defeated (called breaking camouflage) under some circumstances. Most often an object breaks its own camouflage by moving too quickly or by taking up a position that casts a telltale shadow of its outline.

Putting the World Together: Gestalt Principles

Taking the world apart into individual pieces seems like a straightforward way to identify what is out there. However, many times a single object might generate a number of pieces from the segmentation process. In the next example, a light post behind a

Segmentation allows us to see the forest—and the trees.

street sign generates two segments, one above and one below the sign.

Visual perception learns through experience that one continuous light post does generate two or more segments that should be perceived as parts of the same single object. It uses rules to decide if two or more pieces should be considered parts of the same object. The classic collection of this sort of rule is the set of Gestalt principles of *prägnanz*, which includes:[8]

— *Continuity:* Patterns with interruptions at various places are continued across the interruptions.

Sign and lamppost combine to illustrate the Gestalt principle of good continuation.

— *Proximity:* Elements that are closer together are grouped together more than those farther away.

— *Closure:* Perception tends to complete an interrupted closed outline of an object.

— *Similarity:* Elements that are similar are grouped together more than those that are less similar.

— *Common fate:* Elements that move together are grouped together.

In our example, the laws of continuity and similarity would encourage the interpretation of two parts of one information object.

Role of Attention

Our environment contains too much information for us to mentally process. One of the first things vision, hearing, and other senses does is select what might be important in the environment to examine closely. This selection process is called attention. Attention has a number of interesting properties that have been extensively examined. One is that attention is concentrated in one area of the environment at a time (i.e., it doesn't often split into two or more points of focus at one time). Another is that attention can be moved, rather quickly, from one part of the environment to another. Attention also can be tightly focused or spread out more diffusely over a larger area. However, things and events can grab our attention when they are outside current focus.

Attention is also under the control of certain automatic, or unconscious, influences. If something unexpected occurs in the world, we tend to focus our attention tightly and, if that something moves, we move our attention to track it. If an unexpected movement occurs in our peripheral vision, our attention is reflexively redirected to that location. Peripheral vision is, in fact, more sensitive to movement than central vision is. Automatic influences also affect our attention to unexpected auditory and touch events.

Moving over a Scene's Segments

For perceptual interpretation of a particular graphic to occur, the viewer's attention must be focused on it—it first must grab the attention of the viewer. Visual attention is scanned around the environment with movement to a particular location being motivated in complex ways, likely guided to locations where past experience has found important information.

How the eye places its points of fixation when examining a scene is an interesting topic in perceptual and cognitive psychology. A. L. Yarbus, a Russian psychophysicist, recorded patterns of fixations and saccades (a fast movement of eye, head, or other part) as people examined pictures of faces and scenes in the 1950s.[9]

Examination of the elements of the environment, perhaps in search for something in particular, is performed constantly, largely outside of conscious control. This movement over the scene is necessary because the high-resolution part of vision is quite small, about the size of a fingernail at arm's length.

Movement of this high-resolution central vision follows a pattern of alternating fixations and saccades. During a fixation, the eye remains quite still, extracting information from one small part of

For the 2008 Minnesota State Fair Eco Experience Building, transit-focused organizations collaborated with Entropy Design Lab to bring the message of reducing fuel consumption and emissions to life with the message "Kick Gas!"

the scene. Movements between points of fixation are not gradual but are rapid and straight. Perception ignores or suppresses the sensations from the eye during these saccades; this makes sense since the image would be smeared during rapid movement.

Serial Search versus "Pop-out"

Many search tasks require that each element of the scene be examined and processed for a decision to be made about the presence or absence of a figure. A good example of this need for serial search is the images in the popular *Where's Waldo* series of children's books.

Under certain circumstances, however, serial search of a scene is not necessary to perform a particular task. These circumstances are called preattentive processing or pop-out.[10] In the top two panels of the example shown here, the light blue W "pops out" of the background of dark blue X distracters. In the bottom panels, however, the light blue W does not pop out from the light and dark blue Xs. To decide if a light blue W is in the display, the viewer must perform a letter-by-letter, or serial, search to determine if it is present.

In the illustration shown here, we see the pop-out effect. Sometimes just dark blue Xs appear and sometimes a light blue W and dark blue Xs appear. The response time doesn't depend on how many dark blue Xs are in the display; the light blue W is said to pop out. This is taken as evidence that attention does not need to be moved from element to element (called a serial search) to make the decision but that a light blue W, if present, pops out of the background of dark blue X distracters. A different situation is shown in the bottom two panels of the figure. Now the distracter Xs are both light and dark blue. The more distracters there are in

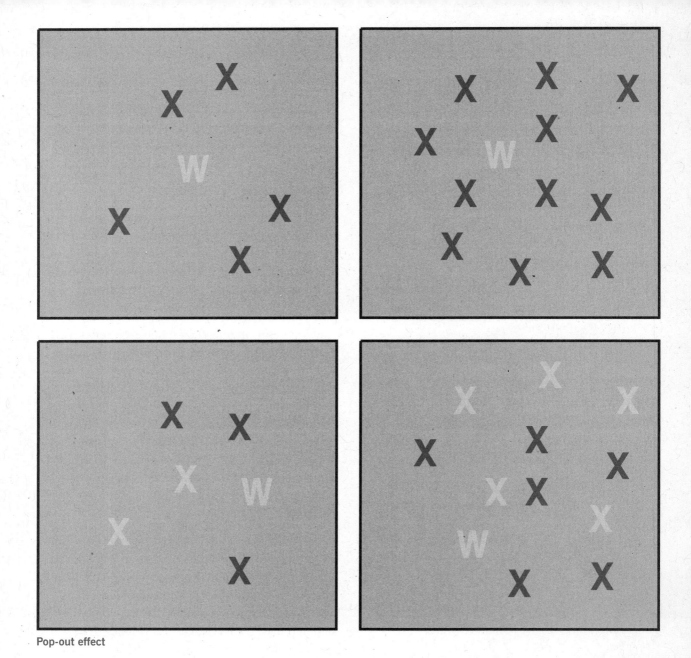

Pop-out effect

Boston design firm Payette makes it easy to see the forest for the trees. Its 2008 promotional sketchbook uses 100% post-consumer board for the cover, around pages made with Paperfect Opaque, a Forest Stewardship Council (FSC) Certified 60% post-consumer paper. The festive belly-band, printed by Reynolds DeWalt, an FSC Certified printer, is Fox River's Evergreen 100% post-consumer paper. The Wire-O binding is manufactured using recycled steel.

the display, the longer it takes the viewer, on average, to decide if a light blue W is present. This is taken as evidence that attention must be moved from letter to letter to make the decision (i.e., a serial search must be performed).

Automatic Processing and the Stroop Effect

Interpretation of information from the environment can require mental analysis of the many elements and their relationships to decode the message it might contain. An example would be the process when we first began reading. Each letter had to be recognized, translated into a sound, and put together with other sounds of other nearby letters, and the collection had to be recognized as a word sound that, it is hoped, corresponded to some conceptual meaning. However, if viewers have extensive experience with a collection of visual

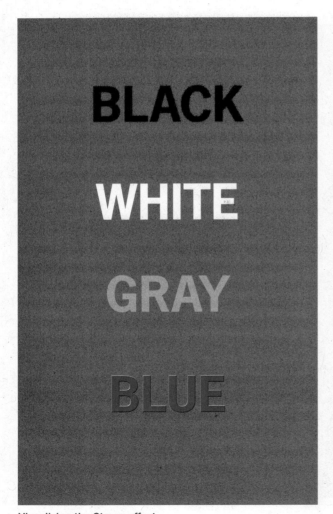

Visualizing the Stroop effect

elements, the interpretation becomes automatic and is said to be overlearned. This overlearning allows rapid information transfer from the environment to viewers that occurs in skilled reading and other tasks. Another example of this is the instant interpretation of icons—for example, a women's room icon on a restroom door—with no required mental effort.

This overlearning is very useful and is the basis of our ability to succeed at increasingly complex tasks throughout our lives. It can, however, cause some difficulties if graphical designs and tasks are not closely matched. A classic example of this is the Stroop effect.

Consider the task of naming the colors of ink for each of the words shown on a display. It's important to note that the task is not to read the words but to name the color of the ink. If the colored words in the first group were shown, performance on this task would be rapid and virtually error-free. However, if the words shown in the second group were shown for the same task, that of naming the color of the ink, performance would be slower and more error-prone than before. People would fight the automatic reading process that would cause them to say "BLACK" while they were trying to produce the correct answer, the name of the color of the text: "WHITE." This finding illustrates two important points:

1. Repeated exposure to a graphic results in an automatic interpretation of that graphic.

2. Graphics should be designed in such a way that the most automatic interpretation is the one that is desired by the designer.

Notice that there is nothing lacking in the graphics (words) making up the second group if the task was to read the *words* themselves. The graphic is poorly designed, however, when the task requires analysis (to name the ink color) although another automatic process is producing a different answer.

The Stroop effect shows that automatic unconscious processes can interfere with performance on nonautomatic analysis tasks. We saw that naming the color of the ink is quick and effortless where no conflict exists. However, when the ink color is different from that of the *word*, the automatic reading process interferes with the color-naming process, slowing it down.

The information in these sections may seem elementary to trained designers, or a whole lot of science to describe common-sense design basics. Yet many pieces fail to serve these very basic ideas because fashion became more important than function, or because designers knew best and completely ignored the audience and environment the end piece would be living and working in. When the design interferes with the function of a piece and causes it to fail, *all* of the resources used—time, energy (electricity, fuel), materials—are wasted. A thing designed sustainably must, first and foremost, do its job well.

Objective Evaluation of Graphics

Evaluation Goals

— Can viewers receive the message from the graphic—do they understand what it is saying? Does the message hold up across generations, disabilities, and cultures?

— Can viewers tell the difference between this graphic and other possible graphics? How confusable is this graphic from those already in use?

— If viewers can receive a message that can be distinguished from others, how quickly can they pick up the message from this graphic?

Evaluation Methods

Since the purpose of a graphical display is to communicate, the effectiveness of a particular display design in passing information to a human observer must be evaluated. This can be done in a number of ways.[11] We are so good at interpretation of visual input that it is often a challenge to arrange situations where people cannot accurately evaluate a display. One method to prevent 100 percent correct performance is to reduce the time the image is displayed. In these cases, a mask—a fragmented similar image—should be presented after the target.[12] Another method is simply to measure the time required to perform the task. Another, used for discrimination trials, is to make the target and comparison graphics more and more similar until errors are made.

Threshold

If we give a human being a task to do—for example, to report whether a light in a darkened room is on or off—we can measure how often the person correctly reports the state of the light. Intuitively, you would think that at low light levels, respondents always would be incorrect because they do not see the light but, above some particular level, they always would correctly report when the light was on. This intuition is often correct when levels are very high or very low, but, at the levels in between, people will make

These Come From Trees sticker: A typical fast-food restaurant with two bathrooms can use up to 2,000 pounds of paper towels a year. There are about 50,000 fast-food restaurants in the United States alone. Launched as a guerrilla public service announcement to raise awareness about resource use, as of early 2009, over 70,000 labels have made their way into the world. Since the campaign's launch, the creators found that a single "These Come From Trees" sticker on a paper towel dispenser reduces consumption by about 15 percent and can save about a tree's worth of paper every year. This label image was captured in the wild at the REI store in Roseville, Minnesota. (thesecomefromtrees.com)
Photo: W. Jedlička, 2009.

mistakes, sometimes reporting seeing the light on when it is off and sometimes reporting it is off when it is on. We much choose some percentage of being correct if we want to determine the threshold of seeing. In psychological studies, usually the light level that results in 75 percent correct performance in this sort of task is taken as the threshold for the task.

Thresholds have been measured for many kinds of visual tasks in the laboratory. Most fall into one of two categories, however: absolute thresholds and difference thresholds.

DETECTION TASKS AND ABSOLUTE THRESHOLDS

One type of threshold is absolute threshold. Measurements of this kind usually ask the question: How big/bright/colorful does the graphic need to be before you see it? This is called a detection task. The example in the last section measures the absolute detection threshold for seeing the light under the conditions present during the test. There are many other kinds of absolute thresholds. The eye chart in the eye doctor's office measures your absolute identification size threshold for black letters of a particular font on a white background under the lighting conditions present in the room at the time. Keep in mind that the value of this type of threshold would shift to larger letters as the brightness contrast between the letters shifts.

DISCRIMINATION TASKS AND DIFFERENCE THRESHOLDS

A discrimination task is used to investigate how much different two stimuli have to be before a viewer can tell that there is a difference. Two patterns are presented to the viewer, one slightly different from the other, and the viewer is asked: "Are these the same or different?" If a person can reliably tell that the patterns are different, when they are, we can say that the person's visual system is sensitive to this type of difference at a particular level. A summary of the results from a discrimination task is often plotted as a curve of the just-noticeable difference (JND).

As an example, two graphical elements could be presented one after the other, and the viewer's task would be to say if there were two copies of the same graphic or if they were different. One example presents viewers with a collection of circles, each slightly different from each other in size. Pairs would be selected at random and presented to viewers one after the other. Half the time, only one of the pair would be shown in both presentations. Viewers would press a button labeled "same" or one labeled "different." Notice in this example there isn't an "I don't know" or "I'm not sure" option; this is called a *forced choice task*. The point at which viewers are 75 percent correct on the task is often taken as the difference threshold (JND).

This type of experiment can be run with differences along many dimensions. Instead of size, the options could differ in lightness, color, roundness, texture, or glossiness. Many of these types of JND's have been measured, reported in research journals, and published in handbooks of perception and human performance.[13]

Reaction Time

Another question psychologists have asked concerns how quickly someone can perform a task. Most of these reaction time measurements are made of either simple reaction time or choice reaction time. Reaction time measurements are more "real world" than threshold measurements, or certainly they can be.

As an example of a choice reaction time task, imagine presenting viewers with two designs for a packaging graphic and asking if they are the same or different. (Note the similarity to a discrimination task.) These pairs would be different in ways that anyone could see, given enough time. Viewers are told to make their decision "as quickly and as accurately as possible." What is measured here is not how often they were correct (nearly 100 percent correct is expected in this case) but how long it took them to decide. To keep them honest, every now and then two designs that are the same are presented. If they get any of these incorrect (by pressing the "different" button), the results may be thrown out since they may not have understood their task. There are many variations on the basic choice reaction time task, but they all want to answer the question: How difficult is it to tell that the two members of the pair are different?

How might this task be useful to a graphics designer? Again, when graphic designs for different applications are being evaluated, it would be important to measure how easily potential viewers can tell the difference between, for example, a client's and a competitor's product on the store shelf. Using choice reaction time, viewers can objectively rate candidate designs on their distinctiveness in a given environment.

Complex Skill Measurements

Some measurements can be made that are closer to everyday tasks than threshold or reaction time tasks. These measure performance of complex skills; two examples are reading[14] and driving performance.[15]

Evaluation Methods for Special Populations

PEOPLE WITH IMPAIRED VISION

Five percent of the world's men have some defect in their color vision. While the term "color blindness" often is used for this condition, it really is closer to "color confusion." Men with defective color vision cannot distinguish between two or more of the fundamental colors, such as blue and green. When these two colors are presented side by side, no difference can be perceived. If information is encoded as color contrast (e.g., blue lines on a green background in which the blue and green have equal lightness values), the graphic will be perceived as blank.

Problems in forming a clear image in the eye are fairly common. Defocusing or diffusing lenses are often used to simulate impaired vision in psychophysical evaluations.[16]

PEOPLE WITH DEVELOPMENTAL DISABILITIES

If some of the potential audience has varying degrees of developmental disabilities, it is a good idea to run a substudy on their performance on various tasks using the design.

OTHER GENERATIONS (CHILDREN AND THE ELDERLY)

Many visual and cognitive (thinking) abilities and characteristics change with age. Children's thought processes are different from those of adults in surprising ways.[17] Visual abilities shift in dramatic ways after age thirty. In addition, the meanings for symbols for societies as a whole shift from generation to generation. An example here would be the meaning of the swastika used by the Nazi party in Germany before and after 1930. Many people are still surprised to find out that this symbol, named from Sanskrit *svástika*, first appears in images dating from the Neolithic period.[18]

OTHER CULTURES

Graphical elements often are uniquely interpreted by a particular culture. For example, Paul Ekman found that most facial expressions of emotion are consistently identified across many cultures.[19] However, there were significant differences in interpretation of some basic emotions (e.g., disgust). Simpler icons may be cross-culturally confusing, as well. Consider the typical gender icons used in western cultures for restroom signage (the male icon has trousers, the female icon has a skirt). It is unlikely that this common icon set of the West would be recognized as readily by someone from a culture in which both genders wear more robe-like apparel (e.g., from Afghanistan or the Pacific islands).

Case Study: Green Map System

New York City resident Wendy Brawer wanted to create a platform to promote inclusive participation in sustainable community development, and mapmaking presented itself as the medium of choice. Looking to take the concept further, she initiated the global Green Map System in 1995.

With the idea of "Think global, map local," the nonprofit Green Map System (*GreenMap.org*) helps support locally led Green Map projects around the world as they create perspective-changing community "portraits." Local Green Maps act not only as comprehensive inventories for decision making but also as practical guides for residents and tourists. Mapmaking teams pair the Green Map's adaptable tools and universal iconography with local knowledge and leadership as they chart green living, ecological, social, and cultural resources.

Hundreds of Green Maps have been published to date, with many more created in classrooms and workshops by mapmakers of all ages. Since launching the project, the Green Map System group has found that the mapmaking process and the resulting Green Maps have tangible effects that:

— Strengthen local-global sustainability networks.

— Expand the demand for healthier, greener choices.

— Help successful initiatives spread to even more communities.

Online since 1995, the Web site *GreenMap.org* has developed a Web2.0 content management system called the "Greenhouse," named for its ability to cultivate and preserve the diverse "garden of Green Maps."

Green Map System is launching a new participatory mapmaking Web site in 2009. Based on open source and familiar mapping technology such as Google Maps, the inclusive Open Green Map has incredible potential for really expanding understanding about countless initiatives as well as eco-challenges.

At the heart of the Green Map System is a set of clear and easy-to-understand icons that help viewers easily spot the features for a given location. The Green Map's icons were collaboratively designed to allow the diverse, locally created Green Maps to be read by a wide variety of people from very different cultures. In their latest icon-set version (v3), the iconography's 12 categories have been refined, and the set has been extended with more climate change, activism, justice, green enterprise, technology, outdoor activities, and indoor greening icons. A poster can be downloaded at GreenMap.org/icons.

As the drive to understand what sustainability means on an individual, social, and environmental level, the Green Map concept offers a platform to allow people from any culture to explore their region, make the ideas of sustainability tangible, and then share that knowledge with their fellow residents as well as newcomers—making for a meaningful experience everyone can enjoy.

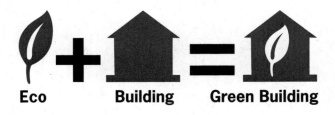

Eco   **Building**   **Green Building**

Taking in the Whole Picture

Graphics within any context deliver a message to viewers. The major challenges of delivering the desired message is first to understand what the message is and then to encode it graphically in such a way that it is most likely to convey that message to the majority of the target audience. Objective evaluation of competing designs is possible using methods developed within experimental and cognitive psychology. Rather than ask what audience members "want" or "think"—results any reputable focus group facilitator will tell you have more to do with the dynamics of the people in the room than true opinions—qualitative methodologies instead offer designers the tools to better understand how people actually will act/react.

In addition, the field of psychology can offer insights into what graphic design techniques may be most compatible with the human visual system. As the population ages, as immigration continues to integrate people from different cultures, and as more people with developmental disabilities are mainstreamed (entering the consumer base for many products), it is important to consider all of these groups in the design and evaluation of any design.

One of the fundamental cornerstones of sustainability is that all human needs are met worldwide. In an ever-globalizing economy, effective communication across borders, cultures, and generations becomes one of the key elements in making those ideas a reality.

A sustainable society is one that satisfies its needs without diminishing the prospects of future generations.

—*Lester Brown, The Worldwatch Institute*

Case Study: Urban Forest Project

In the fall of 2006, the Urban Forest Project, an unprecedented outdoor exhibition, took root in New York City. One hundred eighty-five of some of the world's most celebrated designers and artists employed the idea or form of the tree to make powerful visual statements that were placed on banners and displayed throughout Times Square.

The tree is a metaphor for sustainability, and in that spirit, the banners from the exhibition were recycled into tote bags designed for the project by Jack Spade. Profits from the sale of the tote bags went to Worldstudio AIGA Scholarships and the American Institute of Graphic Artists (AIGA)/NY Chapter Mentoring Program to sustain the next generation of design talent.

The project was conceived by Worldstudio for its client Times Square Alliance, the business improvement district that manages the Times Square area. Worldstudio and the Alliance collaborated with the New York Chapter of AIGA to realize the project. The success of the initiative exceeded the organizers' expectations. When originally announced to the design community, over 300 designers expressed interest in participating within the first two weeks. The exhibition was extended for an additional month from the initial two that were planned.

The educational component of the program involved 22 high school students from the AIGA/NY Mentoring Program. The students, working with their mentors, were guided through the design process, where they came to understand what it means to create a message on a given theme with a specific audience and location in mind.

The thread of sustainability was woven into every aspect of the program, with all solicitation and artwork submission done over the Internet, eliminating the need for printing and delivery. A Web site for the project featured all of the banners and sold T-shirts that were printed on demand. Carbon offsets were purchased to offset shipping impacts for the T-shirts and tote bags.

The project garnered press on television, in print, and online—not only from the design community but from mainstream. The Urban Forest Project was also selected as a top finalist for the Municipal Art Society of New York's prestigious Brendan Gill Prize.

An unexpected outcome of the program was unsolicited interest from the design community, corporations, city governments, urban forestry/tree planting groups, and other civic organizations to mount the Urban Forest Project in their local communities.

In light of this enthusiasm, Worldstudio expanded the project. In April 2007, the Portland, Oregon, chapter of AIGA mounted the Urban Forest Project in celebration of Earth Day, and in October 2007, a coalition of designers in Denver, Colorado, executed the project for the AIGA National Design Conference using banners fabricated from Ecophab, which is

made from 100 percent post-consumer polyethylene terephthalate (PETE beverage) bottles. In June 2008, Tilt Design Studio—working with the city of Baltimore—mounted the project and featured banners by 200 designers and submissions from 285 K–12 students. Through the sale of the tote bags, the program in Baltimore supported local community parks. The Urban Forest Project continues to grow with additional exhibitions planned in cities around the world. It demonstrates the power of design to unite civic leaders, the general public, educators, students, businesses, and the creative community around a common cause to promote sustainability.

Case provided by Mark Randall, Worldstudio (worldstudioinc.com).

STATUARY
WAS 29.99
NOW 24.99
BUDDHA

Price
Cut

Seeking Truth in Marketing

Wendy Jedlička, CPP
Jedlička Design, Ltd.

Jacquelyn Ottman
J. Ottman Consulting

With additional contributions from:
Dr. Paul H. Ray, Arlene Birt, Fred Haberman, Jeremy Faludi, Chad Rea, Dr. Pamela Smith, Green America, Metropolitan Group, Terra-Choice Environmental Marketing, US Federal Trade Commission

With our thoughts we make the world.

—Buddha

People today are looking for products or services that not only whiten and brighten but deliver an intangible extra: ethical values. From production methods, business practices, and stakeholder relationships to corporate giving and vendor associations, more and more people are paying attention to who serves their needs as much as to what they are selling. Successful firms are developing deeper relationships with their target audience, in spite of tightening markets, by learning how to create that extra something to nurture healthy, long-term stakeholder relationships.

Photo: W. Jedlička, 2009

81

Building a Relationship

In the earliest days of humankind, people made or gathered goods and traded them for things they hadn't gathered or couldn't make—and the barter economy was born. People needed stuff, other people developed the skills to make stuff, and each contributed their skills for the betterment of the whole community. You knew the producer of your goods, and they knew you and your needs. Marketing was all by word of mouth, and goods carried the personal guarantee of the maker, making the whole affair a fairly straightforward process.

It's in this simple space that the idea of the market's guiding hand as a benevolent force works well, with localized checks and balances keeping the system in line. Eventually, as mass production and the use of currency, rather than trading for completed local goods, became the norm, producers far removed from markets where their goods would be consumed began to decide what would be made, assuming this attitude: If we make it, they will buy—regardless of the impacts, or how well it fit with the end market, or even if it really needed to be made in the first place. In the beginning years of the Industrial Revolution, the net inflight of people to population centers made demand outpace supply and meant that people bought what was available, not what they really wanted or even what was best for them or their community.

Empowering the Audience

Zip forward through a few hundred years of technological improvements and we find markets becoming more competitive and supply chains more global, opening markets to even more competitors. In contrast to the days of yore, people today are learning they not only have a choice but that these choices have deeper impacts than sales volumes for the producing company. Taking back some of the power they once had in a barter economy, the markets themselves are redefining "needs" and "wants." Through each buying decision, people are molding the market, dictating what goods will be produced. And, more important, they're shaping how these goods are produced and delivered. This choice of how an item is produced breaks down to:

— Made with no regard for the product's impacts, focusing only on the final piece (price, excessive resources used)

— Made with very close attention to the product and its production and afterlife impacts

As populations grow and competition increases, producers find themselves held hostage to the demands of the market rather than dictating its shape. But signaling approval or disapproval with purchases isn't as clear a message as producers need. Are products purchased because consumers are thrilled with the items, or is it just what's there and they can't be bothered finding a more healthful alternative? Is not buying something an indicator that the product is a bad eco-actor, or is it simply a bad product in general? While it's true that buying habits are a pretty good indicator of how willing people really are to participate in change (how far out of their way will they go to find or avoid a product), only a formal boycott speaks loud enough to make the bad actor message clear; the rest is known only to buyers and their consciences.

For producers trying to better position themselves and their products, the realization that markets maybe don't "know best" is what makes current economic trends so dynamic. The importance of connecting with the individuals who make up the market as stakeholders in the production process becomes key to the firm's long-term success. How can we connect with an audience and empower them to help industry make better decisions that will lessen the impacts on our world by the things we create?

Every second of every day, a barrage of advertising reminds us that we live in a market economy that works in a framework where buyer and seller are far removed from each other. Though we don't think about it each day, our buying choices do have a direct impact on how industry shapes our world. All of these choices together decide our collective fate. "Hold on there," a consumer may say. "I'm just making some copies here, not driving an oil tanker into a wildlife sanctuary!" Being so far removed from the production process, consumers naturally fail to make the connection that the memo they're duplicating by the score requires petroleum to make the toner, trees and chemicals to make the paper, as well as oil to fuel the trucks to move the goods they're converting to the store; their purchase is part of the reason the tanker was there. Consumers who are exposed to the deeper supply chain issues by eco-advocates start to feel bad about their choices and helpless to make an impact: "I'm only one person. What can I do?"

Demands of a market-based economy don't always fit neatly within the boundaries of sustainable production models. To be sustainable, goods should be produced, sold, used, and disposed of by and for local consumers. Today, however, the technologies we've come to enjoy consume resources from all around the world, making production today anything but a local affair. Does that mean that to be sustainable we need to turn the clock back before the Industrial Revolution to the ancient days of barter? It's a fairly safe to say that the genie won't go quietly back in the bottle. It's unreasonable to expect all regions to produce all goods for local consumers. Buying choices then become the driving force in determining how green a local market will be, its ripple effect on a global scale, and ultimately how successfully we can shift from being blind consumption machines to being agents of positive change.

Does the Selling Price Really Tell the Story?

Paper is made from trees, a renewable and carbon-sequestering resource. But from where? A plantation, an old-growth sanctuary, or a sustainably managed forest? Trees produce less pulp per acre and require more processing chemicals, than higher-yield annual crops grown to make paper such as kenaf and hemp, and do nothing to help close an ecological and economic loop, as agripulp (field residue fiber) does. Doing something as basic as buying a box of tissues now becomes a test of your forestry practices and supply chain integrity knowledge. What on the surface seemed an easy choice (lotion dipped or extra strong?) becomes a much harder decision with far-reaching impacts. Eco-advocates are working to make complex decisions tangible and are asking consumers targeted questions, such as, "Do you really need to cut down a virgin forest to feel clean?"

Because the true cost of impacts are not yet directly (and universally) attached to the goods we buy, price often makes the decision for us. It is left up to consumers to pay attention (or not) to the goods they buy. This unbridled choice means that every purchase we make, and everything we create, becomes a statement about how we really feel about the environment, whether we mean it to or not. Do we care enough to research our purchases (look for certifications printed on the package), or do we just shop and go? For the designer, the megaconsumer whose choices are magnified by millions of production units, not being familiar with the impacts of their choices is no longer an option.

Brand Loyalty

There was a time when people passed down their shopping habits and favored brands like family traditions. Today competition is fierce, and brands compete in their home markets with competitors from all over the globe. For consumers, these are heady times. Products are diverse, abundant, and—as many producers do not attach the true cost of production to the cost of the product— prices are disproportionately cheap relative to their

actual cost to produce (and distribute, market, and dispose of). It's easy to make cheap goods when lax environment and labor laws in other countries are taken advantage of. And it's easy to leverage that advantage as long as the true cost (e.g., the cost to society of pollution for example) is not applied to the goods being shipped.

Because there are so many ways to avoid paying the true cost of producing a good, almost no product is safe from a competitor introducing a cheaper version that has cashed in on environmental health or taken undue advantage of its citizens. Selling on price alone then seems like a fool's game, because with each new competitor, firms find themselves pushing their profits (and production centers) to the point where they can no longer afford to make the products at all.

Developing and maintaining brand loyalty becomes critical. It's easy to understand that big-ticket items, such as cars, where a manufacturer may sell only a few units to even a loyal consumer over the course of their life, must cultivate a positive user experience and brand loyalty as part of the company's long-term strategy. But price is often the main purchase driver for small, frequently purchased goods—toiletries, packaged food, paper, and the like. Companies have found that developing and sustaining brand loyalty through quality of product and integrity of message allows them a greater range of strategic positioning and pricing options, if they approach the task with the same attention to marketing basics as mainstream products.

The veteran marketers at BBMG put together a white paper titled the *Five Principles of Sustainable*

Seattle's ColorGraphics (now part of Cenveo) is one of a growing number of Forest Stewardship Council Certified printers on the West Coast. To help sell its points of difference, ColorGraphics called on Metropolitan Group to help it better connect with its target audience. The key message is that ColorGraphics' printing process isn't just environmentally responsible—it also produces a better quality product.

The green-printing brochure Metropolitan Group designed became ColorGraphics' main marketing piece. It included an interactive color wheel that let potential customers visualize change by interactively showing them environmental impacts minimized though green printing and printed inserts that contrast vegetable-based and UV ink.

Branding. These principles neatly outline the key elements to consider when producing any effort:[1]

1. Integration: Aligning Promise with Practice.

   Easy access to information means also increased expectations by the consumer and visibility in the market. For each brand today, it's not what you say but what you do that matters.

2. Co-ownership: Leveraging Stakeholders to Create Value.

   Today's companies are co-owned by a variety of stakeholders ready to challenge and authenticate brand promises. According to Nielsen Buzz Metrics, 25 percent of search results on Google for the world's 20 largest brands link to consumer-generated content.

3. Triple Value Proposition™: Delivering Practical, Social and Tribal Benefits.

   Consumers are looking more and more to align their purchases with their values. According to the BBMG Conscious Consumer Report, over one-third of Americans say "conscious consumer" describes them very well, and nearly 9 in 10 say the term describes them well.

4. Inside-Out: Sharing an Authentic Brand Story.

   Increasing transparency as demanded by sustainability practice has led to an increase in certifications and marks. This increase in avenues for differentiation has also provided a vehicle for those just jumping on the green bandwagon. The increase in real efforts, coupled with the increase in "greenwashing," has left consumers confused and cynical. To tell a genuine story, sustainable values and practices must be visible throughout the entire organization. A company's backstory is finally becoming as important as its surface appeal.

5. Empowering: Realizing Our Best Selves and Society.

   "Sustainable brands," BBMG notes, "are not ends unto themselves, but empowering platforms that allow us to meet the full spectrum of our needs, make a difference in the world around us and realize our truest selves and best society."

Ethics-Based Marketing and Business

As connecting with the consumer on a deeper level becomes part of a product manufacturer's long-term strategy, innovators like Ben & Jerry's and Aveda have changed the whole complexion of crowded markets by using ethics as part of their products' point of difference.

> Our mission at Aveda is to care for the world we live in, from the products we make to the ways in which we give back to society. At Aveda, we strive to set an example for environmental leadership and responsibility, not just in the world of beauty, but around the world.

> Since its inception, working with and giving back to nature have been the cornerstones of Aveda's

New York based BBMG (Bemporad Baranowski Marketing Group) "believes that actions speak louder than words and smart cause marketing can improve a company's bottom line while inspiring people to promote social change," says Raphael Bemporad. "When we align our values with our actions, great things can happen."

Living its ethic, BBMG's "It's How We Live Grant" provides a $100,000 package of in-kind communications service to create and launch a breakthrough cause marketing campaign for a visionary nonprofit and its corporate partner.

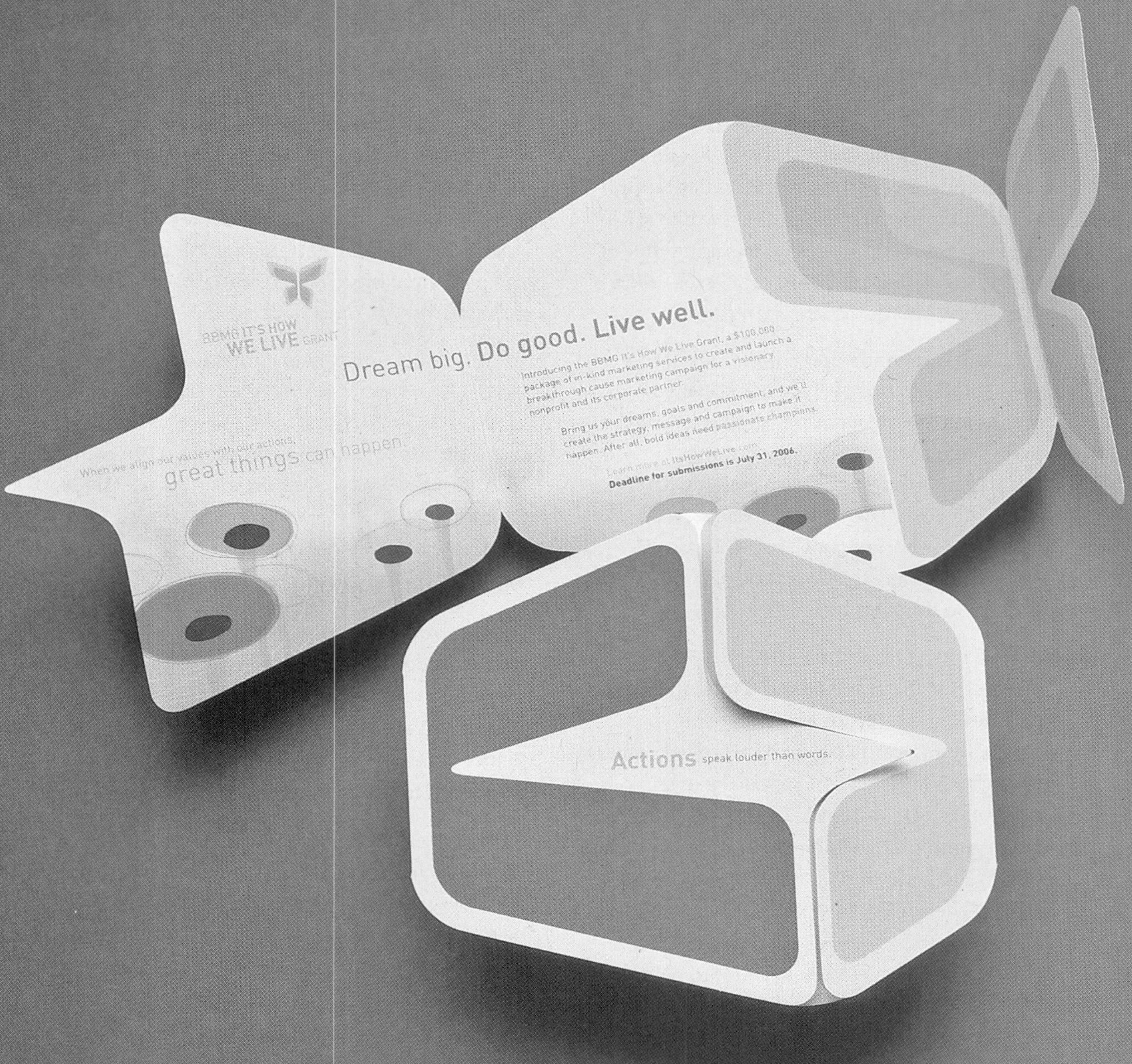
BBMG IT'S HOW WE LIVE GRANT
Dream big. Do good. Live well.
Introducing the BBMG It's How We Live Grant, a $100,000 package of in-kind marketing services to create and launch a breakthrough cause marketing campaign for a visionary nonprofit and its corporate partner.
Bring us your dreams, goals and commitment, and we'll create the strategy, message and campaign to make it happen. After all, bold ideas need passionate champions.
Learn more at ItsHowWeLive.com
Deadline for submissions is July 31, 2006.
When we align our values with our actions,
great things can happen.
Actions speak louder than words.

mission. Taking a systems approach, they partner with their supplier communities to assure not only consistent supply of raw materials, but also work to keep in balance the area's social, as well as environmental health.

Extending this philosophy further, Aveda partners not only with their immediate suppliers, but their suppliers' suppliers, working up and down their supply chain, checking the integrity of all materials and processes undertaken in the creation of their products.

Aveda was one of the first companies in the United States to openly disclose recycled content for their plastics packaging, as well as the recycled content and ink composition of their paper packaging. Not stopping with simply improving existing materials, Aveda looks for new approaches and opportunities to further their goals through design and production innovation.

Empowered by its unique Mission, Aveda believes that authentic beauty is one that works in harmony with the greater web of life. It does not qualify as beauty if it hurts any of the diverse life forms that the best beauty artist of all, Nature, created. Authentic Beauty cares for the environment that we inherited from elders and will leave to generations that follow us. Beauty cares for the society in which we live, enhancing harmony in the way we live and interact with one another as human beings. In order to be Beauty, it also needs to be Good. Beauty is the result, but also the process followed in pursuing that result. Said simply, Beauty Is As Beauty Does.[2]

Due to unflinching attention to quality, healthful products, Aveda enjoys some of the best brand loyalty in the industry. Its customers feel they are getting the best quality possible and are willing to pay a premium for the level of quality assurance Aveda delivers.

Today, one is hard-pressed to find a personal care competitor that doesn't work the nature angle somehow, from corporate giving to basic ingredients. In today's beauty market, few companies openly highlight unnatural ingredients as they did in the past. Imagine a label reading NOW WITH MORE LYE! as hair products once boasted.

Ethics is only one part of a total team. Clever design that relies on ethics alone to attract an audience works only in the short term. As we've been seeing in example after example, the work and the company behind it must all deliver on the promise made to its audience.

Social Justice and Marketing

One of the cornerstones of the Natural Step, a methodology for systems thinking employing four "systems conditions" to weigh efforts, is the concept that there can be no eco-justice without social justice (System Condition 4, see "Chapter 4: Systems Thinking" for more on the Natural Step).

A farmer scratching out a living on the edge of a rainforest has more pressing needs than the fate of a few trees. His family is hungry and his land is becoming unable to sustain crops. He doesn't care that the area he lives in is really only suited to being

---

Origins, an Este Lauder company, chose WindPower Recycled Board to help complete its message of "beauty and wellness through good-for-you products." WindPower Recycled Board is a high-performance product using 50% post-consumer waste and is processed chlorine free (PCF). (*www.recycledboard.com*)

clean comforts

ORIGINS
clean comforts

ORIGINS
ginger accents

Carton made from 50% post-consumer recycled fiber. Paperboard and carton manufactured using only windpower or hydro power, both renewable energy resources. Please recycle where facilities exist.

Seul composé de 50% de fibre à partir de déchets ménagers. Le papier et carton sont fabriqués à partir de l'énergie éolienne et hydrique, deux sources d'énergie renouvelable dans les régions réservés à cet effet.

a rainforest: All he knows is farming—what he can get cash for right now. So each year he clears a little more forestland to help feed his family. But what if the forest itself became valuable if left intact? And what if that farmer were given the tools to help develop the forest's earning potential for what it really is in economic terms—a stable and yet dynamic, millennia-old production facility? A July 22, 2004, *Economist* article, "Saving the Rainforest," weighs in on this question:

> If conservation of tropical forest offers global benefits, ways must be found to charge benefi-ciaries globally. These are beginning to emerge. There is a fledgling market for payments for "environmental services," such as sequestering carbon and preserving biodiversity. Peru, for example, offers "conservation concessions" to groups with the means and know-how to manage forest. A proposal for "compensated reduction" of carbon emissions would discour-age deforestation and give developing countries, which have few commitments under the Kyoto Protocol, a bigger role in reducing greenhouse gases.[3]

So how does all this far-off thinking impact the things we choose to create? We can use the Home Depot Old Growth and Nike Sweatshop lessons as examples of needing to take larger impacts into account.

Home Depot unduly exposed itself to public criti-cism by not taking a more watchful stance on the products it sold. From 1997 to 1999, environmental groups mounted protests against the company in an effort to get the world's biggest buyer of wood to ensure it was not sourceing wood from endangered forests for its stores. Over this period, Home Depot

stores were picketed, banners were hung at its corporate headquarters in Atlanta, and activists demonstrated at shareholder meetings. Home Depot became increasingly afraid the negative publicity would result in consumer backlash and sliding sales, so it took steps to change.

Today Home Depot is part of a growing effort by corporations to work with global activists toward positive change. In this example, Home Depot began by lobbying governments and loggers to stop overcutting forests from its lumber-supplying regions. In Chile, the company helped broker a pact to deter landowners from converting native forests into the very kind of tree farms it depends on.

To meet environmentalists' demands, Home Depot agreed to change its buying practices to select wood logged in environmentally preferable ways. The first guidelines used were from the Forest Stewardship Council, a group that certifies sustainably harvested wood, as well as paper supply chains. But going a step further, as certified supplies would not be enough to meet demand and it needed to better assure the integrity of its supply chain, Home Depot worked to identify endangered forests around the world and persuade suppliers not to log there.[4]

Many retailers find that working with green groups is a fairly inexpensive way to better connect with customers and end negative publicity. Home Depot notes the cost of the new initiatives is small relative to total sales. Many companies that have been forced into change due to citizen action and then pressured their supply chain to help meet those new goals have created a ripple effect throughout their entire industry.

Although Nike and Home Depot both found them-selves in trouble due to lack of supply chain vigilance, Nike's brand was already tied to basic sustainability concepts. When it was revealed that Nike was using sweatshop labor to manufacture its goods, the integrity of its marketing message—in fact, the entire corporate brand—was immediately called into question. This is a serious thing for a company. There are many numbers tossed around, but the general rule of thumb in marketing is: It takes much more money to win customers back than to get them in the first place.

In an effort to realign its supply chain with its core ethics, Nike now encourages third-party verification of factory conditions by trade unions and NGOs. Beginning with its second Corporate Responsibility Report (2004), Nike publicly released a list of the factories it contracts with. This level of transparency is a first in the apparel and footwear industries.

"While we cannot say with certainty what greater levels of factory disclosure will unleash, we know the current system of addressing factory compliance has to be fundamentally transformed to create sustainable change," said Hannah Jones, Nike's vice president of corporate responsibility. "We believe disclosure of supply chains is a step toward greater efficiencies in monitoring and remediation and shared knowledge in capacity building that will elevate overall conditions in the industry. No one company can solve these issues that are endemic to our industry. We know the future demands more collaboration among stakeholders, not less."[5]

Green America's Basics of Fair Trade

The things we create are not just about materials alone. Fair trade is one of the key elements employed by today's sustainability leaders. As the Nike example showed, ethics-based companies need to be sure their talk is walked not just by their employees but by their vendors too. Fair trade practices need to be employed throughout a company's vertical supply chain management system to ensure that the integrity of a company's message is carried through—from the growers in the field and sewers at the factory to the product on the store shelf. Aligning a company's supply chain on more than a simple materials level can seem like a daunting task at first, but finding ethical suppliers (or helping established suppliers realign their priorities) is getting easier every day, and a variety of groups serving various industries can help make the job easier still. Green America (formerly Co-op America) is one of the oldest and most respected groups working with both businesses and consumers. Founded in 1982, Green America is a nonprofit membership organization working to harness economic power—the strength of consumers, investors, businesses, and the marketplace—to create a socially just and environmentally sustainable society.

For a free download of the full version of Green America's Guide to Fair Trade, go to *fairtradeaction. org*. But to get started understanding what fair trade is, a basic overview of fair trade principles and practices from Green America's Guide to Fair Trade follows.

A Fair Price

Fair Trade Certified™ product prices are set by the Fair Trade Labeling Organization. Prices set not only cover the cost of goods but strive to provide a fair living wage for the people involved in the production process.

Investment in People and Communities

Often Fair Trade producer cooperatives and artisan collectives reinvest their revenues back into their communities—strengthening local businesses, building health clinics and schools, supporting scholarship funds, building housing and providing leadership training and women's programs. All work to build stronger, healthier communities.

Environmental Sustainability

Fair Trade producers respect their natural habitat and are encouraged to use sustainable production methods. Example: Nearly 85 percent of Fair Trade Certified™ coffee is also organic.

Empowering Stakeholders

Fair Trade promotes producer empowerment in their communities and in the global marketplace. For Fair Trade coffee producers, their cooperatives or associations are transparent and democratically controlled by their members. For estate-grown products such as tea and bananas, Fair Trade provides revenue that is invested in a fund, managed and controlled by the farmers, and used for the interests of the community—providing education, access to healthcare, and so on.

Empowering Women

Recognizing the untapped potential of all stakeholders in a community, Fair Trade encourages participation by women in local cooperatives and in leadership roles. Fair Trade revenue also often is used to support or promote women's programs.

Direct, Long-Term Relationships

Those who import Fair Trade Certified™ products and other fairly traded goods contribute to the endeavor to establish long-term stable relationships with producer groups. These relations help not only to create healthier communities but provide a more stable and sustainable economic base, allowing entire regions to benefit.

Art Trade as a Tool for Economic Development

As economies become ever more global, art and design have found new international avenues for expansion. Apart from the business end of art production in the graphic arts sense that use more and more outsourced workers (catalogs, direct mail, animators, web design), can art (for example: paintings, illustration, textile arts, sculpture), and its trade become a tool for economic development? Can the developed world nurture growth in developing areas by finding markets for their creative "goods"?

In this article, we consider the global patterns of international trade in art. We also consider differences in the trade of the North (i.e., developed countries) and the South (i.e., developing and less-developed countries). Specifically, for which countries is art trade a significant income-generating activity? How do developing countries participate in the global art market? Motivation for exploring these questions stems from dramatic growth in art trade in recent years. Further, the patterns of art exports and imports across countries are changing. For countries where art is a large and growing share of their overall economic activity, art exports can contribute to economic development. For these reasons, international organizations such as UNESCO have initiated research and promoted policies that support art trade as an income-generating activity.[6] National organizations, such as agencies for the promotion of culture overseas, also support art trade. Countries with active cultural agencies include the United States (Embassy), Japan (Japan Foundation), Germany (Goethe Institute), the United Kingdom (British Council), and France (Institut francais).[7]

When we examine the patterns and growth of art trade for the 125 countries that comprise the international art market, we see some of these countries are currently strong participants (e.g., India) and others are new entrants (e.g., African countries). By exploring the trade of these countries, we seek to stimulate new dialog and policies that focus on art markets in the South. To this end, this article examines trade in artwork (e.g., paintings, engravings, sculptures), collector pieces, and antiques for the year 2005 and growth period 2000–05.

Value of Art Trade in Aggregate

What is the economic value of art trade? In aggregate, the value of world trade in art was $14.6 billion in 2005. To give perspective, this value of art trade is slightly larger than world trade in coffee. It is nearly double world trade in cotton. It is slightly smaller than world trade in manufactured tobacco, and is approximately half of the world's trade in motor vehicles.[8] Further, in terms of growth, art exports increased by 8979 percent for the average country during the period 2000–05. If we omit two unusually high-growth countries, we find that average art exports increased by 285 percent. This growth in art trade is exceptionally high relative to growth in other sectors of the economy, though also highly variable across countries.

Art Trade Between Countries

Which countries are the sources and recipients of art traded in the international market? The world art market is concentrated in a relatively small number of countries. The United Kingdom and the United States are the largest exporters of art, with about 68 percent (or $9.8 billion) of the world's art exports. The United Kingdom and United States also dominate the import market, accounting for approximately two-thirds of the world's imports (65 percent, or $9.0 billion). Beyond these two countries, other significant participants include Switzerland, France, and Germany, together exporting and importing 16.0 percent (or $2.3 billion) of the world's art traded. While the North dominates the export and import markets, prominent exporters from the South, most notably includes South Africa, but also includes India, the Republic of Korea, China. For such developing countries that export significantly more art than they import, art trade can be a significant income-generating activity.

Art Trade as a Percentage of Economic Activity

For which countries are art exports a large percentage of overall economic activity? We answer this question by examining each country's art exports and imports as a percentage of their gross domestic product (GDP). These percentages reveal the magnitude of a country's art trade relative to its total economic activity. Art trade is a relatively important economic activity for the United Kingdom, Switzerland, and Hong Kong.[9] These countries have art exports that are large in absolute terms and relative to other economic activities. This is consistent with the prominence of London (United Kingdom), Basel (Switzerland), and Hong Kong as city/state centers for art. In contrast, art trade is a relatively small share of the total economic activities of countries such as the United States and Germany.

Art trade is a relatively large percentage of the economic activities of developing countries. We also find that developing countries engage in one-way trade—they either export or they import—but not both. Developing countries that rely on art exports include African countries, while developing countries that rely on art imports tend to be island economies.

There are three implications to these findings:

1. The income generated from art exports is more important to countries of the South as a share of their total economic activity.

2. There is a large volume of North-to-North trade within the same group of developed countries.

3. There is a pattern of South-to-North trade across distinct groups of developing and developed countries. For example, artwork traded between countries that differ in level of development may be distinguished by cultural origin, historical period (such as antiquaries), or continental region (such as Asian art).

Growth in Art Exports

Which countries have high growth of art exports? We explore this question to get a sense of trends in art trade over time. That is, growth rates help us identify which countries are likely to be significant contributors to the future international art market. The findings show growth greater than 100 percent for 37 countries during the period from 2000 to 2005. For these countries, art exports have more than doubled in five years. Interestingly, all but two of these are developing countries.[10] These high-growth developing countries include both active participants and new entrants in the international art market.

Active participants with high growth rates include India and the Republic of Korea. India experienced a growth rate in art exports of 18,545 percent from 2000–05 (from $2.5 to $459.4 million). The Republic of Korea experienced a growth rate in art exports of 95 percent (from $22.0 to $174.6 million). These dramatic growth rates far exceed the growth of the overall economies of these countries.

Emerging entrants in the international art market with high growth include many African countries. Indeed, eight African countries experienced more than a doubling of their art exports from 2000 to 2005. These countries include the United Republic of Tanzania, Malawi, Ivory Coast, Uganda, Zambia, Gambia, Namibia, and Benin. Of these high-growth countries, art exports are a relatively large percentage of overall economic activities, particularly in Malawi, Ivory Coast, Zambia, and Namibia. In terms of the value of art exports, Namibia and the Ivory Coast are the leading African countries in the international art market.

Clearly, the international market for art is growing dramatically, particularly in developing countries. The inflows of monies associated with art exports will continue to increase over time with continued growth of their art sectors.

The facts emerge from this analysis are:

Fact 1: International trade in art is highly concentrated between a relatively small number of countries. These countries comprise only one-fifth of the world.

Fact 2: The North dominates the international art market, but there are active participants from the South, and include India and the Republic of Korea.

Fact 3: Art exports are more important to the South when viewed as a percentage of total economic activity rather than in absolute terms.

Fact 4: The direction of art trade tends to be two-way trade between developed countries (North to North) and one-way trade from developing to developed countries (South to North).

Fact 5: The international market for art is growing faster than other economic sectors. Countries with the highest growth in exports are developing countries. Thirty-five developing countries experienced growth in art exports greater than 100 percent from 2000 to 2005. Prominent examples include India, Republic of Korea, Namibia, and Ivory Coast.

Broader Perspective

Is international trade in art a significant economic development activity? The findings here are just the tip of the iceberg. Certainly for developed countries such as the United Kingdom and Switzerland, the value of art exports is large in absolute terms and relative to their overall economic activities. For developing countries such as India and the Republic of Korea, the value of art exports is large in absolute terms, relative terms, and growth. Indeed, many developing countries, particularly in Africa, have growth in art exports that dramatically exceeds the growth of their aggregate economies. The international art market provides a development opportunity, particularly for these high-growth countries, With policy support (such as Fair Trade arrangements and Micro loans), this growth may be fostered in an ethics-based manner.

HELLO
my name is

HELLO
my name is

Case Study: Project Hello

Project Hello was not launched as a company or an organization but as a random act of kindness that began in the fall of 2003. Its core mission was to maximize the creative community's problem-solving talents to instigate social change.

Inspired from overhearing a local homeless man's name on his way to work one morning, Chad Rea, Project Hello founder, stopped looking at the man as a panhandler (his name is Robertson, Rea points out) but as a person he wanted to know more about and help. Rea began to wonder if his own experience could work on a larger scale.

Originally the idea was to distribute, over the course of one weekend, 5,000 oversized "Hello My Name Is . . ." nametags to the homeless in Los Angeles—street corners all over the city would be occupied by people holding a sign with their handwritten name, demanding that they be seen as human beings. Rea wanted the issue of homelessness to be front-page news, to create dialogue, to build awareness by giving homeless people a voice, and to give organizations serving the homeless a platform to offer solutions. For Rea, if he could change the public's perception of homelessness, even if only one person at a time, Project Hello would be a success.

After months of mostly positive meetings with local homeless organizations to help with the distribution of signs, a unified effort proved impossible for a variety of reasons. Rather than let the idea die, though, Rea thought the idea might have even more impact if materials were distributed through thousands of amateur and professional photographers around the world. The idea was to let them bring forward images of homeless people in their own community to be compiled for a Web site, a traveling photo exhibition, a free book, and "whatever else presented itself along the way," Rea adds.

By appealing to the creative community and allowing them to make a difference by donating their time, talent, and materials, Project Hello was able to pull the entire effort off without spending little more than postage.

To date, Project Hello has distributed over 3,500 signs in more than 30 countries; created a comprehensive Web site with over 700 photographs; launched 15 national public service announcements in the United States; mounted a traveling photo exhibition; earned worldwide media coverage in over 50 publications; and was the recipient of the Advertising Community Together (ACT) 2004 Dove Award, the highest honor for socially responsible advertising.

Rea's personal eureka moment came at the 2004 Clio Awards. There he was asked to speak about Project Hello and other cause-marketing initiatives created by advertising and design agencies. Not only were there few examples for him to offer, it occurred to him that the industry's best creative problem solvers were solving the wrong kinds of problems. He thought, "If everyone redirected their energy to the real problems of the world, we might just solve them." It was at that moment that he decided it was time to put his own problem solving abilities to good use. Not 10 percent of the time but 100 percent of the time, with Project Hello being just the beginning. For more information, visit the Web site at *www.projecthello.org*.

Source: Case provided by Chad Rea,
www.ecopop.com.

Design as Bridge or Barrier

A generally accepted industry statistic is that about 70 percent of all purchase decisions are made in the store, and 70 to 90 percent of new products fail each year. These are sobering numbers. Combine this with the fraction of a second one gets to catch an audience's eye in the store, on the Internet, or walking past the trash on the way inside from the mailbox, and one must wonder why anyone would want to sell products at all.

The simple answer is, we have to. Most of us are unable to make all of the goods we need to survive on our own, so we must participate in an integrated and cooperative economic system. Moving product then becomes not just an intellectual exercise but an act of survival.

Given the huge weight involved with decision making, finely tuned and effective design becomes one of the single most important elements a company can engineer to guarantee its survival.

This is pretty intense. So many people making so many of their purchase decisions in the blink of an eye, design can either be the bridge uniting the audience to producer, or a barrier, keeping producer and audience apart.

What Is Good versus Great Design?

A good design is one that does what it's supposed to with a minimum of expense and hassle for everyone involved. Great design, however, takes that even further by delivering maximum "hits" (sales, mouse clicks, response calls, repeat purchases) per market segment with maximum middle- and end-user satisfaction.

Oddly, in spite of all the economic, environmental, and actual weight a piece must carry, decisions about design are still too often driven by people with little or no training in design or production, buyer motivation science, or even an understanding of the real "need" the item must serve. With millions of dollars at stake, why do companies continue to do that? At least in the United States the answer is because they still can. Very few states have enacted the strict producer responsibility laws that are being enacted in markets best positioned to afford U.S. goods: the European Union, Japan, Australia, and Canada.

Also, the United States has not experienced a direct consumer revolt, forcing producers to take responsibility for their products. By contrast, in the 1980s, Germany had a garbage crisis. In an effort to better attach costs to consumption, lawmakers increased all trash-hauling fees. The increase was so high that consumers began emptying their purchase contents into containers from home, leaving the manufacturers' packaging at the end of the checkout line. Not wanting to be left holding the bag, retailers in turn demanded less (or more efficient) packaging solutions from their suppliers, which quickly pulled the whole system into line.

Today, while enjoying a comparable standard of living, "Europeans on average use 47.2 percent fewer resources per person (in oil energy equivalent units) as their North American counterparts."[11]

The things we create do not require those involved in making key decisions to be experts in every point, but they must have a solid enough background to know which questions to ask, whom to seek out for answers, and what to do with the answers once they get them.

A universal lament among designers is: You're only as good as your clients let you be. Yet innovation can happen only when people lose their fear of asking questions. Often a simple "Why do we do it this way?" or "Do we really need it (or this part)?" can spark real and positive change.

Encouraging Choice

With the world's increased focus on green living, companies are clamoring to tell their customers what they're doing to benefit the environment. And consumers are demanding transparent and truthful communication about all aspects of the products they use.

Both groups know that consumer choice is one of capitalism's most powerful tools—and the environment's trump card. How do products communicate to the consumer to encourage good choices?

Communicating a Product's Story

Traditionally, eco-labels or similar stamps of approval by a plethora of certifiers have helped conscientious consumers make purchasing decisions that benefit the environment. But as applied sustainability gains momentum, companies and consumers need a more effective tool to explain how products impact the planet.

Growing segmentation within the sustainability market has brought an array of green-marketing claims (organic, local, fair trade, zero emissions, carbon neutral), causing confusion among consumers. We've all heard examples of something sustainable in one context and environmentally damaging in another.

No product fits a cookie-cutter definition of sustainability. Communicating sustainability requires big-picture connections between the product in your hand and the outside world. The need is greater than a simple, single eco-label can fully address.

Background Stories

One way to arm consumers with the information they need to gauge the eco-worthiness of a product is through visual storytelling.

Born of a master's thesis project, Background Stories is a prototype of a tool that reveals a product's social and environmental impact by visually describing it life cycle—from the production line to the store shelf—with graphics and fact-based captions in a storyline.

Just as nutrition labels provide consistent information (calories, total fat, sodium, etc.), Background Stories can note a product's carbon footprint and other life cycle analysis (LCA) indicators in a framework that also supports existing product labels that certify elements of sustainability, such as organic and Fair Trade. A product's Background Story continues on the company's Web site, where consumers are offered the opportunity to dig deeper into the manufacturer's business practices.

Consumers can choose to explore the information at their own pace or not at all. Just as some consumers are avid readers of Nutrition Facts and others only

Background Stories: Connecting the consumer to their supply chain.

occasionally glance at sodium levels, Background Stories allow consumers to adapt to their own way of navigating a product's social and environmental information.

The system can be customized for any product and speaks to the consumer in a positive way. No scolding fingers are wagged. Consumers do not get told what is right or wrong. They are simply presented with facts through storytelling—a familiar, engaging form of communication.

Why It Works

Background Stories present a win-win situation for the environment, consumers, and business. Consumers are armed with information about a product's environmental impact before purchasing, driving healthy choices for people and the planet. Companies can present their products' sustainability stories—typically buried in sustainability and corporate social responsibility reports—at the point of sale.

Longer-Term Impact Is Even More Promising

Companies with Background Stories on their products will innovate toward manufacturing, transportation, and production practices that reduce negative environmental impact. Consequently, the bar will be raised in sustainability reporting and action. Background Stories can help drive consumers' demand for simpler and more accessible information from companies on packaging, enabling companies to evaluate their approach to preserving the planet and how they share preservation practices.

As they learn from Background Stories on select products, consumers will be better educated on the processes behind those products and inclined to explore the impacts of products without Background Stories.

Compared to other information sources, Background Stories gets stuff right into the consumers hands, allowing companies to put substantive information, not just marketing hype, about their sustainability practices on the back of a box, a hang tag on a garment, or the side panel of a toy package. Where eco-labels mark single attributes, Background Stories put them in context.

Article by Arlene Birt and Fred Haberman. Visit www .backgroundstories.com for more information.

Case Study: Village Green Passport

It's no surprise that *Billboard Magazine* chose Jack Johnson as the number-one green musician activist; even his recording studio is solar powered. Johnson's commitment to the environment carries over to his concerts and worldwide music tours. While typical music concerts and tours can generate tons of waste, including paper, careful planning and partnerships with other eco-minded organizations can make all the difference.

The keepsake pocket-size Village Green Passport for Jack Johnson's 2008 World Tour saves paper, reduces trash, and keeps all of the key tour partners' information and greening actions together in one compact resource. The passport also educates music fans about choices and actions they can take to become active in their local and world community. Johnson partnered with MusicMatters, a marketing agency that specializes in creating innovative and effective campaigns—merging music, marketing and activism—to provide greening services and a vibrant "Village Green" while on tour.

EcoLingo, a green design studio, was commissioned to design the fourteen-page multilingual passport to visually communicate the campaign's tour message, to provide eco resources, and to inspire positive environmental action. Jack Johnson's "Sleep Through the Static" album artwork by Lively + Motch is on the cover, featuring photography and handlettering by Thomas Campbell. Campbell's photos, doodles and background images continue through the passport and collateral materials,

setting the mood for this dynamic project. Translated into six to nine languages/versions, the passport highlights Village Green actions and resources–"your actions," "your voice," and "your choice," with the American version urging fans to register to vote.

Resource saving measures include:

Design: ecoLingo's electronic design and publishing is powered by the sun and wind. The studio purchases renewable energy for studio use, plus offsets all carbon dioxide and global warming impacts through a Green-e® certified provider. During this project, ecoLingo used state-of-the-art paperless and virtual work flows, including project management software that allowed ecoLingo and MusicMatters to share materials and collaborate together via a web browser.

Paper: New Leaf Reincarnation Matte. This recycled paper stock is FSC® certified, contains 100% recycled fiber and 50% post-consumer waste, is processed chlorine free, and is manufactured with electricity that is offset with Green-e® certified renewable energy certificates.

Printing: American and International versions were printed by a Forest Stewardship Council® certified printer using soy-based inks and DtP (Direct to Plate) printing. To save resources, the same cyan, magenta, and yellow plates were used, with only the black ink plate generated and switched between the translations and

versions. While traditional passports use heavy paper stock throughout, the Village Green Passport used lighter-weight paper for the inside pages. This not only conserves paper and resources, it also helps to save on shipping costs and greenhouse emissions associated with transportation.

Additional information about ecoLingo and MusicMatters:

Founded on Earth Day in 2002, ecoLingo is an award-winning graphic design studio. A certified green business, the studio collaborates with people and businesses that share a caring commitment to the environment, good causes, and the community.

MusicMatters™ works closely with leading organic and natural companies to bring their brands to life across the country with experiential and field marketing programs. MusicMatters' innovative programs and dedicated organic-minded Brand Activists™ ensure a meaningful brand experience for target audiences.

Thing or Service?

We can't really begin to understand what the problem is until we step back and look at things from a new perspective. We accumulate things, but is it the thing we want or the service of the thing? When we buy a car, are we interested in the owner-ship of the car (status symbol) or the function of the car (moving people and stuff around)? When we pick up a brochure, do we really want colorful paper or just the information the paper carries?

These are some fundamental questions that lie at the heart of circular and restorative consumption and, by extension sustainable design. In the case of print design, our bird's-eye view tells us that unless some secondary use is built into the thing (a book with pop-out airplanes to fold), usually we're not really interested in the object but in the information the medium carries.

One company that looks at what it creates from a service standpoint is Minnesota-based Restore Products. Restore Products' mission is to serve customers by making it fun, easy, and cost effective to clean and maintain their investments (clothes, dishes, homes, businesses) without harm to the planet or its people. All Restore cleaning products are designed with performance, user safety, and the environment in mind.

Restore's products are made from renewable, plant-based ingredients and use no petroleum solvents, chlorine, ammonia, alcohol, or hazardous ingredients. They don't give off toxic fumes or irritate the skin if used correctly, they contain no known carcinogens, and they are readily biodegradable.

Building on the idea that people are really looking to buy a product's service, not a bottle of soap, the Restore Products system was born.

Restore's products are distributed in specially sized and labeled bottles, created to key into their refill stations. The refill stations will work only for Restore packaging. With this design system, Restore allows consumers to maintain the advantages of the package (use information and product safety warnings—critical for cleaning products, plus branding graphics key for the company) while still helping to keep thousands of tons of plastic out of landfills and incinerators. See *www.restoreproducts .com* for more information.

Eco-Labeling and Eco-Marketing Claims

Many in industry today are talking about a "life cycle facts" label for the things we create. Similar to Nutrition Facts, this label would allow consumers to make important comparisons when choosing which product to buy. To get beyond wild claims and greenwashing, a labeling program of this depth would require standards that do not yet exist (including measurements along the whole of the product's supply chain). This level of detail is currently in the works by many governments and nongovernmental organizations around the world. It may not be in place now, but like the Nutrition Facts panel of the 1990s, we will be seeing this information as standard fare in one form or another very soon.

Nutrition Facts Panel for a Healthier Planet

How do you know what's good to buy? In an age of marketing spin and greenwashing, how can consumers trust a label saying eco-friendly, organic, or Energy Star? Simple yes-or-no systems get trapped by either low standards or excluding good but not great contenders. Even multilevel systems can seem opaque and arbitrary. Customers need objectivity, not just an opinion about quality. Objectivity starts by showing numbers.

Marketers usually try to avoid numbers because they worry that consumers get scared by them and won't make sense to them. (Is 75 kg of carbon emission for a cell phone good or bad?) But nutrition labels are full of numbers, with ingredients lists full of unpronounceable chemical names, and consumers want them for three reasons.

1. They make people feel safer. Even if they don't understand the data, they feel reassured by the level of transparency between them and the producer.

2. If consumers are educated about certain things (e.g., fat, calories, or sodium), the labels are a tool for decision making.

3. Even if people are uninformed, the labels educate them about nutrition, just by seeing what is important to list. Curious consumers may then compare products side by side in the store. After some experience, they know a "good" number of calories for a certain kind of food, without needing to compare. Nutrition labels not only aid consumer decision making but also increase the general public's nutritional awareness.

A Hypothetical Full Life Cycle Label

This section shows a hypothetical Environmental Facts label, modeled after the Nutrition Facts label. The text portion gives quantitative details of production and ingredients—it is the product's life cycle analysis in a nutshell. The graphic portion gives qualitative information at a glance, summarizing the product's impacts in four categories: Resource use, energy use, water use, waste, and labor practices.

Resource use, energy use, water use, waste, and labor practices are the main things you need to know to decide how sustainable a product is. Energy use (including production, transport, and usage) is usually one of the biggest impacts, with consequences for climate change, peak oil (the decline point leading to the end of all oil reserves), and air pollution. Resource use has long been known to be an environmental problem, causing deforestation and other habitat loss as well as pollution and landfills. In addition to listing the resources used, the label would note how to dispose of the product after use (recycling, take-back programs, compost, etc.). Toxins could be a separate section, calling out chemicals known to have human or environmental health impacts, so you can see how healthful the product is to have in your home and how safe it is to produce. Water is becoming an increasingly serious issue in the world as population pressures cause scarcity. The amount of water used to make a product can be surprising. (A pound of U.S. beef requires between 440 and 2,500 gallons of water to produce.) Finally, exploitative trade and labor conditions are unsustainable, while good practices should be rewarded, as should transparency (organizational accountability and openness).

The data listed would include all material ingredients and wastes (with toxic and nonrenewable materials and wastes labeled as such) as well as all embodied energy (all power/fuel used, from resource collection through manufacture and end-of-life) and water, transportation averages (or countries of origin), and social/labor factors. Measuring all this is not simple. Some items do not inherently have numbers (e.g., labor practices) and would be assigned a score based on either internal company metrics (which Nike, Starbucks, and many other companies already have) or a third-party standard, such as the Human Rights Campaign's Corporate Equality Index. The ingredients, waste, and other numbers would require an agreed-on depth of life cycle measurement: Do we measure the product at the assembly stage only, or also include vendors' subassemblies, and their vendors'

sub-subassemblies, or go all the way back to mining the raw materials?

While it is difficult to make these data perfect, it is not difficult to get a decent estimate of a product's impacts using LCA. Many LCA software tools already exist, and dozens of major companies, such as 3M, HP, and Toyota, already practice it. As with anything, more standards will develop as more companies perform LCA. As we saw with nutrition labels around the world, governments may create mandatory standards. Already, the Federal Trade Commission has guidelines for what product labels may legally claim is recyclable, biodegradable, compostable, and so on. The European Commission's new EU regulatory system for chemicals REACH (*registration*, *evaluation*, and *authorization* of *chemicals*) is already pushing companies to investigate and report the materials they use throughout their entire supply chain. Given the complexity of the information, the EU might eventually require a label similar to a Nutrition Facts label be on all products.

A label's graphic elements are designed to make it more accessible. Six-year-olds should be able to read it and get decision-making value from it, even if they don't understand the numbers or the words in the text. The graphic's color scale of good to bad would be relative by product type, grading products on a curve so that computers would be colored on a different scale from sofas, for instance. The colors could also be renormalized every few years, so that the best products continue to stand out even when industries as a whole improve.

A Driver for Change

On a single company's marketing piece, an eco-nutrition label would be a green marketing rocket

Worst | | **Best**

Environmental Facts
Overall Weighted Score _____ 6 / 10

Energy
Embodied energy _____ 2,800kWhr
   Type of energy used: 2,000kWhr coal, 800kWhr solar PV
Energy usage, avg. est. _____ 1,900kWhr/yr
Transportation origin
   Product: USA
   Materials: USA, China, Korea, South Africa

Resources
Product
Mass _____ 10kg
Non-virgin material _____ 5%
Recyclable/Compostable material _____ 30%
   aluminum, steel, plastic #1
Ingredients: Polyethylene terephthalate (PET), aluminum, steel, glass,
   copper, fiberglass, acrylonitrile-butadiene styrene (ABS), lead-free solder,
   nematic liquid crystals, polyimide, indium-tin oxide, Polycarbonate,
   Poly(methyl methacrylate) (PMMA), Styrene-butadiene co-polymer,
   Polyethylene ether, Triphenyl phosphate, polybrominated flame retardant,
   silicon, silicon dioxide, silicon nitride, selenium, cadmium, antimony,
   dopants
Life Expectancy _____ 4-7yrs
End-of-life _____ return to manufacturer

Packaging & Misc.
Mass _____ 800g
Non-virgin material _____ 20%
Recyclable/Compostable material _____ 100%
   cardboard, paper, PLA plastic
Ingredients: cardboard, paper, PLA plastic, soy-based ink
End-of-life _____ recycle, compost

Toxins

Restricted/Toxic ingredients: polybrominated flame retardant, cadmium,
   antimony, dopants
Restricted/Toxic production waste: toluene, mercury oxides, cadmium,
   antimony, arsine, silane, chlorine, phosgene, perfluorocompounds (CF_4,
   C_2F_6, NF_3, SF_6, CHF_3)

Water

Embodied water _____ 2,600L
Water pollution _____ 2/10

Social

Labor Practices _____ 8/10
Fair trade _____ 4/10
Transparency _____ 6/10

engine, propelling it far ahead of the competition. Such labels would be a boon to audience choice within a single industry. On all products everywhere, quantitative eco-labels would embed sustainable thinking into the mental landscape of audiences and industrial purchasers. One of the main barriers to green choice today is simply lack of information.

No system is perfect, and any system can be "gamed," but even a slightly flawed system is vastly better than mass ignorance. Audiences, producers, and investors are already clamoring for measurement systems in many markets, because there is a strong correlation between environmentally and socially responsible companies and companies that make quality products. In the coming decades, labels will become much more ubiquitous and informational.

Source: Article by Jeremy Faludi. Article concept first appeared in "Worldchanging: A User's Guide for the 21st Century," by Alex Steffen, Al Gore, and Bruce Sterling. Harry N. Abrams, Inc. (November 1, 2006)

Carbon Labeling

In addition to the carbon footprint created by the production process, one of a product's larger impacts is in transport to point of distribution. For example, the carbon footprint of fruit shipped from southern climates to northern ones via air is often much greater than fruit grown in the North during appropriate seasons. A 2001 Iowa State University study showed that using conventional food supply chains, the average piece of produce travels

Nutrition Facts for a healthier planet.

1,494 miles to get to the Iowa consumer. Compared to purely locally supplied foods, the conventional system used much more fuel, resulting in the release of 5 to 17 times more carbon dioxide (CO_2) into the atmosphere.[12]

With this impact in mind, the British grocery giant Tesco announced plans to label products with their carbon footprint. Using an airplane icon on products, customers can recognize and then purchase goods based on the amount of CO_2 embodied in their goods and produce as well as the nutrition information they already use to weigh their choices. Combining a variety of emission reduction schemes, Tesco's goal by 2020 is to reduce emissions from existing stores worldwide by at least 50 percent and to restrict air transport to less than 1 percent of its products.

Transportation is only one part of the equation. Produce grown in the South and imported by air may have a lower carbon footprint than those grown in heated greenhouses in the North, according to experts developing carbon labeling in Britain. Ministers are working with the Carbon Trust and British Standards Institution to develop a benchmark for measurements, allowing businesses to calculate the overall carbon load of their goods and label them accordingly.

Ian Pearson, Britain's environment minister, said in 2007, "More and more, businesses are looking for ways to reduce their impact on the environment. To help them achieve that we need a reliable, consistent way to measure these impacts that businesses recognize, trust, and understand."[13]

For more information about carbon and addressing its impacts, refer to Carbon Accounting section in Chapter 5.

Speaking the Truth, and Meaning It

Attitudes are beginning to change. The idea of taking one's global impact personally—that "being part of the global village" is more than a platitude—is starting to become part of our shared psyche. In the more eco-forward countries, strict regulations governing the sustainability (eco-ness) of what one does and how it's done have been a normal part of doing business for years. For U.S. companies, this means getting their arms around the idea that living off loopholes and workarounds does not fly in other markets. In fact, companies have found that if they want to sell on foreign turf, or even maintain positive audience perception at home against foreign brand "invaders," they need to approach their output with the same concern as competitors from more conscientious markets. How profitable is it really to stick to the (lax) letter of the law at home, when hometown buyers begin to find the foreign brand more attractive? The United States has already seen this in the auto industry—with Japanese automakers selling "features" to the U.S. market that are mandated in their home market (higher gas mileage, tougher emissions requirements, etc.).

On the federal level in the United States, current guidelines governing the use of eco-marketing claims are voluntary. The ideas the Federal Trade Commission's (FTC) Environmental Marketing Claims Guidelines (Green Guides) cover are becoming mandatory in the more aggressively green states (e.g., California) and becoming verifiable benchmarks for eco-goals set by large goods buyers and distributors in the United States (e.g., Walmart's scorecards for packaging and electronics). In addition to realigning efforts to meet demands of the domestic audience, firms working in the major trading markets that can afford U.S. goods have already begun to adopt or, in some cases, exceed the demands of the FTC Green Guides. Not only does this better position them for selling abroad; it also is a sound defensive strategy against foreign competitors selling in their home markets. Who wants to be shown up in front of their home-town crowd?

Issued in 1992 and last updated in 1998, the FTC's Green Guides have been around for quite some time. Consumers, and eco-advocacy groups that serve them, have begun to express concern (and confusion) over the new flood of products touting their "greenness" with producers and buyers alike having no real understanding of what that means. In an effort to make the guides more effective, in 2008, the FTC initiated an overhaul of the guides, starting with the hot-button terms "carbon off-sets," "renewable," and "sustainable," which have no definitions under the 1998 guidelines.[14] In addition to defining new terms, the FTC will better define a variety of labels and terms already in the guides.

The FTC's 2008 workshop addressed claims that would appear on packaging and products, but changes adopted would apply to any marketing claim a company makes (mailings, Web sites, promotions, etc.). Topics addressed included:

— Trends resulting in environmental claims

— Terms currently covered by the Green Guides and whether the perception of these terms has changed over the past decade

— New terms not currently addressed in the Green Guides

— Claims based on third-party certification and consumer perception of such claims

— The impact of scientific and technological changes, including the use of new materials and their impact on the environment

— The current state of substantiation for green claims

— The need for new or updated FTC guidance in these areas[15]

Also in 2008, as the FTC began taking comments on improving the Green Guides, Cone LLC and the Boston College Center for Corporate Citizenship released their "2008 Green Gap Survey."[16]

According to the survey, almost 39 percent of Americans are seeking and buying products they believe to be "environmentally friendly," although at the same time, they don't know what the term really means. Nearly half (48 percent) believe a product marketed as "green" or "environmentally friendly" is fully "eco." Only 22 percent surveyed really under-stood that many green marketing terms in use describe a product that is "less bad" than previous versions or competing products. Americans, it appears, simply do not realize a green gap exists.

The survey revealed:

— 47 percent trust companies to tell them the truth in environmental messaging.

— 45 percent believe companies are accurately communicating information about their impact on the environment.

— 61 percent of Americans say they understand the environmental terms companies use in their advertising.

Mike Lawrence, executive vice president of corporate responsibility at Cone LLC, comments:

> The gap creates significant risk of embarrassment for companies and disillusionment for consumers. . . . Activists are closely monitoring green claims and can quickly share information online about the actual environmental impact of a product. The result can be accusations that a company is engaging in "greenwashing" and is misleading the public.[17]

Commitment to their ethic and message has been the common thread shared by all of today's eco-leaders. Not only do they make sure that they understand the impacts of their current efforts as part of their core ethic, but they understand that no one can do it all perfectly right from the start. With this in mind, they continuously look for ways to improve on what they are already doing right as well as staying on top of things they need to work on. But most important, they talk openly about those efforts, keeping appearances and actions transparent, which is a key element of sustainable business practice.

For companies just beginning their journey, the easy answer is: Go for the low-hanging fruit but really mean it. Then make a serious, and public, commitment to working on the rest. As noted, this last part is key. Many companies have been the subject of very public advocacy action in response to their seeming inactivity on (or indifference to) sustainability issues—taking hits to their brand equity in the process—when, in reality, they were working hard on the problem for years before the eco-campaign but did not want to talk about it until they got it "just right."

In contrast to companies actually trying to do well but not talking about it are those companies that have no problem merely "talking." As the Cone study illustrates, many companies are doing almost nothing but talking, treating the shift toward sustainability as just another fad, just more copy to fill up blank space on a box or ad.[18]

Because the United States is such a huge market, and its directives on the use of eco-marketing claims are still voluntary, talking a good game but not walking the talk (greenwashing) is easy, and has left the door open to an epidemic of marketing confusion. According to a 2007 report by TerraChoice Environmental Marketing that solidified the fears and impacts brought out by Cone's study, an overwhelming majority of environmental marketing claims in North America are inaccurate, inappropriate, or unsubstantiated. Using metrics from the FTC and the Environmental Protection Agency, of the over 1,000 products reviewed, TerraChoice concluded that most claims were demonstrably false or at risk of misleading.[19] Even if one believes that TerraChoice's original 2007 study, and broader 2009 study were both horribly flawed, given that the FTC guides for claims, as well as guides in the broader 2009 study markets, have been out since the late 1990s, and too, that information to verify (or dispute) claims today is readily available, why should any product not be what it claims to be? It could be that many well-intentioned people simply don't understand what marketing claims guidelines mean.

Six types of common labeling problems surfaced from TerraChoice's 2007 study, with 2009's study prompting the addition of a seventh. These issues included false claims, true but unverified claims, nonspecific claims, claims that could be true of any product, true claims that are used to mask problems, claims that exceed third-party certification limits, and clams the give the impression of third-party endorsement where no such endorsement exists. Longtime eco-practitioners have found it difficult to accept new members to the eco-club for these very reasons.

"If not forced by regulation with real penalties," they argue, "what's to stop any competitor from just donning a green suit and exclaiming—We're here!—taking away some of our hard-earned market share?" The reality is: Very little. But this is not the Dark Ages, and news about bad behavior can be around the world in seconds. Consumers, bloggers, and eco-advocacy groups are all just waiting to pounce on companies just in it for the "green"—and not following through on what that actually means. Greenwashing does work but only for a little while. As new scrutiny avenues expand, stakeholders at all levels are taking another look at the people they do business with, asking "If they're not taking things that impact the long-term health of my brand (and company) seriously, what else are they doing that needs looking harder at?"

TerraChoice: Sins of Greenwashing

When reviewing the FTC Environmental Marketing Claims Guideline, or any country's marketing claims guideline, before a project, TerraChoice Environmental Marketing's Sins of Greenwashing is a handy heuristic to keep in mind.

Green-wash (green'wash', -wôsh') verb: the act of misleading consumers regarding the environmental practices of a company or the environmental benefits of a product or service.

1. Sin of the Hidden Trade-off

For example, paper (including household tissue, paper towel and copy paper): "Okay, this product comes from a sustainably harvested forest, but what are the impacts of its milling and transportation? Is the manufacturer also trying to reduce those impacts?"

Emphasizing one environmental issue isn't a problem (indeed, it often makes for better communications). The problem arises when hiding a trade-off between environmental issues.

2. Sin of No Proof

For example, personal care products (such as shampoos and conditioners) that claim not to have been tested on animals but offer no evidence or certification of this claim.

Company Web sites, third-party certifiers, and toll-free phone numbers are easy and effective means of delivering proof.

3. Sin of Vagueness

For example, garden insecticides promoted as "chemical-free." In fact, nothing is free of chemicals.

Water is a chemical. All plants, animals, and humans are made of chemicals, as are all products. If the marketing claim doesn't explain itself ("Here's what we mean by 'eco'"), the claim is vague and meaningless. Similarly, watch for other popular vague green terms: "nontoxic," "all-natural," "environmentally friendly," and "earth friendly."

4. Sin of Worshiping False Labels

A product that, through either words or images, gives the impression of third-party endorsement where no such endorsement exists; fake labels, in other words.

5. Sin of Irrelevance

For example, chlorofluorocarbon (CFC)–free oven cleaners, shaving gels, window cleaners, disinfectants.

Could all of the other products in this category make the same claim? The most common example is easy to detect: Don't be impressed by CFC-free! Ask if the claim is important and relevant to the product. (If a light bulb claimed water efficiency benefits you should be suspicious.) Comparison shop (and ask the competitive vendors).

6. Sin of the Lesser of Two Evils

For example, organic tobacco, "green" insecticides and herbicides.

Is the claim trying to make consumers feel "green" about a product category of questionable environmental benefit? Consumers concerned about the pollution associated with cigarettes would be better served by quitting smoking than by buying organic cigarettes. Similarly, consumers concerned about the human health and environmental risks of excessive use of lawn chemicals might create a bigger environmental benefit by reducing their use than by looking for greener alternatives.

7. Sin of Fibbing

For example, shampoos that claim to be "certified organic" but for which our research could find no such certification.

When we check up on it, is the claim true? The most frequent examples were false uses of third-party certifications. Thankfully, these are easy to confirm. Legitimate third-party certifiers—EcoLogo™, Chlorine Free Products Association (CFPA), Forest Stewardship Council (FSC), Green Guard, Green Seal, for example— all maintain publicly available lists of certified products. Some even maintain fraud advisories for products falsely claiming certification.

Sources: "Six Sins of Greenwashing" and "Seven Sins of Greenwashing," by TerraChoice Environmental Marketing Inc. To review their 2007 and 2009 studies as well as future updates go to www.terrachoice.com. "Greenwashing: A Dirty Job?" article concept by Wendy Jedlička, first appeared on www.BrandChannel.com, February 4, 2008.

FTC Green Guides

The Federal Trade Commission began public comment to update its Environmental Marketing Guidelines in January 2008. The guidelines have been out for over a decade, but as the TerraChoice study showed, people were unaware the guides existed, didn't bother reading them, or intentionally ignored them. We present the 1998 guidelines here as a learning tool. They apply to every environmental marketing claim a firm might issue and should be mandatory reading for students and professionals alike.[20]

FTC Environmental Marketing Guidelines

Statement of Purpose (260.1)

These guides represent administrative interpretations of laws administered by the Federal Trade Commission for the guidance of the public in conducting its affairs in conformity with legal requirements. These guides specifically address the application of Section 5 of the FTC Act to environmental advertising and marketing practices. They provide the basis for voluntary compliance with such laws by members of industry. Conduct inconsistent with the positions articulated in these guides may result in corrective action by the Commission under Section 5 if, after investigation, the Commission has reason to believe that the behavior falls within the scope of conduct declared unlawful by the statute.

Scope of Guides (260.2)

These guides apply to environmental claims included in labeling, advertising, promotional materials and all other forms of marketing, whether asserted directly or by implication, through words, symbols, emblems, logos, depictions, product brand names, or through any other means, including marketing through digital or electronic means, such as the Internet or electronic mail. The guides apply to any claim about the environmental attributes of a product, package or service in connection with the sale, offering for sale, or marketing of such product, package or service for personal, family or household use, or for commercial, institutional or industrial use.

Because the guides are not legislative rules under Section 18 of the FTC Act, they are not themselves enforceable regulations, nor do they have the force and effect of law. The guides themselves do not preempt regulation of other federal agencies or of state and local bodies governing the use of environmental marketing claims. Compliance with federal, state or local law and regulations concerning such claims, however, will not

necessarily preclude Commission law enforcement action under Section 5.

Structure of the Guides (260.3)

The guides are composed of general principles and specific guidance on the use of environmental claims. These general principles and specific guidance are followed by examples that generally address a single deception concern. A given claim may raise issues that are addressed under more than one example and in more than one section of the guides.

In many of the examples, one or more options are presented for qualifying a claim. These options are intended to provide a "safe harbor" for marketers who want certainty about how to make environmental claims. They do not represent the only permissible approaches to qualifying a claim. The examples do not illustrate all possible acceptable claims or disclosures that would be permissible under Section 5. In addition, some of the illustrative disclosures may be appropriate for use on labels but not in print or broadcast advertisements and vice versa. In some instances, the guides indicate within the example in what context or contexts a particular type of disclosure should be considered.

Review Procedure (260.4)

The Commission will review the guides as part of its general program of reviewing all industry guides on an ongoing basis. Parties may petition the Commission to alter or amend these guides in light of substantial new evidence regarding consumer interpretation of a claim or regarding substantiation of a claim. Following review of such a petition, the Commission will take such action as it deems appropriate.

Interpretation and Substantiation of Environmental Marketing Claims (260.5)

Section 5 of the FTC Act makes unlawful deceptive acts and practices in or affecting commerce. The Commission's criteria for determining whether an express or implied claim has been made are enunciated in the Commission's Policy Statement on Deception. In addition, any party making an express or implied claim that presents an objective assertion about the environmental attribute of a product, package or service must, at the time the claim is made, possess and rely upon a reasonable basis substantiating the claim. A reasonable basis consists of competent and reliable evidence. In the context of environmental marketing claims, such substantiation will often require competent and reliable scientific evidence, defined as tests, analyses, research, studies or other evidence based on the expertise of professionals in the relevant area, conducted and evaluated in an objective manner by persons qualified to do so, using procedures generally accepted in the profession to yield accurate and reliable results. Further guidance on the reasonable basis standard is set forth in the Commission's 1983 Policy Statement on the Advertising Substantiation Doctrine. 49 Fed. Reg. 30999 (1984); appended to Thompson Medical Co., 104 F.T.C. 648 (1984). The Commission has also taken action in a number of cases involving alleged deceptive or unsubstantiated environmental advertising claims. A current list of environmental marketing cases and/or copies of individual cases can be obtained by calling the FTC Consumer Response Center at (202) 326–2222.

Qualifications or disclosures such as those described in these guides should be sufficiently clear, prominent, and understandable to prevent deception.

General Principles (260.6)

The following general principles apply to all environmental marketing claims, including, but not limited to, those described in 260.7. In addition, 260.7 contains specific guidance applicable to certain environmental marketing claims. Claims should comport with all relevant provisions of these guides, not simply the provision that seems most directly applicable.

(a) Qualifications and Disclosures

The Commission traditionally has held that in order to be effective, any qualifications or disclosures such as those described in these guides should be sufficiently clear, prominent and understandable to prevent deception. Clarity of language, relative type size and proximity to the claim being qualified, and an absence of contrary claims that could undercut effectiveness, will maximize the likelihood that the qualifications and disclosures are appropriately clear and prominent.

(b) Distinction between Benefits of Product, Package and Service

An environmental marketing claim should be presented in a way that makes clear whether the environmental attribute or benefit being asserted refers to the product, the product's packaging, a service or to a portion or component of the product, package or service. In general, if the environmental attribute or benefit applies to all but minor, incidental components of a product or package, the claim need not be qualified to identify that fact. There may be exceptions to this general principle. For example, if an unqualified "recyclable" claim is made and the presence of the incidental component significantly limits the ability to recycle the product, then the claim would be deceptive.

Example 1: A box of aluminum foil is labeled with the claim "recyclable," without further elaboration. Unless the type of product, surrounding language, or other context of the phrase establishes whether the claim refers to the foil or the box, the claim is deceptive if any part of either the box or the foil, other than minor, incidental components, cannot be recycled.

Example 2: A soft drink bottle is labeled "recycled." The bottle is made entirely from recycled materials, but the bottle cap is not. Because reasonable consumers are likely to consider the bottle cap to be a minor, incidental component of the package, the claim is not deceptive. Similarly, it would not be deceptive to label a shopping bag "recycled" where the bag is made entirely of recycled material but the easily detachable handle, an incidental component, is not.

(c) Overstatement of Environmental Attribute

An environmental marketing claim should not be presented in a manner that overstates the environmental attribute or benefit, expressly or by implication. Marketers should avoid implications of significant environmental benefits if the benefit is in fact negligible.

Example 1: A package is labeled "50 percent more recycled content than before." The manufacturer increased the recycled content of its package from 2 percent recycled material to 3 percent recycled material. Although the claim is technically true, it is likely to convey the false impression that the advertiser has increased significantly the use of recycled material.

Example 2: A trash bag is labeled "recyclable" without qualification. Because trash bags will ordinarily not be separated out from other trash at the landfill or incinerator for recycling, they are highly unlikely to be used again for any purpose. Even if the bag is technically capable of being recycled, the claim is deceptive since it asserts an environmental benefit where no significant or meaningful benefit exists.

Example 3: A paper grocery sack is labeled "reusable." The sack can be brought back to the store and reused for carrying groceries but will fall apart after two or three reuses, on average. Because reasonable consumers are unlikely to assume that a paper grocery sack is durable, the unqualified claim does not overstate the environmental benefit conveyed to consumers. The claim is not deceptive and does not need to be qualified to indicate the limited reuse of the sack.

Example 4: A package of paper coffee filters is labeled "These filters were made with a chlorine-free bleaching process." The filters are bleached with a process that releases into the environment a reduced, but still significant, amount of the same harmful byproducts associated with chlorine bleaching. The claim is likely to overstate the product's benefits because it is likely to be interpreted by consumers to mean that the product's manufacture does not cause any of the environmental risks posed by chlorine bleaching. A claim, however, that the filters were "bleached with a process that substantially reduces, but does not eliminate, harmful substances associated with chlorine bleaching" would not, if substantiated, overstate the product's benefits and is unlikely to be deceptive.

(d) Comparative Claims

Environmental marketing claims that include a comparative statement should be presented in a manner that makes the basis for the comparison sufficiently clear to avoid consumer deception. In addition, the advertiser should be able to substantiate the comparison.

Example 1: An advertiser notes that its shampoo bottle contains "20 percent more recycled content." The claim in its context is ambiguous. Depending on contextual factors, it could be a comparison either to the advertiser's immediately preceding product or to a competitor's product. The advertiser should clarify the claim to make the basis for comparison clear, for example, by saying "20 percent more recycled content than our previous package." Otherwise, the advertiser should be prepared to substantiate whatever comparison is conveyed to reasonable consumers.

Example 2: An advertiser claims that "our plastic diaper liner has the most recycled content." The advertised diaper does have more recycled content, calculated as a percentage of weight, than any other on the market, although it is still well under 100 percent recycled. Provided the recycled content and the comparative difference between the product and those of competitors are significant and provided the specific comparison can be substantiated, the claim is not deceptive.

Example 3: An ad claims that the advertiser's packaging creates "less waste than the leading national brand." The advertiser's source reduction was implemented some time ago and is supported by a calculation comparing the relative solid waste contributions of the two packages. The advertiser should be able to substantiate that the comparison remains accurate.

Environmental Marketing Claims (260.7)

Guidance about the use of environmental marketing claims is set forth below. Each guide is followed by several examples that illustrate, but do not provide an exhaustive list of, claims that do and do not comport with the guides. In each case, the general principles set forth in 260.6 should also be followed.

(a) General Environmental Benefit Claims

It is deceptive to misrepresent, directly or by implication, that a product, package or service offers a general environmental benefit. Unqualified general claims of environmental benefit are difficult to interpret, and depending on their context, may convey a wide range of meanings to consumers. In many cases, such claims may convey that the product, package or service has specific and far-reaching environmental benefits. As explained in the Commission's Advertising Substantiation Statement, every express and material implied claim that the general assertion conveys to reasonable consumers about an objective quality, feature or attribute of a product or service must be substantiated. Unless this substantiation duty can be met, broad environmental claims should either be avoided or qualified, as necessary, to prevent deception about the specific nature of the environmental benefit being asserted.

Example 1: A brand name like "Eco-Safe" would be deceptive if, in the context of the product so named, it leads consumers to believe that the product has environmental benefits which cannot be substantiated by the manufacturer. The claim would not be deceptive if "Eco-Safe" were followed by clear and prominent qualifying language limiting the safety representation to a particular product attribute for which it could be substantiated, and provided that no other deceptive implications were created by the context.

Example 2: A product wrapper is printed with the claim "Environmentally Friendly." Textual comments on the wrapper explain that the wrapper is "Environmentally Friendly because it was not chlorine bleached, a process that has been shown to create harmful substances." The wrapper was, in fact, not bleached with chlorine. However, the production of the wrapper now creates and releases to the environment significant quantities of other harmful substances. Since consumers are likely to interpret the "Environmentally Friendly" claim, in combination with the textual explanation, to mean that no significant harmful substances are currently released to the environment, the "Environmentally Friendly" claim would be deceptive.

Example 3: A pump spray product is labeled "environmentally safe." Most of the product's active ingredients consist of volatile organic compounds (VOCs) that may cause smog by contributing to ground-level ozone formation. The claim is deceptive because, absent further qualification, it is likely to convey to consumers that use of the product will not result in air pollution or other harm to the environment.

Example 4: A lawn care pesticide is advertised as "essentially non-toxic" and "practically non-toxic." Consumers would likely interpret these claims in the context of such a product as applying not only to human health effects but also to the product's environmental effects. Since the claims would likely convey to consumers that the product does not pose any risk to humans or the environment, if the pesticide in fact poses a significant risk to humans or environment, the claims would be deceptive.

Example 5: A product label contains an environmental seal, either in the form of a globe icon, or a globe icon with only the text "Earth Smart" around it. Either label is likely to convey to consumers that the product is environmentally superior to other products. If the manufacturer cannot substantiate this broad claim, the claim would be deceptive. The claims would not be deceptive if they were accompanied by clear and prominent qualifying language limiting the environmental superiority representation to the particular product attribute or attributes for which they could be substantiated, provided that no other deceptive implications were created by the context.

Example 6: A product is advertised as "environmentally preferable." This claim is likely to convey to consumers that this product is environmentally superior to other products. If the manufacturer cannot substantiate this broad claim, the claim would be deceptive. The claim would not be deceptive if it were accompanied by clear and prominent qualifying language limiting the environmental superiority representation to the particular product attribute or attributes for which it could be substantiated, provided that no other deceptive implications were created by the context.

(b) Degradable/Biodegradable/Photodegradable

It is deceptive to misrepresent, directly or by implication, that a product or package is degradable, biodegradable or photodegradable. An unqualified claim that a product or package is degradable, biodegradable or photodegradable should be substantiated by competent and reliable scientific evidence that the entire product or package will completely break down and return to nature, i.e., decompose into elements found in nature within a reasonably short period of time after customary disposal.

Claims of degradability, biodegradability or photodegradability should be qualified to the extent necessary to avoid consumer deception about: (1) the product or package's ability to degrade in the environment where it is customarily disposed; and (2) the rate and extent of degradation.

Example 1: A trash bag is marketed as "degradable," with no qualification or other disclosure. The marketer relies on soil burial tests to show that the product will decompose in the presence of water and oxygen. The trash bags are customarily disposed of in incineration facilities or at sanitary landfills that are managed in a way that inhibits degradation by minimizing moisture and oxygen. Degradation will be irrelevant for those trash bags that are incinerated and, for those disposed of in landfills, the marketer does not possess adequate substantiation that the bags will degrade in a reasonably short period of time in a landfill. The claim is therefore deceptive.

Example 2: A commercial agricultural plastic mulch film is advertised as "Photodegradable" and qualified with the phrase "Will break down into small pieces if left uncovered in sunlight." The claim is supported by competent and reliable scientific evidence that the product will break down in a reasonably short period of time after being exposed to sunlight and into sufficiently small pieces to become part of the soil. The qualified claim is not deceptive. Because the claim is qualified to indicate the limited extent of breakdown, the advertiser need not meet the elements for an unqualified photodegradable claim, i.e., that the product will not only break down, but also will decompose into elements found in nature.

Example 3: A soap or shampoo product is advertised as "biodegradable," with no qualification or other disclosure. The manufacturer has competent and reliable scientific evidence demonstrating that the product, which is customarily disposed of in sewage systems, will break down and decompose into elements found in nature in a short period of time. The claim is not deceptive.

Example 4: A plastic six-pack ring carrier is marked with a small diamond. Many state laws require that plastic six-pack ring carriers degrade if littered, and several state laws also require that the carriers be marked with a small diamond symbol to indicate that they meet performance standards for degradability. The use of the diamond, by itself, does not constitute a claim of degradability.

(c) *Compostable*

It is deceptive to misrepresent, directly or by implication, that a product or package is compostable.

A claim that a product or package is compostable should be substantiated by competent and reliable scientific evidence that all the materials in the product or package will break down into, or otherwise become part of, usable compost (e.g., soil-conditioning material, mulch) in a safe and timely manner in an appropriate composting program or facility, or in a home compost pile or device. Claims of compostability should be qualified to the extent necessary to avoid consumer deception. An unqualified claim may be deceptive if: (1) the package cannot be safely composted in a home compost pile or device; or (2) the claim misleads consumers about the environmental benefit provided when the product is disposed of in a landfill. A claim that a product is compostable in a municipal or institutional composting facility may need to be qualified to the extent necessary to avoid deception about the limited availability of such composting facilities.

Example 1: A manufacturer indicates that its unbleached coffee filter is compostable. The unqualified claim is not deceptive provided the manufacturer can substantiate that the filter can be converted safely to usable compost in a timely manner in a home compost pile or device. If this is the case, it is not relevant that no local municipal or institutional composting facilities exist.

Example 2: A lawn and leaf bag is labeled as "Compostable in California Municipal Yard Trimmings Composting Facilities." The bag contains toxic ingredients that are released into the compost material as the bag breaks down. The claim is deceptive if the presence of these toxic ingredients prevents the compost from being usable.

Example 3: A manufacturer makes an unqualified claim that its package is compostable. Although municipal or institutional composting facilities exist where the product is sold, the package will not break down into usable compost in a home compost pile or device. To avoid deception, the manufacturer should disclose that the package is not suitable for home composting.

Example 4: A nationally marketed lawn and leaf bag is labeled "compostable." Also printed on the bag is a disclosure that the bag is not designed for use in home compost piles. The bags are in fact composted in yard trimmings composting programs in many communities around the country, but such programs are not available to a substantial majority of consumers or communities where the bag is sold. The claim is deceptive because reasonable consumers living in areas not served by yard trimmings programs may understand the reference to mean that composting facilities accepting the bags are available in their area. To avoid deception, the claim should be qualified to indicate the limited availability of such programs, for example, by stating, "Appropriate facilities may not exist in your area." Other examples of adequate qualification of the claim include providing the approximate percentage of communities or the population for which such programs are available.

Example 5: A manufacturer sells a disposable diaper that bears the legend, "This diaper can be composted where solid waste composting facilities exist. There are currently [X number of] solid waste composting facilities across the country." The claim is not deceptive, assuming that composting facilities are available as claimed and the manufacturer can substantiate that the diaper can be converted safely to usable compost in solid waste composting facilities.

Example 6: A manufacturer markets yard trimmings bags only to consumers residing in particular geographic areas served by county yard trimmings composting programs. The bags meet specifications for these programs and are labeled "Compostable Yard Trimmings Bag for County Composting Programs." The claim is not deceptive. Because the bags are compostable where they are sold, no qualification is required to indicate the limited availability of composting facilities.

(d) Recyclable

It is deceptive to misrepresent, directly or by implication, that a product or package is recyclable. A product or package should not be marketed as recyclable unless it can be collected, separated or otherwise recovered from the solid waste stream for reuse, or in the manufacture or assembly of another package or product, through an established recycling program. Unqualified claims of recyclability for a product or package may be made if the entire product or package, excluding minor incidental components, is recyclable. For products or packages that are made of both recyclable and non-recyclable components, the recyclable claim should be adequately qualified to avoid consumer deception about which portions or components of the product or package are recyclable. Claims of recyclability should be qualified to the extent necessary to avoid consumer deception about any limited availability of recycling programs and collection sites. If an incidental component significantly limits the ability to recycle a product or package, a claim of recyclability would be deceptive. A product or package that is made from recyclable material, but, because of its shape, size or some other attribute, is not accepted in recycling programs for such material, should not be marketed as recyclable.

Example 1: A packaged product is labeled with an unqualified claim, "recyclable." It is unclear from the type of product and other context whether the claim refers to the product or its package. The unqualified claim is likely to convey to reasonable consumers that all of both the product and its packaging that remain after normal use of the product, except for minor, incidental components, can be recycled. Unless each such message can be substantiated, the claim should be qualified to indicate what portions are recyclable.

Example 2: A nationally marketed 8 oz. plastic cottage-cheese container displays the Society of the Plastics Industry (SPI) code (which consists of a design of arrows in a triangular shape containing a number and abbreviation identifying the component plastic resin) on the front label of the container, in close proximity to the product name and logo.

The manufacturer's conspicuous use of the SPI code in this manner constitutes a recyclability claim. Unless recycling facilities for this container are available to a substantial majority of consumers or communities, the claim should be qualified to disclose the limited availability of recycling programs for the container. If the SPI code, without more, had been placed in an inconspicuous location on the container (e.g., embedded in the bottom of the container) it would not constitute a claim of recyclability.

Example 3: A container can be burned in incinerator facilities to produce heat and power. It cannot, however, be recycled into another product or package. Any claim that the container is recyclable would be deceptive.

Example 4: A nationally marketed bottle bears the unqualified statement that it is "recyclable." Collection sites for recycling the material in question are not available to a substantial majority of consumers or communities, although collection sites are established in a significant percentage of communities or available to a significant percentage of the population. The unqualified claim is deceptive because, unless evidence shows otherwise, reasonable consumers living in communities not served by programs may conclude that recycling programs for the material are available in their area. To avoid deception, the claim should be qualified to indicate the limited availability of programs, for example, by stating "This bottle may not be recyclable in your area," or "Recycling programs for this bottle may not exist in your area." Other examples of adequate qualifications of the claim include providing the approximate percentage of communities or the population to whom programs are available.

Example 5: A paperboard package is marketed nationally and labeled "Recyclable where facilities exist." Recycling programs for this package are available in a significant percentage of communities or to a significant percentage of the population, but are not available to a substantial majority of consumers. The claim is deceptive because, unless evidence shows otherwise, reasonable consumers living in communities not served by programs that recycle paperboard packaging may understand this phrase to mean that such programs are available in their area. To avoid deception, the claim should be further qualified to indicate the limited availability of programs, for example, by using any of the approaches set forth in Example 4 above.

Example 6: A foam polystyrene cup is marketed as follows: "Recyclable in the few communities with facilities for foam polystyrene cups." Collection sites for recycling the cup have been established in a half-dozen major metropolitan areas. This disclosure illustrates one approach to qualifying a claim adequately to prevent deception about the limited availability of recycling programs where collection facilities are not established in a significant percentage of communities or available to a significant percentage of the population. Other examples of adequate qualification of the claim include providing the number of communities with programs, or the percentage of communities or the population to which programs are available.

Example 7: A label claims that the package "includes some recyclable material." The package is composed of four layers of different materials, bonded together. One of the layers is made from the recyclable material, but the others are not. While programs for recycling this type of material are available to a substantial majority of consumers, only a few of those programs

have the capability to separate the recyclable layer from the non-recyclable layers. Even though it is technologically possible to separate the layers, the claim is not adequately qualified to avoid consumer deception. An appropriately qualified claim would be, "includes material recyclable in the few communities that collect multi-layer products." Other examples of adequate qualification of the claim include providing the number of communities with programs, or the percentage of communities or the population to which programs are available.

Example 8: A product is marketed as having a "recyclable" container. The product is distributed and advertised only in Missouri. Collection sites for recycling the container are available to a substantial majority of Missouri residents, but are not yet available nationally. Because programs are generally available where the product is marketed, the unqualified claim does not deceive consumers about the limited availability of recycling programs.

Example 9: A manufacturer of one-time use photographic cameras, with dealers in a substantial majority of communities, collects those cameras through all of its dealers. After the exposed film is removed for processing, the manufacturer reconditions the cameras for resale and labels them as follows: "Recyclable through our dealership network." This claim is not deceptive, even though the cameras are not recyclable through conventional curbside or drop off recycling programs.

Example 10: A manufacturer of toner cartridges for laser printers has established a recycling program to recover its cartridges exclusively through its nationwide dealership network. The company advertises its cartridges nationally as "Recyclable. Contact your local dealer for details." The company's dealers participating in the recovery program are located in a significant number—but not a substantial majority—of communities. The "recyclable" claim is deceptive unless it contains one of the qualifiers set forth in Example 4. If participating dealers are located in only a few communities, the claim should be qualified as indicated in Example 6.

Example 11: An aluminum beverage can bears the statement "Please Recycle." This statement is likely to convey to consumers that the package is recyclable. Because collection sites for recycling aluminum beverage cans are available to a substantial majority of consumers or communities, the claim does not need to be qualified to indicate the limited availability of recycling programs.

(e) Recycled Content

A recycled content claim may be made only for materials that have been recovered or otherwise diverted from the solid waste stream, either during the manufacturing process (pre-consumer), or after consumer use (post-consumer). To the extent the source of recycled content includes pre-consumer material, the manufacturer or advertiser must have substantiation for concluding that the pre-consumer material would otherwise have entered the solid waste stream. In asserting a recycled content claim, distinctions may be made between pre-consumer and post-consumer materials.

Where such distinctions are asserted, any express or implied claim about the specific pre-consumer or post-consumer content of a product or package must be substantiated.

It is deceptive to misrepresent, directly or by implication, that a product or package is made of recycled material, which includes recycled raw material, as well as used, reconditioned and remanufactured components. Unqualified claims of recycled content may be made if the entire product or package, excluding minor, incidental components, is made from recycled material. For products or packages that are only partially made of recycled material, a recycled claim should be adequately qualified to avoid consumer deception about the amount, by weight, of recycled content in the finished product or package. Additionally, for products that contain used, reconditioned or remanufactured components, a recycled claim should be adequately qualified to avoid consumer deception about the nature of such components. No such qualification would be necessary in cases where it would be clear to consumers from the context that a product's recycled content consists of used, reconditioned or remanufactured components.

Example 1: A manufacturer routinely collects spilled raw material and scraps left over from the original manufacturing process. After a minimal amount of reprocessing, the manufacturer combines the spills and scraps with virgin material for use in further production of the same product. A claim that the product contains recycled material is deceptive since the spills and scraps to which the claim refers are normally reused by industry within the original manufacturing process, and would not normally have entered the waste stream.

Example 2: A manufacturer purchases material from a firm that collects discarded material from other manufacturers and resells it. All of the material was diverted from the solid waste stream and is not normally reused by industry within the original manufacturing process. The manufacturer includes the weight of this material in its calculations of the recycled content of its products. A claim of recycled content based on this calculation is not deceptive because, absent the purchase and reuse of this material, it would have entered the waste stream.

Example 3: A greeting card is composed 30 percent by fiber weight of paper collected from consumers after use of a paper product, and 20 percent by fiber weight of paper that was generated after completion of the paper-making process, diverted from the solid waste stream, and otherwise would not normally have been reused in the original manufacturing process. The marketer of the card may claim either that the product "contains 50 percent recycled fiber," or may identify the specific pre-consumer and/or post-consumer content by stating, for example, that the product "contains 50 percent total recycled fiber, including 30 percent post-consumer."

Example 4: A paperboard package with 20 percent recycled fiber by weight is labeled as containing "20 percent recycled fiber." Some of the recycled content was composed of material collected from consumers after use of the original product. The rest was com-

posed of overrun newspaper stock never sold to customers. The claim is not deceptive.

Example 5: A product in a multi-component package, such as a paperboard box in a shrink-wrapped plastic cover, indicates that it has recycled packaging. The paperboard box is made entirely of recycled material, but the plastic cover is not. The claim is deceptive since, without qualification, it suggests that both components are recycled. A claim limited to the paperboard box would not be deceptive.

Example 6: A package is made from layers of foil, plastic, and paper laminated together, although the layers are indistinguishable to consumers. The label claims that "one of the three layers of this package is made of recycled plastic." The plastic layer is made entirely of recycled plastic. The claim is not deceptive provided the recycled plastic layer constitutes a significant component of the entire package.

Example 7: A paper product is labeled as containing "100 percent recycled fiber." The claim is not deceptive if the advertiser can substantiate the conclusion that 100 percent by weight of the fiber in the finished product is recycled.

Example 8: A frozen dinner is marketed in a package composed of a cardboard box over a plastic tray. The package bears the legend "package made from 30 percent recycled material." Each packaging component amounts to one-half the weight of the total package. The box is 20 percent recycled content by weight, while the plastic tray is

40 percent recycled content by weight. The claim is not deceptive, since the average amount of recycled material is 30 percent.

Example 9: A paper greeting card is labeled as containing 50 percent recycled fiber. The seller purchases paper stock from several sources and the amount of recycled fiber in the stock provided by each source varies. Because the 50 percent figure is based on the annual weighted average of recycled material purchased from the sources after accounting for fiber loss during the production process, the claim is permissible.

Example 10: A packaged food product is labeled with a three-chasing-arrows symbol without any further explanatory text as to its meaning. By itself, the symbol is likely to convey that the packaging is both "recyclable" and is made entirely from recycled material. Unless both messages can be substantiated, the claim should be qualified as to whether it refers to the package's recyclability and/or its recycled content. If a "recyclable claim" is being made, the label may need to disclose the limited availability of recycling programs for the package. If a recycled content claim is being made and the packaging is not made entirely from recycled material, the label should disclose the percentage of recycled content.

Example 11: A laser printer toner cartridge containing 25 percent recycled raw materials and 40 percent reconditioned parts is labeled "65 percent recycled content; 40 percent from reconditioned parts." This claim is not deceptive.

Example 12: A store sells both new and used sporting goods. One of the items for sale in the store is a baseball helmet that, although used, is no different in appearance than a brand new item. The helmet bears an unqualified "Recycled" label. This claim is deceptive because, unless evidence shows otherwise, consumers could reasonably believe that the helmet is made of recycled raw materials, when it is in fact a used item. An acceptable claim would bear a disclosure clearly stating that the helmet is used.

Example 13: A manufacturer of home electronics labels its video-cassette recorders ("VCRs") as "40 percent recycled." In fact, each VCR contains 40 percent reconditioned parts. This claim is deceptive because consumers are unlikely to know that the VCR's recycled content consists of reconditioned parts.

Example 14: A dealer of used automotive parts recovers a serviceable engine from a vehicle that has been totaled. Without repairing, rebuilding, remanufacturing, or in any way altering the engine or its components, the dealer attaches a "Recycled" label to the engine, and offers it for resale in its used auto parts store. In this situation, an unqualified recycled content claim is not likely to be deceptive because consumers are likely to understand that the engine is used and has not undergone any rebuilding.

Example 15: An automobile parts dealer purchases a transmission that has been recovered from a junked vehicle. Eighty-five percent by weight of the transmission was rebuilt and 15 percent constitutes new materials. After rebuilding the transmission in accordance with industry practices, the dealer packages it for resale in a box labeled "Rebuilt Transmission," or "Rebuilt Transmission (85 percent recycled content from rebuilt parts)," or "Recycled Transmission (85 percent recycled content from rebuilt parts)." These claims are not likely to be deceptive.

(f) Source Reduction

It is deceptive to misrepresent, directly or by implication, that a product or package has been reduced or is lower in weight, volume or toxicity. Source reduction claims should be qualified to the extent necessary to avoid consumer deception about the amount of the source reduction and about the basis for any comparison asserted.

Example 1: An ad claims that solid waste created by disposal of the advertiser's packaging is "now 10 percent less than our previous package." The claim is not deceptive if the advertiser has substantiation that shows that disposal of the current package contributes 10 percent less waste by weight or volume to the solid waste stream when compared with the immediately preceding version of the package.

Example 2: An advertiser notes that disposal of its product generates "10 percent less waste." The claim is ambiguous. Depending on contextual factors, it could be a comparison either to the immediately preceding product or to a competitor's product. The "10 percent less waste" reference is deceptive unless the seller clarifies which comparison is intended and substantiates that comparison, or

substantiates both possible interpretations of the claim.

(g) Refillable

It is deceptive to misrepresent, directly or by implication, that a package is refillable. An unqualified refillable claim should not be asserted unless a system is provided for: (1) the collection and return of the package for refill; or (2) the later refill of the package by consumers with product subsequently sold in another package. A package should not be marketed with an unqualified refillable claim, if it is up to the consumer to find new ways to refill the package.

Example 1: A container is labeled "refillable x times." The manufacturer has the capability to refill returned containers and can show that the container will withstand being refilled at least x times. The manufacturer, however, has established no collection program. The unqualified claim is deceptive because there is no means for collection and return of the container to the manufacturer for refill.

Example 2: A bottle of fabric softener states that it is in a "handy refillable container." The manufacturer also sells a large-sized container that indicates that the consumer is expected to use it to refill the smaller container. The manufacturer sells the large-sized container in the same market areas where it sells the small container. The claim is not deceptive because there is a means for consumers to refill the smaller container from larger containers of the same product.

(h) Ozone Safe and Ozone Friendly

It is deceptive to misrepresent, directly or by implication, that a product is safe for or "friendly" to the ozone layer or the atmosphere.

For example, a claim that a product does not harm the ozone layer is deceptive if the product contains an ozone-depleting substance.

Example 1: A product is labeled "ozone friendly." The claim is deceptive if the product contains any ozone-depleting substance, including those substances listed as Class I or Class II chemicals in Title VI of the Clean Air Act Amendments of 1990, Pub. L. No. 101–549, and others subsequently designated by EPA as ozone-depleting substances. Chemicals that have been listed or designated as Class I are chlorofluorocarbons (CFCs), halons, carbon tetrachloride, 1,1,1-trichloroethane, methyl bromide and hydrobromofluorocarbons (HBFCs). Chemicals that have been listed as Class II are hydrochlorofluorocarbons (HCFCs).

Example 2: An aerosol air freshener is labeled "ozone friendly." Some of the product's ingredients are volatile organic compounds (VOCs) that may cause smog by contributing to ground-level ozone formation. The claim is likely to convey to consumers that the product is safe for the atmosphere as a whole, and is therefore, deceptive.

Example 3: The seller of an aerosol product makes an unqualified claim that its product "Contains no CFCs." Although the product does not contain CFCs, it does contain HCFC-22, another ozone depleting ingredient. Because the claim "Contains no CFCs"

may imply to reasonable consumers that the product does not harm the ozone layer, the claim is deceptive.

Example 4: A product is labeled "This product is 95 percent less damaging to the ozone layer than past formulations that contained CFCs." The manufacturer has substituted HCFCs for CFC-12, and can substantiate that this substitution will result in 95 percent less ozone depletion. The qualified comparative claim is not likely to be deceptive.

Claims with Clout

Green Seal™ Standards and Certification

Green Seal is an independent organization that certifies a wide variety of environmentally focused products. The Green Seal logo found on paper products must also contain a description of the basis for certification, and the certification criteria for all products are publicly available. Green Seal strives to maintain a standard-setting process that is open, collaborative, fair, and completely transparent. Additionally Green Seal has developed built-in checks that ensure that it is unbiased and realistic, and that the products it certifies are at high levels of performance and quality.

Products marked with the Green Seal meet the criteria of ISO 14020 and 14024, the standards for eco-labeling set by the International Organization for Standardization (ISO); the U.S. Environmental Protection Agency's (EPA) criteria for third-party certifiers of environmentally preferable products; and the criteria for bona fide eco-labeling bodies of the Global Ecolabeling Network (GEN).

Per EPA criteria, the Green Seal Web site notes that a legitimate third-party certifier must have:[21]

— An open, public process that involves key stakeholders (businesses, environmental and consumer groups, states etc.) in developing its criteria or standards

— Award criteria, assumptions, methods and data used to evaluate the product or product categories that are transparent (i.e., they are publicly available, easily accessed and understandable to the layperson)

— A system of data verification and data quality

— A peer review process (with representation of all stakeholders) for developing the standards or criteria

— Criteria that are developed based on a "systems" or life cycle approach (i.e., "cradle to grave")

— An outreach program to educate the consumer, which includes clear communications to consumers that provide key information concerning environmental impacts associated with the product

— An established goal of updating standards or criteria as technology and scientific knowledge advance

— Authority to inspect the facility whose product is certified to ensure compliance with the standards or criteria

— Testing protocols for the products that are certified which ensure testing is conducted by a credible institution

— Access to obtaining the seal by small and medium-size companies (e.g., the cost of the seal is not so high as to prevent access by companies)

— Compliance with the Federal Trade Commission's Guides for the Use of Environmental Marketing Claims

The Green Seal Web site (*www.greenseal.org*) also notes that these criteria are replicated by the GEN admission criteria for eco-labeling bodies.

UL Environmental Claims Validation™

Capitalizing on market greening shifts, as well as the current lack of universal standards for products in many categories in the United States, Underwriters Laboratories (UL) felt it was time to take its 115-year history of product assurance to the next level and announced two new programs to test and certify environmental product claims. Beginning in January 2009, UL invites manufacturers to submit products for testing and environmental claims validation. UL notes "This validation enhances and supports the credibility of sustainability claims, helping to end confusion and giving manufacturers who choose UL validation a competitive edge." To find out more visit UL's Web site at: *www.ulenvironment.com*.

The Story of Stuff with Annie L....

| Intro | Extraction | Production | Distribution | Consumption | Disposal | Another Way |

THE STORY OF STUFF
WITH ANNIE LEONARD

PLAY

free range studios ✿

Over 6 Million Views!

THE STORY OF **STUFF** WITH ANNIE LEONARD

Sponsored by Tides Foundation & Funders Workgroup for Sustainable Production and Consumption

| HOME | MOVIE CREDITS | RESOURCES | MEDIA ROOM | STORY OF STUFF BLOG |

 Get Your Answers (FAQ)

 Tell a Friend

 Order Stuff

 Downloads

 Sign Up for Updates

 Host a Screening

 Help Support The Story

What is the Story of Stuff?

From its extraction through sale, use and disposal, all the stuff in our lives affects communities at home and abroad, yet most of this is hidden from view. **The Story of Stuff** is a 20-minute, fast-paced, fact-filled look at the underside of our production and consumption patterns. **The Story of Stuff** exposes the connections between a huge number of environmental and social issues, and calls us together to create a more sustainable and just world. It'll teach you something, it'll make you laugh, and it just may change the way you look at all the stuff in your life forever.

Other languages? Visit the Int'l Site

Story of Stuff: The Book

The Story of Stuff, the book, will be available March 9, 2010! Click here for more details.

Site design: free range studios ✿

Home :: Movie Credits :: Contact :: Media Room :: Privacy Policy

Visit the Int'l Site

This work is licensed under a Creative Commons Attribution-Noncommercial-No Derivative Works 3.0 Unported License.

Case Study: The Story of Stuff

Originally founded in 1999 as Free Range Graphics, a collaboration between two lifelong friends, Jonah Sachs and Louis Fox, today's Free Range Studios is an advertising and marketing firm that specializes in progressive nonprofit and socially responsible businesses. It is, though, best known for its online storytelling.

Free Range began with a Web site and the idea that it would serve only progressive nonprofits. "It wouldn't be right to spread messages that we did not believe in," said Sachs in a September 29, 2006, Net2 blog interview with Britt Bravo. "We just sort of put it out there. . . . People really responded well to that, and that has been our niche ever since. We've stayed true to that even though some opportunities have come up to leave that, but that [serving progressive nonprofits] is what really gets us excited."[22]

As a way of saying thank you to their clients, as well as a way to get better known in the field, Free Range had an idea to do a Gratitude Grant. Here it would give away a free flash movie to help feature a cause, but the project, too, would provide Free Range an opportunity to really showcase its create thinking. "We don't just serve the movement for a better world; we're a part of it," notes Free Range.[23]

As demand grew for a firm that worked exclusively for a progressive future, the simple collaboration of two friends took on the shape of a design and strategy firm with the addition of their first employee, McArthur (originally a client, now a partner and Free Range's business development and client relations team leader). Today Free Range creates some of the Internet's most effective activism movies and is at the center of hundreds of key campaigns for social change in print and on the Web.

Tackling the issues surrounding the life cycle of goods and services, Free Range's documentary, *The Story of Stuff*, is a 20-minute film, combining stark but whimsically animated line drawings and live action narrated by Annie Leonard, a vocal sustainability activist. It was sponsored by Tides Foundation and The Funders Workgroup for Sustainable Production and Consumption.

Free Range Studios describes *The Story of Stuff* as a:

> Fast-paced, fact-filled look at the underside of our production and consumption patterns, with a special focus on the United States. All the stuff in our lives, beginning from the extraction of the resources to make it, through its production, sale, use and disposal, affects communities at home and abroad, yet most of this is hidden from view. *The Story of Stuff* exposes the connections between a huge number of environmental and social issues and calls for all of us to create a more sustainable and just world. It'll teach you something. It'll make you laugh, and it just may change the way you look at all the stuff in your life forever.

How to Get It Right

What Is "Need"?

Much of what producers offer is in response to a "need" they perceive in the market. But what is need? The reality is, as a species, we really only need things that provide health: warmth, an environment in equilibrium, nourishing food, clean water, sleep, companionship, replications of ourselves to keep the species going, and a way to occupy our day. Everything else is a want. It's wants, not "needs," that are the bulk of what drives our current economy. Targeting wants and pushing them to a level of desire so as to create "need" is how successful products gain market share and how companies serving the market can begin to change end buyer behavior, by *only* supplying choices that keep societal and environmental impacts in mind.

Who Are the People Choosing?

To successfully reshape "need," one of the most fundamental questions we ask when we begin to design is: Whom is the thing supposed to serve, and what do "they" want/need? A pretty basic concept, but one that gets overlooked (or grossly compromised) constantly in the push-pull dynamic that makes up this thing we call the market.

What people want, what they're willing to pay, and what the producer is able to do (time/cost), plus what producers perceive their competitors are doing (or getting away with) are all seemingly at odds with each other. Yet successful products manage to find the sweet spot, riding that wave all the way to the bank.

As we begin to examine the things that make up highly successful or catastrophically bad packaging, defining whom the thing will serve (and so how to define the fulfillment of their need/want) is essential.

Demographics is the statistical characteristics of human populations (such as age or income) used especially to identify markets. There are a variety of ways to zero in on whom potential audiences might be. One is to do the sort of cold calling that has been the bane of civilized dining since telemarketing was invented. Another is to pay people to offer their time and opinions (focus groups, secret shoppers). Focus groups, it must be noted, though a mainstay of today's strategic marketing mix, provide only a sketch of what a potential buyer thinks; at worst they are expensive catastrophes in the making. The conviction that the focus group "knows all" has been the downfall of many otherwise well-intentioned products. Finding the right combination of questions and moderator is key to getting good information. And in all cases, focus group conclusions need to be backed up by other research methods.

As markets began their slow green shift, a demographic committed to sustainability in practice emerged. The LOHAS group (Lifestyles of Health and Sustainability) is a consumer often also referred to as a Cultural Creative, a term coined by Paul H. Ray and Sherry Ruth Anderson in their book, *The Cultural Creatives: How 50 Million People are Changing the World*. This group cares deeply about ecology, the planet, relationships, peace, and social justice. The size of the market ranges from 15 to 30 percent of the adult population in the United States but is much higher in markets the United States exports to.

Although already established in U.S. trading partner countries, the emergence of the LOHAS consumer as a market-driving group in the United States has been unparalleled in its history. These consumers care a great deal about all aspects of the products they buy and are becoming ever more active in using their dollars to push for progressive social, environmental, and economic change.

Going past using their ethics as a product decision-making tool, the LOHAS consumer takes a holistic worldview, believing global economies, cultures, environments, and political systems are all interconnected, so that failure in one area ripples through the whole of society. So too, mind, body, and spirit within individuals are recognized as interconnected, with personal development, spirituality, and personal ethics as their fundamental belief.

With the interconnectedness of all humankind at the core of their ideals, it's no surprise that LOHAS audiences come from all ages, races, religions, and economic classes, making them a difficult group to reach using broad-brush mainstream marketing tactics. Truth and transparency become key tools to making inroads into this highly motivated market. One of the distinguishing characteristics of this group is that it is not an organized movement or "club"; individuals become LOHAS by feeling strongly about something, making up their own minds, and using their personal ethics as their guide to action.

The Natural Marketing Institute breaks U.S. consumers into four categories.[25]

1. The LOHAS Consumer

    63 million adults. Attitudes, behaviors, and usage of goods and services are affected by concern for health—the health of their families, the sustainability of the planet, their personal development, and the future of society.

2. Nomadics

    79 million adults. "A conglomeration of consumers who are in search of their true sense of well-being. As such, they tend to move from place to place with regard to personal ideals, environmental platforms, and the overall relevance of sustainability."

3. Centrists

    52 million adults. "A middle-of-the-road assemblage who congregates toward the central ground when it comes to dealing with health and sustainability. They are more steadfast in their attitudes, behavior, and usage of specific products and services, regardless of their impact on the planet and self."

4. Indifferents

    15 million adults. "A consumer group that sees no need nor recognizes any connection between their consumption patterns and the effect they have on resources. They are caught up in the day-to-day challenges, not necessarily looking out for tomorrow."

Like any demographic breakdown, there are people who fit into several groups at once. As demonstrated by the SUVs in an organic grocer's parking lot, not all people who participate in LOHAS behavior fit wholly into the LOHAS mold.

Marketing to the LOHAS consumer, though, has multiple rewards. Ideas such as fairness, health (for people and planet), and ethical practices—as well as transparency and honest quality—are all ideas that have a long track record of building brand loyalty in all consumer sectors.

Differing from other groups, LOHAS consumers are willing to pay up to 20 percent more for products that fit their ethics. LOHAS consumers are more driven by product honesty than price. Products and services that truly deliver real benefits and solutions, allowing them to act on their ethics, are not as subject to the spiraling drive to the bottom many consumer goods manufacturers find themselves caught in.

Ethnographics

Unlike demographics that paint a portrait of a population with broad strokes, ethnographics is the fine brushwork that brings out detail. Doing just a few focus groups can't paint a complete picture, especially when dealing with a socially charged issue. Who will admit they're not for sustainability on some level?

An ethnographic study, though still more subjective than actual purchase data, can work with each subject in a place with no distractions or outside influences, or observe each audience member in his or her natural environment. Investigators too can key into unspoken communication: Is the person hurried or relaxed? What do they look at before selecting? Do they select alone or are they wrestling with toddlers? All of these are important factors that can color the data.

A bigger problem with understanding market greening is how to interpret the gap between how "eco" people *say* they are and how they ultimately act at selection time. Everybody wants to save the planet—but only if it's convenient—has been the

trend for many years. As markets change and as choices (and competition) increase, learning to target a market well is key to leveraging an increasing variety of materials, structural options, distribution schemes, and supply chain opportunities.

In gathering data for *The Cultural Creatives* Paul H. Ray and Sherry Ruth Anderson amassed an immense amount of survey data from over 100,000 people over 13 years. This work included 500 focus groups and 60 in-depth interviews to reveal personal stories of how people's lives are changing. The authors note that this is the first book on social transformation to offer extensive hard data to back up its conclusions, proving that change is happening right now and that what's going on is much bigger than they expected.[26] The authors ask:

> Are you a Cultural Creative? This list can give you an idea. Choose the statements that you agree with.

You are likely to be a Cultural Creative if you:

1. love Nature and are deeply concerned about its destruction;

2. are strongly aware of the problems of the whole planet (global warming, destruction of rainforests, overpopulation, lack of ecological sustainability, exploitation of people in poorer countries) and want to see more action on them, such as limiting economic growth;

3. would pay more taxes or pay more for consumer goods if you could know the money would go to clean up the environment and to stop global warming;

4. place a great deal of importance on developing and maintaining your relationships;

5. place a lot of value on helping other people and bringing out their unique gifts;

6. do volunteering for one or more good causes;

7. care intensely about both psychological and spiritual development;

8. see spirituality or religion as important in your life, but are concerned about the role of the Religious Right in politics;

9. want more equality for women at work, and more women leaders in business and politics;

10. are concerned about violence and abuse of women and children around the world;

11. want our politics and government spending to put more emphasis on children's education and well-being, on rebuilding our neighborhoods and communities, and on creating an ecologically sustainable future;

12. are unhappy with both the Left and the Right in politics, and want a to find a new way that is not in the mushy middle;

13. tend to be somewhat optimistic about our future, and distrust the cynical and pessimistic view that is given by the media;

14. want to be involved in creating a new and better way of life in our country;

15. are concerned about what the big corporations are doing in the name of making more profits: downsizing, creating environmental problems, and exploiting poorer countries;

16. have your finances and spending under control, and are not concerned about overspending;

17. dislike all the emphasis in modern culture on success and "making it," on getting and spending, on wealth and luxury goods;

18. and like people and places that are exotic and foreign, and like experiencing and learning about other ways of life.

If you agreed with ten or more, you probably are a Cultural Creative.[30]

For more information on Cultural Creatives, a huge breakout of data from the book, other work by Paul H. Ray, as well as new research in Europe and the United States, visit *culturalcreatives.org*.

Building Public Will

Communication that fuels lasting change and creates sticking power for an issue, idea, or point of view is a critical and powerful tool for social change, whether aimed at pushing or supporting decision makers to change policy; altering the voting, buying, or other behavior patterns of private citizens; or triggering a change in the economic, political or social expectations of society.

Twenty-five years ago, organic agricultural products were found exclusively in natural food stores. Today, organic food drives a $16 billion industry, and can be found on the shelves of every major grocery store across the country. What changed? Public will.

Most social change campaigns are designed to impact public opinion and result in quick, short-term attitudinal adjustments rather than create long-term organizational or social change. Building public will means impacting where people rank an issue in their priority of compelling social causes; it is about a long-term or permanent attitudinal shift that is manifested in people's commitment to taking action to create change in systems. Shaping public will on any issue requires a multidimensional approach to changing attitudes and impacting behavior.

Defining "Public Will"

What is public will? Public will building is a communication approach that builds public support for social change by integrating grass-roots outreach methods with traditional mass media tools in a process that connects an issue to the existing, closely held values of individuals and groups. This approach leads to deeper public understanding and ownership of social changes. It creates new and lasting community expectations that shape the way people act, think, and behave.

Public will building:

— Connects people to an issue through their existing, closely held values rather than trying to change people's values.

— Results in long-term attitudinal shifts that are manifested in individuals taking new or

different actions that collectively create change.

— Is achieved when a sufficient number of community members and thought leaders have galvanized around an issue to form a new or different set of fundamental community expectations.

How is public will built? Public will is built by connecting people to an issue through their existing closely held values, triggering long-term attitudinal shifts in people's ranking of issues in their own personal values system, shifts that are manifested in individuals taking new or different actions that collectively create change in systems and societies. This approach to change recognizes the tremendous power of individual and community values in framing individual and community attitudes and behaviors. It recognizes that it is unreasonable to try to change people's values and focuses instead on identifying and understanding how existing values can serve as links to an issue.

Case in point: Thirty years ago, smoking when and where a person chose was considered a right, closely linked to the normative American value of individual rights. Smokers and the tobacco industry were deeply entrenched. However, emerging research about the dangers of secondhand smoke gave advocates of smoke-free public spaces the opportunity to reframe the argument. Using public will building techniques, advocates demonstrated that exposure to secondhand smoke infringed on others' individual rights to protect their health. Leveraging the closely held value placed on self-determination and individual rights, the priority became personal health over personal choice. Today, smoke-free spaces are the norm.

Metropolitan Group, a strategic creative services firm, found that public will building is grounded in four underlying principles, which together form the foundation for the successful development of social change efforts using this model. While each of the principles is independently present in many other forms of social marketing and communication, the synergy and strength of the combined four underlying principles make public will building distinctive.

Four Principles of Public Will Building

1. Connecting through Closely Held Values

   Values trump data when it comes to decision making. People make decisions consciously and unconsciously based on their values, and then utilize data to rationalize and support their choice.

   For individuals to maintain a lasting commitment to an issue as a personal priority, and to hold a conviction that leads to action, the issue must connect to closely held personal values. Individual choices to speak out or take action on an issue flow from resonance between the issue and a person's core value system.

2. Respecting Cultural Context

   To engage in any meaningful discourse involving closely held values and to create ownership of an issue, understanding and working within a person's or group's cultural context is a necessity. It is important for public will organizers to understand the dynamics of power, language, relationships, values, traditions, worldview, and decision making in a given cultural context.

3. Including Target Audiences in Development and Testing

   Building public will is dependent on creating legitimate ownership and engagement in the process by the people impacted by an issue in order to result in action and sustained motivation.

   The public will building process therefore must involve true representation of target audiences in the research, design, development, and testing of key strategies and messages. Inclusion of audiences in all aspects of an effort ensures authenticity, clarity of message, and credibility of messengers. By seeking a deeper level of involvement from their audiences, public will organizers garner perspective and ideas while building a base of grassroots support throughout the planning and implementation process.

4. Integrating Grassroots and Traditional Communication Methods

   Connecting to values is most effectively accomplished through relationships of trust and relies on direct grassroots outreach where peers, friends, neighbors, family members, coworkers, and other trusted community members connect members of their circles of influence or social networks to an issue through a motivating value, and actively seek their support and action.

   Public will building efforts integrate grassroots outreach with advertising and other traditional communication methods to create a fertile environment for outreach and to motivate and reinforce the focus on the issue, key messages, and calls to action. This integrated approach is a major distinguishing factor between public will building and more general public awareness building work.

Building Public Will versus Influencing Public Opinion

Short-Term Wins versus Long-Term Gains

Too often, social change communication is focused on short-term wins and addressing symptoms rather than tackling the root causes of problems or needs. Such efforts are concentrated on changing public opinion (a short-term gain).

Communication to sway public opinion tends to identify a winning message for the short term and drive it home through a concentration of efforts on the most expedient delivery mechanism, often placing the vast majority of resources into mass media. By its nature, public opinion based communication seeks to narrow the discourse and discourage personal exploration of and engagement with an issue.

In contrast, public will based strategies focus on long-term change built over time by engaging broad-based grassroots support to influence individual and institutional change. While public will based strategies also have clear and measurable goals, they focus on developing a sustainable platform for change and thus invest in greater audience engagement.

When the Short-Term Message Does Long-Term Harm

Messages used to fight industrial water polluters have "shut off" many of the big industrial offenders, which means that the primary source of water pollution now comes from nonsource point pollution—the individual actions of the general public. However, the same messages that convinced the public that the main cause of water pollution is big industry have resulted in individuals and families discounting the possibility that they personally have any impact on clean water. In addition, the messages have set up an environment versus economy dichotomy, which has limited common-ground approaches.

Phases of Public Will Building

Public will building is a communication approach that has developed organically through practical experience in social change focused communication campaigns conducted by Metropolitan Group. Over the last decade, Metropolitan Group has been engaged by numerous public sector, nonprofit, and socially responsible business clients to develop communication campaigns to impact attitudes and behaviors and to ultimately create social change. Often the issues in which they are engaged require long-term commitment and reinforcement for the change to last. Through their work, they have learned and refined effective approaches that establish platforms for more sustainable change.

Shaping public will on any issue requires a multidimensional approach to changing attitudes and impacting behavior. Metropolitan

Group defined five phases of public will building: Organizers must go through these steps in order to trigger widespread public will building and audiences must go through these steps in order to change their internal constructs.

Public Will Framework

Phase 1: Framing and defining the issue or problem.

Individuals and organizations define issues and needs in relationship to the context that they are in and the relationship of each issue and need to their personal values. In the early stages of awareness, audiences self-define issues as having relevance and/or impact. The definition phase creates the context in which an issue or problem is viewed.

Phase 2: Building awareness about problems or needs.

Organizers are building awareness about the problem or need through outreach aimed at educating, raising awareness and building interest about the issue by connecting it with existing core value(s) of the priority audiences.

Once an issue or problem is defined, audience awareness and knowledge must increase in order to raise the importance and relevance of the issue. By gaining deeper awareness of the issue, including examples of impact(s), underlying causes, supporters and opponents, and how it relates to core values, audiences become ready to "own" the issue.

Phase 3: Becoming knowledgeable/transmitting information about where and how the problem can be impacted or changed.

During the third phase, organizer outreach moves from focusing on raising awareness of the problem to providing information about how change can occur and what needs to be done to trigger change.

Since audiences are aware of the issue and are seeking ways to have an impact, organizers now focus on providing specific information about how to impact change through personal actions (environmental, parenting, health and other behaviors) and through community and institutional actions (voting, voicing support or opposition to a policy, purchasing behaviors/voting with one's dollars, adopting new policies, practices or procedures, etc.). Once audiences are aware of an issue and are gaining knowledge of its importance, relevancy, and impact, they want to know how to make a difference.

Phase 4: Creating a personal conviction that change needs to occur.

In order to help individuals make a personal commitment, public will building organizers are delivering clear call-to-action messages that encourage both making a lasting commitment and taking specific actions that impact the issue.

In this phase, audiences have a strong awareness of the issue, understand how it connects to their values, and see how they can impact it. Now audiences are moved to make a personal commitment that change needs to occur and that they need to be part of it.

Phase 5: Evaluating while reinforcing.

Public will building organizers must evaluate the approach being used and its impact while continually reinforcing those who have made the choice to take action. By evaluating messages, activities, and results, and linking successes and failures to specific strategies, organizers can make adjustments to strategy and modify the approach to achieve greater impact.

Once individuals in an audience have taken action, they evaluate the results of their action, become increasingly aware of the positions and actions of others in relationship to the issue, and either reinforce their decision and deepen their conviction or question their decision and make adjustments to their actions. The more they feel reinforced in their choice, the more they will take actions consistent with their conviction to help drive change and influence others.

A Powerful Approach to Creating Sustainable Change

Public will building clarifies needs, builds understanding of causes and issues, connects issues with existing values, and identifies the best pathways to change. It develops effective leadership and organizational models, identifies and prioritizes audiences, and integrates traditional media and grassroots outreach. The five-phase process attracts and enlists committed champions and ambassadors. These key influencers are

moved to conviction, their conviction becomes action, and their action garners the conviction and action of others. As change occurs, evaluation and reinforcement support the efforts of early adopters and convert them to ambassadors. Ultimately, this establishes a new set of normative community expectations.

The public will building approach achieves high advancement on mission with high return on investment by leveraging the efforts and resources of supporters, by selecting strategies that have long-term impacts, and by linking issues with existing values to create long-term commitment. It creates a sustainable platform for change and moves an issue to become a touch point for an individual's voting, purchasing, and other decision making.

Advocating and establishing change through the public will building process establishes the values-based commitment and the rationale for the issue as part of the expectations of a community. This makes it more likely that changes will last and that additional and perhaps more difficult challenges will be surmounted in the future. Due to its capacity and movement building nature, the public will building process also grows leaders and networks that have greater voice and power with which to impact other issues and unleash the potential of their communities.

Excerpts from "Public Will Building: A Communication Approach for Creating Sustainable Behavior Change" have been provided with the permission of Metropolitan Group, a full-service social change agency that crafts and integrates strategic communication, creative, and resource development services that empower social purpose organizations to build a just and sustainable world. To download the full article on Public Will Building, additional free resources, tips and tools, and/or to learn more about Metropolitan Group, please visit www.metgroup.com.

Eco-Design in Three Easy Steps

1. Know what the audience expects the design to do, then exceed those expectations.

   — What is your work saying about how you feel about the audience, and the environment?

   — Is it well researched? Do you really understand your audience as well as the thing's use/viewing world?

2. Know what the design actually needs to do.

   — Is it well researched? Do you really understand your supply chain as well as end-of-life and rebirth possibilities?

3. Connect with the audience and foster brand loyalty with the true quality and deep integrity of your work and message. Empower the audience to become a change agent.

I AM HERE I HAVE LEARNED NOW IS MY CHANCE

WRITERS' BLOCK
THE VOICES OF WOMEN IN PROSE

WRITERS' BLOCK
THE VOICES OF WOMEN IN PROSE

Case Study: Writers' Block Zine

Beyondmedia Education collaborates with under-served and underrepresented women, youth, and communities to tell their stories, connect those stories to the rest of the world, and organize for social justice through the creation and distribution of media arts.

Beyondmedia's Women and Prison programming supports formerly incarcerated women and their families to voice their stories through the arts. Beyondmedia engages their issues and experiences to create opportunities for dialogue, healing, and community organizing. Beyondmedia has collaborated extensively with formerly incarcerated women and girls since 1998.

Based on their award-winning video series documenting the lives and stories of America's incarcerated women, Beyondmedia created a public video installation and companion Web site entitled Women and Prison: A Site for Resistance. While the exhibit and site successfully engaged viewers outside prisons, Beyondmedia wanted to reconnect with the women inside by giving them a voice through the tangible media of print.

As the client and project chosen for their first-ever Camp Firebelly design charrette (started as a way to connect fresh talent with nonprofits in need), Chicago-based Firebelly Design brought together Beyondmedia and the Women and Prison Project and 10 of the brightest student designers from

around the country to brainstorm, design, and produce a collection of the women's stories.

Aside from the many technical limitations imposed by the prisons themselves (i.e., no hard covers, rigid spines, spiral binding, etc.) the zine's only legitimate requirement was to create something as engaging and honest as its related DVDs, Web site and installation.

With Firebelly's guidance, the students worked tirelessly and collaboratively to understand the intricacies of the prison industrial complex and create a digest in which women could share their stories in an authentic, meaningful, and humanizing way.

Research started the very first day with a trip to Beyondmedia's studio to screen several of the organization's documentaries and speak with two formerly incarcerated women. The students also heard from Lara Brooks, one of the Midwest's youngest activists involved in the prison abolition movement. After several brainstorm sessions, the students titled their project *Writers' Block: The Voices of Women Inside* and began designing for complex content ranging from drug addiction and prostitution to poverty, racism, and homophobia.

The end result—a compilation of deeply personal narratives, visceral creative writing, and provocative scholarly essays—was supported by a promotional poster and postcard; with printing generously donated by Salsedo Press and Delicious Design League.

By helping make the issues of women prisoners more visible, the students expanded Beyondmedia's efforts to challenge the criminal justice system and work to end the cycle of crisis it creates for women and their families.

Production Specifics: As with most nonprofit organizations, Beyondmedia's budget for print production was incredibly tight. The group kept this in mind from concept to pre-press. Designing the entire zine within a two-color palette meant that it was easy to alter the color combination from issue to issue, in order to deliver a fresh look each time while sustaining a reasonable price per piece.

The print vendor for this project is a local minority-owned, union print shop just around the corner from Firebelly's studio. It used vegetable-based inks and is a Certified Green Business by Green America.

Designed as a "keeper" for multiple audiences, the Writers' Block zine offered contributing participants, their families, educators, social justice advocates, prison abolitionists, and the general public with a permanent archive of imprisoned women's stories, lives, and ideas. It was also designed as a template for future issues. Sized to fit a 6x9 envelope to keep distribution costs down, the zines additionally included a submission form on the back page to encourage future participation by other women.

Case provided by Antonio Garcia, Firebelly Design (*www.firebellydesign.com*).

Systems Thinking

Curt McNamara, PE
Minneapolis College of Art and Design
Sustainable Design Certificate Program

With additional contributions from:
Terry Gips, Dan Halsey, Jessica Jones, John Moes, Biomimicry Guild, Sustainable Packaging Coalition,SM and MBDC's Cradle to CradleSM

Consider life cycle as a means to innovate.

Design is the intentional creation of artifacts (physical or otherwise). It has elements of craft, art, and structured process. Some might say designers use time-tested recipes, combining text and image in ways to communicate effectively. Others might say designers have a holistic view, using multiple perspectives to create solutions.

While there is no contradiction between these two perspectives, the first view sees design as a linear process, combining well-established materials and methods to form an artifact. In contrast, the second view allows us to approach design holistically, combining elements in new ways that interconnect designer, viewer, and the natural world.

Photo: Curt McNamara
(c.mcnamara@ieee.org).

145

The linear view of design can take highly refined elements, assemble them in any way that gives stability, and consider the job done. Unfortunately, these reassembled objects can require the same, or more, effort to take them apart as were used to create them (high heat, pressure, and chemical action). There may not exist in nature the conditions required to reabsorb the materials into natural materials flows. In many cases, objects created in traditional linear ways persist for decades (or even eons), decay into toxic by-products, or release pollutants when incinerated.

Humanity has excelled at taking the world apart and reassembling the pieces to do our bidding. This process, often called reductionism, has brought great benefits yet has also done great harm. Some designers will cling to it as the rest move to a new paradigm and gain new markets.

Reductionism has been an incredible tool; it has allowed humans to harness the atom, ship fuel around the world, cure disease, and visit the moon. How is it possible this could be ending?

Simply put, the damages from reductionism in many cases exceed the benefits gained by it. Often the benefits are short term while the harm is long term. Assembling pieces without considering the whole can yield highly concentrated, inefficient, and damaging materials. Earth systems cannot break down and safely absorb many of these concentrated materials or process wastes. For example, materials from nuclear power plants are unsafe for the environment. They are too concentrated to be broken down safely and must be stored for many thousands of years. They also present an interesting communication problem. How can we be sure, in 10,000 years, future generations will understand the warnings we have written telling them that the stored materials, if unleashed, are life threatening to every being for miles around?[1]

The results of reductionism are the massive environmental changes that are occurring today. Chemicals designed for a specific purpose without regard to their breakdown almost wiped out the bald eagle. There are areas of the world unsafe for habitation due to pervasive pollution. The atmosphere is changing to a new state brought about by our emissions, and the result will be less friendly to the people, animals, and habitation we are accustomed to.

In contrast, living systems continuously recycle materials and regenerate life. Designs modeled after natural systems can repair the damage while adding value to end users, designers, and the company driving the production of the work.

How does a designer do this? One response is to proceed as usual but gain and use more knowledge of material effects. This "do less bad" approach is good as it broadens awareness and expands focus, yet much more can be done.

Holistic Approach and Design

An alternative point of view as old as civilization has been called the holistic approach. This view is represented in Daniel Pink's *A Whole New Mind*,[2] where the age of systems is brought about by design, story, symphony, empathy, play, and meaning. It is design by using a big-picture view that includes other perspectives.

The holistic view is also called the systems view. Rather than seeing design problems as something to be divided down into the smallest bits, the systems view sees them as opportunities for interconnecting the world back together.

While this view can be traced back to early cultures in all parts of the world, R. Buckminster Fuller was a modern designer who epitomized this idea. Fuller came of age in the early part of the twentieth century. His experiences in the Navy led him to consider navigation, efficiency of materials, and energy usage as the key components in a design situation. He was inspired by the elegance of nature's design, and his focus on nature's operating system gave him a dislike for the results of our typical processes.

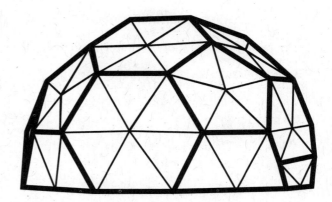

Fuller's geodesic dome design.

We are on a spaceship; a beautiful one. It took billions of years to develop. We're not going to get another. Now, how do we make this spaceship work?

—*R. Buckminster Fuller*

Fuller is best known for the geodesic dome, a high-efficiency, lightweight structure that could span any distance. Domes consist of regular polyhedra coupled together to form a partial sphere. Set on a simple foundation, a dome weighs as little as a pound per square foot. Fuller saw housing as benefiting from the practices of automobile and aircraft manufacture with optimized components and efficient structure.

Yet Fuller was also a philosopher who believed that we all had the capacity to do great things and that the world could work for all if we changed our priorities from weaponry to livingry (using technology to help humanity). During World War II, he cataloged the essential materials of civilization and concluded that there was enough if we simply recycled material and made best use of what we had.

Fuller's designs included a high-efficiency car, low-flow shower (in the 1930s!), and a map that doesn't distort the shapes of the continents.[3] Since this is a spherical world, he taught that we have six degrees of freedom at every instant (radiate/converge, spin, orbit, invert, torque, precess), not the illusory three (xyz) of flat-Earth thinking.

Fuller inspired thousands of designers across several generations and left us with a marvelous catalog of universal principles that can be used to design ever more elegant and sustainable solutions.

Some of the better know practitioners include:

— Jay Baldwin (teaches the ideas of Fuller)

— Paul MacCready (human-powered flight)

— John Todd (water purification systems)

— Hunter Lovins and Amory Lovins (energy systems)

— Stewart Brand (design information for all)

— Medard Gabel and Howard Brown (success for all humanity)

— William McDonough (green architecture, Cradle to Cradle[SM] design)

This brief list shows many of the leaders and ideas in sustainable design. Throughout the last half of the twentieth century, many were aware of this knowledge and contributed to the good work that is still relevant today.

Universal Principles Identified by Fuller

Fuller worked by identifying principles that were true in all situations. Knowing these principles gives design advantage and allows high-efficiency solutions to be found easily. Here are some examples:

"The world is not flat, it is spherical. There is no up and down, just in and out." Humans have a flat-world mentality from time immemorial. However, the world is a rotating sphere whirling around the sun while the solar system moves 52 million kilometers per day along with the Milky Way. Movement is not up in this world, it is out.

TECHNIQUE: The world is not flat. Start design from the center—expanding out or contracting in to fit the problem.

"Nature doesn't calculate pi to 20 decimal places when she designs a flower." Fuller often observed that the basic mathematical "objects" were in fact illusions. There are no straight lines, planes, or circles in the real world. Pi proves that our coordinate system is wrong and that the circle is a mathematical illusion. Sustainable design is aligned with the coordinate system and energy cycles of the universe, enhancing effectiveness by acting in accordance with universal principles.

In the real world, there are no idealized objects but structures whose fine detail comes from individual nodes. As an example, consider the coastline of the United Kingdom. At one level of scale, it appears to be a given length. Zooming in closer reveals more detail, and the length increases. This process occurs to the finest level of detail (the coast is a fractal, an object with similar structure regardless of scale). The coastline is not a "line" but rather an object composed of many nodes. All of nature is constructed this way.

TECHNIQUE: Rather than rectangles, pieces can be structures of fine detail mimicking natural systems. Grow your designs to fit the world by using fine details. There is no flat or square in nature.

Precession: Bees do not intend to pollinate, yet by collecting pollen they ensure that new flowers bloom. In a similar way, Fuller pollinated heads with ideas and expected the universe to provide. If the universe did not provide, he adjusted his pollination strategy.

TECHNIQUE: If the graphic design piece is nectar attracting the buyer/viewer bee, what is the pollen? The brand? Sustainability? If the design fits audience values, it can carry the product along. What else does the audience pick up? How does this information inform their next actions? Can a graphic design element or a logo, a layout, a design piece, or an interactive media experience yield respect and learning about the Earth? How can graphic design change a life?

Synergy: Alloys and composites show material properties not predicted by the behavior of individual components or even the addition of individual component properties. "The whole is greater than the sum of the parts." The most fundamental property of systems is that they can't be understood by taking the pieces apart but only by looking at everything connected. Design done by taking things apart to the smallest level will not result in sustainable design.

TECHNIQUE: Focus on interconnections and relations when designing. Test combinations of design elements to find unexpected gains.

Ephemeralization: Humanity increasingly does more with less. Consider the cell phone network. It has allowed developing countries to gain communications infrastructure without building miles of telephone wires and poles.

Stochastic printing or frequency modulation (FM) screening is a good example of "making more with less." Instead of using evenly spaced dots in a grid like conventional printing, stochastic printing uses smaller, randomly spaced dots that vary in tonal range throughout the image. When used appropriately, this printing technology can offer many advantages of over conventional printing including rich detail, crisper text and lines, and less ink use on the sheet.[4]

TECHNIQUE: How minimal can a piece's substrate and ink coverage be? Can the message be transformed to information? Can the frequency be increased? To Fuller, frequency represented the level of detail: Higher frequency means greater resolution. In

technology, higher frequencies can mean smaller components and less energy.

Trimtab: An ocean liner needs a large rudder. The rudder requires much force to move. Naval designers use a smaller rudder called a trimtab to move the larger rudder.

TECHNIQUE: What are your rudders? The company's rudders? Look for trimtabs to move them. A piece's sustainability story might be able to move the company.

Tensegrity: Most efficient structures use tension and compression in balance. Bridges could be built only so far when they relied on compression columns to support them. Using cables (suspension = tension) allowed structures to span much larger distances using less material.

TECHNIQUE: Graphic elements can use tension and compression to link ideas, creating a web of relations. Look for relations, forces that exist between and not in the elements.

Triangulation: Along with the illusion of a flat world, humans have a "box" mentality that pervades design. Constructing a cube with clay corners shows there is no structural stability in such a design. If a structure is made of triangles, it has stability and strength regardless of what the corners are made of. Rectangles come from a flat-Earth worldview.

TECHNIQUE: Triangulation increases as you add more elements (higher frequencies). Start with the minimal structure and add detail as needed.

Tools not politics: People's behaviors change only when they have the right tools. This book is not about changing minds through legislation but about changing the world through design and tools.

TECHNIQUE: *Design to give advantage and enable users. Emphasize sustainability regardless of the client and project.*

Universal principles are laws that work everywhere and anytime. For example, gravitation pulls inward (contracts) toward the center. It is not a property of either object but exists only as a relation between the two objects.

TECHNIQUE: *What are the forces of relationship that exist between and not in the parts?*

Other universal principles from Fuller:

— Life regenerates itself continually

— Nature runs on loops

— Systems are not static

— Everything is interconnected

To complement these design principles, here are universal principles of life (adapted from Hoagland and Dodson):[5]

　Life:

— *Builds from the bottom up.* Cells form organelles, individuals form societies, and schools of fish emerge from simple rules.

— *Assembles itself into chains.* How do graphic design pieces and their elements link together?

— *Needs an inside and an outside.* One side of a boundary faces in, the other faces out. What is the inside of your design? Does one "side" face the client and the other face the audience?

— *Uses a few themes to create many variations.* Invertebrate, vertebrate . . . Clamshell, nautilus . . . Graphic design, meme . . .

— *Organizes with information and not energy.* The abalone self-assembles in seawater without heat or waste yet is stronger than any ceramic. Graphic designers create pieces that are about information, whether printed, painted, or pixels.

— *Encourages variety by reshuffling information, and creates with mistakes.* Make deliberate and accidental design combinations. Create a set of alternatives and test response.

— *Occurs in water and runs on sugar.* Consider the process first, the end piece second.

— *Works in cycles.* Pieces are born, live, and return to the Earth in some fashion, whether "Frankenstein" or "butterfly."

— *Recycles everything it uses.* There is no waste in nature but food for you or another. Return wastes to Earth safely, or find a partner who can use it.

— *Renews itself by turnover.* Can a piece be refreshed or expire? Don't design for perpetuity, take advantage of decay. The end piece should not last longer than the product it promotes, the event it serves, or the company that initiated the project.

— *Optimizes rather than maximizes.* Optimal is neither worst case nor forever, rather it is a balance of forces and requirements. Design for average, and make alterations for extremes.

— *Is opportunistic.* Look for openings and test with small changes. Experiment. Follow the energy.

Find the free energy in the system and evolve to use it.

— *Competes within a cooperative framework.* Work with peers and team with competitors to increase markets and knowledge. Both parties will gain. "Whatever you want, give it away" (Ford teamwork principle). No design or designer is an island.

— *Is interconnected and interdependent.* Consider the design as a network or web of relationships.

Design Decisions

The preceding section summarized a set of principles that allows a designer to align with the universal coordinate system of universe. Design decisions set the direction for work, people, and the company. To take advantage of the systems view, align your design with universal principles.

TECHNIQUE: Knowing location and orientation allows a designer to move along universal dimensions. Your environment is an ocean and all are sailors.

Changing from the "recipe view" of design is as simple as seeing design decisions as steps along a path. The path leads from the present moment into the future, and each decision point represents an opportunity for change. Many of these decision points are small, yet collectively they are large. For each decision, consider the bigger picture and project the design into the future.

Each design decision can be viewed as the center of nine boxes: At the center is the current situation, above that the environment, and below the elements within/beneath the design.

	Supra	
Past	Design Situation	Future
	Sub	

Nine Boxes: Design in Time and Space. Using this tool gives larger perspective on the design. How does it link into systems above and below? Where does it connect into user time and Earth time?

A design exists in time today: Past time determines the current state, and considering the past as a design element allows sequence design. Example: preparing the audience before the piece to be produced is viewed. Future time is after contact with the design and gives more steps in the interaction. Example: What happens after contact with a design? Does the piece prepare the stage for the next event?

Questions for each decision stage:

— What are the questions this design is answering? Or, what requirements are there?

— What answer to the present design decision allows cycling back into natural systems?

— How can the next decision bring the design closer to the goal of interaction with natural systems?

— Why is the design on the current path?

— What does the current design decision leave behind?

— How can outside resources (see the nine boxes) help solve the situation?

151

— Who are the end users/viewers/customers, and what do they want/need from this decision?

Vertically, the boxes show connections above and below; cycles through space. What resources are available in the larger system? What forces and energy are present in the super-system? Similarly, what resources are available at levels below where the designer is working?

Horizontally, the boxes show connections before and after; cycles through time. What is the system state before the design appears? How is the system changed by the work's contact?

Both dimensions (time and space) emphasize that design isn't a linear processes but links designs above, below, and through time. Works created are interconnected in both time and space, are cyclical, and are not separate. All actions are connected to nature. It is not the work's history but its interconnections that determine future performance.

For the designer, these perspectives are critical in moving from a linear to a holistic view:

Interconnection: How does the design interconnect with Earth systems?

Cycles: What cycles does the design live in, and how can it be tied to the Earth?

Renewal: How does the design allow for new growth?

Evolution: Graphic designs evolve and are selected by the marketplace—how has the designer enabled this?

Adaptation (as in evolution): How has this design piece adapted to the design environment and nature?

Diversity: Sustainable graphic designs are not monocultures. How can a design piece's diversity be enhanced?

Partnership: Rather than singular events, designs are interactions with their viewers and the environment.

Feedback: Systems and works created are not static yet receive feedback from the environment. How can this be enhanced?

Interconnection

Designs draw from natural systems: Substrates, inks, coatings, decorations, and embedded devices all come from the Earth. In many cases, the extraction and processing is energy intensive, produce waste, and may require chemicals that won't break down in nature. The result may be that they can't be recycled and, if incinerated, can produce harmful by-products. This is the result of the linear view. Each component may be excellent when measured by a small set of requirements (high contrast, impervious to moisture, or high reflectance) yet may be poor in overall performance.

To improve interconnection, the design requirements can be expanded so that the work:

— Should not last longer than the product or event

— Can return to nature

— Is appropriate for reuse

The traditional linear view may not be sufficient to answer these requirements, and knowledge of interconnection is required. For example, material properties alone are not sufficient; they need to be augmented by the life cycle impact for creation and knowledge of impact at end of life. This all comes back to interconnection. If this is considered first, then problems do not occur.

Cycles

Nature runs on cycles, while linear pieces ignore or break cycles. If materials and processing are considered at the front end, designs fit into natural cycles and problems are avoided. For example: All materials will return to Earth eventually. The question is, how do they return—with minimal impact, or with toxic components?

Linear works are not circular or closed loop—they use up resources to form an object, then condemn the collection in the form of the final piece to the trash heap. They do not come directly from, nor do they return directly to nature. The production process can also have unintentional results; consider metals and solvents in ink formulations used in printing. At end of life, these and other materials may not decompose readily or may break down into toxic components. At best, printed graphics created in conventional ways stay in landfills and don't decay, locking up valuable materials and resource streams for generations. These are examples of cycles being neglected, with impacts on the Earth and sustainability.

In contrast, works designed with avenues to complete cycles add value for the producer, the consumer, and potentially the Earth. Their impact ranges from minimizing harm to adding value (e.g., factories whose effluent water is cleaner than the water coming into the plant). If designed correctly (as in cradle-to-cradle–inspired approaches), the end of life returns value to the production process or enhances Earth systems.

Cycles should be considered at:

— Material creation

— Processing

— Distribution

— Use

— End of life

Designs have a cycle, intentional or not. Select one design, draw it out on a big sheet of paper, and circulate it for comments. Look for places where the cycle can be improved:

— Reducing impacts

— Getting materials with minimal processing

— Avoiding harmful production steps

— Ensuring materials can be directly composted or recycled after use

— Using material combinations that allow recovery

— Finding ways to return to the Earth directly

— Choosing materials with an appropriate lifetime

— Looking for uses at end of life

— Consider the design's end of life first, then work backward to create conditions in the present that will yield the desired result

Renewal

Life renews itself by continual turnover. Almost all cells in our bodies are replaced every seven years. Essentially the information (DNA) is maintained by renewing the physical components. Designs exist in a particular time and place: A desired lifetime may be brief or long. Often pieces are unintentionally designed for lifetimes much longer than required due to incorrectly chosen materials or overdesign.

Consider the parallels in nature. Birds molt in the spring when it is mating season. Feathers are bright, but fade over the summer from wind, sun, and rain. In the fall and winter, they stay faded, then are replaced once again. Flowers bloom for their season, attracting pollinators. The cherry tree produces thousands of fruits to get a few seedlings started by birds eating and carrying them away, depositing them (complete with starter fertilizer) over great distances. Meanwhile the cherries that remain localized enrich and renew the Earth around the tree.

How can works mimic these kinds of renewal? There are several ways:

Space: Designs change with the environment, using minimal space and energy to perform the function.

Time: Designs change with the seasons, fading as their moment to mate with a viewer goes past.

Cycles: Designs flow back into Earth cycles, enriching the surroundings.

Information: Designs pass on their DNA (i.e., message) by being absorbed, transferred, transformed, or stored.

Consider renewal rather than permanence when designing: How will the message be transferred and transformed rather than how it will persist? The environment changes continuously, and even the best-crafted message may be stale by the time of production. Yet designing for renewal will ensure it persists without the by-products of permanence.

Evolution

Variety comes from changes (or variation) and selection to retain the best. As designs are produced, some are different from the others. The variation can come from the designer, or from the marketplace. Those that best fit the design environment are kept, being selected for continued life. This is evolution.

To design for evolution, allow small changes at every step. Test these changes, internally and externally. Select the most promising, and repeat the process. To serve large markets, consider processes that allow for local optimization to balance volume versus waste generated from unsuitable versions. Example: A user manual in six languages must carry six times the paper needed to serve each individual market.

Evolution is driven by environment yet enabled by variation. The variation can come from your design, or it can come from the competition. This is the larger canvas of evolution: where competing designs clamor for eyes and the best are selected. This environment changes rapidly, and consists of:

— Information (mind-set, culture, media, other designers and artistic mediums)

— Structure (how messages are deployed)

— Energy (what are the costs, what are clients willing to pay for)

— Competitors (each inhabiting their own habitat, none overlapping yours)

— Exchange (designs must give as well as take)

Adaptation

If evolution is variation followed by selection, then what drives variation? It could be random, or in response to a customer or competitor. Yet what are the larger forces?

Designs emerge from designers. For designs to adapt and change, designers must do the same. Some of this is internally driven: Reflection and analysis of practice leads to greater skill and dexterity (mental and physical). Others are externally driven: market forces, changes in product or content, the company mind-set, and management priorities.

For the most part, the designer is unaware of these forces and adaptation is reactive rather than contemplative (based on the larger picture).

To take advantage of adaptation:

— Use the systems view—consider three viewpoints when designing.

— Consider forces outside of the normal (environmental changes).

— Make designs flexible (pieces can adapt).

— Add dimensionality to the design (can work on several levels).

— Decrease cycle time.

— Increase variations.

— Seek out and listen to feedback.

— Use unusual sources.

Diversity

The natural world continually increases diversity as ecological habitats change and organisms adapt. In contrast, the industrial world creates diversity in design, yet often destroys diversity in the natural world. These are not equivalent, as design diversity is short-lived, doesn't necessarily lead to new ongoing species, and doesn't capture and store more solar energy.

How could design diversity model organismal diversity to take advantage of this systems property?

On an individual design basis, coupling more closely to the intended audience creates a better fit than trying to meet all needs with one design. Instead of designing for all, design for the majority, and use modifications to fit the corners of the market.

This process will allow better fit, give better return, and allow producers to sense more closely their environment. As this process unfolds, nearby markets and market movements (akin to environmental changes) will become more obvious, and designs will diversify to meet these newly perceived needs.

Partnership

Life makes conditions conducive to life. In other words, the actions of one species allows others to flourish. In the design world, open source, trade associations, mentoring, and trading arrangements all work toward building together. This building may involve information sharing, scaffolding off another's work, platform designs, using best practice, training, and appreciation.

However it is accomplished, two or more working together create more than each could working separately. Partnership may be at the level of peers, departments, companies, customers, clients, and the Earth.

In a partnership, each gives and each receives. This requires enlarging the scope of design to be a two-way flow: What is given to the viewer as we attract their attention? Design that just takes and takes is not sustainable. Each transaction needs to give, as the flower attracts insects with nectar, allowing its pollen to be distributed and thereby benefiting all.

Could the points of attraction on a graphic design piece represent flowers or kinds of nectar? The intent of a design may be to attract one or multiple species. In the natural environment, there are many kinds of flowers and many kinds of pollinators. There is overlap from one to the other: One flower may attract several species while one insect may visit several species of flowers. The design bridges viewer and producer, client and customer, using maps, attractors, and signs. These tools control perception of image, product/content, and intent in the designed environment.

Feedback

There are no forces in total opposition: Interchanges modify each partner and some energy exits the reaction. The energy alterations and excess are "the force that through the green fuse drives the flower," as the poet Dylan Thomas said.

At a higher level we view this as feedback: either positive (to increase flows) or negative (to decrease flows). Each bit of feedback is fundamental and necessary for life and growth. Biological systems often use one protein to start growth (positive feedback) and another to inhibit it when the correct size is reached (negative feedback). Any system that appears to have a stable state (such as a designer or design firm) has both positive and negative feedback loops. Likewise, controlled growth is positive feedback moderated by negative feedback.

The things we create to sell give implicit feedback: I am like you! Buy me and be happy! Yet the message can be short-lived, and once the interchange is over, an emptiness remains. For any design to be sustainable, the use of feedback needs to be enlarged.

Consider the environment after acquisition of the produced object: How will the audience be enabled by possessing this thing? In what ways will it enlarge and yet limit their space or options?

As the design process unfolds, take into account feedback: from coworkers, clients, customers, and the natural world. Is the design fitting into place, enhancing existing feedback loops or creating new ones? How can feedback be made more prominent in the design?

For one example, a system with feedback would stop filling the tub before it overflows. What is the tub for the current design? The faucet? The sensor? The water?

Feedback will also alter a message. If you see someone with a puzzled look during a conversation, you will modify the message to facilitate communication. How can the design benefit from early feedback about perception? Once delivered, the design can be concrete and unchanging, staying the same as the environment changes. How could the design be enhanced to be more adaptive, responding to feedback in the environment?

Viewing Systems

It is a human tendency to view systems as external and static. In reality, all of us are enmeshed in creating, utilizing, and designing dynamic systems every moment.

Who is your audience or customer?
Photo: Curt McNamara (c.mcnamara@ieee.org).

The movement from reductionism to seeing systems is a change in perspective. Once that change is made, there are several ways to utilize the systems view:

— The properties of systems and how they can improve designs

— Considering work and design itself as a system process

— Using the cycles and properties of natural systems as inspiration for design

Systems as Bridges

How can design leave the world in better condition? One lesson of reductionism is that if designs are improved along just one dimension, other aspects may degrade in ways that were not foreseen. Example: A brochure printed on brilliant white glossy stock that uses toxic materials to produce the paper but uses vegetable inks to appear "eco."

Sustainable design can't be achieved by optimizing just one attribute. As an example, several sustainable accounting methods use a three-part approach that includes social, environmental, and economic factors (aka triple top line and triple bottom line—people, planet, profits). Sustainability is the intersection of these three domains with the economic system embedded in the environment. In the systems view, designs are connected to their environment at all times, from production, to processing, to sale, to end of life. These connections are design attributes—materials they were created with, energy used for processing, connections to the client and end user, and decay at end of life.

In the nested circles image pictured here, objects we create exist inside the economic system yet the

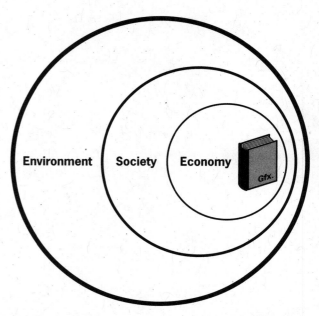

All objects we create exist inside economic, societal, and environmental systems.

economic system is embedded in society and environment. The connections of material, production, and end of life extend out into the environment as they pass through society. A toxic material might appear to have a nice loop within the economic system yet affect workers in the societal system and have negative impacts on the environment.

Contrast this with appropriate materials that benefit the workers and the environment while still fulfilling an economic function. This kind of design builds value at all levels.

The three-part accounting method is a reminder to designers of primary constituencies. However, the parts can't be considered individually. Rather, all must be dealt with at the same time. Connections are the key principle behind the nested circles of sustainability.

Systems Properties

The systems view can be used within multiple perspectives: the end result, the design process, or even the structure and relations of a department or company.

The systems view at the design level focuses on linkages, boundary, and function.

In the natural world, nothing can contract nor expand without limit. A stable system has forces to increase and forces to decrease. The force to increase is termed "positive feedback," while the force to decrease is "negative feedback." Their balance is what creates stability.

System edges and exchange points are at boundaries, the places where they connect to each other and to the world. An object has many boundaries or edges: physical, information, and optical (reflective). The design links client and designer, expanding and contracting to "fill the space" required to communicate the message. Then the design becomes a bridge between client and customer.

Functions are the ways in which a system responds to or modifies the environment. Graphic design pieces or projects identify, instruct, and promote. These functions are mappings from designer to audience. They pass messages using information, color, shape, and arrangement. Functions can be assigned to components of the work. The type of function often gives insight into the structure required to perform that function.

Consider the hierarchy of design elements: Is image stronger than word? How does shape link to message? What is the story of the material? Do oppositions create meaning?

Loops and interconnections are visible when perspective changes from images (a leaf bud or a rusting automobile) to cycles. Designs only appear static: changing perspective from snapshots in time to steps in a cycle that loops from creation to life and return. This is a life cycle, and all objects have one. They are created from the Earth, live on materials and energy from natural systems, and return to nature via landfill or incineration. It is not possible to know the true costs or values or benefits of a design without considering the life cycle.

TECHNIQUE: Seeing the life cycle can inspire a service system where customers pay for the service rather than the thing itself.[6]

The systems perspective looks beyond the current way of doing business and permits designers and managers to imagine future systems that benefit both company and planet. If all current designs are made from primary materials and land-filled, the alternative choices look meager. Instead, a systems perspective allows the company to imagine its design becoming an asset to attract customers, improve the working life of employees and increasing margins and market share. The next few sections show how to move to the systems design perspective.

Sustainability and Graphic Design

Graphic designers apply their skills to a gamut of design needs: from the printed page and packaging; to product graphics and user interface design; to way-finding, signage, and event support; to promotional items, Web pages, advertising and branding, just to name a few. All of these applications have to deal with some sort of base medium (physical materials or Web page screen) and how the "image" gets on to it.

Sustainability approaches certainly must address concerns about materials: Can the object created decay gracefully or be returned to the production process (Cradle to Cradle)?[7] But on another level, it looks deeper at the message being sent: communicating values between the piece's producer and the viewer; or in the case of packaging and advertising, helping consumers make better choices.

Great design encompasses all of these into an integrated unit, including:

— Collaboration between designer and supplier/ service vendor

— Fitting the end piece to the market

— Encouraging positive behaviors

— Giving a visual language to sustainability

— Encoding positive actions (cycling, efficient use, "just enough")

— Moving from a world of things (nouns) to one of actions (verbs)

— Communicating at several levels: design situation, values, style, and market

— Awareness of what and how the design situation is represented

— Identifying sustainability with lifetimes, minimal impacts, and restoration

— Aiding internal changes in the piece's viewer

— Messaging: encoding, channel, transmission, reception, triggering

— Actions: transference, inhibition, activation, transcription, catalysis, growth

Systems and Design

Many things are systems: a chair, a diagram, even a thought. It has been said that three types of information are needed to capture a system: visual, description, and relations. Designers are visual thinkers so the first way comes naturally to them. Description can be text, yet it benefits by using one of these perspectives: dimension (time, space, elements), function (inform, identify, sell), or boundary (flow, exchange, interchange). Relations are linkages, forces, or movements illustrated by graphic elements.

Visualizing Systems Perspectives

To better understand a systems perspective, draw an image of the end piece to be created. Now divide that into components, and connect each design component to the Earth as a source material. Show the materials (ink and substrate) being processed and delivered as a finished piece. The next step is transport—arrival into the viewer's hands. Create an image of the viewer and the finished piece. The information is processed. Now what happens?

The diagram may show a cycle returning materials to the source to create a loop, or it may show a finished piece ending up in a landfill or incinerator. At each stage, diagram the relations of the piece's materials to the Earth and to the people associated with that step in its life. Now write a description of each stage. This is a systems description of the finished piece.

Make a large copy, post it, and invite comments. Document another design option; how does it compare? Does the image show places to add connections? Does the image show system properties, and does it show the potential to use alternative materials?

Dimension, function, boundary, linkages, and interconnection exist in every system and its elements:

Finished Piece

— Materials

Elements: text, color, image

Properties

Substrate (energy use, chemicals to process)

Inks, coatings, finishes, embellishments

— Processing

Prepress

Proofing

Printing

Trimming, binding, die-cutting, etc.

Embedded materials

— Life cycle

(creation ➤ use ➤ end of life ➤ rebirth)

— Stakeholder connections

(company ➤ designer ➤ production staff ➤ supply chain ➤ target community)

— Structure

(differences, shapes, colors, texture)

— Content

Inform

Instruct

Identify

Sell

Link (to calendar)

Trigger response

The design process is also a system with interconnections, loops, feedback, energy, and information flows. Consider documenting the design process and how it connects to the stakeholders.

Design Process

— Design environment (information sources, peers, competitors)

— Finished piece—requirements

— Design tools

— Design representation (design perspective, systems view)

Information design and information architecture

Communication as linking species in changing habitat

— Content design process

— *Design ↔ product/content interconnection* (take it a level higher by considering the larger system)

— Team learning (teaching and learning from each other)

— Company function

Commercial ecology (customers and suppliers)

Industrial ecology (interconnections with other firms)

Departmental ecology (human systems)

System Techniques

There are many systems viewpoints and perspectives. Three that we will investigate are: technical, philosophical, and design guidelines. The next sections cover a range of systems perspectives, the design process, and the relation of design to the environment.

Design as a System

Where does the system perspective start, and how can it be utilized effectively?

As a first step, the designer must ask: What is the intention of the finished piece? If the first thought is to create something to inform, instruct, or promote, then the design has been viewed from a single perspective. The design solution will not be a system but a "point solution." While it may do an excellent job in one area, it might have unintended consequences in others. This type of design solves a situation that is limited in scope, leading to problems in other areas.

Lead paint on children's toys is one example. Although lead paint may have been a good choice for initial cost, the consequences of this material specification went far beyond a product recall. Companies took more steps to ensure safety, suppliers went under, and there were government responses. The total impact is huge and ongoing. Are there any other materials that might have similar risks? This example may make you think only of substances to avoid. While such a list is important, there are many more environmental and competitive *benefits* from sustainably sourced options as well.

A related example is a company with high failure rates on a shipped product. Adding more packaging did not help. The failures continued until the company looked deeper into the product design and found that a rubber stop, costing only a few pennies, positioned inside the product, would keep components from destructively vibrating. Using the rubber stop allowed the company to decrease packaging to the bare minimum, saving material dollars and transportation costs.

These situations are part of a continuum, illustrating how designers and managers have the chance to make decisions from a narrow or wide perspective. In many cases, using the larger perspective takes only a little more time and money, yet the payoff is huge. It has been said that up to 80 percent of a thing's material and energy impacts are determined by the decisions at design time.

How can you enlarge the design practice to make the larger perspective automatic? By considering each design (and its elements) as a system.

Adapt to the Environment

How do we get from here:

Point solutions, doing designs that oppose
    natural systems

to there:

Comprehensive solutions that benefit company,
    society, and the environment?

The systems perspective is an excellent entry point. This may sound surprising if the word "system" brings to mind complex equipment or regimented organizations. This type of system design comes from a view of the world as a static entity with many layers. Such designs can be brittle and unable to adapt as the environment changes.

Buckminster Fuller said, "Extinction happens when the environment changes and the organism doesn't adapt." We are now in times of extreme environmental change, and many designs, organisms, and organizations will become extinct.

What are the environments that a design lives in?

— Regulatory (Coalition of Northeastern Governors, REACH [*r*egistration, *e*valuation, and *a*uthorization of *ch*emicals], Waste Electrical and Electronic Equipment Directive)

— Client (internal images, images of the external world)

— Workplace (company culture and changes)[8]

— Competitive (the company and the competition)

— Marketplace (graphic design pieces are flowers designed to attract . . .)

— Consumer (their mind space)

— Cultural (media, books, art, and music).

— Physical (protection against water, light, and heat)

— Economic (costs and advantages)

— Biosphere or natural environment

Some of these are subsystems of others, and all are changing and evolving. A design can be many things: representation of a system; mapping from one to many; interface between product and consumer; information about an event. In most cases, both sides of the pairing are evolving and changing. The design (and designer!) needs to evolve as well or become extinct. Design is a system when the perspectives of others are included and life cycle is considered.

The creation, distribution, and disposal of every object impacts the physical environment here on Earth. There are many ethical reasons to "do the right thing," including regulations, leaving the planet better for the children, and preserving the health of neighbors.

Adapt to the Biosphere

Typical intentions (requirements) handled through design:

— Buy/sell/promote: Product, company, event, idea

— Inform: Product, company, user

— Identify: Company, product, issue

— Translate/condense/represent

— Amuse/entertain

— Attend

— Trust

Each of these is a complex mapping in two directions: between client and designer and between end piece and viewer. The result of the mapping is a visual surface for the idea, event, or product. This mapping may be static or active: Pieces contain both fixed elements (nouns) as well as encoded movement (verbs). Fixed elements name things and give visual "handles" for quick processing. Movement indicates time and may show loops or cycles. These design elements are known, active, and reviewed by client and designer.

What can be missed—design for the wrong environment?

— Communication function time measured in weeks yet designed piece impacts persist for decades in nature. *Life cycles don't match.*

— Designed to please internal stakeholders yet doesn't connect to audience. *Visual language is not shared.*

— Makes sense to company, end user doesn't understand. *Mappings are not equivalent across the boundaries.*

The design needs to work for all the environmental interfaces. The first benefit of the systems perspective is to enlarge design thinking to include other environmental interfaces. This larger picture makes designing and designs more adaptive, giving competitive advantage.

Note that the design has to fulfill its technical objectives. An Earth-friendly poster or banner that fades early helps no one.

Consider how often designs are updated. Adaptation to the environment happens and improvements occur at the time of design. Just as organisms have new offspring, designers have new projects. The environment acts on them, rewarding the best by:

— Increasing market share

— Bettering the health of planet and people

— Enhancing the career of the designer

To make this work, try several design options and let the market select. Consider one design for the average case and smaller runs for more difficult environmental conditions.

As the environment changes, designs, companies, and designers will go extinct. How does a designer track and adapt as the environment changes? By updating skill sets and being open to new information. Being open to new information means searching outside the current way of doing things

(personal or company). The new information will be from perspectives different from the current one of the designer or company. Beware of the view that it is safe automatically to go back to the tried and true—the old way of doing things has brought us to the troubles we are trying to fix now.

Properties of Systems

Along with the environment, other system properties that can transform a designer's work are:

— Boundary

— Function

— Linkages: Feedback and interchange

Boundary

What is a graphic design? It is an energetic mapping, a boundary or skin between client, designer, and audience that has:

— An information boundary

— An energetic boundary

— A visual boundary

— Representations of ideas or actions

The boundary has layers or levels:

— Text

— Shape

— Color

— Image

— Pigment

— Substrate

— Texture

— Reflection/transmittance

These are patterns of space, time, and energy.

What is a system? Something with a boundary that persists as the environment changes yet is connected to the world.

The boundary of a design serves all the diverse environments just noted. Yet often it is designed for one environment. Is the design boundary alive or dead? Is it seen as an adaptive system, changing as required?

To take a biological example, the cell is a system, and the cell boundary is a system as well. Like every other boundary, the cell membrane divides the world into two: the system inside the boundary and the world outside.

The design project also divides the world in two: on one side the client from designer, on the other side end piece from audience. Seen this way, the project is similar to a cell boundary. It represents the intent of the initiator of the project and the designer's language to the world.

Does this sound familiar? A little more detail: The cell boundary is composed of molecules called phospholipids which have one end that prefers water and the other that rejects water. The molecules snap together with water-loving ends outside and water-hating ends inside. A second layer forms inside the first, and a boundary is created.

The cell boundary protects the contents inside and permits some substances and energies to enter while rejecting others. This idea seems more complex than a print piece, such as a package, yet there are similarities. A boundary could allow

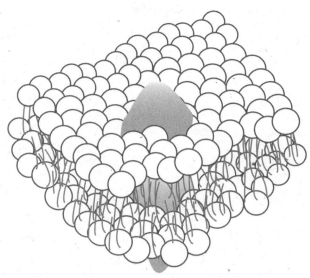

A boundary, showing the interlinked molecules that form the inner and outer layers.

radio-frequency identification (RFID) label signals (and perhaps light) to pass through while keeping moisture out. With the appropriate signal, the boundary can let other signals pass through or trigger events. In a similar way, a print piece can trigger emotional response or recognition.

A cell boundary responds to molecular triggers that fit the shape of its openings. The trigger can initiate an action inside the cell boundary. Cell boundaries maintain one set of environmental conditions inside regardless of the external conditions.

At a larger scale, consider boundaries like the eggshell or the banana peel. Both are elegant design solutions that return to nature and restore the Earth in the process.

What can be learned from recognizing that there are similarities between the cell and a man-made object?

Can the design:

— Be grown?

— Repair itself?

— Trigger?

— Pass information?

— Maintain pressure? (a "Do Not Enter" sign "pushes" outward)

— Respond to stimulus?

— Indicate internal conditions?

An object has a two-part boundary and may also be a boundary between another piece and the external environment.

What does the cell boundary do that the typical man-made object doesn't?

— Renew itself, valve (control flow, or moderate flow)

— Regulate substances and energies

— Decay

— Self-assemble, merge systems together

Things the man-made object and cell boundary both do:

— Signal

— Filter

— Trigger

How can insights from cell boundaries be used to improve an object? The cell boundary has an inside surface (cell to membrane) and an outside surface (membrane to environment). Can items be

improved by considering the two interfaces separately? Start by defining the ideal boundary from the inside looking out and from the outside looking in: between client and designer and between end piece and viewer.

Cell boundaries self-assemble when their fundamental components are close enough to allow interconnection. What materials and processes would mimic this?

To contrast engineered materials and those from nature, engineered materials are monolithic: uniform in all directions. Materials in nature are grown to fit their specific environment, and consist of structural elements replicated over and over, yet changing properties to fit to the boundary.

This is similar to the ideas in the structured creativity tool called Triz, which has dynamization as a fundamental property of innovative designs: moving from monolithic, to segmented, to dynamic systems. For example, computers changed from large shared systems to individual computers for every user. Systems designed with smaller parts may be configured in many shapes.

Apply this by starting with a two-part design. How can you change it to four parts, or to eight? This is similar to the innovative process at 3M, where workers learned that many small lenses are better than just one and then invented technology to create the products and the processes. This idea was then spun off into adhesives and a variety of other product lines.

This cross-fertilization is perhaps best exemplified by 3M's micro-replication process, a technology developed for the manufacture of lenses for overhead projectors. The process enables the creation of tiny, precisely shaped structures that can be used to tailor the physical, chemical and optical properties of a surface.

These perfectly replicated structures, which range in size from nanometers to millimeters, have since been used to create reflective prisms on safety clothing and light enhancement films for display screens, as well as in structural adhesives and a number of abrasive products.[9]

As graphic designers go forward and come into alignment with the dimensions of the universe, they will move from designing for flat squares to webs and skins. This process can start by replication with similar shapes fitting together to cover a surface. Pieces need not be flat or square. If they are unique, then end user and product/company/event are unique by association.

Cell boundaries are composed of organic molecules that need to be renewed, or they will decay and be carried away by scavengers. In the urban environment, valuable materials (e.g., aluminum cans) are carried away by scavengers once the object's primary function has been completed. What other material choices could decay after use or be valuable enough for collection? Perhaps the end piece is of high value, such event programs or special edition packaging, guaranteeing collection and return.

Consider designing the system for collection first: What would make a thing valuable enough for scavengers to take notice? In Brazil, one city rewards residents with food when they bring in recyclable garbage. In her 2002 book *Biomimicry,* author Janine Benyus, tells how she brought secondhand store employees into a manufacturing plant so they could look at wastes and decide which had potential for reuse. The industrial design program at the University of the Arts in Philadelphia sends students out to companies to collect a barrel of whatever they consider waste. The students return and figure out ways to use the material.

Contrast this approach to one that makes the boundary ephemeral and easily decomposed. In one case, make the item valuable and recapture it; in the other, make it easy to return to nature. This is similar to the idea of *biological* and *technical nutrients* described in William McDonough and Michael Braungart's book *Cradle to Cradle.*

Function

The functions of a system are the ways that it reacts to inputs, produces outputs, or responds to the environment. In some cases, these functions are simple: They persist despite environmental changes.

Other functions may be to guard, identify, sell, guide, condense, map, inform, show, communicate, hide, reveal, and draw attention. There are more. Make a list for projects.

For each function, describe whether it is accomplished through materials, processing, or content. Many functions will be a combination or sequence of these elements.

TECHNIQUE: *Describe all functions visually. Break each one down into materials, processing, and information. Show how several functions are contained in one structure. What functions stand alone or are the result of a single processing step or material selection?*

Lightening: *Can the function be accomplished with less material? With lower-impact processing? Moved from material to information?*

Elimination: Are there functions that are not mandatory? Perhaps something designed for worst case can be lightened yet still serve 85 percent of the market. Make a trade-off comparison to see if the savings outweigh the market fit. If necessary, create one design for the majority and another for the minority. Even if serving the targeted needs of the minority might be a bit more expensive, the overall effectiveness of the project can be increased with overall fewer resources.

Splitting: If one material choice, processing step, or element is used to achieve more than one function, split them apart. Does this allow the use of less material or lower-impact processing? How could the secondary function be achieved?

Combining: Look at combining functions in a single material, process, or content step. Perhaps two previously combined functions should be split and each combined with a new, better-fitting partner.

Level-up, Product: In the case of packaging, ask: What are the functions of the package/product combination? Brainstorm with the product team to see if functions could be assigned to the package or even the store signage (Point of Purchase display, shelf talkers). If the graphics can do more, can the product do less? What is the interface between graphics and product? If the graphics component is a subsystem, how does it relate to the product?

Level-up, Content: The end piece is the face or skin of the event/idea/brand. How does this skin fit? Does it transmit the content directly, or does it transform, filter, or phrase it? How can the piece express more of the content by promoting sustainability? There is a design language for the client and event/project/product: Can this also communicate cycles and return to the Earth? Enhance the design language to support more verbs—movement, looping, actions—not things.

Level-down, Product: Can graphics functions be accomplished by the product? Would this make a better product? If the graphics do less, can the product do more?

This process of fine-tuning function relates to life cycle analysis (LCA). The first step in LCA is to define the function, then define the system that bounds that function.

Level-down, Content: Is the end piece too busy and idiosyncratic? Does it reflect more on the designer than what it promotes or identifies? How "thin" and transparent can the design be?

TECHNIQUE: For each function, ask: How would nature do it? Can the function or its expression be minimized? Is it possible to eliminate that function? Can the function be transformed into information?

A typical product design process might view the graphic's function as a decorative skin added at the last minute for user-interface purposes or branding (communication). Yet skin is a complex structure tightly coupled to the tissue underneath: protecting, breathing, growing, and dying. The metaphor of skin (or seed or shell) may spark many ideas, and there may be advantage in coupling the graphic design process more tightly with the product. Similarly, a content team may bring in graphic designers at the end of their process, losing opportunities to codesign a visual language together. This language is a "skin" or fur for the content.

When created separately, the skin doesn't "bond" and the fit is poor. The result is lost information and energy that could be transmitted from the content team to the audience. How many otherwise good products failed to gain a wider audience because the early buyers didn't understand the user-interface graphics provided to aid use? How many really good products stayed on the shelf unsold because the box graphics didn't sell the product?

Function Can Be Reimagined

Graphic Design Function

— Expands out

— Contracts in

— Fits like skin or fur

— Creates a new interface for the content or product

Graphic Design Does

— More functions

— Fewer functions

— How minimal can the graphics be?

— What is the maximum graphics load?

— How valuable can the graphics be?

What is required of the system if the graphics are minimized? In other words, can graphics be rethought in terms of total system design? Perhaps overdesigning can be good if it reduces overall materials or costs, or the system can be designed in a way that minimizes other resource use. The graphics could be grown around the product, be part of the content, or be essential to the end user. Doing the right thing with design carries over to other areas of life and design.

If an object persists, it serves as constant reminder of the company. Sometimes this adds to brand equity if the experience is positive; sometimes it's a "bad ambassador" as in the case of persistent litter. Many companies are thinking of their products and materials as being composed of technical nutrients[10] and want them returned. They reward people for this and gain repeat buyers/users, increasing sustainability.

Graphic design functions can be expanded, contracted, or transformed in ways that increase sustainability.

System Design Strategies

— Look at graphics as part of the product/content system.

— Grow elements, decreasing requirements on the system.

— Shrink elements, increasing system requirements yet decreasing total costs.

— Transform function.

— Survive after sale or event in a useful way?

— Return to the manufacturer in an exchange that benefits both?

Information Design Strategies

— Communicate values that encourage sustainability.

— Show connections, cycles, and loops.

— Give something back for every attraction (pollen and nectar).

— Visualize awareness of the deeper message.

— Create a shared world.

Graphics embody a language and messages that are shared. This shared environment (niche) co-evolves client, audience, and designer, allowing deeper communication.

A design or object that persists after use can be a detriment not only to the environment but also to the company when it becomes trash in the woods or ocean with your logo on it. Create objects that inspire closing the loop.

When designing, consider the object's environments: manufacturing or production, shipment or transport, point of sale, user/viewer transport, home place, and end of life. Each is a different environment with different requirements. Tune in and design for the best case.

Feedback and Interchange

Feedback in design exists at both sides of the boundary: between client and designer, between end product and audience. For one example, certain colors provoke certain associations. While feedback could be used to link the product/idea/event to the buyer, it could also be used to pass on values of sustainability: efficiency, closing loops, appropriate materials, reuse. To be effective, the design needs to communicate core values that resonate with the audience.

One direction of feedback and interchange is end piece to idea/product/event: What is that interface—skin, shell, husk, camouflage, warning, guide? Is it coupled like the banana skin so that it indicates the internal state (the poster fades after the event)?

The other direction is end piece to audience. In some cases, the end piece lets the idea/product/ event shine through and make its own connection to the audience; in other cases, the end piece can aid or obscure it. The idea here is not to think of the design or end piece as a filter but rather another element to create better solutions.

Since a printed piece's function is to absorb/reflect light as an aspect of frequency, it can be seen to "valve," or regulate, energy flows. This has the potential to expand beyond light and tracking. What if the end piece responded to viewers/users or the environment? Then perhaps oxygen could start the piece's decomposition.

The connection to sustainability can be tied to audience mind-set: Pieces can attract viewers/users who already have those values, and pieces can also educate those who have been attracted by some other feature.

In many ways, graphics are the face of the idea/ product/event/enterprise. As noted before, objects created can affirm core values, educate, and include sustainability to expand market share or awareness.

Ideas about feedback that can be used to communicate sustainability:

— Messages and values

— Language of sustainability

— Shared mappings

— Universal principles

— System elements: cycles, binaries, levels, centers, and arrows[11]

— Linkages, loops, belonging, membership, kinship, biophilia

Levels

Point of view determines the structure, order, and relation of a system. For example, the view of a corporation is different from that of a worker,

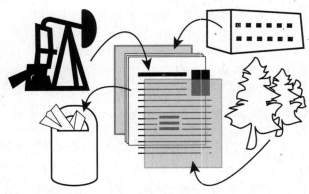

Capturing the impacts of a piece though its life cycle.

— Content

— Messages of sustainability

— Implicit: material types, inks, style, inclusion

Representation

— Product

— Company

— Event

— Idea

manager, owner, and customer audience. For graphic designers, their work is often viewed from outside the idea/event/product and perhaps even outside the larger product design team. Consider the design-level view. Looking out, what does the product/idea/event need and want from its graphics? Looking in, what does the design want back?

This view automatically reminds us of levels, from the product/event/idea, through design, to end user.

Recall that pieces often consists of several levels:

Identification

— Audience

— Company

— Event

Information

— Regulatory

— Use

Levels include instruction, identification, information, labeling, warnings, and guides. Functions may be combined on another level (printing inside external enclosure) that can help or hinder sustainability. For example, an option being considered might require a pigment or process that could contaminate all of the materials.

TECHNIQUE: Make a contents chart of a complex piece. What physical levels are there? What informational levels? Which levels are combined into one physical level? Explore combining or separating the levels.

Can two levels be combined into one? Perhaps the functions of one level can be subsumed in the next, requiring less energy and materials to produce. Conversely, it may be possible that one layer should be split into two. The idea of "platform design" where a standard set of materials is customized for different designs can result in lower impact in a variety of ways: Economy of scale can allow use of more appropriate materials; less time and energy is required for new works; standardization allows refinement instead of inventing the same wheel over and over again.

Taking Advantage of the Systems View

Besides the systems perspective, how can a graphic designer take advantage of systems approaches? There is competitive advantage in considering graphic design as a system. There are several ways to do this: marketing versus the competition, increasing best practice inside the company, and evolving in the product habitat.

Consider the Niche

What is an ecological niche? In ecology, a niche is the area that an organism occupies, and has dimensions for position in the food chain, habitat, life history, and geographic range. The parallels to a particular design are:

— The audience that takes it home

— The places it is sold or is viewed

— Where it goes when it dies

— How it competes against other works

Note that two solutions can't occupy the same niche.

TECHNIQUE: *Map the forces that describe the niche the design lives in. How do these forces link to the audience? To the Earth? What are the commonalities and differences between the end piece produced and the competition's?*

Objects are organisms inside niches where they compete for food (energy or dollars) against other objects. Organisms can't live just anywhere; they are adapted or evolved to the niche they are found in. This could be a kind of soil, a type of insect, a sequence of temperatures, and moisture. Some

birds can live in wider ranges than others, similar to a car that can run on more than one kind of fuel. Many birds migrate between different habitats, using regular movement as a strategy to rediscover optimal conditions.

The niche can be considered in the marketplace:

— Where is the object placed (high or low on the shelves)?

— How does it attract an audience?

— What is the value for price?

Some designs (and their associated product/event/idea) appeal only to a small audience, while others appeal to almost everyone.

TECHNIQUE: *Describe the niche for the design and for the competition. How do they compare and differ? How can your design move away from the competition and toward your audience?*

Questions to consider

How can a design adapt to the niche as it changes?

Niches

— Audience mind-set

— Cultural

— Competitive

— Energetic (money, energy, attendance, belief, loyalty)

Nutrients

— Money

— Information

— Materials

Cycles

— Audience

— Market

— Company

— Earth

What are the design strategies?

— Minimize structure (more efficient in the niche)

— Maximize function (better return versus competition)

— Use cycles (design to utilize cycles in time, density in space)

— Identify with the audience as opposed to compete with others

— Adaptive design (change after release)

— Evolve design practice

— Select design strategy from several options

— Use variation (design alternatives) and let the market select

— Increase iterations of the design system

In other words, is the focus on the audience (the source of energy/dollars) or on competitors? Recall that two organisms that compete for the same resources have to share a niche.[12] This is not a long-term strategy—most companies move products to new niches where there is little or no competition.[13] This forced evolution takes into consideration both audience and product/event/idea characteristics.

Design Practice

How does the process start? A design can be the last thing in the process, or it can be integrated into the broader product or promotion cycle. Early work improves results, and efforts put into the end piece can help optimize the whole system. Design improvements are proportional to effort.

Techniques that encourage excellence and multiple viewpoints:

— Team learning

— Design dimensions

— Using constraints to improve design

— Checklists

— Best practice

— Design language

— Systems design approaches

— Biology as inspiration

The Design Team

It has been said that there are no single brain problems anymore. Rather, excellent design comes from environments where there are multiple diverse viewpoints. Thinking back to the original examples (lead paint and product support), a different viewpoint in the decision process would have saved much time and money.

How can this different viewpoint be accomplished? In many companies, there are reviews and checkpoints where other departments are involved. Unfortunately, these reviews often happen once a design is fairly structured (formalized renderings versus preliminary sketches), and their format can be adversarial so that design decisions are defended instead of allowing space for a new view to evolve. The best solution is to walk around with the design ahead of time. Find a good person in each department to share ideas with. They will really appreciate the effort, and these informal reviews can be much more productive than the formal ones.

This approach comes from biology: acting as a tree, extending roots out into the organization to get nutrients and to give back value. Interestingly, this type of interconnection will benefit all departments that participate.

Team Learning and Decision Making

All effective teams have members with different problem-solving styles. While other styles may not "mesh" with each other, seeing each distinct perspective in action is useful. Knowledge obtained through working together helps with decisions.

Decision-making styles are a mixture of energy source (extrovert versus introvert), information management style, information language, deliberation style, and decision closure style. The bottom line is that if the team leader can recognize and acknowledge these differences, then the team decision will be much stronger than any individual effort.

Note that it may be impossible to obtain consensus on all design decisions. If team members can state the problem clearly along with the decision criteria and why the decision was made, then the team effort has been effective.[14]

Involve the Stakeholders

Each design has several stakeholders: the marketing team, the production team, the product/content team, finance, sales, and the audience. Each design has to work for all these parties, and their needs may be in conflict. The good news is that this wider team will offer more perspective, enabling better and more sustainable solutions.

Stakeholders

— Graphic designers

— Management

— Audience

— Package designers

— Product designers

— Event planners

— Marketing

— Sales

— Regulatory

— Finance

— Production

— Service

— Maintenance

— Manufacturing

With all these people involved, it can feel overwhelming to guide a design to the finish line. To help the process, consider defining design requirements for each stakeholder, and rank or prioritize these requirements to evaluate the design against.

A good tool in this situation is to catalog a piece's "dimensions" or characteristics: for example, weight, material cost, and processing steps. Then you can rank design alternatives by stakeholders (on a scale of 1 to 5) and assign a score. It may be necessary to prioritize dimensions to weigh one characteristic against another.

The best teams are learning teams: teams that work together to advance understanding among all. Since the view of a system (like any design) depends on point of view, the strongest teams have diverse membership and viewpoints. The dialogue that comes from a diverse learning team greatly increases design robustness and viability.

Characteristics of highly successful teams include:

— Positive interdependence

— Individual and group accountability

— Interactions that promote real work

— Team skills (listening, decision making, problem solving, conflict management, and leadership)

The group also periodically reflects on its practice.[15]

Successful teams also use design principles from biology. In *Bioteams*, Ken Thompson lists a variety of tools, including network nurturing, keeping a porous membrane, foraging to find clients and opportunities, and converting opportunities into business by using "live controlled experimentation."[16]

If a design doesn't fit the project's essential goals, sustainable materials alone won't make the project "work."

Design Dimensions

As noted earlier, identifying key characteristics can be critical.[17] If a design doesn't fit the project's essential goals, sustainable materials alone won't make the project "work."

— Physical lifetime

— Use time

— Recognition

— Adhesion

— Economy

— Visibility

— Clarity

As one example, an item may need to last a long time before acquisition (physical lifetime) yet audience use time is very brief (recognition, learning, package information). This leads to a conflict as the designer works toward long physical lifetime, resulting in material choices that don't decompose and return to nature once the use phase is over. In contrast, a seed can travel a long distance (long physical lifetime) yet have a short use phase (water causes the seed husk to open), and it then decays. Sometimes the seed casing (e.g., a workbook) provides materials for the seed (content/idea) to grow, and then returns to Earth.

A structured creativity technique called Triz[18] looks at design dimensions from a variety of perspectives: weight; strength; loss; amount of material and energy; complexity; manufacturability; response to variation; and ease of use.[19]

Human-centered design uses a triad of use, usability, and meaning as design dimensions. *Use* corresponds to function; *usability*, to the ways the viewer interacts with an object; and object's *meaning* is the complex of associations with the design.[20] As an example, a portable MP3 player signifies independence as well as the love of music.

Design Checklists

Having a standard checklist ensures that all critical characteristics (material toxicity, universal design, requirements for new processing) are considered. These should be continuously updated along with examples of how previous teams have used this approach to improve designs. Note that besides the common questions about materials and processing, the checklist should include the design dimensions mentioned earlier and state how each was satisfied. Pieces that meet the most stringent environmental goals but fail to meet the fundamental design dimensions are not sustainable.

Best Practice

To work with best practice, interview designer peers or determine the best case. What is the best design for this type of situation? What characteristics does it have, and what should be carried on to other designs? Keep a chart of design element essentials: cost, processing steps, environmental impact, market attributes. Use this to document design practice and compare new designs to old.

What is the state of the competition? What lessons can be learned from them? How can a better design be marketed against them?

There is good industry buy-in for this approach: The Energy Star[21] rating and International Organization for Standardization (ISO) 14000 require a company's work to be examined against the competition.

Finally, compare design approaches to others. Is one design strategy clearly better than another? Why? Can continuous improvement be done in this area? What are the intangibles? Can an improved design be marketed to give advantage over the competition?

A good way to share best practice is to have design meetings (perhaps over lunch) where each individual shares information about design approaches, new techniques, or his or her current project.

Design Language

Patterns are set ways of seeing and relating to the world. They bestow great power, along with risk. Patterns are a characteristic of the design process, making it possible to transmit previous learning to the next generation of designs and designers.

A design language (style and structure guide) is a set of patterns that describe a standard way of solving problems. Every company has one, whether it is explicit or implicit. A pattern may be as simple as always using postcards for event advertising. This approach may be just "The way things are done around here," or it may be the best solution based on years of experience.

At a basic level, a design language consists of descriptions in three parts:

1. Description of the situation

2. Relational diagram of forces in and outside the design situation

3. Design solution with a visual representation[22]

This example can be mapped:

Design a low-budget, disposable delivery system for a high-volume, low-cost per piece event promotion.

Forces

— Easy distribution: Paper or electronic

— Audience: Clear message/reminder

— Buyer requirement: Low cost, mailable, quick design time

— Content requirement: compelling, intriguing

Solution

— Postcard and Web ad

Readers will note several things. There is still an enormous amount of information left out, for example. What types of materials, coatings, and pigments are appropriate? How are the dimensions selected for lowest-cost manufacture? What design details are required for effective handling?

These specifications are documented in further design patterns, forming a multilevel structure that can be grasped easily by new employees, reveals assumptions about the design that may not have been visible, and draws attention to parts of the design process that can be improved.

As just one example, adding a requirement on ink type (e.g., vegetable) to the inks pattern will create a new set of subpatterns. In a similar way, you can add patterns for separation of a piece's components for recycling or reuse.

A company's design language may not be written, and it may depend on the current mix of employees. Some aspects may be due to implicit understanding of company constraints and expectations. Readers who are in management recognize the difficulties with this situation. Company direction and priorities change, and it can be hard to mold the hidden forces existing within design groups.

The patterns developed this way consist of design solutions to conflicting forces within the situation. Showing how the conflicting forces were resolved gives both context to standard design solutions and inspires new work in documenting new design situations.

Writing down a design language is a very freeing process. Designers and others can see what forces are at work in a particular design, and get feedback. As the language propagates through the company, new patterns and details are added. This becomes a rich repository of design information—it is intellectual property. New employees can be brought up to speed more quickly, and they have a neutral environment in which to express their ideas.

Writing down a design language is a very freeing process. Designers and others can see what forces are at work in a particular design and get feedback.

Client/Designer Relationship

Graphic designers translate needs into artifacts (objects). These needs are expressed through the client, and active management of this relationship is a major way to enhance sustainability. For example, a design that fits the needs (aka requirements) well is more efficient in use, and chances are that its design process will also be more efficient, as each design stage will have been closer to the mark to begin with.

For this relationship to be effective, the designer needs to have a consistent language to describe the design, the requirements, and the functions that will be used to satisfy the requirements. These language elements should be simple and effective. Once they are expressed clearly, the client can understand the design process, which makes communications more effective.

Along with a common language of design, an effective relationship sets project criteria for the design dimensions and accountability for both parties.

This process is two-way education: the designer teaching about the design process, and the client teaching about its market's needs and requirements.

Using Systems Thinking in the Design Process

The systems approach enables many possible views of design.

Co-design. Complement the product/content design by working with that team. This will give advantage to both teams and the end piece, reducing costs on both sides.

Design boundary. What are the boundaries? What passes? What is rejected? How is the boundary created? Can it self-assemble?

Design life cycle. When does the piece decompose? What starts the process? Can the results be used as food for another cycle (Earth or design)?

System feedback. What is the loop from the consumer to the piece? Is there one loop at contact time and another at use time? How about the loop to the seller/distributor? What aspects of the design are most important to each user, and can they be integrated to benefit both?

Design as a level of artifact. Does the design live above, below, or alongside the product/content? Is the piece itself a product or content? Do people want the design more than the product or content (commemorative cereal boxes or baseball cards)?

Design as structure. Does the design have a use apart from the product/content? Does it complement it? Does it have an entirely different use? Will people buy, attend, or believe just for the design?

Design as attachment. Are people attracted more to the design or to the product/content? Is attachment a two-step process?

Shield. Communities often provide a buffer zone between themselves and the surroundings. For example, a forest has an edge area where species can't survive although they flourish in the forest itself. These areas serve as transitions between one kind of environment and another. As one example, there may be high winds outside the forest while it is relatively calm inside. Bird life will differ considerably between these two environments, and species will migrate along the boundary, allowing them access to either environment. How is the design the bridge between product/content and audience? Can the design link to other products/content, creating a community?

Advertisement. Plants advertise themselves to pollinators by a variety of colors and shapes. The arrangement serves both well as the flowers get pollinated while the bees get nectar. The audience is a bee, attracted by the design to the product/content. A good design interaction inclines them to try another (flower) from the garden.

Security. The hard exteriors on some organisms protect them from many predators, yet something always evolves to overcome this defense. The same is true in our networks (spam and computer viruses). A package may have embedded RFID, be bulky, or communicate danger in an effort keep away predators (shoplifters). Each approach is effective in a given environment yet may add high ecological costs to the design. How can we use natural inspiration to fulfill security needs?

Product/content as seed. If the product/content is a seed, how does the graphic catch on (as burdock inspired hook-and-loop fasteners) and connect to the audience, carrying the product/content along? If the end piece is a seed, what causes it to open to the user? (In nature, it may be water or fire). After it opens, the information is transferred, yet what happens to the seed (physical piece)? What are the correct environments for the seed to return to nature? How does the end piece nourish the product/content?

Sustainable Communication

Communication is the key function of graphic design. Whether communicating information, mood, or style, for communication to happen, there needs to be a transmitter, a channel, and a receiver.

What Are the Corresponding Processes in Nature?

A message consists of:

— Intention

— Translation or encoding

— Transmission

— Propagation

— Reception

— Decoding

— Response

What Can Biomimicry Tell Us about These Elements?

Some species that use communications (e.g., ants or bees) have signaling that is readable by members of their own community or species but not by others. This is a language, and the messages are used for organization. Other species use messages to warn other species.

Biological systems consist of highly optimized solutions to local environmental conditions. Signaling or messaging has several roles:

— Attraction (for reproduction or passing on information)

— Warning (for safety and protection)

— Defining pathways (for finding food)

— Dispersal (for reproduction)

Note there are strategies for messaging in space as well as messaging in time.

Attraction. Flowers co-evolve with insects to match their visual systems: advertisement and audience. There are thousands of combinations, and a trip through the local garden will easily reveal a dozen to even the casual observer.

Looking at the image in this section, each flower and each insect is unique, yet all were found in proximity to one another. Clearly nature pays attention to the "audience." Note also that the insects were attracted by shape, color, and fragrance to collect nectar—food critical for their life cycle and propagation. But (almost) all of the insects took away pollen as well, aiding both parties in the action as the flowers took advantage of the distribution system to increase yields for their own species. This observation gives a "law of return": To be successful in propagation, designs need to give as well as attract.

Warning. This technique is optimized with signals that are appropriate for predators. The warning is a function or attribute of the organism.

Pathway. Pathways are defined via visual and olfactory clues, and are found in both bees and ants. Each has a language of scent signals yet also relies on dance or transfer timing. (Heavily loaded bees take longer to unload, indicating greater sources.) This pathway could be related to the density or observational time of a piece.

Dispersal. This technique is practiced via many channels: wind, water, feeding, animal movements. The signals here are the information required for reproduction, and there are many strategies:

— Catch onto fur for dispersal in space

— Ride on wind or water

— Be eaten and then deposited with fertilizer

— Wait for fire to open

— Burrow into host (parasite)

— Be ingested (viral)

Messaging. This technique has many measures and techniques:

— Transference

— Enhanced as enzymes

— Encoded as proteins are on amino acids

— Transcription

— Inhibit other messages

— Activate processes

— Catalyze reactions

— Interfere with pathways

The biological signaling environment depends on wind, water, light, temperature, pH, salinity, conduction, and diffusion. What are the characteristics of a design's message channels? How can biological parallels be used to gain insight and advantage?

The graphic design's message can be seen as a seed, carrying information from one time and space to another. The seed contains the genetic message, food for the development of the seed, protection, triggers to open in the right environment, and a way to break down safely after use.

Many of these techniques are about passing on information in time or space, but few are about passing information from one system to another. In many ways, that is the basic requirement for any design, and consideration of the activities at a cell boundary gives insights.

The cell boundary regulates the internal environment and responds to outside signaling in a variety of ways:

— Buffer

— Exchange

— Trigger

— Response

— Excite

To be successful in propagation, designs need to give as well as attract.
Photos: Curt McNamara (c.mcnamara@ieee.org).

— Repress

— Match shape

— Transfer

For a virus to penetrate to a cellular nucleus, several techniques are needed: The virus must pass the cell wall, travel inside the cell, and then enter the nucleus. How does this compare to the end product or piece? What part of that journey is most appropriate for the project?

Biomimicry

Jessica Jones
Biomimicry Guild

Indentifying Function

A worker honeybee receives many visual cues from a single flower, only a few of which humans can detect. This is because each individual is attuned to different aspects of the flower's design and decodes the signal based on its own sensory and contextual circumstances. For example, the bee's sensitivity to object movement far outstrips our own because the bee is highly tuned to pursue sweet nectar at a flower's slightest movement in the wind. Bees' multifaceted compound eyes produce a mosaic image similar to that of gazing through a kaleidoscope, giving them excellent pattern recognition yet poor resolution. Their eyes perceive wavelengths of light that are hidden signals from us. Bees' senses are honed to prefer flowers with distinct, often symmetrical markings, such as the pentagonal symmetry of the honeysuckle. By visiting and pollinating only the flowers that have the strongest combined sensory appeal, the bee and the flower partake in an elaborate dance of co-evolution that finely tunes each organism to the likings of the other. This dance has persisted for millions of years and is ultimately a metaphor for the refined language that a biomimetic graphic designer strives to emulate with his or her audience.

Symmetry in nature is about language. It provides a way for animals and plants to convey a multitude of messages, from genetic superiority to nutritional information. Symmetry is often a sign of meaning, and can therefore be interpreted as a very basic, almost primeval form of communication. For an insect such as the bee, symmetry is fundamental to survival.

—*Marcus Du Sautoy*

Fortunately, graphic designers, unlike flowers that must spend millions of years co-evolving with their mutualists, have the advantage of more quickly but perhaps less accurately discerning the needs of the viewers. Unfortunately, graphic designers tend to focus solely on the function of attracting the viewer and tend to ignore other functions their piece should have in the context of the entire system. This is akin to a flower focusing solely on landing a bee, with little regard for pollen dispersal, nectar production, and photosynthesis. One of the greatest lessons biologists can teach graphic designers is not only how the flower has adapted to the bee, but also how the flower has adapted to the surrounding ecosystem that supports its life and continued existence. This lesson can teach biomimetic graphic designers to look beyond the biophilic patterns of the natural world and find the deeper principles of how we can fit in with nature.

To bring biomimicry into graphic design, designers must see their profession as an integrated process and a problem-solving discipline. Successful graphic designers correctly define the context of their design, users, and constraints. They stay focused on the original intent of the piece and are attuned and responsive to all factors that affect their design.

Biomimetic graphic design is not the aesthetic mimicry of shapes, patterns, and color palettes found in nature. Instead, biomimicry is a design and leadership discipline that seeks sustainable solutions by emulating nature's time-tested ideas. It is a process where a designer defines a challenge functionally, seeks out a local organism or ecosystem that is the champion of that function, and then begins a conversation about how the design might emulate that function or concept. It is refreshingly cross-disciplinary, allowing not only architects to learn from animal architecture, but graphic designers to learn from animal communication, benign manufacturing, and life's principles.

Life's Principles: Informing All Stages of the Design Process

The Life's Principles conceptual diagram developed by the Biomimicry Guild includes life's deep principles and illustrates their relationship to each other.

These principles capture the strategies that life has used to thrive on this planet. They have application to all types of design, including all stages of the graphic design or visual communication process.

Janine Benyus is obsessed with patterns, connections, and the beauty of life, intertwined. Biomimicry focuses on finding structures, processes, strategies, and mechanisms that nature has been using for a billion years, that we can emulate and use in modern design.

—Terry Tempest Williams

Life's Principles Applied to Graphic Design

Optimizes Rather than Maximizes

Biology: In an effort to attract cows and dominate over intruding bulls, a bull elk's antlers continue to grow larger than the antlers shed in the previous season. However, growing infinitely large antlers (i.e., maximizing) would make escape from predators challenging. The resulting size is optimized based on the simultaneous needs to reproduce and to gather nutrients to grow the antlers, and the desire to not be eaten.

Graphic design: Maximizing the number of pages in a piece or the size of paper probably will allow for a

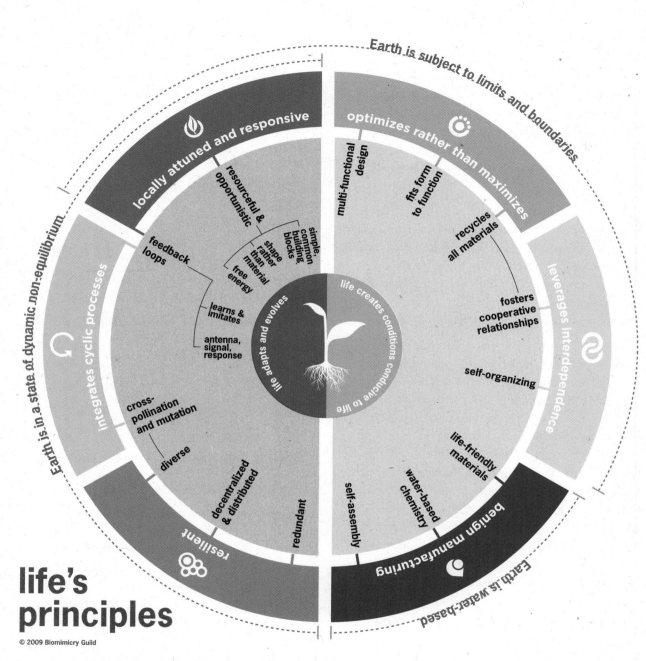

life's
principles

© 2009 Biomimicry Guild

Our understanding of Life's Principles is constantly evolving. Visit *www.biomimicryinstitute.org* to better understand their current representation of life's incredibly elegant and complex systems.
Image used with permission, © 2009 Biomimicry Guild.

more easily achieved eye-catching composition and attract more viewers. However, the functional design of the piece might be compromised because it might not easily fit onto the standard bookshelf or the pages are too burdensome and large for users to flip through quickly. Optimizing all the variables that influence both the functionality and appearance of a design will help designers recognize all the contextual factors that affect its success and will most likely make it more resilient in the marketplace.

Graphic design: Humans tend to maximize when they perceive there is an inexpensive abundance of materials readily available to them. However, the Earth has limits and boundaries, and there is a finite amount of resources at our disposal. It is important to see the entire system and become aware of costs to others when designing or choosing supplies. For example, designers of fonts created for users other than themselves do not have the incentive to design a font that saves them ink. Such disjointed relationships occur across many disciplines and, unfortunately, stifle innovation. Recently, the design firm SPRANQ designed a new typeface called Eco-font, which it claims uses up to 20 percent less ink. Based on Verdana, this font has oblong holes in the text that, when viewed at an optimal size of 9 points, appears to be a solid line. The optimal relationship between ink quantity and visual quality is achieved.

Graphic design: Good designers are brilliant at optimizing space. A good balance of white space and graphical elements can help the viewer effortlessly interact with the piece. Leading, kerning, tracking, and justification are important when designing print materials, especially books weighted heavily with text. In any case, designers need to find the optimal balance between aesthetics and viewer ease and preference.

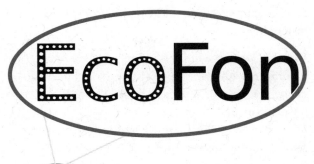

EcoFont-9pt

SPRANQ Creative Communications, the Netherlands (*www.spranq.eu*), designed Eco-font to use up to 20 percent less ink.

Fits Form to Function

Biology: Using the free energy of passing organisms such as sheep or deer, cocklebur seeds travel to new sprouting places. The numerous small hooks protruding from the pod easily attach to moving targets, allowing this opportunistic plant to fulfill its function of reproducing by using a form (the burrs) to achieve its needs.

Graphic design: Print materials can have many functions: to entertain, reference, hang up, pass around, or educate. Depending on the desired function, the form must match and help fulfill the function. Designers frequently achieve function through form subconsciously. Many times, after designing a few mock-ups based entirely on aesthetics, designers will serendipitously find that one of their designs harmoniously lends itself to fulfilling a helpful function for the viewer. Consequently, as designers gain more experience creating as logos, tables, interactive pieces, diagrams, and grouped elements, they become better at strategically designing for function. To strengthen this skill, examine pieces in magazines to find a few examples where a form helped strengthen a function, then think of other alternatives.

Graphic design: Whether designing alone or collaborating with print representatives and packaging designers, graphic designers should be aware of basic forms paper can take in addition to creating form solely by using pigment or die cutting a shape out of a larger piece of material. For instance, Brian Dougherty of Celery Design needed to design a workbook with page dividers that served the function of organization, mental reading breaks, and waste reduction. Usually tab dividers are cut from larger pages producing waste. However, the innovative divider pages have an internal die cut that allows the user to pop out and fold the paper outward to create the tab. The resulting design had no die cut waste and was more interactive, functional, and attractive.

Fosters Cooperative Relationships

Biology: In the rough-and-tumble world of nature, you might expect that competition is the norm. But to the contrary, scientists have found that when times are hard, organisms are more likely to form beneficial and cooperative relationships. For example, a small shrimp might seem to be a likely menu item for many sea creatures; however, the cleaner shrimp is the one that does the dining. The cleaner shrimp sets up shop on a coral reef, advertises itself well as a service, and picks parasites from eels and other organisms. The shrimp gets a free meal and protection from predation, and the sea creatures are free of parasites. Everyone wins, except for the parasites.

Graphic design: A stock photography company allows a printing shop to give its clients access to its stock account. A client can use any photograph as long as it uses the printing shop for printing. The

Burrs ready to hitch a ride.
Photo: Rick Gutierrez (n8studio.com)

stock photography company receives more revenue or exposure, the printer receives more services, and the client receives complementary or reduced-cost photographs.

Graphic design: Today, many graphic designers are expected to increase output with tighter budgets. Creating a piece from scratch using graphic elements created in-house, such as vectors and photographs, is tedious and time consuming. Luckily, the Internet makes it easier for graphic designers, photographers, and illustrators to pool resources. Services such as Flickr make it easy to foster a relationship with a photographer across the globe. *Stock.xchng,* a Web site dedicated to trading vectors or images free of charge, supports cooperative relationships in innovative ways.

Graphic design: The aggressive environment of advertising might be thought of as a competitive ecosystem with highly sought-after scarce resources. Many companies vie for the same audience and try to appeal to that particular segment's values to do so. In nature, competition exists, but it does not persist. Organisms frequently have to depend on other organisms, even their predators, to survive. Larger companies are increasingly using open-innovation strategies where they leverage the resources developed by start-ups, suppliers, and competitors. These companies even have teams dedicated to finding new innovations, usually technology-based ones. In graphic design, many innovations lie in the minds of young designers. Internships, staff cross-fertilization, and mentoring opportunities provide means to foster win-win relationships for all involved.

Learns and Imitates

Biology: The African monarch butterfly, an unpalatable snack to predators, slowly flies in the open so predators can more easily recognize it and have ample warning time to steer clear. Many other butterfly species that are delectable and safe snacks for predators consequently have evolved to resemble the African monarch. The butterflies that look and act the most like monarchs survive and pass on their genes, whereas the butterflies that look least like monarchs end up a nourishing meal.

Graphic design: Many store brands have been successful at mimicking the appearance and packaging of the dominant and flourishing name brand. Their designers use the time saved coming up with and testing the initial brand strategy and positioning

for researching other biomimetic strategies. While designers still have to spend some time learning and imitating, they can stay current on trends when conditions change and can imitate the best designs.

Graphic design: To learn from past designs, designers can look through design magazines, blogs, and other materials that relate to their print specialty. Just as organisms adapt to what works to keep them alive through the process of evolution, graphic designers, through trial and error, learn significantly from past mistakes and successes. Keeping abreast of current design environment context shows how others are responding, or not responding, to these changes.

Graphic design: Just as fake eyespots on wildlife can misdirect or even attract prey by startling them into believing they are something resembling their predator, graphic design pieces can alert users to view a specific element of a target design first. Many direct-mail designers use this strategy, with the eye-catching words or images clearly visible and fine print at the bottom telling the whole truth. However, end users soon learn of the trick, and a new design must then be attempted. If the goal is sustained communication, endeavor to form design solutions that help foster lasting relationships, not ones that cleverly fool the user.

Antenna, Signal, Response

Biology: Living in a bug-eat-bug world, it's necessary for life to highly tune and synchronize antennae, signal, and response mechanisms. Any mismatch among the three can result in the end of the gene pool. A mosquito survives by effectively locating its host. It pursues the most telltale clue of carbon dioxide emitted through its hosts' breathing. In addition to picking up basic signals from the environment, mosquito antennae are highly tuned to detect this molecule—in some cases, up to 50 meters away.

Graphic design: Graphic designers need to be humble students of change because fashion or other aesthetic-based industries are spaces where trends change rapidly. Designers must be attuned to these styles by keeping their antennae out for trend signals. Then they must be able to adapt quickly to make sure their work matches the antennae of the ever-fickle consumer.

Graphic design: As a designer, sending the right message to the right audience is essential. Correctly conduct research and use market statistics to more efficiently identify and distribute only to target markets. Do not make huge assumptions during the scoping phase. Tune your antennae to the signals out there by doing research (due diligence) and looking at the design brief from all points of view.

Graphic design: Often design is associated with aesthetics, not with performance. Just as the mosquito knows when and where to find nourishment, graphic designers need to define their user groups and values accurately to know how to appeal to and fulfill their needs. Designers need to set aside a recurring time to keep fine-tuning their antennae to user needs. Follow the experiences of a user group, watch what the human antennae are attracted to. If they are not looking at what was expected, what other types of pieces are they interacting with?

Biomimicry Approach

Becoming familiar with Life's Principles before starting the design process is one way to learn from life for graphic design. Biology can also be incorporated into all of these design phases: scoping,

creating, and evaluating. Life can inform any or all of these phases, with the greatest success coming from incorporating life at all three phases.

Mimicry is perhaps the oldest and most efficient method for achieving major advances in design.

—*William Lidwell*

Scoping Phase: "Nature as Mentor"

During the scoping phase, designers define their vision and context for the end product. Life's best designs did not evolve in a vacuum. Life's designs are elegant because functional needs are met in context. The designer incorporating life's time-tested strategies at this stage will look to nature as a mentor. By asking what is it the design should *do*, and in what context, a designer will ultimately end up with a broader mind-set, an enhanced solution space, and an increased likelihood that the needs of the design will be met. Ultimately, these contribute to the evolutionary success of the design.

Creating Phase: "Nature as Model"

While in the creating phase, designers discover natural models and abstract the strategies and

---

Organisms use two methods to create color without paint: internal pigments and the structural color that makes tropical butterflies, peacocks, and hummingbirds so gorgeous.
Photo: W. Jedlička.

functions they are trying to emulate and achieve. Usually designers will be looking to life as a model for inspiration in their designs. During this phase, for example, graphic designers specializing in print would most likely ask, "How does nature communicate visually?" Then they would look to environments where visual communication predominates to discover biological strategies that they can then translate into innovative ideas. Through this process, designers will find novel ideas that have been refined over millions of years.

Evaluation Phase: "Life as Measure"

The evaluation phase tends to be brushed over, often due to limited time and resources. Designers should evaluate their design both before and after the user receives it. Biomimetic designers should evaluate their piece based not only on feasibility, such as cost, but also on life's ecological standards. If designers question how well their designed material fits in with life, they will have pretested their product for larger-picture "success," identified missed limits and opportunities, and asked, "What wouldn't nature do?" Through this deeper evaluation, design quality goes beyond aesthetics and becomes timeless good design.

Graphic Design: What's Worth Doing?

Biomimicry is similar to "green" graphic design because it works toward the same goal. However, because biomimicry is another way of viewing and valuing nature, this perspective can help designers brainstorm other ways of being green. A good starting place to incorporating biomimicry into the design process would be to print out the complete conceptual diagram of Life's Principles available at w*ww.biomimicry.net* and post it at hand for brain-

storming. We coexist with at least 30 million species. Imagine how much they have to teach us. It is highly recommended to step outside the workplace in times of creative block to visit just a few of these creatures. In addition to learning about the Life's Principles that organisms abide by, ideas will spring up from their eye-pleasing shapes, patterns, and colors. While this bio-inspired approach makes great stories, ultimately sustainable graphic design seeks to ask the deeper questions of how life has learned to survive and thrive on this planet and, most important, how our designs can do the same.

If success or failure of this planet and of human beings depended on how I am and what I do . . . how would I be and what would I do?

—R. Buckminster Fuller

Visit the discussion forum at *www.asknature.org* to speak with others about bringing biomimicry into the visual communication and graphic design process. *AskNature* is the world's first digital library of nature's solutions, organized by function and is a place where biology and design cross-pollinate to birth bio-inspired breakthroughs. This online community resource is a great place to connect with others. Consider becoming a member of the Bioinspired Graphic Design: Nature as Mentor Flickr group to foster a cooperative nature or photo-sharing relationship.

Ultimately, in our quest to fit in on this planet, biomimetic graphic designers should never forget to thank the natural models that inspired them. Go outside, spend time in nature appreciating her wisdom, and share that wonder with others. More formally, consider donating to Innovation for Conservation, a biodiversity conservation fund formed by The Biomimicry Institute that protects the habitat—the well-spring—from which these well-adapted ideas have emerged. We are surrounded by amazing genius, not just in pattern and form but in strategies that can inform all designers. The beauty of this wisdom is that we can learn as a species to fit in—emulating a practice shared by the 30 million other species that co-inhabit this planet we call home.

Permaculture Principles in Design

Dan Halsey

Nothing exists outside a relationship. Everything is related in the working systems of nature, economics, or design. Designers that do not take into account the effect their plan will have on users, resources, or society deplete the design's potential and future viability. Systems thinking requires a developed awareness and skills to define and design the Functional Relationships,[23] which reduces waste and enhances yield from existing relationships. Permaculture is a practice that uses a set of principles to assure the long-term viability of self-sustaining systems in agriculture. Permanent + Agriculture = Permaculture.

In the 1970s, Australian ecological activist Bill Mollison[24] retreated from popular culture to study and develop a set of principles that would assure success in ecological-minded farming. Over 25

Nature's systems, just waiting to be learned from.
Photo: W. Jedlička.

years of practice, his resulting 34 principles for Permaculture were refined by his close associate David Holmgren.

In his 2002 book *Permaculture: Principles and Pathways beyond Sustainability,*[25] author David Holmgren lays out his refined list of 12 principles for sustainable living systems. These powerful concepts, here applied to design, can open a new worldview of responsibility as designers and possibilities as people. The principles can be viewed as passive, proactive, or progressive in nature and difficulty.

191

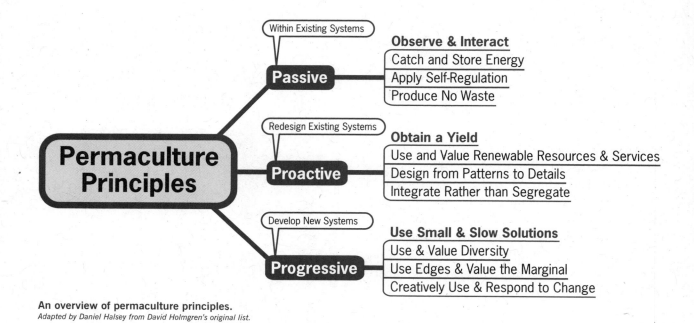

An overview of permaculture principles.
Adapted by Daniel Halsey from David Holmgren's original list.

Passive Principles

Observe and Interact: Omnipresence of Relationships

In the natural world, millions of relationships are occurring. From the lowest levels of living soil to the tops to trees and beyond are the answers to how people can flourish and not just survive. People already interact with everything around. Although not limited to things within close proximity, trying to observe firsthand everything affected is impossible. In permaculture, observing the things around us, such as the cycles of seasons and weather, gives valuable information when designing a garden or ecosystem. For example, where water collects after a rain, how long it stays on top of the soil, and what direction it flows can provide information about the best place for some plants and where to avoid placing others. It also tells where the water is to use, catch, or store it.

To observe successfully means to interact. Stand in the rain, dig a hole, touch the soil, and dig deeper. Stand in the wind on a winter day. Feel the breeze in summer. Where does it come from? Where is it warmest in the winter and coolest in the summer? Where do mushrooms grow? Where do gophers burrow? All these things give important information, but only if we gently interact.

Careful observation of the environment in which a work is used gives power to respond with new ideas for design, materials, and integration. Knowing the environment that materials come from and the ultimate end of the product is an important step in defining the parameters of a design's strategy.

The life cycle of a given design cannot be ignored in the process. Interaction with consumer/viewer or warehouse is not the end of the relationship. The object lives on in an environment as inert or toxic waste, fuel, or a second extended life in another purpose, as an extension of the designer interacting through it.

Catch and Store Energy: Real Life Cycle, Assets, and Waste

For most of us, water, fuel, and electricity flow freely from spigots, pumps, and outlets. The energy is produced somewhere, stored somewhere, and transported (at a huge loss) to places of work or home. Other free energies that exist right outside the door dissipate unnoticed. For economic reasons that are also dissipating, local sources can appear more expensive than mass-generated ones. However, when observers see the energies and resources that wash over their property only to be consumed by the ground or wind, the potential for that energy is realized.

Rain from a season can supply a whole family with bathing and laundry water and then be piped to the garden as part of the morning routine. The water is soft and clean, and needs only limited treatment: the cleanest water that needs no well.

Catching this energy and delaying its passing makes it work and build value. Roof water can also be collected in a fishpond, flushing the accumulating effluents out to an orchard or garden. The fish get fresh oxygenated water and the garden gets nutrient-rich moisture. Add swales (level ditches to collect water), and the water stays even longer, buffering drought and temperature changes.

The sun's energy can also be caught and stored. Evacuated tube solar panels catch enough sunlight to raise their temperatures above 350 degrees (at which point they shut down for safety). An array of these panels then transfers the heat to a large storage tank. One device: free fuel.

As one example, a machining company in Minnesota developed a process to purify lubricating oil used in its milling machines. The oil had been previously filtered but was soon contaminated in the closed system, unusable, and expensive to dispose of. Engineers at the company developed an in-house distilling process that removed the impurities and moisture, making the final oil as pure as new stock. The water from the process was so clean, they ran it to their drinking fountains and the lunchroom. Solving one problem to catch lost resources (energy) brought new opportunities and savings in other areas as well. The company bought less new oil, paid fewer fees for waste removal, and built its reputation using the talent and resources already at hand.

The "paid" time spent in developing designs and the funds invested in the ultimate end object create an asset. If the ensuing object is seen as "stored energy," a potential marketing resource beyond the trash bin, and having a second purpose beyond its initial use, it has additional stored potential for the end user. Harnessing this stored potential for marketing and extended audience interaction increases the return on the object's investment. Being shortsighted leaves lost opportunity if the life of the object is ignored. What can be done with the unused potential? Where is the stored energy potential in the things we create?

APPLY SELF-REGULATION AND ACCEPT FEEDBACK

Imagine limiting consumption, people actually saying "I have enough!" It's almost un-American. From all sides and even in the depths of tragedy, citizens are instructed to shop, buy, and consume. It is what America lives on, ironically consuming itself. Buying everything offered would leave nothing to live on in a very short time. The body self-regulates temperature with perspiration and makes energy available with each heartbeat. If not given the means to regulate with water and healthy food, it cannot. Self-regulation does not mean deprivation. It means knowing the difference between enough and too much, healthy food and empty calories, long-term effects and short-term benefits.

Information needed for self-regulation comes from feedback. Everything can be viewed as positive feedback. Feelings, words, sensations, pain, and happiness are feedback. If it influences change, it is positive. Negative feedback is silence: no message, no response, apathy. If actions or energies are returned with apathy or no response, that is negative. But if a person screams horrid insults, a pipe bursts, or yields increase, these are pretty good doses of feedback and encouragement for change.

In an office setting, years of experience or schooling build in self-regulation. The most creative designer uses internal guides in composition and aesthetics. Innumerable options are assessed, and personal creativity blends with good design. Effort is used to find suitable materials. Personal ethics specify which materials are acceptable, then clients, supervisors, and associates need to give feedback. Pushing the envelope, a proposal is made to use ecologically minded vendors and resources. Questions are asked of consultants and suppliers. Excessive waste is minimized. Attempts are made to have the process self-regulate. All will elicit feedback.

Produce No Waste

Nothing goes to waste in nature. It is not allowed. Everything gets chewed up, spit out, decomposed, and reabsorbed into the relentless cycle of nutrients and biomass. Waste comes from underusing or overusing energy and materials. Most things never have to leave a system if used efficiently. Everything from the kitchen can be composted and made into soil, along with grass clippings, leaves, and weeds. Give something a second use or life and it isn't waste.

Like magic, waste disappears in the shadow of reuse after the recycling bin is full, and the thrift shop or garage sale gets the rest. What could there be? Perhaps the things were unneeded in the first place. Perhaps the consuming of a natural resource and the energy it takes in transport is the real waste. Perhaps the best thing to do when producing no waste is to limit consumption from the start. Do more with what's at hand.

In the electronic age, paper is run through printers as if it came from the sky—which it does, by sunlight, water, nitrogen, and carbon dioxide. From that point, however, waste starts, in processing, trimming, shipping, and disposal. Keeping proofs to a minimum and using electronic documents diminishes wasted paper. Putting the computer to sleep or off when out of the office reduces more. In the quest to produce no waste, one must ultimately limit consumption. Don't buy it, wrap it, bag it, transport it, unwrap it, or toss it. There is no waste. If an item can be sold without a dead-end package (absolute heresy), where is the waste? Again, the second life of all things can extend its useful period and catch and save energy otherwise used in its disposal.

Proactive Measures

Obtain a Yield

When a permaculture designer works on a project, aesthetics is not the main design driver. Each element yields a beneficial if not tangible product. Many produce multiple yields. A few examples are:

— A perennial plant (overwintering) that shields annual plants (vegetables) while itself producing fiber or food

— A ground cover plant that keeps soil moist and attracts pollinating insects, also eaten as salad greens and used as compost

— Alpine strawberries that share nutrients, build soil, and attract bees to flowering fruit trees without competing

Each element yields benefits to the system beyond its initial purpose. Rain falls on a hill; on its way down its energy runs a small hydroelectric generator, its temperature cools a house, its velocity aerates a pond of fish, and its mass carries away nutrients to plants. The more functions it has, the longer it stays on the property working. Each characteristic has a function.

All efforts in producing objects must ultimately produce results. The engineering, marketing, corporate, and government requirements for "allowable" designs must be met. Yet the ultimate function of the thing is not a result of any of these singular dictates. Because of these dictates, the object has multiple functions and thus multiple yields. In the case of packaging, for example, some of these are structure to protect and hold the contents until used, shelf or appetite appeal to increase or keep sales, brand recognition for other products, and regulated or standardized information for public safety. Once these are secured, the designer determines the final yield(s) in the life cycle that few others may be aware of.

Use and Value Renewable Resources and Services

Like trees, renewable resources are in themselves limitless. They grow and grow, yet it takes four to eight years for pulpwood and at least one if not three human generations for building lumber. Corn ethanol is renewable, but as it also occupies food-growing land and resources, is it practical? (Note: New research is looking into ways of using the leftovers [stover] from food production as the biomass for creating fuel. In this scenario, the same field that produces food corn uses the inedible stalks and leaves to produce fuel, making the whole of the growing process exponentially more efficient.)

In his 2007 eBook, *The Essence of Permaculture (permacultureprinciples.com)*, author David Holmgren says, "Renewable resources are like sources of income while nonrenewable resources are like capital needed to generate that income." Assets are to be maintained, increased, and held. A nonrenewable asset like soil is limited and needs maintenance if crops are grown on it. Not maintaining the soil asset will leave no place to grow the renewable crops. To value the renewable resource means taking care of its underlying and supportive asset.

Using renewable resources for transient purposes such as short-lived print pieces may seem practical. However, valuing the materials as limitless is naive. The cheapest paper has value and uses nonrenewable energy to be produced, processed, and shipped. A large portion of renewable material's inherent cost is in production and transportation. Understanding the source of material and its processing methods is central in understanding the ecological cost or sustainable value of the material.

For example, making the piece shape to nest with others reduces partitions and carton materials, which makes more material, money, and time available for other pieces. It also reduces carton size and space used in trucks and warehouses.

In *Beyond Backpacking,* Ray Jardine talks of cascading benefits from using ultra-light backpacking systems.[26] If the backpack weighs less from prudent equipment decisions, the hiker can walk farther in less time and needs less food. Thus the pack itself gets smaller, and the hiker is more comfortable and enjoys the trip more. An eighty-pound pack will cause more injury to the ankles, knees, and back than a twenty-five-pound pack that provides the same features. Pretrip and prepackage decisions cannot be based on a tendency to fear the unknown and overbuild rather than understand and adapt.

Design from Patterns to Details

Permaculture is "the conscious design and maintenance of productive ecosystems that have the diversity, stability and resilience of natural ecosystems. It is the harmonious integration of landscape and people providing their food, energy, shelter, and other material and non-material needs in a sustainable way."[27] Base maps are used in permaculture design to understand a landscape's characteristics. Dimensions are drawn with topography, plants, and soil. As the map develops, structures and information are added with increasing detail. Decisions are made from the patterns of the land and refined as the details are discovered. Placement of ponds, gardens, orchards, and livestock is based on the pattern of the land. Plant and animal species in those groups are chosen from the details in the area placed. Gradually over time, the land is repatterned, enhancing its properties. But it will be the details that change the pattern. A pattern is but the details at a distance.

Changing the pattern in a department or corporation is difficult. Yet one person can make small adjustments each time as opportunity arises and effect change. Broad patterns of corporate culture can be shifted with small details. A pattern is made of small details that repeat over and over. Gradual shifts in materials, modest requirements of suppliers, and eco-options for revisions will set the corporate culture on a course for change. An award for an eco-design goes a long way. Observation of trade trends to eco-minded design can be highlighted in trade journals.

The work flow of design is a pattern. It varies in each company, department, and office. Choices of materials are at times mind-numbingly predictable. Mapping out the patterns in all these can help discover the details and thus the opportunity to make change. Making assumptions about a supplier's materials or techniques without asking for creative solutions wastes a good resource. Let the pattern be innovation in the details. Innovation begets innovation.

Integrate Rather than Segregate

Diversity builds sustainability. Situating landscape plants in close relationships opens opportunities for new efficiencies and added benefits. Although centuries-old European styles of landscape design still influence American landscape design, placing elements in close relationships (rather than isolated areas) helps them integrate and mutually benefit. Large expanses of grass serve only to deplete resources and suppress the natural benefits available from distant companion plants. Experiments with side-by-side planting have shown increased yields. Like people, some plants are proven competitors while others thrive in groups.

Compartmentalized resources in a company also delay potential solutions. Designers working with vendors at the inception of a project can add to the functionality and aesthetics while vendors contribute material options and mechanical parameters. The status quo rationale for production can be opened to other possibilities by simple questions. Designers can understand basic concerns of their vendors. Integrated teams with diverse disciplines add value and understanding, solving problems before they have a chance to exist. Competition from a distance is replaced with appreciation for the talent each area brings to the group.

Progressive Measures

Use Small and Slow Solutions

Wet basements are a problem when surrounded by clay soils with temperate climates. Homeowners are required to put drain tile around foundations to catch the water before it enters the house. Most of this water comes off the roof from rain. Since the house is in the way and built in a hole, the water has an obvious route. Yet moving the water away from the foundation before it has a chance to seep in seems to be problematic.

If a house is built on clay soil and the rainwater overflows the sump pump, options are to add further drain tile, pumps, and buried drainpipe at large expense. It's a quick, expensive solution that will need maintenance and electricity. Or do two other things: Extend the downspout of the gutters ten feet from the house and plant a willow tree or two in the wettest areas. The extensions solve most of the immediate problem, but the long-term solution is the fast-growing willow trees that pull moisture form the soil. Planting more trees as time goes by will reduce further soil saturation. A good-size tree will transpire 2,000 gallons of water a day. The small solution is the downspout extension, using a system that already exists and enhancing it. The slow solution is the tree, which absorbs the water and creates a new route for rainwater.

Using the smallest, cleanest, simplest solution to a problem makes for less waste and faster turnaround. Answering the basic question What does this really need to do? through observation may help define the solution and then gradually make opportunities to advance new design improvements. Build momentum with gradual changes and small efficiencies when revisited. Map future possibilities.

Use and Value Diversity

Solving a problem using a single solution, with no diversity, may make it vulnerable to outside influences. In the 1970s, a drought after intense farming caused rapid desertification of Niger. The sands began to consume the landscape, swallowing up the fertile land and grazing areas. The government acted swiftly with millions of tree plantings. The army was mobilized to achieve a defensive line of sand-catching forests. The solution was heralded as brilliant and ecologically sound. Years later, however, the monoculture of trees, all a single species, was decimated by disease and insects. Since the forest was so limited in diversity, there was no deterrent to either threat. The rapid loss of trees threatened the project's sustainability.

"Mono-" means one. "Poly-" means multiple. A monocrop in agriculture exposes the plants to disease and insects. It provides insects access to needed food sources without natural deterrents, causing the crops to be under stress. When dominoes are set side by side, they fall fast. When spread apart, things are less likely to be affected by other failures. Diverse sources of revenue, supplies, and talent make a strong and interconnected unit.

Using only one supplier, one method, and one material makes design vulnerable to outside forces and internal disturbances. For logistical reasons, it may be easier and comfortable to have all materials come from one warehouse, but any disturbance in infrastructure leading to the warehouse renders it useless and holds all inventory there hostage.

Marketing communicators do not rely on a single sales tool, market sector, or industry for revenue. A diverse source of intelligence and design resources ensures a broad scope of reference. One type of paper may have worked for a series of books but not the next, and a favorite medium may not be the best as new materials evolve. Appreciate diversity in sources and materials, and blend the benefits of each. Keep up with improved and eco-friendly materials.

Use Edges and Value the Marginal

"Clean lines" is a term used to describe style and design. The lines are edges that define space. Most edges are points of transition, from sea to shore, field to woodland, lake to wetland. The edge is a place where energies, nutrients, and biomass collect. Leaves blowing across a smooth field are stopped at the edge of a forest, then the leaves decompose, turn to soil, and feed the forest edge. The forest expands its species into the new soil and increases. Small, quick-growing trees take root, shielding the inner forest from dry winds while slowing the wind's rush, silt, dust, and leaves drop to the forest floor. Floodwaters enter a river island where edge trees slow the current, building soil with each new surge of silty water. The edge collects, protects, and filters.

To be definable one needs to be extreme. To ride the edge of technology, design, and engineering means to be noticed: the leading edge, with all its resistance and polishing; the bleeding edge, where new ideas are tested and challenged. Resources collect at the edges waiting for a purpose or the excitement. Win or lose, there is knowledge to be gained. Nothing is wasted on the edge, the highest point of concentration.

The marginal areas are to be explored. Opportunity missed and resources ignored are in the margins. Both edge and margin are places on transition. The edge is where the action is. The margin where things are waiting for change can be wide or narrow.

Creatively Use and Respond to Change

With all the preceding principles, tactics must be able to change. Change means new life, energy, and purpose. Change can be seen as a roadblock to some and a catapult to others. Most times it's quite obvious, like the weather, seasons, and parenthood. Signs show something is about to need a bit of attention. Signs of change may show the end of one phase of life and the beginning of another. Change can cause stress to those unprepared or unaware of the signals. Seeing the signs of change is almost as important as the change itself. The reflection on the roadway surface signals a need to change speed, steering, and the expected time of arrival. The price of a material drives designers to adapt budgets or technique. Change is opportunity for forward thinking, creatively seeking the benefits the change may bring while mitigating the negative aspects.

If recycled plastics move to corn-based polylactide (PLA) and major fast-food chains want compostable materials, designers see the perceived value and make opportunity, leveraging this change. They take the popular notion from adversity to opportunity. They ride the paradigm shift others avoid.

Some change is about defensive measures. Trying to survive change with the least amount of damage gives the affected parties time to adjust and regroup. Some short-term expenses may need to be taken on in order to protect an asset in the long term: burning forest A to save forest B; flooding a town to keep a dam from failing, destroying more towns; pulling infested vines to stop disease from spreading to the whole vineyard. The Tylenol murder case in the early 1980s is a classic example. Johnson & Johnson, the makers of Tylenol brand pain reliever, pulled millions of bottles off the store shelves and suffered a huge market share loss but ultimately saved the brand. The wake-up call helped expose a distribution weakness, and the standard for packaging for all brands in this sector changed within a year.

Nothing sits still for very long. Everything is moving and adjusting position; the ups and downs are time to be creative. Nature fills all voids. Untapped skills suddenly find use. Solutions shelved long ago find a need. It is an opportunity to be creative while the paradigm shifts and scripts are being written. A disturbance in the "natural order" is an opening for both weed and flower. The seeds have always been there or will soon blow in, catching on the bare soil. Even if the weeds take hold, they are but placeholders while the deeper plants make roots and prepare to emerge. Nothing is wasted, unless there is nothing to respond. In time, something always will.

Change Management

Given the wide variety of information and approaches on sustainability, many readers will wonder how to implement it in their companies.

Change management techniques can help turn what seem like insurmountable obstacles into a logical path for strategic growth.

In many environments, one designer or manager is ready before his or her peers. How can such people serve their organization as change agents and provide an environment for the new information to grow in? Several strategies can be successfully used:[28]

— Teaching each other

— Leading by example

Vertically integrated resource management: A bean vine uses a nearby corn stalk to get off the ground and into more sunlight.
Photo: Dan Halsey (halsey1.com).

199

— Bringing others to the team

— Generating alternative designs on a consistent basis

— Being aware of the process and possible reactions

Change agents often find that the challenge with change is that people are locked in to one way of thinking. The change agent then needs to help them "unfreeze" their old ways of thinking (paradigms) and "refreeze" to operating the new way. It all comes down to patterns.

Humans are "wired" for pattern matching. In fact, brain elements (neurons) learn from real-world situations to recognize familiar shapes and objects such as faces. From an early age, patterns quickly become essential for survival: moving object, door, food, loud animal, stairs. Each of these images provokes strong associations that persist into adulthood and in many cases help survival.

The downside of a dependence on patterns is that humans may keep hold of them where flexibility would give greater opportunities. For example, a sales department may have always done things a certain way, and everyone there is used to the system. Some may see a new way that would offer new opportunities and greater sales, but the change is seen as threatening to those comfortable with the old ways, so change is dismissed without further investigation.

This ties especially well into sustainability, where many things are changing and old patterns no longer fit. How can the change agent present information about change that guides people through the transition to the new way? There are several approaches, depending on what position change agents find themselves in.

Managing change need not be like managing cats.
Photo: W. Jedlička.

Role 1: Change Agent as Peer

Change agents may find themselves in the position of persuading their organizational peers to change their thinking regarding sustainability. In this instance, the change agent may be "self-identified" as an early adopter. What does that mean? Years ago, the United States Department of Agriculture (USDA) spent a lot of time and energy trying to convince farmers to try new techniques and seeds. They were puzzled by the range of responses, and researched it.

They found that in any community, there are several kinds of people:

— Innovators find the next new thing.

— Early adopters will try most any of those new things.

— Early majority or pragmatists pay attention to the early adopters and try what they were successful at.

— Late-majority and laggard farmers would wait until most everyone was doing something before they tried it.[29]

The result for the USDA was to focus on finding and supporting the early adopters, so they got similar results with far less expenditure.

Assuming the reader is an early adopter and wants to reach the early majority of designers or managers, what can be done?

First, avoid triggering the "corporate immune response." Most readers have seen this in action: A new idea appears and is so foreign that employees gang up to defeat it. How to avoid this? Communication to the masses is key. Selling new ideas cannot be overdone at this stage, especially to a peer group. Tie the idea into corporate goals, and reinforce the benefits of doing things more sustainably. Demonstrate to peers how this new way will also benefit them individually. For example, a new design lowers costs and risks. It has inspired designers to create new approaches. Marketing has indicated the new design actually can gain new audiences if appropriately marked.

To communicate the change and propagate ideas, try some of these methods:

— Talk to (and thereby influence) an opinion leader.

— Hold lunch talks to pass on information.

— Use some of the techniques in a project, and publicize the benefits.

— Understand that new ways of doing things challenge old patterns:

— Support those whose ways of working are changing.

— Talk to them about the old patterns dissolving and new ones forming.

— Get management buy-in and use it to advance a key project.

— Share information freely, and praise those who take advantage of it.

— Be flexible about how sustainability can be implemented.

— Ask about best practices. Publicize these, tying them in to sustainability.

— Diagram the forces for and against change. Use the insights to strategize.[30]

— Determine the feedback loops keeping the old system stable. There will be one positive loop tending to grow the system and another negative loop tending to contract the system. It is the interaction of those two loops that creates stability. Use the insights to create or change loops to move the system to a new way of designing.

Role 2: Change Agent in a Position of Authority

Recall that all companies are systems and that departments within the company are systems as well. Systems of people often are referred to as open systems since they are adaptive. So there are two tasks here: Help the individuals change their patterns and help the groups change their systems.

Utilize some of these techniques to influence people regarding organizational change:

— Convincing people (rational approach)

— Changing the social environment (alter norms and values)

— Changing the reward system (use power and implement consequences when necessary)

— Changing the environment (create a new structure for them to move to)[31]

Utilize these twelve ways to change the operation of systems in the organization:

1. *Subsidies, taxes, and standards.* Payback for the good thing, increased cost for the bad thing, rate designs.

2. *The size of buffers, relative to their flows.* Buffers are stored materials, energy, and information. Larger buffers slow down the system but can help in times of change. Faster flows allow the system to respond faster. Consider stockpiles of finished pieces versus the frequency of design updates. Cost versus adaptability?

3. *The structure of material stocks and flows.* Stocks are physical entities like products. What flows increase or decrease a stock?

4. *The length of delays.* Systems have delays that "even out" response yet slow it down and can affect stability. For example, asking for feedback on designs only at release gives stability to the design process while potentially causing problems in other areas.

5. *The strength of negative feedback loops.* Negative feedback brings the system to a set point just as a thermostat controls the temperature. Design reviews and user comments are feedback.

6. *The gain around positive feedback loops.* Positive feedback can move a system to a new state or grow the system until the limits are reached. Positive and negative loops must be balanced for a stable system.

7. *The structure of information flow.* Who sees the information about inventory, sales, and growth? What information is seen? How does the designer know if the work was good?

8. *Incentives, punishment, constraints.* Constraints actually force more creativity since without constraints, things are done the same way they always were or the way things are done in other places. With constraints, designers have to search for new solutions, inspiring innovation.

9. *Adding, changing, or evolving system structure.* Adding new feedback loops or buffers, giving more information to employees.

10. *The goal of the system.* Create a new mission statement for the department. Encourage employees to create their own mission statement.

11. *Work with the mind-set or paradigm out of which the system arises.* A creative services department has a unique opportunity to push change or create new paradigms by repeatedly and consistently pointing out

new avenues to explore. Thinking out of the box should come naturally.

12. *The power to transcend paradigms.* Set up forces to renew vision and direction.[32]

Role 3: Individual in a Changing Organization

Finally, some readers may be in the position of navigating the changes brought about by others or by the marketplace. In this case, you still can be a change agent, but the first task may be to change your own mind-set.

Some possible approaches:

— Consider one new idea each day.

— Find someone in the innovator group and ask for help in adjusting to the change.

— List points of connection to the new system.

— Discover your own reaction to the change: Are you in support of it, or are you resisting it?

— Identify how your actions are supporting or manipulating the change.

— Compose a plan of action for how you will succeed in this change.

— Create an image of the existing system and another of the new system. Consider what it would take to move there.

This last point applies to all the approaches. Change agents need to know the current state of things as well as the desired future state. Knowing these two states gives the end points for a path that is created much as a wide and shallow stream is crossed. Each day the current state and the desired state change, so the path must be updated frequently.

To make this effective, the change agent needs to know:

— What are the new system functions, and how can they be implemented?

— What communication systems keep the old system in place?

— What new communication systems are required?

— How can new channels be created?

It can be important to view the new situation as an opportunity and the current situation as a problem. Doing this can make it easier to identify communication channels. As others get involved in mapping the new and old situations, the change agent gets their buy-in or commitment to the process.

Technical Approaches to Sustainability

Industrial Ecology

While there were many approaches to design for environment before the 1990s, the birth of industrial ecology symbolizes the approaches in place today.

The fields of study in industrial ecology are:

— Systems analysis

— Industrial metabolism: flow of materials and energy, and their transformation

— Using perspectives from other fields

— Study of natural systems

— Closed loop systems

Today we might term these fields as:

— Systems thinking

— Life cycle assessment

— Stakeholder involvement

— Biomimicry

— Cradle to Cradle (C2C) inspired design

Each perspective is useful, and each will attract a different type of designer. For some areas, the industrial ecology descriptions give a larger viewpoint.

Systems analysis is the view of designs as systems, with life cycles, interconnections, boundaries, and relations to the stakeholders. There are a great many tools for systems analysis, and they allow the design team to capture a large amount of information in a structured way and to ensure that this information is part of the process.

As one example, requirements engineering is an excellent tool to capture the needs of the various stakeholders on a complex team. Once the requirements are captured, they can be mapped to parts of the design, and it can be proven that each requirement has been addressed.

Industrial metabolism and the study of natural systems go farther than life cycle assessment by looking at industrial ecosystems to see how complex production processes are structured and interlinked. The study of transformation brings in viewpoints from other industrial processes.

Perspective from other fields includes legal, health, biology, management, engineering, and resource management. Making these groups explicit results in their becoming stakeholders, whether they exist within the company or not.

Closed loop systems are the goal of industrial ecology—moving from I to II to III:

Type I systems take energy from the environment and dump wastes back.

Type II systems have internal process loops so energy and wastes are minimized.

Type III systems have closed loops, utilizing wastes as food and running on solar income.

The field is alive and well with journals[33] and dedicated teaching staff at a variety of institutions.[34] It is out of the scope of this chapter to cover all the facets, so the reader is encouraged to seek out additional sources of information.

Typical design processes from industrial ecology follow the phases of: needs analysis, design requirements, design strategies, and design analysis. The next list provides strategies for meeting environmental requirements.[35]

Design/Product Life Extension

— Extend useful life.

— Make appropriately durable.

— Ensure adaptability.

— Facilitate serviceability by simplifying maintenance and allowing repair.

— Enable remanufacture.

— Accommodate reuse.

Material Life Extension

— Specify recycled materials.

— Use recyclable materials.

— Create closed-loop material strategies (Cradle to Cradle).

Material Selection

— Substitute materials.

— Reformulate designs.

— Change material type.

— Alter material processing.

Reduced Material Intensity

— Conserve resources.

Process Management

— Use substitute processes.

— Map process inputs, outputs, and storage losses.

— Increase energy efficiency.

— Process materials efficiently.

— Control processes.

— Improve process layout.

— Improve inventory control and material handling processes.

— Plan efficient facilities.

— Consider treatment and disposal.

— Perform life cycle assessment.

Efficient Distribution

— Choose the best method transportation.

— Reduce a piece's weight or size.

— Use low-impact or reusable pieces.

Improved Management Practices

— Use office materials and equipment efficiently.

— Phase out high-impact pieces.

— Choose environmentally responsible suppliers or contractors.

— Label properly.

— Advertise demonstrable environmental improvements.

— Measure and manage for sustainability.

Design Service Systems[36]

— Transform from an object to a service.

Design Practice

Good design practice involves multiple viewpoints and is adaptive to new information. Along with this, there are a variety of design aids.

It is essential to eliminate toxic materials, and the sooner material impacts are known, the better the response will be. When looking at materials, it may be difficult to decide on one type of paper versus another, or how to compare dry toner versus inkjet.

As a first step, put some math behind this. What is the equation for a given design problem? Isn't the piece's price just a cost per unit, materials plus process?

This is a typical approach, and gives "cost" at some instant in time without regard to where things come from, what it takes to get them here, and what it takes to retire them. These costs are part of the bigger picture, and the universe takes them into account. Is there advantage in using the universe's viewpoint?

First look at what this would entail. What materials are in the piece, and where did they come from? How much waste and energy was lost in creating the raw materials? Now what happens to the materials?

Were they offset printed? What did that take? A plate had to be created and the art designed, and energy was used for each instance. Next the piece has to be transported. It may seem tiny on an individual basis, but consider the refrigerator, or the millions of portable MP3 players. A tiny improvement in each one gives a huge overall reduction. Now consider the consumer. Is that the final chapter in the piece's life? If thrown away, the landfill is an additional cost. Recycling reduces end-of-life cost, and reuse gives yet another improvement. Litter has a negative impact overall on the company.

This process is called life cycle thinking. In order to quantify environmental impacts a life cycle analysis is conducted. There are more and more public domain and commercial tools becoming available everyday. It is most useful to think of LCA as a comparative tool: Does one approach have less impact than another? There is no single perfect design, just a constantly evolving landscape of designs moving toward our design goals.

The advantage of a LCA is that it gives independent confirmation of material impacts, and designers are forced to consider each step in the process. It is also a key tool in trade-off analysis, allowing designers and management to contrast design approaches (e.g., compare durability and recyclability). LCA is well suited to identify trade-offs and helps to avoid shifting environmental impacts from one environmental compartment to another. It can also be used in combination with multicriteria decision tools (e.g., robust decision making, or the analytic hierarchy process),[37] not only to improve the design strategy but also to communicate with different stakeholders.

Users of LCA find that their design thinking may not have extended to end of life or may not have considered transport costs. Each of these pieces of the puzzle has impacts beyond what the accounting department might consider:

Marketability: Excessive graphics may be confusing, limit the market, and can be seen as a negative by consumers.

Economics: Substrate, ink, printing and transport costs are not in control, rising, and can be a competitive advantage.

End of life: Reduced risks from landfill issues, increased consumer satisfaction from recycling the design (a smaller trash bag).

Growth potential: Just like organic food, sustainable designs are increasing in share much faster than the average.[38]

New audiences: Good design attracts new audiences and makes a statement that inclines buyers toward the company. Bad design may keep old audiences through familiarity but is not a sustainable strategy.

An LCA analysis goes beyond regulation. Looking closer gives improvements against internal designs as well as the competition. Beating those means beating the market. Think the boss is interested? If presented in the right way—with an emphasis on cost reductions, process improvements, and competitive advantage—then most anyone will sign up.

Life Is Cycles

As many have noted, life works in cycles. The Earth rotates, seasons change, and everyone grows up. Material is recycled the same way that water evaporates from the oceans and lakes, condensing in clouds and raining back on the Earth, where it flows to watersheds and starts the cycle over again. Some have said that each of us shares atoms with the Egyptians!

What does this mean for the pieces to be produced? If they are designed without thinking through their whole life, the company is at risk in several ways:

— Unforeseen costs risks

— Material sources

— Design liabilities

— Processing issues

— Regulatory actions

— End-of-life issues

In addition, the designer misses out on one of the most powerful tools for increasing value.

Life cycle management (LCM) is part of the start of the process. Simply put, it follows an object from a pile of raw materials through end of life. It does not attempt to assess impacts; rather, it is a big-picture view of the object's costs over its total lifetime. For example, an LCM approach to a printer would consider the acquisition cost, the cost of supplies (paper and ink), the cost of maintenance, the impact of product downtime, and the costs to dispose of the product at end of life. This approach is popular with managers of large systems, as their true cost is known only when the total life cycle is quantified.

Life cycle analysis is an integrated procedure to quantify the impact of an object's life cycle. After the area of analysis is defined, material and energy flows are identified. Each material and energy flow then has an impact number assigned to it, and the total impact can be calculated. LCA is divided into four major steps:

1. Goal and scope definition (define functional unit and system boundary)

2. Life cycle inventory (allocation procedures and inventory analysis)

3. Life cycle impact assessment

4. Interpretation

In accordance with International Organization for Standardization, a peer review is required if the results of the LCA are communicated to the public. The LCA report should include assumptions and limitations.

LCA Steps

Identify the function of the graphic design piece's system and the functional unit. What is the main use or utility of this piece? Many design pieces have several functions, and this step can help identify aspects that could complicate design decisions. Some companies use this information to pare down functionality, feeling that the most efficient piece is the one that fits a single function.

Define the design piece's system and boundaries. What are the piece's boundaries? Does this analysis include the waste materials? Are all life cycle stages considered? Generally the answer is yes, but it is crucial to document. Only after the boundaries are defined can the material and energy transfers be established. Does the system include transport? Once again, the answer is generally yes, and the results can be surprising. For example, a European study showed that the costs of transporting renewables back to the factory dramatically changed the results.[39]

Perform a life cycle inventory. To assess impacts, the designer needs to know what transfers of material and energy take place over the life of a piece. Using the example from a printer's perspective, the inventory would identify the material components used in the creation of the piece and the energy required to process those materials, including: films, plates, wash-ups, paper, ink, energy, and maintenance supplies. At end of life, the components that make up the job would be classified as recyclable, needing disposal in a landfill, capable of being incinerated, or hazardous waste. The components would be shown entering each of these end-of-life destinations. This step creates a flow diagram showing connections among design processing steps, energy, and materials entering the production system and wastes exiting the production system.

Document material impacts. Use either a public domain or commercial database to quantify the material and energy impacts. The place of manufacture can change the results, as energy in one part of the world may have less impact than energy in other parts. Processes to be considered are acquiring raw material, material conversion into finished parts, transport, use characteristics (consumables and energy), recycle/reuse, and waste management.

Analyze the results. The main value of the LCA is thinking through the process. The number does not indicate either a perfect or a horrible design; rather it allows the designer to compare one design approach to another and to make trade-offs that benefit both the company and the environment. It is also an excellent tool to document design improvements.

Compare alternatives and optimize. As noted, comparing two ways of doing something is one of the more powerful advantages of LCA. Look at recycled substrate versus certified forestry resources, or even tree-free options. The recycled may look better initially yet worse once process steps, such as bleaching, are included. Consider different materials, or change the type of processing to reduce the impact.

Publish and critique. Put the results on a public server, schedule a lunch meeting, or present the findings at a department meeting. Getting others to look at it gives several key advantages:

— Shared understanding of the system

— Ideas about changes that could benefit both the company and environment

— Increased knowledge for study authors and reviewers

— Provides transparency of decision processes

Note on sustainability matrixes. Sustainability matrixes are decision support tools used to compare the impact of one project to another approach. For each project, a variety of dimensions is listed: use of energy, amount of pollution, impact on groundwater, and the like. The alternate designs are rated on each dimension, and the totals are used to get a better picture of overall project impact. While these are more commonly used in building design or development projects, they can be used for other types of design as well. The limitation is that each dimension is ranked using a small range of numbers, sometimes 0:5 or −2:+2. While this does give information about how projects compare at a high level (and it is quick), it doesn't give enough information about the details of a design and it is not tied to the impacts of specific materials. It can be a reasonable way to summarize data for a high-level presentation.[40]

Currently LCA data available in the printing industry is fairly limited. But that doesn't mean that just because a perfect LCA can't be performed, none should be attempted. Understanding and addressing some of a project's impacts are better than ignoring all of them. In addition, some data may be available but not necessarily in a handy form. Printers are required by law to maintain data on many of their materials. Certified printers do this as part of their regular system of monitoring and are happy to help their clients understand their materials impacts per job.

Eco-costs Approach

An LCA is a somewhat complex tool that requires the material characteristics of a piece to be known before analysis can proceed. This creates difficulties for designers in several ways:

— Components of a piece may not be known when the design process is started.

— Composition and chemistry of a piece's components may not be known.

— There may not be support (staff and software) for the LCA process.

The result is that designers often look for nontechnical approaches to a piece's impacts, either with a philosophic approach or with higher-level tools. One higher-level tool is eco-costs.

An eco-cost summarizes all the effects on the environment from a given material. The eco-cost for a material is the "extent to which a product or production process is not yet environmentally sustainable."[41]

Why does a business use an eco-cost? To fulfill this mission:

The delivery of competitively priced goods and services that satisfy human needs and bring "quality of life," while progressively reducing ecological impacts and resource intensity, throughout the life cycle, to a level at least in line with the Earth's estimated carrying capacity.[42]

Eco-costs may be in the same range as material costs and include the impact of emissions, energy, and materials. Similar in a way to an LCA, however, eco-costs give one total number for each component of the design over the whole range of a piece's life, which simplifies calculations.

In design decisions, it is useful to relate the eco-costs to the (audience) value. The ratio of eco-costs to value is the eco-costs to value ratio (EVR). Pieces with low EVR numbers have large impact or low value compared to the environmental impact. Conversely, pieces with high EVR numbers give good value for their impact. Design decisions can be made based on EVR: The element can be dropped if the EVR is low; material substitution or increase value if it is medium; keep as a core design element if it is high.

Value (to the audience) often can be increased faster than eco-costs. Labor has lower eco-costs than materials or energy, so reducing high-impact materials while increasing labor content will improve EVR.

Teaching materials on the Delft University of Technology Web site (*www.ecocostsvalue.com*) note that in design decisions, environmental sustainability is a second-level filter after quality and price. This finding reinforces the earlier point that sustainable designs have to meet quality goals along with reduced impact.

At this time, eco-costs are an optional exercise allowing a company to evaluate design decisions in terms of environmental impact. However, these voluntary calculations will become a matter of regulation in the future.

Graphic design products with high eco-costs may appear profitable today but are not good investments in the long term. Rather, look for options with lower eco-costs and a good value to cost ratio. For existing design pieces, decrease eco-costs where they are high and increase a piece's value where it is high (impact value, collectors value, reuse value). A piece with increased value may have a lower eco-cost to value ratio and be a better design even if its eco-costs are higher than the original design.

Note that life cycle costs or whole life costs are the total amounts from an LCA analysis, and compare to an eco-cost calculation. Also, the eco-costs are the marginal prevention costs of making materials sustainable. They are not the same as the external costs, which represent damage to the environment.

In summary, an eco-cost is an LCA-based indicator for environmental burden. Each material has an associated eco-cost, which is the cost required to make use of that material sustainable. The eco-costs to value ratio is an easy way to visualize which designs have the best strategic fit. The eco-costs are "virtual": These are measures to make (and recycle) an object "in line with the Earth's estimated carrying capacity."[43]

Watertown, Massachusetts, design firm Zen Kitchen took a fresh approach for its client Olive and Bean, to reflect the whimsical yet elegant nature of the boutique's brand. Printed by Zen Kitchen's local union eco-printer, the smaller, square business card makes a dynamic impact while minimizing materials use. The background pattern of thin-lined circles for the stationery system allows for visual interest without relying on heavy ink coverage.

Systems Approaches

LCA is a powerful tool to measure and compare the impacts of a particular design. What way of thinking will guide designs to the opportunities beyond the current situation? The Sustainable Packaging Coalition[SM] draws on a number of philosophies that address sustainability, including industrial ecology, natural capitalism, the Natural Step, and Cradle to Cradle, to name just a few. Their definition of what a sustainable package could be is an easy to understand and actionable outline for how to address any man-made effort.

Sustainable Packaging Coalition[SM]

A project of the nonprofit institute GreenBlue[SM], the Sustainable Packaging Coalition (SPC)[44] is an industry group committed to creating and implementing sustainable packaging solutions. Its vision for a sustainable package though can easily be applied to any effort.

The SPC envisions a world where all packaging:

— Is sourced responsibly.

— Is designed to be effective and safe throughout its life cycle.

— Meets market criteria for performance and cost.

— Is made entirely using renewable energy.

— Once used, is recycled efficiently to provide a valuable resource for subsequent generations.

SPC Approach

— Provide a forum for supply chain collaboration.

— Share best practices and design guidelines.

— Support innovation and effective, new technologies.

— Provide education, resources, and tools.

The SPC is made up of leading companies seeking consensus on approach and best practice in packaging design. The SPC seeks to engage the entire packaging supply chain; members include raw materials suppliers, converters, consumer product goods companies, design firms, retailers, and recyclers.

In addition to the packaging guidelines, other SCP projects include:

— Case studies that document the strategies, business justification, and environmental impacts of sustainable packaging.

— Environmental briefs that summarize the environmental impacts related to the production, use, and end of life of packaging materials.

— COMPASS (Comparative Packaging Assessment), an online software application that allows packaging professionals to compare the environmental impacts of their package designs using a life cycle approach. It provides profiles for packaging based on metrics such as fossil fuel consumption, water consumption, and greenhouse gas emissions.[45]

Definition of Sustainable Packaging

The definition of Sustainable Packaging[46] is reprinted here with the permission of the Sustainable Packaging Coalition. To get up-to-the-minute information on sustainable packaging and to get a copy of their *Design Guidelines for Sustainable Packaging*,[47] visit their Web site at: *www.sustainable packaging.org.*

Sustainable packaging:

1. Is beneficial, safe and healthy for individuals and communities throughout its life cycle;

2. Meets market criteria for performance and cost;

3. Is sourced, manufactured, transported, and recycled using renewable energy;

4. Maximizes the use of renewable or recycled source materials;

5. Is manufactured using clean production technologies and best practices;

6. Is made from materials healthy in all probable end-of-life scenarios;

7. Is physically designed to optimize materials and energy;

8. Is effectively recovered and utilized in biological and/or industrial Cradle to Cradle cycles.

Paper and packaging accounts a huge share of the waste stream in developed countries. How can that be reduced while increasing market share and brand loyalty?

In many ways, "doing the right thing" lets customers feel good about their product choices, reinforcing brand loyalty. Keep the buyer, eliminate the remorse.

What does that take?

— Use the right materials by considering the health of workers, customers, and the planet.

— Restore the Earth: Put back resources.

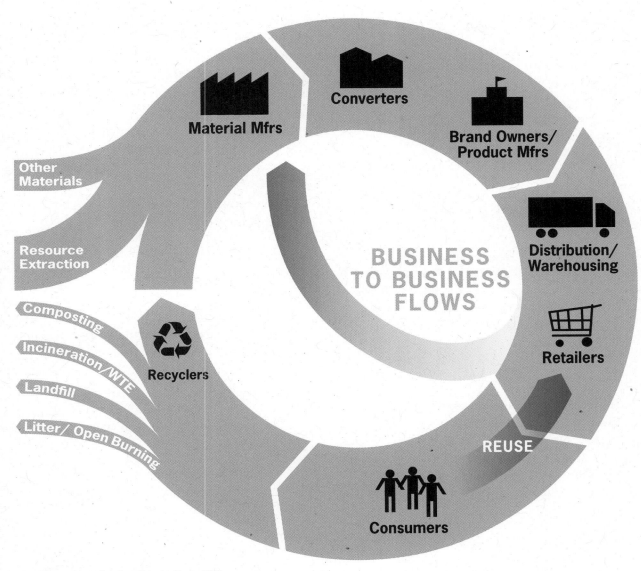

Cycle from Material Creation to End of Life
Used with permission of Sustainable Packaging Coalition[SM], © Green Blue[SM].

— Create systems and solutions that are long term and forward thinking.

— Use renewable resources (energy and materials).

— Favor reuse rather than virgin sources.

— Increase efficiency of all costs: logistics, materials use, transport, end of life.

— Confirm that all components are doing what they're supposed to do.

— "Protect/inform/sell" is the base criteria for packaging. Protect though should include the planet.

The criteria are a goal, not gospel. As new products are designed or systems are improved, the criteria provide a benchmark. Sometimes all the marks are hit, sometimes just a few. But in all cases movement is in a forward direction.

Design Guidelines from the SPC

The next concise reminders of key design guidelines are presented as an overview with permission from the Sustainable Packaging Coalition "Design Guidelines for Sustainable Packaging."[48] It is recommended that readers download the complete book from the SPC Web site to get the full utility of the work.

Design with a larger view of the product: Expand the definition of quality (traditionally, package design quality is based on a small set of dimensions):

— Technical performance (how the package does its job: protect, inform, and sell)

— Cost

— Appearance

— Regulatory compliance

Looking closely at these parameters and continually doing a better job can be one way to make a better package. However, the parameters are limited in the same ways mentioned before. For example: Optimizing for costs alone may be shortsighted and impact environmental performance and therefore increase risk at the corporate, manufacturing, and consumer levels of the system.

Expand the definition of quality to:

— Optimize resources—use less materials and energy, use better materials and energy.

   — Practice source reduction.

   — Use recycled content.

   — Design for transport.

— Conduct responsible sourcing—talk to vendors and make judgments as to who is best.

   — Use environmental best practice as a yardstick.

   — Confirm vendors adhere to fair labor and trade practices.

   — Design with virgin renewable materials from sustainably managed sources.

— Material health

   — Know the chemistry of the materials of the piece.

— Ask questions, research, compare approaches. Use an LCA.

   — Know the potential health and environmental impacts over the life cycle of the piece.

— Resource recovery

— Design for reuse, recycling, composting, or energy recovery.

The definition of a "design well done" is bigger but also better. Employees, stakeholders, and the customer base will appreciate the focus.

Do the right job: Avoid overengineering. The Industrial Revolution mind-set didn't care about material and energy usage if the job was done. As a result, packages often are more than needed. They are: stronger (older people can't open them), longer lasting (decades or centuries in the landfill or ocean gyre), and larger (excess packing material buffering empty space in a huge box or a huge poster no one will display when a card would have done the same job).

Consider Carefully and Design Appropriately

— What physical product protections are required?

— Consider the package life cycle.

— Can the product protect itself?

— What are the actual constraints and requirements in manufacture, transport, and storage?

— Can transport packaging reduce package requirements?

— Chart all the environments the package lives in between birth and death.

— Optimal designs use less resources and energy, saving money for the producer.

— Consider the channel (distribution, point of sale) the product lives in.

— Consider add-ons (RFID, foil, electronics) as added burdens at end of life.

Design simply. Sometimes we simply add more rather than designing well:

— Move marketing and other information from packaging to signage.

— Add recovery/recycling signage on all packaging.

— Design appropriately for the product target markets.

— Check regulations.

— Consider costs for packaging and disposal.

— Verify design requirements for content.

— Confirm prohibitions on materials.

— Use appropriate labeling.

— Consider using the strictest set of requirements to reduce design variety and increase volume.

Checklist of Design Strategies for Sustainability

Practice Continuous Source Reduction

— Use materials with lower production energy levels.

— Use the minimum number of materials.

— Choose the best suppliers and converters.

— Work with the product designer to reduce one and/or the other.

— Reduce size, weight, and thickness.

— Minimize void space.

— Optimize primary versus transport packaging.

— Consider the transport energy.

Expand the Use of Recycled Content

— What are the package requirements, and can they be met with recycled content?

— Change the package design so requirements meet capabilities.

— Consider the markets for recyclables in your markets.

— Work with marketing to help advertise and avoid conflicts.

— Set internal goals for content.

Design for Transport at the Front End

— Optimize primary versus transport packaging.

— Change one design to minimize the other; calculate savings.

— Eliminate primary or transport packaging through design.

— Use source reduction.

— Use all the transport package space.

— Consider truck and container dimensions for most efficient packing.

— Make transport packaging reusable or recyclable.

— Choose transport suppliers with good environmental performance.

— Work with logistics experts.

Adapt and Expect Environmental Best Practice

— Demand compliance with all reporting requirements.

— Set goals to minimize hazardous and increase reusable and recyclable materials.

— Use of closed-loop systems in production processes.

— Set goals for continuous improvement beyond compliance.

Practice Design for Equity

— Ask suppliers to provide their labor and trade practices.

— Check how often compliance is verified.

— Confirm their policies match the one at your company.

Use Renewable Virgin Material from Sustainable Sources

— Require certification for sustainable management.

— Where possible, use local or regional sources.

Support Green Chemistry

— Choose a supplier that practices it.

— Know your material impacts, and choose the lowest-impact materials.

Know Your Materials

— Use an LCA tool.

— Ask for contents of each material you use.

— Use confidentiality agreements if necessary to get details.

— Choose vendors that are easy to work with.

— Check material impacts both in use and end-of-life phases.

— Scan for updated materials of concern.

- Check plasticizers, heat stabilizers, compatibilizers, dyes, pigments, fillers, ultraviolet stabilizers, antioxidants, and flame retardants.

- Consider all package components, including add-ons such as RFID, inks, coatings, and adhesives.

Design for Reuse

- Confirm if it will work for your package requirements (food in particular).

- It can result in overdesign if the customer or transporter won't close the loop.

- Create incentives to help close the loop.

- Consider the transport costs for reuse versus one way.

- Consider end of life for reusable packages.

- Work with suppliers and process personnel from the start on a reuse design.

Design for Recycling

- Select the best materials.

- Consider add-ons, as they can affect recycling.

- Use appropriate labeling.

- Check with suppliers in the design process.

- Use single materials, or design for disassembly.

- Design projects to increase recycling rates.

- Design a take-back program so customers return and recycling rates increase.

- *Paper/cardboard:* Watch for plastic films, foil stamping, adhesives, inks, wax.

- *Plastic:* Watch for single or compatible materials, attachments, inks, foils.

- *Biopolymers:* Watch for additives such as coupling agents, plasticizers, fillers, dyes, and pigments.

- *Steel:* Watch for inks, added features, plastic components, paints, and coatings.

- *Aluminum:* Watch for coatings and laminations.

- *Glass:* Watch for pigments such as cobalt blue, metal rings, and inks for on-glass printing.

Design for Composting

- Degradable may mean only "separates into small pieces."

- Biodegradable means "it will be consumed by microorganisms."

- Compostable means "biodegradable within constraints." Check standards.

- Can compostable packaging meet technical needs?

- Confirm that all components (add-ons, printing) are compatible.

- Test the package to confirm biodegradability.

- Check for infrastructure.

- Possible materials suitable for composting where facilities exist include natural fibers and fiber products, such as hemp, kenaf, wheat straw, palm fiber, agripulp, kraft paper, molded fiber, paperboard, and plant-based plastics such as poly-3-hydroxyalkanoate (PHA), polylactide (PLA), and starch-based products.

The approaches used by the Sustainable Packaging Coalition are made up of ideas, philosophies, and frameworks that have a long history of providing real and actionable solutions. The world is a very complex place, so there can be no one-size-fits-all solution for putting sustainability into practice. Rather than blindly following the SPC definitions as gospel, the SPC asks everyone to dig deeper, to discover for themselves how they arrived at their definitions and formed the ideas put into their design guidelines, and then join with the SPC in taking these ideas to the next level. "The criteria presented here blend broad sustainability objectives with business considerations and strategies that address the environmental concerns related to the life cycle of packaging."[49] They are a goal, a guide, and are themselves organic—growing and developing over time as our understanding grows.

Natural Step Framework

The Natural Step Framework (NSF) is a compass or guide to sustainability. It can be viewed at many levels: as a tool for creating a shared understanding, vision, and a sustainability action plan among everyone in an organization; as a checklist for assessing current status; as a yardstick to measure design against; and as a way of seeing into the future and responding proactively.

One of the most elegant ways to enhance each design is to examine it against basic sustainability principles, breaking difficult and intertwined systems down into actionable choices. This simple step takes much of the uncertainty out of the process and frees designers up to do the thing they do best: create.

To allow this to happen, the designer has to be forward looking, making sure each design decision holds up in the light of future society. Typically a designer is tied tightly to the present moment and to the demands of the design situation as it exists today.

The beauty of the NSF is that the key principles are easily recalled, allowing the designer to quickly assess options and create breakthrough work.

The NSF uses four lenses to focus attention on the effects of any decision: TAKE, MAKE, BREAK, and NEEDS. This high-level approach can be used easily to examine actions, improve strategies, and make choices that can save money while being environmentally and socially responsible.

Natural Step Framework: Four Sustainability Principles

Terry Gips
Sustainability Associates

The Natural Step Framework is based on scientific consensus principles developed by Dr. John Holmberg (physicist) and Dr. Karl Henrik Robert (medical doctor and founder of the Natural Step), and consists of four basic *system conditions* for sustainability.

The principles state that in a sustainable society, nature won't be subject to systematically increasing:[50]

1. Concentrations of substances extracted from the Earth's crust.

The Natural Step—a nonprofit research, education, and advisory group that helps corporations and communities move toward sustainability—wanted an updated brand as it opened its first U.S. office. Celery designed a comprehensive identity and collateral system that walks the talk of eco-innovation. The logo references the mythological symbol of regeneration: a serpent eating its own tail. The letterhead is perforated and scored for easy self-mailing, which eliminates the need for envelopes for day-to-day mailing.

2. Concentrations of substances produced by society.

3. Degradation by physical means.

And, in that society,

4. Human needs are met worldwide.

In other words, not systematically increasing:

— What we TAKE from the Earth: mining of metals and burning of fossil fuels.

— What we MAKE: pesticides, plastics, and chemicals.

— What we BREAK: ecosystems and biodiversity.

— While meeting human NEEDS worldwide.[51]

Design strategies include:

— Dematerialization or ephemeralization (using less resources to accomplish the same task)

— Substitution of alternatives

— More efficient use of materials

— Better materials and material processing

— 3 Rs and 1 C: Reduce, Reuse, Recycle, and Compost

The simplicity of the four system conditions allows the designer to quickly evaluate options and make a decision on the best approach.

1. What Is Taken from the Earth (Take)

MINING AND FOSSIL FUELS

Avoid systematically increasing concentrations of substances extracted from the Earth's crust.

Use renewable energy and nontoxic, reusable materials to avoid the spread of hazardous mined metals and pollutants. Why? Mining and burning fossil fuels release a wide range of substances that may continue to build up and spread in our ecosphere. Nature has adapted over millions of years to specific amounts of these materials. Cells don't know how to handle significant amounts of lead, mercury, radioactive materials, and other hazardous compounds from mining. Unwanted chemicals can lead to learning disabilities, weakening of immune systems, and improper development of the body. The burning of fossil fuels creates smog, acid rain, and global climate change, and living things cannot evolve fast enough to adjust to such changes: millions of years versus hundreds of years for such dramatic human-created changes.

PRINT DESIGN ACTIONS

Use lower-impact materials, reduce energy use, and create designs that conserve energy and/or use renewable energy.

— Material selection.

Use renewables instead of fossil fuels.

Use reused materials instead of primary sources extracted from the Earth.

Replace metals with materials that require less energy and pollution.

— Reduce energy use.

Choose materials that require less energy to produce.

Use local materials as transport costs are lower.

Increase processing efficiency.

Increase efficient use of materials.

— Reduce transport costs.

Lighten the load—saving a gram on a million pieces is a ton!

— Recycle.

Design for disassembly.

Choose materials with the largest markets for their recycled versions.

Select recycling processes that don't downcycle materials to a lower quality.

Overall, the aim is to reuse and reduce consumption. Use the general principles to guide actions: Choose the renewable energy source over the coal plant, the renewable biomaterial over metals from across the world.

2. What Is Made (Make)

CHEMICALS, PLASTICS, AND PESTICIDES

Nature must not be subject to systematically increasing concentrations of substances produced by society.

Use safe, biodegradable substances that don't cause the spread of toxins in the environment. Why? Since World War II, our society has produced more than 85,000 chemicals, such as DDT and polychlorinated biphenyls (PCBs). Many of these substances don't go away, but spread and bioaccumulate in nature and the fat cells of animals and humans. Cells don't know how to handle significant amounts of these chemicals, often leading to cancer, hormone disruption, improper development, birth defects, and long-term genetic change. This system condition tells designers not to use these chemicals in anything they create at any level. Perform design differently to keep these things out of the system.

PRINT DESIGN ACTIONS

— Consider the lifetime of the printed material.

If it ends up in the ocean or woodland how long does it last?

If it is landfilled or incinerated, will toxic components escape?

— Support green procurement policies. Work with better vendors.

— Replace high-impact materials with biobased, reusable, or compostable ones.

— Design for disassembly and recyclability.

— Utilize recycled materials.

— Design production processes that minimize air and water pollution.

— Use nontoxic inks.

— Materials processing.

Low-impact forming (check LCA databases for details).

Minimize production steps.

Minimize material waste.

3. What Is Done to the Earth (Break)

BIODIVERSITY AND ECOSYSTEMS

Nature must not be subject to degradation by physical means.

Protect soils, water, and air, so all are able to eat, drink, and breathe. Why? Forests, soils, wetlands, lakes, oceans, and other naturally productive ecosystems provide food, fiber, habitat and oxygen, waste handling, temperature moderation, and a host of other essential goods and services. For millions of years, they have been purifying the planet and creating a habitat suitable for human and other life. Destruction or depletion of these systems endangers current livelihoods and the likelihood of human existence. Make design decisions that enhance diversity. Choose materials that enhance the Earth instead of depleting it. Consider material sources: Did it come from virgin timber or sustainable forestry? Perhaps it doesn't need to come from a slow-growing tree but could from an annual plant source.

PRINT DESIGN ACTIONS

— Reduce paper use during the design process.

— Use Earth-friendly processes for printing.

— Purchase certified, sustainably harvested forest products and products manufactured with certified renewable energy

— Use 100 percent post-consumer recycled content paper.

— Decrease water use and runoff by carefully examining the impacts of production processes, and review whitening and bleaching methods.

— Encourage smart growth in the company and community.

— Examine material choices carefully to minimize impact on natural systems.

4. Meeting Basic Human Needs (Needs)

MINING AND FOSSIL FUELS

Use less stuff and save money while meeting the needs of every human on this planet. Why? Developed countries make up only a small percentage of

the world's population but consume a disproportionately high percentage of its resources. Just to survive, people in underdeveloped countries see no choice but to cut down their rain forests, sell off endangered species, and use polluting energy sources. As a designer, act to reduce the impact of designs by choosing materials and energy sources that benefit human systems.

PRINT DESIGN ACTIONS

— Designs can be examples of meeting goals while minimizing impact on the Earth.

— Being public about design approach spreads design knowledge and promotes the company.

— Encourage the company and peers to make socially responsible investments and purchase fair trade products.

— Create works with an understanding of the market in which they will be sold.

— Gear projects to add value to the user and their community.

— Create works that educate the audience about eco-impacts and actions (i.e., the appropriate use of eco-labels and eco-audits on materials).

— Create works that aid the local economy.

Tools to Implement the Natural Step

The sustainability "tunnel" shows society moving from using resources without regard into a region where these materials appear scarce, expensive, or regulated. The other side of the tunnel has light coming from increased product efficiencies, worker-friendly processes, design innovations, and a more sustainable work environment.

Designers often are focused on the current design situation and the forces at work today, along with knowledge of past designs. It is an inspiration to have awareness of the upcoming situation, but it is more powerful to imagine being on the other side of the tunnel where the solutions have been implemented. These ideal designs can then be projected back to today (back-casting from a desired future).

This powerful technique pulls the design team through the current situation. Companies that use this approach report impressive gains—with decisions made today benefiting both current and future efforts.[52]

The Next Level in the Picture

The Natural Step provides four ways of seeing the impact of design decisions. These ways are qualitative, allowing nearly anyone in the company to add value to the process. From a systems viewpoint, the Natural Step is a philosophical framework focused on the interaction between design and environment. To focus in on putting these ideas into action, we begin to examine frameworks that take a more prescriptive approach to design impacts and strategic thinking.

o2's 5Rs of Great Design

Many years ago, the o2 International Network for Sustainable Design (*www.o2.org*) undertook the task of updating the classic three Rs of reduce-reuse-recycle. Initiated by the United States Upper Midwest chapter (*www. o2umw.org*), its goal was to tap into ideas already in common use, create a resource-ordered list (least to most energy/resource intensive), and have the Rs include ideas that would help shift from a world where designers are asked only to do less "bad" to one where they can create more "good," moving toward a restorative economy.

The sustainability "tunnel" moving into the future.

223

A restorative economy is:

— A way to add diversity back into natural systems.

— Industrial plants where the water coming out is better than the water going in, or that clean the air.

— Products whose life cycle aids natural cycles, allowing the designer to calculate restoration instead of quantifying impact.

— Organizations that rebuild themselves to a higher level of functioning as employees increase their own capabilities.

The expanded 5Rs help guide actions of an organization, from one end to the other: energy sourcing, to design and marketing, to end product and its afterlife plan. Here the organization is viewed as an organism that takes in food, produces a useful product, emits waste, and has an internal structure to respond to the environment. While not as metrics oriented as the SPC's eight criteria for a sustainable package, the 5Rs represent the next level in thinking about impacts and are used as a tool for quickly moving through design ideas in the brainstorming (early design) phase. The 5Rs consist of:

1. Restore

2. Respect

3. Reduce

4. Reuse

5. Recover

Restore

Ecological systems create new information and continually expand diversity. Use biological inspira-

tion for design to create end product diversity. For example, use variation and selection, allowing end product environments and energy sources to determine the parents for the next generation. Choose suppliers and sources that add diversity back to natural systems, particularly where it has been depleted.

Other sources of biological diversity are:

Variation (recombination): Genetic mixing produces new organisms that have differing abilities.

Selection: The environment acts on those organisms to favor the ones that best match the niche.

Food sources: Waste materials and unused energy can become food sources, allowing some designs to propagate more widely and fill the niche.

Migration: As the niche changes, organisms migrate to follow the changes.

Boundary regions: Allow intermixing of species, leading to competitive exclusion where two organisms try to occupy the same niche, with evolutionary changes as a result.

Using all the biomes: In the tropics, there are species at each level, from tree canopy to undergrowth.

Succession: Other species can colonize new territory, while a mature ecosystem has few spaces for new designs. The new territory changes as some species win out over others, creating an environment with gradations from full sun to shade.

The world as it exists is the result of millions of years of evolution and interconnection. Over many thousands of years, the processes just mentioned will bring products of the industrial economy into natural systems.

To make this happen in human lifetimes, restoring the state of the world will require positive actions to bring industrial and natural cycles back together. Designers are in a unique spot to take these actions since their decisions affect as much as 90 percent of energy and material impacts over the design lifetime.

Pick raw materials from sustainably managed sources, and design to return the end product at its end of life into either the production process or the biosphere.

In other words, use materials (and support firms) that help reverse damage or add to natural capital. Natural capital represents the embodied information and energy in natural systems. What did it take to grow that tree, and how much value does that tree add to the local environment in its intact state? Along with cleaning the air and recycling water, the tree gives habitat to animals, reduces the impact of the sun on hot days, and provides useful materials (leaves and twigs) to develop new soil. Natural capital is the bank account humanity has inherited from the Earth, to be used wisely by all beings and their descendants. The value of genetic information in the rain forest is one way to visualize natural capital.

Other actions that help restore include:

— Retiring carbon credits.

— Purchasing renewable energy and using vendors who do also.

— Supporting organizations that do ecological restoration.

Respect

Design like you give a darn.[53] This means thinking of all the people in the supply chain, from material extraction, to manufacturing, to assembly, to sales, to end user, to end of life. Is mining required to obtain the raw material, potentially damaging streams from which others make their livelihood? What chemicals are required in the production process that could impact health today or generations from now (bioaccumulation)? Does the production process involve chemicals that are harmful to workers? Is it possible for an older person to open that package or print piece, or navigate that Web site (Universal Design)?[54] Is rushing to an "easy" answer creating an economic shift with broader socioeconomic impacts (such as the move to a corn economy)? In other words, examine impacts the item will have on all stakeholders as well as ecosystems. Examine the triple top line for economic health, environmental restoration, and social equity.

Bring images of nature and world citizens into the design environment. Update them monthly. Get outside every day. Put a face on your supply chain. Make it personal.

Reduce

Buckminster Fuller said, "Do more with less!" Make the structure minimal by using triangulation instead of a massive thing. Use compression and tension to create minimal structures. Examine all of the functions of a piece and reduce the material and energy needed, including less raw feedstocks, less weight to transport, and less energy to manufacture, less energy to store (store flat and pop up for use), less energy to use (light-emitting diode [LED] bulbs versus incandescent). Combine layers of a complex piece, reducing total layers and material use.

Examine all materials and choose ones with reduced toxicity (moving toward zero).

In the natural world, "extra" requires more energy to create and support. The peacock is an exception, not the rule.

Reuse

The best use of energy in a manufactured item is reuse. Each pass through the material recapture system takes energy and can result in materials being downcycled. (Most plastics do not become the same thing again.) Design for reuse by making the object robust and creating a system to take advantage of that durable good: Even though it may cost more the first time, the overall life costs are lower and the end user becomes a participant in satisfying a need rather than just in consuming goods. Identify the reusable item and reward those who return it. Yet consider the system carefully: If the item is not reused, energy and materials were wasted. Returnables work well only when systems are in place for them to be returned. Do not create durable garbage under the guise of "reuse" as a clever marketing ploy. A reusable thing is useful only if it actually gets reused.

Recover

Recover replaces recycle in this last slot, as recycle-*able* without recovering those resources is just waste. Recovery can happen in one of two ways: (1) The materials are fed back into the production process or (2) the materials can be returned to Nature directly. Design the pathways intentionally and label the item to aid the end user. To do so, you must create the item to fit needs with the production process or Nature in mind. Recovered materials that return to Nature are noteworthy and will increase brand equity. However, jumping a manu-

factured good over the reuse or closed-loop recycling level and going right to compost, just to leverage the image of "back to nature," is not taking resource use processes seriously.

PLA and paperboard are good examples: Can the item be used to make a few rounds of goods before returning that resource to the Earth?

The minimum level of recovery is to use recycled substrates in the first place, decreasing loads on Earth systems, increasing the market for materials, and increasing marketability. However, just because materials *can* be recycled doesn't mean they will be.

Strategies to increase recovery/recycling include:

— Teaming with other companies to increase market demand for the recycled material.

— Designing with materials with maximum recovery/recycling potential. These have the most value to manufacturers and the largest markets.

— Giving customers an incentive to put the item back into the resource loop via rebates, recognition, and rewards.

— Designing for recyclability using noncomposite materials and easily separable components.

— Labeling correctly as to material type. Clearly communicate disassembly instructions.

The last resort for a recovered product is incineration (waste to energy). If this is the end case, design carefully to avoid any toxic trace materials. A few milligrams of a toxin multiplied by many millions of pieces can cause serious contamination.

Recycle has no meaning unless the material is selected to fit an actively functioning recycling market and the material actually is collected. Recover/recycle is last on the 5R list, as remanufacture (without any interim reuse) is the most energy intensive of the Rs.

When manufactured free of toxins, paper, paperboard, and pulp (wood, kenaf, bamboo, agripulp, etc.) are great examples of renewable, biodegradable resources that make many useful reuse and/or remanufacture trips (C2C technical nutrient) before it's time to retire the item as compost fodder or animal bedding on the way to the next growing cycle (C2C biological nutrient).[55]

Walmart 7Rs

Over the past several years, Walmart has learned that working toward sustainability makes good business sense from a variety of perspectives: less risk, increased profits, and increased customer goodwill and market share. As just one example, Walmart made a commitment to sell 100 million compact fluorescents in the first year of its greening effort, benefiting the company, customers, and the environment—the classic *win-win-win* of eco-business.

This business direction has extended into other areas where costs can be decreased while also reducing toxins and impact on the environment. In the first of many initiatives, Walmart initiated its "scorecard" rating systems for packaging and then followed with one for consumer electronics. Here the company asks suppliers to enter product information into a program to determine their impacts. Understanding the workings of the scorecard is important to all vendors, as Walmart's Global Supply Chain Initiative will be extending ideas and lessons learned from its early scorecard efforts and applying them across the whole of the company's product offerings and operations.

In a major partnership with the Environmental Defense Fund, Walmart has outlined its long-term goal as one of raising environmental performance standards throughout its supply chain. The Global Supply Chain Initiative will include targets for the reduction of energy and water use, reductions in packaging (already in place with the scorecard) as well as commitments to develop more sustainable products and supply chain practices.

Even if a company is not directly involved with Walmart, the sheer size of Walmart (with an annual budget larger than that of many nations) and the magnitude of its effort, have already had impacts on the packaging and electronics industries. As Walmart's scope broadens to include all parts of its operations, scarcely an industry in business today won't eventually be moved into action.

Like many sustainability ideas in use today, Walmart's 7Rs are goals, subject to continual improvement and change. To get a feel for what Walmart is looking at with its scorecards, let's look at the one evolving to target packaging.[56]

Here suppliers are to consider these seven Rs for the packaging of products sold at Walmart:

1. *Remove packaging:* Eliminate unnecessary packaging, extra boxes, or layers.

2. *Reduce packaging:* "Right-size" packages and optimize material strength.

3. *Reuse packaging:* Use round-trip, recycled, or reusable pallets (CHEP, IFCO, etc.) and reusable plastic containers (RPC).

4. *Renewable packaging:* Use materials made of renewable resources; select biodegradable or compostable materials.

5. *Recyclable packaging:* Use materials with highest recycled content without compromising quality.

BUILDING WITH VISION

Optimizing and Finding Alternatives to Wood

A Watershed Media Book

PAPERORPLASTIC

Searching for Solutions to an Overpackaged World

Daniel Imhoff

"I foresee the time when industry shall no longer denude the forests which require generations to mature, nor use up the mines which were ages in the making, but shall draw its materials largely from the annual produce of the fields." —Henry Ford, 1934

6. *Revenue:* Achieve all preceding principles at cost parity or cost savings.

7. *Read:* Get educated on sustainability and how we can all support it.

The official scorecard is embodied in Walmart-approved software, which creates a score weighting these factors:

— Greenhouse gas emissions (15 percent)

— Amount of materials used (15 percent)

— The ratio of the product to the packaging (15 percent)

— Efficient packing into shipping containers (cube utilization) (15 percent)

— Amounts of recycled content (10 percent)

— Innovation (5 percent)

— Quantity of renewable energy used in manufacture (5 percent)

— Value of the raw materials that could be recovered (10 percent)

— Calculations of emissions used for transport of the package (10 percent)

Note: Categories and percentages are subject to change as the scorecard evolves.

There is, and will continue to be, a vigorous debate about the scorecard. On one side, some will say that it doesn't go far enough and should not become a standard; others argue that it goes too far and is not realistic.

"The Wood Reduction Trilogy" is a series by Watershed Media that takes a hard look at one of the planet's key resources for economic and environmental health. (*www.WatershedMedia.org*)

The truth will be somewhere in the middle, and the main benefit will be that these factors are now visible to suppliers, purchasers, and end users. It is likely that, over time, the debate will cool down. As suppliers comply with the scorecard system, they will benefit from decreased costs, increased market share, and a motivated workforce.

Readers will also observe that the 7Rs can be matched to the fundamental principles outlined throughout this book: Removing levels, reducing weight and size, and creating minimal structures are examples of ephemeralization (doing more with less) as well as triangulation (designing with minimal structures) and tensegrity (using tension and compression in tandem).

Design for Environment

A large body of material is available under this name. How can it inform the design process?

The Minnesota Pollution Control Agency researched best practice and created a product design guide that covers biomimicry, the basics of LCA, checklists, and information on how to design for recyclability.[57]

Design for disassembly: To be recycled effectively, objects must be able to be taken apart with minimal effort. How are materials joined in the design? Can parts be separated and discarded (safely!)? Can adhesives be eliminated?

Design for recyclability: Similar to the last item, are the components recyclable in the local system? Can they be disassembled easily to allow this to happen?

Design inspiration: Note the biomimicry section; can the design use these principles to reduce material or energy costs?

Reduce process steps: Each step adds energy.

Confirm that the piece:

— Avoids the need for using hazardous or restricted materials.

— Optimizes assembly (relates directly to disassembly).

— Avoids energy-intensive processes (e.g., multiple heat/cool cycles).

— Minimizes waste (avoiding surplus coating, cut-aways, trimming, by-products).

Consider changing printed pieces to information services or Web pages. Some copier makers have changed their business model from selling copiers, to leasing machines that make copies.

> The core idea is that nature, imaginative by necessity, has already solved many of the problems we are grappling with. Animals, plants, and microbes are the consummate engineers. They have found what works, what is appropriate, and most important, what lasts here on Earth. This is the real news of biomimicry: After 3.8 billion years of research and development, failures are fossils, and what surrounds us is the secret to survival.

—Janine M. Benyus, *Biomimicry: Innovation Inspired by Nature*

Design for the environment surprisingly coincides very well with design for manufacturability. (With) design for the environment, we have a lot of components and pieces of the hardware that snap together or can come apart easily, and that also benefits our manufacturing assembly time as well as the throughput rate of all of our products on the production floor. So not only do we get the environmental benefits, but we get the manufacturing benefits at the same time.

—Greg Vande Corput, Hardware Development Engineer, IBM (Better by Design video, 2004)

Cradle to Cradle[SM]

Cradle to Cradle is the idea of nature's systems made tangible by William McDonough and Michael Braungart in their book, *Cradle to Cradle: Remaking the Way We Make Things*.[58] The basic precept is that items of human use can be manufactured so that the biological and synthetic components are retained and reused safely and independently in endless recycling loops. The C2C approach is being used on design projects ranging from packaging to buildings but can be applied to any effort. A building using C2C ideas, for example, focuses on the effective use of energy and resources along with the creation of safe and uplifting environments for human occupation.

McDonough and Braungart define the "eco-effective" design methodology of C2C as one that strives for products and places that are "more

---

ecoEnvelopes began with the simple idea: Why use two envelopes, when the first one is still good? RSVPs and return billings can be sent in a single reusable, two-way envelope, reducing environmental impact and saving money with each mailing cycle. ecoEnvelopes are manufactured exclusively with Forest Stewardship Council and Sustainable Forestry Initiative certified papers, can be made with 100 percent post-consumer waste content, uses environmentally responsible inks and window films, and is recyclable when the final return trip is made. (ecoenvelopes.com)

To REUSE the envelope remove perforated patch carefully.

To REUSE the envelope remove perforated patch carefully.

ecoenvelopes

ecoenvelopes

ecoenvelopes

Presorted
First-Class Mail
US Postage PAID
ecoenvelopes

NO POSTAGE
NECESSARY IF
MAILED IN THE
UNITED STATES

Customer Name
1122 Second St.
New City, MN 55082

Place postage here

Place address here

reusable envelopes for people, profit, and the planet.

good," in distinction from "eco-efficient" design, which strives for products that are "less bad." A truly C2C product is considered to be 100 percent good in every category of evaluation.

Life works in cycles, yet it is all too common for a product's life to end in the landfill or be incinerated. This approach to design is called *cradle to grave*. Recall that many materials:

— Do not break down in the environment.

— Are captured in a landfill where decomposition is not possible.

— Only break down over decades or centuries.

— Emit harmful wastes or toxins if incinerated.

This end of life does not close a loop. Rather, it locks up materials and energy in forms that are not usable in the cycles of nature or technology and often pollute.

The alternative strategy is for object end of life as a new beginning, looping back either into the production process or into the biological system.

This is the idea of C2C: Model industrial cycles on natural processes, and ensure that these cycles are tied safely back to the Earth.

A life cycle analysis shows a negative cost at object end of life if it ends up in the landfill and a positive cost if it is recycled. Costs also can be higher for materials that come from nonrenewable sources.

In contrast, a C2C-modeled process intentionally reuses or recycles materials for another round of production, avoiding the life cycle costs of landfill or incineration and reducing the manufacturer's costs for source materials. To take this design approach further, it is possible to have positive impacts if end of life results in materials that are returned directly to the Earth and enrich soils.

Using this systems approach means that market growth is good, as objects created actually could improve ecosystems instead of just doing less damage to them.

A systems approach example is Rohner, a Swiss manufacturer of industrial textiles. Its processes required many dyes produced by chemical manufacturers that were always straightforward about the chemicals used, which put Rohner into a difficult position, as Swiss authorities then designated its process scraps as toxic waste. In addition to disposal and handling requirements, a toxic waste designation also meant the company could not use its scrap to fuel its internal heating system.

Luckily for Rohner, their customer Susan Lyons of Designtex was looking for a low-impact line of materials, and employed William McDonough and Michael Baungart Design Chemistry (MDBC).[59] They contacted all the dye manufacturers and finally were able to find one willing to share data on dye composition. After analyzing many thousands of dyes, they found enough that met the C2C requirements for human and ecological health to start the new product line. The results:

— New market opportunity

— Elimination of a regulatory burden

— Production scraps now sold as compost

— Reduced health risk for factory workers (since the new dyes are safe)

— Effluent water cleaner than the water coming into the factory

It is possible to create products with lower negative or even positive impacts by careful design and appropriate information about materials, without new inventions or custom processes.

A key perspective from C2C is that the original Industrial Revolution was not designed to create waste and pollution. Rather, these were side effects as easy access to energy and improved machinery allowed processing of materials in new ways. The results were effective economically, but since there was no design intent other than efficiency, there were many unforeseen results.

Today the impacts of material production, processing, and disposal are known. Using ideas such as C2C, it becomes possible to design objects with positive impact on Earth systems. This is a huge benefit psychologically, enabling designers to see sustainable design as a creative tool, a way to expand design freedom and see that growth can be good.

Cradle to cradle looks at two cycles: the *technical cycle* and the *biological cycle*. A key viewpoint in C2C is that product life cycles should not end by materials simply dumped into natural systems. C2C provides two alternative approaches:

1. *Technical cycle (technical mutrients):* The technical cycle uses products at end of life, or production waste, as input to a new production cycle. This creates a technical metabolism similar to the biological metabolism of the Earth.

2. *Biological cycle (biological nutrients):* Alternatively, create objects so the materials can be returned safely to the ecosystem in a way that improves natural systems. This is the biological cycle, and these are products of consumption since they get used up in the object's life cycle. An example is the banana peel returned to the compost pile.

Key Design Goals of Cradle to Cradle

Waste = food. Traditional industrial production saw waste as extra, not useful, to be thrown away. Today industry knows there is no "away." Everyone lives in the same biosphere, and what goes out one pipe comes in another. The result is that waste is now risk and cost. C2C ideas take note that nature continuously evolves to take advantage of material and energy flows. Instead of waste being cost and risk, can it be transformed into something useful that reduces risk and cost? What can waste be used for? Can it be transformed into something safe? Perhaps it can be looped back into the production cycle to make new objects. Waste then becomes an asset. Consider having the user return the object. Even if this is not as profitable in the short term as other approaches, it brings people back, increases their satisfaction, and can help with operations in other parts of the company. Consider the scavenger, living on the scraps that other species do not want.

Use current solar income. Virtually all variety on Earth was created with energy from the sun. The Industrial Revolution discovered stored solar energy as fossil fuel. For the past century, society has been on a wild ride spending down the bank account (natural capital). The by-products of this are climate change, increased energy costs, and vulnerability to supply disruptions. C2C ideas suggest that designers examine all processes to increase efficiency or lower energy usage. Move operations progressively toward a balance with current solar income. Enough sunlight hits the Earth every day to fuel society for a year.[60]

233

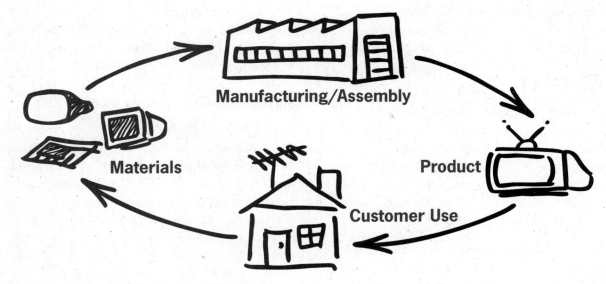

A product moving through a Cradle to Cradle^{SM}
Technical Nutrient Cycle.
Source: © MBDC

Celebrate diversity. In the rain forest, there are species at every level, from the ground to the treetops. This diversity allows the ecosystem to maximize capture of solar energy, and the interconnections make the system stronger and less vulnerable to changes. In contrast, a company with a single product is a monoculture and is very sensitive to environmental changes, in some cases becoming extinct with just the smallest shift.

Encouraging diversity benefits both the human and the natural community. There are a multitude of approaches to encourage diversity. Start by considering the kinds and sources of materials used in a project. Are they all from the same basic sources? Does the extraction of that material affect ecosystem diversity? Specify material sources that are more diverse and that enhance diversity in natural systems. A more diverse system is more robust and resilient to change.

C2C Design Strategies

To move a design toward a C2C strategy, it is essential to examine these process steps:

— Material sources

— Material processing

— Object creation (putting it all together)

— Object transport: To/from manufacturer, to distribution center, to end user

— Object use

— Object end of life

The "dimensions" of each process step are:

— waste = food

— solar income

— diversity

234

As one example, material sourcing may require the use of natural resources. Are these sources managed in a way that is sustainable and that will encourage diversity? What about the energy used to extract the materials? Can this be done on a solar equivalent basis (e.g., the energy comes from wind power)?

Similar examinations are done with material processing, considering the other chemicals entering the process. Where do they come from, what are their impacts?

It is useful to draw a process diagram showing where materials and energy come into the process at each step. Then move outside the product cycle and create a process diagram for each of these external inputs.[61]

Along with the process diagram for the overall product, consider assembly of components, how items are attached to each other, and what types of inks and extra materials are in the package. These items can affect the end phase of the package by impeding recycling or reuse.

Another perspective on C2C is to view the product life cycle and look for areas where particular tools can be employed. For example:

— Consider material impacts (toxicity, source reduction) in material acquisition, processing, manufacturing, and end of life.

— Design for reuse, recycling, and composting in material selection, acquisition, processing, and end of life.

— Consider energy use in material processing, material acquisition, and transport.

— Use recycled materials in materials acquisition, processing, and end of life.

— Consider biological diversity in material acquisition.

— Work toward weight reduction and design for transport in manufacturing and end of life.

— Choose best practices when selecting materials and suppliers.

— Know the chemistry of your package. Ask about green chemistry and engineering when checking supplier performance.

C2C Strategies to Close the Loop

Return to nature. To make a return to nature possible, the materials, processing, and any extra components in the item created have to be benign and able to break down readily in normal environments. Returning the object safely to the Earth enhances biological productivity, as in the Rohner textile company example.

Reuse of object. Reuse gives the highest return value, as no extra energy is needed and there are no landfill or incinerator costs. Objects must be designed to withstand being cycled through the distribution system.

Recapture of object. This method uses the object as a technical nutrient and requires coordination with manufacturing personnel. For example, virgin paper has one set of process conditions while recaptured paper has another. It is important to design this cycle effectively so the recaptured material is not downcycled (changed into material of lower value).

As one example of this recapture of technical nutrients, Shaw Contract Group leases its carpets to maintain a closed-loop system. Besides the positive environmental impacts, it gets return customers, who gain benefits from using a better product.[62]

When presenting the C2C concept to others, recall that present-day design processes are based on a world where constraints, impacts, and the end of the cycle weren't considered. This is not so much wrong as a simple view based on a past version of the world. Now more is known. This knowledge does not restrict design freedom; rather, it gives new paradigms and approaches to benefit both the company and the Earth.

C2C ideas suggest that designers move away from "doing less bad" to inventing new systems where the product life cycle is tied to natural cycles and the results improve Earth systems. This is a deeper and more powerful approach than merely sustaining. Imagine an industrial system where the waste products actually improved the Earth's ability to grow the crops required to build the product. This is an example of the carbohydrate economy, getting raw materials from plant-based systems.[63] The Carbohydrate Economy Web site notes:

> Carbohydrates, the building blocks of plant matter, can be converted into chemicals, energy, textiles, building materials, paper, and many other industrial products. We call this new materials base a "carbohydrate economy." A carbohydrate economy reduces pollution, builds stronger rural communities, and supports a rooted farmer-owned manufacturing sector.

The C2C approach sees intelligence and learning in natural systems ranging from sensitive use of materials, to efficiency, to solar energy. All works can benefit from that knowledge and create new loops that benefit the Earth.

As with Shaw Contract Group, a variety of other manufacturers have learned that getting materials back from customers minimizes production costs

and risks while also giving another point of contact that encourages repeat business and brand loyalty.

Checkpoints for C2C-Inspired Design

When considering the original source of materials and the impacts of processing, the next points are critical in the object creation system:

— What systems are needed to procure and process a design's materials?

Do the material systems use C2C guidelines?

— What are the material characteristics, and what is the impact on ecological and human health?

Use C2C design protocol[64] or LCA data.

— Design the object to aid recycling and recovery.

— Think of the object as a resource instead of a waste product.

— Reuse the object instead of recycling it.

Reuse retains more value.

— What systems are required for reuse?

— Return the object to a biological cycle by composting.

— Eliminate anything impacting reuse or recycling.

— Design the object to be an asset with user value.

RePruduct™ greeting cards and envelopes use synthetic paper vetted for both human and environmental health. Cards reach their first destination in a prepaid two-way envelope that can, with their greeting delivered, direct the card and envelope to Shaw Industries Group, which then converts 100 percent of the collected material to create carpet backing for new carpet tiles.

— Worst case: Design the object so it can be burned safely to recover energy.

— Make customers your partners when they return or compost the package.

— Work with other companies to:

Educate clients and distributors.

Increase market share of recycled and/or recyclable materials.

Create larger recycling opportunities.

Teach each other about inks, additives, labels, and decoration that hurts recycling.

Take a proactive stance, avoiding regulation.

Summary of Cradle to Cradle

Sustainability requires that the three domains of economy, society, and environment are satisfied. To aid in remembering this requirement, C2C uses a "fractal triangle" that illustrates the interconnection of ecology, economy, and equity (a society sharing resources equally among its members). The larger triangle is divided into smaller triangles, each of which is a combination of the aspects along that edge of the triangle. By using several triangles along each edge, the designer considers multiple interactions with the paired principles in each triangle alternating in strength, such as Economy/Equity or Economy/Ecology. In this way, two kinds of interaction are gained from each pairing. The essential question of each pair is: How can these two forces be resolved to add value? In practice, the areas with the most conflict offer the most opportunities for improvement.

C2C design principles are:

— Waste = food (evolve a system to use it).

— Use current solar income (don't spend down the bank account using limited mined or drilled resources, or irreplaceable old-growth diversity).

— Celebrate diversity (the world is full of niches).

Your Nearest Advantage May Be Behind You

Is sustainable design a new set of requirements and processes, or can it be related directly to things a company is already doing? Design is the first stage in a set of operations to create and deliver an end product. Designers pass their art on to others for production, and they in turn deliver their work product to the next stage. On the production side, many techniques have advanced sustainability in practice.

As just one example, production has always considered material sources and characteristics. The "dimensions" considered can be enlarged just as the definition of quality was enlarged earlier. Bottom

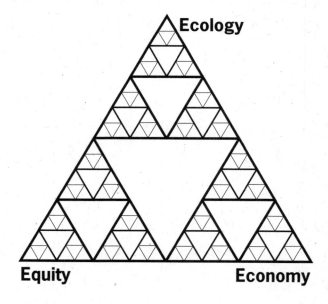

The fractal triangle of economy, environment, and society.
Text adaptation of Sierpinski Triangle to reflect triple-top-line ideas © MBDC.

line: Any of these practices can be a way to implement sustainability. With a few exceptions (materials bans, changes in pollution laws, etc.), nothing requires that companies must start from scratch or add new processes; they can start simply by reexamining their current systems.

Bad blueprints make bad houses, regardless of vision. Yet a good blueprint becomes a great house only when there are good workers to build it. An excellent architect learns from the workers (people who are actually touching the materials being used) what is practical and how to design for success. Since hindsight is 20/20, why not take advantage of it? If the ideas discussed next sound familiar, your company already may be on the path to making sustainable design part of its business model.

Note: A "Parallel from Nature" is provided for each production or quality approach. It is hoped that readers will connect these ideas with systems presented throughout this book and integrate the core principles into their design insights and strategies.

ISO 14000

Just as many companies in the late 1970s joined the quality revolution by embracing ISO 9000 as a quality system, many have now embraced sustainability by becoming ISO 14000 certified.

In a December 2008 *Package Design Magazine* article, ISO 14000 consultant and author Mariann Zanardo introduced (or reintroduced) readers to the ideas behind the certification:[65]

ISO 14001 is based on the Plan-Do-Check-Act (PDCA) Cycle, introduced in the 1950s by W. Edwards Deming. PDCA helps businesses improve customer satisfaction by analyzing and measuring sources of variations that cause products to deviate from customer requirements. When PDCA is applied to a process, the feedback given to managers helps them identify those parts of the process that can be improved upon. The cycle has four steps:

1. PLAN: Design or revise business process components to improve results

2. DO: Implement the plan and measure its performance

3. CHECK: Assess the measurements and report the results to decision makers

3. ACT: Decide on changes needed to improve the process

Coming on the scene in the 1990s, and gaining whole new followers today as companies push for eco-certified vendor partners, ISO 14000 encompasses a range of eco-activities. At its heart, though, is the requirement to do life cycle assessment on the whole of a company's efforts. While the detailed impacts of each material are beyond the standard, the requirements are clear: Define the system, identify the functions, perform life cycle assessment continuously as an improvement practice, record the results of the LCA and make them available to outside auditors.

A requirement of certification is that a company has an environmental management system (EMS) with the following characteristics:

— Document and manage the environmental impact of activities, products, or services.

— Continually improve environmental performance.

— Establish a system to set environmental goals, to accomplish them, and to document the performance.[66]

Levels of environmental performance are specific for each business and type of activity so they are not specified in the standard. The intent of the standard is to enable a consistent framework for reporting and managing environmental issues.

There are many other ISO standards for environmental issues, but ISO 14001: 2004 specifically is intended to provide a comprehensive and consistent approach on environmental issues, with generic requirements, as effective EMSs are the same regardless of business type or activity.

Given a consistent approach to EMSs, there is now a consistent approach to the communication of environmental issues.

Since the levels of environmental performance are not specified, organizations in a variety of fields and stages of development can use the standard. As with other quality standards, organizations must commit to comply with all applicable environmental legislation and regulations. In addition, the standard requires continuous improvement as a practice and that each company adopt continuous monitoring and improvement policies with regard to the environment.

PARALLEL FROM NATURE

In the wild, organisms can get away with an unfair advantage (taking more than an ecosystem can support for example), but not for very long. Being able to show verifiable eco-efforts is one way to attract like-minded partners and to continue to evolve as the environment (and the market) changes

in response to increases in ecosystem damage and resource demand.

Total Quality Management

In total quality management (TQM), or the house of quality, practitioners focus on continuous improvement of processes (visible, repeatable, and measurable in both production and design). Yet they also check to make sure the right product is being built and that all parts of the company are in agreement on that product. There is focus on making created objects work as they are supposed to, improving designs by looking at how people use them, and making an excellent design aesthetically. In agreement with TQM practice, sustainability means listening more closely to users and bringing their concerns into material and processing choices.

PARALLEL FROM NATURE

TQM can be seen as adaptation between organisms. In the natural world this is known as symbiosis. To survive, every organism must changes as the niche changes.

5S

This is an improvement process involving five steps (sort, set in order, shine, standardize, and sustain) to create and maintain a clean, neat, and orderly workplace. Some organizations add a sixth "S" for safety.

PARALLEL FROM NATURE

Scavengers reduce the waste materials in the bloodstream, creating an environment where the desired recombination can take place. Most biological processes take place by diffusion, requiring the presence of the correct materials in all locations without direct control of their motion.

Standard Work and Visual Controls

Standard work represents the best ("least-waste") way to perform a given operation. Visual controls are used to reinforce standardized procedures and to display the status of an activity so every employee can see it and take appropriate action. This is similar to the design language example where best practice is written down for all to see and learn from.

Organisms using the least materials and energy can survive in more environments. Visual cues (leaves sprouting, flowers blooming, and reflections of fish in water) trigger actions.

Cellular Manufacturing

Manufacturing work centers (cells) have the ability to produce an item or group of similar items. Changes in production requirements can easily be handled by adding parallel cells to produce more product.

PARALLEL FROM NATURE

All life is divided into cells, and work is distributed in parallel between them. Nutrients arrive "just in time" for absorption.

Just in Time/Kanban

The scheduling concept of just in time (JIT)/kanban requires that any item needed for an operation—raw material, finished product, or anything in between—is available precisely when needed. Kanban (signals) are used to control levels of inventory and work in process. In effect, this reduces the buffers in the system, allowing the production system to respond more precisely to changes.

PARALLEL FROM NATURE

Living systems use only what is present in front of them. Growth and change occur when triggered.

ANTIPARALLEL

Although squirrels are well known for their ability to store food (and body fat) for the long winter ahead, humans excel at storing materials and energy "for a rainy day" with no mechanism for the "forgotten nuts" reintegrating themselves back into natural systems.

Total Productive Maintenance

In total productive maintenance (TPM), enlist operators in the design, selection, correction, and maintenance of equipment to ensure that every machine or process can perform its required tasks without interruption. The TPM process puts the production stakeholders in charge of the most critical parameters of production. Knowledge of production capabilities enables optimal designs.

PARALLEL FROM NATURE

Cells persist by continually renewing each element, avoiding decay. Most human cells are replaced within seven years. This requires both a cell regeneration process and a scavenger process. The scavenger process can find unused materials and resources in your organization, improving efficiencies and increasing profitability.

Six Sigma

Six sigma reduces variation and thereby scrap, yet it is also a design practice that looks carefully at choice of materials, the fit between design and user need, material processing, and how to minimize variation. Six sigma has experts (black belts) who move from project to project, doing optimization and spreading knowledge.

PARALLEL FROM NATURE

RNA/DNA copying is amazingly precise in general and has an error rate similar to six sigma. Bees pollinate (spread flowers' DNA) as they move from flower to flower.

Advanced Lean Enterprise Methods

Pre-production planning (3P) is the lean method for product and/or process design. It designs and implements production processes, tools, and equipment that support one-piece flow, are designed for ease of manufacturing, and achieve appropriate cost, quality, and lead time. Minimize energy and material use in the manufacturing process by looking at every step of the process, from design, to material acquisition, to material processing, to product quality. For every step, determine where efficiencies can be improved, material reused, or energy use decreased. Doing this reduces costs along with environmental impact.

PARALLEL FROM NATURE

Evolution (variation and selection) produces organisms with minimal materials and energy use. Consider some hummingbirds, which migrate nonstop across the Gulf of Mexico.

Lean Enterprise Supplier Networks

Lean enterprise supplier networks are sets of buyer-supplier relationships where organizations apply lean production concepts across the supply chain to reduce costs, delays, and other wastes.

PARALLEL FROM NATURE

Consider the mollusk, which grows its shell in seawater using available chemicals and generates no toxic waste.

Backstory on Production Processes

Life evolves by recombination of functional units. For example, there are only twenty amino acids but hundreds of proteins. The English language has twenty-six letters and a few rules of grammar. Yet out of it comes Shakespeare and rap!

Designers create using the existing functional units, combining them to come up with new solutions. When the design is approved, it heads to production, where the rules are different. Now the design needs to be replicated reliably over and over again. If the design calls for capabilities that aren't present in the production process, it will not succeed. Design must be done in an environment of full production knowledge.

If design is sexual recombination, production is the DNA/RNA transcription happening in our cells constantly.

Innovation Heuristics

The systems approach can be used to transform designs from static "things" into flows within natural cycles. This is the basis of innovation in design. The flow is the system—from material creation through processing, assembly, distribution, and recycling.

Flow is dynamization, making a process more dynamic or flexible. Design the system first and then the object to live within it. This dynamic process starts by dividing the object into pieces (segmentation) and moves through ever-finer gradations until objects are replaced by services.

Lightness is closely related to flow. How light can the end product be? Can the materials be chosen for the lowest impact? The material in this section covers a variety of approaches to transform design.

Design Rules

— *Stop the use of inappropriate materials:* Objects created shall not last longer than the thing they were created to serve.

— *Expand the space of design knowledge:* Use the power of teams and diversity.

— *Use evolution as a guide:* Experiment continuously.

— *All things live in ecological niches:* Listen and be guided by the user.

— *Move beyond local limits:* Harness the power of open source to improve knowledge and networks.

TECHNIQUE: Create your own set of five to seven innovation heuristics and share them.

Basics of Innovation

Innovation is applied creativity. Some fundamental areas for innovation:

— *Location:* Where (design, designer, user).

— *Direction:* Why (what your principles are).

— *Materials:* What they are (good and bad).

— *Cycles:* How to use them.

— *Users:* Who they are, their needs, desires, and interactions.

Innovation occurs in:

— *People:* Changing design practice, changing an object's use.

— *Process:* New ways to produce objects.

— *Objects:* Providing a function with greater advantage.

Innovation can be:

— *Incremental:* Increasing the good qualities, decreasing the bad qualities.

— *Transformational:* Providing a service instead of a product.

— *Disruptive:* Changing the nature of the industry.

Movement toward a goal or ideal design can occur at the level of people, process, or end piece.

At the level of people, designers need to know where they are. This can happen only when their methods and means of interaction with the world—the design principles—have been documented.[67]

TECHNIQUE: Create your own set of design principles.

Ecological Design Principles

According to Sim van der Ryn:[68]

— *Solutions grow from place:* Keep it local.

— *Ecological accounting informs design:* Know your material and energy flows.

— *Design with nature,* not against it

— *Everyone is a designer:* Take advantage of different viewpoints and knowledge.

— *Make nature visible:* Let it shine in the design.

According to John Todd:[69]

— The living world is the matrix for all design.

— Design should follow, not oppose, the laws of life.

— Biological equity must determine design.

— Design to reflect bioregionality.

— Base projects on renewable energy.

— Use the integration of living systems to design.

— Design as evolution along with the natural world.

— Design to heal.

Process Innovation

At the level of process, designers need to know material qualities and transformations.

Materials are the world of form. What can be made? What effect does it have? Can it be cycled back into production or left in the environment? Is it possible to let it "evaporate," leaving a web?

Transformations occur via energy, organization, or information. For example, plastics can be transformed with heat and pressure (energy). Companies can be transformed by organization as levels of hierarchy are reduced and interconnections formed. Societies can be transformed as information about the results of processes (industrial or political) is made available.

Design Innovation

At the level of design, consider function, system, and end users. To innovate with function, consider providing the design as a service rather than a tangible good.

Systems can be designed to transform the world as it exists or to create new structures via interconnection. For example, sharing products (e.g., power tools) creates new systems as well as new opportunities for design.

The practice of user-influenced design requires that designers forget their unique knowledge of typical techniques and solutions. Instead, they should explore and define the functions users are most interested in. Ask users how they are using the existing design and what features are missing.

Designers can learn to place themselves into the users' world, and then project user needs and desires back to innovate. Alternatively, users can be interviewed (lead user process)[70] to find out preferences and how they use the design.

Innovations can be classified as quality improvement, new market creation, design range extension, reduction of labor or material or impact or energy, improvements in process, replacing products with services, or adapting to constraints (including regulation).[71]

Design Mindfulness

According to John Thackara:[72]

— Think about the consequences of design.

— Most impacts come from design decisions.

— Consider the material and energy flows of creation and use.

— Give priority to humans.

— Deliver value to people.

— Know that place, time, and cultural differences are positive values.

— Create services, not things.

Other design strategies from Thackara:

Learn from users: Innovation is becoming user led, as exemplified by Wikipedia and open source solutions. Use that same power of multiple intelligences by being open to design solutions from users. Enlarge design thinking by including the Earth and the end user. Quiet down the "maker" mind-set that knows all about solutions and jumps to design decisions.

Follow user needs: Users have needs. How does the design satisfy the need? What is excess? What is an irritant about the design? The creativity tool Triz[73] notes that there are two ways to improve a design: Increase the good factors or decrease the bad factors.

Study how the object lives: Use context. How is the end piece used? Get it home, read it, toss it? Consider egg carton packaging loaded with seeds that the kids want to plant. Think they will remember that brand?

Solution space: Enlarge the thinking space in the company. Bring in ideas from Nature (biomimicry). Encourage others to see the design as a spaceship or alien.

Mobility: The Internet has sped up the material economy and its flows. Now a book arrives overnight and goods come from the other coast. On an individual basis, lower environmental impact by thinking more and driving less. From a company perspective, the same holds true—this is the lesson from operations research, where the activities at a company are studied to make optimal decisions about resource allocation. Consider where materials come from, the processing location, and how designs get from the company to the next step in the chain. Perhaps transport markings aren't a layer on top of individual pieces. Make all designs local.

Locality: Instead of moving things faster, make them closer. Local products are a growing market, and the things we create are a big part of that. Make the thing itself locally, and it will sell the product (made right here in Lake Wobegon!). Consciously design for going deeper instead of searching farther. Everything is particular: Design for each situation.

Experiment: Design implies intent, knowing the outcome. Evolution shows that variation and selection lead to variety and solutions that optimize fit into the local environment. Practice experimentation, not design. Start with small experiments. Try several, don't invest everything in one.

Appropriate-use case models: Don't design for the worst case. Eighty percent of all traffic is local, 15 percent is continental, and 5 percent is international. This holds for everything from cars to the Internet. Consider the time cycle of the design: Design to represent ideal life.

Connect designs, content, and people: Life is structured via connections—use webs, chains, and networks. Most people want big-city amenities and a small-city pace.

Design Approaches

— Design tends to converge on single (point) solutions. Rather, diverge outward from the center (Fuller's dimensions).

— Innovation thrives in adversity, creating novel adaptations. Design without constraints can look like last year's or, worse, a competitor's works.

— Requirement changes are part of life. Learn how to adapt to, and anticipate, changing requirements.

— Pay attention to flow: design, information, mind-set of peers, changes in the economy. Emulate the flexibility of agile software development strategy. Teams meet every morning for a few minutes to determine top priorities for the day and to track requirements changes.

— Create friendly design—pieces that bring people together and create community.

— Move from design of objects to creation of service.

— Consider local exchanges and trades, sharing resources, time, and skills: Extend family to community. Use social and business networks to enlarge your design community.

— Design using the universals of culture. If the design seems to fit in one market, consider what other context it is used in. For example, household articles might be used in play and recreation, or a beautiful sustainable design could define a new market.

— Consider how a design fits one or more of these areas outlined by Alice Ann Cleaveland, Jean Craven, and Maryanne Danfelser, who have extended the work of George Murdock on cultural universals:[74]

  — *Material culture:* Food, clothing, tools, housing, transportation, possessions

  — *Arts, play, and recreation:* Music, arts, design

  — *Language and nonverbal communication:* Books, language, video

  — *Social organization:* Societies, families, networks

— The information space of the designer and user are different: Consider how to make messages "sticky" and how to represent the message of sustainability.

Design Using Universal Principles

Gravitation: What pulls the design into the Earth? What grounds the design and designer?

Dimension: Spin, radiate/converge, orbit, invert, torque, precess.

Trimtab: Use a small rudder to change the big rudder.

Boundary, flows, and loops: Chart design flows.

Use viral or meme design techniques: What would cause a message or piece to attach to a user? Consider hook and loop tape or sticky seeds.

Similar to these examples, a meme is a behavior or piece of information that passes from one person to another. For memes to propagate, one user exhibits a behavior that others copy. The rapid popularity of white MP3 player earbuds is a good example. The idea jumps from one mind to the next, and behavior is copied and reinforced.

Other Design Strategies

Consider how the user interacts with the design and end product. Consider design as a teacher: How can the design promote learning or literacy in general terms or for sustainability?

Biomimicry asks us to follow nature by exchanging complication for biological inspiration.

Consider the state of the industry: How does it mirror the ecosystem's maturity level? Is it a stable mature forest, or are there open areas where new species are growing rapidly? Should the design (and business) move toward or away from areas like these?

⑤ Materials and Processes

Wendy Jedlička, CPP
o2 International Network for Sustainable Design

Dion Zuess
ecoLingo: earth friendly graphic design

With additional contributions from:
Paul Andre, Sharell Benson, Jeremy Faludi, Carbonless Promise, Chlorine Free Products Association, Eureka Recycling, Environmental Paper Network, National Recycling Coalition, Organic Design Operatives, Great Printer Environmental Initiative, Sustainable Green Printing Partnership,[SM] Sustainable Packaging Coalition[SM]

Creativity can solve almost any problem. The creative act, the defeat of habit by originality, overcomes everything.

—*George Lois*

Resources are Earth's gifts to be shared with the future.
*Photo: Halsey1.com,
Paper Art: Amalia Benlian.*

We've seen that, in theory, picking an eco-material is a better move than picking an un-eco one. But if one doesn't know why a material is eco, how to use it correctly, or even if it actually is eco, taking a typically shallow replacement approach can end up with impacts far worse than the thing being replaced.

Materials

Paper or Plastic? Neither!

Like so many things humans have made over time, what was once a handy nicety has become an environmental nightmare. Eco-minded businesses, communities, and even whole countries around the world, are banning limited-use (disposable, one-use) totes with increasing frequency, particularly plastic bags. Unlike paper bags, which do break down on their own like most wood-based products, plastic bags stay in the environment for 400 to 1,000 years, clogging up drainage (making flooding worse) and killing wildlife. Due to their longevity in the environment, plastic bags accumulate (both in whole form and as bioavailable particulates), and have gone "from being rare in the late 1980s and early 1990s to being almost everywhere from Spitsbergen 78° North [latitude] to Falklands 51° South [latitude]," notes David Barnes, a marine scientist with the British Antarctic Survey.[1] "Trashing the Oceans," by Thomas Hayden, in the November 4, 2002, U.*S. News & World Report*, gives a particularly sobering account of plastic's impact on marine life.

As the debate rages on, when the question of paper versus plastic comes up, careful examination of the "facts" are in order.

Comparing the Numbers

Published on May 19, 2000, in the *Government Gazette*, South Africa undertook to study the question of paper versus plastic as part of proposed new plastic bag regulations under Section 24 of the Environmental Conservation Act (73/1998). Two life cycle studies—from production to disposal—of paper versus plastic bags showed contradictory results.[2]

Study 1: 1/6 barrel grocery sacks (plastic)

— Primary energy: Plastic life cycle uses 23.08 percent less

— Solid waste: Plastic life cycle produces 75.68 percent less

— Abiotic resource depletion: Category not considered

— Global warming: Category not considered

— Acidification: Category not considered

— Nutrient enrichment: Category not considered

— Photochemical ozone formation: Category not considered

— Aquatic ecotoxicity: Category not considered

— Air emissions: Plastic life cycle contributes 57.45 percent less

— Water emissions: Plastic life cycle has 96.58 percent fewer.

Each FEED 100 bag provides 100 school meals to hungry children in Rwanda through the UN World Food Program (WFP). FEED Projects started in 2006 when model and activist Lauren Bush designed a bag to benefit the WFP's School Feeding operations. All FEED products are made as eco-friendly and fairly as possible, are produced with 100 percent organic cotton and natural burlap, and are manufactured by audited and certified fair labor facilities. The hangtags for the FEED 100 bags shown here were printed by Greg Barber Printing (gregbarberco.com) on 100 percent post-consumer waste (PCW) recycled, and certified processed chlorine-free (PCF) stock.

Study 2: 25 kg (capacity) distribution sacks (paper)

— Primary energy: Paper life cycle uses 80.00 percent less

— Solid waste: Category not considered

— Abiotic resource depletion: Paper life cycle depletes 85.00 percent less

— Global warming: Paper life cycle contributes 95.69 percent less

— Acidification: Paper lifecycle contributes 53.79 percent less

— Nutrient enrichment: Plastic life cycle 55.36 percent less

— Photochemical ozone formation: Paper life cycle contributes 64.04 percent less

— Aquatic ecotoxicity: Paper life cycle contributes 37.04 percent less

— Air emissions: Paper life cycle contributes 52.23 percent less

— Water emissions: Paper life cycle contributes 28.79 percent less

An analysis of the two studies showed that location and scope of the assessments can result in drastically different conclusions.

Deeper review would require addressing who funded each study; the disposable tote industry is huge. There is also the issue of deeper life cycle issues (cradle-to-cradle solar cycle), which is not illustrated in the comparison given. Paper bags are usually recycled wherever paper-recycling facilities exist (very common). Plastic bags and plastics in general don't enjoy the same recycling rates that paper manages. Limited-use paper bags sequester carbon from today's carbon/solar cycle for the whole time they remain as paper, no matter how many times they are reused and recycled. When burned, paper bags release what they had sequestered from today's carbon/solar cycle. Limited-use plastic bags, made from a nonrenewable fossil fuel, simply add in the ancient carbon they had been sequestering for millions of years on top of today's carbon and toxin load when burned, as is their fate in many markets. It should be noted, though, when talking about burning fossil fuels, plastic bags are lighter and thinner for the same carrying capacity, and so less petroleum is used to move them around and to store them versus paper. So again, the debate rages on. Or does it?

In reality, when the question is paper or plastic for a product with a very limited use life, the answer is, should be, and should have always been: Neither.

What Are We Trashing?

What we throw away says a lot about a society. Archeologists spend whole careers finding and analyzing ancient peoples' castoffs. What will future generations think of us when they crack open a landfill? Today discards range from packaging, food scraps and grass clippings, to old sofas, computers, tires, and refrigerators. In 2007, the United States Environmental Protection Agency (EPA) released its most recent review of municipal solid waste (MSW). Of the 254.1 million tons of things we throw away, paper and paperboard made up over a third of the waste, the largest portion of waste generated. In all, Americans recovered 85 million tons of resources through recycling. An impressive figure, but this is only 33.4 percent of the total waste.[3] Recovery figures, though improving, are still way lower than other developed countries. In addition, though these figures now include organics for composting, this is still a resource recovery system that is way under-supported in the United States, though very popular in other countries.

2007 U.S. RECYCLING RATES	%
Yard trimmings	64.1
Paper and paperboard	54.5
Metals	34.8
Other materials	26.2
Glass	23.7
Textiles	15.9
Rubber and leather	14.7
Wood	9.3
Plastics	6.8
Food	2.6

Paper and paperboard recovery in the United States, according to the EPA report, rose to over 54.4 percent; metals were recycled at a rate over 34 percent, while about 64 percent of yard trimmings were recovered. Commonly used metals like aluminum and steel can be recycled into new products and packaging nearly indefinitely. Their low recovery rate then adds insult to injury, locking up otherwise super valuable materials in landfills, rather than keeping them in a useful closed-loop system (Cradle to Cradle *technical nutrient*). In addition to maintaining access to these valuable resources, by recycling nearly 7 million tons of metals the EPA calculates Americans eliminated what would otherwise have been about 6.5 million metric tons of carbon equivalent (MMTCE) greenhouse gas (GHG) emissions. This is equivalent to removing more than 5 million cars from the road for one year. Imagine the impacts if the recycling rates for metals were at 100 percent!

In an effort to encourage better consumer participation in recycling, starting in 2009 many of the pet food brands manufactured by Purina (the largest maker of canned pet food in the Unites States) will begin allocating label space for stronger recycling messages. Given the small physical size of some of their canned products this is a really big deal. Purina packaging with a bit more area to play with will feature "did you know" facts to help further consumer's recycling awareness. Facts like, "Did you know making a 'new' aluminum can from recycled aluminum takes 95 percent less energy than producing the same can from virgin ore?"—will help the consumer better connect with their part in a product's life cycle, and how their participation really does make a significant difference in resource use.

Mark Brodeur, Director of Sustainability for Purina PetCare North America notes, "It's our responsibility to educate and engage consumers on the many benefits of recycling our cans . . . As the largest manufacturer of wet pet food in the U.S., we produced over 3 billion aluminum and steel cans last year, which are 100% recyclable."[4]

Looking further at how to improve recycling rates, individual states are taking a much more aggressive stance on resource management, with higher than national average results.

According to the California Department of Conservation's *Six-Month Report of Beverage Container Recycling and Significant Carbon Reductions,* the state's beverage container recycling rate rose to 76 percent over the study period of January to June 2008, up from 71 percent in 2007, which in turn was up from 65 percent for the same period in 2006. In addition, California figures for glass container recycling continue to be much higher than the national average for the United States. In the United Kingdom, recycling rates for glass containers (e.g., bottles and jars) is around 50 percent. The figure has doubled in recent years but still lags behind other countries—for example, Switzerland and Finland recycle more than 90 percent of their glass containers.

According to the 2008 *Six-Month Report,* each year California consumes 714 million barrels of oil (up from 657 in 2007) and emits 479 million metric tons of greenhouse gases (down from 492 in 2007). California's beverage container recycling effort from January through June 2008 saved the equivalent of 3.3 million barrels of oil and reduced the equivalent of 311,000 metric tons of carbon in greenhouse gas emissions.[5]

As both citizen and industrial demand increase, governments will be forced to implement new, more forward-thinking, and more egalitarian systems for resource use.

Imagine what it would be like if the successes in California could be duplicated all over the United States. Using California's example to show what can be done within a U.S. market system, the nation might begin to approach the impact reductions other countries have already achieved.

If It Can't Be Grown, It Must Be Mined

Where does your cell phone, your furniture, your shoes—all your stuff come from? Before the store, before the factory, where is the real beginning? If it isn't made of wood, cloth, or other living matter, it was dug out of the ground. The first of the Natural Step's four system conditions is: "In the sustainable society, nature is not subject to systematically increasing concentrations of substances extracted from the Earth's crust." Ultimately, one day our industrial economy will be made up entirely of recycled and biologically grown material. That day, however, is a long way off. How do we get there, and what is the world of mining like today? How rapidly are we depleting the minerals we have, and how do we get to sustainable mining?

Current Usage

The Robinson Mine in eastern Nevada (also called the Liberty Pit mine) was one of the biggest copper mines in the world. Today a shadow of its former self, the mine is now mostly piles of tailings (leftover rock and dirt that doesn't contain ore). Climbing up a pile of tailings, one can see they are gigantic, stretching over a mile wide and over four miles long. A future civilization stumbling on them might think them earthen-mound architecture. According to literature available at the site in 2005: "Every year 40,000 pounds of minerals must be provided for every person in the United States to maintain [his or her] standard of living." According to 2007 statistics from the Mineral Information Institute (*www.mii.org*), the United States requires about 46,000 pounds of minerals for each person, each year, to maintain their standard of living.

UNITED STATES PER CAPITA LIFETIME MINERAL USE:

911 lb lead

1,398 lb copper

1.546 Troy oz gold

32,654 lb iron ore

5,417 lb bauxite (aluminum)

773 lb zinc

18,447 lb phosphate rock

31,909 lb salt

20,452 lb clays

75,047 lb cement

82,169 gal petroleum

578,956 lb coal

5.71 million cu ft natural gas

1.72 million lb stone, sand, and gravel

Plus 68,0341 lb other minerals and metals

These numbers do not include tailings; the ratio of tailings to ore can be huge. The concept of an "ecological rucksack" measures how many kilos of material must be mined (or grown) to produce one kilogram (kg) of end product.

According to a report by NOAH, the Danish Friends of the Earth, every 1 kg of gold in the hand carries an invisible history of 540,000 kg material in its ecological rucksack.[6] A few other notable metals in the report: Polyethylene's rucksack is a mere 2.4 kg "abiotic" material per kg end material; copper's is 356 kg/kg; stainless steel's is 23 kg/kg; and virgin aluminum's is 66 kg/kg; while recycled aluminum is just 1.2 kg/kg. Ecological rucksack calculations in NOAH's report also include water and air. In addition to the ecological rucksack, there is sometimes a social cost as well.

Everyone is familiar with "blood diamonds," but gold often is mined under inequitable circumstances. In the 1990s, tantalum, used in high-temperature applications such as aircraft engines; electrical devices, such as capacitors; surgical implants; and handling corrosive chemicals, was responsible for much bloodshed and endangered species habitat loss in the Congo.

The phrase "maintaining the standard of living" is often called out as a reason for continuing certain practices. Most people probably assume that using fewer minerals means lowering our standard of living, but the phrase is carefully neutral. If we find organic alternatives to these materials, our standard of living might even improve. For instance, as *ScienceDaily* has pointed out, carbon nanotubes can exhibit "electrical conductivity as high as copper, thermal conductivity as high as diamond, strength 100 times greater than steel at one sixth the weight, and high strain to failure."[7] Although nanotubes are currently very resource intensive to make, the field is still in its infancy, and the carbon used to make them is the most common element on earth.

A more immediate example is renewable energy. Over 22,000 pounds of the mining listed earlier is for energy: oil, gas, and coal. Growing biodiesel from algae to replace petroleum mined from the Earth shows how our standard of living could actually improve with less mining, by having safer vehicle emissions and less carbon dioxide buildup in the atmosphere. Wind power replacing coal shows how our lives could improve while radically reducing mining impacts. The Mineral Information Institute offers some interesting facts on mineral use in daily life. Did you know a computer screen uses feldspar and a hair tie uses clay and phosphorus?

The U.S. Geological Survey has an excellent report, "Materials in the Economy—Material Flows, Scarcity, and the Environment," with legions of data.[8] While much of it seems grim, it offers hope as well. For instance, today only about 5 percent of material used in the United States is from renewable sources, but in 1900, 40 percent was renewable, showing that using renewable energy is possible and doesn't even require high technology. Much of the nonrenewable material in use is invisible to us: "Crushed stone and construction sand and gravel make up as much as three quarters (by weight) of new resources used annually." The average person probably doesn't go out and buy gravel; it's used mostly to build and repair the roads we drive on. One of the simplest ways to reduce mining impact is simply to drive less, reducing the need for more or expanded roads as well as reducing the demand for fossil fuels.

The report also has some good news about metal recycling:

Recycling contributed 80.7 million tons of metal, valued at about $17.7 billion, or more than half of metal apparent supply by weight in 2000 . . . recycled sources supplied 63 percent of lead; 55 percent of iron and steel; 50 percent of titanium; more than 30 percent of aluminum, copper, and magnesium; and more than 20 percent of chromium, tin, and zinc.

Peak Minerals

How much mining can the Earth sustain? The answer is not quite zero, as one might think from the Natural Step principle. Mineral compounds can slowly return to the Earth's crust on their own. Steel can rust away in a few decades, and aluminum takes between 200 and 500 years to degrade. Estimates vary widely, but the State of Nevada presents a list of how quickly various materials degrade; compare an aluminum can's degradation rate (500 years) to that of a Styrofoam cup ("May be around forever").[9] But minerals and ores are clearly a nonrenewable resource on the time scale of our lives—they are not current solar income by any stretch of the imagination. Some researchers have begun to argue that just as we are hitting peak oil, we will soon be hitting peaks for other mined resources and have already passed peaks for some. The Italian chemist Ugo Bardi published a research paper, "The Oil Drum: Europe," an abstract of which follows.[10]

We examined the world production of 57 minerals reported in the database of the United States Geological Survey (USGS). Of these, we found eleven cases where production has clearly peaked and is now declining. Several more may be peaking or be close to peaking. Fitting the production curve with a logistic function, we see that, in most cases, the ultimate amount extrap-

Surface mining operation.
Photo: Jeremy Faludi.

olated from the fitting corresponds well to the amount obtained, summing the cumulative production so far and the reserves estimated by the USGS. These results are a clear indication that the Hubbert model is valid for the world-wide production of minerals and not just for regional cases. It strongly supports the concept that "peak oil" is just one of several cases of worldwide peaking and decline of a depletable resource. Many more mineral resources may peak worldwide and start their decline in the near future.

The resources Bardi and coauthor Marco Pagani found to be peaking were mercury, tellurium, lead, cadmium, potash, phosphate rock, thallium selenium, zirconium, rhenium, and gallium—most of which are key components in computers and other electronics. How serious is the issue of "peak minerals"? *New Scientist* released a report with excellent charts plotting expected years to depletion for twenty of the most-used minerals as well as the percent recycled, the amount an average U.S. consumer will use in a lifetime, and a map of the world showing where the various metals are mined.[11] According to the report, copper has between thirty-eight and sixty-one years left before depletion, indium (used in liquid crystal display [LCD] monitors) has between four and thirteen years, silver (used in catalytic converters and jewelry) has between nine and twenty-nine years, and antimony (used in flame retardants and some drugs) has between thirteen and thirty years. The market already knows this in a dim way—copper prices have tripled in the past decade, and as the report points out, indium is even worse: "In January 2003 the metal sold for around $60 per kilogram; by August 2006 the price had shot up to over $1000 per kilogram."

As with peak oil, the economics of this situation both help and hurt. They hurt because higher ore prices make it more economically viable to do larger-scale mining at lower rates of return, causing more destruction per unit of product. The economics of scarcity help because mining for virgin materials becomes more expensive, so alternative materials and recycling become more economical by comparison. British geologist Hazel Prichard discovered in 1998 that platinum dust from cars' catalytic converters covers roadsides in the United Kingdom in high enough concentrations that sweeping up road dust and extracting the platinum will soon be cheaper than mining and refining the ore. The *New Scientist* article mentioned earlier says Prichard and fellow researcher Lynne Macaskie are "developing a bacterial process that will efficiently extract the platinum from the dust." The report also suggests pulling copper pipes out of buildings and replacing them with plastic, effectively mining buildings.

Greening the Mining Industry

How sustainably run are mines? It varies wildly, both by country and by industry. A 2006 *Geotimes* article described the current situation in the United States as being a mess, but several other countries were doing well:[12]

The current impasse between environmentalists and industry, however, is unique among advanced nations. The United States conflict contrasts especially sharply with policy in Sweden, where a dynamic mining and mineral industry coexists with a strong national environmental commitment in a high-wage, strong economy. The Swedish policy model, as well as Canadian and Finnish models, may not be applicable to current United States sociopolitical conditions, but they offer important perspectives on potential ways to break out of the current standoff.

Pressure is being put on mining companies, thanks to organizations like the Environmental Working Group, which makes information more available to activists. The group has a Google Maps mash-up of the western United States that maps literally hundreds of thousands of mines and mining claims; existing mines can even be viewed in Google Earth on its three-dimensional terrain maps. The group points out that there are "815 mining claims within 5 miles of Grand Canyon National Park." And the Grand Canyon is hardly unique: Arches, Dinosaur, Capitol Reef, Death Valley, and many other parks are in areas where mining is the backbone of the local economy.

Mining is already getting cleaner, though it has a long way to go. In 2000, the United States EPA's Toxics Release Inventory[13] listed metal mining as responsible for a whopping 47 percent of all toxic waste released by industry in the country; its 2005 report listed metal mining at just 27 percent. The increase is not due to other industries dumping more; 2000 releases were a nationwide total of 7.1 billion pounds, while 2005's total was 4.34 billion pounds, over 30 percent less. A significant amount of this savings is no doubt due to offshoring environmental burdens to mines and manufacturing facilities in poorer countries, but a significant amount is due to better practices as well, and recycling is growing. The *Encyclopedia of Earth* talks about one of the world's largest mining companies, Noranda, Inc., of Canada, which investigated ways to make its smelters more profitable. Through its study, it found recyclable materials to be as important to the operation's profitability as essential ore concentrates.[14]

Several organizations are dedicated to more sustainable mining. Good Practice (*www.goodpracticemining.org*) is an informational Web site. The Initiative for Responsible Mining Assurance (IRMA) is a multisector effort to develop a voluntary system to independently verify compliance with environmental, human rights, and social standards for mining operations. Participants in IRMA include Walmart, World Wildlife Fund, DeBeers Group, Oxfam America, and Tiffany & Co. (*www.responsiblemining.net*).

The strategies for sustainable material use are the classics: reduce, reuse, recycle on a massive industrial scale. The USGS report recommends the classic three Rs (Reduce, Reuse, Recycle) as well as remanufacturing (a mixture of reuse and recycling) and landfill mining. Landfills will soon have higher concentrations of useful ores than virgin ground; for some elements, they already do. We must also look to grow alternatives to many of the materials we now mine. This is where McDonough and Braungart's concepts of "technical nutrients" and "biological nutrients" come into sharp focus.

Technical nutrients are things that at some point needed to be mined but in the long run must be used in a closed loop, not combined with biological nutrients (because separate they are useful, but conjoined they are garbage). Biological nutrients are those that can be farmed or otherwise grown, but these also need not to exceed the available land's carrying capacity. Even if we could replace all minerals in industry with functional equivalents grown from organic matter, it still might not be the wisest course of action. The wisest course is to close the resource loops and keep them easily separable, so all ingredients can retain their value. Both sustainable harvests and closed-loop recycling are needed to create a viable system. There is no single answer to meet all needs.

In 1900, 40 percent of United States materials used were renewable; now the standard of living is much higher, but renewable materials have fallen to 5 percent. In many poor rural parts of India and Africa today, the vast majority of materials used are renewable and local, but the standards of living are low, and much of the younger generation leaves for cities when given the opportunity. We must find ways to make the best of the resources we have, to create a universal quality of life even higher than today's and shared by all.

Article by Jeremy Faludi. Original article concept appeared on www.worldchanging.org, *December 25, 2007.*

The wisest course is to close the resource loops and keep them easily separable, so all ingredients can retain their value. Both sustainable harvests and closed-loop recycling are needed to create a viable system.

Paper

Paper provides an important role in our society yet its current sourcing and manufacturing from tree fiber puts forests and indigenous peoples at risk. Deforestation affects habitats and ecosystems and globally contributes to climate change. Trees naturally remove carbon dioxide (CO_2) from the atmosphere and store or sequester it as carbon within their trunks, branches, leaves, roots, and surrounding soil.

Nearly half of the trees cut in North America go to papermaking,[15] and according to WoodWise, a forest area the size of twenty football fields is lost every minute to paper production.[16] Ironically, much of this valuable resource is trashed after use—paper products and paperboard are the largest component of the nation's municipal solid waste.[17] Purchasing papers from tree-free or alternative fibers offer options worth considering and can take pressure off forests.

It is important to ensure that wood-based paper is not sourced from ancient or endangered forests or from indigenous communities that have been impacted by logging and land right conflicts. Sustainable forest management and third-party certification programs with their corresponding logos, trade names, marks, or seals are valuable guides for purchasing a variety of wood products, including paper.

Papermaking is resource intensive. Chlorine effluents and water quality issues abound, as do air quality and pollution issues. Paper recycling plays a vital role not only in conserving trees and wood fiber; the recycling process also saves water, reduces the need for chemicals, and decreases energy usage compared to manufacturing virgin pulp into paper. Paper mills are exploring and using methods to

Photo: Halsey1.com

generate energy from waste generated from manufacturing, and several mills are switching to renewable energy or are purchasing carbon offsets to reduce their carbon footprints.

In the United States alone, graphic designers purchase or specify billions of dollars for printing and paper annually.[18] As such, designers have the potential to play a powerful role as change agents and market leaders, guiding sustainable design practices and responsible paper choices.

Designers have the potential to play a powerful role as change agents and market leaders, guiding sustainable design practices and responsible paper choices.

Recycling 1 ton of paper saves

— 17 trees (35-foot tall)

— 7,000 gallons of water

— 2 barrels of oil (enough fuel to run the average car for 1,260 miles or from Dallas to Los Angeles)

— 4100 kilowatts of energy (enough power for the average home for 6 months)

— 3.2 cubic yards of landfill space (one family-size pickup truck)

— 60 pounds of air pollution

— 4.2 megawatts of energy (enough energy to power a computer for almost a year)

Statistics from *www.recyclebank.com*

Benefits at a glance

— Paper and paperboard can be made from a variety of pulp fiber plants, including annual crops and field waste, alternative pulp source streams like animal waste, and from minerals or recycled plastics.

— Recycled papers and certified papers from well-managed forests are readily available.

— Recycled paper sequesters carbon through to end of life.

— Paper is readily recycled in most markets.

— Recycled paper is lightweight and durable.

— Many virgin annual agri-fiber crops typically require little bleaching.

— Paper mills are exploring and using methods to generate energy from waste created during manufacturing: steam, methane gas, "black liquor" (a recycled by-product formed during the pulping of wood in the papermaking industry), and others.

Walking the talk. Since the company was founded in 1998, San Francisco–based New Leaf Paper's mission is to be the leading national source for environmentally responsible, economically sound paper. To help further its goals, it called on Chambers Design to create guides to serve the technical and aesthetic demands of both printers and designers. New Leaf's "Eco-Audit" chart for its papers provides a tangible overview of savings in terms of trees, water, energy, solid waste, and greenhouse gases when recycled paper is used versus virgin sources.

Every paper dec...

Certifications and Environmental Standards

Reincarnation

DO YOU BELIEVE
IN REINCARNATION?

Inventory Items

V4

REINCARNATION (FSC)
PRIMAVERA (FSC)
NEW LEAF SAKURA
EVEREST (FSC)
NEW LEAF IMAGINATION (FSC)
NEW LEAF OPAQUE (FSC)

NEW LEAF
PAPER

NEW LEAF PAPER
ENVIRONMENTAL BENEFITS STATEMENT

Paper with a past, and a future.

— More and more mills are switching to renewable energy or are purchasing carbon offsets to reduce their carbon footprints to meet additional reduction goals.

— Closed-loop paper mill technologies are being researched to reroute or eliminate wastewater and air emissions.

— A renewable resource though responsible management assures long-term viability of supply as well as opportunities for better managing carbon loads (current solar income strategies).

Drawbacks at a glance

— The supply chain is not universally certified as sustainable.

— The industry is still very dependent on one slow-growing pulp source: wood.

— Heavy reliance on a single pulp source coupled with monoculture and nonsustainable forestry practices deepens catastrophic risks to industry (and ecosystems) from disease, fire, and mismanagement.

PRIMARY USES: Extremely versatile, serving a vast array of functions from communication to packaging, to decorative needs.

TYPICAL TOXINS: Dioxins (bleach for virgin wood pulp or recycled pulp), furans and biocides (prevent bacterial growth).

ENERGY USE IMPACTS: In the United States, the forest products industry is the third largest industrial consumer of energy behind petroleum and chemicals, with pulp and paper processing consuming the greatest share.[19] Though many mills generate energy from process waste, mining/drilling impacts and combustion pollution from electricity generated by fossil fuel are part of this industry's energy use impacts. Deforestation and CO_2 emissions from paper and pulp manufacturing as well as fossil fuel combustion to create electricity increase carbon dioxide emissions and contribute to global warming.

RECYCLING IMPACTS: Although recycled paper takes pressure off forests, reduces waste, uses less resources such as energy and water, and produces fewer toxic releases, it still produces waste and pollution. Paper sludge from the deinking process contains solids, impurities, and sometimes hazardous chemicals. Paper sludge must be properly disposed of or treated as waste, with care taken to keep it out of waterways and food chains.

WATER QUALITY AND USAGE IMPACTS: Water is one of the major resources used in the paper-making process. Water pollutants from pulp and paper processes include particulates, effluent solids, biochemical oxygen demand (amount of oxygen required by aerobic microorganisms feeding on solids), and colorants.

AIR QUALITY AND POLLUTANT IMPACTS: Fine and coarse particulates, nitrogen oxides, ammonia, sulfur gases, and VOCs are some of the major types of air pollutants released from pulp and paper processes.

LANDFILL AND WASTE ISSUES: Although paper and paperboard enjoy comparatively high recycling rates, they still make up a large share of municipal solid waste. When paper decomposes in the anaerobic conditions of a landfill, like any organic matter, it releases methane, a greenhouse gas nearly twenty-five times more powerful than CO_2 at trapping heat in the atmosphere.

HABITAT IMPACTS: Paper manufacturing, conventional logging, and conversions of forests to tree plantations destroys indigenous habitats, reduces biodiversity, damages wetlands and soils, and decreases carbon storage or terrestrial carbon sequestration (a process through which CO_2 from the atmosphere is absorbed by trees, plants and crops through photosynthesis, and stored as carbon in biomass (tree trunks, branches, foliage, and roots).

SOCIAL AND INDIGENOUS CULTURE IMPACTS: Deforestation of virgin forests and rainforests not only affects the animals and species living in them, it affects the health of indigenous peoples and their livelihoods, culture, and economy.

Why What's in Your Paper Matters

Making responsible paper choices is one of the most significant environmental choices we make on a daily basis. The world's still-growing appetite for paper and the climate, forest, and social impacts of its production are one of the planet's greatest environmental challenges. Global paper consumption is currently running at more than 350 million tons per year and fast approaching an unsustainable 1 million tons per day. Right now, paper production is expanding deeper into the world's last endangered forests and more frequently coming in conflict with local and indigenous communities over land, water, and public health. However, when we examine our paper choices, we can find opportunities to be more efficient and to choose high-quality paper with environmentally advantageous qualities that add value to our design work. Making these responsible paper choices is something we all must do if we desire a sustainable future.

Paper is a wonderful asset to all of us, from designers to just about any other person in the world. Its natural texture, versatility, and availability are among its many positive attributes that make it so abundant in our lives, and will continue to be so for the foreseeable future, despite the "digital revolution." At times paper will be the appropriate material for a project, and that's why knowing what's in your paper matters.

Much like the urban cliché of the child who responds, "The grocery store," to the question "Where does food come from?" most of us don't really know where paper comes from. Unfortunately, if we don't ask ourselves what is in the paper we are using, there is a very good chance it is coming from unsustainable sources, resulting in major negative impacts such as the loss of endangered forests, pollution to air and water, and accelerating climate change.

Paper still comes primarily from trees. The industry accounts for over 40 percent of the world's industrial wood harvest, threatening the world's last endangered forests and the habitat they provide for endangered species. Paper companies are currently cutting deeper into ancient and endangered forests, such as the Canadian Boreal Forest, the Russian Taiga, and the tropical rain forests of Indonesia. They are replacing native forests with sterile, monoculture tree plantations across biologically significant areas in the southern United States, Tasmania, and South America. With less than 20 percent of the world's original forest still intact and undisturbed (less than 5 percent in the United States), the situation is critical for the world's endangered forests. These forests provide unique habitat for endangered species, store carbon and regulate the global climate, and ensure fresh water for millions, among many other benefits.

The paper industry is the fourth largest greenhouse gas contributor among manufacturers and a huge consumer of energy, making it a major culprit in climate change. In addition, paper that ends up in landfills releases methane, a greenhouse gas with twenty-three times the heat-trapping power of carbon dioxide. Landfills are the largest human source of methane, and paper is the single largest component of our landfills, despite the fact that about half of paper waste is recovered for recycling.

Paper choices don't affect just the fate of our climate and our forests, they also impact the immediate livelihoods and health of people around the world. As paper companies seek cheap land, cheap labor, and limited regulation in new regions of the world, they are increasingly directly impacting the land, air, and water of local and indigenous communities. The land rights of indigenous peoples and rural communities must be respected, but in some regions, these rights are violated in the course of activities by pulp and paper corporations. When paper companies are granted concessions to log forests and/or establish fiber plantations without gaining the full and informed prior consent of local communities or indigenous peoples with customary rights on that land, this is an abuse of the land rights of those people and communities. Unfortunately, these abuses are far too widespread. Indigenous people are struggling for their rights in many paper-producing regions, from the Sami in Finland, to the Maori in New Zealand, from the Haida in western Canada, to the Udege in the Russian Far East.

In Brazil, for example, there is bitter conflict in the state of Espírito Santo, Brazil, surrounding the acquisition by Aracruz Cellulose, the world's biggest producer of eucalyptus pulp, on land claimed by indigenous peoples. In Brazil, more than 5 million hectares (11 million acres) of eucalyptus plantation are growing in vast monocultures, termed "green deserts" by their opponents, who complain that the plantations consume vast quantities of water, causing rivers to dry up and leading to erosion, deterioration of water quality, and loss of fishing and water resources to local communities. The pressure on our planet from paper production is clear, but what can we realistically do about it?

FIRST, BE EFFICIENT. Designing paper-use efficiency into products has the most significant impact. It can also result in significant cost savings for manufacturers and clients and set products apart from others in a competitive marketplace. Just as a unit of conservation/efficiency is the most economically valuable unit of "alternative/clean energy," the same applies to paper use.

SECOND, MAKE A RESPONSIBLE CHOICE. Today, like never before, opportunity abounds to find high-quality paper produced with responsibility in mind. Today, there are more products containing recycled paper content than ever, with new innovations demolishing old perceptions and bringing quality and performance on par with virgin-fiber paper. Today, there is the Forest Stewardship Council, third-party certifiers that can provide a credible assurance that forest fiber was harvested in a sustainable manner and local communities were not negatively impacted. (Note: Beware of other certification schemes that have not yet established credibility.) Today, there is paper produced without chlorine bleaching. Today, there are paper products produced using clean energy, reducing the impact on our climate. Today, it is not just a nice idea; it is truly possible to choose socially and environmentally responsible paper.

The Environmental Paper Network is a community of conservation organizations that can connect designers with tools and resources to make socially and responsible paper choices. Their Web site, *www.WhatsInYourPaper.com*, provides a wealth of information and people ready to help. When thinking about the next project, remember to think about and ask, "What's in your paper?"

Article by Joshua Martin, Director, Environmental Paper Network. For more information, visit the Web site www.environmentalpaper.org.

Wood-based Papers

Wood as a fiber source for paper is a relatively new phenomenon. It was introduced in the 1850s when publications could no longer keep up with the demand for cotton and linen rags used to manufacture paper. During this time, the quest for new fibers for papermaking grew intensely in the United States and Europe, and contests were held to encourage the growth of paper made from new materials. Straw, hay, swamp grass, potatoes, corn-husks, old paper, barks and shrubs, marsh mallow, and asbestos were put to use to make paper.[20]

The development of the Fourdrinier paper machine[21] accelerated the papermaking process, with experiments in wood as a pulp source occurring shortly thereafter. Wood quickly became the raw material of choice as it was seen to be abundant and provided a consistent source of fiber, plus it was much less labor intensive to work with than removing contaminants from old rags or used rag paper at that time. Paper quantity become more important than quality, especially when there was a shortage of rags and cotton during World War I. For a brief time during World War II, the focus was shifted to waste-paper as an important fiber source. Old paper, newspapers, and even books were reused in the mills, and deinking technology was explored to meet demand.

After the war, the continued growth of wood pulping technology and vast supplies of wood from standing forests took precedence over reuse, and the use of virgin pulping methods became dominant.[22] Time marched on, and the lack of economic constraints, wartime shortages, or major demands to find better, alternative pulp fibers stalled the impetus for alternative papers. Fiber from trees was considered to be "abundant," "renewable," and "cheap."

As we noted in the beginning of this section, today nearly half of the trees cut in North America go to papermaking,[23] with a forest area the size of twenty football fields lost every minute to paper production.[24] Ontario Canada's boreal forest supports vital habitats, and the boreal ecosystem supports the largest fresh water system in the world, holding almost a third of the world's fresh water.[25] However, less than 10 percent of Ontario's Boreal Forest is protected. It is being logged at a rate of "an acre a minute, 24 hours a day, much of it to make things like catalogs, junk mail, magazines, newspapers and toilet paper."[26] Consider these ideas along with a quote commonly sourced to Scott Ewen of Emigre: "Designers make the world's most beautiful trash."[27] Paper products and paperboard compose the largest component of the nation's municipal solid waste.[28]

Papers made from ancient and vital forests are being used for single-use, throwaway products.

Paper Steps

Taking the Steps to Environmentally Responsible Paper

In the Steps below, 'environmental attributes' are defined as:

- Post-consumer Recycled Fiber
- Pre-consumer Recycled Fiber
- Agricultural Residue Fiber
- Forest Stewardship Council (FSC) Certified Virgin Fiber[1]

TRANSITIONAL **IMPROVED** **SUPERIOR**

INFERIOR

ENVIRONMENTALLY INFERIOR PAPER

This paper has no, or very minor, environmental attributes

MEETS NO MINIMUM CRITERIA:

- No/minimal recycled content
- Virgin tree fibers not FSC-certified
- Paper bleaching not: Totally Chlorine Free (TCF), Process Chlorine Free (PCF), or Enhanced Elemental Chlorine Free (EECF)[2]

ENVIRONMENTAL IMPACT:
100% virgin paper emits 5,483 to 6,855 pounds of greenhouse gases and consumes 15-26 trees per short ton.[3]

TRANSITIONAL PAPER

Meets the minimum criteria below and at least 10-30% of fiber has environmental attributes

MINIMUM CRITERIA:

- 10% post-consumer OR may be 100% virgin only if it has FSC certification
- Virgin fiber cannot be from controversial sources[4/5]
- Paper bleaching not: Totally Chlorine Free (TCF), Process Chlorine Free (PCF), or Enhanced Elemental Chlorine Free (EECF)[2]

ENVIRONMENTAL IMPACT:
30% post-consumer recycled paper emits approx. 10-15% less greenhouse gases, and saves the equivalent of 4 to 8 trees per short ton.[3]

ENVIRONMENTALLY IMPROVED PAPER

Meets the minimum criteria below and at least 50% of fiber has environmental attributes

MINIMUM CRITERIA:

- Minimum 30% post-consumer recycled
- FSC certification required on papers with more than 50% virgin content
- No controversial sources[4/5]
- Process Chlorine Free (PCF), Totally Chlorine Free (TCF), or Enhanced Elemental Chlorine Free (EECF)[2]

ENVIRONMENTAL IMPACT:
50% post-consumer recycled paper emits approx. 19-25% less greenhouse gases, and saves the equivalent of 8 to 13 trees per short ton.[3]

ENVIRONMENTALLY SUPERIOR PAPER

Meets the minimum criteria below and all fiber (100%) has environmental attributes

MINIMUM CRITERIA:

- Minimum 50% post-consumer recycled
- Virgin fiber can not have controlled wood content[6] or controversial sources[5]
- Processed Chlorine Free or Totally Chlorine Free (PCF or TCF)

ENVIRONMENTAL IMPACT:
100% post-consumer recycled paper emits 25-50% less greenhouse gases, and consumes no trees.[3]

CLEANER PRODUCTION is also a key element in environmental paper and while there are many variables, the Paper Steps focuses on bleaching technologies in its Minimum Criteria.

What's in Your Paper?

presented by environmental paper network

To find a list of Environmentally Improved and Environmentally Superior Papers visit **www.WhatsInYourPaper.com.**

1. Refers to virgin from FSC certified forests.
2. Enhanced Elemental Chlorine Free paper is made using technologies such as oxygen delignification and ozone bleaching prior to bleaching with chlorine dioxide.
3. Source: Paper Calculator from Environmental Defense, based on national (US) averages and varies by paper type. Does not include emissions for the burning of biomass.
4. FSC paper may contain pure, mixed or recycled sources. A 'transitional paper' does not include virgin fiber from controversial sources.
5. Controversial Sources include Endangered Forests as defined in the Ecological Attributes of Endangered Forests (reference), and those sources dealt with in FSC under the Controlled Wood Standard, including fiber sources from High Conservation Value Forests or Ecosystems, or where

there is a risk of illegal logging, violations of traditional or civil rights, ecosystems subject to conversion, or fiber from genetically modified organisms.
6. To qualify for 'Environmentally Superior Paper,' no controlled wood content is allowed.

- The comparisons in this chart are assumed to be applied to a consistent grade of paper. Shifting from one grade to another, particularly from papers made from chemical pulp to those made from mechanical pulp may produce quite different comparisons of environmental impacts.
- The criteria above correspond to the pulp rating system for: www.Pulpwatch.org
- The Paper Steps is based on the Hierarchy of Environmental Papers developed by Canopy, formerly Markets Initiative: www.canopyplanet.org

Clearcut hillside in North Carolina. An area that was once able to boast about being part of the oldest and most diverse forest system in the world.
Photo: W. Jedlička, 2009

North Pacific, southern, and mid-Atlantic coastal American forests are also at risk, as well as rain forests and endangered forests around the world. Each year millions of acres are logged and clear-cut to feed the pulp and paper industry, including pulp for packaging.

Of particular concern is single use, throwaway packaging and wrappers, including those used by

"Taking the Steps to Environmentally Responsible Paper," provided by the Environmental Paper Network.

fast-food industry giants. The Dogwood Alliance estimates that fast food packaging makes up 20 percent of all litter, and that three fourths of all food and drink packaging comes from forests.[29] The beauty and music industries are other heavy consumers of paper, again packaged with endangered Southern forests.

Although new trees are planted to replace those logged, monoculture crops are no substitute for the rich habitats and ecosystems that true forests provide. Harvard biologist and Pulitzer Prize winner Dr. E. O. Wilson estimates that "pine plantations in the south of the United States contain 90 to 95 percent fewer species than the forest that preceded it."[30]

Sterile pine plantations and monocrops typically rely on forestry practices that are unsustainable, including the use of toxic fertilizers and herbicides. Other potential issues and problems arise with genetically engineered trees that could become invasive and threaten forests and ecosystems.[31]

Interestingly enough, wood fiber is not as wholly ideal a fiber source as one might think. It does not offer the same quality as linen, cotton, or rags, the cellulose content of wood is around 50 percent by weight, which is much less than linen or cotton. Wood also contains lignin, which must be removed from the wood pulp to keep paper from deteriorating and yellowing.[32] Trees are slow to harvest and require much mechanical effort to transport, stockpile, debark, cut, and turn into a manageable form that then requires resource intensive "cooking" and chemical processing. The papermaking process, including whitening or deinking for recycling, also results in the discharge of toxic substances, pollution and waste. Furthermore, trees provide many more valuable functions than wood and paper pulp and may be worth considerably more as forests instead of fiber. Again, "true-cost" accounting is important to consider with any fiber source. The Canadian Boreal Initiative makes the case that "Canada's Boreal is worth more intact than harvested. Canada's boreal forests store 67 billion tonnes of carbon, a 'bank account' for the future preservation of Earth worth an estimated $3.7 trillion."[33]

Clearly, a return to the heyday of alternative fiber experimentation and agri-based pulps can not only protect forest ecosystems but incorporate agricul-

tural waste and yield innovative markets for sustainable products and papers. Read on to see how the alternative fiber revolution is slowly gaining momentum once more.

In the meantime, designers can take opportunities to learn more about paper manufacturing and sourcing. It is imperative to understand the value of recycled paper, sustainably harvested wood and certified paper products, and alternatives to wood-based papers. Designers can use their knowledge and purchasing power to help prevent deforestation and protect endangered habitats and to share this knowledge with customers.

The wonder is that we can see these trees and not wonder more.

—*Ralph Waldo Emerson*

Responsible Forests and Fiber

One of the core principles of choosing environmentally preferred paper includes the responsible sourcing of fiber. Ensuring that wood-based paper is not sourced from ancient or endangered forests or from indigenous communities that have been

---

Glama Natural is the only translucent paper currently available that uses a mechanical rather than chemical process. In addition, it is one of the only translucent papers to come in recycled grades and is readily recyclable. It has earned Forest Stewardship Council certification as well.

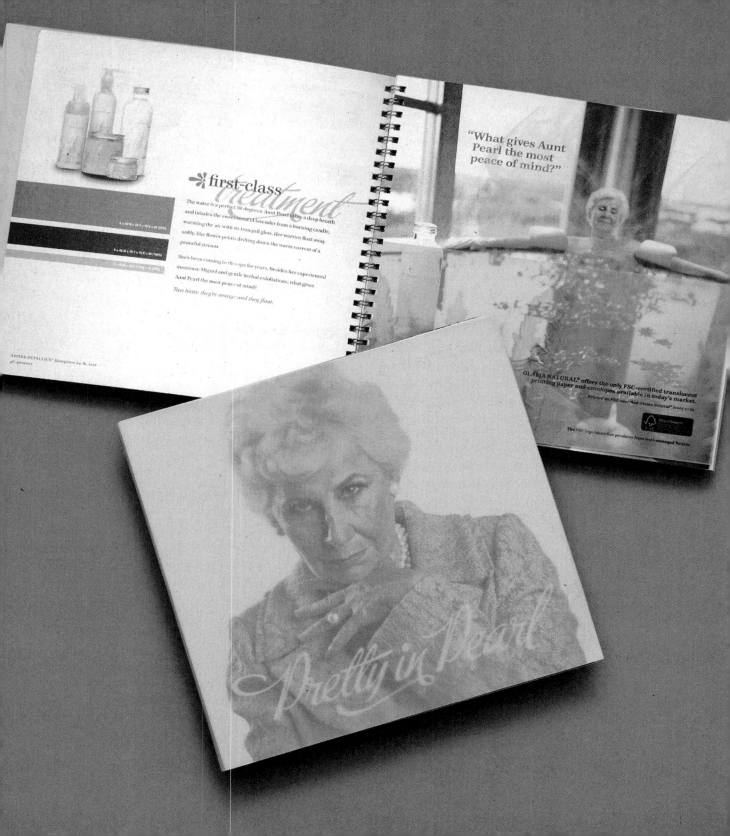

impacted by logging and land right conflicts are issues of paramount importance. Sustainable forest management and third-party certification programs with their corresponding logos, trade names, marks, or seals are valuable guides for purchasing a variety of wood products, including paper.

Designers have more options than ever before to specify eco papers with confidence, and to ensure that papers come from well-managed forests or fiber sources that have been verified or certified via sustainable forestry standards and chain-of-custody (CoC) programs. Whether designing and specifying paper for small projects, such as business cards, or for large-scale publication projects, such as magazines or books, there are numerous varieties of high-quality, third-party-certified papers from which to choose—many of which are available from major brands that designers are already familiar with.

Forests, habitats, and indigenous cultures are not the only ones who benefit from using certified papers. Closer to home, designers, clients, customers, companies. and stakeholders also benefit. Approved use of an appropriate forest certification logo demonstrates sustainability awareness and leadership, which in turn can raise the bar for business practices, enhance customer awareness and market recognition, and create new business opportunities.

One of the core principles of choosing environmentally preferred paper includes the responsible sourcing of fiber.

Designers who specify independent or third-party-certified papers also ensure that the market momentum for responsibly sourced and manufactured papers continues. Furthermore, specifying certified papers for design and print projects allow designers to integrate smart business practices with sustainable or environmentally preferable purchasing programs and to share these same smart choices and strategies with customers to foster environmental stewardship and change. Awareness and change can spread across borders, especially in today's global marketplace.

International Forest Certification with Third-Party Verification

FOREST STEWARDSHIP COUNCIL (FSC)

In the early 1990s, meetings between timber users, traders, and representatives of environmental and human rights organizations identified the need for a credible system of identifying well-managed forests and products. The Forest Stewardship Council (FSC) was named, and shortly after, with support and intensive consultation with other countries, the worldwide certification and accreditation process was born.[34]

The Forest Stewardship Council is an independent nonprofit organization devoted to encouraging the responsible management of the world's forests. The FSC sets high standards that ensure forestry is practiced in an environmentally responsible, socially beneficial, and economically viable way. The FSC logo identifies products that contain wood from well-managed forests certified in accordance with the rules of the Forest Stewardship Council. Products carrying the FSC label are *independently certified* to assure consumers those products come from forests that are managed to meet the social, economic, and ecological needs of present and future generations.[35]

USING THE FSC LOGO

In order to use the FSC logo, trademark, initials "FSC" or phrase "Forest Stewardship Council" on printed materials, the printer must have chain-of-custody (CoC) certification. Without this certification, no claims can be printed regarding the FSC-certified content of the paper. Certification ensures that the wood product, including paper, has flowed from the FSC-certified forest to a FSC-certified manufacturer or paper mill, merchant, and printer[36] and that the product can be tracked or traced from one operation to the next.[37] Use of the logo shows an awareness of conservation, high environmental standards, and social responsibility values. It also assures purchasers that the products contain wood from socially and environmentally responsible forests.[38]

FSC labels currently include the following three categories and several variations of the on-product claim.[39] Furthermore, each label is related to the fiber content and has specific design elements that differentiate one label from another. Look for these on wood products and paper swatch books, and consult with a FSC-certified paper representative and FSC-certified printer to ensure appropriate use and labeling.

FSC PURE LABEL

This FSC product group contains 100 percent FSC-certified materials and states "100%—From well-managed forests." These products are made exclusively from materials originating in FSC-certified forests.

FSC MIXED SOURCES LABELS

These FSC product groups contain a mixture of FSC-certified material, recycled material, and other company-controlled sources. There are currently five mixed label combinations, with statements and label design elements unique to each combination, including text information relating that the product group comes from well-managed forests, controlled sources, and/or recycled wood or fiber.

Controlled wood is non-FSC-certified virgin material that has been controlled to avoid sources with: illegally harvested wood; wood harvested in violation of traditional and civil rights; wood harvested in forests where high conservation values are threatened by management activities; wood harvested in forests being converted to plantations or nonforest use; and wood from forests in which genetically modified trees are planted.[40]

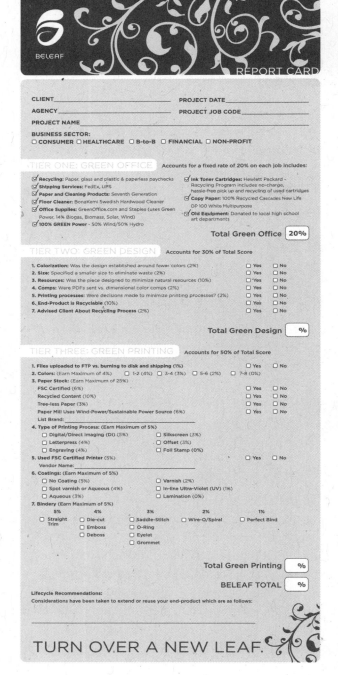

FSC RECYCLED LABEL

This FSC product group contains 100 percent post-consumer reclaimed material and states "Recycled—Supporting responsible use of forest resources."

FSC-certified products are readily available in North America from both small, independent paper companies and large paper mills. To learn more about appropriate use of the logo and the chain-of-custody certification process, visit the FSC Web site (*www.fscus. org*). Also note that the site provides regularly updated lists of FSC-certified papers, paper merchants, paper manufacturers, printers, and pulp suppliers.[41]

Additional Third-Party Paper Verification

ANCIENT FOREST FRIENDLY™

Ancient Forest Friendly paper purchasing policies help safeguard ancient and endangered forests, and protect their biodiversity and ecosystems.[42] They also help stimulate the development and

---

Rizco Design created a three-tiered environmental program to extend the sustainability efforts of the Forest Stewardship Council's (FSC) chain of custody to measure decision-making impacts throughout the creative process. The effort starts with how its office operates, then extends to how it approaches a design, and finally, to how projects are printed, linking up with the rest of the chain-of-custody process.

growth of the eco-paper market and sustainable supply chains. [43]

The Ancient Forest Friendly™ logo is a designation that represents the highest ecological qualities in the paper industry. In order to be Ancient Forest Friendly, a paper must be manufactured with a high percentage of post-consumer recycled fiber or agricultural residue. Any virgin fiber used in the paper must be both FSC certified and assessed as not originating from endangered forests. Bleaching must be chlorine free. Ancient Forest Friendly™ papers conserve intact forest ecosystems and their functions such as climate stabilization, water regulation and species habitat. [44]

The Ancient Forest Friendly™ logo and wordmark is managed by Canopy (formerly Markets Initiative), a Canadian not-for-profit that works collaboratively with large paper consumers (book, magazine or newspaper publishers) to guide them to change paper-buying habits and to develop and implement paper policies that help safeguard ancient and endangered forests.[45] Companies that have an eco-paper policy with Canopy may use the logo on applicable papers.

To learn more about the Ancient Forest Friendly™ designation and approved logo usage, or to view a database of papers with AFF designation, visit *www.canopyplanet.org.*

RAINFOREST ALLIANCE CERTIFIED™

The Rainforest Alliance is an international, non-profit conservation organization that was founded in 1987 to conserve biodiversity and to ensure sustainable livelihoods by transforming land-use practices, business practices, and consumer behavior. In 1989, the Rainforest Alliance launched the SmartWood program and became the world's first global forestry certification program.[46]

The Rainforest Alliance's SmartWood program is the world's leading FSC forest management certifier, working with both large forestry companies and small communities and cooperatives throughout the world to ensure that their products and services meet strict standards for social and environmental responsibility. The Rainforest Alliance Certified seal, which appears on a variety of agricultural products, including bananas, coffee, and chocolate, is recognized around the world as an indication that those products come from farms that meet the standards of the Sustainable Agricultural Network. The Rainforest Alliance Certified seal can also be used in tandem with the FSC trademarks on forestry products such as flooring, decking, guitars, and paper when they have been certified by the Rainforest Alliance's SmartWood program in accordance with the FSC standards.[47]

Both the FSC on-product label and the Rainforest Alliance Certified seal may appear on FSC-certified products or printed pieces if an FSC-certified printer with Rainforest Alliance Chain-of-Custody certification is used. To learn more about the Rainforest Alliance Certified seal, visit *www.rainforest-alliance.org.*

Ancient Forest Friendly,™ SmartWood, and the Rainforest Alliance certification program go hand in hand with the leading global forest certification system, the FSC.

ISO 14000 AND PAPER

The International Organization for Standardization (ISO), through the 14000 family, addresses various aspects of environmental management. It works as a management tool to enable organizations of any size to identify and control the environmental impact of its activities, products, or services; to improve its environmental performance continually; and to implement a systematic approach to setting environmental objectives and targets, to achieving these, and to demonstrating that they have been achieved.[48] ISO certification relates more specifically to the environmental quality of forest management rather than through forest certification programs.

ISO 14001:2004 can be used as a tool to meet both internal and external objectives. Regarding the latter, it can provide assurance to customers that companies that have been certified comply with regulations and have environmental policies, plans, and actions in place. Designers may see the ISO certification statement in a variety of applications, not only in regard to sustainable forest management but also in context with vendors and suppliers—several printers and paper mills now have ISO certification.

Intra-Industry Verification

SUSTAINABLE FORESTRY INITIATIVE® (SFI INC.)

SFI Inc. is an independent, non-profit charitable organization with a science-based, internationally recognized forest management standard developed specifically for North American forests. It is one of the fastest growing certification programs, with over 160 million acres (65 million hectares) of SFI-certified forests across Canada and the U.S. Supported by conservation groups, the SFI Standard is based on principles and measures that promote sustainability, including measures to protect water quality, biodiversity, wildlife habitat, species at risk and forests with exceptional conservation value. SFI Inc. is governed by a three-chamber board of directors representing environmental, social and economic sectors equally.[49]

For more information on the SFI certification program, visit the official Web site: *www.sfiprogram.org*.

PROGRAMME FOR THE ENDORSEMENT OF FOREST CERTIFICATION SCHEMES (PEFC)

The PEFC Council (Programme for the Endorsement of Forest Certification schemes) is an independent, non-profit, non-governmental organization, founded in 1999, that promotes sustainably managed forests through independent third-party certification.

PEFC is a global umbrella organization for the assessment of and mutual recognition of national forest certification schemes developed in a multi-stakeholder process. These national schemes build upon the inter-governmental processes for the promotion of sustainable forest management, a series of ongoing mechanisms supported by 149 governments in the world covering 85 percent of the world's forest area.[50]

The PEFC logo must be used with license registration number, and claim "Promoting Sustainable Forest Management"—for more info: *www.pefc.org.*"

Factors to Consider When Choosing Certification Systems

Designers and print buyers play a key role in advancing environmentally responsible and socially sustainable paper production and consumption. Designers are also some of the most active participants in creating the market indicators that guide the direction of certification standards. Forest certification standards and systems are evolving and changing, so it is important to review and compare current certification criteria based on: objective, independent and performance-based standards, including both environmental and social criteria; independently funded and governed standards with balanced and broad stakeholder participation; a labeling system that includes a credible chain of custody system; transparency and accountability confirmed through independent, third-party assessment and field audits.

Other basic requirements for forest certification include: forest management unit level certification (rather than certification at the country or regional level); systems that are cost-effective and voluntary; forest management improvement goals that demonstrate positive commitment from the forest owner or manager; objective standards that are adapted to local conditions; and stakeholder consultation and participation in the certification and accreditation process. Additionally, a forest certification system should be applicable on a global level to a variety of tenure systems, to provide equitable market access, as well as other criteria.[51]

As found in other industry certification programs emerging and evolving today, some forest certification programs reflect an industry bias. For forest products, some of these efforts may be funded largely by industry groups, such as logging and sawmill companies, or have management boards that predominantly consist of representatives of the forest industry and forest owners rather than a more balanced group including independent members and stakeholders.[52]

Today, as is occurring in other industries, forest certification has become a competitive, multibillion-dollar international industry, with certification organizations creating intense promotional campaigns to win customers. However, many buyers of certified products lack awareness of the differences in standards and certifications, believing that all forest certification programs and their accompanying eco-logos or sustainability statements promise the same level of forest management and sustainability, when this is not always the case.

As a global umbrella organization, PEFC standards and schemes vary from country to country, particularly with some standards allowing logging in ancient forests or areas with high conservation value, the conversion of forests to plantations, and the labeling of content from genetically modified sources.[53] Additionally, as is happening in several industries' certification programs, many programs lack standards or assessments regarding social issues, such as providing measures to respect and protect indigenous peoples' rights.

As standards and systems evolve in tandem with knowledge, experience and participation, it is important to keep up to date and carefully review criteria (and the certifying body) for *any* certification or certified product being considered.

For the forest products industry, currently FSC certification is the only system with broad conservation group support.[54] SFI and PEFC originally came out of forest industry efforts, (SFI is under the umbrella of PEFC in the United States, as is CSA, the Canadian Standards Association), unlike FSC, which was developed by stakeholder groups bringing together social, environmental, and business concerns. The Environmental Paper Network, a coalition of nearly 100 non-profit organizations working on sustainability in the paper industry, holds FSC as the gold standard for forest certification, and as of 2009, the only one deemed credible in structure, chain of custody, and standards. The Environmental Paper Network strongly encourages paper purchasers and designers to look for the FSC logo and work with their suppliers to achieve FSC certification.[55]

In an effort to serve their clients on a variety of levels, some paper mills, merchants, and printers are applying for Triple Certification (FSC, SFI, and PEFC) to meet customers' expectations for sustainability, and to meet requirements for a range of customers, both domestically and internationally (i.e., if a mill is located overseas and obtains pulp or fiber under a different standard).

What we are doing to the forests of the world is but a mirror reflection of what we are doing to ourselves and to one another.

—Mahatma Gandhi

To learn more or to compare forest management certification systems in North America refer to "Environmental Paper Procurement: Review of Forest Certification Schemes in Canada,"[56] an independent research study carried out by ÉEM (*www.eem.ca*) available through Canopy (formerly Markets Initiative, *www.canopyplanet.org*). Additional reports and publications of interest can be found there as well.

Recycled Papers

Currently there is no global consensus on what the term "recycled paper" means beyond the fact that it may contain either post- or pre-consumer fiber or waste. Saying that paper is "recycled" is not enough, as this could vary from 1 percent to 100 percent, but not necessarily from post-consumer waste (PCW) paper that actually has been used and then recycled. Furthermore, to add to the confusion, recycled paper in the past included pre-consumer waste instead of post-consumer waste or secondary fiber. Common terms and definitions follow.

— *Pre-consumer waste* consists of paper or scraps left over from manufacturing, converting, or trimming paper in the mill or print house. It may also include unsold magazines and newspapers. Although the paper and scraps are being reused, this paper has never made the journey to the consumer and back again.

— *Post-consumer recycled or post-consumer waste (PCW)* refers to paper that was printed on or used for its intended purpose, put into a recycling bin, and then recycled into new paper or products. It also refers to a finished material that normally would be disposed of as a solid waste.

An Environmental Protection Agency (EPA) guideline governs purchases of paper made by federal agencies and helps promote paper recycling by using government purchasing to expand and maintain markets for recovered paper. The "Paper Products Recovered Materials Advisory," Notice II (Paper RMAN II), revises the EPA's 1996 recommendations for purchasing specified printing and writing papers containing post-consumer fiber. Under section 6002 of the Resource Conservation and Recovery Act, which establishes a buy-recycled program for federal agencies, the EPA designates items that are or can be made with recovered materials and provides recommendations for government procurement of these items. Under Executive Order 12873, federal executive agencies are required to purchase specified printing and writing papers containing 30 percent post-consumer fiber.[57]

In 2007, an executive order from the president (in the footsteps of other United States presidents since 1989) required these goals for federal agency acquisitions of goods and services to strengthen the environmental, energy, and transportation management of federal agencies:[58]

> (i) use of sustainable environmental practices, including acquisition of biobased, environmentally preferable, energy-efficient, water-efficient, and recycled-content products, and (ii) use of paper of at least 30 percent post-consumer fiber content.

In the absence of other national standards, many paper mills adopted the EPA's purchasing policy recommendations for defining recycled content, and have introduced and marketed grades using this guideline as a minimum standard for recycled content.[59]

While only the federal government in the United States requires its purchasers (and contractors who pay more than $10,000 a year for paper) to procure writing paper with recovered materials, many local and state governments now have policies or mandates to purchase recycled paper and other products. Some state governments offer a price preference for purchasing recycled paper, and others have redefined the requirements of recycled content, as many viewed the EPA's guideline as an ineffective model for a national standard.[60]

For example, the state of California has one of the strictest definitions of a recycled paper product, stating that paper and wood pulp products must contain a minimum of 50 percent, by fiber weight, of "secondary" and "post-consumer material" with not less than 10 percent of fiber weight consisting of post-consumer material.[61]

Although there appears to be a disconnect between state and federal recommendations in the United States and worldwide, recognized third-party certifications and criteria for recycled paper, it is still a straightforward choice for designers: Choose papers with the highest recycled PCW fiber content available. This is not as difficult as it sounds, as now many papers mills are selling high-quality papers with 30 to 50 percent PCW, and others offer 100 percent PCW content papers with other environmental attributes and certification as well.

Keep in mind that recycled content is now stated according to recycled *fiber* content, not weight. For example, coated paper has filler materials, thus making its total weight higher than its fiber weight. A comparison of recycled fiber content to total fiber provides a more accurate view of the true recycled content of the paper. Look for sheets that provide the breakdown of post-consumer waste and pre-consumer waste content. Naturally, papers that are 50 to 100 percent PCW are more significant environmentally.

Private groups or government-sponsored environmental logo or seal programs have taken care to establish specific criteria for printing and writing papers, including Green Seal and the EcoLogo program, now recognized worldwide. The latter goes beyond recycled fiber content, with a multi-attribute, life cycle approach. Included are strict criteria regarding resource material, energy consumption, chemical oxygen demand (COD), aquatic toxicity, and the generation of solid waste.

EcoLogo

Founded in 1988 by the government of Canada, EcoLogo is one of North America's most respected environmental standard and certification marks. EcoLogo provides customers—public, corporate, and consumer—with assurance that the products and services bearing the logo meet stringent standards of environmental leadership. EcoLogo certifies environmental leaders in over 120 product categories, helping customers find and trust the world's most sustainable products. To learn more about the product specific requirements that must be met for products to carry the EcoLogo[CM] or to view environmentally preferred paper products, visit the EcoLogo Web site.[62]

Green Seal

Green Seal, Inc. is an independent, nonprofit organization whose mission is to create a more environmentally sustainable economy by identifying and promoting environmentally preferable products and services. Green Seal has developed environmental leadership standards for dozens of product and service categories, including printing and writing paper, and its certification program verifies that products meet this stringent standard.[63]

Having papers certified by Green Seal signifies that recycled papers meet standards for recycled content, with a minimum of 30 percent post consumer fiber, and that the mill manufacturing processes, including packaging, meet stringent process control standards and are environmentally preferable.[64]

Recycling Symbol and Usage

Recyclable

Recyclable

The very first Earth Day celebration took place in the spring of 1970. As part of a public relations campaign, the Container Corporation of America, a paperboard company, sponsored a nationwide contest for graphic design students to create a design that could be used to promote the recycled content of the containerboard packaging. More than 500 students entered, and designers, including Saul Bass, Herbert Bayer and Eliot Noyes, judged the design competition as part of the Aspen Design Conference. University of Southern California student Gary Anderson submitted the winning entry, drawing inspiration from the Möbius strip. His design featured three chasing arrows within a continuous loop.

The three arrows are symbolic of three steps in the recycling process:

— Separating and collecting recyclable materials

— Processing and manufacturing these materials into new products

— Purchasing and/or using recycled products

The American Forest and Paper Association recommends the usage regarding the recycling symbol as follows:[65]

— Products that are recyclable, with a qualifying statement regarding the availability of recycling programs in a substantial majority of communities for that product or package. Making a "recyclable" statement is not generally recommended, as the above criteria may be difficult to meet.

— Products made from 100 percent recycled fiber, accompanied with either the "100% Recycled Fiber" or "Recycled" statement.

— Products made with a percentage of recycled fiber, accompanied with a legend identifying the total percent (by weight) of recycled fiber.

Other industries have adopted recycling symbols or codes specific to their industry. Industry associations for plastic, paperboard, and corrugated materials have all developed, and in some cases trademarked, unique recycling symbols. For example, plastics use a recycling symbol along with a numbering system (1–7) to help distinguish the plastics used in that product.

RECYCLED CONTENT CLAIMS

The Federal Trade Commission (FTC) has issued guidelines for the use of environmental marketing claims that can be helpful to designers. These guidelines can not only guide recycled paper purchasing choices but can assist designers or marketers in making accurate and lawful statements about recycled content on printed materials for customers and clients. Note that a recycled content claim may be made only for materials that have been recovered or otherwise diverted from the solid waste stream and that distinctions must be made between pre-consumer and post-consumer materials if asserted on products or packaging.

Guidelines also exist for marketing packages or products as "recyclable." Designers and printers must label products clearly, and where recycled content distinctions are made, claims about the pre-consumer or post-consumer content of a product or package must be substantiated. In addition, any claim of recyclability must made clear to consumers whether it refers to the product, packaging, or both.[66] To learn more about the FTC's Green Advertising claims and Environmental Marketing guides, visit the Federal Trade Commission's Web site: *www.ftc.gov.*

Virgin Papers

Virgin paper is paper made from fiber sources used for the first time in the manufacturing process. In the case of wood-pulp papers, it is produced from trees and tree parts (chips, sawdust, branches, etc.) that were harvested in order to make lumber or paper.[67] Wood fibers (like all fibers used for paper) have finite recycling rounds. At each cycle they degrade (break), eventually becoming unusable, requiring fresh infusions of virgin fibers to strengthen the pulp mixtures.[68]

Modern paper mill technology and pulp processing are geared primarily toward the use of wood-based pulps rather than other fibers. Thus, this technology drives the need to use forests or tree plantations (tree farms) to generate the pulp to meet the demands of consumers. Sustainable nonwood fiber though is an excellent source of virgin pulp and may yield even higher fiber content. However, new pulping methods and infrastructure are needed to fully develop the potential of nonwood fibers for papermaking.

Today, tree plantations are being planted to generate large volumes of small-size logs as quickly as possible, primarily for the paper and pulp industry. Single species of trees are grown, many of which are not native to the area. An invasion of these foreign trees can pose serious problems for the local ecosystem and community. Other environmental impacts associated with tree farms or plantations include threats to biodiversity (with many forests clear cut to be replaced with plantations), water pollution and water table impacts, as many tree crops require vast amounts of water. Erosion too is a serious impact from harvesting using clear cutting methods. Here precious topsoil washes away before new growth can take hold, requiring chemical fertilizers to maintain soil that, had more sustainable harvesting methods been used, would have allowed the land to replenished itself.

Another lesser-known impact is the increase in rural poverty, especially in indigenous communities. Since the work is largely mechanized, few jobs are created, and the ones that are tend to be the most dangerous or are related to the most health problems.[69] "The worst safety and health situation is usually found in forestry," according to the UN International Labor Organization and other forest industry experts.[70]

Some paper companies are proposing that the term "renewable" be used to describe the virgin paper logged from managed tree plantations. However, according to the Environmental Paper Network[71] and other environmental organizations, though the term "renewable" looks good on paper, this does not ensure an environmentally sound product.

Progress in forest certification programs now makes it possible to ascertain if virgin papers have been made with fiber or pulp from well-managed or certified forests (i.e., designated with the FSC "Pure Label"). Virgin fibers can be processed "Totally Chlorine Free"; however, keep in mind that papers with recycled content are considered by many to be the environmentally preferred choice.

Chlorine Concerns

Core principles of choosing environmentally and socially responsible paper go beyond selecting recycled fiber content, certified fiber, or alternative fiber content; they also include choosing chlorine-free papers. Papers often are identified or classified according to bleaching technology and certification. Designers need to understand the types of bleaching processes and weigh a sheet's whiteness and brightness factor against the corresponding impacts on the environment.

Several bleaching processes are used to whiten paper or to enhance the removal of lignin. Chlorination is a common whitening process. Its use in papermaking can produce dangerous organochlorine compounds and toxic by-products, such as chlorinated dioxins and furans. These compounds can get into waterways and cause harm to humans and aquatic life.[72] A Green Seal report in 2006 estimated that 1.5 trillion gallons of organochlorine compound contaminated wastewater are released by the paper manufacturing industry each year.[73]

There is convincing evidence that dioxins cause cancer plus strong indications they disrupt hormonal, reproductive, and immune systems. Developing fetuses and breastfeeding infants are particularly sensitive to dioxins, with studies also indicating that dioxins are endocrine disrupters; thus dioxins must be added to a list of toxic chemicals found to mimic natural hormones and block or disrupt their normal function.

Chlorine dioxide has largely replaced elemental chlorine and has reduced toxic releases greatly; however, the use of chlorine in general still poses risks and continues to be harmful to aquatic life, humans, plants, and animals. Alternatives include using hydrogen peroxide, ozone, and oxygen.

Chlorine Use: Certifications and Basic Definitions[74]

TOTALLY CHLORINE-FREE (TCF)

Certified TCF: These products require that no chlorine or chlorine compounds were used in the papermaking process, that all virgin components need to be certified as totally chlorine free and require a chain of custody for all fiber, that the mill has no current or pending violations, and that the

mill does not use old-growth forest for any of the virgin pulp.

PROCESSED CHLORINE-FREE (PCF)

Processed Chlorine-Free (PCF) is recycled paper made with a bleaching process that uses no chlorine-based compounds.

Certified PCF: In addition to the certified TCF criteria, certified PCF products require the product contains at least 30 percent post-consumer content and that the mill details post-consumer content sources.

For more information about TCF, PCF, and Chlorine Free Products Association Certification, visit the Web site *www.chlorinefreeproducts.org.*

Additional Terms

Elemental Chlorine-Free (ECF) often is used to label products that have substituted chlorine dioxide for another type of chlorine called elemental chlorine. Compared to bleaching processes using elemental chlorine, ECF chlorine dioxide processes reduce the formation of many chlorinated organic compounds. However, as chlorine is still used, effluent quality remains an issue that mills using replacements that still contain chlorine must address.

Enhanced ECF with extended or oxygen delignification is a process that removes more of the lignin from the wood before bleaching. This reduction helps reduce energy and chemical demands for the bleaching process.

Enhanced ECF with ozone or hydrogen peroxide delignification is a process that also removes more of the lignin from the wood before bleaching but substitutes ozone or hydrogen peroxide for chlorine or chlorine dioxides in the early stages of the bleaching process.

For both Enhanced ECF processes however, the final or near-final stages still use chlorine in some form, making TCF and PCF preferable options.

The Natural Resources Defense Council offers visitors to its Web site an order of preference for bleaching processes, on the basis of environmental criteria:[75]

1. PCF (preferable to TCF for wood-based papers because product includes recycled content; TCF is used to refer only to 100 percent virgin paper)

2. TCF

3. Enhanced ECF with ozone or hydrogen peroxide

4. Enhanced ECF (ECF with extended or oxygen delignification)

5. Traditional ECF

For more information about chlorine, see "Chlorine and Bleaching" later in this chapter.

Papermaking and Green Power

As most of the electricity in the United States (and elsewhere around the world), is generated by coal-burning power plants, pollution, greenhouse gases and global warming concerns are an issue for all manufacturers, including paper manufacturers. Coal use, primarily for the generation of electricity, now accounts for roughly 20 percent of global GHG emissions.[76] A Sierra Club article, "Clean Air: Dirty Coal Power" explains:

Power plants are a major source of air pollution, with coal-fired power plants spewing 59 percent of total U.S. sulfur dioxide pollution and 18 percent of total nitrogen oxides every year. Coal-fired power plants are also the largest polluter of toxic mercury pollution, the largest contributor of hazardous air toxins, and release about 50 percent of particle pollution. Additionally, power plants release over 40 percent of total U.S. carbon dioxide emissions, a prime contributor to global warming.[77]

Papermaking is an extremely energy intensive process, with the papermaking industry earning a spot with some of the top users of electricity in the United States. It is refreshing, then, to see that paper mills and paper companies are working hard to increase energy efficiency or are converting waste into energy. Others are purchasing renewable energy to manufacture their papers.

In essence, several leading paper companies and their mill partners are tackling climate change. They are using innovative methods to conserve energy and reduce paper manufacturing emissions, or are supporting renewable energy projects via Renewable Energy Credits (RECs) or Verified Emissions Reduction credits (VERs). The latter enable paper manufacturers to claim that some or all of their product lines are "carbon neutral." Many conservation groups, however, take issue with the authenticity of this claim, so careful consideration should be undertaken when deciding to use this claim as part of a brand's marketing initiative. (See: *www.environmentalpaper.org/carbonneutralpaper*).

In regard to renewable energy, mills are using hydropower, windpower, biogas, and even using "black liquor" or "green steam" energy methods.

Here's an example from Neenah Paper in Wisconsin, which projects that using "green steam" will reduce its annual natural gas usage by 80 percent.

Using a patented and award-winning method, 5,000 tons of sludge from all of the company's paper brands is converted to steam, electricity and glass aggregate every year. The primary purpose of this recycling process is to reduce the load on landfills, which carries out a corporate environmental directive. Neenah then purchases the steam back to dry paper during manufacturing and also to heat its Neenah, Wisconsin mill.[78]

Another paper mill, French Paper, aptly states in a promotional poster: "Some call it environmentalism, we call it common sense-ism." This small, family-owned paper mill has used its own hydroelectric generator to power its mill for over 84 years, with an estimated savings of 1 million of barrels of oil during this time. The generator also provides surplus energy back to the local energy company.

Mohawk Fine Papers became the first paper mill in the United States to power part of its manufacturing with emission-free wind energy in 2003. It now offers a complete portfolio of business papers made from windpower and offset with VERs.

Monadnock Paper Mills is certified with an ISO 14001: 2004 management system, and its graphic arts and packaging papers are made with a renewable energy combination of low-impact hydroelectric power and purchased wind energy. The company also has invested in methods to reclaim fiber that normally goes into the waste stream and use it instead as a soil amendment and for animal bedding and nutrient-rich compost.[79]

New Leaf Paper's entire inventory is manufactured with certified renewable energy, with RECs purchased from Sterling Planet, one of the nation's leading retail providers of solar, wind, and other renewable energy. New Leaf Paper's mill partner uses biogas generated from a local landfill in a process that coverts methane, a key greenhouse gas, into an energy source.[80]

Cascades Fine Papers' in Canada produces all of its papers using biogas energy, a step that enables the company to reduce its greenhouse gas emissions directly instead of by purchasing third-party offsets or RECs. Reported savings on its Web site show that using biogas at the Rolland mill reduces annual CO_2 emissions by 60,000 tons. This is equivalent to a regional reduction of 50 percent, or the emissions from 15, 000 cars.[81] Visit *www.environmentalbychoice .com* for more information.

Other sustainability commitments made by paper companies and mill partners include the use of biodiesel fuel in transportation (Mohawk Fine Papers and New Leaf Paper), the purchase of carbon offsets for fleet mileage (Mohawk Paper), and involvement in nonprofit conservation or greenhouse prevention initiatives (Domtar Paper, Smart Papers, etc).

Others are members of the EPA Climate Leaders program and the Chicago Climate Exchange (CCX®), the world's first and North America's only voluntary, legally binding greenhouse emission reduction, registry, and trading system to track, report, and reduce greenhouse emissions. More information about these organizations is presented next.

Renewable Energy Certification

GREEN-E

Green-e is the nation's leading independent consumer protection program for the sale of renewable energy and greenhouse gas reductions in the retail market. Green-e offers certification and verification of renewable energy through Green-e Energy, and greenhouse gas mitigation products (also known as carbon offsets) through Green-e Climate. Green-e is a program of the Center for Resource Solutions, a national nonprofit working to mitigate climate change.[82]

The Green-e logo means that an independent third party certified that the product meets strict consumer-protection and environmental standards. Businesses participating in Green-e Marketplace that purchase or generate a significant amount of certified renewable energy can also display the Green-e logo in order to communicate their commitment to certified renewable energy: *www.green-e.org/find*.

Paper manufacturers that are using renewable energy or purchasing renewable energy certificates to offset part or all of the electricity used in their operations include:[83]

— Grays's Harbor Paper

— Mohawk Fine Papers

— Monadnock Paper Mills

— Neenah Paper

— New Leaf Paper

— Sappi Paper

— The Paper Mill Store (Online paper merchant)

Additional Related Labels or Verification

BIOGAS

Use of the biogas logo verifies that energy is sourced from the decomposition of waste in a landfill and transported to the paper mill for use in the papermaking process. Typically biogas (aka "green gas") is used as thermal energy to replace traditional combustible fuels such as natural gas in the papermaking process, and helps reduces greenhouse emissions.[84]

Renewable Energy Partners

CHICAGO CLIMATE EXCHANGE

Chicago Climate Exchange (CCX®) operates North America's only cap and trade system for all six greenhouse gases, with global affiliates and projects worldwide.

CCX Members are leaders in greenhouse gas (GHG) management and represent all sectors of the global economy as well as public sector innovators. Reductions achieved through CCX are the only reductions made in North America through a legally binding compliance regime that provides independent, third-party verification by the Financial Industry Regulatory Authority (FINRA, formerly NASD).

CCX emitting members make a voluntary but legally binding commitment to meet annual GHG emission reduction targets. Those who reduce below the targets have surplus allowances to sell or bank; those who emit above the targets comply by purchasing CCX Carbon Financial Instrument® (CFI®) contracts.[85] To learn more, visit the CCX Web site: *www.chicagoclimatex.com.*

EPA CLIMATE LEADERS

Climate Leaders is an EPA industry-government partnership that works with companies to develop comprehensive climate change strategies. Partner companies commit to reducing their impact on the global environment by completing a corporate-wide inventory of their greenhouse gas emissions based on a quality management system, setting aggressive reduction goals, and annually reporting their progress to the EPA. Through program participation, companies create a credible record of their accomplishments and receive EPA recognition as corporate environmental leaders.[86] To learn more, visit the EPA Climate Leader Web site: *www.epa.gov/climateleaders.*

How wonderful it is that nobody need wait a single moment before starting to improve the world.

—Anne Frank

Environmental Paper Calculators and Eco-Audits

Designers make strides in sustainability when they specify environmental-preferred papers and vegetable or agri-based inks, especially when printing publications, packages, catalogs, reports and multipage brochures that can be resource intensive. There is also an extra bonus when using eco-papers and highlighting their related eco-labels (recycling logo, forest certification logos or labels, Soy Seal and renewable energy logos, etc.): Designers have an opportunity to educate clients and readers alike about positive environmental choices and resource saving options.[87]

One of the most powerful methods to visually convey paper conservation strategies and leadership in environmental sustainability is to use a paper calculator and related "eco-audit." Interactive, Web-based environmental paper calculators are valuable tools to evaluate paper choices and to measure environmental impacts of different papers in the context of recycled fiber content and energy. Resource savings in trees, wastewater, energy, solid waste, and greenhouse gases are provided as part of the calculations. The metrics or values used for calculating the savings are based on the percentage of recycled content, the source of energy, basis weight, and actual weight of paper used.

Designers can use these paper calculators to easily compare the resource savings that can be made by specifying papers with PCW recycled fiber content and renewable energy instead of papers made with virgin fiber and fossil fuel–generated electricity. This in turn can guide paper choices and assist clients or customers in reducing their eco-footprint. When the calculations are followed up with a printed eco-audit or environmental savings or benefit statement, resource savings can be provided at a glance in the front of a publication or elsewhere on a printed project.

CONTENTS

tips & demonstrations
page 5

speaker schedule
pages 6-9

Cinema Verde
Sustainable Film Festival
pages 10-11

exhibitor directory
pages 70-75

green market place
page 77-79

GREEN BUILDING EXPO · CELEBRATING 10 YEARS! · SCOTTSDALE CENTER FOR THE PERFORMING ARTS · OCTOBER 5 AND 6, 2007.

NEW LEAF PAPER®
ENVIRONMENTAL BENEFITS STATE
of using post-consumer waste fibre vs.

The Green Building Expo saved the following resources by using New Leaf Reincar
manufactured with electricity that is offset with Green-e® certified renewable ene
100% recycled fiber and 50% post-consumer waste, and processed chlorine free.

trees	water	energy	solid waste
29	6,329	13	1,384
fully grown	gallons	million Btu	pounds

Calculations based on research by Environmental Defense and other members of the

©2007 New Leaf Paper   www.newleafpaper.co

10th Annual
GREEN BUILDING
EXPO

October 5-6, 2007
Scottsdale Center For
The Performing Arts

City of Phoenix
City of Scottsdale
City of Tempe

Urban Sustainability in the Desert Southwest

GREEN BUILDING EXPO DIRECTORY AND PROGRAM

The Environmental Defense Fund (EDF) developed "The Paper Calculator" in 2005. The interactive tool is based on research done by the EDF and the Paper Task Force, a peer-reviewed study of the life cycle environmental impacts of paper production and disposal. To learn more about the Environmental Defense Fund, the Paper Task Force or the "Paper Calculator," go to *www.papercalculator.org.*

Several paper companies also provide environmental savings calculators, and share the same reference data as the EDF Paper Calculator. Additional environmental impact estimates for savings relating to the use of energy are gathered from several sources, including the EPA's Green Power Profiler and e-Grid database.[88] Refer to the Web site for each paper company that offers this type of service.

New Leaf Paper led the paper industry in quantifying the benefits of using post-consumer recycled fiber to translate resource savings. The New Leaf eco-audit shows environmental savings in a visual format with related certified eco-logos. Its appearance in 2003 in J. K. Rowling's *Harry Potter and the Order of the Phoenix* by Canadian publisher Raincoast Books indicated the environmental savings of printing on paper with 100 percent post-consumer waste. With an initial press run of 935,000 copies, the Raincoast edition saved 30,000 trees, 12 million gallons of water, 1 million pounds of solid waste, and 2.7 million pounds of greenhouse gases by using New Leaf EcoBook 100.[89]

New Leaf Paper provides a customized, print ready eco-audit to display on projects printed with New Leaf paper. To learn more, visit the New Leaf Paper Web site: *www.newleafpaper.com.*

Neenah Paper Inc. provides an environmental calculator that compares papers and related savings made with 100 percent of renewable energy. Savings are stated in hours of continuous electricity saved by a single-family home and/or the amount of waste in pounds that are recycled instead of being landfilled. Again, values and metrics are based on the EDF Paper Calculator and other publicly available information sources. Visit the Neenah Papers Web site for more information: *www.neenahpaper.com.*

Mohawk Fine Papers' calculator provides resource savings plus specific savings related to windpower use. For example, calculations stating the pounds of air emissions not generated and unused crude oil, which are then further stated as equivalent to not driving a number of miles or to planting a number of trees. Mohawk provides eps artwork for the icons to accompany the saving statement for publication. Also offered is a downloadable desktop version of its Environmental Savings Calculator. Visit the Mohawk Fine Papers Web site for more information: *www.mohawkpaper.com.*[90]

Cascades Fine Paper Group also provides a "Cascades Eco Calculator" to compare the resource savings from printing with its environmental papers compared to virgin papers. Again, savings can be demonstrated in the amount of trees used, solid waste generated, water use, suspended particles in the water, air emissions, and natural gas use. The

---

This full-color program and educational resource directory was designed by ecoLingo: earth-friendly graphic design to reflect the goals and values of the Green Building Expo. The publication was printed by a FSC-certified printer with light ink coverage using low-VOC, vegetable-based inks on recycled stock—"Reincarnation Matte" from New Leaf Paper. A customized eco-audit was also printed inside the directory to show the tangible, positive effects of using post-consumer recycled paper instead of virgin paper—showing savings in trees, water, energy, solid waste, and greenhouse gases.

online calculator (*www.environmentalbychoice. com*) quickly shows the savings and relays them into interesting comparisons. For example, the tree(s) saved are compared to the equivalent of American football field(s), water usage is compared to a shower of a number of day(s), and the air emissions are compared to emission of number of car(s) per year.

Words mean more than what is set down on paper. It takes the human voice to infuse them with shades of deeper meaning.

—*Maya Angelou*

Tree-Free and Alternative Papers

Interest in tree-free or alternative papers has waxed and waned throughout the years. The availability of tree free or alternative fiber paper products has been largely dependent on the opportunities (or lack thereof) to mill fibers from agricultural by-products or from plants such as kenaf, hemp, and wheat. Large-scale impacts of agri-pulp to replace wood pulp for papermaking are still unknown. Resource-intensive farming and land management practices used to meet demand (water usage, agrochemicals), currently practiced in many parts of the world, may outweigh the environmental benefits. However, recent trials have shown that when managed as part of a more holistic approach, agri-pulps and alternative fiber pulps have enormous potential.

Designers can play a role in keeping the interest and demand for tree-free or alternative fibers high by using or requesting these papers and supporting new products when they become available. Although interest in these papers is somewhat cyclical, there is certainly a steadily growing preference for environmentally preferred products.

A 1998 100% Recycled Paperboard Alliance (RPA-100%) national survey of U.S. primary shoppers indicated that preference for 100 percent recycled paperboard products had reached an extremely high level: 92 percent believe they are doing something for the environment when they buy it, 84 percent feel better about companies that use it as packaging material, and 73 percent are more inclined to buy products from companies that use it.

With such high, and long-established, consumer support for forest-free (100 percent recycled) or even virgin pulp reduced (partially recycled) packaging documented over 10 years ago, the opportunities are ripe for companies looking to integrate the positive consumer perception advantages found in tree-free products. The fact that no trees were used at all, and that most alternative pulp products come from annually harvested crops and residue (agripulp), is a simple idea consumers can easily understand. In this time of transition, with companies issuing varied and confusing eco-marketing claims, companies that find simple ways of connecting with the consumer are best positioned to profit the most in an ever-greening market.

For its 2009 promotional journal, Payette used paper embedded with wildflower seeds for the book's belly band to encourage people to get out, participate in, and enjoy nature.

-plant

water

grow

FROM PAPER TO FLOWERS — ENJOY!
HAPPY HOLIDAYS FROM PAYETTE

This plantable paper is embedded with wildflower seeds.

In its 2000 report, *Toward a Sustainable Paper Cycle*, the International Institute for Environment and Development talk about nonwood fibers in developing countries, where nonwood fibers account for over half the virgin pulp production and are important to the paper industry. In addition to importance as a materials resource, the report notes that there may be social and economic benefits to be gained by expanding paper production from nonwood fibers.[91] Closer to home, a 2006 report confirms another benefit: Some agricultural residues have smaller ecological footprints than using virgin wood-fiber pulps from the same region in Canada.[92]

As with any other material, though, a single simple substitution should not be the primary go-to mode in the decision-making process. Materials selected should be ones that will provide advantages on a variety of levels. Is the material considered special for the purpose? Do the environmental advantages continue if demand and production grows? Will forests be displaced if the land is converted to agricultural use? What are the greater impacts of selecting this material (i.e., water usage, agrochemical use, climate impacts from shipping materials or pulp around the globe, energy usage, waste management, etc.)? What does the material's process and supply chain look like? What effects, positive and negative, does it have on local and indigenous peoples and their local economies?

The selection of any material needs to be undertaken with considerable thought. One high spot in otherwise bleak discussions of rampant consumption is that to meet increasing demand, both in the developed and developing world, all pulp sources will require serious attention. In his 1999 book, *The Guide to Tree-free Recycled and Certified Papers*, author Dan Imhoff explains:[93]

. . . a tree-free paper industry promotes the goal of keeping old-growth forests and trees growing on United States federal forest lands out of the paper stream. A tree-free paper industry could greatly benefit rural economies as well.

Imhoff goes on to describe several regions in the Unites States (the world's biggest consumer of paper) that could support pulp demand, and talks about the development of mini-mills to keep transport fuel use down. Local crops serving local needs is one of the cornerstones of sustainability systems thinking. Couple that basic idea with the notion of looking at all viable pulp sources as part of a comprehensive pulp use cycle, and suddenly we begin to see resource options explode. In this section we look at alternative papers from past and current pulp cycles to help open up ideas for new avenues of creativity. Numerous tree-free, specialty, and novelty papers are available; keep in mind that not all papers serve every need the same. Many of the product examples or paper companies listed here have been included because they offer papers that can be printed with conventional presses or because they provide papers for smaller projects, including office stationary or promotional materials. Paper selection should be based on providing the best material for the desired outcome.

Agricultural Residues

Straw and husks left over from agricultural harvests are marvelous sources of tree-free fiber for paper. Wheat, barley, oat, rice, flax, and sugarcane bagasse all provide high-quality fiber for paper pulp and require much less energy, water, and chemicals than pulps derived from tree fiber. Furthermore, these agricultural fibers need no additional production, as they make use of harvest by-products that would normally be burned or wasted, so using the residue for paper fiber and pulp makes perfect sense. Historically, high-quality papers have been made from linen, a textile made from the fibers of the flax plant. In Canada and the U.S. Midwest, wheat in particular has great potential, as it is grown and harvested in abundance. China already uses these harvest resources wisely; apparently more than 20 percent of its paper fiber is sourced from wheat and rice.[94]

In 2008, *Canadian Geographic's* June issue was printed on paper made from wheat and other fibers, using 60 percent fewer trees.[95] "The Wheat Sheet" trial and magazine issue was the result of a lengthy experiment by Markets Initiative in partnership with the magazine and the Alberta Research Council, NewPage, and Dollco, a printer of leading publications.[96] Note that this was a one-time trial, and wheat sourced from China was used after the partners could not secure a large enough volume of wheat pulp in Canada. "Pulp" is the operative word here. While wheat fiber is readily available in Canada, currently there are no mills to turn this valuable resource into pulp, which made outsourcing necessary. The partners clearly understood that this is not a long-term solution nor a sustainable one, given the eco-ramifications of transportation and shipping. However, the results of the trial clearly showed the potential of using wheat as an alternative fiber. The next step is to reconfigure traditional mills to be able to locally process wheat fiber and other alternative fibers instead of only tree fibers for papermaking.

Greenfield Paper in Southern California uses agricultural residues in its papers, including garlic and coffee chaff. It also creates handmade journals, sketchpads, cards, invitations, and stationary sets with matching envelopes made from embedded-seed papers and other alternative fibers and post-consumer waste from junk mail, denim, and hemp.

EcoPaper, also known as Costa Rica Naturals, sells tree-free journals, note pads, stationary, and sheets for desktop publishing made from agricultural fibers. Its line includes Banana Paper, Cigar Paper, Coffee Paper, Hemp Paper, Lemon Paper, and Mango Paper.

New Leaf Paper recently launched the New Leaf's Farm Fiber collection of premium business and resumé papers with matching #10 envelopes made from banana and palm fiber. The collection is made up of sustainable farm fiber and 100 percent recycled fiber, with a minimum of 35 percent post-consumer content, and is processed chlorine free. The collection and other business papers and notebooks are being carried in Office Depot stores nationwide.

Benefits at a glance:

— Agricultural fibers yield high-quality fibers, and decreases pressure on forest-based pulp sources.

— Harvesting and production produces no additional environmental impact, while harvesting of crop residue for use prevents waste and increases per acre profits. Additionally, greenhouse gas emissions are decreased if residues are used instead of burned.

— Annual plants have a quick growth and maturity rate, and sourcing goes hand in hand with many sustenance crops already planted.

— Like recycled paper, they require less water, energy, and chemicals to produce.

— The PCW fiber content of fiber mix can be processed chlorine free.

— Rural communities and economies benefit, and the use of local resources helps decrease the ecological footprint.

Drawbacks at a glance:

— No certification is available to ensure that the fiber is harvested with social and environmental concerns in mind.

— Fiber availability and storage issues exist.

— Possible resource-intensive farming and land management practices used to meet demand (water usage, agrochemicals) may outweigh the environmental benefits. Knowing the full life cycle of products will be key to selection.

— Unlike wood fiber and pulp, the supply and demand for alternative or agri-based pulp is not well established. Considerable capital invest-ment is required to retrofit or develop mills to handle agri-pulp to become an integral part of meeting consumer demand.

— Distance from point of growth to production facilities may require disproportionately high fuel use versus established materials and supply chains.

Product Examples:

— EcoPaper, also known as Costa Rica Naturals: *www.ecopaper.com*

Paper products and sheets for desktop publish-ing made from agricultural fibers. Line includes Banana Paper, Cigar Paper, Coffee Paper, Hemp Paper, Lemon Paper, Mango Paper.

— Greenfield paper: *www.greenfieldpaper.com*

Paper products made from garlic and coffee chaff, as well as handmade specialty papers made from embedded-seed papers and other alternative fibers and post consumer waste from junk mail, denim and hemp.

— Gmund: *www.gmund.com*

Bier (beer) paper made with malt, yeast, and hops leftover from brewing, plus recycled beer labels and TCF virgin pulp.

— Neenah Paper: *www.neenahpaper.com*

Neenah Environment® Alternative fiber paper in "Mesa White" and "Tortilla." Manufactured with 50 percent sugarcane bagasse pulp (the fibrous material remaining in the sugarcane after the sugar is removed), and 50 percent recycled paper, including 30 percent post-consumer fiber.

Grasses, Wild Plants, Tree Products (Naturally Shed), Shrubs

Bamboo, mulberry, and bulrush all have a long and rich history in papermaking. For example, *sa,* or mulberry tree bark and branches, are well known in handmade specialty paper circles, and mulberry flowers and petals are often clearly recognizable when embedded into art papers.

New purposes are for these and other alternative fiber sources are now being explored, including the use of fiber extracted from the leaves of sisal (agave)

This box from Distant Village Packaging is made of 100 percent post-consumer recycled (PCR) content paperboard, covered in woven, wild grass paper. (distantvillage.com)
Photo: tnphoto.com

that is native to Central America and bulrushes harvested from wetlands and marshlands from southeast China on land that is normally unsuitable for food crops. The fast-growing wild plant is being used to produce organic, 100 percent biodegradable and compostable disposable food containers by biopac in the United Kingdom. The company also makes products out of palm, cane, cornstarch fibers, potato-starch, FSC-certified wood and recycled post-consumer waste.

Bamboo's quick growth rate has made it a popular nonwood fiber, now readily found in flooring, chopping blocks, bowls, utensils, and even clothing and skateboard decks. Although bamboo is technically a member of the grass family, the tall, treelike plant grows in the form of biologically diverse forests, and deforestation and loss of habitat remain an issue if bamboo is not sourced responsibly.

In the mid-1990s, several domestic papermakers introduced lines with bamboo fiber content sourced from plantations in Thailand. In 1997, ReThink Paper, a guiding light in developing a sustainable pulp and paper industry at the time, issued a public alert to warn consumers about environmental issues related to bamboo. It was learned that some of the mill operations in Southeast Asia had displaced or mistreated local people and significantly disturbed native ecosytems, including polluting the surrounding watershed.[97] At that time, industrial use of bamboo as a replacement for wood fiber was jeopardizing some of the world's last bamboo forests. Also, transportation of bamboo pulp, including plantation-grown bamboo, from this ecologically sensitive area was not considered to be environmentally sound. Since then, many U.S. paper manufacturers have stopped importing bamboo pulp. As of 2008, there are no

certification policies for bamboo as a pulp source to ensure that bamboo for paper is harvested in accordance with social and environmental certification schemes.[98]

Today, consideration of bamboo as a pulp to meet global consumer demand still poses environmental concerns. Although bamboo plantations are replacing harvests from endangered or protected areas, they are still pulped overseas, where certification and environmental regulations are lax. The use of plantation-grown bamboo poses many of the same issues as using virgin wood as a paper source. Since bamboo can be chipped in existing wood-based pulp mills, it discourages the much-needed conversion of mill technology to incorporate alternative pulp technologies, in particular those from agricultural fiber sources.[99]

Given that this member of the grass family (Poaceae) has such a high-quality fiber yield and an ability to grow in many geographic locations around the world, it offers opportunities closer to home with more research and market development in the future.

Benefits at a glance:

— High-fiber-yield bamboo can be pulped and manufactured like traditional printing papers.

— Bamboo enjoys quick growth and maturity rate and can reach heights of fifty feet or more in four years. Other sources have various harvest seasons and maturity rates.

— "Tree-free" bamboo contributes as much as 50 percent of tree-free fiber in some commercial paper lines. Other fiber materials in paper mix may come from PCW wood fiber.

— No certification is available to ensure that harvesting and production processes are socially and environmentally sound.

— Distance from point of growth to production facilities may require disproportionate fuel use versus established materials streams.

— Chipping and pulping processes for some paper types share many of the same environmental impact issues of wood-based paper.

Product example:

— A wide variety of handmade and artisan papers are available at art and craft stores. With the increase in popularity of scrapbooking, new specialty papers are becoming available all the time.

— Suitable for graphic arts demands, Neenah Environment® EverGreen 50/50 (Formerly Fox River) is manufactured with 50 percent bamboo fibers and 50 percent post-consumer fibers. (*www.neenahpaper.com*)

Fiber Crops or "On-Purpose" Crops

Crops that require land allocated for their use are often termed "on-purpose" crops when it comes to obtaining fibers for papermaking. These include cotton, hemp, plantation bamboo, and kenaf.

COTTON

Cotton fiber has enjoyed a rich history and often has been used for quality papers and correspondence. Combined with linen, the strength and durability of the fibers have made them the choice for printing America's paper currency. Cotton is grown primarily for the textile industry, and papers come from a by-product of cotton production known as cotton linters. These are the small fibers left on the cottonseed when a cotton gin separates the cotton from the seedpod. If papermakers didn't use these linters, they likely would end up in the landfill.

Given that the linters are an agricultural by-crop, they can also qualify as recycled fiber, and the production process produces no additional environmental impact. Unlike wood, cotton fibers do not contain lignin that needs to broken down by chemicals, nor do they require intense bleaching to make the paper pulp whiter. The drawback to cotton production is that the majority of cotton crops are farmed with considerable use of pesticides or may not meet Fair Trade standards.

Benefits at a glance:

— Cotton fiber papers impart a sense of premium quality and tradition, with soft and luxurious textures.

— Strong, durable fibers make cotton the top choice for majority of fiber used for paper currency in the United States.

— Cotton fibers can be made from fibrous residuals. Cotton linters can also qualify as recycled fiber. Harvesting and production produces no additional environmental impact, and prevents waste (linter fibers on cotton seeds are used, which normally would be landfilled).

— They are lignin free, so chemicals are not required for softening.

— Little bleaching of cotton fibers is required.

Drawbacks at a glance:

— Mainstream cotton crops use many agrochemicals that can damage the environment. This danger can be mitigated by using organic cotton or species of cotton that are more resistant to insects.

— Cotton is a "thirsty crop"—it requires much water to cultivate.

— Cotton is an important commodity around the world, and social and environmental standards may be lacking, especially in undeveloped or developing countries.

Product examples:

These paper companies offer products made with different percentages of cotton:

— Crane & Co: *www.cranepaper.com*

Crane's Crest: 100 percent cotton; Crane's Bond: 100 percent cotton; Cranes' Choice: 25 percent cotton; Crane's Lettra Letterpress: 100 percent cotton developed expressly for letterpress printing; Crane's Palette: 100 percent cotton

— Gmund: *www.gmund.com*

Kaschmir: 50 percent cotton, and Act Green Collection includes paper made from 100 percent cotton

— Greenfield Paper: *www.greenfieldpaper.com*

Hemp Heritage Paper, Stationary and Envelopes, plus paper by the ream, with 25 percent hemp fiber and 75 percent post-consumer waste

— Mohawk Fine Papers: *www.mohawkpaper.com*

Mohawk Via: 25 percent cotton; Strathmore Pure Cotton: 100 percent cotton; Strathmore Writing: 25 percent and 100 percent cotton; Strathmore Writing: 25 percent cotton i-Tone (for digital presses)

— Neenah Paper: *www.neenahpaper.com*

Classic Cotton: 25 percent, 50 percent and 100 percent cotton; Gilbert Cottons: 25 percent and 100 percent cotton; Capitol Bond: 25 percent cotton; Neutech Cotton: 25 percent and 100 percent cotton; Fox River Select: 25 percent and 100 percent cotton

— Smart Papers: *www.smartpapers.com*

Synergy 25 percent cotton: 25 percent cotton; Nekoosa Bond/25 percent cotton: 25 percent cotton (with exception of Carrara White)

— Southworth (recently acquired Esleeck Papers): *www.southworth.com*

Cotton Wove Paper: 25 percent and 100 percent cotton; Connoisseur Collection: 100 percent cotton; Credentials Collection: 25 percent cotton

— Wausau Papers: *www.wausaupapers.com*

Royal Cotton: 25 percent cotton

HEMP

Hemp has been grown for thousands of years, and its fibers have been used for numerous materials, including textiles and paper. Hemp and tobacco were important cash crops to the early American settlers, and it has been said that Thomas Jefferson wrote rough drafts of the Declaration of Independence on hemp paper.

Hemp grows quickly and, per acre, yields from two to four times the fiber of pine and has the potential to take pressure off forests to obtain paper fiber and pulp. The plant has a natural resistance to pests. Its fast-growing canopy suppresses weeds and can easily be grown organically without pesticides and herbicides. The fibers are strong and are naturally acid free, meaning that papers made from hemp pulp have archival qualities. The light, creamy color of the fibers mean that little or no bleaching is required. Because hemp cultivation is illegal in the United States, pulp must be imported.

Benefits at a glance:

— Industrial hemp provides promising pulp source potential to take pressure off forests, as well as providing a variety of other commercial uses (oil, fabrics, bioplastics, health food, and fuel).

— Hemp is fast growing, yielding two to four times more fiber than trees in a much shorter period of time.

— It is naturally resistant to pests and can be part of sustainable agricultural practices.

— Hemp has strong, durable fibers, is naturally acid free, and offers archival benefits.

— Its light-colored fiber requires little or no bleaching depending on the paper type being made.

Drawbacks at a glance:

— Hemp is a controversial crop. Its cultivation currently is illegal in many countries (the United States, for example). Importing processed hemp fiber from countries where its cultivation is legal (Canada, France, and China, for example) increases cost and the product's eco-footprint.

— Few pulping and manufacturing mills can process fiber for papermaking in United States, though such facilities do exist in countries where hemp is actively grown.

Product examples:

— EcoPaper, also known as Costa Rica Naturals: *www.ecopaper.com*

Hemp paper made from hemp and PCF and PCW fibers.

— Ecosource paper: *www.islandnet.com/~ecodette/ecosource.htm*

Eco-21: Completely tree-free paper with 40 percent hemp, 40 percent flax, and 20 percent cotton.

— GMUND: *www.gmund.com*

Act Green collection includes "Cannibis" made from 30 percent cannabis and 70 percent FSC paper from mixed sources.

— Greenfield Paper: *www.greenfieldpaper.com*

Hemp Heritage Paper, Stationary and Envelopes, plus paper by the ream, with 25 percent hemp fiber and 75 percent post-consumer waste. The Hemp Thread-Green paper is handcrafted with 100 percent recycled hemp fabric.

— Living Tree Paper: *www.livingtreepaper.com*

Déjà Vu Coated C2S: 10 percent hemp/flax, 40 percent post-consumer waste, 20 percent pre-consumer waste, and 30 percent certified sustainably harvested wood; Vanguard Recycled Plus: 10 percent hemp/flax and 90 percent post-consumer waste, processed totally chlorine free.

KENAF

Kenaf is an annual crop and member of the hibiscus family, related to cotton and okra. Cultivated for thousands of years, it has recently been "rediscovered" as a viable alternative for paper pulp. Since it is grown for fiber only, not for flowers or fruit, it can be grown without the need for pesticides in many parts of the world, including southern areas of the United States.

In 1963, the United States Department of Agriculture identified kenaf as being the fiber source with the most potential to replace wood. Kenaf crops grow quickly and can produce 6 to 10 tons of dry fiber per acre annually, which is approximately three to five times greater than pine. It rotates well with other crops and legumes, has lower production costs, and uses less energy and chemicals to manufacture it into pulp. Papers made with 100 percent kenaf are a beautiful, creamy, pale taupe color.

Benefits at a glance:

— Kenaf provides promising potential to take pressure off forests.

— Kenaf is fast growing, yielding three to five times more fiber than trees.

— It is naturally resistant to pests and can be part of sustainable agricultural practices.

— It has excellent papermaking characteristics; it is stronger, whiter, and uses less energy and chemicals than paper made from trees.

— Kenaf is water and energy efficient.

— Bio-energy can be generated from processing of by-products during manufacturing.

— For other than the brightest white paper types, kenaf's naturally light-colored fiber requires little or no bleaching.

Drawbacks at a glance:

— Few pulping and manufacturing mills can process kenaf fiber economically for papermaking at the present time.

Product examples:

— Vision Paper: *www.visionpaper.com*. The company produced several kenaf papers made from 100 percent kenaf fiber or kenaf and PCW paper, much heralded by corporate clients and environmental organizations. However, these papers currently are not available due to third-party mill closures. The company's focus has shifted to develop leading-edge pulping technology to produce environmentally superior and quality products.

Textile, Rag, and Artisan Papers

Recycled clothing, textiles, and fabric scraps for papermaking have a long history in papermaking, and perhaps will reemerge as a vital fiber source in the future. Papers made from textile fibers are not only tree-free, they take recycling and reuse to another level.

In the twenty-first century, paper companies have used industrial textile scraps to make high-quality papers, including denim that yields beautiful blue-hued sheets. Many of these paper products are available in writing papers for stationary use.

Other usages of textile or rag papers are for specialty or art papers. For example, St. Louis based Arch Paper offers opportunities for fibers from cast-off clothes to live again in the form of beautiful, high-quality paper. The company separates fabrics by color and material to eliminate the need for bleaches, solvents, or dyes. Custom colors can be created, or artists can purchase "shred" to use in their own handmade papers.

Product examples:

— Greenfield Paper Company: *www.greenfieldpaper.com*; Denim Paper Evolution Stationary, 100 percent recycled denim fabric trimmings

— Arch Paper: *www.archpaper.net*; art papers made from recycled cotton clothing and textiles

Stone or Minerals

Papers made from stone or minerals, specifically calcium carbonate plus a plastic polymer binder, have recently emerged on the market and have been marketed as tree free. It should be noted that minerals have been used in papermaking for some time and that calcium carbonate and kaolin (clay) have been used as whiteners and as additives to make coated papers. The mining of these minerals and other finite resources and their environmental impact is being questioned. The trend to replace tree fiber with minerals continues to rise, especially in Europe, where wood fiber is scarce and expensive.[100] Companies that produce "stone papers" state that the calcium carbonate used for their products mainly comes from building and construction material waste as well as marble and limestone scraps. These are ground into a chalklike consistency with polyethylene (PE) used as a binder, with high heat applied to bond ingredients together. This process requires no water and requires much less energy than traditional papermaking. The end result is a product that is naturally white without the use of bleaching compounds, is acid free, durable, and water and tear resistant.

These papers could be a useful part of the mix to help take pressure off forests to meet a variety of paper demands. However, other questions arise about the long-term effects of mining resources and the issues surrounding the recycling of materials composed of several resources.

Benefits at a glance:

— Papers made from stone or minerals are completely tree-free, combining calcium carbonate and PE or other binding agents.

— Often no water is used in the production process, there are fewer emissions, and half the energy of paper production is required.

— Some of these papers require 20 to 30 percent less ink than conventional papers.

— Many are chlorine free and naturally bright white from the minerals used.

— Many are water and tear resistant.

— These papers can be considered recyclable once facilities become available. Some are not considered to be a contaminant in recycling streams.

Drawbacks at a glance:

— The binder may be composed of petroleum-based plastic.

— Some require transport from a great distance, adding fuel impacts to footprint.

— Not all of these papers work well with all printer types, including ink-jet printers and laser printers. Some manufacturers/distributors prefer printing to be done at their facility.

BURT'S BEES
NATURAL
SKIN CARE FOR MEN
BAR SOAP
4 oz / 113 g
99.72% NATURAL
BURT'S BEES
Fabulously Fresh
Peppermint & Rosemary
BODY BAR
4 oz
NEW
BURT'S BEES
Radiance
EXFOLIATING BODY BAR
with royal jelly
100% NATURAL
4 oz / 113 g
NEW
Extra
Energizing
Get naturally clean, soft, supple, beautiful
toe with Burt's Bees line of Citrus & Ginger
This wrapper is made from TerraSkin™, a paper made of minerals
and produced without the use of toxic bleaching chemicals, so it
will degrade back into its source: the powder of stone.
Please discard normally; do not recycle with regular paper.

— End-of-life issues: These papers may require specific recycling or composting facilities not common in all markets, so often they are landfilled or incinerated.

Product examples:

— TerraSkin: *www.chameleonpackaging.com*

— FiberStone™: *www.naturalsourceprinting.com*

— XTerrane Stone Photo Paper: *www.xterrane.en.ecplaza.net*

— ViaStone: *www.viastone.net*

Synthetic Papers

Consider author William McDonough's thoughts about the "elegance" of trees and the shortsightedness of using wood pulp for paper. The following is quoted from a TED (Technology, Entertainment, Design) talk filmed in 2005.

> Imagine this design assignment. Design something that makes oxygen, sequesters carbon, fixes nitrogen, distills water, accrues solar energy as fuel, makes complex sugars and food, creates microclimates, changes colors with the season, and self-replicates . . . [shrugs, pauses and then wryly adds]—Why don't we knock that down and write on it.

In the book *Cradle to Cradle,* by William McDonough and Michael Braungart, the introduction is titled "This Book Is Not a Tree." The book is printed on synthetic paper, made from plastic resins and inorganic fillers. The book is durable and waterproof, and the authors consider the book a "technical ingredient," referring to a product that can be broken down and circulated infinitely in a closed loop industrial cycle.[101] The book, though heavier and more fuel intensive to ship than a natural fiber–based book, was created to get people thinking beyond just ink on paper to word delivery systems. Were facilities in place, the authors envisioned synthetic paper that could be easily washed of ink and then recycled, reused, and recycled again without losing material quality.

Benefits at a glance:

— Synthetic papers are completely tree-free.

— Use "technical nutrients" and recycled plastic trimmings from polypropylene (PP) or high-density polyethylene (HDPE). Labels made from PP are used for packaging and can be processed along with the object they are adhered to, facilitating recycling.

— Durable and water, chemical, and tear resistant. Such papers are useful for some outdoor applications, waterproof maps, wipeable menus, tags, and long-lasting goods.

— Recyclable where facilities accept PP in this form, although currently there are very few markets with these facilities.

Drawbacks at a glance:

— Many of these synthetic papers are derived from petroleum.

— Manufacturers have specific ink and cutting recommendations. Some require specially formulated inks, primers, and spray powders to reduce static on press.

Burt's Bees pioneered the use of TerraSkin™ paper in personal care for wrapping bar soaps. TerraSkin™ is an environmentally conscious, treeless and bleach-free paper alternative. It also has a lower absorption rate so 20–30 percent less ink is used when printing.

— Synthetic papers should not be used in laser printers or photocopiers where heat would fuse paper to the imaging mechanism.

— End-of-life issues require specific recycling facilities that are not readably available in all markets.

— Such papers can weigh more than natural fiber papers, adding additional costs for transportation and shipping with related emission of greenhouse gases.

Product examples:

— DuPont Tyvek®: *www2.dupont.com*

— Polyart®: *www.polyart.com*

— Yupo®: *www.yupo.com*

Animal "Processed" or Dung Fibers

Vegetable fiber consumed, preprocessed, and then "eliminated" by a variety of animals makes for a truly novel and resourceful fiber for papermaking. Although some of these papers may be considered novelty papers, lacking true potential to replace wood pulp to meet global market demand, they are included here to demonstrate conservation and innovation in process. Elephant, panda, and bison waste can now be found in several novelty or specialty papers. Given that these animals live almost exclusively on fibrous plants, the waste product is essentially raw cellulose. Once it is cleaned and processed, the pulp often is mixed with recycled post-consumer waste materials to give them added printing and handling properties, making for beautiful and unusual papers.

Paper pulp from animal waste (aka: poop-paper or dung-paper) makes great use of a waste product and in some cases can bring attention to conservation efforts or help raise funds. Beloved panda couple Chuang Chuang and Lin Hui produce around fifty-five pounds of feces daily. This waste processed into paper has proven to be a highly popular product at the zoo's gift store. Better yet, the profits from the panda poop paper, made in conjunction with Thailand's Chiang Mai Zoo's panda unit, where the pair lives, helps balance the costs of the pandas' keep.[102] In the case of elephant paper, the gathering of dung may help provide solutions for resolving human-elephant conflicts in Sri Lanka by changing minds about the "value" of the animals for humans.[103]

Benefits at a glance:

— Paper pulp from animal droppings uses waste resourcefully.

— Harvesting and production produces no additional environmental impact.

— Like recycled stocks, these papers require less water, energy, and chemicals to produce.

— The PCW wood fiber content of the fiber mix can be processed chlorine free.

— Rural communities and economies benefit and the use of local resources decreases the ecological footprint. These papers provide fundraising options and help conservation efforts.

Mr. Ellie Pooh paper uses nature to "preprocess" naturally growing fibers for papermaking. They are made up of 75 percent elephant dung and 25 percent post-consumer paper. No toxic chemicals are used in this papermaking process; instead, natural vegetative binding agents are used, along with water-soluble salt dyes for coloring. "Mr. Ellie Pooh's papers are handmade, acid free and as organic as it gets." (*www.mrelliepooh.com*)

— May provide solutions or reduce conflicts for shared areas among agricultural crops, animals, and humans.

Drawbacks at a glance:

— No certification is available to ensure that animals are treated fairly and humanely or that waste is gathered without encroaching on important or protected habitats, or eco-systems that rely on specific dung levels.

— Fiber availability and storage issues exist.

— Some suppliers are using chlorine to sterilize or lighten papers until more sustainable options are found.

— These papers are not viable options for large-scale paper demands. Most papers are handmade and are not available for conventional graphic design projects requiring large press runs or for publications and books.

— Distance from point of growth to production facilities may require disproportionate fuel use versus more established materials streams.

This pulp source is growing, and many of these papers are emerging as tie-ins to conservation projects. A Web search will help designers find sources to use these papers for small, special projects or for use as journals, greeting cards or stationary sets. The efforts of the Mr. Ellie Pooh company have been recognized with a Green Business Leader Award by Green America. This Brooklyn-based company uses its position in the marketplace to organize consumers and businesses to build a more socially just and ecologically sustainable economy. Visit *www.mrelliepooh.com* to learn more about the paper and the plight of Asian elephants living in Sri Lanka.

What to Look for in an Alternative Fiber Paper

Green Seal offers a "Green Report" and checklist for alternative papers on its Web site:[104]

— Look for paper that contains at least *50 percent tree-free content.*

— Seek out papers that incorporate *fibers that would traditionally be burned or wasted* in other ways (e.g., banana stalks; recovered cotton, denim, or currency; tobacco leaves; coffee bean residues; and other types of agricultural or manufacturing remainders).

— If a paper is chosen that is not entirely tree free, look for paper that makes up the balance with *post-consumer waste (PCW).*

— If choosing a paper that has been bleached, choose a paper that is classified as either *TCF (Totally Chlorine Free)* or *PCF (Processed Chlorine Free).*

— Look for paper fibers that are *grown and processed locally.* This cuts down on transportation and environmental costs.

Worth the Paper It's Printed On

In a speech delivered to attendees at an American Institute of Graphic Arts conference in 2003, Susan S. Szenasy, editor of *Metropolis Magazine*, encouraged graphic designers to start asking questions and learn more about environmental sustainability.

Designers today stand on the brink of being seen by society as essential contributors to its health, safety, and welfare. If you—together with the other design professions—decide to examine the materials and processes endemic to your work, as well as demand that these materials and processes become environmentally safe, you will be the heroes of the twenty-first century.[105]

Key Considerations for Specifying Paper

MATERIAL SOURCES: Whether papers are made from recycled paper, wood or agri-fibers, animal dung, stone, or plastic, it is important to understand how raw materials and their sourcing, manufacturing, distribution, and end life have environmental, social, and climate impacts. The designer's role is to be aware of these impacts and to carefully choose papers to mitigate these impacts by, for example, purchasing paper with high post-consumer content or alternative fibers, paper made with pulp from suppliers that can prove that it was sustainably sourced, or paper made with renewable energy. Designers also play a role in encouraging the growth, marketability, and use of alternative papers and the development of more sustainable supply chains.

WATER USAGE AND BLEACHING METHODS: The manufacturing of paper consumes more water per ton of product than any other manufacturing process.[106] The use of recycled paper saves resources and decreases water usage by 50 to 60 percent.[107] Bleaching processes and the chemicals used directly impact both water usage and water quality. Bleaching chemistry uses enormous amounts of water during the whitening process and renders the water unsafe and toxic afterward. Wastewater and mill effluent wreak havoc on habitats, and additional chemicals and water pollutants from the pulp and papermaking processes require intensive treatment. Give preference to post-consumer recycled, Totally Chlorine Free (TCF), or Processed Chlorine Free (PCF) papers. Learn more about bleaching methods, definitions, and certifications.

ENERGY USAGE: Paper mills and paper companies are working hard to increase energy efficiency, convert waste into energy, and use or purchase renewable energy to manufacture their papers. Source papers from mills that use certified green energy, whether it is wind, low-impact hydroelectric, biomass or biogas, and/or mills and companies that purchase third-party, certified offsets or renewable energy credits to become carbon neutral. Also note: Compared to virgin paper manufacturing, post-consumer recycled paper requires 40 to 64 percent less energy.[108]

WISE USE OF RESOURCES: Designers have numerous options to conserve resources, whether they include the use of digital workflows, paper reduction strategies, or smart layout and design. Consider these strategies:

— Utilize double-sided or default duplexing features for in-house printing and copying.

— Use digital delivery systems, including Web-based FTP services to upload files and Direct to Plate (DtP) pre-press and soft-proofing to save film and paper.

— Make efficient use of standard parent sheets and standard press sheets and envelopes to reduce paper waste, or utilize edges of paper for smaller projects (i.e., minicards or belly bands).

— Gang multiple projects on one press run to decrease proofs, make-readies, and ink and paper use.

— Choose the lightest weight of paper required for the project while maintaining quality to conserve resources, and to reduce paper shipping costs and related greenhouse emissions.

— Match scale to content, and choose the best medium to deliver the design message (i.e., an e-mail can take the place of a postcard, a postcard can take the place of a brochure, etc.).

— Avoid bleeds that create trim waste, and refrain from spreading design content to additional pages, folds, or signatures that are not needed (i.e., French folds that double paper usage).

— Consult with printers to determine which printing technology will suit each project best with the minimal environmental impact.

— Respect resourceful design over artful excess.

TRANSPORTATION AND ECO-FOOTPRINT: As always, locality is a core element of sustainability. Specifying a fabulous eco-paper from across the world will yield little benefit if the shipping cost and carbon footprint of transportation exceeds the benefits. Designers can keep informed about paper companies, distributors, and printers that best serve their region or the location of the customer's final shipping destination. For example, online proofing or "soft proofing" can aid designers and customers with reducing carbon footprints on a variety of levels. The "Distribute then Print" model for sharing digital files that can be printed on-demand in local geographic regions can prevent overprinting, plus save time and shipping costs, as does the selection of a printer near the final shipping location. Careful consideration of the basis weight of paper needed for projects can also make an impact, not only in regards to saving pulp, water, and energy resources but also for transportation. For example, an uncoated or lighter paper stock still can meet professional quality expectations yet can dramatically save resources and money by decreasing related shipping weights, fuel use, and distribution costs.

END OF LIFE: Specifying paper for a project goes beyond color, weight, texture, gloss, whiteness, and the like. Designers must also consider that the paper is appropriate to the life of the project and has a minimal eco-impact once it has run its course. Work backward and ask these questions:

— Can the paper for this project be readily recycled in typical recycling facilities?

— Can the paper be reused?

— Is the paper degradable or compostable without harmful releases?

— Can the paper be deinked easily, or does it pose recycling issues and add to recycling sludge if it has full ink coverage, contains coatings or laminates, or is made from brightly or deeply colored paper stock?

— Papers made from stone or plastic may tread lightly on forests and use little or no water;

If you—together with the other design professions—decide to examine the materials and processes endemic to your work, as well as demand that these materials and processes become environmentally safe, you will be the heroes of the 21st century.

—*Susan S. Szenasy*

---

however what are the end-of-life consider-ations? Are the papers truly biodegradable? Can plastic papers readily be recycled along with other plastics of the same type?

— Will the paper chosen last longer than the life of the project? Carefully consider and research papers backward from their end-of-life use, and educate others along the way.

Paper Resources

Online Databases of Environmentally Preferred Papers and Grades

— Ancient Forest Friendly™ paper database: *www.canopyplanet.org*

— Celery Design Collaborative: Ecological Guide to Paper: *www.celerydesign.com*

— Conservatree: *www.conservatree.org*

— Design Can Change "Green Paper Guide": *www.designcanchange.org*

— Forest Stewardship Council: Lists of certified papers, paper merchants, paper manufacturers, certifed printers, and certified pulp suppliers: *www.fscus.org*

— Paper Specs: This powerful, first of its kind online paper database was specifically devel-oped for the design and print industries. With over 4,300 paper products to choose from (including a selection of packaging grades), the Basic Search function selects paper by weight, color, finish, and brand name. The Advanced Search however can look for any combination of recycled content, FSC, TCF/PCF and other key certifications and eco-features. Users can

also receive the latest swatchbooks, order newly released mill promotions and have easy access to in-depth paper facts and tips: *www.paperspecs.com*

— Rainforest Alliance SmartGuide to Paper: global list of paper, pulp, converters, merchants, printers, etc.: *www.rainforest-alliance.org*

Web-Based Environmental Paper Calculators:

— The Paper Calculator, developed by the Environmental Defense Fund, and based on research done by the Paper Task Force: *www.edf.org/papercalculator*. (Note: Several paper companies also provide environmental savings calculators or eco-audits, based on data compiled by the Paper Task Force)

— Mohawk Fine Papers: Environmental Calcula-tor: *www.mohawkpaper.com*

— Neenah Paper: ECO Calculator: *www.neenah.com*

— New Leaf paper: Provides "eco-audit" artwork with environmental benefits and eco-logos when New Leaf papers are used: *www.newleafpaper.com/ecoaudit.html*

Resources, Overviews, Glossaries, and Purchasing Guides:

— AIGA Design Business and Ethics, "Print Design and Environmental Responsibility" Brochure, *www.aiga.com*

— Ancient Forest Friendly™: *www.canopyplanet.org*

— Celery Design Collaborative, Ecological Guide to Paper: *www.celerydesign.com*

— Chlorine Free Products Association (CFPA): *www.chlorinefreeproducts.org*

— Conservatree provides detailed fact sheets about papermaking, environmental issues, and ways to reduce waste. Purchasing guides include the "Paper Master List" for professional paper buyers and "Recycled Copy Paper Listings" containing national and regional retail store lists: *www.conservatree.org*

— Design Can Change "Sustainable Design Checklist": *www.designcanchange.org*

— Dogwood Alliance: Brings together the voices of thousands of individuals, local and regional grassroots partners, and national and international organizations: *www.dogwoodalliance.org*

— ecoLingo: Earth-friendly graphic design "Label Lingo" and other resources and links: *www.ecolingo.com*

— EcoLogo Program: *www.ecologo.org* or *www.environmentalchoice.com*

— *EcoPackaging.net*: Sustainability articles, books and links: *www.EcoPackaging.net*

— EPA Guide to Purchasing Green Power: Renewable Electricity, Renewable Energy Certificates, and On-Site Renewable Generation: PDF available online: *www.epa.gov/greenpower/documents/purchasing_guide_for_web.pdf*

— Environmental Defense Fund, "Tips for Selecting, Buying and Reducing Paper" and other guides: *www.edf.org*

— Environmental Paper Network, "Paper Steps: Taking the Steps to Environmentally Responsible Paper" and a "Purchaser Toolkit": *www.whatsinyourpaper.com* or *www.environmentalpaper.org*

— ForestEthics: *www.forestethics.com*

— FSC Forest Stewardship Council: *www.fscus.org*

— Green-e: *www.green-e.org*

— Green-in-Print, "A Guide to Environmentally Friendly Choices in Photographic Paper": *www.conservatree.com/paper/Choose/GreenInPrintApril08.pdf*

— Green Press Initiative, "Toolkit for Responsible Paper Use." Green Press Initiative helps those in the book and newspaper industries better understand their impacts on endangered forests, indigenous communities, and the Earth's climate: *www.greenpressinitiative.org*

— Green Seal: *www.greenseal.org*

— MBDC Cradle to Cradle Certification: *www.c2ccertified.com*

— Monadnock, "A Field Guide": *www.mpm.com/graphicarts/environment/field_guide*

— ODO (Organic Design Operatives)—"eco-design toolkits": *www. themightyodo.com*

— Paper Recycling Coalition: *www .paperrecyclingcoalition.com*

— Treefree Paper "Treefree 101" Primer: *www.treefreepaper.com*

— Rainforest Action Network: *www.ran.org*

— Rainforest Alliance: *www.rainforest-alliance.org*

— Re-nourish—"Recipe for Sustainable Paper": *www.re-nourish.com*

— Sustainable Forestry Initiative (SFI): *www.aboutsfi.org*

— Watershed Media—"The Guide to Tree-Free, Recycled, and Certified Papers" book excerpts and listing of paper companies: *www.watershedmedia.org*

— WoodWise™ Consumer Guides and Glossary of Terms are available on the Green America (formerly Co-op America) Web site: *www.coopamerica.org/programs/woodwise*

— World Wildlife Foundation (WWF)—"WWF Paper Scorecard": *www.panda.org/paper*

Paper section contributing editor Dion Zuess, ecoLingo: earth friendly graphic design.

Inks

Whether it is black ink on plain white paper or rainbows of saturated color, our modern world would not be the same without ink to form letters and images on printed substrates: books, packages, labels, food wrappers, credit cards, and more. We have magnetic inks that can be recognized by specialized electronic equipment to increase the efficiency of handling bank checks; inks that are alkali-resistant for soap wrappers; inks that resist smearing by alcohol for liquor labels; metallic inks that simulate gold, silver, and other metals; we even have near-infrared dyes for "security printing" as a means of protecting documents from counterfeiting and fraudulent use.

From an environmental viewpoint alone, many innovations in ink formulations have altered the printing landscape over the past thirty years. Some of these developments include new combinations of agri-based inks, inks with minimal volatile organic compounds (VOCs), water-based inks, and solid, light-curing ink formulations that dry instantly. Other inks are being made from renewable, bio-derived raw materials or have been formulated to speed up make-ready and reduce start-up waste. Many new ink formulations require less waste management or come in reusable containers, reducing the need for special disposal of drums as hazardous waste. Best of all, European and North American ink manufacturers and experts have stated that inks formulated with heavy metals (referred to as "toxic inks" in the past) have been phased out of common commercial usage in their home markets for some time.[109] (Note: This is not always the case for inks made or used in other countries; more information follows.) Looking ahead, there are discussions in the industry regarding eco-labels or seals for inks and carbon footprint data that could be made available for different printing technologies.

Given these strides, there are still challenges with all new print technologies and ink formulations. Gary Jones, director of environmental health and safety affairs for Printing Industries of America/Graphic Arts Technical Foundation (PIA/GATF), states:

> There's no silver bullet when looking at best practices or when looking at environmental claims made from an environmental perspective. There are positives and negatives with all technologies.

He cites an example of the move from analog to digital, direct-to-plate printing technology.

> This has been a step in the right direction, eliminating the metal and film chemistry required to make and develop film/plates in the

311

printing process. However, digital processing has a trade-off, as this process generates a high pH that can be considered hazardous waste unless neutralized or handled appropriately.[110]

Also known as computer-to-plate (CtP), direct-to-plate systems enhance digital productivity and workflow, and offer customized short-run jobs on demand.

There's no silver bullet. . . . There are positives and negatives with all technologies.

—Gary Jones, director of environmental health and safety affairs for Printing Industries of America/Graphic Arts Technical Foundation

---

Another trade-off is the use of soy-based inks. These and other agri-based inks are made from renewable sources and emit fewer VOCs. Soy crops have sustained North American farmers and diminished the dependence on nonrenewable foreign resources, such as petroleum. Yet now that soy growing is on the rise in other geographic areas, new issues are springing up. Advocates for sustainable forestry and rain forest protection are concerned that the expanding cash crops of palm oil and soy are contributing to rainforest deforestation and global climate change. Clear-cutting and burning forests to make way for soy farming damages ecosystems, displaces indigenous peoples, and exposes farmers, communities, and surrounding fragile ecosystems to herbicides and pesticides.[111]

Other critics of agri-based materials and biofuels maintain that on a global front, soy and corn crops are better suited for sustenance crops rather than for ink and fuel.[112] The future may bring more research and development into soy inks and alternative agri-based ink and pressroom material options, including methods such as deriving ethanol from cellulosic feedstocks like prairie grass and wood chips or even from the field waste left from growing food crops.

Despite these innovations, industry changes, and proposals, can there truly be labeling of any ink formula or printing process as "earth friendly" or "environmentally friendly" at this time? The answer may lie in definitions of those terms and others, and a more complete understanding of the inherent chemical and industrial nature of inks and the related pre-press, printing, cleanup, and disposal of these and related chemicals and materials. As we learn more about applying sustainability ideas, systems thinking, and life cycle analyses to this industry and many others, we find that we are at the start of a very long yet exciting journey.

The first step of this journey includes learning not only about the current state of the ink industry and options to choose from, but reviewing the past so that designers can make informed choices and have clear conversations with printers and ink representatives. The second step requires designers, print buyers, printers, and ink manufacturers all to work together to move the process forward.

On the Road to Better Inks

David Savastano, editor of *Ink World*, gathered thoughts from ink manufacturers regarding key trends in waxes, solvents and additives in his article of that name in 2007.[113] Green initiatives and sustainability were listed as one of the key issues of importance to manufacturers. Bob Lieberman, global market manager for Cognis Corporation, was quoted as saying:

> To be successful in the future, companies will need to offer improved products that meet these needs—sustainable, lower carbon footprints, based on renewable resources, environmentally more friendly, etc.

Joon Choo, vice president of Shamrock Technologies echoed that sentiment:

> There is more focus towards being 'green' with environmentally friendly products and practices. We are continuing with design of new additives for aqueous and UV inks.[114]

Other additive manufacturers noted that there is more of a push toward low-VOC and formaldehyde-free options.

A year later, Sean Milmo, the European editor of *Ink World,* wrote about key topics and technologies that were the focus of Drupa, the world's biggest printing exhibition, held in Dusseldorf, Germany.

> Sustainability is becoming the major issue confronting the printing industry at the moment, with the emphasis on lower CO_2 emissions, less pollution, greater conservation of resources like water and reduced waste.

> Energy efficiency is fast becoming the biggest challenge among the industry's sustainability objectives. This is not only because of the urgent need to cut emissions of greenhouse gases,

but also to cut costs because of escalating energy prices.[115]

Other ink and printing industry manufacturers, exhibitors, and industry conventions and seminars are starting to shift their focus not only to greener supply chains, technology, and equipment but also to sustainable business strategies and marketing as it is becoming clear that the rising costs of raw materials and energy usage not only impacts their industry but the environment as well. For others, product stewardship and striving to meeting customers' goals to minimize their environmental impact also play a role.

"Sustainability is the biggest thing on the mind of our customers," Michelle Hearn, director of marketing of Sun Chemical said in a phone interview in 2008. She predicts we will see four key trends in the next few years: bio-based inks, energy-efficient inks, inks and press materials that release fewer VOC emissions into the environment, and energy usage for drying inks.[116]

Each of these industry snapshots emphasizes several key details that designers need to pay attention to when specifying inks and printing for projects: VOCs (volatile organic compounds) and HAPs (hazardous air pollutants) in inks and press-room materials; heavy metal compliance; the sourcing of raw materials, including bio-derived renewable materials; energy usage; biodegradability; and the impact on recycling and life cycle.

Inks: Eco-basics

It's important to remember that the materials and products of the current commercial ink and printing industry are comprised of chemicals and use industrial processes. As such, they are not considered inherently "healthy" or "environmentally friendly."

The National Association of Printing Ink Manufacturers (NAPIM), in conjunction with the National Printing Ink Research Institute's Environmental Impact Committee, has noted at least six possible characteristics or properties that would indicate that an ink has a reduced environmental impact. These include inks or products that are made from bio-derived renewable resources products that reduce emissions, do not result in any waste that is classified as hazardous, are more readily de-inkable after printing, produces de-inked sludge that is not classified as hazardous, and are more biodegradable.[117] The last three properties are difficult to determine, as there have been limited studies and data.

In the future, it will be foreseeable to have other eco-indicators for inks, including water conservation and energy usage (for setting or curing inks), raw material sourcing and formulation techniques, carbon or eco-footprint measurements, life cycle analyses, and more.

Overall, sustainability efforts and milestones in the ink industry lag behind other industries in such areas as: using certified renewable energy or offsets for manufacturing, using biodiesel or alternative fuel for transportation, providing transparent supply chain accountability, manufacturing with eco-based closed-loop systems, or participating in nonprofit conservation or climate change initiatives and making this progress and information publicly available.

The printing process relies on a variety of compounds and chemicals, many of which are petro-leum based: pigments and metals used for colorants, additives used to accelerate drying, and solvents used in press washes or plate-making. While environmental impacts can be minimized along the supply chain and pre-press and printing process, the fact remains that some of these materials have been linked to health problems, are classified as "hazardous waste,"[118] and require strictly regulated handing and disposal.[119]

Just as ink formulations are important when considering environmental impact, so too is working with a printer that understands the impacts of the chemicals and solvents used in other pressroom materials.

Cleanup and disposal are a part of printing that those on the design side don't often think about. Just as ink formulations are important when considering environmental impact, so too is working with a printer that understands the impacts of the chemicals and solvents used in other pressroom materials. The primary source of VOC emissions in any printing facility are solvents used to clean press blankets and ink rollers.[120] Press washes outnumber fountain solutions[121] three to one in a typical pressroom.[122] Since the cleaning of components is an important task undertaken not only between jobs but sometimes between colors of inks for the same run, cleanup requires a variety of products and is one of the greatest points of exposure to chemicals in a print house. Care with usage, storage, and disposal is key.

In general, "good housekeeping" practices and specific wastewater and waste management protocols,[123] ink-recycling guidelines, and other pollution prevention efforts are all part of the modern printing process. Each year, at least 2 billion pounds of ink are used by the printing industry,[124] so one can imagine the importance of toxin mitigation, ink recycling and waste management, plus the additional efforts that are put forward to deal with the rest of the materials used in the printing process.

Waste management for the printing process includes: wastewater, solid waste (empty containers, damaged plates, developed film, damaged products and spoilage), recycling, and air pollution or air emissions in the form of VOCs and HAPs.

Fresh Ink versus Fresh Air: Understanding VOCs and HAPs

Pressroom chemicals and materials (inks, fountain solutions, coatings, adhesives, additives, and solvents) and other materials used in printing facilities are sources of air pollutants and emissions of VOCs,[125] the precursors of ozone and a component of urban smog.[126] VOCs often are derived from petroleum and are found in chemicals used for ink formulations, plate or film processing chemicals, additives, solvents containing alcohols and esters, press washes, floor cleaning products, and other pressroom materials.[127] Naturally, the amount of VOCs released during the printing process depends on several factors, including the type of ink used; the pre-press and printing method used; the drying or curing process; the type of ventilation, collection or burn-off system used; the solvents used in press washes for cleanup; and so on.

Press chemicals are by far the greatest contributors to the release of VOCs from printing establishments.

Biochemicals for the Printing Industry; The Institute for Local Self-Reliance

In addition to air quality and pollution issues, VOCs and HAPs have been linked to health problems for humans, animals, and plants.[128] VOCs have been found to be a lung irritant for pressroom workers.[129] In the 1990s, environmental and health regulations limited the use of VOCs, in particular the federal Clean Air Act.[130] Also during this time, the United States Environmental Protection Agency (EPA) developed the EPA Test Method 24[131] as a standard test method to measure the amount of volatile matter content in inks, paints, varnishes, lacquers, fountain solutions, and other related materials.

VOC emissions are measured in pounds per gallon, grams per liter, or percentage by weight.[132] To learn more about the VOC content of inks to be considered for a job, or the VOC content of specific pressroom materials, consult with the printer, contact the manufacturer, or ask to see the product's material safety data sheet (MSDS). VOC information and other physical and chemical properties are required to be listed on the MSDS.

Typical petroleum or solvent-based formulations can have VOC levels as high as 25 to 40 percent.[133] Soy-based inks, vegetable-based inks, or other

Learn more about the VOC content of inks or the VOC content of specific pressroom materials by consulting with the printer, contacting the manufacturer, or asking to see the product's material safety data sheet.

agri-based inks are naturally lower in VOCs since they are made from renewable, nonpetroleum resources. However, the amount of vegetable oil content in inks can vary wildly. For example, some inks containing as little as 7 percent nonpetroleum content are still labeled as a soy ink.[134] Sometimes petroleum products or additives are included in ink formulations to assist with drying or as part of the pigment. John Adkin, Sun Chemical's product director in Europe, states that: "It is difficult to build a colored pigment without petroleum . . . it will be a long-time, probably 5 to 10 years, before we move away from this."[135]

Metals and Toxins

Metals connected with printing inks can be found in pigments, driers, or impurities and contaminants in the formulation process, such as the superfine particles that can form from the abrasion of the mixer and container during mixing.

Local and national regulations and legislation in the past twenty years have been quietly yet dramatically improving the ink and printing industry's performance with regard to reductions in heavy metals in ink formulations. Rather than list every law and regulation, we'll review some of the most relevant changes to the industry that relate to metals and toxins.

Local and national regulations and legislation in the past twenty years have been quietly yet dramatically improving the ink and printing industry.

Beginning in the 1970s and formalized in the 1990s, due to increasing concern about man-made concentrations of heavy metals in the environment, regulations in the United States and Europe began to come into force. Regulations, such as the Coalition of Northeastern Governors (CONEG)/USA, with restrictions on metals in packaging were adopted in key states, and the European Packaging and Packaging Waste Directive 94/62 EC was put in force for all members to better regulate all packaging impacts. These pieces of legislation made the commercial use of highly toxic metals (i.e., lead, arsenic, selenium, mercury, cadmium, and hexavalent chromium or compounds based on these metals) no longer viable.

In the late 1980s, pigments, raw materials, stabilizers, coatings, and other materials and chemicals found in inks came under scrutiny. In 1995, it was reported that more than 41 million pounds of toxic compounds were being transferred or released into the environment by the printing industry.[136]

Vibrant yellows, oranges, and warm reds containing barium in particular were a cause for concern, and it was determined that several inks were in use that contained heavy metals such as chromium, cadmium, and lead.[137] While the inks were considered safe in their bound form on paper and paperboard, the release of heavy metals through end-of-life processes (recycling, landfilling, burning) was of concern. Because of these dangers, CONEG, representing nine eastern states, including New York, New Jersey, and Connecticut, proposed model legislation that would strictly restrict the use of lead, cadmium, mercury, and a form of chromium in packaging. The Model Toxics in Packaging Legislation was developed in 1989. As of 2004, legislation based on this model was adopted only by nineteen states in the United States, but it has inspired action and influenced legislation in other countries.[138] The European Union used the model in 1994 as the basis of its packaging requirements for EU member states.

In 1988, the U.S. Congress passed the Title III of the Superfund Amendments and Reauthorization Act of 1988 (SARA). This "Section 313 List" or "SARA 313" contains a Toxic Release Inventory (TRI)[139] and requires states, communities, and industries to work together to plan for and respond to chemical accidents, to develop inventories of hazardous substances, track toxic chemical releases, and provide public access to information on hazardous substances.

When the EPA began regulating heavy metals, color formulators "typically turned to high-performance organic pigments to replace heavy-metal-based pigments."[140] During this time, many eco-minded graphic designers avoided warm red ink colors purported to contain heavy metals or barium, referring to the reporting requirements of SARA 313, and used CMYK blends to achieve approximate spot colors. In addition, designers fine-tuned their work to eliminate the use of inks commonly referred to as metallics (meaning inks used to replicate the look of metal).[141] As Sun Chemical in Europe has pointed out, however, metallic inks have far less of an environmental impact than other metallic effects, such as metal foils.[142]

Progressive ink manufacturers took early steps to prevent pollution and toxicity in their ink formulations. Others made the change after SARA 313 reporting and CONEG legislation were put into place. Some of these improvements included the replacement of color pigments containing heavy metals with organic pigments. In 1994, Ecoprint, a printer with an environmental focus, undertook a study with the EPA to determine if specific ink colors could be reformulated to avoid using undesirable metal-based pigments.[143] The twelve target metals selected for testing and replacement were antimony, arsenic, barium, cadmium, chromium, copper, lead, mercury, nickel, selenium, silver, and zinc. The study found that undesirable metals could be eliminated by creating new mixes of existing preferable inks with no loss of performance.

Each year, commercial formulators use millions of pounds of chemical ingredients that one way or another find their way into the environment.

—Alexis Golini, "The State of Ink"

At the time, the overall cost for the reformulated inks was higher as small batches would be made to order. However, today, ink makers serving a variety of print processes are responding to the demand for more environmentally favorable inks and are making reformulated inks a more accessible choice for printers and the designers they serve. Ecoprint notes: "Cleaner inks mean a cleaner recycling and de-inking process, and less impact on our land and water."[144]

In 2007, a representative of the National Association of Printing Ink Manufacturers stated: "There are no known carcinogens in the metallic and fluorescent inks currently manufactured by United States printing ink companies."[145] In addition, representatives from one of the world's largest producer of printing inks and pigments, Sun Chemical, state that, as a rule, there are no SARA 313 materials in their formulas or global supply chain.

However, do all ink markets, such as those in Asia and even the European Union, have the same access to materials and formulations that meet metals in inks compliance? Unfortunately not.

Access to ink markets passes through a variety of geographic borders, and often ink manufacturing and printing companies choose economics over the environment.

Even though regulation and legislation in Europe and North America have made dramatic improvements in ink formulations and have made inks safer for the personnel who create or work with them, this may not be the case elsewhere in the world. In 2007, for example, lead found in ink, paint, toys, jewelry, clothing (including coatings on snaps and zippers), and packaging materials (with recalls reported to number in the millions) caused worry and doubt about products that consumers buy or use every day.[146]

Also in 2007, the Toxics in Packaging Clearinghouse (TPCH) released a groundbreaking report describing how toxic heavy metals in packaging are still an issue overseas.[147] The greatest threat to the quality of packaging materials and compliance with state laws appears to be packages of imported products, namely polyvinyl chloride (PVC) packaging, and inks and colorants used on plastic shopping or

Even though regulation and legislation in Europe and North America have made dramatic improvements in ink formulations and have made inks safer for the personnel who create or work with them, this may not be the case elsewhere in the world.

Toxic heavy metals in imported packaging are still an issue almost 15 years after many major markets enacted laws prohibiting these substances in packaging.

—*Toxics in Packaging Clearinghouse*

mailing/shipping bags—both largely imported from Asia, where solvent-based inks and colorants are still used. Furthermore, the TPCH report states: "Given the amount and short-lived nature of packaging, lead and cadmium, in particular, are being continuously fed into the solid waste and recycling streams via discarded packaging, and potentially released into the environment."[148]

The TPCH report and other recent recalls and tests[149] remind us that we must continue to address on a global scale issues of supply chain documentation, correspondence with safety agencies, manufacturing, testing, and disposal of both everyday and recalled products.

Until there is worldwide acceptance of regulations (from the most restrictive markets) for metals in ink formulations and solvents, designers and print buyers may well extend the adage of "buy local" to inks, packaging, and printing in addition to food and other products, especially if local laws favor more responsible manufacturing. Regardless of where inks are manufactured and sold though, it is important to check the MSDS that comes with ink and pressroom materials to see exactly what's in the products they'll be using to represent their brand. (See the section "MSDS: An Eco-Design Tool Kit Essential" for more information.)

For example, a recent look at several MSDSs from ink manufacturers in major markets from 2004 to 2007 show "hazardous ingredients" or metals (barium, copper, cobalt, and zinc) in their ink formulations, with some ingredients listed under the SARA section of the MSDS. Furthermore, on several MSDSs viewed, the "Ecotoxicological Information" and "Chemical Fate Information" was listed as "No Data Available" or "Unknown," leaving

Until there is worldwide compliance about heavy metals in ink formulations and solvents, those working in areas with more forward-looking environmental laws may well want to extend the adage of "buy local" to inks.

designers or print buyers to wonder what this means both in the short and long term.

In addition, while proponents of metal pigments note that some of the pigments in question are not considered hazardous under the U.S. Occupational Health and Safety Association (OSHA) standard for Hazard Communication (29 CFR 1910.1200), OSHA's standards are not necessarily as extensive, as comprehensive, or as considerate of interactions and recombination in the body as one might need to fully capture the level of regulation needed to address the scope of the issue. Just as permissible arsenic levels for drinking water is a moving target depending on the current political climate, so too should "good enough" levels of known hazardous materials be considered with caution when assessing materials for environmental performance. Simple compliance with a particular standard in one market does not ensure compliance with standards in other markets.

It should be noted that while barium, one of the metals in question, is administered for ingestion in medical applications, it is not considered wholly "safe" by the medical community. In fact, according to the report "Chemtrails and Barium Toxicity" a form of barium is used in rat poison, with a variety of physical impacts on mammals from mild irritation, to chronic illness, to death, depending on the levels of exposure and type of barium compound encountered.[150] In nature, trace amounts of various forms of barium are widely found. However, the report notes that the most likely source of barium in the atmosphere is from industrial emissions. While the study this report refers to is several years old, barium is still actively used in industry. AquaMD.com, a Web site owned by the Connecticut-based American Water Trust, LLC, reports that: "[i]n 2002, the Environmental Protection Agency reported more than 222 million pounds of barium and barium compounds were legally released into the air, landfills, and waterways such as water wells, lakes, and rivers."[151]

It makes one wonder whether the compounds and chemicals deemed safe now are they likely to be deemed otherwise in the future. We need to fast forward and ask ourselves these questions and others:

— What happens when trash is landfilled or incinerated and the components on printed materials become bioavailable?

— Should the finite supplies of Earth's metals be dispersed into ink formulations and printed on paper and packaging, to then become irretrievable as a resource in landfills and incinerator ash when nonmetal alternatives might be available?

— Are landfills really as secure as we are led to believe to prevent leaching of ink compounds, chlorine, solvents, and metals such as cadmium, chromium, or lead?[152]

— Why do we continue to assume that ink and printing chemicals are benign and negligible compared to the impact of paper in the design and printing process?

Chain-of-custody protocols exist for responsible forest management and paper production; it will take efforts from designers, their clients, and printers to push for environmental stewardship and supply chain management for inks. One of the cornerstones of sustainability thinking is to go beyond compliance and take measures beyond regulations that may at best be the result of compromise legislation. Until regulations catch up with actions and impact studies, it is important to work with printers and suppliers to use materials better than the law demands. Doing so will help lay the groundwork for tomorrow while providing improved environmental performance today.

The Role of Renewables

The National Association of Printing Ink Manufacturers (NAPIM), a U.S.-based printing industry group, defines bio-derived renewable materials as "any material originating from plants, animals or naturally derived sources (such as water) that can be replenished in the short term. . . . There are well over sixty types of bio-derived renewable materials that can be used in printing inks."

One of NAPIM's objectives is to provide a universal labeling program for the printing ink industry in regard to bio-derived renewable content (BRC). The BRC label or seal will be based on the percent of bio-derived, renewable materials of an ink as delivered to the printer.[153] The National Association of Printing Ink Manufacturers notes:

> We will have an actual percentage on that label so that when our ink member companies supply this ink to their customers they're going to know what the percentage of renewable materials are within the ink as it sits in the can as a compositional factor.[154]

NAPIM's Web site maintains a list of renewables to be used in place of petroleum options; these renewables are generally considered a more environmentally preferable option, but the Web site notes that "there have been very few life cycle studies conducted on materials used by the ink industry due to the complexities, cost and time involved."[155] Many life cycle programs designed to assess packaging impacts coming onto the market today leave inks out of their assessments due to these complexities. Still, while not all of the impacts of renewables are known, a great deal is known about the economic, health, and environmental impacts of petroleum-based products in general, and the need to phase their use out when advantageous.

It's important for people considering any material or process to look at a variety of alternatives with the whole of the outcome in mind. Consulting with printers and ink representatives are an important part of job planning, especially when it comes to reducing environmental impact. In some cases, a specially formulated low-VOC petroleum ink may deliver better overall environmental performance than a renewable alternative with less favorable VOC levels or more resource-intensive drying needs. Simply saying "print it with soy" is not the beat-all answer. It's a very good answer for a great number of applications and a well recognized symbol of effort and eco-intent,

but it's not the only answer or even the most currently advantageous one in all cases. The question always to ask at the beginning of the job is: What option will deliver the best environmental performance for this application? Then design to maximize that option's environmental and functional performance.

Impacts on Recyclability

To understand what impacts inks and other applied materials have on substrate recyclability, a basic understanding of the recycling process is in order. As this book is focused primarily on paper, and since ink impacts on biodegradability and recycling studies are scarce, we'll look briefly at the paper recycling process to get an overall feel for where concerns will pop up. The basic paper recycling process consists of three main steps:

1. Paper and paperboard are collected and sorted. Contaminants such as plastic, paper clips, staples, bindery, sticky notes, and other waste materials are removed. This initially cleaned material is then sent to the paper mill.

2. At the mill, the paper is soaked in a combination of water and chemicals to separate out the useful fibers, creating pulp. This pulp is then filtered through screens to remove smaller impurities, such as coatings, additives, fillers, and loose ink particles.

3. Any remaining ink in the pulp must be removed. The pulp enters a flotation device where soapy chemicals and air bubbles blown into the mixture lift the ink particles to the top to be skimmed off.

Materials and processes added to a printed piece that disturb the smooth running of any one of these basic processes can make that piece unsuitable for recycling. In many areas, milk cartons are not taken for recycling because that market doesn't have the required equipment to grind the cartons to the size needed to release the paperboard from the polyethylene laminate. Other areas refuse pizza boxes or produce cartons, as these are coated with a waxy substance. Still other areas are finding papers imaged with dyes rather than inks difficult to deink as dye soaks into paper while inks sit on top.

Complicating matters, recycling is currently a regional issue, one answer does not work for all markets. A look at what could be recyclable for a given target market must be considered on a market-by-market basis. To better understand what companies active in recovery and recycling are doing, in the section titled "Closer Look at the Riches of Waste" we look at RockTenn, a company that's been converting post-consumer waste into high-quality packaging since 1908.

Inks, Coatings, Processes

Inks are made by combining colorants, vehicles, solvents, and additives. The largest portion in an ink formulation is the solvent. It gives the ink its fluidity and helps determine its viscosity. Some examples of solvents are water for water-based ink and hydrocarbon solvents (i.e., mineral oils, toluol, etc.) for solvent-based ink.

The vehicle is usually the second largest portion in an ink but is the most important ingredient because it acts as a carrier to help bind the ink to the substrate. Vehicles are made of resins and/or emulsions (except in ultraviolet (UV)/electron beam (EB) inks, which are made of monomers and oligimers). Besides binding the ink to the substrate, the vehicle also gives the ink its characteristics, such as gloss, resoluability, water resistance, drying speed, and transfer.

The vehicle is the main area where formulators can improve an ink's environmental performance. Typically most resins are petroleum based. Petroleum-based resins can be replaced by some, if not all, agri- and/or pine tree rosins.

Typically, the third largest ingredient in an ink is the colorant. Colorants determine an ink's color strength, transparency, and opacity. Some inks are made from dyes, but most printing inks are made of pigments. Pigments are organic or inorganic compounds ground into a very fine powderlike consistency.

Additives are anything else put in to enhance the ink's characteristics. Minimal amounts of additives are used in an ink formulation. Examples of additives are wax to help increase the rub resistance and defoamer to help reduce an ink's foam.

Pigments and Dyes

PIGMENTED INKS

Pigmented inks are colored particles (metal oxide or organic substances), suspended in what is commonly referred to as resins (in solvent-based inks) or binding agents (in water-based inks). These substances help ensure the pigment will stick to the surface being printed and prevent it from being rubbed off. Pigmented inks remain on the paper's surface, so less ink is needed to create the same intensity of image printed than with dye-based inks. The composition of pigmented inks allows it to be more resistant to fading as well.

DYE-BASED INKS

Dye-based inks are color in a liquid medium. They can soak into the printing surface, creating uncontrolled bleed at the edges of an image. This produces poor-quality printing on common porous printing surfaces like uncoated paper. Dye-based inks, though, often can deliver more saturated color than pigment-based inks per unit of mass applied.

To make dye-based inks more useful for paper imaging, they are commonly solvent based to allow for quick-drying methods of printing (e.g., air driers). Other methods to improve print quality for dye-based inks include harder paper sizing and optimized paper coatings. To conform to tighter toxicity and emission controls, special coatings commonly are used in nonindustrial settings, such as in a home or studio inkjet printer setup. On the industrial side, a technique to improve dye-based ink performance employs a charged coating for the paper. Oppositely charged, the dye is attracted to and retained by the coating, leaving only the solvent to soak into the paper.

Ink Types

The most common printing inks can be broken down into two main categories: standard printing inks and specialty inks, such as metallics, fluorescents, or security inks. Web offset ink (heatset and non-heatset), sheet-fed, soybean, vegetable or agri-based ink, process ink for color printing, and others are considered to be standard inks. Included in this category would be UV or EB inks and water-based inks.

Not all ink types in each category use the same technologies or formulations to achieve a more environmentally acceptable product. It is important for designers to work with their printers to deliver a result that is, on the whole better, rather than merely going to a screen printer, for example, and demand that they print with soy inks. In this case,

gravure, pad-printing, or screen printing inks with soy formulations have been slower to market (if available at all) than lithographic inks. A designer who assumes that only one option is possible and insists on a specific ink formulation based on this misconception limits options that would deliver both the result the designer is looking for and good environmental performance.[156]

Each printing process uses different types of ink formulations, and of course, inks perform differently on a variety of substrates. The next section touches on just a few of the standard ink types and is by no means comprehensive. To learn more about the wide range of inks, characteristics of inks, ink types, and their related printing technologies, consult with printers and ink representatives as well as up-to-the-minute industry fact sheets and publications.

WEB OFFSET NON-HEATSET INK

Web offset printing is lithographic printing using a rotary (web) press and paper in roll form. Paper and ink requirements differ between non-heatset and heatset inks in the web offset printing process. Non-heatset inks are commonly used on high-speed web presses for uncoated paper stocks, such as newspaper and business forms printing, as this type of paper is very absorbent. Coated stocks are not recommended, as the inks do not fully penetrate the paper and the ink may smudge and smear.

WEB OFFSET HEATSET INK

The heatset variety of web-offset inks contains varnishes to assist the ink drying process when heat is applied via drier units. These units must be specially built and properly maintained for optimal printing performance, safety, and pollution prevention. The inks and varnishes used in this printing produce higher-quality results, especially on coated paper, but they result in VOC emissions that must be recaptured for reuse or for burning during the drying and evaporating process.

SHEET-FED INK

Sheet-fed presses print sheets instead of rolls, and the inks and drying mechanisms differ between this and web-fed offset lithography. Sheet-fed litho inks are specially manufactured for sheet-fed presses, and these inks contain the highest proportion of pigment. They dry by polymerization, absorption into the paper, and some evaporation.[157] Compared to web printing, only small amounts of emissions escape the page upon drying.

FLEXOGRAPHIC INK

Flexography is a high-speed printing process that uses a flexible printing plate to image a substrate. Four types of inks are commonly used in flexography; solvent, water, UV, or EB with water-based inks. The ink must continuously stay wet on the printing plate but must dry instantaneously on the substrate before moving through to the next print station on the press. The flexographic process has been undergoing many new developments in the past years, allowing for improved environmental performance in many areas of the process, from plate-making to inks and wash-ups.

SPOT AND PROCESS INK COLORS

Printers reproduce color on press in two ways. Spot color requires blending different inks into one ink, resulting in one hue. This method resembles blending paints for household use.[158] Spot inks can be used for precise color matching, as they are based on standardized, premixed formulations and color palettes. They are often used for corporate logos to ensure that exact matches are made rather than trying to match color achieved via process printing.

Process color inks are used in four-color printing or CMYK (cyan, magenta, yellow, and black [K]). These are formulated differently for each printing process, and use halftone plates to produce a rainbow of intermediate shades, hues, and tonal values. The four-color printing process typically requires one ink station per color in a commercial press, with press cleanup between colors for some printers.

Agri-Based Inks and Materials

Agri-based inks were once the standard, as was the case with many materials before synthetics were found. Two main factors signaled the reintroduction of vegetable-based inks into the marketplace: the oil and gas crisis of the 1970s and 1980s[159] and the introduction of stringent environmental regulations that affected the printing industry. Flaxseed, canola oil, soy, and other vegetable oils were common ingredients in inks prior to the 1960s. When petroleum-based inks were introduced, printers discovered that they dried more quickly than vegetable-based inks. Many considered petroleum-based inks to be "high-performance" inks, since printers could turn around jobs faster with increased productivity.

Events surrounding the oil crisis of the 1970s meant that prices fluctuated widely, and there were tight supplies and cutbacks.[160] In 1979, the board of directors of the American Newspaper Publishers Association, now known as the Newspaper Association of America, directed its technical staff to develop an alternative to the petroleum-based ink long used by the newspaper industry.

The main impetus for the development and use of soy-based inks and other agri-based inks to replace petroleum-based inks on a large scale was the oil embargo and gas crisis of the 1970s and 1980s.

—*United Soybean Board*

After years of research, soy ink was introduced to the newspaper industry in 1987 by the American Soybean Association in conjunction with General Printing Ink (now Sun Chemical Corporation), which agreed to produce it.[161] This formula was made from nontoxic soybean oil, the same oil found in cooking oils, salad dressings, mayonnaise, and other foods. The ink performed well on press and gained the acceptance of newspaper publishers, who appreciated its vibrant color saturation and clarity.[162] Although early soy ink formulations took longer to dry on press, ink experts today state that there is no significant difference in drying time for modern soy-based ink formulations.

In the mid-1990s, researchers at the Agricultural Research Service (ARS), National Center for Agricultural Utilization Research in Peoria, Illinois, found that soy-based ink formulations were more degradable than petroleum-based commercial inks in one study.[163] Other studies found that soy ink could be removed more effectively from newsprint than petroleum ink during the deinking phase of the

recycling process, resulting in less paper fiber damage and a brighter paper. Since then, there have been limited studies to verify the actual biodegradability and deinking aspect of current soy ink formulations. Others have suggested that the biodegradability of printed material depends more on the biodegradability of the substrate, rather than on the dry ink film. John Adkin of Sun Chemical aptly states that:[164]

> Biodegradability statements can be misleading, since so many papers now contain PCW content. There is no published evidence in the difference between the biodegradability of either vegetable-based inks or petroleum inks. However, from a point of view of waste, there is a difference of disposing of 100 percent vegetable waste, clearly.

The marketing and growth of soy ink has been phenomenal, and now more than 90 percent of the nation's newspapers are printed with soy ink. In 2005, the National Soy Ink Information Center closed; there was no longer a need to continue to promote the use of soy ink since it is now so widely accepted.

It should be noted that while soy oil has dominated the market in the United States, in Canada, oilseed crops such as canola and flax (also known as linseed) are more commonly used for inks. To meet demand for this versatile crop, soy is being grown in tropical rainforests and temperate forests as a new cash crop and is impacting the environment in many ways. Several leading green printers are moving from soy inks (which, although naturally low in VOCs, may contain little soybean oil content) to inks made with non-soy, vegetable-content inks that have lower VOCs[165] or are printing with instant-drying UV inks that have minimal VOCs.

Although designers now have a bigger range of ink choices, soy inks continue to enjoy broad acceptance among mainstream printers as well as solid public recognition. If soy inks offer a logical "next step" away from higher-VOC options, they can provide a readily available interim transition away from petroleum products. For an ink manufacturing company to be eligible to apply the "Printed with Soy Ink" SoySeal to its packaging or literature, the soy products used must meet certain minimum requirements for soybean content. The percentage of soy oil content varies, from 7 to 40 percent, depending on the type of ink formulation and printing process. With the help of the ink manufacturing industry, the American Soybean Association (ASA) established standards for soybean content for printing and asks those interested in using the SoySeal to complete the ASA's SoySeal User Agreement and follow the criteria for use.[166] To understand the basics, ASA asks candidates to consider these points:[167]

> Soybean oil must be the predominant vegetable oil, with vegetable drying oils added as needed, but not to exceed the level of soybean oil set out in the respective formulation. Alcohol esters of soybean oil may be substituted directly for soybean oil in news, sheet-fed, cold-set and business forms inks to obtain the minimum concentration standard. The minimum soybean oil concentration for heat-set inks increased to 15 percent (by weight) when alcohol esters of soybean oil replace soybean oil in this formulation.

The ASA owns the SoySeal copyright and handles requests for the license agreements, collection of fees, and use of the seal.[168]

Forest-based Inks and Materials

Another renewable resource option besides soy or other types of agri-based inks are forest-based inks made from pine tree rosins. Tall oil, gum, and wood are the three types of rosins produced from pine trees. Gum rosin is collected from live pine trees while wood rosin is obtained from the dried, aged stumps of pine trees.

Tall oil is a viscous liquid obtained as a byproduct of the Kraft process of wood pulp manufacture. The name comes from the Swedish "tallolja" ("pine oil"). During the paper pulp-making process, toxic black liquor is extracted. The invention of the recovery boiler in the 1930s allowed the paper pulp-making mills to recover and burn most of the black liquor. Previously it was discharged into rivers, lakes, and streams, which created an environmental issue. The recovery boiler helped reduce the pollution in the waterways and allowed the mills to produce and run energy self-sufficiently. Besides being able to generate energy, black liquor distillation allowed the recovery of chemicals that produced tall oil rosin.

UV/EB Cured Inks and Printing

Ultraviolet inks and electron beam cured inks and coatings have excited many print professionals and print buyers from both an environmental and productivity point of view. This technology continues to grow quickly, especially in the digital and inkjet area. New UV hybrid presses and hybrid inks provide printers with the option of combining UV technology with conventional press equipment.

UV inks are solids that dry instantly when exposed to ultraviolet light or a beam of electrons. UV and EB inks and coatings have minimal solvents, meaning in their solid form negligible VOCs are released into the atmosphere since they cure or dry instantly during inline printing.[169] Naturally, this speeds up printing turnaround and productivity and can also save significantly on energy costs[170] compared to thermal drying costs for other printing methods. Common applications include printing by wide-format inkjet printers on signs, banners, plastics, vehicle graphics, textiles, and even difficult-to-print-on substrates such as glass, metal, and wood. UV/EB inks provide a high-quality, crisp, bright, high-gloss appearance, contributing to the shelf appeal of these inks.

It must be noted that many of the substrates used in signage are far from eco-friendly themselves. For example, banners or vehicle graphics printed on vinyl have recently come under fire for toxicity.[171]

"The newest trend in printing is using UV inks on uncoated stocks," comments Dave Anderson of Shapco Printing, Inc.

> Since many designers love uncoated stocks but find the "dry-back"[172] undesirable, our UV presses cure the UV inks immediately after the dots hit the press sheet. This results in more vibrant printing (not allowing the ink to soak in), and with no dry time, it speeds up production and eliminates any worry of "offset" or scuffing. Since the UV ink dries as the sheet passes under the light, the sheet is ready for the next production step as soon as it comes off the press.[173]

As with other ink formulations currently available, there are drawbacks to using UV/EB inks. Although the process reduces some waste and maintenance costs, the start-up and energy operating costs can be much higher.[174] UV technology requires staff training, and the purchase of curing lamps and other special equipment required to focus the UV

energy onto the sheet can represent a significant up-front cost. As technology develops and grows (and becomes more affordable), low-watt, long-lasting light emitting diodes (LEDs) could become an alternative to conventional UV lamps.[175] Until reduced energy technology comes on line to help level the playing field, though, it would be a good idea to include energy sourcing for the printer using UV/EB inks, as coal-generated electricity could play a role in determining the final eco-footprint of this technology compared to other options (See "If It Can't Be Grown It Must Be Mined" in this book). Here a UV/EB printer using windpower would offer the designer a more comprehensive eco-advantage for this technology over another competitor using coal-generated power.

In addition to energy use/sourcing, UV inks contain acrylate components, which can cause press workers to develop allergic reactions, experience irritation, redness, dermatitis, or burns.[176] Questions have been raised about other materials used in the UV process, namely 4-methylbenzophenone (4MBP) and isopropylthioxanthone (ITX). 4MBP and benzophenone (which 4MBP can be used with or replace) were the focus of studies by the European Food Safety Authority (EFSA), which noted with regard to UV-printed packaging: "Given their highest levels reported so far, both substances may migrate into the package and contaminate even solid foodstuffs." These concerns are triggering possible restrictions by the European Commission.[177] In 2005, concerns over ITX migration into food triggered the recall of several packaged products that used this material in the printing process.

UV/EB are fairly new technologies. Time will tell if this print technology causes other health and worker safety issues, including the exposure to UV itself.

There is still some discussion regarding the true recyclability of UV inks; some believe that UV inks are more difficult to deink than conventional inks. Others suggest that the hybrid UV ink formulations may be appropriate for recycling.

Water-based Inks and Printing

Many chemicals in the pressroom are derived from petroleum or crude oil. Water-based inks and coatings, like all other inks and coatings, are industrial chemicals. However, the use of water-based alternatives can dramatically reduce the use of solvents and reduce special handling disposal costs and VOC emissions. Water-based inks are replacing conventional inks in the flexography printing process, as they readily absorb into paper and paperboard. These inks are an alternative to conventional, solvent-based inks. There is little or no exposure to alcohol, and they generally have lower VOCs than other inks.

The drawbacks to these inks are that they may not work well on nonporous substrates, may require more frequent press and equipment cleaning, and can require additional energy to dry the ink on press. Here again, as with UV/EB inks, it would be a good idea to consider energy sourcing for the printer using water-based inks, as coal-generated electricity to feed increased energy needs in the drying processes could play a role in determining the final eco-footprint of this technology compared to other options.

Overview of Coatings

Coatings typically are applied after printing to protect the printed surface from dirt, smudges,

fingerprints, and abrasion. They commonly are used for pieces that would receive considerable handling, such as packaging, postcards, business cards, and brochures. Coatings also allow for additional visual interest. For example, applying selective gloss or dull areas to a piece can deliver a certain feel (spot varnish); a gloss applied only to the water spray areas of a surfing image would heighten the visual excitement of the "splash."

Coatings, however, may impact recycling. It is important to look carefully at what the coating will be doing for the project and assess its importance as part of a holistic approach. People tend to avoid damaged-looking packages. If a coating will help maintain the visual quality of a package to ensure its appeal to consumers, then all of the resources going into both package and product will not be wasted. Here, though, the type and amount of coating need to be considered carefully. For example, does there need to be printing on the bottom of the box? If not, then this whole panel can be left uncoated. Other examples can be found in various print forms, with just the outside or one side of the piece that gets the most handling getting coated. Postcards are a good example of selective coating; the image of value is on only one side, leaving the uncoated side easy to write on.

AQUEOUS OR WATER-BASED COATING

An aqueous coating is a clear, water-based coating applied in-line on press. It is available in gloss, dull, and satin, and is fast drying.

The coating is applied to the printed sheet directly after the final inks have been laid down, then sent through a heated air system to quickly dry the coating. Aqueous coatings dry by removal of water and ammonia from the coating solids through evaporation and absorption into the print substrate. Due to the quick-dry nature of this coating, pieces can move on to finishing stations much sooner than pieces treated with traditional varnishes. Nevertheless, pieces still may require 24 to 48 hours to develop their full properties.

Fuji Hunt Photographic Chemicals, Inc. notes that "some aqueous coatings make an excellent primer for offline UV jobs, but more and more 'specialty' jobs require foil stamping, gluing (pocket folders), ink jet (address labels), or the ability to go through a laser printer."[178]

Water-based coatings vary depending on their intended use, but most water-based coatings contain:

— *Polymeric resin* used as a base provides a gloss film and is made from styrenated acrylic, acrylic, or polyester.

— *Wax and/or silicone* added to the base provides either rub resistance or slipperiness.

— *Surfactants* are added to provide improved flow and leveling.

— *Additives* are used in small amounts to enhance particular properties. Additives include solvents, defoamers, and optical brighteners.

Water-based coatings offer a variety of advantages over traditional varnishes. These advantages include:

— Reduction or elimination of the need for spray powder commonly sprayed onto the wet ink film surface to prevent set-off

— Improved environmental performance: water based instead of oil or solvent based, with insignificant VOCs

— Reduced waiting time for finishing

— Glueable and UV-able

— Nonyellowing

— Nonflammable

Varnish

Varnishes used in the printing industry are commonly petroleum based and come in gloss, dull, and satin. They can be tinted by adding pigment and are, in fact, basically ink without pigment. They can be wet-trapped if the primary imaging inks chosen are compatible (run at same time as inks) or dry-trapped (run as an additional pass through the press after the initial ink coating has dried). Petroleum-based varnishes share many of the same environmental impact issues as petroleum-based printing inks and present other issues not shared by water-based or UV coatings. Varnishes, like other coatings, can be harder to deink or recycle and may add contaminants to the deinking sludge, a solid waste that must be disposed of properly.

UV Coating

A UV coating is a clear coating applied in-line on press and cured instantly with ultraviolet light. Available in gloss or dull finishes, it can deliver more protection and sheen than either varnish or aqueous coatings. UV coatings provide color stability and sharper graphics, higher gloss, scuff resistance, and better outdoor endurance. The instant curing process speeds up production time and enables in-line die cutting. Cured with light and not heat, little or no solvents are released into the atmosphere in the drying process. The drawback is that these highly protective coatings and their hardness characteristics make the pieces they are applied to more difficult to deink or recycle.

Laminates can be either film or liquid, and are available in gloss or matte finish. Film laminates are a clear plastic film adhered to the target surface. Liquid laminates are spread or printed over the base substrate and dry (or cure) like a varnish. Laminates are used to protect the underlying substrate and to extend its function. For example, to make a milk carton waterproof, a laminate of polyethylene over a paperboard core is used. In the past few years, laminates made from bioplastics have appeared on the market. These provide many of the advantages of their petroleum-based plastic cousins but can be removed easily in the repulping process. They are intended to increase the ease of recycling of the underlying substrate as well as decrease petroleum use and its associated resourcing and waste-handling issues.

Functional coatings, such as liquid laminates, are applied like a varnish and are used to extend the functionality of the underlying substrate. Some of these coatings are falling out of use as they can render the underlying substrate completely non-recyclable. Wax coatings on cartons used to sell produce would be one example.

Think Beyond Ink

To VOC or not to VOC? Though a serious question to ask at the start of each job, keep in mind that ink composition is only one tool in the eco-designer's tool kit. There is no substitute for smart, sustainable design practices, such as using less ink coverage, using resources wisely, and designing for reuse and recovery. A designer can minimize ink coverage by designing smaller documents and reducing bleeds. Eye-catching and tactile embossing and die-cutting methods can add interest and reduce ink usage.

> There is no substitute for smart, sustainable design practices, such as using less ink coverage, using resources wisely, and designing for reuse and recovery.

MSDS: An Eco-Design Tool Kit Essential

One way to learn more about an ink formulation or pressroom material and the variety of chemicals used in its manufacture is to obtain a material safety data sheet from the manufacturer. An MSDS is an informational document that contains information about hazardous ingredients, the potential health effects of the exposure to ingredients and chemicals, and precautions and recommendations for the correct use, storage, and disposal of chemicals.[179] Information about the total volatile content can be found, and "Section II—Ingredients" lists any hazardous ingredients or toxic chemicals subject to the reporting requirements of SARA Section 313 or other hazards communications standards.[180] Note that a MSDS is intended for use in an occupational setting, and use varies in different countries. It is a resource geared toward health and safety information rather than a comprehensive environmental data sheet. In the United States, Occupational Safety and Health Administration (OSHA) requires that the MSDS be easily accessible to employees as well as made available to local fire departments and local and state emergency planning officials under Section 311 of the Emergency Planning and Community Right-to-Know Act.[181]

MSDS summaries and forms can be obtained directly from ink manufacturers or printers. The "MSDS on File" Web site provides nearly 10,000 MSDS for various print industry manufacturers.[182] "How to Read and Use an MSDS for Environmental Purposes" is another extremely helpful resource put out by the Printers National Environmental Assistance Center (PNEAC) and can be found at: *www.pneac.org*.[183]

One way to learn more about an ink formulation or pressroom material and the variety of chemicals used in its manufacture is to obtain a MSDS from the manufacturer.

Green Printing in the Future

In just three decades, the pre-press and printing industry has changed dramatically. Remember hand-cutting masking film, or waxing and cutting galleys to fix on boards? Remember dot matrix printers? Floppy disks? Typically today, designers and others have personal inkjet printers that deliver high-resolution, print shop–quality photos and text to their desktops, and more and more have access to printing facilities that use the latest in low-eco-impact technologies for inks, coatings, and other pressroom materials. Common to eco and non-eco printers alike, today's digital pre-press and direct computer-to-plate processes conserve resources and are free of the chemical baths of former years while also dramatically enhancing workflow and productivity. Managing impacts in the studio, designers can choose from computers and desktop printers that have been designed to meet Energy Star certification[184] or can purchase hardware by companies that offer recycling services.

The next decade is likely to see even more remarkable changes in ink and printing technologies driven by environmental stewardship.

As in other industries, in printing, both short- and long-term change will likely be driven by cost-cutting methods, efficiency gains, and sustainability efforts. For example, reducing ink color palettes in packaging using color harmonization software could save manufacturers millions of dollars per year by streamlining ink usage and cleanup as well as reducing waste on various levels.[185] Also on the horizon from NAPIM and the National Printing Ink Research Institute (NPIRI) are initiatives to evaluate and minimize printing inks' environmental impact via the NPIRI Environmental Impact Task Force.[186]

Change will also be driven by environmental standards and mandatory regulation. For example: The International Organization for Standardization's ISO 14000 standards, which is a series of international standards on environmental management,[187] and European Union (EU) laws and regulations. RoHS (Restriction of Hazardous Substances Directive) is a mandatory EU regulation, introduced in 2006, for the "restriction of the use of certain hazardous substances in electrical and electronic equipment regulations."[188] RoHS bans new electrical or electronic equipment containing more than agreed levels of lead, cadmium, mercury, hexavalent chromium, polybrominated biphenyl (PBB), and polybrominated diphenyl ether (PBDE) flame retardants.[189]

How does this electrical equipment mandate relate to inks? Inks are found in electronic components and packaging, including the variable-data ink printed on product packaging.[190] Noncompliance with legislation in the United Kingdom means that manufacturers will be unable to export or market these products to the European Union, which could result in "dire" financial consequences for manufacturers or suppliers.[191]

Although meeting these standards can be time consuming, the rewards are great. Compliance ensures that manufacturers meet health and environmental targets, improve worker safety, and reduce waste and environmental impact. The standards also encourage accurate reporting and record keeping, and compliance can help companies mitigate risk and avoid costly fines and legal actions. Meeting these regulations also can help manufacturers and companies differentiate their products and processes from those of competitors and enhance positive company perception and value to customers by aiding them to meet their sustainability goals, which in turn can help increase prospects and sales.[192]

Numerous American companies have already made their products RoHS compliant, and RoHs has spurred other legislation addressing harmful chemicals in various countries.[193] Furthermore, new laws and regulations will undoubtedly continue to come into effect as the result of accidents and controversies as well as the emergence of new technology and results of long-term studies.

Noted sustainability practitioners William McDonough and Michael Braungart, coauthors of *Cradle to Cradle: Remaking the Way We Make Things*, have described environmental regulations as "a signal of design failure." It is not that these authors oppose or reject regulations; rather they believe that regulations are not the long-term answer and that heavily regulated industries offer opportunities for "redesign." Furthermore, "redesign is a chance to make energy and manufacturing systems so inherently healthful, productive and socially beneficial [that] regulations become unnecessary."[194]

Regardless of where one stands regarding regulation, it is imperative that all choices are considered carefully. It's important that everyone stays informed about materials, supply chain sources, legislation issues and emerging technology. Again, liaison and consultation with printers and vendors are key, as is using common sense and the "Precau-

---

Ink manufacturers, printers, designers, and print buyers all play a valuable role—to seek and strive for eco-innovations, to guide colleagues and customers with sustainable design choices, and to foster environmental awareness and change.

---

tionary Principle," which guides us to take action now, as individuals and as a society, to prevent harm to human health and the environment before it happens.[195]

It's been a long and winding road, and we have a long way yet to go, but change is afoot. The next decade is likely to see even more remarkable changes in ink and printing technologies driven by environmental stewardship. According to a recent survey conducted by PIA/GATF, more than 90 percent of printers believe that their customers will require "green" printing in the future.[196]

Until then, ink manufacturers, printers, designers and print buyers all play a valuable role—to seek and strive for eco-innovations, to guide colleagues and customers with sustainable design choices, and to foster environmental awareness and change.

Learning more about design ecology is one of the most effective ways to make decisions that have the least environmental impact.

Ink Tips and Better Practices

For this section, "Best Practices" in the common vernacular is not a place we can point to yet. Sustainability in practice is a constantly evolving process, with new "Best Practices" superseding old ones at an ever-increasing rate. Naturally, new

technology and the sourcing of raw materials always will mean that this industry is growing and changing, and it is important to keep up to date. Yet learning more about design ecology is one of the most effective ways to make decisions that have the least environmental impact. Design for Environment (DfE), Cradle to Cradle (C2C), and other sustainability systems thinking processes can help designers think cyclically instead of linearly.

Designers also need to stay informed. Ask questions. Obtain general information sheets, technical data, and MSDSs from suppliers and manufacturers to learn more about the contents of a specific ink or for particular solvents used in the pressroom. Consult with printers about which ink and printing process will have the least environmental impact or eco-footprint for projects.

Resources, Tips, and Better Practices
(Courtesy of ecoLingo: earth friendly graphic design)

— *Consult with print partners and other vendors early in the design process* to explore energy and resource saving options, (ink type, availability of eco papers, document sizes to prevent paper waste, availability of soft proofs, etc.).

— *Less is more.* Full bleeds, floods or high ink coverage, and oversize designs use more resources and can add to the cost of the print job. Keep ink coverage to a minimum. Paper must be deinked before the pulp can be recycled into new paper, so less ink coverage is better for the environment than covering an entire sheet with color.

— *Review fact sheets and MSDSs* for inks, coatings, and other pressroom materials. Look for VOC content, hazardous ingredients, or toxic chemicals subject to the reporting requirements of SARA Section 313 or other hazards communications standards. See the MSDS sidebar for more information.

— *Specify low-VOC inks.* Some new ink formulations are lower in VOCs than soy-based ink formulations.

— *Ask printers about printing with ultraviolet or electron beam inks.* UV inks are thick, solid inks that contain minimal solvents and hence have negligible VOCs. The ink ingredients are instantly cured when exposed to UV light or beams of electrons. Note the energy sources for this process though. Using coal as the electricity source may impact the total environmental footprint.

— *Choose inks made from local, bio-derived or renewable, responsibly grown sources,* such as linseed, soy oil, canola oil, or other agri-based inks. (Conversion of forests to soy plantations has been linked to both temperate and rainforest deforestation and climate change.)

— *Explore a variety of options for desired outcomes.* Water-based inks are a viable option for flexography and can reduce costs from lower emission treatment of inks. Paper and paperboard readily accept water-based inks and coatings; however, other substrates may not. In that case, UV and EB inks might be a viable option. Consult with printers and vendors at the start of the project to get the best ideas of what's possible. Likewise, when screen printing on textiles or other substrates, look into water-based or bio-based inks instead of inks containing vinyl or other petroleum products.

— *Ask printers about the newest information and legislation regarding metals in inks (including barium),* and take extra care to ensure that inks for food and children's products meet requirements for safety. Note: Attention to heavy metal compliance is especially important when printing overseas, where regulations are less stringent. Review the MSDS if in doubt.

— *Use metallic inks sparingly, if at all.* Metallic inks often are printed on papers that lack environmentally preferred attributes (i.e., coated, glossy stocks), in an effort to help emphasize the inks' reflective and metallic qualities. Furthermore, they are often varnished or laminated afterward to prevent them from scuffing, a step that can hinder recycling and adds more material to the recycling sludge. Most laminates are not recyclable.

— *Come unglued.* Glues and other adhesives for binding or affixing labels can contain petroleum and also can cause problems with recycling. Instead, choose water-based, biodegradable adhesives or gum arabic (like the lick-and-stick type on postage stamps).

— *Skip inks altogether.* Embossing and die cutting add interest, dimension, and texture. Both work especially well on uncoated, recycled paper stock.

— *Think local with a twist.* North America and Europe have legislation to prevent the addition of heavy metals to inks and coatings, but other countries may not. Cadmium, lead, chromium, and zinc have recently been found on imported products and packaging. Ask to see a MSDS for the inks specified.

— *Adopt paperless office practices and use a digital work flow where possible.* PDF soft proofs can often replace blue lines, laser proofs, and color printouts in the print work flow.

— *Haste makes waste.* Take extra care in the final approval stage of design, proofreading, and pre-press to prevent mistakes and to avoid generating extra proofs, plates, film, or reprints.

— *Allow adequate scheduling to obtain permissions* and artwork for appropriate eco-labels or logos to be displayed on the printed projects, and for the calculation of educational environmental benefit saving statements or eco-audits.

— *Work with a certified green printer, and encourage local printers to go green,* lower their environmental footprint, or put more pollution prevention strategies into place.

— *Design for reuse and recycling.* Thermography, foil stamping, and UV-cured or water-based catalyzed varnishes can be harder to deink or recycle plus may add contaminants to the deinking sludge. For optimum recycling, design with the project's end of use / end of life in mind.

— *Educate colleagues, clients, customers, and vendors about green options,* and partner together to ensure that projects have minimal impact on the environment. Remember, most printed pieces will eventually end up in the recycling bin or will be thrown away, and there really isn't any "away"—it's here on the Earth to stay. Leave a legacy, not a landfill.

Ink Resources: Fact Sheets and Reports

— Consolidated List of Chemicals Subject to the Emergency Planning and Community Right-To-

Know Act (EPCRA) and Section 112(r) of the Clean Air Act, *www.epa.gov/ceppo/pubs/title3.pdf*

— EPA's Toxics Release Inventory *www.epa.gov/tri/chemical/index.htm*

— EPA's Laws, Regulations and Executive Order *www.epa.gov/tri/lawsandregs/index.htm*

— PNEAC Printing Inks Fact Sheet *www.pneac.org/sheets/litho/inks.cfm*

— MSDS on File. Web site provides nearly 10,000 MSDS for various print industry manufacturers, *www.msdsonfile.com/mctx/msds/msdsonfile.jsp*

— Plain Language Guide to Regulations *www.paintcenter.org/peg/pegnew.cfm*

— PNEAC "How to Read and Use an MSDS for Environmental Purposes" *www.pneac.org/sheets/all/msds.cfm*

— Toxics in Packaging Clearinghouse *www.toxicsinpackaging.org*

The Inks section was written by Dion Zuess, Wendy Jedlička, and Rob Calif.

Processes

Chlorine and Bleaching

Not all paper pulp sources are the same. To create a paper that will deliver qualities a designer might be looking for, from brilliant white to natural tones, some pulps require a bit of bleaching, some a lot, and others none at all. Like a stereotypical salesman flashing an overbleached smile to induce people to buy his product, picking the whitest possible white paper for every job will not make a mediocre design "sparkle." For any design, one must ask: What is the

message we're trying to convey? What resources are needed to achieve that? And are we using those resources because they are the best possible answer, or just what's always been done?

Before designers began to be confronted with the impact realities of their design decisions, choosing materials and process was a carefree indulgence in assigning importance to things that maybe really didn't matter all that much. When completely flooded with ink, will a mailer printed on stock labeled as 100 brightness really sell better than one labeled 88? Will giving it a high-gloss finish make it that much more effective? Were those decisions based on quantitative evidence or claims on a sales brochure, or something overheard once?

Going deeper into the problem, brightness and whiteness of paper are seemingly perpetual points of confusion to professional creatives and consumers alike. *Brightness* refers to the paper's ability to reflect light. Measured on a scale of zero to one hundred, the brightness units indicate the volume of light reflected—the higher the number, the brighter the sheet. A brighter paper will reflect more light, afford more contrast, and allow four-color process colors to appear, under more varied lighting conditions, to "snap" or "pop."[197]

Whiteness refers to the paper's shade (inherent color). There are three primary paper shades: *balanced-white*, *warm-white*, and *blue-white*. Coated papers tend to be blue-white because the eye perceives this tone as "brighter," and the added coating on the stock increases the actual brightness, or ability of the paper to reflect light.

"Bright" Does Not Always Make Right

Whiteness can be broken down into a very easy-to-understand list of basic characteristics:[198]

— Blue-whites appear "brighter" to the eye and allow colors to be perceived as standing out, when used appropriately.

— Warm-whites have a lower perceived "brightness" and are easier on the eye for reading or extended viewing.

— Balanced (or neutral) whites reflect the total color spectrum equally and so would deliver the truest color. A balanced white paper does not become part of the ink's color-read "mix."

Select a paper's "whiteness" and "brightness" to best present the message. For example: Skin tones rendered on a blue-white page would make the person pictured look an unhealthy gray, while warmer-tone papers would help enhance the same image and require less ink coverage to overcome the paper's color.

With a basic understanding of how people perceive color bouncing back to them from a page, selecting paper types becomes a bit easier. With such knowledge, designers can ask questions with an eye on better harmonizing paper and design: What kind of white is required, and what resources must be expended to achieve that? What will be the impacts of those expenditures?

Understanding Chlorine

Although banned in some parts of the world (e.g., Europe), chlorine in various forms continues to be used as both a whitener and purifying agent in many places. Europeans are understandably sensitive to the use of chlorine; it was used during World War I as a choking gas and as a component of more lethal mustard and phosgene gases. Today, chlorine is widely used to purify America's drinking water and keep swimming pools clean. Other forms of chlorine, such as the chlorofluorocarbons that have been proven harmful to the Earth's protective ozone layer, have been banned worldwide.[199]

"If it's used in drinking water (and swimming pools) in the United States then what's the big deal?" one might ask. This is a very good question. Inertia (overcoming the obstacles to change), and expense to convert to other technologies would be the simple answer. According to a variety of studies done in the United States, Canada, Norway, Australia, and Belgium, chlorine by-products found in swimming pools are linked to higher incidences of asthma, lung damage, stillbirths, miscarriages, and bladder cancer. In Europe and elsewhere, nonchlorine systems (ozone or ultraviolet light) have been in regular use to purify water since the 1950s.[200] When chlorine is used in the paper bleaching process, harmful chemicals such as dioxins and furans can form, both of which are known to cause cancer in humans.

In addition to convincing evidence that dioxins cause cancer, there are also strong indications that they disrupt hormonal, reproductive, and immune systems. Developing fetuses and breast-feeding infants are found to be particularly sensitive to dioxins, with studies additionally indicating dioxins are also an "endocrine disrupter," adding dioxins to a list of toxic chemicals found to mimic natural hormones and block or disrupt their normal function. Concerns about endocrine disrupters found in some types of plastics have led to a ban on their use for many common products like bottles and toys, while whole classes of chemicals found to be endocrine disrupters have been banned for any use in many parts of the world. Mounting U.S. EPA evidence shows that current dioxin levels in our bodies in general are at or near

tipping point levels for adverse reactions—any additional dioxins in the environment should be of significant concern.[201]

Chlorine Use: Basic Definitions[202]

— *Totally Chlorine-Free (TCF):* Paper made with a bleaching process that uses no chlorine-based compounds; currently TCF refers only to 100 percent virgin paper.

— *Certified TCF:* These products require that no chlorine or chlorine compounds were used in the papermaking process, that all virgin components need to be certified as totally chlorine free and require a chain of custody for all fiber, that the mill has no current or pending violations, and that the mill does not use old-growth forest for any of the virgin pulp.

— *Processed Chlorine-Free (PCF):* This recycled paper is made with a bleaching process that uses no chlorine-based compounds.

— *Certified PCF:* In addition to the certified TCF criteria, certified PCF products require the product to contain at least 30 percent post-consumer content and that the mill details post-consumer content sources.

For more information about TCF, PCF, and Chlorine Free Products Association Certification, visit the Web site *www.chlorinefreeproducts.org*.

— *Elemental Chlorine-Free (ECF).* This term often is used to label products that have substituted chlorine dioxide for *elemental chlorine*. Compared to bleaching processes using elemental chlorine, ECF chlorine dioxide processes reduce the formation of many chlorinated organic compounds. However, as chlorine is still used, effluent quality remains an issue that mills still must address.

Note: Companies displaying claims of ECF as an improvement feature must document that this new product replaces the company's previous one that contained elemental chlorine or run the risk of violating the U.S. Federal Trade Commission's Environmental Marketing Claims Guideline as well as other marketing claims guidelines around the world. In many markets, elemental chlorine has already been phased out, so no papers in that market would have used this substance in their bleaching process. Featuring the removal of elemental chlorine as an "improvement" would be in violation of most eco-claim guidelines, as no papers would have used that substance in that market anyway. It's not a "feature" if all players are mandated to comply with a minimum standard.

— *Enhanced ECF with extended or oxygen delignification.* This process removes more of the lignin from the wood before bleaching. This reduction helps reduce energy and chemical demands for the bleaching process.

— *Enhanced ECF with ozone or hydrogen peroxide delignification.* This process also removes more of the lignin from the wood before bleaching, but it substitutes ozone or hydrogen peroxide for chlorine or chlorine dioxides in the early stages of the bleaching process.

For both Enhanced ECF processes, however, the final or near-final stages still use chlorine dioxide.

The Natural Resources Defense Council offers visitors to their Web site an order of preference for bleaching processes, on the basis of environmental criteria:[203]

1. PCF (preferable to TCF because product includes recycled content; TCF is used to refer only to 100 percent virgin paper)

2. TCF

3. Enhanced ECF with ozone or hydrogen peroxide

4. Enhanced ECF (ECF with extended or oxygen delignification)

5. Traditional ECF

Not included in the list, as the bulk of paper produced in and for Western markets is still made from trees, are the growing options found in tree-free papers. Many pulps and substrates are naturally white and require little or no bleaching at all. Reduction in bleaching demand not only reduces or eliminates the need for chemicals, but cuts out whole levels of energy and process water demands as well. As with any other material or process, weighing design decisions to also favor third-party certified papers (and vendors) becomes the key to helping drive change in a healthier direction for everyone.

Future Trends

Decades ago, European paper mills abandoned conventional pulp-bleaching sequences using chlorine and have been producing quality paper products ever since. In North America, mills lag behind their European counterparts when it comes to eliminating chlorine in their bleaching processes. Mills operating today using conventional bleaching processes are based on 1950s technology requiring multiple stages of chlorine-based chemistry. In contrast, modern pulp bleaching sequences, as used in most mills in the European Union, use pulp bleaching technology that works with oxygen-based compounds, hydrogen peroxide, ozone, or other nonchlorine processes.

Besides chemicals used in any process, additional cause for concern arises from the amount of water consumed during the paper production process. Depending on the technology, making a single sheet of copy paper bleached with chlorine chemistry can use over thirteen ounces of water—more than what is used to manufacture a typical soda can.[204] By comparison, certified TCF or PCF papers use only two ounces of water to make the same sheet of paper.

In a United Nations press release for the 2003 International Year of Freshwater, the availability of clean freshwater is called "one of the most important issues facing humanity today." The UN points out that as growing demands outstrip supplies and pollution continues to contaminate rivers, lakes, and streams, the water crises will become ever more difficult to address.[205] Already an unacceptably large percentage of the world's population—one in every five people—does not have access to safe and affordable drinking water.[206]

In industrialized and newly industrialized countries alike, industry is finding itself increasingly at odds with populations when it comes to water demand; water for basic human consumption as well as for agricultural use all require a share. In the Ogalla aquifer (High Plains Aquifer) of the United States, groundwater is being extracted in excess of its rate of natural recharge, with some areas already having exhausted their underground supply.[207] Even in the Great Lakes regions—which make up the largest

surface freshwater system on Earth and contain about 84 percent of North America's surface fresh water and about 21 percent of the world's supply— plans to sell and truck water to regions outside of the Great Lakes water-cycle area are being quashed, as researchers warn that the ancient glacial waters that make up the Great Lakes would never be replaced given current (and increasing) use levels.[208]

As both citizen and industrial demand increase, governments will be forced to implement new, more forward-thinking, and more egalitarian systems for resource use. In order to do so, governments will have to implement more aggressive, and verifiable, rules for transparency, operations accounting, and reporting.

In an effort to get ahead of the curve and move toward greater sustainability, some paper manufacturers are voluntarily seeking out and enjoying the benefits of third-party certification. The logo of a third-party, standard-setting organization assures customers that the products and services meet stringent environmental standards that have been verified, independent of the applicant's influence. In an increasingly skeptical marketplace, third-party certification is building needed trust by providing verifiable proof of claims made.

Examples of such multi-attribute, standard-setting and certification organizations include EcoLogo and Chlorine Free Products (CFP). Environmental leadership standards such as these address multiple environmental impacts of a product and offer the most comprehensive certification available.

CFP, founded in 1993, is a leader in third-party chain of custody for raw materials and audits of process. For a mill to be certified TCF/PCF, it must be audited under the Sustainability Index, which looks at environmental policy, environmental management, mill process, forestry certification, environmental risk management, product stewardship, public information, environmental compliance, and employee recognition.

CFP's audits measure the impact of a manufacturing process on the environment, taking into account everything from water and energy use to chemistry and carbon gas releases. These audits also review permit compliance, ethical management practices and compliance, financial performance, and funding of research and development.

Only processes or products that are manufactured free of chlorine chemistry and also meet broader sustainability criteria are identified with the TCF or PCF Certification marks.

The EcoLogo Program also takes a multi-attribute, life cycle approach to developing its standards. Environmental impacts examined for paper include: recycled content, solid waste, resource and energy consumption, and measure of organic pollutants in water (COD-Chemical Oxygen Discharge) and aquatic toxicity.

Moving forward, manufacturers will want to take a careful look at the amount of chlorine and other chemicals they consume and at the water used in their bleaching processes. Chlorine chemistry uses an intolerably large amount of water that is then rendered unsafe to use again. To meet increasing future demand, annual crops will play an ever more important role as part of an expanded and better-managed pulp cycle. In this new scenario, trees will also be used less and less in the future of papermaking, with fast-growing alternatives such as

bamboo, kenaf, hemp, and agri-pulp, to name a few, providing a nontoxic and renewable supply that virtually eliminates the need for bleaching.

With an eye on minimizing future costs, companies that adopt third-party certification and eliminate chlorine use from their bleaching processes today will be best positioned to gain competitive advantage and increased market share in the future.

"Future Trends" section of "Chlorine and Bleaching" courtesy of Archie Beaton, executive director of Chlorine Free Products. www.chlorinefreeproducts.org.

Printing

Printing as we know it today is a long way from the earliest days of carved wooden characters, rolled with ink and pressed on paper. Today, digital on-demand printing as well as paperless virtual publishing—from Web sites to e-books—have made the distribution of knowledge and ideas nearly universally accessible. With platforms such as the One Laptop per Child project (*www.laptop.org*), even the poorest areas are slowly connecting to the wealth of information available. In addition, previously inaccessible works (out of print, rare) are becoming more readily available through the efforts of the Internet Archive (*www.archive.org*).

Although great strides have been made to become "paperless," printing continues to be an important and vibrant form for distributing information and ideas. The Printers' National Environmental Assistance Center, the Great Printer Environmental Initiative, the Sustainable Green Printing Partnership, and other groups in the United States and around the world, provide resources to encourage printers to move in a more sustainable direction. In addition, material safety data sheets as well as support from materials and equipment vendors offer printers the opportunity to better understand their processes and impacts. As clients press their designers for solutions that better fit with their eco-ethics, designers are looking to their print vendors to help them deliver the best possible product, opening new avenues for creativity and collaboration. Designers looking for printers that not only produce consistent quality but are taking (or have taken) steps to become eco-certified can participate in chain-of-custody schemes (e.g., FSC) and create works that fit well in a sustainable production process.

Lithographic Printing

PROCESS OVERVIEW

In lithography, a planographic plate is used where the image areas and the nonimage areas are on the same plane (image areas and nonimage areas are neither raised nor depressed) and are defined by differences in their physiochemical properties. There are several subtypes of lithographic printing defined principally by substrate feeding mechanisms and ink drying, but they all use a planographic plate.

PRE-PRESS

Lithographic printing relies on the fundamental property that oil and water do not mix. As a result, lithographic inks are oil based, and fountain solution provides the water that makes the process work. The key to the lithographic process is the plate. Lithographic plates can be made from several different base materials including metal, paper, or plastic. The plates are coated with a light-sensitive chemical that hardens and becomes ink receptive when exposed to ultraviolet light. The nonimage areas are washed off the plate with a developing solution and are treated with a finisher containing gum arabic or a synthetic equivalent to become water receptive. The developer and finisher are aqueous based solutions and contain little or no solvent. In the case of digitally imaged plates, the film-negative step and its associated processing chemistry are eliminated altogether.

Occasionally a job will call for bimetallic plates. Here, plates are composed of two metals, usually an aluminum base or stainless steel base covered with a copper layer. Once exposed, the plates are etched with acids to produce the image. These plates are treated in the same manner in that the nonimage area receives gum arabic or its synthetic equivalent to become water receptive.

In waterless printing, silicone in the plate material is a natural ink repellent, thus negating the need for fountain solution. Waterless plates are exposed in the same manner as conventional plates, but they are developed with solvent-based materials. These processes may not release significant quantities of emissions as they are in a contained environment.

PRINTING

A wide variety of inks have been developed for lithographic printing, with new formulations making their way to market all the time. Although these criteria apply to all print jobs, here especially due to the wide range of variables, inks, the specific press and process, and desired final outcomes (cost, quantity, quality, turnaround, stock, ink coverage) all play a role in how best to maximize design advantages. Working with the printer starting at the concept phase becomes a vital element of the design process.

During the actual printing process, ink film from the lithographic plate is transferred to an intermediate surface (blanket), which, in turn, transfers the ink film to the substrate. Fountain solution is applied to the plate to maintain the hydrophilic properties of the nonimage area.

Fountain solution is a mixture of water and other volatile and nonvolatile chemicals and additives that maintain the quality of the printing plate and reduce the surface tension of the water so that it spreads easily across the plate surface. The fountain solution wets the nonimage area so that the ink is maintained within the image areas. Nonvolatile additives include mineral salts and hydrophilic gums. Alcohol and alcohol substitutes, including isopropyl alcohol, glycol ethers, and ethylene glycol, are the most common VOC additives used to reduce the surface tension of the fountain solution. Fountain solution may contain 5 to 10 percent isopropyl alcohol or alcohol substitutes that meet the same needs but with a much lower VOC content.

Through the use of inking rollers, ink is applied to the plate, adhering only to the image areas. The image is transferred, or "offset," from the plate to a rubber roller (the blanket), which then transfers the image to the substrate being printed. To accelerate drying and control ink flow characteristics, lithographic inks contain solvents. These solvents are referred to as ink oils and have very low vapor pressures and very high boiling points. Some lithographic inks are curable using ultraviolet energy or electron beam and do not contain solvents.

Depending on the type of press and ink drying, the lithographic process is further divided into three subprocesses: sheet-fed, heatset web, and nonheatset web. On a sheet-fed press, the substrate is fed into the press one sheet at a time. A web-fed press prints on a continuous roll of substrate, known as a web, which is later cut to size.

The inks that can be used on lithographic presses include conventional, UV, and waterless. Conventional and sheet-fed conventional inks dry by a combination of penetration and oxidation, with very little solvent (i.e., ink oil) loss. Nonheatset web inks dry by a combination of penetration and oxidation, and the inks do not represent a significant source of VOC emissions. In the heatset process, the ink is dried through evaporation of the ink oil with indirect hot air dryers. This process is potentially the most significant source of VOC emissions in lithography. Waterless inks, while having a higher VOC content, dry in the same way as conventional inks.

Ultraviolet inks consist of pigments, monomers, oligomers, additives, and modifiers. The photoinitiator reacting to the UV light source produces free radicals that initiate a chain reaction, resulting in polymerization of the monomers and oligomers. There are usually very little, if any, VOC emissions from UV inks as they are virtually 100 percent solids.

A variety of chemicals, including cleaning solvents, solution additives, printing inks, and coating materials, can be used in the sheet-fed offset printing process. Due to the nature of the printing equipment though, most of the air emissions happen as a general nonspecific part of the process. Add-on measures to control air emissions would require creating a closed system, not currently part of printing process systems. Due to more specific emissions sources though, heatset web offset emissions can use add-on control technology, and

seh+s
sustainable environments for health + shelter
sustained Note
T 202 360 5999 E info@SustainedNote.org W SustainedNote.org
A 5239 Western Ave. NW, Washington DC, 20016 USA
from the garden to the table
g2t.org
Jeffrey Smith
from the garden to the table
Berkeley CA 94709 510 841 4335 jsmith@g2t.org
eat and live green
YOGA IN THE VINEYARD
a moving retreat for the senses
Christie Dufault
P+F 415.682.4369
C 415.519.1150
29a Downey Street
San Francisco, CA 94117
christie@yogainthevineyard.com
Cheri Larsh-Arellano
Creative Director, Photographer
T 510 540 4800 M 415 377 9349
cheri@consciouscreative.com
conscious
CREATIVE
DESIGN • WEB • VIDEO • PHOTO

use either a catalytic or thermal afterburner, and enjoy a control efficiency of 95 to 99 percent.

POST-PRESS

Finishing activities in commercial printing include but are not limited to folding, cutting and trimming, die cutting, inkjet application, embossing, debossing, foil stamping, and a variety of binding approaches. The binding approaches can be mechanical (e.g., saddle stitching, spiral binding, stapling, etc.) or chemical, which involves the use of adhesives. There are several different types of adhesives, including hot melts, solvent-based, and water-based animal glues. In addition, post-press operations, like press operations, may also include cleaning operations.

Conscious Creative started in 2001 to support the community of entrepreneurs who handle business in a more sustainable manner. Highly targeted graphics and resource minimization as well as high post-consumer waste content stocks and vegetable inks are some of the natural choices Conscious Creative uses to help deliver client messages. (*www.ConsciousCreative.com*)

Yoga in the Vineyard was looking to strike a balance between the two seemingly disparate worlds of yoga and fine dining to attract people to eco-conscious retreats that provided guided yoga practice in the vineyards of California, with organic wine and meals that feature the rich diversity of the region.

From the Garden to the Table is a nonprofit that works with inner-city schools in Oakland, California, to teach children how to garden, grow organic vegetables, and cook for themselves.

Sustainable Environments for Health + Shelter provides solar-powered sustainable energy, heating, and water filtration systems to charitable and other organizations that provide for the care of disadvantaged, homeless, orphaned, or disabled children.

Sustained Note Records (now known as Sustained Note World) is a marriage of music, architecture, and sustainability whose mission is to improve homeless shelters around the world in a sustainable fashion.

Paper dust can be a by-product of the binding and finishing activities, and is generated from the cutting and occasionally die-cutting operations, and perfect binding (flat-back printed products) operations. For many printing operations, the paper dust is not released into the atmosphere but is contained in the facility. Some larger printers use cyclones and/or air pumps to generate negative air flow for a centralized paper trim collection system. In some instances, bag houses are used to collect paper dust from the centralized system or machines. In most instances, the air from the centralized systems is ducted back into the facility and not to the ambient air outside the building.

WATERLESS PRINTING

Waterless or dryography printing offers a low-impact alternative from a water conservation point of view. This offset lithographic printing process eliminates the water or dampening system used in conventional printing. (Dampening solutions often contain high amounts of solvents, contributing to VOC emissions.) According to the Waterless Printing Association:

> Waterless printing plates offer quick roll-up to color and thereby reduce set-up (make-ready) paper waste. Chemically tainted wastewater from traditional offset printing is also eliminated. Waterless plates are capable of extremely high screen rulings and, as a result, apply more ink to the printed piece. The result is a much larger range of colors in four color process printing.[209]

Warren's Waterless Printing, Inc. talks about the environmental potential of this process on its Web site: *www.warrenswaterless.com*.

With the world facing serious water shortages by the year 2025, over half the world's population could be living with serious water shortages. We believe passionately that it's up to each of us to save this resource.[210]

The Web site further states that the company's waterless printing helps it conserve an estimated 200,000 liters (about 52,835 gallons) of water annually. Vibrant color, sharper images with less dot gain, low eco-impact printing, and the ability to print on a wider variety of substrates, especially uneven, uncoated, recycled paper stocks, make this lesser known printing process a favorite among customers looking for high-quality press runs and archival art prints.

While this process conserves water and does not require the use of fountain solutions, there are other drawbacks to consider, especially from another resource consideration: energy. Waterless printing requires a temperature-controlled inking system and thus use a great deal of electricity. Here, alternative energy as part of the mix makes for a much better overall environmental impact reduction.

Flexographic Printing

PROCESS OVERVIEW

Flexographic printing is a widely used printing process applied to corrugated containers, folding cartons, multiwall and paper sacks, plastic bags, milk and beverage cartons, disposable cups and containers, labels, adhesive tapes, envelopes, newspapers, wrappers (candy and food), and a variety of substrates.

A flexographic press can run at higher speeds than a lithographic press and is geared for repeatable items with comparatively lower printing plate costs.

Waterless printing is a favorite among consumers looking for high-quality press runs and archival art prints.

Although flexographic printing may deliver lower quality when compared to other processes, this technology is improving. Some presses and print shops now produce lithography-like results.

Flexographic plates carry raised images (relief) that make contact with the substrate to be printed. Printers offering flexographic services use a press appropriate for the job. The press types include: stack type, central impression cylinder (CIC), in-line, newspaper unit, and dedicated four-, five-, or six-color commercial publication press. Each flexographic press uses a plate cylinder, an application cylinder (anilox roll) that applies ink to the plate, and an ink pan. Some use an additional roller to draw ink from the ink pan, and others will use a doctor blade to improve ink distribution.

PRE-PRESS

Flexographic plates are made of plastic, rubber, or UV-sensitive polymer (photopolymer). The flexible nature of the plate allows it to be attached to a roller or cylinder, allowing it to print on substrates not practical on other presses. Flexographic plates are created through photomechanical, photochemical, and laser-engraved processes.

Traditional flexographic platemaking (photomechanical, photochemical), like any traditional photo process, relies on chemicals that require specific handling. Digitally imaged sheet photopolymer flexographic platemaking offers environmental advantages with no film or associated processing chemicals but has relied on solvents for the wash-out process. Water-washable digital plates are in development.

In 2008, label converter Rako Etiketten in Germany announced that it had begun field-testing a water-washable and digitally imagable flexographic plate from Asahi Photoproducts. If the trials are successful, these plates will prove suitable for all types of inks (solvent-based, UV curing, and water-based) yet still be washed out with water and a simple soap commonly known as soda (sodium carbonate).

For the plates under trial, the entire manufacturing process from imaging, to exposure, to wash-out, drying, and post-exposure takes only an hour. Printing companies able to use digital-quality, eco-compatible flexographic plates that are also ready in short turn times can take advantage of new options for job and resource management. In addition, water wash-out is proving to provide truer register, even after several mounting operations, in contrast to plates that are washed out in solvent, reducing waste and providing additional run-time opportunities.

PRINTING

Four types of inks can be used in flexography; the most common are solvent, water, UV, or EB with water-based inks. Ink is transferred from the pan to the anilox roller delivering a uniform thickness of ink onto the plate cylinder. The substrate to be printed moves between the plate cylinder and the impression cylinder, transferring the image onto the substrate. The printed substrate moves onto an overhead dryer before moving to the next operation. After being printed with all colors specified for the job, the piece may move through an additional dryer to remove residual solvents or water.

POST-PRESS

Finishing activities for flexographic printing are similar to those for most forms of commercial printing, including folding, cutting and trimming, die cutting, inkjet application, embossing, debossing, foil stamping, and a variety of binding approaches.

Gravure

PROCESS OVERVIEW

Gravure printing has a long history and is still part of the selection mix when designers have print needs requiring high volumes or high quality. Due to the high cost of presses, plates, and components though, there are few printers offering this service. However, as a process noted for the long service life of plates, and the large number of high quality impressions possible before the plate needs replacement, gravure printing remains an attractive option for many applications.

PRE-PRESS

Gravure printing uses fluid inks with a very low viscosity. To dry the inks to prevent smudging, the printed substrate must pass through a gas- or electric-fired drier after each printing station. Air from these driers is then passed through either a solvent recovery system or a solvent vapor incinerator. About 95 percent of the solvents can be recovered using this process for reuse or managed disposal. Packaging and products using water-based inks on a gravure press may require a higher temperature and longer dry time at each drying station.

PRINTING

A type of intaglio printing, a gravure plate cylinder rotates in a bath of ink, with the raised areas of the cylinder making up the areas that will not be printed. Excess ink is removed from the plate cylinder by a flexible steel doctor blade, and the ink image is then transferred to the print substrate. When gravure is the printing method used for publication, packaging, and product applications, web-fed gravure presses are the main press type. To serve special printing applications, sheet-fed, intaglio plate, and offset gravure presses may be employed.

POST-PRESS

Finishing activities for gravure printing are similar to those for most forms of commercial printing, including folding, cutting and trimming, die cutting, inkjet application, embossing, debossing, foil stamping, and a variety of binding approaches.

Letterpress

PROCESS OVERVIEW

Letterpress printing is one of the oldest forms of printing and traces its roots all the way back to the earliest forms of relief printing, such as Chinese woodblock printing using characters or images carved in relief, which was widespread in Asia centuries before it was used in other parts of the world. Originally used to print patterns on textiles, it was later used to reproduce text as well as images. (Currently the earliest known work is the Pure Light Dharani Sutra from Korea, about 750 CE). In Europe,

Johannes Gutenberg's movable type press first appeared on the scene in 1450. Using a raised surface to carry the inked image, the image is pressed directly onto the printing surface (paper). In the twenty-first century, commercial letterpress has been experiencing a revival through the use of "water-wash" photopolymer plates versus traditional handset lead or wood type. Several organizations have grown over the years to help preserve traditional printing and book crafts including hand papermaking, letterpress printing, and hand bookbinding, as well as to encourage the use of these traditional techniques to create new books and fine art works.

PRE-PRESS

Handset with lead or wood type as well as cast metal, photopolymer plates, or hand-cut blocks, images are composed on a flat marble stone within a frame. Objects are arranged within the frame, surrounded by nonprinting spacers, and tightened along with the frame to form the image surface.

PRINTING

There are three main types of letterpress presses: platen, flatbed, and rotary, with additional variations found within a press type. Typical pieces created using letterpress presses include business cards, letterhead, forms, posters, announcements, imprinting, and embossing. Eco-options available to letterpress printers include vegetable-based and low-VOC inks, low-VOC and citrus-based solvents,

---

Firebelly Design takes advantage of the paper's tooth to really make an impression. These pieces are printed on French Paper's Frostone with vegetable-based inks at Chicago's Wildflower Letterpress. (*www.firebellydesign.com*)

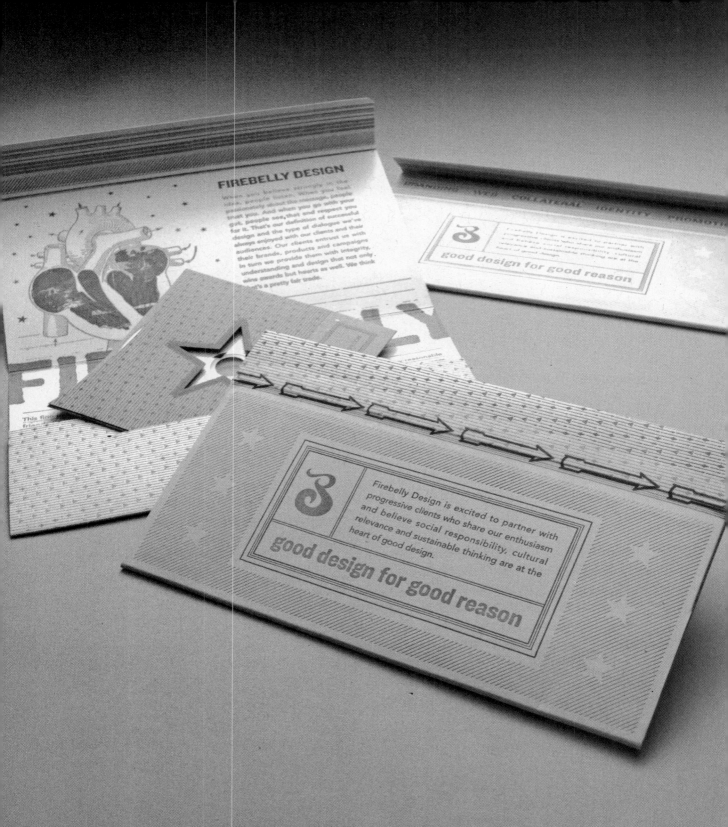

FIREBELLY DESIGN

When you believe strongly in the ideas, people listen. When you feel passionately about the message, people trust you. And when you go with your gut, people see, hear and respect you for it. That's our definition of successful design and the type of dialogue we've always enjoyed with our clients and their audiences. Our clients entrust us with their brands, products and campaigns. In turn we provide them with integrity, understanding and design that not only wins awards but hearts as well. We think that's a pretty fair trade.

3

Firebelly Design is excited to partner with progressive clients who share our enthusiasm and believe social responsibility, cultural relevance and sustainable thinking are at the heart of good design.

good design for good reason

as well as a variety of handcrafted or highly textured papers not practical for use on higher-volume output presses.

POST-PRESS

Finishing activities for letterpress printing are similar to those for most forms of commercial printing. Due to the craft nature of this print form, finishing activities tend to be more fine art in nature (one of a kind, limited run) than suited to mass production.

Screen Printing

PROCESS OVERVIEW

Screen printing is an extremely versatile printing process and can be used to print on a wide variety of substrates, including paper, plastics, glass, and metals, as well as synthetic and natural fabrics, to produce a wide variety of products including, posters, labels, fleet decals, signage, all types of textile garments, and membrane circuits.

PRE-PRESS

The screen printing process uses a porous mesh as its image transfer device. The mesh is stretched tightly over a frame, and a stencil, which defines the image to be printed, is applied to the mesh. The stencil material, referred to as an emulsion, is a chemical based on silver halide that, once exposed, creates the image for printing.

PRINTING

Whether operated by hand or by machine, a squeegee blade sweeps across the surface of the pretensioned, preimaged screen, pressing the ink through the areas of the screen not blocked by the stencil and onto the substrate. The printed substrate then goes into a drying unit. This similar process is used regardless of the type of product produced via screen printing technology.

The major chemicals used in screen printing process include organic solvents, adhesives, and inks. The chemical composition of the ink used varies depending on the substrate printed and the end product produced. There are five main categories of inks used within the screen printing process: UV curable, solvent-based, and water-based for graphic applications; plastisols, and water-based for textile applications.

Ultraviolet inks consist of pigments, monomers, oligomers, additives, and modifiers. The photoinitiator reacting to the UV light source produces free radicals that initiate a chain reaction, resulting in polymerization of the monomers and oligomers. Water-based ink systems use water as part of or as their entire solvent component. These ink systems all contain organic pigments, resins, and additives, such as flow promoters, retarders, and other performance enhancers. Water-based systems require the use of water-soluble resins and contain up to 65 to 70 percent solids.

Conventional solvent-based ink systems are still widely used within the screen printing industry. These ink systems consist of pigments, resins, solvents, and additives. They are dried by the

---

Architects at Payette Associates in Boston and Seattle-based software company Bee Docs teamed up with Portland, Oregon, creative services firm Prolabro to create these eco-responsible shirts printed on EDUN LIVE 100 percent organic cotton shirt using water-based inks. Prolabro is a petroleum-free studio utilizing soy-based cleaners, and specifies sustainably produced garments and paper stocks for its print medium. (*www.prolabro.com*)

AIACONVENTION
BOSTON2008

evaporation of the solvent from the system, leaving behind a thin film of resins and pigments. These ink systems are used on virtually all substrates. The amount of volatiles emitted by these different ink systems depends on the resin system utilized and the amount of volatile additive required.

Inks are rarely used as supplied by the ink manufacturers. Because of variations in temperature and humidity, the screen printing facility generally uses ink additives (usually solvents). The three general categories of solvents used in the screen printing industry are aliphatic hydrocarbons, aromatic hydrocarbons, and oxygenated solvents that are miscible in water. These additives perform various functions. Thinners hold the resin in the binding agent and reduce the viscosity of the inks. Retarding agents slow the drying time of the ink, so that the ink does not block the mesh openings of the screen.

The majority of emissions associated with a screen printing happen as a general nonspecific part of the process. Add-on measures to control air emissions would require creating a closed system, not currently part of printing process systems. However, product reformulation has been adopted as a control measure for this printing process.

SCREEN/STENCIL RECLAMATION

Depending on the ink system utilized during the printing process, screen reclamation activities can be undertaken with organic solvents or water-based systems. During the screen reclamation process, the ink residue is removed after all excess ink is removed from the screen. Water-soluble ink degradents or appropriate solvents are used for this purpose. The fabric/stencil must then be degreased. Any chemical or solvent residue left on the stencil will impede the effectiveness of the stencil remover.

After the stencil remover has been applied, the emulsion begins to dissolve and is completely removed using a high-pressure washer. After repeated uses, hardened ink and removed stencil material appear as a ghost image from previous stencil applications. Ghost/haze removers are used to remove this unwanted condition. After using the haze removers, the screen fabric must be degreased again to prepare it for reuse.

Digital Printing

PROCESS OVERVIEW

Digital printing (direct-to-media printing) refers to the transfer of electronic files directly from the computer to an electronically driven output device that prints the image directly on the selected media (substrate). Electronic images and four-color process images can be printed virtually any size. There are several different types of direct output devices: inkjet devices, dry toner, and wet toner. Digital imaging of printing plates is generally not considered digital printing, as it is a technological evolution, not a production process.

PRE-PRESS

To produce a "digital" image, elements are converted to digital files that can be manipulated on a computer system. This includes scanning analog artwork, or using digital files created with art/layout software.

PRINTING

Digital images can be produced from a wide range of output devices using various technologies. The primary technologies used today are liquid inkjet, electrostatic, solid inkjet, thermal-transfer and photographic. Digital images can be applied to paper, vinyl, fabric, plastics, and many other materials. Depending on specific requirements, the job's service provider can help select the best output device. Here is a brief introduction to several digital printing technologies:

DROP-ON-DEMAND INKJET: For this type of printing, ink is released by applying pressure to force a drop of ink onto the media as needed to create the image.

CONTINUOUS INKJET: In this process, ink is continuously under pressure, forming a stream of droplets. The droplets required to form the image are channeled to the media while the unused droplets are recycled.

THERMAL INKJET: Here, a gas bubble is created in the nozzle, creating pressure to force a droplet of ink onto the media.

SOLID INKJET: Unlike liquid inkjet processes, ink is stored in a solid format, melted as needed, and applied to media using methods similar to liquid inkjet.

THERMAL WAX/RESIN TRANSFER: In this method, wax or resin is applied to a film carrier, usually in a roll format. The wax or resin is transferred to the media using heat. Each color must be transferred individually.

DYE SUBLIMATION: Similar to thermal transfer, in dye sublimation, dyes are transferred from a carrier roll and applied through the use of heat. When a controlled amount of heat is applied, the dye is vaporized and transferred to the media.

ELECTROSTATIC: Here special media is imaged with an electronic charge that attracts toner particles.

Typical electrostatic printers image each color individually.

SPRAY JET: In this process, individual ink colors are applied directly to the media through a spray nozzle.

Inks used for inkjet applications can be water based, dye based, UV curable, or solvent based. Solvent-based ink systems used for this printing process generally have a high solvent content due to the nature of the system. UV-curable ink systems are new to the market.

Similar to the screen printing process, air emissions happen as a general nonspecific part of the process. Add-on measures to control air emissions would require creating a closed system, not currently part of printing process systems. However, depending on the equipment used, ventilation hoods can be employed to control indoor air quality issues.

POST-PRESS

Finished prints often are laminated with a top coat for outdoor durability. These laminates can be applied with a dry system or a wet system. The wet system uses liquid laminates that are hand-applied to the final print. These systems do contain solvent materials.

Article provided by the Sustainable Green Printing Partnership Program, with additional content by Wendy Jedlička, and Paul Gutkowski, and Dion Zuess.

Foil Stamping and Embossing

As designers look for ways to reduce materials use, embossing and debossing (pressing paper or board into a form so it raises above or below the base surface) are becoming very attractive options. These techniques enable designers to get more impact from the same piece of paper or board, adding another element to the design without adding any extra materials at all. Foil stamping is another story, as a thin layer of metal or other solid is added to the paper surface. The Foil Stamping and Embossing Association (FSEA) is the first to admit that some designers and converters have gone a little crazy with foil applications. Using foil-covered boards and printing opaque ink over the top so just a bit of the foil shows through, rather than spot stamping the desired area, is one of the more glaring examples.

In an effort to better understand just what sort of impacts foil stamping has in sustainability terms, FSEA commissioned an independent research firm, Pira International, of Surrey, England, to do an assessment. "It has become quite apparent that this study is extremely important to the long-term health of our industry and association," noted FSEA executive director Jeff Peterson.

As part of their 2008 study for FSEA, "Repulpability of Foil-decorated Paper," Pira foil-stamped paper/board with the more traditional hot foil stamping process and with the cold foil process, and included foil-decorated products that represented 25 percent PCW up to 100 percent PCW waste.

The study describes the pulping and screening methods used in the research and provides a complete analysis of the reporting results from the testing methods. The main conclusion of the study is that paper products selectively decorated by both the traditional hot stamp and new cold foil processes are still very much recyclable. Repulping facilities that use centrifugal cleaners (hydrocyclones) to better remove all types of adhesives, laminates, bindery remnants, and labels—a process

used in many markets—have little problem removing applied foils.

FSEA is committed to providing its members and the industry at large with the tools to address the expanding number of questions regarding the topic of sustainability. FSEA will continue to stay abreast of changes, as well as develop resources to help designers and converters use stamping options in better ways. For more information, and to keep up on the industry's eco-efforts visit its Web site at: *www.fsea.com.*

Printing and Certification

Like many other industries, the graphics arts industry is going through sweeping changes. From major customer initiatives forcing vendors to reassess their operating practices (Walmart's Global Responsible Sourcing Initiative) to stiffening environmental laws in key markets (RoHS, European Union Directive on Packaging, Producer Responsibility Laws), there is no aspect of the printing process that will not be, or has not already been, affected.

In an effort to better manage the requirements being placed on them, print buyers are increasingly looking to their vendors to become active partners in meeting their environmental goals. With this in mind, certifications are becoming an increasingly

When Anatomy Communications had to change its phone number, the idea of tossing away a huge stack of beautifully printed and embossed, and otherwise perfectly correct, cards really bothered them. Instead, a simple rubber stamp impression was applied over the old phone number. Not only did it announce that there had been a phone number change, but it added a touch of whimsy everyone could appreciate.

ANATO
COMMUNICAT

laurie varga • creative project m
laurie@anatomycommunication
~~416-651-9310~~ • messages that res
416-465-1173

ANATOMY
COMMUNICATIONS

important tool to help print buyers determine whom to choose for their work.

It should be noted that, sustainability standards and verification (certification) systems are evolving and changing as new information and technology becomes available. As a front-end "mega-consumer," designers and print buyers play a key role in guiding the direction and depth of standards that are applied to printers and print products. It is important then to keep up with certification criteria changes, and favor products and vendors measured on objective, and verifiable criteria inclusive of a broad range of stakeholder concerns, from the environmental, to social and economic.

In Europe and increasingly in the United States, ISO 14000 has been one path firms can pursue to assure existing and potential customers that they are what they claim to be. Industry-specific certifications also are available to printers. In the United States, the Great Printers Project and the Sustainable Green Printing Partnership Program℠ are two programs that focus specifically on the printing industry.

Great Printer Environmental Initiative

The Great Printer Environmental Initiative, also known as the Great Printer Program, began in 1992 as a joint effort of the Printing Industries of America, the Council of Great Lakes Governors, and the Environmental Defense Fund. This partnership was designed to promote waste prevention and encourage lithographic printers to become more environmentally responsible.

The program is managed today by the Printing Industry of Minnesota. A key effort launched in 2001 was the addition of a third-party audit requirement to certify that Great Printers are not only in compliance with environmental, health, and safety regulations, but take those ideas a step further. Although the program has evolved over the years to take advantage of new technologies, it works to encourage those earning Great Printer status to go beyond simple compliance.

To qualify for the Great Printer Environmental Initiative, a printer must meet these criteria:

A. COMMIT TO THE GREAT PRINTER ENVIRONMENTAL INITIATIVE PRINCIPLES

These principles simply state that a printer that is participating in the Great Printer Environmental Initiative commits to:

— Complying with all applicable environmental, health and safety requirements

— Going beyond compliance by minimizing wastes, reusing, or recycling waste that cannot be prevented and maximizing energy efficiency

— Pursuing continuous environmental, health and safety improvements.

B. COMPLETE AN ENVIRONMENTAL, HEALTH AND SAFETY COMPLIANCE AUDIT

The company must have conducted a facility environmental, health, and safety (EHS) compliance audit in accordance with the Great Printer Environmental Initiative EHS Compliance Audit Requirements and corrected the issues identified in that audit. Companies must conduct a facility EHS audit annually or once every thirty-six months if they have a written and effective environmental management system (EMS) plan in place that meets the Great Printer Environmental Initiative EMS Plan Requirements.

C. PURSUE BEYOND-COMPLIANCE PROJECTS

The company must have completed at least one beyond-compliance project within the last five years and must currently be working on at least two other beyond-compliance projects (one beyond-compliance project if a company is renewing its participation in the initiative). Beyond-compliance projects are those projects that a company undertakes that have either an environmental or an employee health or safety benefit to them. Toward this effort, printers have purchased wind energy from their local utility (some have purchased 100 percent of their energy from the program), and some have undertaken additional greening projects, including installing more energy-efficient roofs. Another effort is to look for secondary uses for their by-products, for example, send waste newsprint to a dairy operation for animal bedding. Looking in-house, some printers recycle their own waste solvents to prevent the need to purchase new chemicals while others are reducing toxin loads by reworking their printing processes to use solvents that are lower in VOCs right from the start.

Together, the printers that make up the Great Printer Environmental Initiative see their role as not just passive compliance, but an opportunity to help move the whole of the printing industry in a more positive, and sustainable direction. Though located in the Midwest (close to the paper mills, helping to reduce fuel demand in the early part of the supply chain), Great Printers serve national as well as international accounts, to find a Great Printer, visit *www.pimn.org*.

*Sustainable Green Printing Partnership Program*SM

The Sustainable Green Printing Partnership SM (SGP) advocates the idea that sustainable printing is the incorporation of green business practices that provide environmental stewardship and corporate social responsibility. These ideas include protection of employee health and safety through the efficient use of renewable resources, energy, and recycling. Green initiatives and sustainable production practices in manufacturing operations are gaining considerable momentum. For the printing industry, sustainability has reached a critical mass of interest due to the demands of customers, environmental groups, investment firms, government agencies, and consumers.

Launched in August 2008, the SGP Partnership program provides a pathway for printing facilities to begin their sustainability journey. The program was the brainchild of three major printing trade associations: Specialty Graphic Imaging Association, Printing Industries of America, and the Flexographic Technical Association. The SGP Partnership program was conceived, created, and launched to help the printing industry across the United States establish itself as a sustainability leader and advocate for change, and focuses on a facility's entire operation rather than one piece.

Similar to other certification programs, the SGP Partnership program requires third-party certification. Developed through a stakeholder group process, the program adopted an approach that mimics the triple bottom line: people, profit, and planet. A sustainable business is one that shows a profit while protecting the environment and

One of the original Great Printers, Johnson Printing and Packaging (*www.JPPcorp.com*) has been staying ahead of the curve since 1921. This promotional set from JPP shows off its certifications, as well as a glueless envelope design that adds no contaminants to the pulp mix at recycling time.

improving the lives of the people with whom it interacts. Sustainability requires that the entire system be evaluated. The SGP Partnership program embodies these principles by asking facilities to adopt a systematic approach to certifying their facilities based on a series of best management practices. The goal of the SGP Partnership is to define sustainable printing and identify steps that help the printing industry establish manufacturing practices and products that are more environmentally sustainable. This serves as the foundation for a broader sustainability initiative that also encompasses social and economic elements.

The SGP provides a central location for information on recognized printers and sustainable green printing activities, utilizing the Web site *www.sgppartnership.org*. The registry assures the print customer that the registered printing facilities have made significant commitments toward sustainability. The SGP Partnership strives to be the central focus for "sustainable green" registration for the printing industry to harmonize and strengthen sustainability efforts.

The SGP Partnership has taken a particular approach in describing what sustainability means for the printing sector and uses the terms "product," "process," and "envelope." Taken together, these terms provide printers with a useful road map of sustainability in their activities, products, and services. All of these elements are important when defining sustainable printing operations.

Product includes the design aspects and input material management to create the product.

Process includes all manufacturing steps (e.g., pre-press, press, and post-press) involved with converting raw materials into a finished product including process by-products (e.g., solid wastes, air pollution, and wastewater) that have an environmental, health, and safety impact.

Envelope includes all the manufacturing support activities and includes the building, grounds, utilities, employees, and other functions at an individual site.

As sustainability efforts are part of a continuous improvement process, the criteria used by this recognition program will expand and evolve over time as new techniques and technologies become available. New program requirements will be developed and implemented. Printing facilities will be asked to certify that they have met any newly adopted criteria.

Sustainability is not limited to the environmental dimension. The scope of the SGP Partnership is intended go beyond environmental considerations to include "corporate social responsibility" and "corporate citizenship" elements. These are still-evolving concepts. In subsequent versions, the SGP Partnership will issue the latest approaches and additional best practices.

Further iterations of SGP criteria will be developed through a specific process, including a technical advisory committee, that will identify additional best practices and make recommendations for adjustments to the partnership's Guiding Principles, management system, reporting, and verification components.

Since printers do not manufacture their own equipment and consumables and suppliers are an integral part of the industry's efforts, the SGP Partnership will work with the supplier network and others to address issues such as recyclability, biodegradability, compostability, recycled content, and VOC/HAP content.

SGP Guiding Principles

Participants in the SGP Partnership program are asked to observe a specific set of Guiding Principles. These principles reflect the key elements of sustainable business practices that will ensure continued viability and growth in a responsible manner. The SGP Guiding Principles serve to provide a framework of commitment to sustainable green practices and form the basis for how an SGP printer should strive to operate its business. Once accepted into the program, printing facilities are requested to print, sign, and prominently display a set of the Guiding Principles as a commitment to not only the SGP Partnership program but to incorporating sustainable business practices into its operation. A full

version of the SGP Partnership program Guiding Principles can be found on the SGP Web site at *www.sgppartnership.org.*

SGP Printer Categories

Within the SGP Partnership, there are two categories of printer recognition. A printer can initially apply for either category. Candidate Pending Verification (CPV) is an optional, provisional category and a precursor to SGP Printer status. It is not a requirement that a printer become CPV prior to full SGP Printer status. This category is meant to allow facilities that are not yet eligible for full SGP Printer recognition the time to develop their program and demonstrate their commitment to sustainability. Applying for CPV status is more than a placeholder formality; it requires a significant commitment to implementing the program.

An SGP Printer is a full participation level within the SGP Partnership registration program and has substantial requirements relating to sustainable business practices. Recognition under this program is on a facility-by-facility basis. Companies with multiple locations must seek recognition for each site separately. Conformity with SGP participant criteria will be verified by an on-site verification conducted by a SGP Partnership–qualified auditor. It is valid for a two-year period. SGP Printers will be required to submit an annual progress report using the partnership's official template. For a complete listing of SGP Partnership Program Requirements, visit the SGP Web site.

SGP Certification

One of the cornerstones of the SGP Partnership program is the requirement to undergo a third-party certification process by demonstrating to a third-party auditor that the printer meets the SGP registration criteria. The SGP certification process comprises three stages: precertification activities, on-site certification, and followup activities.

All printers that seek to become a certified SGP Printer must undergo the same verification process. This rigorous, third-party review provides both credibility and consistency to the SGP Partnership program. A print buyer wanting to do business with a sustainable green printer knows that a company displaying the SGP logo has demonstrated to an objective auditor that it meets the SGP registration criteria. For a complete listing of SGP certification criteria, visit the SGP Web site.

Article provided by the Sustainable Green Printing Partnership Program. For more information about certification or to find an SGP certified printer, visit the Web site www.sgppartnership.org.

Printing Checklist

This overview for creating and managing a print job is offered by the Organic Design Operatives (*www.themightyodo.com*). [211]

1. **Define the Problem**

   Begin by answering a few questions about the project. Purpose (inform, sell, and so on)? Audience (social, economic, and so on)? Restrictions (budget, format, regulations, and so on)? Special requirements? Useful life span (a week, a year)? Quality of life (durable versus consumable, fixed versus changeable)?

2. **Plan the Life Cycle**

   Everything we create has a past, present, and future. Now that the problem has been defined,

begin planning for a closed-loop, sustainable life cycle.

Resources. Source reclaimed (used, recycled) and renewable (for any virgin content) resources that are sustainably managed. Resources should also be recoverable after end use. Don't just use recycle "-able" materials; use materials that actually will be recycled in the target market.

Production. Seek out socially responsible manufacturers that utilize clean production technologies, resources, and practices. When practical, choose manufacturers that are nearest the end user to reduce transportation impacts.

End use. Seek out the cleanest, most efficient, and most effective solution.

Recovery. Begin to plan for project's end of life. Think about how to enable end users to complete the cycle by designing for resource recovery (i.e., label recyclable materials and include any needed instructions).

3. **Design the Solution**

   Designers have far more positive impact at the creative stage, long before any end of life scenario is played out.

   Start with a powerful idea. Creative, deliberate solutions can be considerably more effective than those that rely solely on a frivolous use of resources.

   Carefully select a medium/format. Take what's learned from defining the problem and brainstorm the most effective and least resource-intensive medium/format in which to solve it. For instance, a problem may be resolved just as well with an e-mail as with a postcard. For packaging, is a polybag with header card needed to sell a T-shirt, or would a simple hangtag and a reusable hanger that stays at point of sale work just as well?

Estimate scale based on content. Using volume of content as a guide, determine the approximate scale of a chosen format. For example, it would be wasteful to design a twenty-four-page brochure for twelve pages of content. For packaging, avoid overpackaging. The consumer doesn't appreciate it, landfills are bulging with it, and it just adds cost.

Determine actual size. Working backward from standard press sheet sizes, determine the most efficient final dimensions for the job. Minimize trim waste through optimal imposition or by avoiding bleeds.

Ask the printer for help with special requirements, such as gripper margins, grain direction, and so on. Consider transport needs from the start. Can we make the product just a bit stronger to avoid exponentially larger packaging to move too fragile an item? Can a book's layout be just a bit tighter, but still highly readable, to allow for a smaller size and so more books per case?

Use resources wisely. Utilize both sides of paper, limit the number of inks and ink coverage, gang projects together on press when possible, and so on. Choose materials appropriate to function, life span, and quality of life. Use what you need, but *need* what you use.

Maximize functionality. Combine otherwise separate functions into a single piece (i.e., brochures that incorporate a mailing panel, eliminating the need for an envelope). Expand function by building in a second use (i.e., paper swatch books that double as sketchbooks). Extend the useful life of resources by designing the piece for reuse (i.e., refillable milk jugs) or employing the idea of modularity (i.e., blank stock boxes combined with easily updatable applied labels). Be careful not to use expanded functionality as an excuse to make a piece overly engineered, overly durable, or overly materialized.

Avoid frills. Don't add needless extras, or go crazy with their application if used (i.e., foil stamping, thermography, coatings, lamination, varnishes, embossing, and die cuts). Extras are there to enhance a good idea and to greatly extend the functionality or effectiveness of a design. Extras can be overkill from a design standpoint, can consume additional energy and resources, and, in some cases, can create problems come recycling time.

Work smart. Evolve your creative process to include sustainability criteria. (see "The Nature Factor": *www.themightyodo.com/html/ resources_designtools.htm*). Proof on-screen. Use e-mail, PDFs, and the Internet where appropriate. Print on both sides of office paper and/or use for sketch paper. Don't print e-mail. Create an office purchasing policy to buy sustainable products. Turn off idle computers and utilize/support renewable energy sources such as wind and solar. (For more ideas see chapter 6, "Working Smarter.")

4. **Specify Resources**

Paper. Specify papers containing a high amount of post-consumer recycled content and pro-

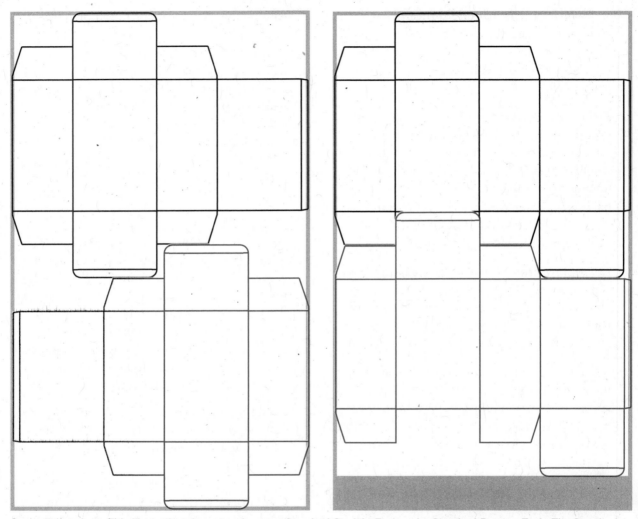

Space is the place. This illustration shows two boxes: a Standard Straight Tuck and a Standard Reverse Tuck. The Standard Straight box on the same width stock requires 6.83 percent more board to deliver the same size box as the Standard Reverse.

cessed chlorine free. Any virgin content should be derived from tree-free fibers (kenaf, hemp, etc.) or Forest Stewardship Council certified wood fibers and whitened totally chlorine free (TCF). Look for cleanly produced papers (i.e., wind power, carbon neutral) and vendors that have ISO 14001 or other third-party certifications.

Ink. Specify low-VOC inks. Avoid colors that contain heavy metal compounds. Use recycled inks where possible.

Adhesives and bindings. Specify pasted binding (similar to saddle stitch binding but without metal staples, which must be removed during recycling) over saddle stitching when possible. Ask the printer to source paste that is water- or vegetable-based, and nontoxic, and that disperses in water (better recyclability). When saddle stitching is a must, consider specifying one instead of two staples. Keep in mind that anything made from metal must be mined and processed, and so should be used sparingly. When perfect binding is appropriate, specify water-soluble over solvent-based glues, hot-melts, and toxic vinyl acetates (found in many padding compounds).

Labels. Look for alternatives to crack-and-peel labels that may hinder recycling and employ a throw-away (backer paper). Consider silicone-coated backerless labels, starch-based gum arabic adhesive (i.e., lick-and-stick), and low/no-VOC inkjet labeling.

5. Get It Produced

Preparation. Work closely with the job's vendors throughout the process. A well-conceived production plan minimizes surprises, waste, added costs, and mistakes.

Before sending the final design out to be produced, create a list of instructions and specifications. This is a chance to double-check dimensions, ink, paper, and so on while also providing the vendor with clear written instructions.

Carefully determine quantities to be printed in order to avoid overruns or reprints. Miscalculation here can be a huge source of waste and cost.

Printing. Work with certified printers (*www.PIMN.org, SGPpartnership.org*, ISO 14000).

These printers go beyond compliance with environmental, health, and safety requirements to reduce waste and pollution in day-to-day printing plant operations.

Reduce the negative impacts of printing process: Use dryography (waterless), computer-to-plate (CTP), direct imaging (DI), low-VOC dampening solutions, and press washes.

Specify embellishments with restraint: Choose only those processes that increase functionality or effectiveness—die cutting, embossing, engraving (specify water- or vegetable-based ink), aqueous varnish (water-based), spot varnish (vegetable- or water-based).

Avoid embellishments that may make paper unrecyclable: Avoid excessive use of foil, lamination, coatings, thermography.

6. Send It Out

Use targeted, updated mailing lists and request address corrections. A clean mailing list is not only more profitable and easier on the environment, but makes for a more successful campaign. (Refer to the Direct Marketing Association's "Green 15" environmental performance resolution at: *www.the-dma.org*).

Avoid air and rush delivery when possible.

Specify addresses to be applied directly onto pieces via inkjet. Demand water-based, high-resolution inkjet technology over solvent-based methods.

7. Follow Up

Seek feedback. Talk to the client, vendors, and others about what was successful and what could be done better next time.

Stay up to speed. To make wise choices, know facts and options.

Keep learning. Get active, and exchange information with others; support and participate in relevant organizations—like ODO!

Energy Changes Everything

Understanding Energy

The term "embodied energy" refers to the total energy needed for an entire product/service life cycle. The life cycle includes all raw material extraction, all transport, manufacture, installation, disassembly, and decomposition. When reviewing options, these are a few ideas to help weigh not only materials choices but structure options.

WEIGHT: Heavier weight means more transport energy costs. If the transport fuel is a fossil fuel, every gram of extra weight means that much more energy is needed to move the thing at every point of its life from manufacture through end of life. PDFs of a user manual on a CD deliver all of the information at a fraction of the weight of a printed paper manual, downloading the PDF manual from a dedicated Web site carries no physical weight, and less delivery energy "weight."

SIZE: How many units will fit in a case? Case optimization has impacts for both transport energy demands (how many per truckload) as well as warehouse space/energy demands. How many will fit on a shelf? Must the product also inflate distributor and end user's space/energy demands? Again we ask: Why spend the fuel, time, money, and space to move a manual around, when the consumer can download the most up-to-date version from a dedicated Web site?

DISTANCE: The farther a good has to travel from materials sources, to manufacturer, to buyer, the more energy it uses. A Leopold Center study of energy use in the food system[212] found that, for a Des Moines, Iowa, processing plant to make a tub of strawberry yogurt using current food distribution systems, it brings in strawberries from California (1,811 miles), milk from out of state (205 miles), and sugar from Minnesota and North Dakota (524 miles). A total of 2,540 miles were expended to make a product that could have been produced from local sources in-season.

QUALITY: Create goods that will do the job well. How many "cheap" products have we all purchased to meet a need—with all the associated manufacturing, transport, and disposal impacts attached to each purchase—when one very good but more expensive version would have served in place of the string of broken wannabes?

EFFICIENCY: Over 90 percent of the energy that goes into an incandescent bulb is converted to heat energy. That's why a child's toy oven functions with only a 100-watt bulb as its heat source. Compact fluorescent lamps (CFLs) deliver the same light output as incandescent lightbulbs but use 75 percent less energy. A typical household can save $200 to $500 in a year by switching to more energy-efficient lighting and appliances. In his February 2005 TED talk, "On Winning the Oil Endgame," Amory Lovins, cofounder of the Rocky Mountain Institute notes that for cars: less than one

The Footprint Chronicles Web site by apparel maker and longtime eco-advocate Patagonia was created to help consumers connect with the firm's products on a very tangible level. It details all stages of product and materials use as well as the pros and cons of the product's production. (*www.patagonia.com*)

percent of the fuel energy ends up moving the driver. For an event, what would deliver the best impact for resources used? Can what is needed be delivered on a two-sided half-sheet rather than a one-sided full sheet? The end result is the same amount of information, using the same font sizes, but requiring half the paper.

ENERGY USE: For packaging, this would mean the total amount of energy to deliver a good. An example of a product that eliminates a whole level of energy use is aseptic packaging and canned goods. Milk packaged in aseptic bricks is shelf stable and doesn't require refrigeration for months until

opened. Traditionally-packaged milk, however, needs to be refrigerated from the moment it's packaged and through all of its short shelf life, requiring larger refrigerated storage areas for the store and more frequent trips to the store for the consumer. How much energy and resources are expended to send a mailing? Would a smaller "teaser" piece, like a bookmark, have been just as effective to drive people to a more comprehensive Web site that does the actual selling?

SOURCE: Papermaking is one of the largest users of electricity in the United States. Mining/drilling impacts and combustion pollution from electricity generated by fossil fuel is at issue. Eco-minded paper mills, as well as the eco-printers that use their products, are switching to windpower to eliminate one of their biggest manufacturing impacts: energy usage. For areas that use the mining technique known as mountain topping (a particularly impactful method common in the southeast region of the Unites States that is environmentally destructive with lingering long-term regionally destructive economic impacts), power used to extract coal this way carries additional negative perceptions. Companies in these coal-burning regions that go out of their way to generate their energy using renewable resources would be easily looked on as comparative superchampions.[213]

With energy at the heart of everything we do, things that may seem like minor annoyances, when multiplied by many units, become staggeringly alarming impacts. U.S. computer-security company McAfee, as part of a study it commissioned, found that about 62 trillion unsolicited emails (spam) were sent in 2008. These mails use 33 terawatt hours of electricity: the amount of energy used by 1.5 million American homes or 3.1 million cars over a year. As so much of the energy in the U.S. (and elsewhere in the world) is generated by coal-fired power plants, this mean a release of 17 million tons of carbon dioxide—0.2 percent of the global carbon dioxide greenhouse gas emissions load. Unsolicited e-mail isn't just annoying, it's adding to global warming.[214]

Carbon Accounting

Eric Jackson

www.carbonlesspromise.com

Global warming is the first pan-world issue that humans have ever faced. No disease or resource shortage has ever had the potential to touch every human being the way that significant climate change will. Like most issues, the first human impacts will be felt by those who can least afford it—those in equatorial Africa and low-level coastal communities in Southeast Asia, for example. Animal populations will be affected before humans—the polar regions and shallow-water sea life, for example. But if our current greenhouse gas emissions trajectory remains unchanged, here are some possibilities that everyone should consider.

By 2100, Chicago will have 30+ days per year over 100°F. In fact, the weather in central Illinois will be similar to current-day southeast Texas. Not much corn or soybeans grow in southeast Texas. At the same time, the southern edge of the great boreal forests, currently in Minnesota, will be pushed northward some 500 miles. No more pine forests in the northern United States? The range of estimates of how much of Florida will disappear due to rising sea levels varies, but it is generally agreed that none of the current coastal cities south of Jacksonville will remain on dry land. And don't forget Manhattan—

It was a restaurant, now it's just a roof. Biloxi, MS.
Photo: Jeremy Faludi

the entire island will likely be covered by water: great for the boating industry, not much good for everyone else.

Therefore, the counting of carbon has become a popular idea. "What's your carbon footprint?" really is one of the hottest phrases in the news today. The image of a footprint in wet sand is a great visual aid in communicating the idea, but the discipline of carbon accounting actually has become quite complicated. A whole new industry has sprung up to advise, measure, and report organizational activities as they relate to greenhouse gases. Carbon has become a whole new branch of EHS (Environmental

Health and Safety) departments. Universities, landowners, transportation companies, municipalities, states, nations, manufacturers, and even individuals are being called to account for their carbon impacts.

Motivations

So what does this mean to an organization? The motivations for developing a GHG (greenhouse gas) strategy and embarking on carbon accounting are many, but they seem generally to fall into the categories of enviro-ethics, marketing, economics, or regulation.

ENVIRO-ETHICS: DOING THE RIGHT THING

It is the rare organization that starts concerning itself with its carbon impact solely due to enviro-ethics. More often than not, a carbon initiative is catalyzed by an organization's customers, investors, or some other critical stakeholder group. Once the process begins, however, it often leads to a heightened understanding that in turn leads to a new and true environmental ethos within the company or institution. If an organization already "believes," then the next step is taking action.

MARKETING: GREENWASHING?

Unfortunately, but not surprisingly, many organizations seem to be eager to do anything to paint themselves with a greener hue. That's not quite accurate though. They want the greener hue, but they don't want to spend any time or money making real changes. This can work for a while, poking at projects and making them a bit "greener," but the whole point of sustainability in action is to create meaningful and measurable long-term change. As carbon reporting methodologies become more standardized and transparent, organizations motivated simply by greenwashing will be exposed for the frauds that they are.

Things are already heading in that direction. The U.S. Federal Trade Commission has already begun the process to better define "green claims" (FTC Green Guide basics are in Chapter 3 of this book). This action is in response to studies such as that completed by TerraChoice, which state that a huge majority of green product claims are misleading or nonfactual.

ECONOMICS: DOING WELL WHILE DOING GOOD

Walmart has once again shown everyone how to save money. By making reduced carbon emissions and reduced energy consumption part of its management strategy, Walmart is driving energy costs and carbon emissions out of its supply chain. The company's economic motivations stay intact, and it gets to make greener performance claims that, for the most part, can be backed up with data.

It's also fascinating to see that many corporations listed on "socially responsible" indices, such as the Dow Jones Sustainability Index, outperform their peers in almost every business segment: coincidental or causal? At the very least, having a GHG Strategy seems to coincide with a deep and broad understanding of how apparent externalities can impact businesses across all sectors.

REGULATION: SMOKESTACKS BEWARE

If an organization has a smokestack, concerns about being regulated for carbon emissions are well founded. Utilities, cement, steel, and other heavy industries are going to be the first to feel the direct teeth-marks from carbon-constraining regulations. Most other organizations will not be directly regulated, or will be regulated in the second or third wave of rules.

This will surprise some institutions, such as universities or cities that have their own central power facilities. They are likely to fall under the same axe as the largest coal-fired power plants across the country. They might also struggle with compliance more because they can't pass along rate hikes to their customers—they are their own customers. Large hospitals with incinerators might also feel the pinch.

Professionals in the field of GHG management may be less concerned about what a company's motivation is, but they still need to know what it is in order to help the company achieve the desired outcomes. Perhaps environmentalists shouldn't care what motivations are either, as long as actions lead to real, meaningful, and measurable reductions in carbon emissions. But even if motivations are known, and it usually is a combination of two or more, there is still a lot of work to do.

Stakeholders

Every organization has them. Some are more easily identified than others. Customers are often the first stakeholder group that comes to mind. Or investors. But the list is much longer than that. Consider all of these groups of potential stakeholders in an organization;

— *Employees:* both current and future

— *Banks:* as lenders

— *Board of directors:* as fiduciaries

— *Insurance companies:* as risk assessors and coverage providers

— *Media:* the press

— *Academia:* the pundits

— *Bloggers:* the unruly

— *Customers:* the obvious

— *Investors:* the owners

— *Students:* both current and future

— *Alumni:* funders of future university growth opportunities

— *Regulators:* both current and future

It's true that not all stakeholder groups are equal and it is highly dependent on the type of organization being analyzed. Rather than trying to appeal to all stakeholder groups when first developing a GHG strategy, it is more efficient to identify the first group or two that is likely to hurt the organization without a GHG strategy. It is the rare organization that hasn't heard some murmurs about how a particular stakeholder group views the organization's global warming efforts.

Developing knowledge about stakeholders' concerns isn't difficult in concept, but it takes some time and some expertise. To get beyond the buzzwords like "carbon footprint" or "carbon neutral" to find out how deep stakeholder concerns are and what they expect an organization to do to assuage those fears. So the first step is to do a stakeholder analysis with the identified critical stakeholder groups.

The Plan

Armed with the insights and information that the stakeholder analysis provides, one can next develop a GHG strategy that makes sense for the organization. Again, each organization is unique and will be driven by different motivations and stakeholder requirements. And it is likely, or rather almost certain, that any GHG strategy will continue to evolve over time as more is learned and those involved become more fluent and comfortable with the risks and opportunities that a carbon-constrained world presents to the organization.

Don't be scared by the term "GHG strategy." It doesn't need to be complicated. Too many large consulting firms try to make a mountain out of a molehill so they can charge exorbitant fees for producing hundreds of pages of stuff. The best plans are relatively short and to the point. The primary sections of the plan are to articulate the stakeholders' interests, the organization's motivations, broad objectives, and specific goals. To help identify those goals, we enter the world of carbon accounting.

Measuring

Once broad objectives have been determined, setting goals and measuring carbon impacts are done more or less together. It becomes an iterative process, and both processes and goals are revisited several times in order to get it right. Let's demystify this a little bit.

For those with a business mind-set, think of a balance sheet: assets and liabilities. The current balance sheet likely doesn't have any entries for carbon. And a formal balance sheet possibly never will, although some banks are asking clients to do just that. The notion of carbon assets and carbon liabilities is instructive. All organizations have carbon liabilities; some organizations also have carbon assets.

STEP ONE — ENTERPRISE ACCOUNTING VERSUS PRODUCT ACCOUNTING

The stakeholder analysis should have revealed whether the carbon analysis should be an enterprise approach or a product approach. If a firm doesn't make any products, the choice is quite simple. But many organizations do have products, and they obviously also have an enterprise. To explain the differences, let's use the simple comparison of horizontal and vertical.

An enterprise (company or effort) is a vertical system, a silo if you will. Its shape and size is determined by how one sets the boundaries as discussed in the next section. But a visual of a silo is a good place to start. Activities happening within that silo lead to carbon emissions. Stuff comes into and out of that silo that lead to more carbon emissions. The silo has a resulting carbon footprint that includes the sum of all of these activities.

The enterprise's product has a horizontal life. It starts somewhere as a bunch of trees, corn, ore, petroleum, and so on, and winds up as a toaster in a landfill or a recycled paperboard box of corn flakes. To analyze the carbon emissions created by products, one would have to undertake a carbon life cycle assessment (LCA) of the products. Done properly, the LCA would calculate the carbon emissions resulting from raw material extraction all the way to the end of life of that product.

Again, *enterprise accounting* is about the activities of the organization. *Product accounting* is about the inputs, processes, and uses associated with a specific product.

STEP TWO — SCOPES AND BOUNDARIES

The process of establishing an organization's scope and boundary for purposes of carbon accounting is critical. It's impossible to measure everything, but something has to be measured. The scope of the measurement relates to how many activities are included in the calculations. The boundary of the measurement refers to what portion of the organization (enterprise or product) will be included. The GHG protocol developed by World Resources Institute and World Business Council for Sustainable Development puts together a series of documents that describe these scopes and boundaries.[215] The brief summary that follows might save several hours of reading and rereading by boiling the protocol down to what is essential.

When considering the organizational boundary, the primary determination is about what the organization owns (the equity approach) versus what the organization effectively controls (the control approach). For example, a chain of fast-food stores that are operated as independent franchises is different from a chain of stores directly owned and operated by the company itself. Boundary setting is a choice made, based on broad objectives and informed by stakeholder input.

The two terms used regarding boundaries are the "equity approach" and the "control approach." The first focuses strictly on the ownership category while the second considers the broader context of the domain that the organization controls contractually. Back to the fast-food example: If the independent franchisees are contractually required to operate certain machinery and equipment a specified number of hours every day, then those activities would be included in the control approach, but not in the equity approach.

Scope 1 Emissions cover all direct combustion in activities. If fossil fuels are burned within the defined boundary, this activity is included. For many organizations, this might only be the natural gas that heats the building or boiler. If a school has a large campus, it could include the fuel burned in the fleet of vehicles used on that campus. Except for industrial manufacturers, Scope 1 emissions are not likely to represent more than 5 to15 percent of total carbon emissions. All organizations doing carbon accounting do Scope 1 analysis.

Scope 2 Emissions cover all energy used in all activities within the defined boundary but not generated on site. It is an upstream calculation of carbon emissions that result from the electricity used or steam received from another entity. For most organizations, Scope 2 can represent a significant portion of the overall carbon emissions; 50 percent or more is not uncommon. All organizations doing carbon accounting do Scope 2 analysis.

Scope 3 Emissions are everything else one could possibly imagine. Taken to an extreme, a paper manufacturer might choose to include emissions resulting from tree-harvesting activities or the emissions resulting from transporting the tree-harvesting equipment to the harvesting site, or even the emissions resulting from the manufacturing of the equipment used in tree harvesting, and so on. At a more practical level, the Scope 3 emissions should include any GHG emissions arising from activities that the enterprise has control over. This could include emissions resulting from business travel, purchased supplies, and the transportation of finished goods, among others. Doing Scope 3 analysis as part of a carbon accounting exercise varies widely among organizations.

So now we've identified the need to do enterprise or product accounting, and whether to use the equity approach or the control approach to set organizational boundaries. Plus a choice has been made as to what portion of Scope 3 emissions accounting to add to the "mandatory" accounting for Scope 1 and Scope 2 emissions. Now we are ready to calculate emissions to determine carbon impact.

Calculating Emissions

The precision with which emissions are calculated is highly dependent on the tools used. Some organizations choose to use a spreadsheet coupled with general averages for emission coefficients that they get from a data bank somewhere or that they find in an online resource. This approach is usually effective to within +/- 30 percent of accuracy. A more accurate approach would use emission coefficients received directly from a local utility coupled with sophisticated calculation software.

Larger organizations tend to hire consultants to help them do this work. The reasons are twofold. The first time through the exercise can be frustrating; it helps to have an experienced professional walk the client firm through the process. Another reason is to get third-party verification or at least the sense of impartiality in the numbers that are generated. Larger organizations sometimes believe they need the same stamp of objectivity that they feel they get from a large accounting firm in their annual audit.

As methodologies become more standardized and transparent, it will become easier for organizations to do this work themselves. But in a voluntary carbon accounting system, such as that which currently exists in the United States, there are no rules about which methodology should be used. Some widely accepted best practices have emerged, but these will change over time as more calculation data is developed and more software is vetted for accuracy and thoroughness.

Do not let all of these uncertainties thwart forward progress. Any measurement of carbon emissions is better than no measurement. Depending on the broad objectives and on which stakeholder groups are being responded to, some of the simpler and less sophisticated tools and methodologies might be sufficient for the first-pass attempt. Nevertheless, it is still recommended that a professional help those new to carbon accounting with the process.

Some combination of calculation process and emissions data to get starting carbon measurements is called the "baseline." Any declared carbon reduction goals are referenced against that baseline. For example, if there is enough data to accurately calculate various carbon emissions for 2005, one might use that as the baseline year. The firm then might declare that it is going to reduce emissions by 25 percent by the year 2015. So regardless when the reduction plan gets implemented, everyone understands that by 2015, carbon emissions will have been reduced by 25 percent from what they were in 2005. If carbon emissions become directly regulated, the regulations will define what the baseline year is.

Direct Action versus Offsets

Using stakeholder input, a plan was created that describes broad objectives, current carbon inventory has been measured, and reduction goals have been developed to satisfy stakeholders concerns. How to achieve those goals?

Some combination of direct action and offsets will be used to achieve any goal set. "Direct action" simply refers to steps an organization takes to measurably reduce carbon emissions within the determined boundary and across the chosen scopes. Direct action could be as simple as changing lightbulbs and dialing down the heating and cooling activities. It could include replacing old heating, ventilation, and air-conditioning (HVAC) systems or buying a new on-campus fleet of vehicles that are more fuel efficient. It might mean buying supplies from organizations that have done their own carbon analysis and are offering a line of low-carbon paper or inks.

Direct action can help reduce carbon emissions by a significant amount, but one cannot "get to zero" through direct actions alone unless the organization is shut down and goes out of business. Enter the world of offsets.

Offsets are basically credits on a firm's carbon balance sheet, used to make up for debits. In fact, "carbon credits" are the most common type of offset that an organization will purchase. There are two basic considerations regarding the use of offsets.

1. The cost associated with buying offsets (carbon credits)

2. The philosophical implications of using of offsets

Let's examine these two areas in a little more depth.

Most organizations tend to take direct action when the cost of doing so can be expensed rather than capitalized. Compact fluorescent lightbulbs, for example, save an organization energy use and reduce an organization's carbon footprint, and the purchase can be expensed on the organization's income statement. Most organizations can take several such first-tier direct actions to reduce energy usage and carbon impact up to 15 percent from their baseline. An alternative method would be to buy carbon credits directly. Since there are no additional savings (from reduced energy use) associated with the purchase of credits, most organizations do not use offsets alone as the means by which to achieve Tier 1 reductions.

Tier 2 reductions can be achieved by making larger investments, to replace outdated HVAC system, for example. The cost of this expenditure would get capitalized, not expensed. Significant energy savings and carbon emission reductions can occur in Tier 2, but the costs are much higher than in Tier 1. The savvy accountant will also look at purchasing carbon credits as an alternative to making the investments necessary to reduce this next tranche of carbon emissions, which could be as much as 50 percent. A true return on investment analysis often is used to determine the best mode of achieving Tier 2 reductions.

Tier 3 reductions include any steps taken to get down to a carbon-neutral position. The last 30 to 40 percent of potential carbon reductions rarely can be achieved through direct action; they only can be achieved through the purchase of carbon credits to offset the remaining carbon impacts.

In addition to the financial calculation, the use of offsets to achieve Tier 2 or Tier 3 emission reductions becomes a philosophical question. Due to the unregulated nature of carbon credits in a voluntary system, there are concerns about the validity of what carbon credits really represent. Several protocols have evolved that describe the "rules" that must be followed to generate a carbon credit. Some protocols are more widely recognized than others, and most organizations that consider using carbon credits to offset some or all of their carbon emissions struggle with determining the best system to use. Again refer to the stakeholder analysis created for the firm for guidance.

Outcomes

What outcomes should an organization seek to achieve? Remember the stakeholder analysis—at least part of the answer should be discovered during that process. There are several different methods for describing outcomes.

An *absolute* goal of carbon emission reductions can be set. If this is the intent, then establish goals that state a specific quantity of emissions reduction, say 100 tons per year. This is the most common type of outcome required of organizations that face emissions regulations.

A *relative* goal of carbon emission reductions can be set. As in the example in the prior sections, goals are established that compare some future period to some baseline period. This is the most common type of outcome chosen by organizations that are voluntarily reducing their carbon emissions.

Another outcome that some organizations seek is referred to as *intensity*. There are several different variations, but these are goals set as units of carbon per units of something else. Some examples would be tons of carbon per dollar of sales, or per number of employees, or per units of product produced, and so on.

It's pretty apparent that the story that gets told and the emissions reductions that get achieved can vary significantly depending on what type of outcome is desired. Let the stakeholder analysis inform GHG strategy. Part of that strategy will be an articulation of the outcomes necessary to keep stakeholders happy. Set goals, determine the scope and boundary of accounting, and develop the baseline carbon footprint. At the very least, this is good management preparation for the carbon-constrained world that we will be living in. And it quite possibly might change followers into leaders.

Carbon Offsets

Although the debate about climate change has been going on for decades, 2006 was considered a pivotal year with the publication of the *Stern Review on the Economics of Climate Change*, and the release of Al Gore's film *An Inconvenient Truth*. Now the question of climate change is no longer just a theoretical exercise for the select few; public and business attention finally has become focused on the realities of what that debate means today on a personal and business level.[216]

Concerns over how to deal with the very real issues of climate change have given rise to an ever-growing selection of schemes promoting carbon offsets. These plans use a variety of methods, including using monies collected to help support renewable energy development and implementation; carbon sequestering, helping to make old-growth forests economically attractive left intact; and carbon trading, which allows eco-forward companies a chance to recoup more quickly the costs of their improvement investments.

Many companies around the world have announced plans to become carbon neutral. In January 2007, United Kingdom retail giant Tesco announced its intention to put carbon labels on all of its products to provide information on their carbon footprint from production to consumption. In the United States, Frito-Lay has added the Green-e logo, a designation from the Center for Resource Solutions used to indicate that a product offsets its carbon emissions, across the full line of its SunChips® snacks.

One of the problems facing companies trying to meet various guidelines and scorecards, and then adding carbon issues into the mix, are the complexities involved in minimizing the environmental impacts of a product. There is no straight line to "goodness," and there may be significant trade-offs to weigh between recycling or energy consumption that look good on a particular scorecard but overall may have impacts that are outside of that metric. Recycling, for example, a common feature for favorable scores, is only part of the story, and must not be considered in isolation. Recycling, like any decision variable, must be weighed as part of a comprehensive environmental objective to achieve goals for reductions in pollution, greenhouse gas emissions, and better resource management throughout the whole product life cycle.

Carbon labels have received a lot of attention in recent years. A 2007 study from L.E.K. Consulting in the United Kingdom found that more than half of UK consumers want information about the carbon footprint of the products they purchase, with nearly half indicating a willingness to switch to brands with smaller carbon footprints.[217] In July 2007, Carbonfund.org launched a CarbonFree Certified Product label that companies can use to promote their products as being climate neutral.

Paying attention to carbon impacts needs to be added to the overall impact strategy with the same care as any impact variable. As Timberland found out, impacts are complicated to calculate and to articulate to give a complete picture. Today, Timberland footwear carries a "nutrition facts" label detailing the product's impacts:

— *Manufactured Section:* Gives the name and factory location where the product was made as a tool for maintaining production transparency.

— *Environmental Impact:* Reports how much energy was needed to produce Timberland footwear and the amount of Timberland's energy generated from renewable resources, such as the sun, wind, or water.

— *Community Impact:* Details the percentage of factories assessed by the company's code of conduct standards, the percentage of children in the workforce, and total number of hours Timberland employees volunteer in the community.

To measure the true environmental costs of Timberland's products, though, one would have to go all the way back to the cow that supplied the leather. In fact, Timberland found the vast majority of its products' carbon footprints is accrued before its shoes are even produced.

Today there exist a variety of carbon-offset schemes but no comprehensive regulation. In a 2007 article, Team TreeHugger asks:[218]

What will your offsets go to? Are their projects certified? Does any independent authority audit them to ensure your money is going to the projects mentioned in the marketing? Do they have a solid client list? Contact some of those clients and see what they thought of the service? What is the price per ton? How does this compare? Do they use any recognized guidelines to prepare their calculations? Are your funds supporting new projects, not "business as usual"? As The Guardian newspaper put it, "There is nothing but the customer's canniness to stop a company claiming to be running a scheme which does not exist; claiming wildly exaggerated carbon cuts; selling offsets that have already been sold; charging hugely inflated prices.

For more information on carbon offsets, review "Clean Air-Cool Planet Guide: A Consumer's Guide to Retail Carbon Offset Providers."[219]

Wonderful World of Waste

Economic and Environmental Benefits of Recycling

Recycling creates economic and environmental benefits at the local, state, and national levels. The National Recycling Coalition's Recycling Economic Information Project demonstrated the importance of the recycling and reuse industries to our national economy.

Consider these facts:

— Well-run recycling programs cost less to operate than waste collection, landfilling, and incineration.

— The more people recycle, the cheaper it gets.

— Two years after calling recycling a $40 million drain on the city, New York City leaders realized that a redesigned, efficient recycling system could actually save the city $20 million, and they have now signed a twenty-year recycling contract.

— Recycling helps families save money, especially in communities with pay-as-you-throw programs.

— Well-designed programs save money. Communities have many options available to make their programs more cost effective, including maximizing their recycling rates, implementing pay-as-you-throw programs, and including incentives in waste management contracts that encourage disposal companies to recycle more and dispose of less.

— Recycling creates 1.1 million U.S. jobs, $236 billion in gross annual sales, and $37 billion in annual payrolls.

— Public sector investment in local recycling programs pays great dividends by creating private sector jobs. For every job collecting recyclables, there are twenty-six jobs in processing the materials and manufacturing them into new products.

— Recycling creates four jobs for every one job created in the waste management and disposal industries.

— Thousands of U.S. companies have saved millions of dollars through their voluntary recycling programs. They wouldn't recycle if it didn't make economic sense.

Recycling is one of America's best environmental success stories. Consider these facts:

— Recycling results in a net reduction in ten major categories of air pollutants and eight major categories of water pollutants.

— Recycling saves energy, which can help the United States reduce its dependence on foreign oil.

The amount of lost energy from throwing away aluminum and steel cans, plastic polyethylene terephthalate (PET) and glass containers, newsprint, and corrugated packaging each year is equivalent to the annual output of fifteen medium-size coal power plants.

— Increasing the recycling rate of these commodities by 10 percent would save enough energy annually to heat 74,350 million American homes, provide the required electricity for 2.5 million Americans, and save about $771 million in costs for barrels of crude oil.

— Manufacturing with recycled materials, with very few exceptions, saves energy and water and produces less air and water pollution than manufacturing with virgin materials.

It takes 95 percent less energy to recycle aluminum than it does to make it from raw materials. Making recycled steel saves 60 percent; recycled newspaper, 40 percent; recycled plastics, 70 percent; and recycled glass, 40 percent. These savings far outweigh the energy created as by-products of incineration and landfilling.

— A national recycling rate of 30 percent reduces greenhouse gas emissions as much as removing nearly 25 million cars from the road.

— Recycling conserves valuable natural resources, which are often dangerous to obtain, while protecting natural habitats and ecosystems.

Mining is the world's deadliest occupation. On average, forty mineworkers are killed on the job each day, and many more are injured. Recycling reduces the need for mining.

In the United States, processing minerals contributes almost half of all reported toxic emissions from industry, sending 1.5 million tons of pollution into the air and water each year. Recycling can significantly reduce these emissions.

Recycled paper supplies more than 37 percent of the raw materials used to make new paper products in the United States. Without recycling, this material would come from trees.

Every ton of recycled newsprint or mixed paper is the equivalent of twelve trees. Every ton of recycled office paper is the equivalent of twenty-four trees.

When one ton of steel is recycled, 2,500 pounds of iron ore, 1,400 pounds of coal, and 120 pounds of limestone are conserved.

"The Economic and Environmental Benefits of Recycling" was provided with permission by the National Recycling Coalition.

The National Recycling Coalition (NRC) is a 501(c)(3) membership organization of recycling professionals and advocates from every region of the country, in every sector of the waste reduction field. Local recycling coordinators, state and federal regulators, corporate environmental managers, environmental educators and advocates, and waste management professionals are all members of NRC. Founded in 1978, NRC's objective is to eliminate waste and promote sustainable economies through advancing sound management practices for raw materials in North America. NRC hosts the Annual Congress & Exposition each year in a different city to bring its members and others together for several days of outstanding educational and networking opportunities. NRC also works closely with nineteen affiliated state and regional recycling organizations around the nation.

Since 1908, RockTenn has been turning waste paper and paperboard into packaging.
Photo: www.tnphoto.com.

Leave a legacy, not a landfill.

Greenhouse Gas Emissions and Waste

Currently the U.S. Environmental Protection Agency defines four main stages of product life cycles, all of which provide opportunities for GHG emissions and/or offsets: raw material acquisition, manufacturing, recycling, and waste management.[220]

RAW MATERIAL ACQUISITION. All products use inputs of raw materials, such as metal ore, petroleum, trees, and so on. Extracting and transporting these materials entails the combustion of fossil fuels for energy, which results in carbon dioxide emissions. These fossil fuels must be extracted themselves, which requires additional energy use.

MANUFACTURING. The processes that transform raw materials into products require the combustion of fossil fuels for energy. Again, energy use produces GHG emissions, both directly from the combustion of fossil fuels (mainly in the form of carbon dioxide) and from the upstream energy used to obtain and transport those fossil fuels. In addition, some manufacturing processes release other GHGs, although the type and amount of these emissions are specific to the manufacturing processes for each material.

RECYCLING. Once a product has been used, it can be recycled into new products. While manufacturing products from recycled inputs still requires energy, fewer raw materials are necessary. GHG emissions are therefore offset by the avoided fossil fuel use for raw material acquisition. In addition, for products that require wood or paper inputs, recycling reduces the need to cut down trees, increasing carbon sequestration in forests.

WASTE MANAGEMENT. If a product is not recycled at the end of its useful life, it goes through one of three waste management options: composting, combustion, or landfilling. All three use energy for transporting and managing the waste, but they produce additional GHGs to varying degrees.

COMPOSTING. Composting is an option for organic materials such as food scraps and yard waste. It releases some nonbiogenic carbon dioxide associated with transporting and turning the compost. However, some of the carbon contained in organic materials is returned and stored in the soil and therefore not released into the atmosphere.

COMBUSTION. When waste is burned, both CO_2 and nitrous oxide (a GHG that is 310 times more potent than CO_2) are released. However, some of the energy released during combustion can be harnessed and used to power other processes, which results in offset GHG emissions from avoided fossil fuel use.

LANDFILLING. This is the most common waste management practice and results in the release of methane from the anaerobic decomposition of organic materials. Methane is a GHG twenty-one times more potent than CO_2. However, landfill methane is also a source of energy, and some landfills capture and use it. In addition, many materials in landfills do not decompose fully, and the carbon that remains is sequestered in the landfill and is not released into the atmosphere.

In an effort to reduce methane emissions from landfills, the EPA's Landfill Methane Outreach Program (LMOP) is a voluntary assistance program that encourages the recovery and use of landfill gas as an energy resource. LMOP forms partnerships with communities, landfill owners, utilities, power marketers, states, project developers, tribes, and nonprofit organizations to overcome barriers to project development by helping them assess project feasibility, find financing, and market the benefits of project development to the community. The EPA launched LMOP to encourage productive use of this resource as part of the U.S. commitment to reduce greenhouse gas emissions under the UN Framework Convention on Climate Change.[221]

Landfill tapping (extracting methane from landfills as fuel) and landfill mining (extracting resources literally just sitting there) are some of the ways people are starting to look at garbage as a new revenue stream rather than a burden.

Books are but waste paper unless we spend in action the wisdom we get from thought.

—Edward G. Bulwer-Lytton

Closer Look at the Riches of Waste

Established on a forty-five-acre site in Minnesota, midway between the downtowns of Minneapolis and St. Paul, and operating over the past 100 years under four names, today's RockTenn–St. Paul has been recycling and converting scrap paper since 1908. RockTenn–St. Paul is the oldest and largest paper recycler in Minnesota, and buys over 1,000 tons of scrap paper daily, recycling it into coated paperboard and corrugating medium for use in printing and converting into 100 percent recycled packaging. In 2007, RockTenn's eleven mills recycled over 1.9 million tons of recovered paper, 5 percent of the U.S. total. Given the tight integration of supply chains in RockTenn–St. Paul's area, paper picked up at curbside can be available again as a cereal box on local grocers' shelves in as little as three weeks.

GLOBAL MARKET FOR RECOVERED FIBER

Feeding ever-increasing foreign demand (mostly in China), in 2007 scrap paper was the largest single U.S. export at 19.9 million tons, or about 37 percent of all paper recovered in the United States. Many companies on both sides of the ocean have done very well by recognizing that the same containers that bring goods to the United States are more profitably returned fully loaded with raw materials.

Historically, recovered-paper markets were regionally based with material moving according to transportation cost limitations. In 2007, 54.3 million tons of scrap paper was collected for recycling in the United States. While it sounds like a lot, the recycling rate was only 56 percent for all available paper fiber. Today, competition for recovered materials from foreign mills continues to escalate as additional mills continue to come on line. Of the collected papers in the United States, only 63 percent found its way to domestic use, with the remaining exported to foreign mills.

ROCKTENN-ST. PAUL DIGS DEEPER

Despite an excellent paper recovery rate in RockTenn–St. Paul's home market (2006 figures for Minnesota, 66 percent, 10 percent above the national average), RockTenn knew from experience there were more ways to connect with the local community and collect additional fiber sources.

From the 1920s to the 1980s, volunteer paper drives were a very popular way for schools, scouts, and youth groups to earn money and were the primary vehicles for collection of newspapers for recycling at the time. The 1990s brought the convenience of curbside collection of recyclables and a strong secondary market for selling newspaper to newsprint paper mills. But as circulation for print periodicals continues to decline as the media converts to nonprint distribution methods, Rock-Tenn made a capital investment to update its boxboard mills to include recovered fibers from a broader variety of business and household recoverable papers.

Instead of accepting only newsprint and old corrugated containers, the company expanded options to include direct mail, magazines, office papers, catalogs, telephone books, paper grocery bags, and folding cartons such as cereal, cake mix, pasta, tissue boxes, and so on. RockTenn's ability to take mixed household and business papers opened options for local cities and recyclers involved in managing curbside recycling programs as well as provided a clean fiber stream for producing food grade-paperboard for packaging.

In 2008, RockTenn rejuvenated volunteer paper-drive fundraisers and launched two additional strategies for digging deeper into the recoverable paper mix: document destruction day and obsolete book collection.

VOLUNTEER PAPER DRIVES

Volunteer paper-drive efforts have long been fundraisers that the entire family can be involved in. More than fun and easy fundraisers with no risks or up-front costs, they connect organizations with their communities and help build leadership skills for youth volunteers. Encouraged to create teams, volunteers get involved in a variety of actions, from marketing to get the word out to their surrounding community to save recyclable paper for them, to

getting a firsthand look at logistics and transport. Kids have fun and gain a sense of pride as they watch the collection container fill. Several groups have been conducting quarterly community-wide paper drives for more than a decade, making thousands of dollars every year for their groups.

DOCUMENT DESTRUCTION DAY

RockTenn has been doing "document destruction" as a normal part of the recycling process for decades, so it seemed a logical next step to offer the service formally. Document destruction day was initiated as a neighborhood service. Advertisements detailing the idea instructed participants to put sensitive and confidential documents into paper grocery bags, roll the top down, and then either staple or tape the bag shut. The paper bags were collected securely, placed in large corrugated boxes, sealed, and then dumped into pulpers (blenders), where they were quickly destroyed and reduced to paper fiber slurry. Destruction by recycling within a controlled system is easy and eliminates the time and energy required for shredding documents.

OBSOLETE BOOKS RECYCLED

RockTenn–St. Paul began accepting hardbound and paperback books that are damaged and cannot be reused. Considering the important role that books play in education, groups wishing to participate in the book fiber recovery program are first asked whether all avenues have been exhausted to donate books to schools or libraries, or resold through a variety of outlets, before they are accepted for recycling.

Once deemed ready for recovery, books present a variety of challenges. But over the years, RockTenn developed methods to remove glue used for bindings and covers, dealing with contaminants (adhesives and other "stickys") from an ever-expanding variety of business and household papers.

EYE ON THE FUTURE

All producers of 100 percent recycled content packaging are delighted that dialogue has turned from a focus on high-gloss and disposable, to effective, green, and sustainable life-cycle-loop-oriented products. For decades, 100 percent recycled paperboard packaging was considered a cheap-looking, low-grade choice when compared to bleached-white virgin-board options. In any era, though, makers of packaged goods always look for function, value, and cost savings from materials when choosing options for their brand's packaging. Today, more than 36 percent of all fiber used to make new paper products in the United States comes from recycled sources. Now 100 percent recycled paperboard is readily available and meets or exceeds stringent specifications for graphics and distribution requirements.

As RockTenn–St. Paul looks to a more sustainable future, local fiber sources are enjoying renewed interest. From 1920 to 1950, for example, Rock-Tenn used flax straw from the Dakotas as part of its fiber mix. In Asia, where trees have long been in short supply, paperboard is commonly made from rice agri-pulp—one of paper's original fiber sources. As mills take a more forward-looking approach, new ways of working supply chains takes on greater importance. Paper recycling is dependent on scrap paper as well as a regular supply of new fiber. Trees, as well as other local fiber sources such as agri-pulp, are crops (or residue from crops) that are planted, harvested, processed, pulped, and printed for distribution and use. With an eye on the future, all well-managed fiber sources become an important part of the strategic mix, adding value to local as well as global economies for continually striving to develop a sustainable fiber market.

Statistics for this article were provided by the American Forest and Paper Association and the Minnesota Pollution Control Agency. "A Closer Look at the Riches of Waste" by Sharell Benson (www.sharellbenson.com) and Rock-Tenn St. Paul (www.rocktenn.com).

Recycling
Paper & Cardboard
RETHINK
RECYCLE
REDUCE
REUSE
Recycling
Paper & Cardboard
Newspapers with inserts
Magazines, Catalogs & Phonebooks
Mail, Paper & Notebooks
(spiral binding and staples OK)
Shredded Paper
(must be contained in a bag!)
Cardboard & Boxboard
(please flatten)
No frozen food boxes
No paper cups, plates, or napkins
No pizza boxes
No tissue or wrapping paper
Recycling really does matter!
The things you throw away don't really go away. They will be burned in an incinerator or buried in a landfill, both of which contribute to global warming.
MAKE DIRT
NOT WASTE
We compost here!

Case Study: Eureka Recycling

Eureka Recycling is a nonprofit recycler and waste-reduction organization serving Minnesota's Twin Cities Metro area communities. Its mission is to demonstrate that waste is completely preventable: absolutely, entirely preventable. In other words, it believes that there really is no such thing as waste. Eureka feels that with a little research and creativity, as well as by working closely with designers and printing partners, they can move past status quo and closer to zero waste using what we already know. Innovation doesn't always require new technology or new materials. In fact, great strides in sustainability can be made by simply rethinking routine decisions.

Even when designing bins for homes or office, most automatically choose plastic. However, as Eureka began working with office and schools to increase their recycling, it began to rethink the bin. Eureka asked, "What happens if we don't use plastic?" Working with local designers and manufacturers, Eureka created a container that ships flat but folds out. Not new technology, but certainly a new idea for recycling. The risk for paperboard as a choice was that the box wouldn't last forever . . . but then again, that was exactly the intention: Do we really need a recycling bin forever? Wouldn't it be okay if it lasted ten years, we recycled it, and then replaced it if needed? The benefits of switching to paper far outweighed the drawbacks. Not only was a nonrenewable petroleum product replaced with a renewable, but a custom educational message could be printed on the box. This further reduced the need for labels (usually vinyl), making the container completely recyclable when it reached its own end of life — and the paperboard box proved more than sturdy enough for use in offices, classrooms, apartments, and dorm rooms.

Following the idea of making more with less, each year, Eureka Recycling creates a mailing to help people understand its program, including a personalized calendar for each recipient's recycling collection day. With eight cities and up to five collection days each, Eureka faced the challenge of creating twenty-seven versions to serve its area communities as well as pack it full of information and resources to help encourage participation.

In 2007, Eureka produced a 24 x 9.125-inch trifold self-mailer with sixteen versions of a calendar insert — an improvement over the brochure from the previous year sent in an envelope. Eureka consulted with its print and design vendors to find ways to cut back on paper usage, leading to a 50 percent reduction in paper usage for a mailing that was already top notch for the environment. For its next piece, though, Eureka wanted to do even better. Keeping the critical educational information, the total piece was reduced to a 8.5 x 11-inch two-color, trifold self-mailer by using variable data inkjet technology. For this new version, the piece was designed so that customer address, specific city logos, and collection schedule could be printed right on the cover of each piece. By eliminating the need for multiple versions, Eureka saved paper immediately. Reducing the number of inks significantly reduced plate numbers, test runs, and resources to create and run those additional colors.

Eureka used the lightest text-weight paper (100 percent post-consumer recycled content) that would still render a quality print and meet postal standards, and carefully considered design to minimize bleed trim and waste—fitting more brochures on a single press sheet. In addition, by using only two colors but taking advantage of their full tonal range and mixing options, Eureka was able to create a finished piece with the feel of a full-color brochure that only required two plates and the resources needed to run two colors.

Projects and Services

In this section, we look at whole classes of things where materials and processes are interdependent.

Photography

Dan Halsey
Daniel Halsey Photography

2009 marked the end of an era as Kodak announced the retirement of its classic film: Kodachrome. With the wide adoption of digital photography and the market-driven pursuit of hardware, software, and increasingly complex design solutions, the digital environment forces new expectations for artists. Digital is here to stay, but what has changed since the "old days"? Here we take quick look at the relative impact of digital photography in a summary of comparative effects for the film and digital eras.

Categories of Change

We start with **capital investment.** Equipment costs for start-up studios and entry-level photographers has risen exponentially since the end of the film era. However, the **capacity** of the studio to shoot and deliver a higher number of images has increased, reducing shot fees.

The **learning curve** has steepened as digital skills and previously outsourced production services are now required of the photographer while educational expenses for initial and ongoing training increase.

The **externalized costs** of toxic manufacturing processes, the specter of disposal of obsolete mechanisms and valuable metals (e-waste), stands in comparison to the silver halide era. While e-waste is a problem in all sectors, niche service industries serving photography that dealt with these specialized disposal needs, such as the labs that collected and sold the silver sludge of film processing, are gone.

Equipment longevity/life span is diminished in the digital world as new technology becomes constantly available, pushing upward the base level of what's acceptable. Where at one time a photographer may have had a few cameras over a career, now they must upgrade annually to stay current with client expectations. Although much of these annual upgrades are support equipment, such as printers, drives, and imaging backs, these purchases increase overhead as well as the environmental burden from e-waste.

Aside from economic issues such as client budgets and volume of sales, **profitability** for digital is tied to project management skills and the ability to deliver quickly, sometimes in hours, what would have been expected over days previously.

Artists have a history of creative seclusion, occasionally gathering together for social and trade events with associates. Less free time and increased competition for a shrinking client base has reduced what **community** may have existed.

Marketability may be the least changed aspect in the digital era. With expanded services, delivery options, and markets via the Internet, increased market range encompasses more prospects. Adding in the previously mentioned external costs, **resources** needed by a digital studio, though on many levels much lower per job, when multiplied by the increase in output are consumed at a higher rate. Decentralized services also broadens the demand for soft goods.

The combination of complex production tasks with digital and reduced profitability overall has increased **stress** on artist and client. Pressure to deliver more complex images in a shorter time frame using technology carries less creative/time

Comparing photography's tools and consumables, then and now.
Photo: tnphoto.com.

risk than analog film only because the real-time results are evident and obvious as work progresses. Business risk for the photo studio may be higher due to overhead and investments but are no greater than with film. The big change for artists using digital imaging is expressing *creativity*. This two-edged sword of techno filters and automated effects reduces some to innumerous drop shadows and clip paths, but others have been able to bring otherwise impossible film imagery to view with great experimentation. Finally, there is the *adaptability* issue, though digital has a much lower barrier to entry for creative expression. For those using film, skills often required decades to hone, with many photographers collaborating with darkroom technicians to realize their vision.

Signage and Environments

Paul Andre
Minnesota Pollution Control Agency

When talking about the stuff graphic designers can produce—the tangible deliverables—we are all familiar with the huge amount of material that goes into creating printed publications and packaging. Coming in under the radar for material use is signage and display. These short-term use pieces designed for trade shows, retail events, and public environments also have measurably huge environmental impacts. But like most industry side processes, these impacts go completely unnoticed by the general public.

The challenges are considerable for signage designers wanting to incorporate a sustainable approach into their work. There's a wide range of possible materials and processes—as well as objectives and end uses—that neither print work or packaging have to tackle. With much less information readily available to the designer than for print or packaging, the quest for an environmental approach often feels daunting and not worth the time. Yet with many possible ways to get a job done comes the opportunity for experimentation and innovation.

Strategy: Design Away Waste and Toxicity

For clients who come to the designer and say they need a 10 x 3-foot banner with six grommets at the top and bottom, the request is so to the point that stepping back and applying eco-strategies is often forgotten. In the field of architecture, however, like all other creative trades, it is during the concept phase when most of a building's ultimate energy and material use and overall impact on the environment are determined. Architects doing cutting-edge green building don't wait until the design is finished and then try to source eco-friendly materials. Instead of trying to specify the most efficient boiler, they might be able design away the need for a boiler at all, instead relying on passive solar gain, heat sinks, and superinsulated walls.

Before decisions about form (a 10 x 3 banner) and material choices are made, there are questions whose answers can dramatically change the envisioned form and materials while still achieving client objectives.

— *How much does the sign or display need to say?* Often the temptation is to incorporate too much information. Instead, the detail could come from an existing printed brochure available at the display location or be available online. In the case of a trade show, the best source of more information is the person staffing the booth. Having to present only an image or a succinct message could increase the usable life span of

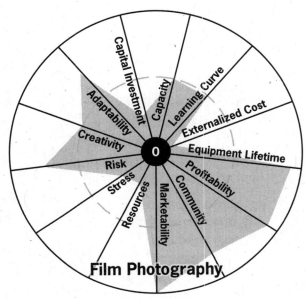
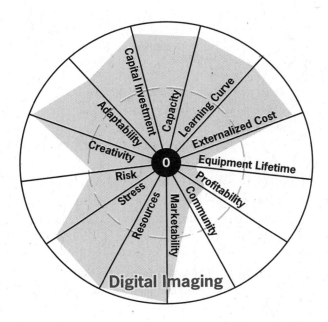

Relative impact of digital: A spider diagram.

the signage. More important, it could broaden options for processes and materials. With less copy to display, there's more flexibility for placement and form.

— **How durable does it need to be?** Durability is often an unquestioned virtue, but the reality is that people change their minds—often. The marketing plan that looked awesome two months ago seems embarrassing now. The downside of durability is often more material (heavier weight), mixed materials (laminate on top of substrate), and more toxicity.

— **Does it conform closely to a style guide?** Longevity can be a function of how well the piece works with other program pieces. Over time, an out-of-sync design becomes more obvious and can doom a display to the back of the closet. Similarly, consider a signage element that doesn't say too much—just sticks to general

messages and leaves details (which are more likely to change) to other media.

— **How will it be stored?** What will happen to the display or signage in between events? Plenty of current signage turns into solid waste when it gets warped, crimped, or scratched. Nearly all "soft" signage (plastic film, fabric) survives best when hung. Rigid signage nearly always does best in flat, horizontal storage.

— **Where will it be displayed?** Whether it's wall-mounted, hanging from the ceiling, having to endure wind, or subjected to changing humidity can affect material choice and cost. If a banner can be attached flat to an exterior wall instead of strung between two columns, more eco-options will be available because less strength will be needed. Also, if it's possible to rely on existing site structures to support signage, a large amount of material can be removed from sustainability calculations. (See the section titled "Experiments in Sustainable Signage.")

— ***Who will set up and install?*** If it will be someone who is directly connected to the sign, such as the client, the designer, or the signage production company, then more nonstandard (often greener) approaches can be tried. Easy-to-use portable displays that can be set up by people outside of the direct ownership chain, although appealing, can add a lot of cost that might preclude taking an environmental path. Those with a vested interest in the sign's longevity who are willing to take a more hands-on approach can help bring new techniques and materials to the mainstream.

Materials and Processes for Signage and Display

In the realm of printing, designers have demanded more environmental choices. Paper companies have responded by offering better products. Here a relationship has developed between the designer and the material producer or distributor, with the printer merely getting told what to use for the job.

For signage and display creation, very little dialog has developed between designers and material producers. There has been little marketing of signage materials to designers, with significant ambiguity and jargon used to describe these materials complicating the process. How can designers specify a material or use type if they don't know what it's called? In addition, the printing and process technologies have advanced and multiplied at a pace rivaling the publication printing industry. Consequently, designers tend to rely heavily on the advice of signage vendors for material and process choices, narrowing the discussion to a handful of

vendors who are convenient rather than those who would be willing to help move the job in a more sustainable direction.

Given these limitations, designers intent on moving toward more sustainable deliverables need a snapshot of what's available in the market.

VINYL: IT SEEMS LIKE THE ONLY OPTION

Polyvinyl chloride (PVC, "vinyl") is king of the signage media market. It's usually the default choice—the media that signage vendors specify on cost proposals when the designer doesn't indicate material type. PVC is ubiquitous in flexible signage—available in thin films, impregnated into fabrics, and the primary constituent of nylon-reinforced heavy-duty banner media.

PVC, though, carries with it some significant environmental costs. It's inexpensive because the true costs of its impacts are not reflected in its selling price. One of the primary ingredients is chlorine—a toxic by-product from manufacturing high-value chemicals, such as sodium hydroxide. In most places in the world where chlorine and PVC are produced, dioxins and other related compounds are emitted into the environment. Dioxin has been identified as a human carcinogen and developmental toxin (see the section titled "Chlorine and Bleaching") and also bio-accumulates upward in the food chain.

PVC is by nature a rigid plastic. To be made into banner media, it needs chemical softening additives, such as phthalates. Phthalates frequently off-gas from vinyl and are responsible for the characteristic odor of new shower curtains or similar vinyl products. Ever wonder what's in that "new car smell"?[222] From a human health perspec-

Fabrics for printing.

product's end of life, incineration liberates these toxic metals (as well as dioxins) into the air, where they eventually enter the food chain.

Better Plastic: Simply Hydrocarbon

While signage vinyls are a mixture of many chemicals (and in some cases heavy metals), most other plastics available for signage are much better. Polyethylene and polypropylene are hydrocarbon polymers (no chlorine) and are useful without additional toxic additives. Their manufacture creates less toxic emissions than vinyl production, but since they are petroleum-based, they carry their own life cycle burdens. Some types of polyethylene (PET #1, HDPE #2, LDPE #4) are widely recycled, but at present this is primarily only in food and beverage packaging forms; recycling options for signage plastics are still near zero. In terms of disposal, however, these types of hydrocarbon plastics in a municipal waste incineration present fewer concerns than PVC.

Polyethylene and polypropylene can be made into film banner media, woven into fabrics, or formed into rigid or semirigid board. (The latter is mostly marketed and sold only in the building products sector.)

A third type of hydrocarbon plastic, polystyrene, is made into a readily available semirigid signboard, usually referred to as styrene.

Specialized Synthetic Products

Tyvek, familiar to most as the plastic used for express envelopes and building wraps, is a polyethylene film made from spun fibers. It has good strength (for indoor applications) and has an attractive appearance owing to a subtle swirling pattern of the fibers. It's available with and without a

tive, pthalates are cause for concern. American and European toy makers have largely phased out their use in infant toys because of evidence that phthalates can disrupt functioning of the endocrine (hormone) system.

One further concern is PVC manufactured outside of the United State and Europe, where additives such as cadmium, chromium, and lead still are used to modify the physical properties of the plastic. At the mineral coating to accommodate various printing technologies.

Polyolefin film, also a type of polyethylene, offers high strength for outdoor applications.

FABRIC: A FLEXIBLE OPTION

Woven fabrics can provide some unique advantages over plastic films and rigid boards. There are more material choices and they can be woven from a wide variety of fibers, from recycled-content polyethylene to organic cotton. Fabric also offers more finishing and final display options: It can be hemmed or heat-cut, supported with pipe or dowels, grommetted, or sewn and fitted around tables and other objects. Fabric wears well too, and it doesn't crimp or scratch. Depending on the printing technique, some fabrics can be washed if they get dirty or steamed if they get wrinkled.

At the end of their useful life, fabric signage can go into the reclaimed textile market, an established recycling industry. Uses for post-consumer textile waste include insulation, furniture padding, fill materials, wiping cloths, and absorbent pads (for chemical spills). And they are all the rage right now for reusable tote bags to replace paper or plastic shopping bags.

PAPER AND PAPERBOARD: A HAPPIER END OF LIFE

Paper is an environmentally preferable option for some signage applications, such as short-term indoor use. Like any material, though, paper can be ecologically positive or negative, depending on factors such as recycled content, sustainable certification (e.g., FSC), whether it has a coating compatible with recycling, and whether it actually gets recycled at end of life.

Compared to plastics, a paper sign has a better chance of getting routed into a recycling stream, simply because paper recycling is readily available in most markets. Therefore, a paper sign can realize material and energy savings advantages.

An ideal scenario might read like this:

1. Source a minimally coated, 75 to 100 percent post-consumer content paperboard from a local recycler or paper mill.

2. Print signs without laminate or varnish.

3. At end of life, the sign goes to an established and local recycling system (to minimize the eco-costs of transportation).

Paper's drawbacks, though, need to be looked at carefully. Lack of durability can lead to increased waste. Paper signage is easily crimped, bent, or warped. Paperboard is also highly unstable in environments where humidity is high or fluctuating.

FOAM BOARDS AND ALTERNATIVES: RIGID THINKING

Standard rigid foam boards consist of blown polystyrene foam sandwiched between layers of paper or paperboard. Polystyrene is another simple hydrocarbon polymer, and, like its cousins polyethylene and polypropylene, is typically not manufactured with many additives. Originally, the polystyrene used in foam boards was blown using a chlorofluorocarbon (CFC) gas. This gas is being phased-out worldwide due to its ozone layer–depleting properties. Foam board manufacturers in the United States and Europe today have largely switched to using more benign blowing agents. Manufacturers outside these geographic areas might still be using ozone-depleting CFCs.

Recycling of polystyrene is nearly nonexistent in the United States, and foam board is an even less likely candidate for recycling because it is polystyrene bonded to paper. In environmental terms, multi-material products, especially those not designed for disassembly, nearly always have more end of life challenges.

Some all-paper options are emerging, especially a type using a honeycomb internal structure. This is board-making technology is ported over from the world of large-product packing and shipping, so ultimately such boards could be lower in cost than foam-filled boards. They also have the eco-benefit of being recyclable via established corrugated recycling schemes or compostable through emerging organics recycling options.

PROCESSES: ENVIRONMENTAL PROS AND CONS

DIRECT PRINT UV: This process involves a machine that sprays a viscous ink directly onto the target signage material. The ink stays on the surface and dries (cures) only when exposed to a strong ultraviolet (UV) light source. The fact that the ink stays on the surface and doesn't interact with the substrate means that these machines can print on almost any material, as long as it's flat. Newer machines have increased the distance from the ink nozzle to the intended printing surface, allowing for media with uneven surfaces. This has opened the door to customer-supplied materials, allowing designers to move beyond the scant environmental offerings of signage vendors. Vendors with these new machines could print projects on FSC-certified plywood, reclaimed glass, refrigerator-box paperboard, or a high post-consumer content polyethylene wallboard from a builder's supply store.

INKJET: Essentially scaled-up versions of printers found in any home office, these printers use alcohol-based inks that sink into the surface of the media. Many commercial inkjet machines can provide photographic levels of resolution, but they are limited to inkjet-specific papers and media, and there are few environmental options at present.

DYE SUBLIMATION: Dye sublimation, the type of printing employed mostly for fabrics, uses solid dyes that briefly get heated to a gaseous state. The gas diffuses into the fabric and fuses onto the fibers. The image is created by tiny heating elements on the dye sublimation printer's head, which change temperature rapidly, laying different amounts of dye depending on the amount of heat applied. This process can produce a wide gamut of color, wider than either standard inkjet or UV direct printing. The primary environmental advantages to dye sublimation are:

— The ability to create durable, flexible banners without the use of vinyl

— A broad selection of fabric options, including some with high recycled content and other natural fibers

EXPERIMENTS IN SUSTAINABLE SIGNAGE

The Living Green Expo and the Eco Experience are two of the largest dedicated environmental events in the United States. Common to any large show, these yearly events require intense signage for way-finding and display work. Some of the signage gets reused from the previous year, while some is one-time use. Here are some of the strategies for design and planning used by these events to mitigate the environmental downsides of their banner and display needs.

— Maintaining a do-it-yourself orientation to graphical environments has saved money and

---

Balancing act: Issues with nonpermanent signage

Eco-issue at hand	Common un-eco argument
Waste: Resources lost, embodied energy lost, landfill and incineration ecological issues.	Sometimes signage has only one use, and recycling isn't available, even if it is theoretically possible.
Polyvinyl chloride: Biologically persistent toxins from manufacturing and end of life incineration.	Is inexpensive and always available.
Recycled content (post-consumer): Saves energy, keeps materials out of waste stream.	Sometimes hard to source and can be of inferior quality compared to virgin-content products.
Recyclable: Keeps materials out of the waste streams, salvages some of the embodied energy, and helps maintain local jobs.	Recyclable in theory is different from recyclable in practice, and sometimes getting retired signage to a recycler is too arduous if not impossible.
Least material used: Saves embodied manufacturing energy, transportation costs, and eco-impacts, and yields less to dispose or recycle at end of life.	May force limited or single-use of sign because it's not durable enough to reuse. Can look cheap.

---

increased staff knowledge of signage physics and material properties. This, in turn, has allowed more budget flexibility, leading to more experimentation with (greener) materials of unknown characteristics.

— Signage elements are designed to be hung or supported by what will be at the site. Planners may rent scissor lifts and other equipment to accommodate rigging of signage on nearly any building truss, balcony, or exterior facade. This has greatly reduced the need for material-intensive custom structures to hold the signage.

— Large signage or banners that need to be closer to eye level are designed to be hung directly from the horizontal pipe and vertical stanchions that are part of the standard "pipe and drape"

present at most trade shows. The events often rent these structures as part of the booth and flow-setting plan, so further working this support option yields a significant cost and material savings.

— A post-consumer polyethylene fabric called EcoPhab™ is made from recycled beverage containers and is frequently used for multiyear applications. Both the fabric and its fiber are made domestically, adding to its sustainability credentials. Banners and display can be printed using a dye sublimation process, are easy to hang, and have functioned well both indoors and out.

Sharing the eco-experience at the Minnesota State Fair.

— For one-time signage, paper has been used exclusively. Paper recycling options are available and easy. (The events partner with area recyclers.) Paper and paperboard are used, even for very large applications, where paper isn't usually considered. For example, 10 x 8-foot sponsor recognition banners were created using a heavy paper, seamed with tape, and finished with top and bottom pole pockets to accommodate metal pipe fittings.

— Outdoor signage has been made for years without using the standard choice, reinforced PVC. EcoPhab and standard polyethylene duck woven fabrics have been printed via dye sublimation. Since some of these were used only for one event, dye sublimation, instead of direct print UV, was seen as a way to preserve fiber quality for reclamation. Natural canvas (using direct print) was hard to find but has proved itself workable for four to five event cycles. This signage was designed to be hung or mounted in ways that minimized wind load, with special attention to hanging and mounting strategies to eliminate the use of vinyl.

Case Study: Seward Co-op

Background: The Seward Co-op is a community grocery store that has been serving its Minneapolis, Minnesota, community since the 1970s. As membership and needs grew, it was clear that a larger location was necessary. The co-op chose an old building to renovate and added an addition to meet space needs. As one of the Twin Cities' early advocates for greener living, from the very start it was important to the co-op to make the move and building as environmentally sensitive as possible. Spunk Design Machine, a local graphics firm, worked with the co-op's architects to design a look for the building that carried a feeling of "fresh produce."

Problem: Create a colorful window graphic that doesn't use traditional vinyl but communicates the vibrant "fresh" look the co-op was looking for. The dominant solution is vinyl graphics. This decoration form is not collected for recycling (window graphics for grocery stores typically are changed several times a year, generating waste), plus the off-gasing of the vinyl window treatment would impact the building's indoor air quality and overall LEEDs points (U.S. Green Building Council green building guidelines), and would negate some of the hard work and eco-sensitive efforts the co-op had invested in, such as a white roof that did not absorb heat and allowed water to flow into a rain garden, and solar hookups.

Solution: Jeff Johnson, owner of Spunk Design Machine (*www.spkdm.com*), looked at the problem closely. Nontoxic graphics were the first priority, but visual impact too was crucial. Jeff, an award-winning graphic artist with a strong background in screen printing, turned to this medium as an option. Peet Fetsch, Lucas Richards, and Craig Johnson started doing the research and testing. Ink manufacturers were contacted, graphics were tested on windows and were washed, and a variety of screen printing shops were questioned as part of the process. Speedball's nontoxic water-soluble inks, though not endorsed for this use by the manufacturer, held up well enough for this application while being the most environmentally responsible choice. Tests were carried out under various conditions (including a car), and the final graphics were applied over two days with very little mess or cleanup.

Conclusion: The semitranslucent, nontoxic, water-soluble inks allow the Seward Co-op's brand colors to be applied throughout the structure with a crisp clean look while adding a nice glow to the inside space as light shines though the windows. The graphics are easily removed with a common scraper and can be easily replaced to fit the co-op's changing needs with minimal cost and eco-impact.

Promotional Products Industry

Jocelyn Azada
Promotional Product Solutions

Promotional products are products such as a tote bag, a pen or a T-shirt, imprinted with a company's logo or brand message. In an industry rife with products affectionately referred to as "trinkets and trash" and "cheap plastic stuff," concerns about sustainability and social responsibility are rarely at the forefront.

According to the 2008 Promotional Products Association International (PPAI), *Promotional Products Fact Sheet*, in 2007, the top five categories of promotional items were apparel, writing instruments, bags, drinkware (e.g., coffee mugs and water bottles), and desk or office accessories. For many companies, promotional products are important communication vehicles because they are tangible expressions of a brand, reinforcing a company's message and providing interaction with the brand. Certainly, universities use promotional products with great effect to extend their brand and further create a sense of belonging and community around the brand.

The promotional products industry is a $19.4 billion industry in the United States, according to the *2007 PPAI Estimate of Promotional Consultants Sales*. This amount exceeded spending in these media categories: point-of-purchase advertising, cable television, the Yellow Pages, couponing, and product placement in movies and film. It is primarily a business-to-business industry, with the top five buyers by volume representing the educational, financial, nonprofit, healthcare, and construction industries.[223]

The promotional products industry is highly fragmented, with several layers of distributors between a few makers of goods and the end buyer. There are more than 20,000 distributors in the United States but only about 3,500 supplier companies that manufacture, import, or imprint logoed items. These supplier companies make approximately 500,000 different products, including such familiar items as plastic lanyards, ceramic coffee mugs, writing instruments, sticky notes, magnets, water bottles, chocolate, flashlights, and flash drives.

Increasing customer demand and public interest in environmental issues has prompted a green revolution in the industry. From the fourth quarter of 2007 throughout 2008, the industry has seen an exponential increase in the number of promotional products being touted as green. For example, in 2005, a product search in an industry database using the keywords "organic," "recycled," "recyclable," "environmentally friendly," "environmentally responsible" and "eco" yielded approximately 400 products out of 500,000 products available. By contrast, in 2008, the term "organic" in the same industry database resulted in almost 3,000 entries. The terms "recycled," "recyclable," and "eco" in 2008 returned over 10,000 options.

The industry remains, by and large, unsustainable. Although a variety of environmentally friendly products are now available (many with questionable environmental claims, particularly as there are no enforceable standards), the bulk of products still are made from inexpensive, unsustainable, and often toxic materials (e.g., PVC). Many of the items are highly commoditized with little differentiation and are manufactured outside of the United States, increasing carbon emissions from transport. Finally, many products have a short life span for use, being disposed of quickly but remaining in a landfill indefinitely.

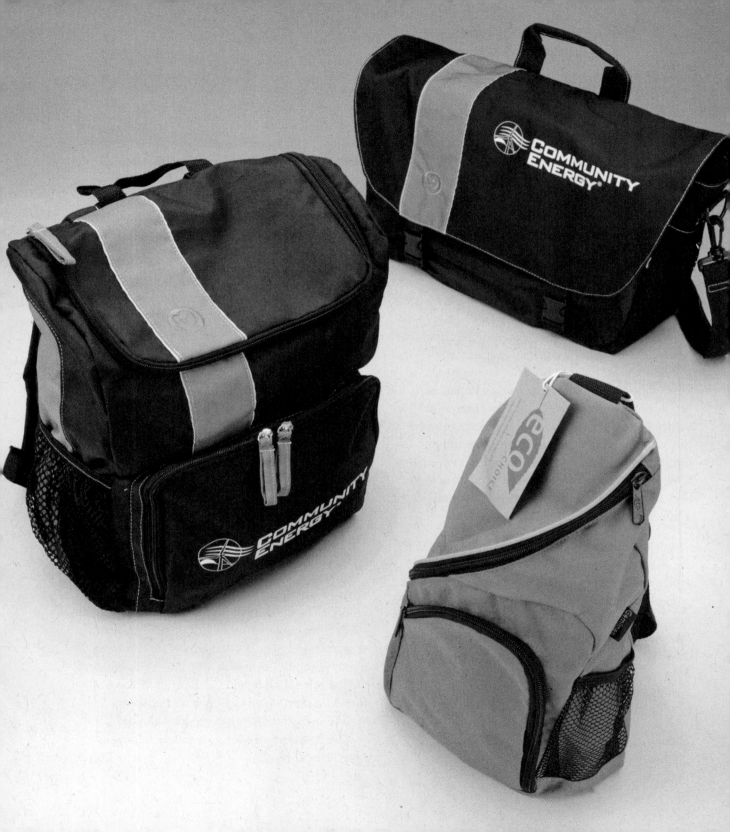

Some product offerings do stand out as well-designed, sustainable, and high-quality alternatives to more typical promotional products. For example, a private-labeled Fair Trade certified coffee can be a great communication vehicle for the right business: The label has a lot of room for information and graphics, it lasts for some time in the office or the home for repeated impressions, and it is both socially and environmentally responsible.

As consumer attitudes change about products in general, how a company chooses to follow through on its image becomes more and more of an issue.

Today, people have no problem saying out loud, "It's a good thing this was free, because it's just another cheap give-away thing." If the idea was to put the company's brand in the hands of potential customers and have them take away that contact and make a positive connection, just what does "just another cheap give-away" say about the company?

Companies looking to tell an honest story and make a positive connection with potential customers don't need to spend more, just spend smarter. More than just "better swag," making every dollar and effort count are two key elements of sustainability systems thinking.

Product promotion may be about image, but to make connections that lead to something more than just awareness, companies need to deliver substance, too. Promotional Product Solutions has been an industry leader in the promotional product industry and was the first to create corporate promotional marketing solutions that are socially conscious and earth friendly. Unlike the usual giveaway that becomes garbage, these bags are made *from* recycled soda bottles. (*www.ppsolutionsllc.com*)

6 Working Smarter

Dion Zuess
ecoLingo: Earth-friendly Graphic Design

Sustainable design is smart design.

Smart design can boost innovation, efficiency, ecology, and the economy at the same time. You've probably heard the expression "Green is the new black." "Green"—whether it is called sustainable, eco, or any other word—is here to stay. There's no turning back. For graphic designers, it's no longer enough simply to choose eco-papers and vegetable-based inks; it's time to step back and look at the bigger picture of design and the role it plays in long-term social and environmental sustainability. It's time (and even past due) to become more aware of the impacts of the graphic arts industry and to take advantage of the marvelous tools and resources that are available to green creative processes, workflows, and workspaces.

Photo: Halsey1.com

As designers become more eco-minded, new creative and innovative ways to conserve energy, resources, and money will be discovered. Designers will be able to translate and share this information with colleagues and become better able to guide clients toward more environmentally aware choices. Designers will grow their businesses in new ways and will be able to effect social change at the same time.

The sections in this chapter contain information about smart, sustainable design workflows, eco-products, best (or better) practices, and much more. This includes environmentally preferred purchasing programs; efficient, paperless, digital processes; and virtual tools. Tips are included on how to choose greener electronics and carbon offsets, how to conserve energy in the studio, and how to dispose of e-waste. Designers can learn more about measuring and changing their ecological footprint as well as their studio's or office's carbon footprint. Working greener and smarter can help keep businesses in the black, provide a competitive edge, and make work environments healthier and more sustainable.

New developments, eco-products, and state-of-the-art technologies are emerging everyday, alongside traditional, time-tested lore and practices. Essentially, this chapter contains a bit of each, with straightforward environmental facts and information. Each is matched with resources and actions designers can take to work smarter and make a difference—step by step, but with a smaller eco-footprint than ever before.

Getting Started

Take a look around your work or creative environment: the desk or table, chairs, cabinets, and office equipment. Much of what you see has been designed for the workplace. It may serve you right now, but does it really "work" for the Earth in the long term? How about you as an eco-conscious designer? Does your creative workspace reflect your ideals, values, and goals for greener living and environmental stewardship?

Products are specially designed for the workplace, but do they really "work" for the Earth?

Does your creative workspace reflect your ideals, values, and goals for greener living and environmental stewardship?

Look further—how does your workspace impact your own health and that of the world at large? Does the paint on the walls contain harmful volatile organic compounds (VOCs) and other solvents? Is the flooring from an endangered forest? Does the carpet, rug, or vinyl flooring off-gas toxic chemicals? What kind of lighting illuminates your tasks—energy-hungry incandescent and halogen bulbs, or old-style energy-inefficient fluorescents? Are your desks, counters, cabinets, or shelving made with medium-density fiberboard (MDF) or compressed wood products held together with glues containing formaldehyde and other carcinogens?

What about the information technology side of your business? For example, take the removable media file of the client file you've just created, plus your computer, hard drive, mouse or tablet, and keyboard, as well as the office chair you're sitting in: What type of valuable resources were mined to manufacture them? Do they also contain toxic materials or chemicals? And what happens to your office equipment and materials when they've reached their end of use and go out your door? (Consider this, even if you are technically savvy and use one of the many online file-sharing or server storage options available: Does the lack of physical storage media and transfer to digital or Web-based storage mean that you are using less resources, or are you simply using energy resources in a different way?)

Now that we're starting to see some of the dilemmas and issues common with work environments, let's focus on solution talk and strategies. Part of working toward sustainability goals means being willing to look all production systems. Taking a minute to review your working environment and determine if your workspace—whether it is a cubicle, a corporate building, or a home-based studio—treads lightly on the Earth's ecosystem or burdens it is integral to meeting long-term goals. Taking a systems approach, ask:

— Do you know the provenance of your everyday working materials, tools, and office equipment and furniture?

— What about the impact these goods have made or will make during their sourcing, manufacturing, shipping, assembly, disassembly, recycling, remanufacturing, degradation, or journey to the landfill?

— How can your supply chain purchases, waste management, or creative workflow be enhanced to make the most of the emerging new green technologies and products?

Investigating and taking steps to make changes that support eco-goals today will make your work environment healthier, more productive, and more Earth-friendly for the long haul. Smart, sustainable office policies and protocols save resources *and* money, making your business more profitable. For example, office equipment power management features not only save energy, they can also put money in your pocket—saving $75 or more per computer annually.[1] Many small changes add up to big impacts, and collectively firms can save millions of dollars per year. Whole industries can save billions of dollars annually and greatly reduce greenhouse emissions at the same time. All of this can happen when workers start to do simple things like power down their computers at night or switch to more efficient light bulbs.[2]

Other statistics show that a typical office generates about 1.5 pounds of wastepaper per employee per day.[3] When paper waste is reduced, there remains more money to spend on business growth. Eliminating paper waste also plays a dramatic part on a larger scale. Paper products and paperboard are the largest component of the nation's municipal solid waste.[4] Businesses that include paper conservation strategies become part of the solution instead of remaining part of the problem. Customers are looking for suppliers who "walk their talk" and who are willing to take a lead in sustainability issues. Each step and environmental action (or nonaction!) we make reflects our core values. What are your actions saying about you and your business?

Each time we purchase a socially aware, environmentally preferred product or office supply, we trigger change or reinforce eco-efforts on a variety of levels.

Shop Green

Environmentally Preferable Socially Responsible Purchasing

Each time we purchase a socially aware, environmentally preferred product or office supply, we trigger change or reinforce eco-efforts on a variety of levels. We promote sustainability, we protect the environment, and we help protect the health and wellbeing of those around us. Most of all, we put our purchasing power to work to foster market change and environmental stewardship.

Environmentally preferable purchasing goes beyond choosing products that have environmental attributes; it also combines purchasing with social justice in mind. Socially responsible purchasing aspects include buying goods that are manufactured with standards regarding safe working conditions, payment of living wages, labor rights (especially about exploitive or child labor concerns), human and animal rights, and community welfare. Some examples include purchasing Fair Trade coffee for the break room or electronics manufactured with reduced toxins. Going further to avoid products with brominated flame retardants (BFRs) helps protect

the health of the workers who dismantle the products at the end of the product's useful life (see the section titled "E-waste and Technotrash" for more details).

Create a "Green Team"

To jump-start or build on a firm's environmentally preferable purchasing program, designate an eco-leader or green team within the workplace. To ensure success, involve management and gain chief executive approval and support. Roles of the eco-leader or green team include reviewing current supply chain purchases, developing and outlining environmentally preferable purchasing goals, creating a mission statement or policy, and working with suppliers and vendors to find healthier, environmentally preferred products.

Putting an EPP Policy into Action

Start and maintain an environmentally preferable purchasing (EPP) policy or program to ensure that the products the firm purchases meet key environmental and social standards. Ensure that the guidelines are available for review for all team members, employees, and new hires.

For samples of EPP policies or guidelines, visit the "Green Business Guides" and "Greening Advisor's" pages of the Natural Resources Defense Council's (NDRC) Web site: *www.nrdc.org.*

The Environmental Protection Agency (EPA) has developed five guiding principles to provide broad guidance for applying environmentally preferable purchasing in the federal government setting that also can be applied to other settings. Visit *www.epa .gov* and type in EPP in the search line to find numerous resources and publications for all business types.

Several core concepts are the basis of EPP policies; these include:

— Comparing environmental impacts, quality, and performance

— Product life cycle perspectives and analysis

— Review of industry standards and certifications

— Resource conservation

— Pollution prevention

— Full or "true cost accounting"—considering environmental, economic, and social impacts or costs

For example, life cycle analyses show that recycled paper is better for the environment. Recycled paper reduces demand on forests, reduces waste, uses fewer resources such as energy and water, and produces fewer toxic releases.[5] Yet because the greater benefits of recycled papers aren't reflected back in the selling price, recycled paper or paper from certified or well-managed forests sometimes (but not always) is more expensive. Cost is often cited as the key reason customers do not purchase recycled stocks, but smart designers know that effective paper usage and paper reduction plans can offset the price of any paper option. In addition to cost objections, there is an outdated notion that all recycled papers are coarse, inferior, or fiber flecked, even though today's eco-papers are some of the most beautiful, high-performance papers on the market.

Using sales price to determine the value or cost of recycled paper does not provide the "true cost" of

the resources or take into account the social and eco-impacts that revolve around deforestation and paper manufacturing. Deforestation of virgin forests and rain forests not only affects the animals and species living in them, it affects the health of indigenous peoples (due to the release of toxic pollutants and pesticides from paper-making processes), their livelihoods (human rights and land rights), and culture (if evicted from their geographic homeland by paper companies, and by changes in the local economy).[6]

Furthermore, using recycled paper plays a larger role in the economy on another level. Several recent reports, including the Intergovernmental Panel on Climate Change, have demonstrated that "saving forests is one of the most cost-effective and immediate options for combating climate change."[7]

If we step back and look at the bigger picture, we see that recycled or certified paper sometimes costs more at the checkout line, but virgin paper from endangered and old-growth forests costs the Earth.

Recycled paper is just one example of true cost accounting. Environmentally preferable purchasing programs in general not only save resources, they also provide designers and firms with strategies to

Recycled or certified paper sometimes costs more at the checkout line, but virgin paper from endangered and old-growth forests costs the Earth.

make supply chain decisions and to create opportunities to provide or expand markets for eco-based products. EPP programs also encourage product stewardship and can push suppliers and manufacturers to:

— Use recycled content in their materials.

— Reduce pollution.

— Use fewer resources (i.e., paper made from annual crops or other tree-free materials).

— Minimize waste.

— Create energy-efficient products.

— Develop healthier, less toxic products.

— Design with life cycles in mind (i.e., design for end of life via reuse, recycling, or upcycling).

These organizations help businesses develop environmentally preferable purchasing programs:

— EPA's Environmentally Preferable Purchasing Policy and Guidance was geared first to help federal purchasers. Today this site can help eco-minded vendors, businesses large and small, and consumers. The site includes tools, databases, calculators and case studies. Visit *www.epa.gov/epp/*.

— The Responsible Purchasing Network (RPN), staffed and managed by the Center for a New American Dream, provides purchasing guides that include social and environmental issues associated with a variety of product categories. *www.responsiblepurchasing.org*.

— INFORM—Strategies for a Better Environment. Visit *www.informinc.org* for more information and to view materials related to "extended producer responsibility," a policy that "requires manufacturers to accept responsibility for all stages in a product's lifecycle, including 'end-of-life' management when people discard it."

— The Pacific Northwest Pollution Prevention Resource Center provides a guide titled "Product Stewardship for Manufacturers." Visit *www.pprc.org*.

— EnviroCalc: Environmental Benefits and Energy Cost Savings Calculator for Purchasers. "This calculator is a downloadable spreadsheet tool designed to estimate the environmental benefits of purchases of recycled-content and energy efficient products." The official Web site of the Commonwealth of Massachusetts also has a variety of other tools and resources. Visit *www.mass.gov* and type in "EnviroCalc and other tools" in the search feature.

— The Environmentally Preferable Purchasing Database is a tool to make it easier to purchase products and services with reduced environmental impacts. Environmental information on over 600 products and services is included in this database provided by U.S. Environmental Protection Agency. Visit *www.epa.gov* and type "epp database" into the search feature.

— Worldwatch Institute provides a comprehensive list of resources on environmentally preferable purchasing on its Web site: *www.worldwatch.org*.

— ENERGY STAR, a joint program of the U.S. Environmental Protection Agency and the U.S. Department of Energy, provides a variety of purchasing and procurement resources online at *www.energystar.gov*.

— The Electronic Product Environmental Assessment Tool (EPEAT) helps purchasers compare and select computers, notebooks, and monitors on their environmental attributes: *www.epeat.net*.

— Green Seal™ certified products, services, and publications can be found on Green Seal's Web site, *www.greenseal.org*, including the publication "Benefits of Green Purchasing Decisions."

— The Natural Resources Defense Council has developed an in-depth guide series called "The NRDC Greening Advisor" with tools and resources for businesses. Visit *www.nrdc.org* to learn more.

Keep this question at the forefront of any EPP: *Is this product or service needed in the first place or could less be used?* The best environmental purchasing plan is to purchase less, use less, and use wisely. Before purchasing a product or service, ask whether you could upgrade, trade, repair, mend, or update existing equipment or use it more efficiently.

The best environmental purchasing plan is to purchase less, use less, and use wisely.

EPP Best Practices

Paper

Buy paper and stationary with this criteria in mind: High PCW (post-consumer waste) content, Forest Stewardship Council (FSC) certified from well-managed forests, certified Processed Chlorine Free (PCF) or Totally Chlorine Free (TCF), and manufactured with renewable energy. See Chapter 5 for more details, including information about alternative and tree-free paper options.

Nearly half of the trees cut in North America go to papermaking.

Designers take note: According to figures from Conservatree, a project of Social and Environmental Entrepreneurs (SEE), nearly half of the trees cut in North America go to papermaking,[8] and recycling paper requires 60 percent less energy than making paper from raw materials. One ton of recycled paper saves:[9]

— 4,100 kilowatts of electricity

— 380 gallons of oil

— 54 million BTUs of energy

— 3.3 cubic yards of landfill space

— 7,000 gallons of water

— 17 trees

It also creates 74 percent less air pollution and 35 percent less water pollution. Or, put it another way, research shows that each ton of recycled fiber that displaces a ton of virgin fiber used in coated groundwood paper (stock used in magazines) reduces:[10]

— Total energy consumption by 27 percent

DISCLAIMER

Any recommendations made in this book regarding regulatory compliance should be considered as suggestions based on our understanding of industry practices in effect at the time of the recommendations. They are not intended as legal opinion or advice. In all matters concerning federal, state, or local regulations, we advise readers to seek proper legal counsel to verify that their business practices comply with all applicable statutory requirements.

COPYRIGHT

©2008 A. Cook Associates, Inc. All rights reserved. No part of this publication may be reproduced, transmitted, stored in a retrieval system, or translated into any language in any form by any means without the written permission of Andrew Cook and A. Cook Associates, Inc.

PUBLISHED BY
A. Cook Associates, Inc.
PO Box 229, 4155 Route 113
Thetford Center, VT 05075
www.storeservicessoftware.com

BOOK DESIGN BY
Jess Sand, Roughstock Studios
PO Box 460010
San Francisco CA 94146
www.roughstockstudios.com

This book is printed on 100% recycled paper using soy inks and wind power.

ACKNOWLEDGMENTS

There are too many people in the industry who challenged my assumptions, and helped me. individually I owe thanks to them all. their insight to what I know; without have little information to share.

Finally, and most importantly, and has visited many more in the industry should ha business and my dreams

SUPERMARKET
FACILITIES
A BLUEPRINT
BY ANDREW

SUPERMARKET
FACILITIES MANAGEMENT
A BLUEPRINT FOR BEST PRACTICES
BY ANDREW COOK

— Net greenhouse gas emissions by 47 percent and particulate emissions by 28 percent

— Wastewater by 33 percent

— Solid waste by 54 percent

— Wood use by 100 percent

Resources:

— Conservatree provides detailed fact sheets about papermaking, environmental issues, and ways to reduce waste. There are helpful purchasing guides, such as the "Paper Master List," for professional paper buyers, and "Recycled Copy Paper Listings," which includes national and regional retail store lists. Visit *www .conservatree.org.*

— The Environmental Paper Network has numerous resources and fact sheets, including "Paper Steps: Taking the Steps to Environmentally Responsible Paper" and a "Purchaser Toolkit." Visit *www.whatsinyourpaper.com* or *www .environmentalpaper.org.*

— The Forest Stewardship Council is an independent, nonprofit organization devoted to encouraging the responsible management of the world's forests. The U.S. chapter's Web site offers links to FSC-certified paper stocks (papers in all categories: coated/uncoated, text/cover, newsprint, packaging, envelopes and digital), plus FSC-certified paper merchants, paper manufacturers, printers, and pulp suppliers. Visit *www.fscus.org* to learn more.

— The World Wildlife Foundation (WWF) provides a "WWF Paper Scorecard." Visit *www.panda.org* and type "WWF paper scorecard" in the search feature.

— WoodWise™ Consumer Guides and Glossary of Terms are available on the Green America (formerly Co-op America) Web site: *www .coopamerica.org/programs/woodwise.*

— "Tips for Selecting, Buying and Reducing Paper" and other guides are available in the Environmental Defense Fund's online archives: *www .edf.org.*

— The Paper Recycling Coalition: *www.paper recyclingcoalition.com.*

Use an interactive, Web-based tool environmental paper calculator to evaluate paper choices and measure environmental impacts of different papers.

Resources:

— The Paper Calculator, developed by the Environmental Defense Fund, and based on research done by the Paper Task Force: *www.edf .org/papercalculator/.*

Note: Several paper companies also provide environmental savings calculators or eco-audits, based on data from the cited sources.

Author Andrew Cook turned to San Francico's Roughstock Studios to see the sustainability issues addressed in his book reflected in the printing itself. Roughstock selected a final page size that would make use of the entire press sheet, reducing typical trim waste for a book of this type from 25 percent to 9.1 percent. A. Maciel, the printer tapped for this project, is, like Roughstock, a Green Business certified by the city of San Francisco. A. Maciel's electricity powering its energy-efficient equipment is 100 percent offset by wind-power credits, and its printing plates are recycled after use. The inks for this run were Toyo Hyplus 100 series inks, a soy-based ink that produces less than 1 gram per liter of VOCs. In addition to the low VOC count, these inks cover well and require less ink usage overall.

Use 100 percent cotton rag paper or FSC certified recycled papers with at least 30 percent PCW content if you are a photographer or exhibitor.

Resources:

— Green-in-Print: A Guide to Environmentally Friendly Choices in Photographic Paper: *www .conservatree.com/paper/Choose/GreenInPrint April08.pdf.*

Other Paper Goods and Mailing Supplies

Choose envelopes and mailers with the same environmental criteria as paper. High PCW content, FSC certified, certified Processed Chlorine Free or Totally Chlorine Free, and manufactured with renewable energy.

Select business window envelopes that are made from biodegradable polymers instead of petroleum-based plastic. For example, some grades of cellulose acetate (a clear plastic made from trees) are often biodegradable. In addition, PLA, a corn-based plastic, is being used for window applications as it doesn't interfere with the recycling quality of the paper it is used with. In packaging, it actually adds to the overall performance qualities.

Use water-based, "removable adhesive" or biodegradable mailing labels and adhesives. Typical pressure-sensitive label adhesive formulations contain petroleum, acrylics, or solvents and are printed on coated support sheets or release liners.[11] Once these labels are affixed to envelopes, they can be very difficult to separate from the envelope or other substrate. Furthermore, during recycling, adhesive bits can clog processing equipment and contribute to recycling sludge along with waste ink or dyes, clays, fibers, and chemicals. Sludge is considered an industrial waste that requires proper disposal to prevent environmental degradation or contamination; disposal can be expensive.

Resources:

— Dolphin Blue, an online office supply store, offers recycled office supplies, including Pinnacle Recyclabels™—a line of cut sheet, self-adhesive label stock made with FSC-certified 100 post-consumer recycled face stock that is certified processed chlorine free, with 100 percent recyclable adhesive that can be recycled with mixed office papers. See *www .dolphinblue.com* to learn more.

— Plan It Green, part of R&D Print and Packaging in Southern California, offers 100 percent corn labels/biopolymer, tree-free and dissolvable labels printed with soy or vegetable-based inks. For more information, visit *www.planitgreen printing.com.*

— GoGreen Labels: FSC-certified labels with recyclable adhesive, manufactured with renewable energy, with 100 percent recycled corrugate packaging, and "carbon-free" delivery. See: *www.gogreenlabels.com.*

Reconsider sticky notes, repositionable notes, or plastic markers. Although very convenient for making temporary notes, papers with even low-tack adhesive on the back can cause problems in the recycling process for some recycling mills. Some consider the self-adhesive notes and plastic markers as paper contaminants,[12] and other recycling mills will not recycle the brightly colored self-adhesive notes at all.[13]

Replace packaging tape, plastic bags, and packaging films with biodegradable cellulose-based packing and packaging products. Reuse loose-fill

packaging materials and use biodegradable packing peanuts or paper-based void-fill options for shipping.

Resources:

— Green Earth Office Supply offers cornstarch packing peanuts and many other eco office supplies, including food service, janitorial, and kitchen supplies: *www.greenearthofficesupply .com.*

Magazines Subscriptions and Magazines in Waiting Rooms

Subscribe to magazines that print on eco-papers or are on a "responsible magazine list." According to Woodwise™: "More than 95 percent of all magazine paper is made from virgin tree fiber requiring hundreds of dangerous chemicals and threatening both forests and the health of communities. Every second one tree is logged to produce magazine paper—about 31 million trees each year."[17]

— Green America (formerly Co-op America) provides paper production and consumption facts, including "The Better Paper Project." To learn more, or to encourage magazines to switch to recycled paper and sustainable production processes, visit *www.coopamerica .org/programs/woodwise.*

— Catalog Choice is a free service that assists people in deciding what gets in their mailbox and helps reduce the number of unwanted or repeat catalog mailings. Visit *www.catalogchoice .org* for more information.

— Ask suppliers to replace their paper catalogs with e-catalogs.

Office and Desk Supplies

The selection and range of eco-conscious offerings for office supplies grows every season. The simplest way to keep abreast of cutting-edge, sustainable office products is to visit or shop online at a dedicated green office supply site.

Environmentally preferable purchasing note: For all goods, but especially durable goods, which enjoy fewer recycling options than consumables such as paper in many communities, recyclability means that the item could be recycled—if a recycling program were available to do so. Choosing a product only because it says "recyclable" on the box is not looking at the whole story a product has to tell. Consider life cycle as part of the purchasing process.

Purchase notepads, planners, calendars, sketch-pads, and binders made with recycled content. Avoid buying and using laminated binders (including metallic, foil-coated, or holographic) and plastic- or vinyl-coated ring binders that have no end-of-life recycling options. Also consider the binding on notebooks and pads during your purchases: Where will the binding go once you're finished with the notebook or pad? Can it be recycled without contaminating recycling streams? You can throw it away, but first ask yourself, "Where is away?"

Resources:

— Sustainable Group (*www.sustainablegroup.net*) and Treecycle Recycled Paper (*www.treecycle .com*) offer recyclable three-ring binders, pocket

You can throw it away, but first ask yourself, "Where is away?"

folders, and other office supplies and food service items.

Use recycled paper in badge nametags and ask recipients to return the plastic protector badge for reuse. Avoid one-use, removable sticky nametags, due to the problems mentioned earlier regarding adhesives. Alternatively, look into reusable, compostable, plant-based PLA badge holders for events, trade shows, and security badges.

Resources:

— "REBADGE" from Sustainable Group (*www.sustainablegroup.net*), or use the search term "PLA name badge" to find more options.

Ensure that everyday office materials purchased contain recycled content or can be easily recycled. For example, use paper clips without plastic or vinyl coatings,[14] metal thumb tacks rather than plastic-tipped tacks, scissors with steel blades and recycled plastic handles, recyclable letter trays or sorters (look at plastic polymer codes before purchasing), and so on.

Keep an eye out for clever office accessories that use fewer resources or have positive end-of-life uses. Items include stapleless staplers, clocks made from recycled detergent bottles or bicycle parts, mouse pads made from recycled paper or recycled rubber, and desk calendars made from biodegradable, plantable seed paper.

Filing Supplies

Use digital file options where possible. For other paper storage, choose file folders and manila folders that contain at least 30 percent post-consumer content.

Resources:

— Recycled file folders and other office products are available from Recycled Products Cooperative: *www.recycledproducts.org*.

Writing Instruments

Avoid disposable writing instruments and use refillable pens or pencils. Choose erasers that contain 100 percent natural rubber or other biodegradable content over plastic or polyvinyl chloride (PVC; vinyl) erasers.

Purchase pencils made with recycled or alternative content or those made from certified wood from well-managed forests. Refillable pens can be easily found, as can pencils that have outer shells made from newsprint, jeans, and old currency. See the next section for markers and highlighters.

Art Supplies

Choose nontoxic art supplies, paints, markers, pigments, and fixatives. Many graphic designers are also talented in other art mediums, including illustration and painting. Carefully choose solvent-free markers, certified nontoxic or ASTM paints, and pigments free of heavy metals. Limit paint waste and store unused quantities in glass containers.

Clean paintbrushes with nontoxic, solvent-free, or biodegradable cleaners.

Carefully select fixatives and adhesives, especially aerosol spray adhesives commonly used for mounting artwork or printed projects onto boards or portfolios. Review labels for the product's safety precautions or review the Material Safety Data Sheet (MSDS)[15] regarding hazards, potential health effects, toxicological and environmental information, and disposal considerations for these and other studio materials.

Presentations and Promotions

Portfolio Cases, Briefcases, and Laptop Bags

Look for carry cases that are PVC free (vinyl free) and have recyclable content. Alternative fabrics and materials include canvas, wool felt, hemp, bamboo, aluminum, cardboard, recycled rubber, recycled soda bottles, and repurposed boat sails.

Presentation Boards and Signage

Choose paperboard or "eco-boards" instead of plastic-based foam-center boards to mount projects for displays, presentations, or signage.

Resources:

— PlyVeneer: Makes boards from lightweight corrugated materials (kraft honeycomb): MiracleBoard®/PlyCorr and BioBoard.™ These are 100 percent recyclable, 63 percent PCW, with a white printable surface (including digital). *www.plyveneer.com.*

— Xanita: X-board, X-board Plus, and Mondi Xtreme are a foam-free, particleboard alternative for flat branding applications, bus and train interior graphics, or side and rear framed bus graphics. The company's manufacturing process combines recycled paperboard and sugar cane bagasse with VOC-free organic starch-based adhesives, resulting in kraft-based boards that weigh as little as one-seventh the weight of formaldehyde-based MDF and particleboard. *www.xanita.com.*

Banners and Signage

Apply sustainability thinking to business signage and way finding. Specify and use vinyl-free banners and signage where applicable. For those who need to take business or product signage on the road, carefully review eco-options for portable signage and trade booths.

Resources:

— Green Banners creates high-resolution, full-color photo-quality graphics and text on a wide variety of materials using ecologically sound renewable and recycled/recyclable materials and water-based inks. *www.greenbanners.com.*

— Banner Creations, Inc. prints banners on "Eco-Phab,™" a fabric made from 100 percent post-consumer polyethylene terephthalate (PET) soft drink bottles. *www.bannercreations.com.*

Promotional Products, Gifts, and Giveaways

Eco-minded promotional products, corporate gifts and giveaways. Do colleagues and clients really need another plastic item emblazoned with your logo as a promotional giveaway or holiday gift? Numerous "green" or "eco" promotional product companies are springing up daily. First, though, always consider if the recipient (and the Earth) really "need" another pen, T-shirt or promotional whatchamacallit, even if it manufactured in a less toxic way. If objects must be created, produce ones the receiver will value or use.

Consider eco-minded ideas or services instead of products, or gifts that educate or help others make

a difference. Gift ideas include paperless e-cards with resourceful, educational, content, reusable shopping bags, reusable drink bottles, or a membership or subscription to a local community supported agriculture (CSA) program. Carbon offsets and donations to environmental organizations and nonprofits are also a great way to give. Sources for socially conscious gifts include Global Exchange (*www.store.gxonlinestore.org*) and Pristine Planet (*www.pristineplanet.com*).

Awards and Certificates

Give thoughtful, eco-minded awards and certificates instead of typical ones made from wood or plastic. Alternatives include tree-free paper certificates, glass awards, or plaques made from recycled or FSC content, bamboo, sunflower hulls, and post-consumer materials.

Recyclable Gift Bags, Packages, and Wrapping Paper

Use recyclable or reusable bags or packages for gifts. Reusable handmade boxes tied with colorful ribbons, mini paint tins, glass containers, or even a fabric remnant or kitchen towel make for an appealing and refreshing change from paper bags. Reusable cloth bags can become the wrapping for another gift tucked inside. Alternatively, extra poster reprints or press sheets make great gift-wrapping and matching tags.

Rethink wrapping paper, bows, and tissue paper. Americans toss out an extra 25 million tons of trash over the holidays, largely due to packaging.[16] Foil or metallic printed bows, ribbons, gift papers, and bags are not recyclable in many markets, nor are wrapping tissue papers. (See Chapter 5 for more information about metals in metallic inks.)

Kitchen and Break Room

Green the break room. Think organic, shade-grown, Fair Trade coffees and teas, organic milk and coffee creamers, and locally grown honey and natural sweeteners.

Resources:

— World Fair Trade Organization: *www.wfto.org*

— Fair Trade Federation: *www.fairtradefederation.org*

— TransFair USA: *www.transfairusa.org*

— Equal Exchange: *www.equalexchange.coop*

The average American office worker goes through around 500 disposable cups every year.

—Clean Air Council

Substitute single-serving plastic water bottles with pitchers, coolers, or filtered tap water, or best of all, encourage employees to use their own washable drinking bottle or coffee cup.

Encourage employees to bring in their own lunch or meals (to save costs and prevent take-out container waste) and use reusable bags, cutlery, and napkins in their lunch bags or containers.

Replace single-serving disposable plastic utensils or dishes with reusable or compostable items, or provide washable china, glassware, and flatware if sink facilities are available.

Many green office supply stores carry biodegradable or compostable items. But more important, encourage the use of washable reusable items that stay onsite, or use portable, reusable utensils. For example, consider To-Go Ware's CONSERVE organic bamboo flatware set: *www.to-goware.com.*

When shopping for supplies, use reusable bags made of canvas or recycled content to reduce plastic bag use.

Bulk order to save on costs and delivery/shipping costs.

Initiate a waste reduction and composting plan.

Provide recycling bins and posters to educate and remind staff about items accepted for recycling.

Use trash bags made from biodegradable plastic or recycled content plastic.

Use washable linens or recycled paper goods for cleanup.

Purchase napkins and paper goods made with recycled content.

If every household in the United States replaced just one package of virgin fiber napkins (250 count) with 100 percent recycled ones, we could save 1 million trees.

—*Natural Resources Defense Council*

Janitorial Goods

Purchase biodegradable, nontoxic or natural cleaning products and toiletries to reduce employees' and cleaners' exposure to harmful chemicals, solvents, and contaminants.

Look for products that use bio-based solvents or renewable resources; are low in corrosive, carcinogenic, or hazardous chemicals and compounds; have a low VOC content or no ozone-depleting compounds; have low flammability; are cruelty free; and are formulated to work in cold water to save energy.

When in doubt, consult a material safety data sheet (MSDS) to learn more about the ingredients used in the product—there are many MSDS databases online.

Alternatively, handmade, natural mixes can be made that combine baking soda, vinegar, and other common yet highly effective ingredients together for cleaning purposes.

Resources:

— "Greening Your Purchase of Cleaning Products: A Guide for Federal Purchasers" is available on the EPA's Web site in the Environmentally Preferable Purchasing Guides section. Visit *www.epa.gov* to find this and other resources.

— "Green Cleaning Toolkit"—a variety of fact sheets and resources, including an ingredients checklist. Prepared by INFORM: Strategies for a Better Environment. *www.informinc.org.*

— "Buy Green: Cleaning Supplies"—a resource posted on Planet Green's Web site: *www.planetgreen.discovery.com.*

Use eco-cleaning services or housekeeping companies that use natural, nontoxic, and biodegradable cleaning products as part of their service.

Switching to green cleaners can help reduce the more than $75 million a year U.S. institutions spend to address the chemical-related injuries of custodial workers.

—The Janitorial Products Pollution
Prevention Project (JPPP)

Choose washable linens or recycled content paper goods for restrooms. Toilet tissue, facial tissues, napkins, paper towels, or paper hand towels are all items that we use daily in the home and the office. Unfortunately, these throwaway products are commonly sourced from virgin paper from ancient or endangered forests.

Resources:

— "A Shopper's Guide to Home Tissue Products: Shop Smart. Save Forests." Prepared by the NRDC. View the guide online, print out a card for your wallet, or give to the eco-leader in charge of the EPP program: *www.nrdc.org/land/ forests/tissueguide/walletcard.pdf.*

— Consider installing a paper-free hand dryer in the restroom, such as an energy efficient Dyson® Airblade or similar product.

Green Catering and Events

Be mindful of how dietary choices impact the environment when planning menus. Diet considerations today are a regular part of questionnaires used to calculate environmental footprints. The UN Food and Agriculture Organization (FAO) estimates that direct emissions from meat production account for about 18 percent of the world's total greenhouse gas emissions. This figure includes "greenhouse gases released in every part of the meat production cycle—clearing forested land, making and transporting fertilizer, burning fossil fuels in farm vehicles, and the front and rear end emissions of cattle and sheep."[18]

The UN estimates that direct emissions from meat production account for about 18 percent of the world's total greenhouse gas emissions.

—Food and Agriculture Organization
of the United Nations

Extend purchasing policies to include event, meeting, or conference catering that is eco-minded. Local, organically grown produce, vegetarian offerings, or natural, free-range poultry or sustainable fish, organic beverages and Fair Trade coffee and teas, all served with washable china, flatware, linens and napkins (instead of disposables), recycling stations, and options for donating leftover food are just a few of the things that can be done as part of an eco-conscious corporate event. Remember that it is also possible to purchase carbon offsets for events, including the travel. See the section titled "Carbon Offsets" in this chapter for more information.

Prevent waste. Catered events, conferences, and trade shows generate enormous amounts of waste. Some tips include: Plan ahead to minimize impacts. Ask attendees to R.S.V.P. to help event planners buy appropriate amounts of food. Consider renting washable plates, cups, and cutlery instead of using disposable items. (In many cases they won't need to be washed, just scraped clean before returning to rental services.) Provide recycling bins for bottles and plastic catering platters or lids.

Resources:

— "Greening Your Event" is a Green Business Guide on the Natural Resources Defense Council's Web site. Visit *www.nrdc.org* and type in "Greening your event" to gather more information and tips to lighten the environmental impacts of gatherings.

— The Green Meeting Industry Council (GMIC) is a nonprofit organization whose mission is to transform the meetings industry through sustainability. GMIC encourages collaboration within the meetings industry toward the development of green/eco-standards that will improve the environmental performance of meetings and events on a global basis. Visit *www.greenmeetings.info* to learn more.

Promote natural environments and green building awareness and development. Host events in "green venues"—natural outdoor settings, certified LEED® buildings, ecotourism resorts, and the like.

Office Furniture, Flooring, Shelving, and Storage

Timber from endangered or tropical forests often is used to make flooring and furniture, and both of these industries contribute to deforestation and global warming. According to Global Forest Resource Assessment 2005, tropical rain forests are disappearing at a rate of 100,000 acres per day.[19]

Carefully choose products that have clear stated origins and are made from well-managed forests with FSC certification. The Forest Stewardship Council (FSC) is an independent, nongovernmental, not-for-profit organization established to promote the responsible management of the world's forests. Look for products with the FSC logo when making purchases. Visit *www.fscus.org* to learn more or to search the database for a certified product or manufacturer.

Purchase desks, task chairs, and other office furniture that can be disassembled easily and can be recycled. Aluminum table legs and chairs can last over 100 years. A good product example is from Emeco, a company that sells aluminum chairs that are 100 percent recyclable (*www.emeco.net*). Additionally, the Think® chair by Steelcase, Inc. is made from 44 percent recycled materials and is 99 percent recyclable by weight (*www.steelcase.com*). Steelcase recently forged a partnership with the Institution Recycling Network (IRN) to find ways to reuse old office furniture. IRN is a cooperative that focuses its recycling efforts in colleges, universities, hospitals, schools and state agencies. To learn more visit: *www.ir-network.com*.

Resources:

— Look for C2C (Crade to Cradle) certified products or furniture that can contribute to LEED credits for green building certification.

— To learn more about C2C certification and for a list of certified products: visit *www.mbdc.com*.

— Note: Allsteel, Hayworth, Herman Miller, and Steelcase, Inc. all offer C2C certified chairs, office tables and desks, storage, and work stations.

Look for recycled content or reclaimed, refurbished materials and certified woods for furniture, shelving, countertops, flooring, and storage cabinets in the studio and workplace.

Consider flooring and furnishings made from alternative materials: bamboo, cork, kirei, wool, recycled glass, cardboard, or rubber.

Consider flooring, furnishings, and storage cabinets made from alternative materials: bamboo, cork, kirei, wool, recycled glass, cardboard, paper, rubber, corn stover, or other agricultural wastes.

Product examples:

— Furniture designed by Iannone Design is made with reclaimed kirei, cork, bamboo, and certified materials: *www.iannonedesign.com*. This and other sustainable furniture offerings are available at Vivavi Modern Green Furniture and Furnishings: *www.vivavi.com*.

— Baltix Sustainable Furniture offers a rich palette of eco-material options including pre- and post-consumer recycled content, biocomposite wheat and sunflower, rapidly renewable bamboo, and FSC hardwood veneers. The products contain no harmful adhesives, formaldehydes, or VOCs: *www.baltix.com*.

— PaperStone™ or IceStone® surfaces are both made from recycled materials and contribute points toward LEED® certification: *www .paperstoneproducts.com* and *www.icestone.biz*.

Other sustainable furniture choices include buying durable goods that last longer and are less likely to end in landfills; buying furniture that is made with less toxic materials, finishes, and glues; and purchasing vintage or refurbished furniture. Others propose purchasing easy-to-assemble (and disassemble), resourcefully packaged flat-pack furniture to reduce shipping costs and related greenhouse emissions.[20]

Resources:

— Top Green Furniture Tips: Planet Green: *www .planetgreen.discovery.com*.

Look for furniture that is untreated (including the upholstery fabric) or has natural wood finishes. Hormone-disrupting fire retardants, air-polluting formaldehydes and VOCs and other harmful chemicals are commonly used in glues, finishes, coatings, and fabrics. (See the "Healthier, More Sustainable Work Environments" section of this chapter for more information on the impact of VOCs on air quality and the environment.)

Groups that provide indoor air quality certification for indoor furnishings and offer product databases:

— GREENGUARD: *www.greenguard.org*.

— Scientific Certification Systems (SCS): *www.scscertified.com*.

— Ensure that flat-pack furniture that needs assembly is made from fiberboard or MDF that is formaldehyde-free.

— Use natural oils or beeswax to clean, seal, and polish wood.

Carpet disposal is a major solid waste issue. Over 60 percent of the new carpet installed is replacing old carpet, amounting to about 1 billion square yards, or 3.5 billion pounds, of discarded carpet every year.

—*BuildingGreen.com*

Avoid purchasing carpets and rugs made from synthetic fibers. Instead, choose floor coverings made from natural fibers or recycled materials.

Look for carpets or floor coverings that can be recycled.

— "Environmentally Responsible Carpet Choices" is a publication provided by the Sustainable Practices and Opportunities Plan of the Pacific West Region of the U.S. National Park Service. Visit *www.nps.gov/sustain/spop/carpet.htm* for more information and a list of recycled carpet vendors or for companies that lease carpets.

— Product sample: FLOR® carpet squares by Interface Inc. are made with renewable and recyclable materials. FLOR also has an innovative return and recycle program: *www.flor.com*.

Look for the RugMark® seal when purchasing rugs and carpets to ensure that they are made without illegal child labor: www.rugmark.org.

Limit the use of plastic containers for storage. Plastic is sourced from petroleum, and many plastic storage containers are made from mixed plastic polymer sources that cannot be recycled as well as some that leach chemicals into food when heated.

For additional information about lighting, electronics, computers, inkjet cartridges, and related office supplies, see the "Energy Efficiency in the Workplace" and "Pollution Prevention" sections.

Smart Communications and Digital Workflow

Designers have never had it better in terms of efficient workflow and digital tools. Each computer is a digital hub that allows the operator to transact business without ever needing to leave his or her chair. Gone are the days of the mad dash out to postal or overnight services to get an important file or document to a client. Today we can send works faster via FTP (file transfer protocol) technology or secure digital transfer or delivery systems that offer tracking and file storage. A computer, e-mail application, and other Web technology enables most of us to use the Internet as a phone book; as a "mailbox" to send letters worldwide without actual postage or handling stickers; and as a platform to talk or collaborate with colleagues, customers, or vendors via video conference services, voice over Internet protocol (VoIP), and Web-based project management software. We use our computers to check the weather, make travel arrangements, or view a soft proof from a printer in another time zone. Of course, we can also shop or order office supplies online and make a paperless Web archive of the receipt transaction. A computer can also act as an alarm clock, an address book, a paperless fax machine, a basic stereo system, and a digital file cabinet.

Being an eco-minded designer goes beyond the paper and ink specified for clients. It also includes the everyday greening efforts and actions taken within the creative space and workflow.

All of these innovative technological functions and software applications not only save time and boost efficiency, they conserve natural resources as well. Uploading a digital file to a printer via a Web browser saves considerable resources compared to methods of the past: burning a compact disk or other type of removable storage media (metal/plastic/petroleum), labeling the media with a waterproof marker (petroleum/pigment/solvents) or a label (paper/trees and petroleum/adhesive), putting it into a padded envelope (plastic/petroleum padding or paper/trees) or a small box (paper/trees), and dropping it off at a postal office or arranging for delivery service—either method uses fossil fuel (petroleum/pollution and carbon dioxide [CO_2]

generation)—then sorting, collecting at the facility (electricity/pollution and CO_2 generation), and final delivery—plane, truck, or mail vehicle (petroleum/pollution and CO_2 generation)—to the customer. Being an eco-minded designer goes beyond the paper and ink specified for clients. It also includes the everyday greening efforts and actions taken within the creative space and workflow.

Paper Reduction Strategies

Initiate a paper reduction strategy for the workplace. Again, this is where the "eco-leader" or "green team" mentioned previously can work together to create guidelines for best (or better) practices. Look to these sources for guidance:

— "Toolkit: How to Create a Smart Paper Plan for Your Business" and the "Smart Paper Policies Are Good for Business" guides from the Natural Resources Defense Council. Visit the NRDC site to find a Paper Reduction Worksheet, Office Paper Use Questionnaire, sample paper procurement policy, and more. Learn more about how an eco-friendly paper policy can boost employee morale, be good public relations, and give your business an edge against the competition at: *www.nrdc.org/cities/living/paper/toolkit.asp.*

Expressing the idea that sustainable design is, at its root, a discipline requiring foresight and ethical responsibility, Chicago nonprofit Foresight Design Initiative expanded the definition of function for its day-to-day print needs. Each piece is designed for extra duty. A single print piece, for example, can function as a letterhead, folded card, or notepaper, depending on how it's folded or cut at the time of use.

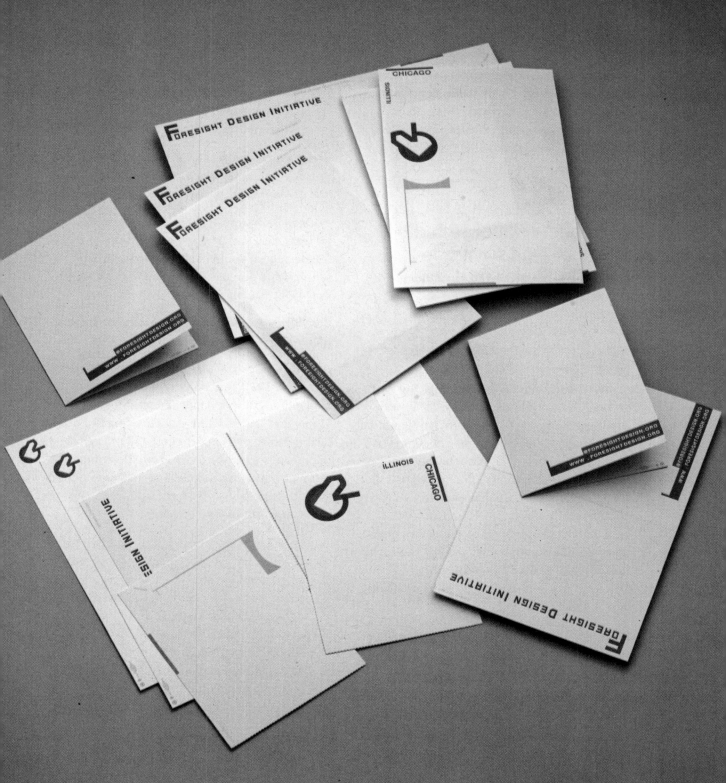

— **Purchase all-in-one electronic equipment with the most capabilities as possible.** For example, consolidate printers, scanners, fax machines, and copiers into one device and potentially reduce energy costs by a third.[21]

Each year, Americans trash enough office paper to build a twelve-foot wall from Los Angeles to New York City.

—*Clean Air Council*

— **Reduce wasted pages when printing.** The "print preview" feature found within most software applications provides a preview of how pages will look when they are printed. Look under the "File" menu to generate a review window prior to printing. Use this feature to print only pages that are needed, or use it as a guide to reformat pages for more efficient printing. Before printing, consider reducing point sizes, removing graphics, or printing multiple pages on one sheet. The "Save as PDF" feature allows for editing of unwanted pages from PDF files to create smaller files or for more controlled printing.

Resources:

— GreenPrint® provides free page saving-software to reduce wasted pages and save time and money: *www.printgreener.com.*

— "Save Paper, Save Money: 5 Free Software Downloads that Spare Your Printer" by Jaymi

Heimbuch, as posted on the Treehugger Web site. Visit *www.treehugger.com* and type the article name into the search feature to learn more about these free downloads.

Remind all employees to "think before you print." Post signs at copier machines to foster awareness and to remind employees to conserve resources.

Print on both sides of the paper and use duplexing features. Set computer and printer settings to the "duplexing" or double-sided option as default settings, and purchase replacement models with duplexing print options.

Consider digital or e-mail fax options instead of paper-based fax machines.

Provide printer-friendly pages for Web sites or archival PDFs. "Text-only" versions increase readability and save paper and resources. (Also see "Paper-free Digital Filing and Archiving" for more techniques to prevent printing at all.) Next, take the opportunity to educate viewers to incorporate resource-saving techniques into their own Web surfing. Sample ideas for further education include these tips courtesy of ecoLingo:[22]

> Please consider the environment when printing web pages. And if you absolutely must print, take these steps to save paper and to reduce waste. Try changing your print settings so that you can print more than 1 page view per paper, and click the double-side printing (duplexing) option if your printer has one. Better yet, save screen documents as web archives by using the "Print to PDF" option to save a copy to your computer. This creates a handy digital reference that requires no paper or metal filing cabinets.

Encourage paper recycling to prevent waste.
Make it easy for employees to recycle and gather scrap papers. Provide individual paper recycling bins or decorative containers at each desk that are easy to empty into larger recycling bins. Post signs with information about materials that can be recycled to encourage action and to prevent recycling contaminants from being added to the recycling containers.

Junk mail in the United States accounts for one-third of all the mail delivered in the world. Even though 44 percent of that mail goes to the landfill unopened, Americans still spend eight months of their lives dealing with it all.

—donotmail.org

Reuse scrap press sheets, paper, file folders, and envelopes into mini-notebooks and scratch pads.

Choose recycled paper to fill copiers and other printers. Every 20 cases of recycled paper purchased saves 17 trees, 390 gallons of oil, 7,000 gallons of water, and 4,100 kilowatts of energy. It also eliminates 60 pounds of air-polluting emissions and saves 8 cubic feet of landfill space.[23]

Choose the lightest-weight paper needed for the project while maintaining quality to conserve

resources, including paper shipping costs and related greenhouse emissions.

Keep address book and recipient lists up to date. Whether correspondence is posted via snail mail or e-mail, save time, energy, and resources by keeping lists up to date.

Lessen the eco-impact of direct mail advertising campaigns and learn more about the impact of direct mail advertising. Read the next list and then consider that a "designer" most likely designed or prepared these "design pieces":

— "Every person in the U.S. receives the equivalent of one and a half trees per year or approximately 560 pieces of junk mail per year."[24]

— "These days Americans get an average of 18 pieces of junk mail for every personal letter. In fact, junk mail in the United States accounts for one-third of all the mail delivered in the world. Even though 44 percent of that mail goes to the landfill unopened, we still spend eight months of our lives dealing with it all."[25]

— "More than 100 billion pieces of junk mail are delivered in the United States each year, which comes out to 848 pieces per household."[26]

— To review environmental impacts and resources of direct mail advertising and to get off direct mail advertising lists, use these resources:

— ForestEthics' campaign to support a "Do Not Mail Registry" includes resources like "The Facts about Junk Mail," plus ways to stop junk mail via the Do Not Mail campaign. Visit *www.donotmail.org* and *www.forestethics.org.*

— Read "Reducing Unsolicited Mail at Your Business," a Web guide prepared by the

California Integrated Waste Management Board: *www.ciwmb.ca.gov/BizWaste/Office Paper/MailReduce.htm.*

— The Ecological Mail Coalition can help design firms or businesses stop receiving bulk mail, catalogs, and magazines addressed to former employees: *www.ecologicalmail.org.*

— The Direct Marketing Association's Mail Preference Service or DMAchoice™ helps people manage mail, including catalogs and credit, magazine, and other mail offers. It's also possible to reduce the number of unsolicited e-mails received via the DMA-choice™ e-mail Preference Service. To learn more or register, visit *www.dmachoice.org.*

— The nonprofit organization 41pounds.org (named after the amount of junk mail a typical adult receives per year) also offers a junk mail and catalog reduction service. For more information, visit *www.41pounds.org.*

Paper-free Digital Filing and Archiving

With the advent of "Web archiving," "screen captures" and "print to PDF" options, combined with portable laptops, thumb/jump drives, and Web-based file storage, rarely do we need to print the volume of materials that we did in the past.

Save paper and physical filing cabinet space by using computers and related software to archive files.

— Digital screen captures: Using the computer keyboard to capture an image of the entire screen or part of a screen is easy: Command+Shift+3/Command+Shift+4 on a Mac, or the PrtScn ("print screen" keyboard option and save process on a PC), or use free or commercial screen capture software.

The average worker prints 10,000 pages per year and wastes 1,410 pages.

—Copy This! Results of the Citigroup-Environmental Defense Partnership to Improve Office Paper Management

---

— Product sample—TechSmith's® SnagIt software (*www.techsmith.com*) can capture specific screen regions, scrolling windows and cascading menus, and video screen and text screen captures.

— "Digital File Cabinet"—Runningman Software for PCs allows users to scan documents with a scanner and organize them into file cabinets, drawers, and folders on your computer: *www.rmsft.com.*

— PDF software or PDF distilling options can generate PDFs of desktop publishing files, photo image files, and other documents. Save these to a drive instead of printing them. This includes Web content—you can even save online receipts via the "Save PDF to web receipts folder" option. The "Printing to PDF" option preserves the original document look and format, and creates a compact, platform-independent file that is searchable and easily shared with colleagues.

- Product sample—Adobe® Acrobat. Visit *www .adobe.com* for more information about the Adobe family of software and about the integration of Postcript and PDF language formats.

- Enterprise Content Management (ECM) technology can dramatically reduce paper usage, handling, and storage by transitioning documents into digital forms that can be archived. To learn more, visit *www .ecmconnection.com.*

Digital Productivity

Become familiar with digital productivity software or applications to reduce paper usage. Time tracking software, online bookkeeping and expense tracking, digital calendars, "to-do lists," "sticky notes," and other time project management or productivity software can not only reduce paper usage, they can help anyone work smarter by improving efficiency and organizational functionality.

Virtual File Exchange, File Sharing, and Project Management

Explore virtual project management software, virtual whiteboards, digital mind-mapping software, and other virtual collaboration tools to brainstorm ideas, organize thoughts, and share ideas with colleagues and clients. Benefits include portable information that can be stored off-site and accessed from secure Web browsers while traveling.

Product Examples:

- Web-based software from 37signals includes Basecamp® (project management and collaboration), Highrise® (online contact manager and CRM), Backpack® (intranet, group calendar and organizer) and Campfire® (real-time chat for business) software. Visit *www.37signals.com.*

- LiquidPlanner offers task management, project scheduling, and team collaboration in one central place. Visit *www.liquidplanner.com* for more information.

Utilize Web-based FTP or digital file transfer services to send files and documents over the Internet instead of sending hard copy via surface delivery services.

Product Example:

- YouSendIt is an FTP replacement and e-mail attachment solution that allows users to zip and send folders securely from their desktop. Users can send up to 2 GB with resumable upload with file tracking notification. Package plans include fully branded dropboxes, multiple dropboxes, and unlimited bandwidth. See *www.yousendit.com.*

The greenest paper is no paper.

Digital Documentation and Contracts

Share documents electronically for review and edit digital copies using file actions like "track changes" or adding digital "sticky notes."

Use digital contracts, with the optional use of forms, cyber or digital signatures (via PDF or a third-party signature software) to keep documents secure, paper free, and easy to archive. Another advantage of digital paperwork is that it's easy to create paperwork with security settings and send it via e-mail or upload it via a file transfer service—the latter can track the delivery and notify senders when the file transfer has been completed.

Product Examples:

— Adobe® Acrobat®: Visit *www.adobe.com* for more information.

— Docusign® e-signature (electronic signature) services and a paper-free contract service: *www.docusign.com*.

— Echosign™ provides services to file, manage, and store documents and also offers electronic or cyber signatures: *www.echosign.com*.

Virtual Presentations and Communications

Look into virtual, Web-based technology to communicate online, host meetings, or share digital workspaces. Virtual tools save time, money, resources, and travel costs. Slide shows, live streaming video and audio, polls and surveys, screen sharing, and annotated whiteboards are just some of the features available in Web conference applications.

Product Examples:

— Adobe® Acrobat® Connect™: *www.adobe.com*

— GoToMeeting®: *www.gotomeeting.com*

— Microsoft® Sharepoint: *www.microsoft.com*

— Skype™: *www.skype.com*

— WebEx: *www.webex.com*

Consider screen-sharing technology to review comps and drafts with clients. For screen sharing tips[27] visit the CreativePro.com Web site and type "screen sharing" in the search feature.

Smart Design and Production

Utilize design and production methods and tools that enhance productivity, increase speed and efficiency, and reduce file size and versions. While designers can choose from different options of industry standard design software, look for software and program applications that do these things and also seamlessly work together. This saves time sorting and managing files, reduces physical (or virtual) storage space, and decreases time and energy needed to manipulate and transfer files (via uploads, etc). For example, some graphic design software workflows can utilize native image files or link directly to original images for edits within the file being worked on rather than requiring users to "click out" and return to other file creation applications and back again.

Use commercial software to easily store, sort, and adjust photographs for streamlined access for design projects.

Use pre-press and pre-flighting software to save time, avoid pre-press glitches, and reduce proofs generated from files that contain mistakes and errors.

— Acrobat® PDF X/-1a[28] format is currently the gold standard for delivering reliable and efficient press-ready files. This format prevents font issues, wrong color spaces, missing images, and over-printing or trapping issues since the fonts are embedded in the file and colors must be encoded as CMYK or Spot, trapped or not trapped. To learn more about it and other PDF X formats see the Adobe® Web site: *www.adobe.com*.

Liaise with print vendors to obtain color printing profiles or Acrobat® Distiller settings for best color results and to avoid costly proofs and reprints.

Consider using digital PDF "soft-proof" options for proofing to save paper. Preview soft proofs to confirm separations, overprints, transparency, and color assignments.

Use less intensive pre-press technology. Computer to plate (CtP), Direct Imaging (DI) chemical-free plates, and digital presses reduce film and chemical usage.

Factor in parent sheet sizes when determining layout and sizes of documents to reduce paper waste and trim size. Work backward from available envelope sizes to ensure that final document sizes fit stock envelopes. Gang projects on press to maximize resources.

Match scale to content, and choose the best medium to deliver the design message. For example, an e-mail can take the place of a postcard, a postcard can take the place of a brochure, and so on.

Use digital photography as part of the graphic design workflow to reduce both chemical processing and paper waste.

Consult with print vendors to determine which printing technology will suit the project best with the minimal environmental impact.

Respect resourceful design over artful excess. Avoid bleeds that create trim waste, and refrain from spreading design content to additional pages, folds, or signatures that are not needed. Consumers are increasingly aware and discerning about appropriate paper usage.

Digital Correspondence

Utilize electronic mail services and electronic correspondence, but in a smart and sustainable way. Many people are under the impression that paperless letters via e-mail are eco-friendly. While it is true that valuable paper resources and the pollution derived from the papermaking process is prevented with paperless correspondence, digital correspondence is still energy intensive.

Use "opt-in" e-newsletter services to provide recipients with the option to unsubscribe from missives and publications. And remember, no matter what you call it, even in the name of paperless communication, unsolicited bulk e-mail or SPAM is unwanted, annoying, and costs the Earth in terms of energy usage, pollution, and wasted productivity.

Energy Efficiency in the Workplace

Electricity is a precious resource, yet it is often taken for granted. We flick the switch and bring power and life to appliances and computers in a seemingly magical and effortless way. Flick the switch or press the button to "off," and the magic current stops, or so we think. In this section, we look more closely at "vampire" or "phantom energy." But first let's take a closer look at electricity in general to set the tone. Conservation and smart usage of this energy resource is an important part of any workflow.

Electrical energy can be generated from a variety of sources, including renewable sources such as solar, wind, and hydropower. However, much of the electricity in countries around the world is still largely based on energy derived or converted from limited or finite energy sources, including coal and other fossil fuels. Naturally, these methods of generating electricity also impact the Earth on another level: pollution. According to the Natural Resources Defense Council's "Global Warming Basics" article posted on its Web site: "Coal-burning power plants are the largest U.S. source of carbon dioxide pollution—they produce 2.5 billion tons every year."[29]

An Energy Dilemma

Electricity generated mainly by polluting, coal-burning power plants is used to power the nation's data centers and servers. Data centers are home to the electronic equipment, servers, switches, routers, and data storage devices that store, manage, process, and exchange digital data and information.[30] It is these data centers, or server farms, that keep Web-based software, services, and data flowing via the Internet. Think of all the Internet searches and Web sites, downloads, smart phone Internet services, and e-mail, all moving through cyberspace.

According to the EPA, it is estimated that approximately 61 billion kilowatt-hours (kWh) were consumed in 2006 for data server consumption—a total electricity cost of $4.5 billion. This estimate also indicates that energy usage from data centers has more than doubled since 2000. Furthermore, forecasts indicate that national energy consumption for this purpose could nearly double again in another five years (2011), to more than 100 billion kWh. In terms of annual electricity cost, this represents an estimated $7.4 billion.[31]

Other forecasts point to the dilemma posed by this unchecked growth for energy and power. We only have to look over our shoulder to remember the recent power grid failures on both the East and West coasts. Some experts recommend that we focus on alternatives to coal and natural gas, renewable energy, and nuclear power and to look to the "fifth fuel": efficiency.[32] Other experts contend that data

servers are not the issue but that energy consumption is much closer to home (or office): Leaving computers on overnight and power-hungry "standby mode" products that continue to consume energy even while electronics are turned off collectively use vast amounts of energy every day.

While companies are searching for innovative ways to increase data server energy efficiency or use alternative energy to power data centers, anyone can take part in reducing electricity-based workloads.

Electricity Usage and Electronics

Modern technology, information technology (IT), data servers, and electronic devices and gadgets all place an increased demand for electricity, and each person's creative or work area plays a role. For example, today's designers rely on computers to power most of their designs and digital workflows. Computers in general use more energy than all office equipment combined.[33] They and other office equipment and other powered machines, including printers, fax machines, and photocopiers, are the fastest-growing users of energy in the business world, accounting for 7 to 15 percent of all electrical energy used in offices.[34] This figure is expected to double to 30 percent by 2020.[35]

The irony is that every day, part of this valuable energy in the form of electricity is wasted: Power is drawn when it is not needed, or power is leaked or sucked away in the form of "vampire" or "phantom" energy. Many electrical appliances and electronics that use "standby power" or have power adapters, and "power brick" or "wall wart" power supply devices continue to draw current while they are plugged in, even if the gadget or appliance is turned off. In the average home, 75 percent of the electricity used to power home electronics is consumed while the products are turned off.[36] Additional studies have shown that standby power or vampire power consumes between 5 and 25 percent of a typical household's annual electric bill, adding up to billions of dollars per annum around the world.[37] For example: A laptop computer or cell phone charger is likely to use less energy to charge the electronics than the energy consumed while the charger is left unused but plugged in low power mode.[38]

In addition to standby power, we waste electricity by letting our computers run without power management settings activated or by neglecting to turn them off at night. A Lawrence Berkeley Lab study from 1999 estimated that

> one workstation (computer and monitor) left on after business hours is responsible for power plants emitting nearly one ton of CO_2 per year. That could be cut by 80 percent if the workstation is switched off at night and is set to go to "sleep" during idle periods in the day. If every US computer and monitor were turned off at night, the nation could shut down eight large power stations and avoid emitting 7 million tons of CO_2 every year.[39]

A decade later, it seems that we still haven't wised up. A recent study suggests that PCs worldwide consume around 80 billion kWh of electricity per year, and as much as two-thirds of that electricity is wasted[40]—again due to lack of power management as well as leaving computers on when they are not needed. It's not enough to power down; you need to unplug as well.

Power down computers and office equipment when not in use—especially overnight. A typical PC

> ### Screen savers are not energy savers. Using a screen saver may in fact use more energy than not using one, and the power-down feature may not work if a screen saver is activated.
>
> —*U.S. Department of Energy*

operating nine hours a day will use only 38 percent of the power consumed by a computer operating twenty-four hours a day.[41]

Prevent phantom loads—unplug appliances, computers, and electronics when they are not in use. Plug cords and adapters into a power strip that has an "on" and "off" feature, then simply turn off the switch to cut the all power to the strip and related equipment. Purchase a "smart" power strip that senses power use and auto-switches devices on or off.

Power Management

Power management features are standard in Windows and Macintosh computer operating systems. Note, however, that these features require manual setup. It only takes a couple of mouse clicks to activate the energy-saving features that place monitor, computer, and hard drive into a low-power "sleep mode" after a designated time of inactivity. A computer that actively uses power management burns half the energy of a computer without power management,[42] keeps equipment running cooler, and prolongs the life of equipment, especially monitors and laptop batteries.[43]

Power management features reduce energy better than screen savers. Screen savers are not energy savers. Using a screen saver may in fact use more energy than not using one, and the power-down feature may not work if a screen saver is activated. In fact, modern liquid crystal diode (LCD) color monitors do not need screen savers at all.[44]

Use power management features on computers and electronics to save energy and reduce global warming emissions.

— ENERGY STAR (*www.energystar.gov*) provides power management overviews, calculators, tools, product guides, and activation instructions for both individual computer users and organizations with IT managers.

— The Climate Savers Computing Initiative brings together consumers, manufacturers, system buyers, and environmental and consumer organizations. The nonprofit organization offers information on how to slow climate change with computers, provides power management energy-saving calculators, and offers a "smarter computing catalog." For more information, visit *www.climatesaverscomputing.org.*

Look for energy-efficient electronics, computer hardware, lighting, appliances, and other electrical goods. These can easily be identified by certified eco-labeling programs, such as ENERGY STAR. In order to earn the ENERGY STAR label, products must meet strict efficiency guidelines set by the U.S. Environmental Protection Agency and the U.S. Department of Energy. According to the ENERGY STAR

Web site: "If all computers sold in the United States meet the ENERGY STAR requirements, the savings in energy costs will grow to about $2 billion each year and greenhouse gas emissions will be reduced by the equivalent of those from 2 million cars."[45]

— Visit *www.energystar.gov* for more information and to find qualified office equipment, including computers, printers, scanners, fax machines, and monitors.

An **ENERGY STAR** computer uses **70 percent less electricity** than computers without this designation. If left inactive, **ENERGY STAR** computers enter a low-power mode and use 15 watts or less.

—ENERGY STAR

Prolong the life of monitors by turning them off completely at night, on weekends, or if they will go unused for two hours. For more information on how to buy an energy-efficient monitor, visit the U.S. Department of Energy's Federal Energy Management Program (FEMP) energy-efficient products Web site: *www1.eere.energy.gov/femp.*[46]

Measure and monitor the energy consumption of electronics and other household appliances.

— For example, "Kill A Watt™" is a small device that measures energy consumption the same way a local utility does, by the kilowatt-hour. Visit *www.p3international.com* for more information.

Compare the amount of energy used with others and gain tools to reduce consumption.

— WattzOn is a free online tool to help quantify, track, and compare energy usage and to reduce power consumption footprint: *www.wattzon.com*.

Replace single use batteries with rechargeable batteries for gadgets, remote controllers, and cordless computer mice.

Consider using a solar or kinetic charger for small electronics or laptops.

— Solio (*www.solio.com*) offers a hybrid charger that works with multiple gadgets, including mobile phones, digital cameras, global positioning systems, and the like.

— For laptops, try the "Voltaic Messenger" — a messenger bag that charges laptops and handheld appliances (*www.voltaicsystems.com*).

Switch to clean, renewable energy or offset energy use. Naturally, you can reduce your business's reliance on electricity partially or altogether if you add clean or renewable energy to the energy mix. In addition, purchasing carbon offsets reduces eco footprints and helps to provide capital to build new renewable energy projects.

Explore options for purchasing renewable energy or "green power" (solar, wind, geothermal, biomass, etc.) from local utilities providers.

Research the availability and options of installing solar panels or wind turbines for office buildings or home-based studios.

Eco-Conscious Web Sites

Choose Web-hosting companies wisely. Some Web hosts use renewable energy to help meet their high energy demands in a more farsighted way. Also, many are committed to improving data center energy efficiency via new technology or more efficient equipment and innovative cooling systems, or by installing shade structures or green roofs to reduce server cooling costs. It is becoming more common for hosting companies to purchase carbon offsets or renewable energy credits (RECs) to offset their conventional energy usage. Ask potential Web hosts for details about their environmental initiatives and carbon offset providers to ensure that they purchase from verified providers. Hosting and business operations can be carbon offset directly by the business alone, without having to wait for vendors to "see the light."

— Clean Air-Cool Planet provides "A Consumers Guide to Retail Carbon Offset Providers." Visit *www.cleanair-coolplanet.org* for more information.

Look into ways to reduce a Web site's total energy consumption, especially if it is a high-traffic site. Suggestions include using black backgrounds to reduce the number of kilowatts required to view sites[47] and to reduce repeating, animated advertisements and banners in order to reduce power drawn by moving images on the Internet.[48] However scientific data has not confirmed that these methods are effective, especially for computer users who have LCD monitors and displays rather than older cathode ray tube (CRT) monitors.[49] One tradeoff with black or dark gray Web pages is poor readability in some conditions; taking longer to read the page may negate energy savings.

Others suggest designing and programming Web sites to load pages quickly and to use the most efficient file size needed to convey the information most effectively with the least amount of power. Again, this method is not confirmed at this stage, and others disagree, thinking that intense multimedia content in Web sites serves their function best—to encourage viewers to visit and spend time on the site. Perhaps the most practical thing to do goes back to smart monitor and computer use in the first place: Decrease the brightness setting on each monitor/display, use sleep mode and power management settings, and power down. Turning off the monitor, computer, and other peripherals and electronics—including the power strips and adapters each night—is the best and smartest way to save computer energy usage.

— CO2Stats, *www.co2stats.com*, offers opportunities to make Web sites carbon neutral without changing Web hosts. CO2Stats software and coding monitors a Web site's energy usage, provides tips on how make to the site more energy efficient, and automatically calculates and purchases the appropriate amount of audited renewable energy credits. Information can be gained about the make and model of the computer the visitor is using to view a site and what its electrical usage is, the type and quantity of energy the host server uses, as well as the related networks that connect visitors' computers with host servers.

Lighting

Electricity costs for lighting accounts for 30 to 50 percent of the electric bill for a typical business. Again, much of this energy usage and cost can be prevented by adopting smart usage policies and switching to energy-efficient lighting systems. Design or photography studios in particular often use halogen-based task lighting, spot lighting, or track lighting to display photos, artwork, or projects, yet these bulbs are more expensive to operate and produce heat, which in turn can increase cooling costs.

Replace incandescent light bulbs and halogens (where appropriate—consult with an electrician if needed) with energy-efficient compact fluorescents or light emitting diodes (LEDs) to provide energy savings and reduce maintenance costs.

Use timers or computerized sensors to reduce wasted electricity. For example, occupancy sensors can detect lighting requirements in conference rooms or little-used rooms such as storage rooms or closets.

Make use of natural lighting.

Contact local utility companies to gain more information about both manual and computerized lighting control options and strategies for businesses.

Heating and Cooling

Whether you work in a home-based studio or in a large office building, there are numerous tips and resources available to help any business save energy on heating and cooling costs. Installing ENERGY STAR qualified equipment and programmable thermostats can save money; the latter can save up to 15 percent on heating and cooling costs.[50] Ceiling fans, blinds or shades, or caulking or sealing windows and doors can all save energy and increase worker comfort. Perhaps the best place to start is to consult with a skilled contractor to look for leaks and drafts or to get an energy audit to provide specific information and recommendations to improve energy efficiency.

The "Green Buildings and Interiors" section of this chapter has more information on saving electricity, energy, and resources.

Carbon Offsets

Purchasing carbon offsets or renewable energy credits (RECs) is another option available to help reduce the impact of global warming pollution generated by a home or business. This includes energy usage, carbon emissions from commuting and travel, and much more. Although some people oppose offsets as a means of counterbalancing global warming, it is important to keep in mind that offsets purchased from reputable providers also help provide capital to finance clean, renewable energy projects. Note, though, that not all offsets are the same, nor are they regulated at this time. Look for Web hosts that purchase carbon offsets from providers that meet criteria for "transparency," "additionality," and other industry-specific benchmarks, including the use of third-party verification and certification.

Purchase carbon offsets or renewable energy credits (RECs) to offset electricity or power use.

Resources:

— Clean Air-Cool Planet provides "A Consumers Guide to Retail Carbon Offset Providers." Visit *www.cleanair-coolplanet.org* for more information.

— NativeEnergy: Carbon offsets for individuals and businesses, lifestyle, travel and event

calculators and education via the Web site: *www.nativeenergy.com.*

— Bonneville Environmental Fund (BEF): "Green Tags" or BEF carbon offsets for business, home, event, travel, building or ski trip: *www.b-e-f.org/renewables.*

— TerraPass: Carbon offset calculator and carbon offsets for individuals or businesses, including driving, flying, home energy, wedding, conference or event offsets: *www.terrapass.com.*

Energy Audits, Energy Savings Calculators, and Office Carbon Footprint Tools

Obtain an energy audit for a design studio space or a business workplace based on LEED™, ENERGY STAR, and ASHRAE (American Society of Heating, Refrigerating and Air-Conditioning Engineers) standards. An audit will assess energy usage, show problem areas (such as air leaks, heat loss, and insulation and ventilation issues), and reveal ways to conserve energy or resources that can provide significant savings over time.

Use energy savings calculators or office carbon footprint tools to make informed energy decisions and to discover ways to reduce energy.

— ENERGY STAR provides resources and energy savings calculators that cover a variety of appliances and electronics, as well as thermostats, light fixtures, commercial heating and cooling products, and much more. Visit the ENERGY STAR Web site for more information: *www.energystar.gov.*

— The EPA provides an "office carbon footprint tool" designed to assist offices in making decisions on how to reduce greenhouse gas emissions associated with their activities. Visit *www.epa.gov* and type "office carbon footprint" in the search feature to locate the Microsoft® Excel® spreadsheet.

— "Working 9 to 5 on Climate Change: An Office Guide" by the World Resources Institute provides calculation tools and offers office-based organizations practical steps to measure and reduce CO_2 emissions. Visit *www.wri.org* for additional details.

— David Suzuki's "Nature Challenge at Work" is an easy to use tool kit in PDF format that contains fun activities to inspire workers, customers, and suppliers to green their lives. Visit *www.davidsuzuki.org* and search "nature challenge at work." The site contains a myriad of environmental information and resources.

Ecological Footprint Tools

"How many planets does it take to support your lifestyle?" asks the first question in the online quiz as part of the Earth Day Network's Footprint Calculator. It is one of the many environmental footprint calculators available to help measure and compare how much land and water (or how much of the biological capacity of the Earth's resources) is required to support consumption choices.

Other footprint tools are available to measure how your electrical energy consumption (including appliance usage) or carbon footprint affects the planet. Although footprint tools typically are aimed more at personal or household consumption rather than business use, they contain impacts related to work environments and cover diet and public transportation or commuting. Footprint tools are valuable ways to bring awareness of energy conservation into the workplace or to open dialogues and conversations with workers, colleagues, and customers. Footprint tools can also help businesses predict market trends goal setting for strategic action.

Calculate your ecological footprint to help you gain information and resources to live and work more sustainably.

— Earth Day Network Footprint Calculator: *www.earthday.net*

— Global Footprint Network: *www.footprintnetwork.org*

— The Bonneville Environmental Foundation (BEF) provides a "Shrink Your Foot" carbon calculator: *www.b-e-f.org.*

— Act on CO_2 Calculator: Although this calculator is UK based, it provides educational content and a personalized action plan (including information about appliances) with recommendations about how you can help tackle climate change. Visit *http://actonco2.direct.gov.uk/index.html.*

— The World Wildlife Foundation Footprint Calculator in association with *The Independent* (UK) offers a tool that incorporates "Stuff" into the calculations. Items under the "Stuff" category includes electronics, jewelry, and pet care. Visit *http://footprint.wwf.org.uk* for more information.

— Carbon offset providers also provide carbon footprints calculators—see the "Carbon Offset" section for more details.

Speaking of "Stuff"...

No discussion about energy impacts, footprints, and consumption would be complete without taking a closer look at how the production, sale, and disposal of material goods and "stuff" impact the planet and global communities. Consider the fact that most "stuff" is made or packaged by a designer at some point (whether it is by an industrial designer, a package designer, a graphic designer, or other). It is highly recommended, therefore, that designers and design teams become familiar with the impacts of production and consumption. A review of the "Systems Thinking" chapter of this book is invaluable in understanding these impacts. In addition, add the next resource to your library, and consider it a required element for any professional development or training curriculum.

Resource:

— An educational and thought provoking video, *The Story of Stuff,* is a twenty-minute, fast-paced, fact-filled, Web-based look at the underside of our production and consumption patterns. *www.storyofstuff.com.*

Pollution Prevention and End of Life

E-waste and Technotrash

Most people might expect a section dedicated to office/design studio recycling and waste management to begin with paper or toner cartridge recycling. First, however, let's start with some of the most important tools used for business and design: office electronics. Computers and most other digital visual communication tools and gadgets—monitors, phones, hard drives, laptops with LCD displays,

printers, and even cables and cords—contain a variety of valuable metals and trace elements as well as a slew of toxic materials and components. When these types of electronics reach the end of their useful life or are discarded, they are called electronic waste, or e-waste.

E-waste is the fastest-growing stream of municipal waste not only in North America but worldwide.

—Natural Resources Defense Council

The average life span of computers, printers, audio equipment, and mobile phones has dropped significantly in just two years.[51] This fact, combined with the surge in sales in new electronics and consumables, contributes to our growing mountains of e-waste. It is now commonly accepted that e-waste is the fastest-growing stream of municipal waste worldwide. Allen Hershkowitz, a senior scientist and authority on waste management at the Natural Resources Defense Council, stated on CBS's *60 Minutes*: "We throw out about 130,000 computers every day in the United States."[52] Hershkowitz also said that over 100 million cell phones are thrown out annually.

Hazardous Waste

Many consider e-waste to be "hazardous waste," as many electronics contain mercury, lead, cadmium, PCB (polychlorinated biphenyl), PVC (polyvinyl chloride) and other hazardous materials. These electronic components pose enormous health risks, hazards, and social justice issues for the people who are exposed to them when the items are dismantled for precious metal recovery, a task undertaken mostly by people in developing nations. (Note: It has been documented that up to 80 percent of e-waste is illegally shipped to Asia,[53] with most of that ending up in China. Laborers, including child workers who have developed lead poisoning as a result, dismantle the e-waste by hand.)[54] Other environmental and health concerns include issues arising when toxic chemicals are leached into waterways from landfills or illegal dumpsites, and the release of toxic furans and dioxins that can occur when e-waste components are burned to release the metals for extraction or are incinerated as part of waste disposal.[55] When e-waste is incinerated, the opportunity to recover valuable metals and minerals, such as gold, silver, palladium, platinum, and copper used in the manufacturing of the electronic product is lost. Cell phones alone contain about a dollar's worth of precious metals each, mainly gold.[56]

Techno Trash

Even if computers and related hardware and software are used in a mindful paperless or virtual workflow, it's likely that businesses still generate "cyber trash" or "techno trash" from their activities. Hard drives or digital files burned to disks—CDs, DVDs, or other removable electronic media storage disks—become part of techno trash, as do the myriad of spent supplies such as printer cartridges, and a variety of computer accessories, including digital cameras, MP3 players, cables, cords, boards, and chips. Again, it is imperative that these items are recycled or disposed of properly and that each person looks for ways to reduce this type of trash.

For example: Consider the ink cartridge used in printers, fax machines, or copiers. According to Earth911.com's Web site, over 13 cartridges are disposed of in an American trash can every second, totaling an estimated 375 million each year.

> The average toner cartridge is composed of 40 percent plastic, 40 percent metal and smaller amounts of rubber, paper, foam and toner. The plastic takes at least 1,000 years to decompose and is mixed resin, one of the most difficult plastics to recycle. The average cartridge also requires almost a gallon of oil in its production.[57]

Yet the potential to reduce waste and retrieve and remanufacture ink cartridges is great, as up to 97 percent of the cartridge components can be reused. Remanufactured toner cartridges also cost less, conserve resources, and save energy.[58] Naturally, the best way to conserve is to reduce consumption and waste.

Making Responsible Choices

Computer users around the world want it all. They want the latest, sleekest, fastest, coolest gadget, capable of high storage capacity and memory, and at the same time they lament that electronics and software are "obsolete out of the box." This issue hits close to home for graphic designers and their print vendors, who are encouraged to update computer operating systems and design software programs on a regular basis. Granted, while many of these upgrades offer improvement to workflow, speed, and productivity, it could be argued that the time spent on frequent software upgrades with related program learning curves and the transferring of files to new computers, hard drives, or servers takes valuable time and energy, as does locating reputable recycling services for old equipment.

There is yet another factor to be mindful of: the "true cost" of electronics (and indeed most things you can purchase these days). In order to keep prices low and to encourage consumption, in the past manufacturers did have not include the true, big-picture cost in the price tag, one that includes the costs of mining and eventual depletion of the Earth's finite supply of resources, the disposal and environmental impact of e-waste, and the health or well-being of workers who assemble or disassemble the components and equipment. Furthermore, it's a strange world indeed when it costs people extra to recycle or return electronics for recycling, or when it "costs less" to throw something away than it does to collect, recycle, or remanufacture the item, as is particularly the case with many portable electronic gadgets. It is not too hard to see how shortsighted the status quo is, using materials that contain toxic compounds without providing resource recovery and end-of-life protocols. Fortunately, change is on the horizon. The European Community is making strides in this area, with the creation of directives and laws to address the disposal of e-waste and the restriction of hazardous substances in electrical and electronic equipment. Directive 2002/96/EC includes collection strategies and schemes allowing buyers to return their used e-waste free of charge. The directive also sets targets for e-waste treatment and for safer substitutes and alternatives for heavy metals and toxic flame retardants.[59] Although this is not yet legislated in all markets (including the United States at this time), electronics manufacturers are taking note and complying.

Until legislation shapes and changes the electronics industry, individuals play an important role in making informed choices and eco-conscious

Individuals play an important role in making informed choices and eco-conscious decisions about the electronics they use in their workflow.

decisions about the electronics they use in their workflow.

Steps to Reduce E-waste

Before upgrading or making a new electronics purchase, carefully consider if it is necessary. This also applies to new design, illustration, and photography software upgrades. Consult with printers, colleagues, vendors, and clients to determine the best timeline to upgrade software to stay in sync and have compatible workflows for file prep and pre-press.

When purchasing printers, copiers, and fax machines, take environmental attributes into account, including research into consumables. Inkjet cartridges, toners, or other ink systems will need to be replaced, refilled, remanufactured, or recycled during a printer's life span. Eco-impacts can be reduced by purchasing hardware or supplies from manufacturers that provide products that get great ink "mileage," offer recycling or take-back options, or have models that accept refillable or remanufactured ink cartridges. (An alternative option is to consider printers that use compact and cartridge-free solid ink sticks—they save storage space and reduce packaging waste.)

— Earth911.com's Web site is the go-to environmental resource for reduction, reuse, and recycling information. Categories include paper, metal, hazardous, plastics, glass, electronics, automotive, household, garden, and construction. Visit *www.earth911.com* for more information and to find local recycling services.

Support companies that make greener electronics. For example, choose EPEAT®-registered products that are compliant with international directives, including the European Union's Waste Electrical and Electronic Equipment (WEEE) and Restriction of Hazardous Substance (RoHS) directives.

— EPEAT (Electronic Product Environment Assessment Tool) helps consumers evaluate, compare, and select desktop computers, notebooks, and monitors based on their environmental attributes. For more information and a registry of products meeting verified IEEE 1680 criteria, visit *www.epeat.net*.

— Greenpeace provides an electronic "report card." The "Guide to Greener Electronics" provides rankings of top electronic manufacturers based on their policies on toxic chemicals, recycling, and climate change. Go to *www.greenpeace.org* and type in "Guide to Greener Electronics" in the search feature.

— ClimateCounts provides the "ClimateCounts Company Scorecard" comparing companies on their commitment to stop climate change. The scorecard includes an electronic sector as well as an Internet/software sector. See *www.climatecounts.org* for more details.

Select computer hardware based on manufacturer recycling and take-back policies. Again, this is part of EPEAT's criteria under "Design for end of life" and "End of life management."

— The Electronics Take-Back Coalition provides a report that lists the type of take-back programs electronic manufacturers provide. Visit *www.computertakeback.com* for more information.

Choose reputable e-waste and techno trash recycling providers.

— E-stewards (The Basel Action Network and Electronics Take-Back Coalition) have partnered to create rigorous criteria and certification standards to identify recyclers or "e-stewards" that maintain standards of environmental and social responsibility. For more information, visit *www.e-stewards.org*.

— The National Resources Defense Council provides a helpful guide about e-waste and includes resources to help keep electronics out of landfills: *www.nrdc.org*.

Other Hazardous Waste

Carefully dispose of paint, photographic chemicals, compact fluorescent lightbulbs, batteries, solvent-based household cleaners, aerosol and spray fixatives, and other hazardous materials.

The listed products are examples of common hazardous household waste (HHW) that require proper storage and disposal.

— Check your city or state HHW collection service to find out about collection events or services, or find local resources in the United States quickly and easily by visiting *www.earth911.com* and typing in the target ZIP code.

— Choose rechargeable batteries over single-use batteries and see that they are responsibly recycled at their end of life. For more information, contact the Rechargeable Battery Recycling Corporation: *www.rbrc.org*.

Once you know better you must do better.

Waste Audits

A waste audit is an important and valuable step to undertake when developing any recycling plan or program. Waste audits can provide insights into the type of waste generated and also can provide strategies as to how to RRR (reduce, reuse, recycle) the amount of waste generated.

Complete a waste audit to provide insight into the type of waste generated and to develop strategies to prevent waste and conserve resources.

Sample forms and interactive waste audit tools are available online: *www.wasteaudittool.com* and *www.dep.state.pa.us/dep/deputate/airwaste/wm/ recycle/FACTS/ComRec.htm*.

Recycling Tips

Check with local city or state recycling collection services to find out about accepted materials for recycling and collection dates or services. Local resources in the United States can be found quickly and easily by visiting *www.earth911.com* and typing in the target ZIP code.

Establish an office recycling or solid waste reduction program based on research from links provided in this book. Items to be recycled may include paper, paperboard, toner cartridges, glass, plastics, cans and metals, appliances and durable goods, techno trash, e-waste, and hazardous waste (electronics, monitors, televisions, batteries, paint, aerosol fixatives or adhesives, mercury-containing compact fluorescent lightbulbs, etc.).

Note: If recycling services are not available through regular channels, partner with other groups to share recycling options or services. In addition, several recycling companies provide mail-in services or on-site drop box options for batteries, inkjet cartridges, and small electronics.

Post information and signs about accepted recycling content next to bins to encourage recycling and to reduce contaminants. See the next item.

Keep recycling bins free from contaminants. Explain to coworkers the importance of keeping recycling containers free of contaminants (e.g., chewing gum, food waste, paper napkins/paper towels/tissues, waxed paper, metallic wrapping paper and gift tissue paper, pizza boxes, aluminum foil, plastics, paper clips, sticky notes or hardcover books). Note: Staples are not considered a contaminant;[60] in many markets, however, check with your local recycling service.

Keep paper clips out of the waste bin, and avoid purchasing and using coated clips. These may pose recycling or end-of-life issues, as many brightly coated paper clips are covered with vinyl or plastics.

A paper clip tidbit: These little marvels made out of shaped, recycled steel often wind up in the trash, yet steel is 100 percent recyclable and can be recycled over and over again without losing quality (in areas that accept paper clips with steel cans for recycling).

Provide all employees with small recycling bins or decorative containers to put waste and scrap paper into while they work. These small containers can then be dumped into a central paper-recycling container at the end of the day or workweek.

Americans throw away enough plastic bottles each year to circle the Earth four times.

—Clean Air Council

Recycle glass. Bottles, jars, and other glass containers for products can be recycled in most facilities. Inquire about the ability to recycle glass from durable goods as well, such as glass found in furniture, appliances, and even new laptop displays.

Recycle cans and metal. Steel cans often contain 25 percent recycled content and are completely recyclable where facilities exist.

Learn about plastic content and recycling symbols to sort for recycling and to guide your product packaging purchases. Every hour, we throw away 2.5 million plastic bottles or (22 billion plastic bottles per year),[61] yet these bottles can easily be recycled or "upcycled" into other items, including clothing. It is estimated that it takes twenty-six recycled polyethylene terephthalate (PET) bottles to make a polyester suit and five recycled PET bottles to make enough fiberfill to stuff a ski jacket.[62] This

Web site has information about plastic polymers/resins and related plastic symbols: *www.earth odyssey.com/symbols.html.*

Recycle overhead transparencies. Here's a little-known fact: Overhead transparencies made by 3M can be returned to the company for recycling. Simply ship used 3M transparencies (no paper) to 3M's recycling partner (a polyester recovery company). Visit *www.3m.com* to download a shipping label.[63]

Healthier, More Sustainable Work Environments

The buildings where we meet, work, and learn play a key role in human health and well-being. According to the *American Time Use Survey*, employed persons worked 7.6 hours on average on the days they worked in 2007, with 87 percent of people doing some or all of their work at a workplace.[64]

Hence, nearly a third of our lives are spent at work in buildings (yes, to some no doubt it feels like more!). A healthy work environment boosts wellness, morale, and productivity. We've all heard of sick building syndrome (SBS) or building-related illness (BRI), and the role of poor ventilation and chemical compounds or contaminants on workers' health and job-related stress. (The term "BRI" is used when symptoms of diagnosable illness are identified and can be attributed directly to airborne building contaminants.)[65]

Air Quality and Indoor Pollution

Numerous studies show that the air quality within homes and buildings can be considerably more polluted than the air outdoors. Exposure to environmental tobacco smoke, biological contaminants, household chemicals, and solvents in paints, varnishes, pesticides, and cleaning and disinfecting products all contribute to air quality issues and pose health risks. [66] Even our work attire and wardrobe can impact our health and the environment if clothes are dry-cleaned by a cleaner that uses perchloroethlylene. [67]

Another source of indoor air pollution is formaldehyde. It is mentioned specifically here since it is often found in building materials and pressed-wood products for common office furniture such as cabinets, shelving units, drawer fronts, and furniture tops. Medium-density fiberboard (MDF) typically emits the most formaldehyde, as it is comprised of wood chips bound with adhesives that contain urea-formaldehyde (UF). MDF has a high ratio of adhesives or resin to wood and can release formaldehyde over time. Other formaldehyde-emitting products are flooring and carpets (again, due to the adhesives used in installation or the manufacturing process for laminated or engineered wood planks, carpets, and vinyl flooring).

Other common air pollutants that most people have more control over is the choice of paints used in their workplace. Paint formulations, preservatives, biocides (to prevent mold or mildew growth), and even the pigments used to color paints can contain harmful chemicals and VOCs (volatile organic compounds). Given their volatile nature, VOCs off-gas during application and create various problems after exposure.

VOCs have been linked to a variety of health problems, including nausea, dizziness, heart and lung damage, and even cancer. [68]

Look for natural, water-based, and other paint formulations that are certified and meet stringent VOC standards. Remember to use appropriate storage and disposal methods for all paints and cleanup materials.

Groups that provide indoor air quality certification for paints and coatings and offer product databases include:

— GREENGUARD: *www.greenguard.org*

— Green Seal: *www.greenseal.org*

— Scientific Certification Systems (SCS): *www .scscertified.com*

To learn more about indoor air quality issues and sources of indoor air pollution, access the statement by the Consumer Product Safety Commission and Environmental Protection Agency: "The Inside Story: A Guide to Indoor Air Quality." Visit *www.cpsc.gov* for more details and to view other safety guides.

Impacts of Building Construction

Naturally, in addition to health issues, office buildings and the related sourcing and manufacturing of building materials, the construction and deconstruction process, and materials and energy used in construction also impact the environment on many levels. In the United States, buildings use one-third of our total energy, two-thirds of our electricity, and one-eighth of our water, and transform land that provides valuable ecological resources. [69]

Looking at global impact, 40 percent of the world's materials and energy are used by buildings, and 55 percent of the wood cut for nonfuel uses is for construction, as reported by Worldwatch Institute in 1995. [70] Furthermore, buildings account for one-sixth of the world's fresh water withdrawals and two-fifths of its material and energy flows. [71]

For example, commercial buildings use close to 20 percent of U.S. drinking water supplies. Reducing total commercial building water consumption by just 10 percent would mean saving well over 2 trillion gallons of water each year.[72]

Reducing total commercial building water consumption by just 10 percent would mean saving well over 2 trillion gallons of water each year.

—ENERGY STAR

These and other studies reflect the need to make buildings healthier and more sustainable. The surge in "green" building design and the interest and commitment to sustainability has led to an expanding green building movement.

Green Buildings and Interiors

The EPA defines "green building" or "sustainable building" as the practice of

> increasing the efficiency with which buildings and their sites use and harvest energy, water, and materials; and protecting and restoring human health and the environment, throughout the building life-cycle: siting, design, construction, operation, maintenance, renovation and deconstruction.[73]

LEED®, the Leadership in Energy and Environmental Design Green Building Rating System,™ is a third-party certification program and the nationally recognized benchmark for the design, construction, and operation of high-performance green buildings.[74]

A sustainable building maximizes operational efficiency while minimizing environmental impacts.

—*LEED® for Existing Buildings:
O & M rating system*

Recycling and waste management, ventilation and indoor air quality, site and landscape management, integrated pest management, sustainable purchasing plans, and efficient water and energy strategies are just some of the areas of voluntary performance standards covered. LEED® currently offers rating systems for New Construction, Existing Buildings, Commercial Interiors, Core and Shell Construction, Schools, Retail, Healthcare, Homes, and Neighborhood Development.

Although few design firms or studios can afford to start fresh with a new green build, the LEED "Existing Buildings" category offers guidance and provides an opportunity to green current worksites by increasing operational efficiency and reducing pollution and carbon emissions.[75]

Whether undertaking a remodel or just updating office decor, consult a LEED Accredited Professional, (LEED AP) or a green designer for advice on healthier options for paint, carpet, and furniture.

"A green interior designer brings an awareness to the project about materials and processes that are better for the health of the client and the health of the planet."[76] Anne Bertino of the Bertino-Baumann Group in Phoenix, Arizona, recommends: [77]

> At the very least the firm should implement a recycling program and use recycled content materials as much as possible. Consider energy-efficient options on lighting, heating and cooling and also consider water efficient plumbing fixtures. These are some visual signs that show the client a commitment to environmental awareness.

Green interior designers not only create beautiful spaces, they create beautiful and healthy spaces for the client and the planet.

—Anne Bertino, LEED AP, Allied ASID,
and owner/principal designer,
Bertino-Baumann Group

Resources:

— REGREEN by ASID (American Society of Interior Designer's Foundation) and USGBC (U.S. Green Building Council) is the nation's first set of resources and tools for green home remodeling projects. The REGREEN program can help increase understanding of sustainable renovation project practices and provide information regarding best practices. Visit *www.regreen program.org* for more information or to download "Residential Remodeling Guidelines, 2nd Edition," plus a green product checklist and slideshow presentation.

— BuildingGreen.com provides green product categories, including interior finish and trims, flooring, furniture, and furnishings. Visit *www .buildinggreen.com* for news, product reviews, and green product listings.

— The Green Building Pages is a "sustainable building materials database and design tool for the environmentally and socially responsible designer, builder and client." Visit *www.green buildingpages.com* for more information and links and resources.

Numerous books are available on green interiors and green building. Here are just a few actions to make work and living spaces healthier and more efficient inside and out. Many actions are also found in the "Shop Green" and "EPP Best Practices" sections and other parts of the chapter. And naturally, just as you wouldn't ask a public relations or marketing team do the job that Web programmers or developers do best, find the right person for the job, or consider hiring an accredited, experienced green building consultant or green interior designer to guide greening decisions.

Integrate components of green building into the design studio or workplace. According to LEED®, "A sustainable building maximizes operational efficiency while minimizing environmental impacts."[78]

Learn more about green building and standards and strategies. The Leadership in Energy and

Environmental Design (LEED®) and the U.S. Green Building Council® (USGBC) are the go-to resources for guiding green building principles. Utilize these rating systems for design, construction, remodels, and renovation.

— The Leadership in Energy and Environmental Design (LEED®) Green Building Rating System™: *www.usgbc.org/leed/*

— U.S. Green Building Council®: *www.usgbc.org*

— GBCI Green Building Certification Institute: *www.gbci.org*

— "Green Building Basics," a Web-based guide provided by the California Integrated Waste Management Board: *www.ciwmb.ca.gov*

Improve energy performance and develop energy saving strategies.

— The ENERGY STAR Service and Product Directory can provide guidelines, free tools and resources, including "Guidelines for Energy Management Overview" and an "Energy Program Assessment Matrix" tool.[79] Visit *www.energystar.gov* for information.

Make building, landscape, and interior design purchases based on an environmentally preferable purchasing (EPP) policy or a green purchasing program to reduce the social, health, and environmental impact of goods and services. For example, base building materials and office supply purchases on recycled content, renewable materials, sustainably harvested or certified criteria, and where possible, with locally sourced/harvested/manufactured criteria. For additional information about office papers, office supplies, break room and cleaning supplies, computers, and electronics, see the "EPP Best Practices" section in this chapter.

Follow a regular maintenance schedule for building ventilation and exhaust systems, and regularly check and replace air filters.

Protect workers, ventilation systems, and wall surfaces from tobacco smoke. Provide designated smoking areas. Better yet, provide employee health and wellness programs and incentives to quit smoking.

Utilize blinds, curtains, or shade structures to screen the sun and deflect radiant heat in the summer. Ceiling fans can improve airflow and reduce energy consumption and costs.

Make use of natural lighting, and utilize energy-efficient lighting systems and timers.

Replace incandescent lightbulbs with compact fluorescents or LEDs. LEDs in particular can provide energy savings and maintenance cost savings, especially for signage and exit lighting.[80]

Establish an office recycling or solid waste reduction plan.

Purchase nontoxic cleaning products to improve indoor air quality and to reduce employee and cleaners' exposure to hazardous chemicals, solvents, and contaminants. (See the "EPP Best Practices" section for more details.)

Review opportunities for installing alternative energy technologies, such as solar panels. Alternatively, purchase renewable energy from a local utility provider, if available.

Purchase carbon offsets or renewable energy credits to offset power use. (See the "Carbon Offsets" section of this chapter for more information.)

Track and monitor water use. This can include indoor and outdoor use, gray water or wastewater, and efficient use of heated water. Regularly check for drips, leaks, or faulty equipment.

Choose water-conserving fixtures when replacing old bathroom sinks, toilets, or urinals. Visit the EPA's Web site to find products and tips—type "WaterSense" in the search field: *www.epa.gov*.

Integrate landscaping strategies that reduce water, pesticides, and maintenance. Use native plantings and groundcovers. Use compost and mulches to save water and reduce weeds.

Learn more about integrated pest management (IPM) to manage pests in a more sustainable or environmentally sensitive manner.[81]

Keep in mind common sense and use the precautionary principle to guide decisions and policies. "The precautionary principle guides us to take action now, as individuals and as a society, to prevent harm to human health and the environment before it happens." Visit *www.takingprecaution.org* for more information.

How You Get to Work Matters

Of course, a discussion about green or sustainable studios or offices wouldn't be complete without touching on commuting and traveling to work. Environmental impacts include pollution, carbon/greenhouse emissions, and the use of fossil fuels. Transportation emissions currently account for one-third of U.S. greenhouse gas emissions.[83]

Congestion and traffic jams waste fuel and steal valuable productive hours. According to *GRIST*, Americans drive 734 billion miles to and from work each year—and spend an average of 47 hours stuck in rush-hour traffic.[84] A 2007 Urban Mobility Report states:

> Traffic congestion continues to worsen in American cities of all sizes, creating a $78 billion annual drain on the U.S. economy in the form of 4.2 billion lost hours and 2.9 billion gallons of wasted fuel—that's 105 million weeks of vacation and 58 fully-loaded supertankers.[85]

While some independent, virtual, or home-based designers have the option simply to stroll down the hall or up the stairs to get to work, others will be commuting to their workplace or traveling as part of their job description. We've already discussed purchasing offsets to cover emissions for both studio power and travel; now let's consider eco-conscious commuting.

Eco-Conscious Commuting

Utilize strategies to help keep vehicles well maintained. This includes regular auto maintenance and tune-ups to ensure that all vehicles achieve optimal fuel efficiency. This in turn will help save money and lower emissions. Check air pressure on tires regularly to extend tire life and to reduce fuel usage and costs.[86]

Encourage employees and fleets to purchase fuel-economic vehicles and alternative-fuel vehicles. To find and compare gas mileage (miles per gallon), greenhouse gas emissions, air pollution ratings, and safety information for new and used cars and trucks, visit *www.fueleconomy.gov*, an online resource by the U.S. Department of Energy's Energy Efficiency and Renewable Energy and U.S. Environmental Protection Agency.

Provide employee incentives or vouchers for carpooling, hybrid driving, or using a bike or public transportation.

Here are a couple of smart reasons to ride-share or take public transportation. Carpooling can save around $3,000 per year, reduce stress, and improve mental acuity.[87]

Many commuters who take public transportation enjoy the time to relax, read, or catch up on work. Others who walk or ride their bikes can multitask and charge their electronic gadgets along the way by using wheel-driven chargers or portable solar units. (Refer to "Energy Efficiency in the Workplace" section for more details about solar chargers.)

When traveling or renting cars, look into options for hybrid vehicles or "green taxis."

Consider additional strategies to reduce travel and commuting. Telecommuting twice a week can save 40 percent in gas costs and save an average of 53 minutes of commuting each day.[88] Other strategies may include compressed workweeks and using teleconferencing technology, office sharing, and virtual studios and offices.

Telecommuting twice a week can save 40 percent of gas costs and saves an average of 53 minutes of commuting each day.

—*The Telework Coalition*

Resources:

— The Telework Coalition provides fact sheets, tools, and resources, including an Emissions Calculator. Visit *www.telcoa.org* for more information.

— "How Virtual Offices Work" discusses the advantages and disadvantages of virtual offices. This and other related articles are posted on the "How Stuff Works" Web site: *www.howstuffworks.org*.

Thinking Green

Working smarter entails thinking green. Environmentally preferable purchasing polices can guide industry growth to a more sustainable place. Smart, virtual workflows save time and energy and conserve natural resources. Energy conservation strategies prolong the useful life of equipment and save money. Environmental footprint tools, energy waste audits, and office carbon footprint tools help measure an effort's impact and help to provide feedback and guidance to make adjustments. Design firms and personal workspaces can be healthier, more productive, and more sustainable.

Becoming more eco-minded not only leads to ways to conserve energy, resources, and money, it provides creditability and gives design firms or studios an edge. Designers will be able to translate and share new information with colleagues and become better able to guide clients toward more environmentally aware choices. Designers can grow their businesses in new ways and effect social change at the same time.

Thinking green requires a flexible mind open to challenges and creative problem solving. Keep up to date with the latest news and information regarding eco-products, green gadgets, sustainable developments, design and marketing. Just a few of the Web sites that offer free online e-newsletters and information to spark your thinking are listed next.

Resources:

— Greener World Media. Includes Green Biz: *www.GreenBiz.com*; Greener Buildings: *www.GreenerBuildings.com*; Greener Computing: *www.GreenerComputing.com*; Greener Design: *www.GreenerDesign.com*; Climate Biz: *www.ClimateBiz.com*; and more. Visit *www.GreenerWorldMedia.com/brands*.

— Inhabitat: *www.inhabitat.com*

— Planet Green: *www.planetgreen.discovery.com*

— Sustainable Life Media; includes *Sustainable Brands Weekly* and more: *www.sustainablelifemedia.com*

— Treehugger: *www.treehugger.com*

— Worldchanging: *www.worldchanging.com*

Professional Development and Education

Join organizations or participate in forums that promote awareness, education, and sustainability strategies. The next sites are especially helpful for graphic designers:

— AIGA Center for Sustainable Design: *www.sustainability.aiga.org*

— Design Can Change: *www.designcanchange.org*

— o2: The International Network on Sustainable Design, *www.o2.org* and *www.o2-usa.org*

— ODO (Organic Design Operatives): *www.themightyodo.com*

— Re-nourish: *www.re-nourish.com*

— Designers Accord: *www.designersaccord.org*

Learn more, study sustainable design online: Minneapolis College of Art and Design's Sustainable Design Online Certification Program: visit *www.mcad.edu*.

The resources in this chapter have been gathered to assist you with exploring, reviewing, sharing, and putting sustainable ideas and methods into practice. There is no doubt that some of these may change quickly or be updated in the future. However, let's make a start now and work together to create a healthier and greener (work) environment for ourselves and for those around us.

As Milton Glaser says, "Good design is good citizenship."[89] Designers play a key role in environmental stewardship. Thinking and working green is well within the realm of design and social responsibility, and designers are in a unique position to educate others and work for change. In short, sustainable design is smart design, and smart, eco-savvy design can change the world.

Good design is good citizenship

—*Milton Glaser*

7 Innovation Toolbox

A quick and handy *Field Guide* to ideas and resources referred to throughout this book

Eco-Design in Three Easy Steps

1. Know what the audience expects the design to do, then exceed those expectations.

    — What is your work saying about how you feel about the audience, and the environment?

    — Is it well researched, do you really understand your audience as well as the thing's use/viewing world?

2. Know what the design actually needs to do.

    — Is it well researched, do you really understand your supply chain as well as end-of-life and rebirth possibilities?

3. Empower the audience to become a change agent.

449

— Connect with the audience and foster brand loyalty with the true quality and deep integrity of your work and message.

Definition of "Sustainable Effort"

The definition of a sustainable package from the Sustainable Packaging Coalition[SM] is a great benchmark to apply to any effort. To get a copy of its Design Guidelines for Sustainable Packaging to put these ideas into action, visit *sustainablepackaging.org.*

Sustainable packaging:[1]

1. Is beneficial, safe and healthy for individuals and communities throughout its life cycle;

2. Meets market criteria for performance and cost;

3. Is sourced, manufactured, transported, and recycled using renewable energy;

4. Maximizes the use of renewable or recycled source materials;

5. Is manufactured using clean production technologies and best practices;

6. Is made from materials healthy in all probable end-of-life scenarios;

7. Is physically designed to optimize materials and energy;

8. Is effectively recovered and utilized in biological and/or industrial Cradle to Cradle cycles.

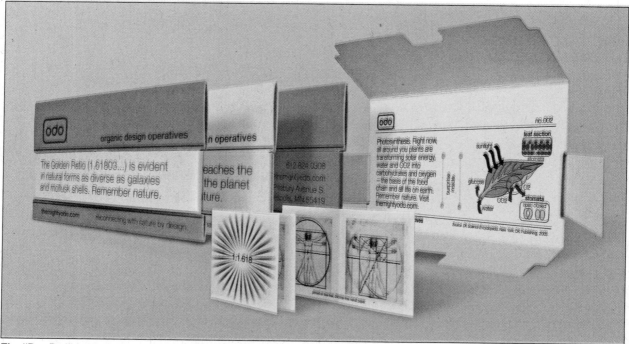

The "Pea Pod" business card for **Organic Design Operatives** takes the opportunity to educate on sustainability issues as well as provide information about the firm.

The criteria blend broad sustainability objectives with business considerations and strategies that address the environmental concerns related to the life cycle of packaging. Many working in packaging believe that by addressing these criteria successfully, packaging can be transformed into a C2C flow of packaging materials in a system that is economically robust and provides benefit throughout the life cycle: a sustainable system.

Shopping List for Change

Consumer advocates use these ideas to help buyers better align their purchases with their ethics:[2]

— *Choose products/packaging that use sustainably renewable or recycled materials first.* Encourage manufacturers to do the right thing. Help make those eco-choices part of their competitive advantage.

— *Buy locally.* Help cut down on fuel for transportation and keep jobs in local communities.

— *Choose products currently recycled in your area, and look for those that close the loop.* Stay familiar with the recycling rules; not all areas take all materials. Give preference to products that allow you to close the loop.

— *Use common sense.* Concentrates are more cost effective than ready to use. Do you really need cheese in individually wrapped slices? If the package is plastic, is it adding a positive user feature, such as shampoo in a shatter-proof bottle for safety? If it looks wasteful, it is.

— *Be an advocate for change.* If you regularly buy a product that's overall really good, but has un-eco packaging, drop the company a letter. Be an eco-purchasing activist. Say you'd like to keep buying the product but its un-eco packaging is making it hard for you. If there's a competing product packaged in a more responsible way, point that out too. Support manufacturers that are proud of their eco-efforts (usually printed right on their packaging with more details on Web sites).

At home: Encourage family and friends to use eco-alternatives. Teach your kids why good buying choices and recycling are important.

At the office: Give your company's purchasing department alternatives for more eco-preferable products. Most people will pick a more eco product if given the option. Make it easy for them.

Innovation Heuristics

The systems approach can be used to transform designs from static "things" into flows within natural cycles. This is the basis of innovation in design. The flow is the system—from material creation through processing, assembly, distribution, and recycling.

Flow is dynamization, making a process more dynamic or flexible. Design the system first and then the object to live within it. This dynamic process starts by dividing the object into pieces (segmentation) and moves through ever-finer gradations until objects are replaced by services.

Lightness is closely related to flow. How light can the end product be? Can the materials be chosen for the lowest impact? The material in this section covers a variety of approaches to transform design.

Design Rules

— *Stop the use of inappropriate materials:* Objects created shall not last longer than the thing they were created to serve.

— *Expand the space of design knowledge:* Use the power of teams and diversity.

— *Use evolution as a guide:* Experiment continuously.

— *All things live in ecological niches:* Listen and be guided by the user.

— *Move beyond local limits:* Harness the power of open source to improve knowledge and networks.

TECHNIQUE: *Create your own set of five to seven innovation heuristics and share them.*

Basics of Innovation

Innovation is applied creativity. Some fundamental areas for innovation:

— *Location:* Where (design, designer, user).

— *Direction:* Why (what your principles are).

— *Materials:* What they are (good and bad).

— *Cycles:* How to use them.

— *Users:* Who they are, their needs, desires, and interactions.

Beer importer All Saints Brands tapped Jedlička Design to create this first introduction of its own branded Belgian ale. With no other budget available for promotion other than the packaging, All Saints wanted a look that would sell itself. Produced and bottled at the brewery, under the strict rules for packaging in Europe, the bottles' labels used water-based adhesive to easily facilitate reuse or recycling.

Innovation occurs in:

— *People:* Changing design practice, changing an object's use.

— *Process:* New ways to produce objects.

— *Objects:* Providing a function with greater advantage.

Innovation can be:

— *Incremental:* Increasing the good qualities, decreasing the bad qualities.

— *Transformational:* Providing a service instead of a product.

— *Disruptive:* Changing the nature of the industry.

Movement toward a goal or ideal design can occur at the level of people, process, or end piece.

At the level of people, designers need to know where they are. This can happen only when their methods and means of interaction with the world—the design principles—have been documented.[3]

TECHNIQUE: *Create your own set of design principles.*

Ecological Design Principles

According to Sim van der Ryn:[4]

— *Solutions grow from place:* Keep it local.

— *Ecological accounting informs design:* Know your material and energy flows.

— *Design with nature,* not against it.

— *Everyone is a designer:* Take advantage of different viewpoints and knowledge.

— *Make nature visible:* Let it shine in the design.

According to John Todd:[5]

— The living world is the matrix for all design.

— Design should follow, not oppose, the laws of life.

— Biological equity must determine design.

— Design to reflect bioregionality.

— Base projects on renewable energy.

— Use the integration of living systems to design.

— Design as evolution along with the natural world.

— Design to heal.

Process Innovation

At the level of process, designers need to know material qualities and transformations.

Materials are the world of form. What can be made? What effect does it have? Can it be cycled back into production or left in the environment? Is it possible to let it "evaporate," leaving a web?

Transformations occur via energy, organization, or information. For example, plastics can be transformed with heat and pressure (energy). Companies can be transformed by organization as levels of hierarchy are reduced and interconnections formed. Societies can be transformed as information about the results of processes (industrial or political) is made available.

Design Innovation

At the level of design, consider function, system, and end users. To innovate with function, consider providing the design as a service rather than a tangible good.

Systems can be designed to transform the world as it exists or to create new structures via interconnection. For example, sharing products (e.g., power tools) creates new systems as well as new opportunities for design.

The practice of user-influenced design requires that designers forget their unique knowledge of typical techniques and solutions. Instead, they should explore and define the functions users are most interested in. Ask users how they are using the existing design and what features are missing.

Designers can learn to place themselves into the users' world, and then project user needs and desires back to innovate. Alternatively, users can be interviewed (lead user process)[6] to find out preferences and how they use the design.

Innovations can be classified as quality improvement, new market creation, design range extension, reduction of labor or material or impact or energy, improvements in process, replacing products with services, or adapting to constraints (including regulation).[7]

Design Mindfulness

According to John Thackara:[8]

— Think about the consequences of design.

  — Most impacts come from design decisions.

— Consider the material and energy flows of creation and use.

— Give priority to humans.

— Deliver value to people.

— Know that place, time, and cultural differences are positive values.

— Create services, not things.

Other Design Strategies from Thackara

Learn from users: Innovation is becoming user led, as exemplified by Wikipedia and open source solutions. Use that same power of multiple intelligences by being open to design solutions from users. Enlarge design thinking by including the Earth and the end user. Quiet down the "maker" mind-set that knows all about solutions and jumps to design decisions.

Follow user needs: Users have needs. How does the design satisfy the need? What is excess? What is an irritant about the design? The creativity tool Triz[9] notes that there are two ways to improve a design: Increase the good factors or decrease the bad factors.

Study how the object lives: Use context. How is the end piece used? Get it home, read it, toss it? Consider egg carton packaging loaded with seeds that the kids want to plant. Think they will remember that brand?

Solution space: Enlarge the thinking space in the company. Bring in ideas from Nature (biomimicry). Encourage others to see the design as a spaceship or alien.

Mobility: The Internet has sped up the material economy and its flows. Now a book arrives overnight and goods come from the other coast. On an individual basis, lower environmental impact by thinking more and driving less. From a company perspective, the same holds true—this is the lesson from operations research, where the activities at a company are studied to make optimal decisions about resource allocation. Consider where materials come from, the processing location, and how designs get from the company to the next step in the chain. Perhaps transport markings aren't a layer on top of individual pieces. Make all designs local.

Locality: Instead of moving things faster, make them closer. Local products are a growing market, and the things we create are a big part of that. Make the thing itself locally, and it will sell the product (made right here in Lake Wobegon!). Consciously design for going deeper instead of searching farther. Everything is particular: Design for each situation.

Experiment: Design implies intent, knowing the outcome. Evolution shows that variation and selection lead to variety and solutions that optimize fit into the local environment. Practice experimentation, not design. Start with small experiments. Try several, don't invest everything in one.

Appropriate-use case models: Don't design for the worst case. Eighty percent of all traffic is local, 15 percent is continental, and 5 percent is international. This holds for everything from cars to the Internet. Consider the time cycle of the design: Design to represent ideal life.

Connect designs, content, and people: Life is structured via connections—use webs, chains, and networks. Most people want big-city amenities and a small-city pace.

Design Approaches

— Design tends to converge on single (point) solutions. Rather, diverge outward from the center (Fuller's dimensions).

— Innovation thrives in adversity, creating novel adaptations. Design without constraints can look like last year's or, worse, a competitor's works.

— Requirement changes are part of life. Learn how to adapt to, and anticipate, changing requirements.

— Pay attention to flow: design, information, mind-set of peers, changes in the economy. Emulate the flexibility of agile software development strategy. Teams meet every morning for a few minutes to determine top priorities for the day and to track requirements changes.

— Create friendly design—pieces that bring people together and create community.

— Move from design of objects to creation of service.

— Consider local exchanges and trades, sharing resources, time, and skills: Extend family to community. Use social and business networks to enlarge your design community.

— Design using the universals of culture. If the design seems to fit in one market, consider what other context it is used in. For example, household articles might be used in play and recreation, or a beautiful sustainable design could define a new market.

— Consider how a design fits one or more of these areas outlined by Alice Ann Cleaveland, Jean Craven, and Maryanne Danfelser, who have extended the work of George Murdock on cultural universals:

  — *Material culture:* Food, clothing, tools, housing, transportation, possessions

  — *Arts, play, and recreation:* Music, arts, design

  — *Language and nonverbal communication:* Books, language, video

  — *Social organization:* Societies, families, networks

— The information space of the designer and user are different: Consider how to make messages "sticky" and how to represent the message of sustainability.

Design Using Universal Principles

— *Gravitation:* What pulls the design into the Earth? What grounds the design and designer?

— *Dimension:* Spin, radiate/converge, orbit, invert, torque, precess.

— *Trimtab:* Use a small rudder to change the big rudder.

— *Boundary, flows, and loops:* Chart design flows.

— *Use viral or meme design techniques:* What would cause a message or piece to attach to a user? Consider hook and loop tape or sticky seeds.

Similar to these examples, a meme is a behavior or piece of information that passes from one person to another. For memes to propagate, one user exhibits a behavior that others copy. The rapid popularity of white MP3 player earbuds is a good example. The idea jumps from one mind to the next, and behavior is copied and reinforced.

Other Design Strategies

Consider how the user interacts with the design and end product. Consider design as a teacher: How can the design promote learning or literacy in general terms or for sustainability?

Biomimicry asks us to follow Nature by exchanging complication for biological inspiration. Consider the

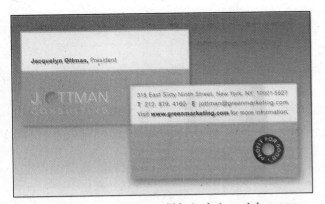

Sometimes it's not what you add but what you take away. This fun take on J. Ottman's logo by Celery Design adds visual impact without requiring additional inks.

state of the industry: How does it mirror the ecosystem's maturity level? Is it a stable mature forest, or are there open areas where new species are growing rapidly? Should the design (and business) move toward or away from areas like these?

Consider life cycle as a means to innovate.

Fair Trade Essentials

Green America's Basics of Fair Trade

The things we create are not just about materials alone. Fair trade is one of the key elements employed by today's sustainability leaders. As the Nike example showed, ethics-based companies need to be sure their talk is walked not just by their employees but by their vendors too. Fair trade practices need to be employed throughout a company's vertical supply chain management system to ensure that the integrity of a company's message is carried through—from the growers in the field and sewers at the factory to the product on the store shelf. Aligning a company's supply chain on more than a simple materials level can seem like a daunting task at first, but finding ethical suppliers (or helping established suppliers realign their priorities) is getting easier every day, and a variety of groups serving various industries can help make the job easier still. Green America (formerly Co-op America) is one of the oldest and most respected groups working with both businesses and consumers. Founded in 1982, Green America is a nonprofit membership organization working to harness economic power—the strength of consumers, investors, businesses, and the marketplace—to create a socially just and environmentally sustainable society.

For a free download of the full version of Green America's Guide to Fair Trade, go to *fairtradeaction. org*. But to get started understanding what fair trade is, a basic overview of fair trade principles and practices from Green America's Guide to Fair Trade follows.

A Fair Price

Fair Trade Certified™ product prices are set by the Fair Trade Labeling Organization. Prices set not only cover the cost of goods but strive to provide a fair living wage for the people involved in the production process.

Investment in People and Communities

Often Fair Trade producer cooperatives and artisan collectives reinvest their revenues back into their communities—strengthening local businesses, building health clinics and schools, supporting scholarship funds, building housing and providing leadership training and women's programs. All work to build stronger, healthier communities.

Environmental Sustainability

Fair Trade producers respect their natural habitat and are encouraged to use sustainable production methods. Example: Nearly 85 percent of Fair Trade Certified™ coffee is also organic.

Empowering Stakeholders

Fair Trade promotes producer empowerment in their communities and in the global marketplace. For Fair Trade coffee producers, their cooperatives or associations are transparent and democratically controlled by their members. For estate grown products such as tea and bananas, Fair Trade provides revenue that is invested in a fund, managed and controlled by the farmers, and used for the interests of the community—providing education, access to healthcare, and so on.

Empowering Women

Recognizing the untapped potential of all stakeholders in a community, Fair Trade encourages participation by women in local cooperatives and in leadership roles. Fair Trade revenue also often is used to support or promote women's programs.

Direct, Long-Term Relationships

Those who import Fair Trade Certified™ products and other fairly traded goods contribute to the endeavor to establish long-term stable relationships with producer groups. These relations help not only to create healthier communities but provide a more stable and sustainable economic base, allowing entire regions to benefit.

Airside UK wanted each aspect of its rebrand to be environmentally considered. CD and DVD cases were replaced by fully recycled and recyclable slipcases and wallets. Printers were chosen based on their eco-processes for inks, wash-ups and waste management. With branding items such as a show-reel DVD case that needs to be refreshed every few months, rather than specify dates and risk having to discard unused, out-of-date stock, Airside designed cases with a choice of dates and simply blacks out the others with a matching pen. This ensures the cases will be usable for several years, about the right time for another rebrand (*http://airside.co.uk*).

Overview of Environmental Marketing Claims

TerraChoice: Sins of Greenwashing

TerraChoice Environmental Marketing's Sins of Greenwashing is a handy heuristic to keep in mind. To review current and past marketing claims studies as well as find future updates go to *www.terrachoice.com.*

> Green-wash (green'wash', -wôsh') verb: the act of misleading consumers regarding the environmental practices of a company or the environmental benefits of a product or service.

1. Sin of the Hidden Trade-off

   For example, paper (including household tissue, paper towel and copy paper): "Okay, this product comes from a sustainably harvested forest, but what are the impacts of its milling and transportation? Is the manufacturer also trying to reduce those impacts?"

   Emphasizing one environmental issue isn't a problem (indeed, it often makes for better communications). The problem arises when hiding a trade-off between environmental issues.

2. Sin of No Proof

   For example, personal care products (such as shampoos and conditioners) that claim not to have been tested on animals but offer no evidence or certification of this claim.

   Company Web sites, third-party certifiers, and toll-free phone numbers are easy and effective means of delivering proof.

3. Sin of Vagueness

   For example, garden insecticides promoted as "chemical-free." In fact, nothing is free of chemicals.

   Water is a chemical. All plants, animals, and humans are made of chemicals, as are all products. If the marketing claim doesn't explain itself ("Here's what we mean by 'eco'"), the claim is vague and meaningless. Similarly, watch for other popular vague green terms: "nontoxic," "all natural," "environmentally friendly," and "earth friendly."

4. Sin of Worshiping False Labels

   A product that, through either words or images, gives the impression of third-party endorsement where no such endorsement exists; fake labels, in other words.

5. Sin of Irrelevance

   For example, chlorofluorocarbon (CFC)–free oven cleaners, shaving gels, window cleaners, disinfectants.

   Could all of the other products in this category make the same claim? The most common example is easy to detect: Don't be impressed by CFC-free! Ask if the claim is important and relevant to the product. (If a light bulb claimed water efficiency benefits you should be suspicious.) Comparison shop (and ask the competitive vendors).

6. Sin of the Lesser of Two Evils

   For example, organic tobacco, "green" insecticides and herbicides.

Is the claim trying to make consumers feel "green" about a product category of questionable environmental benefit? Consumers concerned about the pollution associated with cigarettes would be better served by quitting smoking than by buying organic cigarettes. Similarly, consumers concerned about the human health and environmental risks of excessive use of lawn chemicals might create a bigger environmental benefit by reducing their use than by looking for greener alternatives.

7. Sin of Fibbing

    For example, shampoos that claim to be "certified organic" but for which our research could find no such certification.

    When we check up on it, is the claim true? The most frequent examples were false uses of third-party certifications. Thankfully, these are easy to confirm. Legitimate third-party certifiers—EcoLogo™, Chlorine Free Products Association (CFPA), Forest Stewardship Council (FSC), Green Guard, Green Seal, for example—all maintain publicly available lists of certified products. Some even maintain fraud advisories for products falsely claiming certification.

Eco Seals, Certifications, and Claims

Compounding the confusion of what is "eco/green/sustainable" is a long list of terms and "seals." Many are signs of actual third-party verified efforts, but many more were created as a marketing tactic with no official meaning.

To help better communicate valuable information to the consumer, presented here is a list of commonly accepted terms and certifications in current use for print and packaging. This is not a complete list by any means, and, like the nutrition facts panel found on food packaging, disclosures must accurately reflect the claims of any product. This means all attributes called out must be carefully researched and correctly applied for disclosure to be in compliance with marketing claims guidelines in each distribution market.

As standards and systems evolve in tandem with knowledge, experience and participation, it is important to keep up to date and carefully review criteria (and the certifying body) for *any* certification or certified product being considered.

This list was compiled from resources found at *greenamerica.org*, *ecoLingo.com*, and *greenerchoices.org*. Please visit these Web sites for additional information.

Alternative or Tree-free Papers

Tree-free fibers for papermaking include: bagasse, cotton, flax, old jeans, mulberry, kenaf, hemp, agri-pulp (wheat, rice, corn, straw), banana, and bamboo, with more fibers coming to market all the time. Currently, however, there are no official certifications for tree-free fibers, though certified organic growers for these fibers are becoming more common.

Green Seal offers a "Green Report" and checklist for alternative papers on its Web site:[12]

—   Look for paper which contains at least *50% Tree-free Content*.

—   Seek out papers that incorporate *fibers which would traditionally be burned or wasted* in other ways (e.g., banana stalks;

recovered cotton, denim, or currency; tobacco leaves; coffee bean residues; and other types of agricultural or manufacturing remainders).

— If a paper is chosen that is not entirely tree free, look for paper that makes up the balance with *pos-consumer waste (PCW)*.

— If choosing a paper that has been bleached, choose a paper that is classified as either *TCF (Totally Chlorine Free)* or *PCF (Processed Chlorine Free)*.

— Look for paper fibers that are *grown and processed locally*. This cuts down on transportation and environmental costs.

Ancient Forest Friendly (AFF) (www.canopyplanet.org)

Ancient Forest Friendly paper purchasing policies help safeguard ancient and endangered forests, and protect their biodiversity and ecosystems. They also help stimulate the development and growth of the eco-paper market and sustainable supply chains.

The Ancient Forest Friendly™ logo is a designation that represents the highest ecological qualities in the paper industry. In order to be Ancient Forest Friendly, a paper must be manufactured with a high percentage of post-consumer recycled fiber or agricultural residue. Any virgin fiber used in the paper must be both FSC certified and assessed as not originating from endangered forests. Bleaching must be chlorine free. Ancient Forest Friendly™ papers conserve intact forest ecosystems and their functions such as climate stabilization, water regulation and species habitat.).

The Ancient Forest Friendly™ logo and wordmark is managed by Canopy, (formerly Markets Initiative), a Canadian not-for-profit that works collaboratively with large paper consumers (book, magazine or newspaper publishers) to guide them to change paper buying habits and to develop and implement paper policies that help safeguard ancient and endangered forests. Companies that have an eco-paper policy with Canopy may use the logo on applicable papers.

Biodegradable/Compostable

The Federal Trade Commission (FTC) has issued general guidelines on how the terms should be used. Claims that a product is "degradable," "biodegradable," or "photodegradable" mean that the materials will break down and return to Nature within a reasonably short time after customary disposal. What a "reasonably short time" is depends on where the product is disposed. In addition, it is important to understand the difference between the terms "biodegradable" and "compostable."

A material labeled as "biodegradable" can be broken down completely under the action of microorganisms into carbon dioxide, water, and biomass. It may take a very long time for a material to biodegrade on its own, depending on its environment (e.g., hardwood in an arid area), but it ultimately breaks down completely without human assistance.

Compostable materials biodegrade substantially with the help of specifically designed systems into carbon dioxide, methane, water, and compost biomass and are a subset of "biodegradable." Compostable materials for packaging usually require the controlled environment of an industrial composting facility. Unlike a backyard/home composter, the industrial composting facility generates much higher temperatures and maintains other specifically monitored conditions that include attention to microbe types plus carefully controlled moisture and air levels not possible in a home compost setup.

Biogas

Use of the biogas logo verifies that energy is sourced from the decomposition of waste in a landfill and transported to the paper mill for use in the paper-making process. Typically biogas (aka "green gas") is used as thermal energy to replace traditional combustible fuels such as natural gas in the papermaking process, and helps reduces green-house emissions.

Blue Angel

The Blue Angel is the first and oldest environment-related label in the world for products and services. About 3,850 products and services from approximately 550 label users in Germany and abroad are entitled to bear the Blue Angel seal.

Carbon Labeling

Currently several products have begun carrying a label disclosing their carbon footprint. This disclosure is still in its early stages with several labels in use. Carefully research any label before committing to its use. *Carbonfund.org* offers a CarbonFree Certified Product label that companies can use to promote their products as being climate neutral.

Contains no CFCs or Other Ozone-Depleting Substances

Regulations in countries around the world prohibit chloroflurocarbon (CFC) propellants in aerosols. Companies that wish to use the claim are required to submit a notification to the U.S. Environmental Protection Agency for review. There are additional qualifications for adding the claim "or other ozone-depleting substances."

Chasing Arrows

Recognized around the world, the three chasing arrows are symbolic of the three main steps in the recycling process:

— Separating and collecting recyclable materials

— Processing and manufacturing these materials into new products

— Purchasing and/or using recycled products

Variations of this symbol can provide important information at a glance—or be extremely mislead-ing. Unfortunately, the common impression is that any item carrying a chasing arrow logo is recyclable and has recycled content; this impression couldn't be further from the truth on both counts.

Chasing-Arrow Variations

Since the first recycling symbol was designed and plastic resin codes were introduced, certain groups have developed unique symbols specific to their industry. For example, industry associations for glass, paperboard, and corrugated materials have all developed, and in some cases trademarked, their own recycling symbols.

On plastics, the chasing-arrow logo is used along with a numbering system (1 to 7) to help designate plastic resins used in the product, but this does not mean the item has been recycled or is even accepted for recycling in the market in which the product is sold.

For aluminum, steel, and glass, it is common to find a note "(X) Recycles." This generic statement can be used only for items that are commonly accepted for recycling, but it does not provide buyers with information about recycled content. This can be confusing to consumers who are asked to "buy recycled" but then are not provided with information about whether an item has been recycled. Information is becoming available now from more forward-looking aluminum, steel, and glass suppliers. Buyers whose corporate ethics require transparency and disclosure should give preference to vendor partners willing to provide recycled content detail.

For industries using paper products, the American Forest and Paper Association recommends the usage regarding the recycling symbol as follows:

— Products that are recyclable, with a qualifying statement regarding the availability of recycling programs in a substantial majority of communities for that product or package. Making a "recyclable" statement is not generally recommended, as the above criteria may be difficult to meet.

— Products made from 100 percent recycled fiber, accompanied with either the "100% Recycled Fiber" or "Recycled" statement.

— Products made with a percentage of recycled fiber, accompanied with a legend identifying the total percent (by weight) of recycled fiber.

Keep in mind that recycled content for paper is now stated according to recycled *fiber* content, not weight. For example, coated paper has filler materials, thus making its total weight higher than its fiber weight. A comparison of recycled fiber content to total fiber provides a more accurate view of the true recycled content of the paper—papers that are 50 to 100 percent PCW are more significant environmentally.

Chlorine Free (PCF/TCF/ECF)

The Natural Resources Defense Council offers visitors to its Web site an order of preference for bleaching processes, on the basis of environmental criteria:[11]

1. PCF (preferable to TCF for wood-based papers because product includes recycled content; TCF is used to refer only to 100 percent virgin paper)

2. TCF

3. Enhanced ECF with ozone or hydrogen peroxide

4. Enhanced ECF (ECF with extended or oxygen delignification)

5. Traditional ECF

Totally Chlorine Free (TCF) is paper made with a bleaching process that uses no chlorine-based compounds; currently TCF refers only to 100 percent virgin paper.

Certified TCF: These products require that no chlorine or chlorine compounds were used in the papermaking process, that all virgin components need to be certified as totally chlorine free and require a chain of custody for all fiber, that the mill has no current or pending violations, and that the mill does not use old-growth forest for any of the virgin pulp.

Processed Chlorine Free (PCF) is recycled paper made with a bleaching process that uses no chlorine-based compounds.

Certified PCF: In addition to the certified TCF criteria, certified PCF products require the product contains at least 30 percent post-consumer content and that the mill details post-consumer content sources.

For more information about TCF, PCF, and Chlorine Free Products Association Certification, visit the Web site: *chlorinefreeproducts.org*.

Additional Chlorine Claims

Elemental Chlorine Free (ECF) often is used to label products that have substituted chlorine dioxide for another type of chlorine called elemental chlorine. Compared to bleaching processes using elemental chlorine, ECF chlorine dioxide processes reduce the formation of many chlorinated organic compounds. However, as chlorine is still used, effluent quality remains an issue that mills using replacements that still contain chlorine must address.

Enhanced ECF (EECF) with extended or oxygen delignification is a process that removes more of the lignin from the wood before bleaching. This reduction helps reduce energy and chemical demands for the bleaching process.

Enhanced ECF (EECF) with ozone or hydrogen peroxide delignification is a process that also removes more of the lignin from the wood before bleaching but substitutes ozone or hydrogen peroxide for chlorine or chlorine dioxides in the early stages of the bleaching process.

For both Enhanced ECF processes however, the final or near-final stages still use chlorine in some form, making TCF and PCF preferable options.

Earth Smart, Eco-Concious, Eco-Safe

Of this group *eco-conscious*, while still "unofficial" is gaining ground in common usage as a term that highlights environmentally positive (or at least benign) efforts, while acknowledging that the effort still has need for improvement. However, there are no official definitions for these terms and no organization behind these claims other than the company marketing the product displaying this term.

Eco

While, *eco* (short for ecological) has a long history of common use as a way of indicating environmentally positive efforts, and is a quick and handy shorthand to indicate very complex ideas, there are no universally binding definitions for this term and no organization behind these claims other than the company marketing the product displaying this term.

EcoLogo (www.ecologo.org)

Founded in 1988 by the government of Canada, EcoLogo is one of North America's most respected environmental standard and certification marks. EcoLogo provides customers—public, corporate, and consumer—with assurance that the products and services bearing the logo meet stringent standards of environmental leadership. EcoLogo certifies environmental leaders in over 120 product categories, helping customers find and trust the world's most sustainable products. To learn more about the product specific requirements that must be met for products to carry the EcoLogo^{CM} or to view environmentally preferred paper products, visit the EcoLogo Web site.

Eco Mark (www.ecomark.jp)

The Eco Mark program by the Japan Environment Association is managed in accordance with the standards and principles of International Organization for Standardization (ISO) 14020 and ISO 14024. Certification criteria for every product category has taken the environment and product life cycle (resource extraction, manufacture, distribution, use, disposal, recycling) into consideration.

Environmentally Friendly, Environmentally Safe

There are no official definitions for these terms and no organization behind these claims other than the company marketing the product displaying this term.

Environmentally Preferable

This term is gaining ground in common usage as a way to highlight environmentally positive (or at least benign) efforts, while acknowledging that the effort still has need for improvement. However, there are no official definitions for this term and no organiza-

tion behind these claims other than the company marketing the product displaying this term.

Fair Trade Certified (www.transfairusa.org)

TransFair USA is currently the only certifier of Fair Trade goods in the United States. It is a nonprofit organization, one of twenty members of Fairtrade Labeling Organizations International (FLO), the umbrella organization based in Bonn, Germany, that sets certification standards.

Forest Stewardship Council (www.fscus.org)

The Forest Stewardship Council (FSC) is an independent, nonprofit organization devoted to encouraging the responsible management of the world's forests. The FSC sets high standards that ensure forestry is practiced in an environmentally responsible, socially beneficial, and economically viable way.

The FSC Logo identifies products that contain wood from well-managed forests certified in accordance with the rules of the FSC.

Products carrying the FSC label are independently certified to assure consumers those products come from forests that are managed to meet the social, economic, and ecological needs of present and future generations.

FSC has offices in more than forty-six countries, and provides standard setting, trademark assurance and accreditation services for companies and organizations interested in responsible forestry.

Of interest to those who specify paper and paperboard, FSC-certified products are now readily available in North America from both small, independent paper companies as well as large paper mills.

To view links to certified paper merchants and certified printers with FSC chain-of-custody certification, visit the FSC Web site.

Green

Like *eco*, *green* has a long history of common use as a way of indicating environmentally positive efforts, but there are no universally binding definitions for this term and no organization behind these claims other than the company marketing the product displaying this term.

Green-e (www.green-e.org)

Green-e is the United States' leading independent consumer protection program for the sale of renewable energy and greenhouse gas reductions in the retail market. Green-e offers certification and verification of renewable energy through Green-e Energy, and greenhouse gas mitigation products (also known as carbon offsets) through Green-e Climate. Green-e is a program of the Center for Resource Solutions, a national nonprofit working to mitigate climate change.

The Green-e logo means that an independent third party certified that the product meets strict consumer-protection and environmental standards. Businesses participating in Green-e Marketplace that purchase or generate a significant amount of certified renewable energy can also display the Green-e logo in order to communicate their commitment to certified renewable energy.

Green Seal (www.greenseal.org)

Green Seal, Inc. is an independent, nonprofit organization whose mission is to create a more environmentally sustainable economy by identifying and promoting environmentally preferable products and services. Green Seal has developed environmental leadership standards for dozens of product and service categories, including printing and writing paper, and it's certification program verifies that products meet this stringent standard.

Papers certified by Green Seal signifies that recycled papers meet standards for recycled content with a minimum of 30 percent post consumer fiber and that the mill manufacturing processes, including packaging, meets stringent process control standards and are environmentally preferable.

Grüne Punkt/Green Dot (www.gruener-punkt.de)

In Germany, producer responsibility has been served through the Green Dot license program in response to the 1991 German Packaging Ordinance. Once packages have served their purpose, manufacturers, vendors, and importers are required to take them back, arrange for eco-friendly recovery, and document the procedures involved. The Green Dot logo now used throughout Europe has a different meaning from recycling symbols commonly used in North America. The Green Dot indicates that the manufacturer of that package has purchased a license for the right to use the Green Dot trademark and is obliged to abide by the regulations that license imposes, with fees funding the recovery and recycling system.

ISO 14000

The International Organization for Standardization (ISO), through the 14000 family of certifications, addresses various aspects of environmental management. It works as a management tool to enable organizations of any size to identify and control the environmental impact of its activities, products, or services; to improve its environmental performance continually; and to implement a systematic approach to setting environmental objectives and targets, to achieving these, and to demonstrating that they have been achieved.

Natural

The U.S. Department of Agriculture has defined this term, holding manufacturers accountable for proper use, but it does not yet have a verification system. The Natural Products Association (NPA), though, is helping address this issue for personal care products through its certification program.

Nontoxic

The claim "nontoxic" implies that the product will not cause adverse health effects. There are no specific standards for the "nontoxic" claim.

Post-Consumer Recycled (PCR) or Post-Consumer Waste (PCW)

These terms refers to paper that was *printed on or used for its intended purpose*, put into a recycling bin, and then recycled into new paper or products. It also refers to a finished material that normally would be disposed of as a solid waste.

Pre-Consumer Waste

This term refers to paper or scraps left over from manufacturing, converting, or trimming paper in the mill or print house. It may also include unsold magazines and newspapers. Although the paper and scraps are being reused, this paper has never made the journey to the consumer and back again.

Programme for the Endorsement of Forest Certification schemes (PEFC) (www.pefc.org)

Programme for the Endorsement of Forest Certification schemes (PEFC) The PEFC Council (Programme for the Endorsement of Forest Certification schemes) is an independent, non-profit, non-governmental organization, founded in 1999 which promotes sustainably managed forests through independent third party certification.

PEFC is a global umbrella organization for the assessment of and mutual recognition of national forest certification schemes developed in a multi-stakeholder process. These national schemes build upon the inter-governmental processes for the promotion of sustainable forest management, a series of on-going mechanisms supported by 149 governments in the world covering 85 percent of the world's forest area.

Rainforest Alliance Certified™ (www.rainforest-alliance.org)

The Rainforest Alliance is an international, non-profit conservation organization that was founded in 1987 to conserve biodiversity and to ensure sustainable livelihoods by transforming land-use practices, business practices, and consumer behavior. In 1989, the Rainforest Alliance launched the SmartWood program and became the world's first global forestry certification program.

The Rainforest Alliance's SmartWood program is the world's leading FSC forest management certifier, working with both large forestry companies and small communities and cooperatives throughout the world to ensure that their products and services meet strict standards for social and environmental responsibility. The Rainforest Alliance Certified seal, which appears on a variety of agricultural products, including bananas, coffee, chocolate, is recognized around the world as an indication that those products come from farms that meet the standards of the Sustainable Agricultural Network. The Rainforest Alliance Certified seal can also be used in tandem with the FSC trademarks on forestry products such as flooring, decking, guitars, and paper when they have been certified by the Rainforest Alliance's SmartWood program in accordance with the FSC standards.

Both the FSC on-product label and the Rainforest Alliance Certified seal may appear on FSC-certified products or printed pieces if an FSC-certified printer with Rainforest Alliance Chain-of-Custody certification is used.

Recyclable

This claim means that products can be collected, separated, and recovered from the solid waste stream and used again, or reused in the manufacture or assembly of another package or product through an established recycling program. Unless otherwise third-party certified, there is no organization behind this claim other than the company marketing the product.

The phrase "Please Recycle" is likely to convey to consumers that the product is recyclable, where in fact it may not be. Some labeling laws allow for this statement's use when recycling is available in a majority of areas.

Recycled

Recycled claims may be used for products or packaging that contain either pre-consumer or post-consumer recycled materials. Unless the entire product is recycled, the percent of recycled material should be indicated. However, listing the type of recycled material or the portion of post-consumer content is not required. True recycled content papers, though, are defined as papers containing a minimum of 30 percent post-consumer fiber by weight.

Currently there is no global consensus on what the term "recycled" means beyond the fact that it may contain either post- or pre-consumer materials. Just saying that a thing is recycled is not enough, as this could vary from 1 percent to 100 percent, but not necessarily from post-consumer waste that has actually been recycled. Look for data sheets that provide the breakdown of pre- and post-consumer waste content. For paper, those that contain 50 to 100 percent PCW (post-consumer waste) are more significant environmentally.

Renewable

Generally this term refers to something that is generated or grown using current solar income, either continually, or at least in a short period of time (usually one season). However, there are no universal standards for this claim in all categories, and so does not ensure an environmentally sound product in all cases. For example: Unless certified organic, vegetable-based inks, while made from seasonally-grown resources are often better on many environmental levels than some of their petroleum-based counter-parts, these inks are made from crops using industrial farming practices that employ petroleum-based chemicals and intensive farming techniques resulting in a wide-range of local and downstream environmental and economic impacts. When referring to energy, hydropower is generated from redirecting the natural flow of water renewed with each rain or snowmelt. However, many of these efforts leave deep impacts on river ecosystems and local economies, as well as contributing to local species extinctions.

In addition, some makers of recycled products are attempting to attach the "renewable" claim to non current solar income materials as the resource is "renewed" from collected cast-offs, rather than from newly mined sources. This use of the term pushes it beyond its ability to carry real meaning, and adds to general confusion.

Social Accountability 8000 Standard (SA8000) (http://www.sa-intl.org)

Social Accountability International (SAI) works with Social Accountability Accreditation Services (SAAS) which licenses qualified auditors to certify workplace compliance with social accountability standards. SAAS regularly audits the auditors.

Sustainable

Unlike *eco* and *green, sustainable* is a more recent term in general use to indicate positive efforts. Gaining ground as the term to describe efforts that are broader than purely environmental, it asks that efforts be simultaneously socially, environmentally, and economically beneficial. Refined definitions for sustainability, based on the idea of meeting all three criteria, are appearing within specific industries and regions. However, whether all three core criteria are actually served all the way through the supply chain to the point of resource extraction must be judged on a case by case basis. Currently there are no universally binding legal definitions for this term to assure all criteria are met, and there is no single organization to certify this claim.

Sustainable Forestry Initiative (SFI) (www.sfiprogram.org)

SFI Inc. is an independent, non-profit charitable organization with a science-based, internationally-recognized forest management standard developed specifically for North American forests. It is one of the fastest growing certification programs, with over 160 million acres (65 million hectares) of SFI-certified forests across Canada and the US. Supported by conservation groups, the SFI Standard is based on principles and measures that promote sustainability, including measures to protect water quality, biodiversity, wildlife habitat, species at risk and forests with exceptional conservation value. SFI Inc. is governed by a three chamber board of directors representing environmental, social and economic sectors equally.

Vegetable-Based/Soy-Based

Vegetable-based inks and solvents contain varying amounts of oil from annual crops, such as soy and citrus, to replace petroleum in the mix, often making it lower in volatile organic compounds (VOCs), which react with other atmospheric pollutants and pose potential health risks. However, a material marked as having vegetable content can actually be mostly petroleum, or have a higher VOC index than a VOC-reduced petroleum product or process. Do not automatically assume that because a material is marked with vegetable content that it is automatically "safe." Those wishing to specify these materials should obtain the material safety data sheets (MSDSs) to understand the specific makeup of the material they are considering. The American Soybean Association has developed standards for soybean content in soy inks and the appropriate use of the Soy Seal or "Printed with Soy Ink" logo.

Materials Choices at a Glance

When it's time to pick materials, ask yourself these simple questions:

— Are you picking your material because it's the best one for your application or the same as it's always been done?

— Are you picking your material because it's the best one for your application or because your competitor is using it?

— Are you choosing materials that have long-term benefits and a solid systems approach or just grabbing from a list of happy-sounding buzzwords?

— What are the end-of-life materials-handling systems currently in place for your material choice in your target market?

— If you're displacing an actively recycled material, are you ready to help create a new materials stream for your product?

— If you're not able to accept responsibility for the full cycle and true cost of your product, can you provide an alternative that makes better use of the existing infrastructures?

Eco-Resources at a Glance

This list, provided by *EcoPackaging.net*, will help you find groups and resources that will go deeper into topic areas that impact the graphic arts industry. Each is a gateway to even more resources, materials options, and service vendors.

E-News, Online Publications, and Resources

AIGA Center for Sustainable Design
www.sustainability.aiga.org

Biomimicry Institute
www.biomimicryinstitute.org

Based in New York City, Seltzer, a maker of fun and playful eco-conscious greeting cards, graphic T-shirts, gifts, and stationery, takes minding the impacts of its materials, packaging, and production methods very seriously. According to its eco-audit environmental savings as of July 2007, by using 100 percent post-consumer recycled paper, the company has saved 375 trees, 65,914 gallons of water, 87,967 btus of energy, and 13,357 emissions. (*www.seltzergoods.com*)

BrandChannel.com
www.brandchannel.com

Carbonfund.org
www.carbonfund.org

Consumer Reports: Greener Choices
www.greenerchoices.org

Cradle to Cradle[SM]
www.mbdc.com/c2c

Designers Accord
www. designersaccord.org

EcoPackaging.net
Sustainable packaging, marketing, and print
www.ecopackaging.net

Environmental Defense
Alliance for Environmental Innovation
www.environmentaldefense.org

GreenBiz
www.greenbiz.com

GreenBlue[SM]
www.greenblue.org

Green Marketing
www.greenmarketing.com

The LOHAS Journal
www.lohas.com

The Natural Step
www.naturalstep.org

o2 International Network for Sustainable Design
www.o2.org

Package Design Magazine
www.packagedesignmag.com

Packaging Strategies
www.packstrat.com

Rocky Mountain Institute
www.rmi.org

Roper Report
National report cards on environment attitudes, knowledge, and behavior
www.neefusa.org

Sustainable Is Good
www.sustainableisgood.com

Sustainable Packaging Coalition[SM]
www.sustainablepackaging.org

Treehugger
www.treehugger.com

Watershed Media
www.watershedmedia.org

Life Cycle Analysis/Life Cycle Inventory Tools and Databases

COMPASS
www.sustainablepackaging.org

NREL U.S. Life-Cycle Inventory Database
www.nrel.gov/lci

SimaPro
www.simapro.com

Sustainable Minds
www.sustainableminds.com

UNEP International Life Cycle Partnership for a Sustainable World
www.lcinitiative.unep.fr

Walmart Stores Package Modeling
www.packagemodeling.com

Materials

Inks

PIMN Great Printer Environmental Initiative
www.pimn.org/environment/greatprinter
.htm

Printing Industries of America, Inc.
Graphic Arts Technical Foundation (PIA/GATF)
www.gain.net

The Printers' National Environmental Assistance
Center (PNEAC)
www.pneac.org

Sustainable Green Printing Partnership
www.sgppartnership.org

The National Association of Printing Ink Manufacturers (NAPIM)
www.napim.org

Glass

Glass Packaging Institute
www.gpi.org

Metals

Aluminum Association
www.aluminum.org

American Iron and Steel Institute
Steel Packaging Council
www.steel.org

Steel Recycling Institute (SRI)
www.recycle-steel.org

Paper and Paperboard

Paper Tools

Calculate the environmental impacts of your paper
choice:
www.environmentaldefense.org/papercalculator

Green America Better Paper Project
www.coopamerica.org/programs/woodwise

Ecological Guide to Paper
www.celerydesign.com

Paper Term Glossary
http://glossary.ippaper.com/default.asp?req=glossary/
termlist/Paper

PaperSpecs
Paper Selection Database
www.paperspecs.com

Rainforest Alliance
A SmartGuide to Paper and Print Sources
www.rainforest-alliance.org/programs/forestry

Paper Groups

100% Recycled Paperboard Alliance
www.rpa100.com

Ancient Forest Friendly (AFF)
www.canopyplanet.org

Chlorine Free Products Association
www.chlorinefreeproducts.org

Environmental Paper Network
www.environmentalpaper.org

Forest Certification Resource Center
www.certifiedwood.org

Forest Stewardship Council (FSC)
www.fscus.org

Programme for the Endorsement of Forest Certification schemes (PEFC)
www.pefc.org

Sustainable Forestry Initiative (SFI)
www.sfiprogram.org

Technical Association of the Pulp and Paper Industry (TAPPI)
www.tappi.org

Plastics: Biodegradable, Biobased, Recycled

Association of Postconsumer Plastic Recyclers
www.plasticsrecycling.org

Biodegradable Plastics Society
www.bpsweb.net

Biodegradable Products Institute (BPI)
www.bpiworld.org

BioEnvironmental Polymer Society (BEPS)
www.beps.org

Biopolymer.net
www.biopolymer.net

Center for Biodegradable Polymer Research
www.bprc.caeds.eng.uml.edu

National Association for PET Container Resources (NAPCOR)
www.napcor.com

Packaging and Packaging Design

IoPP Sustainable Packaging Technical Committee
www.iopp.org

Packaging Association of Canada
www.pac.ca

Sustainable Packaging Alliance (SPA)
www.sustainablepack.org

Sustainable Packaging Coalition^{SM}
www.sustainablepackaging.org

World Packaging Association
www.worldpackaging.org

Printing and Print Design

AIGA Center for Sustainable Design
www.sustainability.aiga.org

Institute for Sustainable Communication
www.sustaincom.org

PIM Great Printer Environmental Initiative
www.pimn.org/environment/greatprinter.htm

Printer's National Environmental Assistance Center
www.pneac.org

Sustainable Green Printing Partnership
www.sgppartnership.org

Organizations

Governmental

Environnement Canada
www.ec.gc.ca

European Commission Environmental Marketing Claims Guidelines (EU)
www.europa.eu.int

U.S. Environmental Protection Agency
www.epa.gov

Nongovernmental (NGO)

Biomimicry Guild and Institute
www.Biomimicry.org

Carbonfund
www.carbonfund.org

Center for a New American Dream
www.ibuydifferent.org

Earth 911
www.earth911.org

Environmental Defense
Alliance for Environmental Innovation
www.environmentaldefense.org

Environmental Paper Network
www.environmentalpaper.org

GrassRoots Recycling Network
www.grrn.org

GreenBlue^SM
www.greenblue.org

International Standards Organization
www.iso.org

The Natural Step
www.naturalstep.org

o2 International Network for Sustainable Design
www.o2.org

Rainforest Action Network
www.ran.org

Rocky Mountain Institute
www.rmi.org

Union of Concerned Scientists (UCS)
www.ucsusa.org

World Resources Institute
www.wri.org

Sustainable Business

Businesses for Social Responsibility
www.bsr.org

Center for Environmental Leadership in Business
www.celb.org

Caux Round Table/Principles for Business
www.cauxroundtable.org

Ceres
www.ceres.org

Ethical Consumer
www.ethicalconsumer.org

GreenBiz
www.greenbiz.com

Natural Capital Institute
www.naturalcapital.org

Sustainability Consultants

Biomimicry Guild
www.Biomimicry.org

Celery Design Collaborative
www.celerydesign.com

ecoLingo
www.ecolingo.com

Jedlička Design Ltd.
www.jedlicka.com

Organic Design Operatives
www.themightyodo.com

J. Ottman Consulting
www.greenmarketing.com

RegRelief International
ISO 14000 Consulting and Training
www.regrelief.com

Sustainability Associates
www.SustainabilityAssociates.us

Sustainability Education

AIGA Center for Sustainable Design
www.sustainability.aiga.org

Biomimicry Guild and Institute
www.biomimicry.org

Design:Green
www.designgreen.org

Designers Accord
www.designersaccord.org

ecoLingo
*www.ecolingo.com*IDSA Ecodesign
www.idsa.org/whatsnew/sections/ecosection

Minneapolis College of Art and Design
MCAD Online: Sustainable Design Certificate
www.mcad.edu/sustainable

The Natural Step
www.naturalstep.org

Sustainability Associates
www.sustainabilityassociates.us

Sustainable Packaging Coalition[SM]
www.sustainablepackaging.org

Environmentally Preferable Purchasing

Certified Forest Products Council
www.certifiedwood.org

Environmentally Preferable Purchasing (EPP)
www.moea.state.mn.us/lc/purchasing

Natural Resources Defense Council's (NDRC)
"Green Business Guides" and "Greening
Advisor's" pages
www.nrdc.org

Solid Waste Management Coordinating Board
www.greenguardian.com/businessWaste Issues

The Annenberg/CPB Project
www.learner.org/exhibits/garbage

Bureau of International Recycling
www.bir.org

Container Recycling Institute
www.container-recycling.org

Eco-Cycle
www.ecocycle.org

EPA/WasteWise
www.epa.gov/wastewise

Eureka Recycling
www.eurekarecycling.org

"If not you, then who?" / MPCA
www.moea.state.mn.us/campaign

Natural Resources Defense Council
www.nrdc.org/cities/recycling

New York WasteMatch
www.wastematch.org

Recycling Laws International
www.raymond.com

RecycleBank
www.recyclebank.com

Recycler's World
www.recycle.net

SEEK / Sharing Environmental Knowledge
www.nextstep.state.mn.us

Solid Waste Association of North America
www.swana.org

Strategies for Waste Minimization
www.cfd.rmit.edu.au/waste

Waste News
www.wastenews.com

Waste Wise / EPA Program
www.epa.gov/wastewise

Knowledge Is Power

By educating ourselves, we can in turn educate our clients, suppliers, and the consumer, the driving force behind it all. Sustainable design simply becomes great design, and suddenly the whole landscape has changed—quite a lot to demand of a little lunchtime reading, but every journey starts with the first step. For reading list updates, visit: o2-USA/Upper Midwest (*o2umw.org*).

The Big Picture

Biomimicry: Innovation Inspired by Nature
Janine M. Benyus

Cradle to Cradle: Remaking the Way We Make Things
William McDonough and Michael Braungart

Design for the Real World: Human Ecology and Social Change
Victor Papanek

Earth in Mind: On Education, Environment, and the Human Prospect
David W. Orr

Ecodesign: The Sourcebook
Alastair Fuad-Luke

Eco-Economy: Building an Economy for the Earth
Lester R. Brown
www.earth-policy.org

Ecological Design
Sim van der Ryn and Stuart Cowan
www.serve.com/ecobooks/ecodesig.htm

Eternally Yours: Visions on Product Endurance
Edited by Ed van Hinte, Liesbeth Bonekamp, Henk Muis, and Arnout Odding
www.eternally-yours.org

Green Marketing: Opportunity for Innovation
Jacquelyn A. Ottman
www.GreenMarketing.com

The Landscape of Man: Shaping the Environment from Prehistory to the Present Day
Geoffrey Jellicoe and Susan Jellicoe

Natural Capitalism: Creating the Next Industrial Revolution
Paul Hawken, Amory Lovins, and L. Hunter Lovins
www.natcap.org

The Nature of Design: Ecology, Culture, and Human Intention
David W. Orr

The Natural Step for Business
Natural Step Publications
www.naturalstep.org

Trespassers: Inspirations for Eco-Efficient Design
Conny Bakker and Ed van Hinte
www.010publishers.nl

Architecture and Community Development

Building with Vision: Optimizing and Finding Alternatives to Wood
Dan Imhoff
www.watershedmedia.org

Dimensions of Sustainability: Architecture, Form, Technology, Environment and Culture
Andrew Scott, editor

From Eco-Cities to Living Machines: Principles of Ecological Design
Nancy Todd, John Todd, and Jeffrey Parkin, illustrator

Sustainable Ecosystems and the Built Environment
Christopher McCarthy and Guy Battle

Packaging and Print Design

The All New Print Production Handbook
David Bann

Design Guidelines for Sustainable Packaging
Sustainable Packaging Coalition
www.sustainablepackaging.org

Getting It Printed: How to Work with Printers and Graphic Imaging Services to Assure Quality, Stay on Schedule and Control Costs (Getting It Printed), 4th edition
Eric Kenly and Mark Beach

Getting it Right in Print: Digital Prepress for Graphic Designers
Mark Gatter, Harry N. Abrams

Graphic Designer's Digital Printing and Prepress Handbook
Constance Sidles

Green Graphic Design
Brian Dougherty
www.celerydesign.com

The Guide to Tree-Free, Recycled and Certified Papers
Dan Imhoff
www.watershedmedia.org

Package Design Magazine: Sustainability Update
www.packagedesignmag.com/ sustainableresource

Packaging Sustainability: Tools, Systems and Strategies for Innovative Package Design
Wendy Jedlička, contributing editor
www.packagingsustainability.info

Paper or Plastic: Searching for Solutions to an Overpackaged World
Dan Imhoff
www.watershedmedia.org

The Printing Ink Manual
Robert Leach and Ray Pierce, editors, 5th edition (1999)

Printing Technology
J. Michael Adams and Penny Ann Dolin

Real World Print Production (Real World)
Claudia McCue

Product Design

Design + Environment: A Global Guide to Designing Greener Goods
Helen Lewis and John Gertsakis, with Tim Grant, Nicola Morelli, and Andrew Sweatman
www.greenleaf-publishing.com

Sustainable Solutions: Developing Products and Services for the Future
Martin Charter and Ursula Tischner, editors.
www.greenleaf-publishing.com

The Total Beauty of Sustainable Products
Edwin Datschefski
www.biothinking.com

Notes by Chapter

Chapter 1: Making the Business Case

1. Wikipedia contributors, "Tylenol," *Wikipedia, The Free Encyclopedia*, http://en.wikipedia.org/w/index.php ?title=Tylenol&oldid=293464539.
2. Dave Tilford, "Sustainable Consumption: Why Consumption Matters," Sierra Club Sustainable Consumption Committee Web site, 2000; www.sierraclub.org/ sustainable_consumption/tilford.asp.
3. Data from www.footprintnetwork.org.
4. Annie Leonard, *The Story of Stuff*, video, Free Range Studios (2005); storyofstuff.com.
5. Tilford, "Sustainable Consumption."
6. Ibid.
7. Redefining Progress, "Genuine Progress Indicator," www .rprogress.org/sustainability_indica tors/genuine _progress_indicator.htm. Other GNH/GPI links: www .calvert-henderson.com, www.gnh-movement.org/.
8. Tilford, "Sustainable Consumption."
9. Neva Goodwin, "Economic Vitality in a Transition to Sustainability," Civil Society Institute, 2008. www .civilsocietyinstitute.org/reports/GEGWS-Goodwin Chapter.pdf.
10. Business Role Focus Area Team, *Sustainable Consumption Facts and Trends: From a Business Perspective*, World Business Council for Sustainable Development (November 2008); www.wbcsd.org/DocRoot/ I9Xwhv7X5V8cDIHbHC3G/WBCSD_Sustainable _Consumption_web.pdf.
11. To download the entire report, visit the WBCSD Web site at: *2007 Cause Evolution & Environmental Survey*, Cone LLC, www.coneinc.com/files/ 2007ConeSurveyReport.pdf.
12. United Nations NGO Committee on Sustainable Development, www.unngosustainability.org/.
13. Ron Romanik, "The Wal-Mart Sustainability Scorecard Becomes Interactive, Competitive Reality," *Package Design Magazine* (November 2006. www .packagedesignmag.com/issues/2006.11/special. walmart.shtml.
14. GreenBiz.com. "Wal-Mart's Newest Green Goal: Cleaner Supply Chains" (September 2007); www.greenbizleaders. com/NewsDetail.cfm?NewsID=35966.
15. Tilford, "Sustainable Consumption."
16. Mindy S. Lubber, letter in Ceres Annual Report, "2006 & Beyond" (August 2007). www.ceres.org/ NETCOMMUNITY/Document.Doc?id=137.
17. "Playing Games with the Planet," *The Economist*, Septem-ber 27, 2007. www.economist.com/finance/displaystory .cfm?story_id=9867020.
18. Robert Axelrod and William D. Hamilton, "The Evolution of Cooperation," *Science*, New Series, 211, no. 4489, Mar. 27, 1981), pp. 1390–1396; www.cscs.umich.edu/ Software/ComplexCoop.html.
19. Wikipedia contributors, "Code of Hammurabi," *Wikipedia, The Free Encyclopedia*, http://en.wikipedia.org/w/ index.php?title=Code_of_Hammurabi&oldid=293643618.
20. Science and Environmental Health Network, "Precautionary Principle," www.sehn.org/precaution.html.
21. Tim O'Riordan and James Cameron, eds., *Interpreting The Precautionary Principle* (London: Earthscan Publications, 1994); www.dieoff.org/page31.htm.
22. World Charter for Nature, 48th plenary meeting, October 28. 1982; www.un.org/documents/ga/res/37/a37r007 .htm.
23. The Body Shop International, Chemicals Strategy, August 2006.
24. Michael Pollan, "Precautionary Principle," *New York Times Magazine*, December 9, 2001; www.michaelpollan .com/article.php?id=61.
25. Bay Area Working Group on the Precautionary Principle, "The Precautionary Principle in Action"; www.taking precaution.org/inact.html.
26. City and County of San Francisco Environment Code, Ord. No. 279–07, File No. 070678, approved December 12, 2007 (added by Ord. 171–03, File No. 030422, App. 7/3/2003); www.municode.com/Resources/ gateway.asp?pid=14134&sid=5.
27. Blue Planet Village, www.blueplanetvillage.com/article. php?a=read&aid=22.
28. "Japan's Sustainable Society in the Edo Period (1603–1867)," *Japan for Sustainability Newsletter* 7 (March 2003).
29. C. M. Boardman and H. K. Kato, "The Confucian Roots of Business Kyosei," *Journal of Business Ethics* 48, no. 4 (December 2003): 317–333.
30. The Caux Round Table, excerpts reprinted with permission; www.cauxroundtable.org/history.html, /about .htm, /principles.html.
31. Canon Global, Environmental Activities, www.canon .com/environment, www.usa.canon.com/html/ templatedata/pressrelease/20071022_iso14001.html.
32. "Dow Jones Sustainability Index," *Economist*, September, 11, 1999. p. 24; Andrew Crane, *Business Ethics*, The Economist publication, Deceber 2006, Introduction.

33. Wikipedia contributors, "Overview of Triple Bottom Line," *Wikipedia: The Free Encyclopedia*, htpp://en.wikipedia.org/wiki/Triple_bottom_line.

34. Joel Makower, "The New Value Prop," March 18, 2006, www.makower.typepad.com/joel_makower/2006/03/the_new_value_p.html.

35. As cited in Lisa Eunson, "Blending Profit and Nonprofit Values," Stanford University, Graduate School of Business (May 2003); www.gsb.stanford.edu/news/bmag/sbsm0305/ideas_emerson_social_innovation.shtml.

36. Ceres, www.ceres.org.

37. Anya Kamenetz, "Building a Sustainable Design Community," Fast Company, Wed Sep 17, 2008. www.fastcompany.com/magazine/129/100000-and-counting.html. (Accessed June 15, 2009).

38. Innovest Strategic Value Advisors, "Carbon Beta and Equity Performance: An Empirical Analysis" (October 2007); www.innovestgroup.com.

39. William Baue, "List of Global 100 Most Sustainable Companies Highlights Alcoa, BP, and Toyota," Sustainability Investment News, SRI World Group, Inc. February 02, 2005. www.socialfunds.com/news/article.cgi/1628.html.

40. John Kalkowski, "State of 'Green Packaging,'" *Packaging Digest*, December 1, 2007; www.packagingdigest.com/article/CA6505215.html?q=state+of+green+packaging.

41. "Playing Games with the Planet."

42. Rachel Lianna Davis, "Around the world in . . . record time," *Wal-Mart Shareholders Souvenir Edition 2009 Benton County Daily Record.* June 2, 2006. walmart.nwanews.com/wm_story.php?storyid=35569&section=shareholder.

43. Don Carli, "The Footprint of Print and Digital Media Supply Chains," Institute for Sustainable Communication, April 11, 2009; Energy Information Administratio, www.eia.doe.gov/fuelelectric.html.

44. Don Carli, "The Footprint of Print and Digital Media Supply Chains," Institute for Sustainable Communication, April 11, 2009.

45. Don Carli, "The Footprint of Print and Digital Media Supply Chains," Institute for Sustainable Communication, April 11, 2009.

46. http://greenormal.blogspot.com/2007/05/green-marketing-manifesto-it-is.html.

47. McCann-Erickson World Group, "Can Sustainability Sell?" www.eaca.be/_upload/documents/ResponsibleAdvertising/Sustainabiblity_Brochure.pdf.

48. Jacob Gordon, "Tom Friedman: 'Living Green is not for Sissies." Treehugger.com, January 12, 2006. www.treehugger.com/files/2006/01/tom_friedman_li.php.

49. Carbon Disclosure Project, www.cdproject.net.

50. Global Reporting Initiative, www.globalreport ing.org.

51. "Washington State Joins the West's War on Warming: Five Governors Target Pollution," *Seattle Post-Intelligencer*, February 27, 2007; www.heatisonline.org/contentserver/objecthandlers/index.cfm?id=6290&method=full.

52. Moira Herbst, "Investors Call on Congress to Go Green," *Business Week*, March 20, 2007; www.businessweek.com/bwdaily/dnflash/content/mar2007/db20070320_535194.htm?chan=top%25.

53. Knowledge Networks, July 26, 2007; www.knowledgenetworks.com/news/releases/2007/072607_MIT.html.

54. LOHAS online, www.lohas.com.

55. E. L. Plambeck and L. Denend, "The Greening of Wal-Mart," *Stanford Social Innovation Review* (Spring 2008); www.value-networks.com/Articles/Wal-Mart%20Value%20Networks.pdf.

56. John Elkington, *Cannibals with Forks: Triple Bottom Line of 21st Century Business* (Stony Creek, CT: New Society Publishers, 1998), chap. 1, "Enter the Triple Bottom Line," www.johnelk ington.com/TBL-elkington-chapter.pdf.

57. Denis Du Bois, "Carbon Neutral Is Oxford Dictionary 2006 Word of the Year," *Energy Priorities*, November 14, 2006; http://energypri orities.com/entries/2006/11/carbon_neutral_oxford_word.php.

Chapter 2: The Psychology of Graphics

1. Jeremy Faludi, "If It Can't Be Grown, It Must Be Mined," in Wendy Jedlička, *Packaging Sustainability* (Hoboken, NJ: John Wiley & Sons, 2008.

2. Wendy Jedlička, *Packaging Sustainability* (Hoboken, NJ: John Wiley & Sons, 2008).

3. E. R. Tufte, *Visual Explanations: Images and Quantities, Evidence and Narrative* (Cheshire, CT: Graphics Press, 1983).

4. Colin Turnbull cited in Roger R. Hock, "What You See Is What You've Learned," in *Forty Studies that Changed Psychology* (Upper Saddle River, NJ: Prentice-Hall, 1999).

5. G. E. Legge, Y. Gu, and A. Luebker, "Efficiency of Graphical Perception," *Perception & Psycho-physics* 46 (1991): 365–374.

6. W. L. Braje, "Illumination Encoding in Face Recognition: Effect of Position Shift," *Journal of Vision* 3 (March 2003): 161–170; http://journalofvision.org/3/2/4/, DOI10.1167/3.2.4.

7. J. Walraven, C. Enroth-Cugell, D. C. Hood, D. I. A. MacLeod, and J. L. Schnapf, "The Control of Visual Sensitivity," in L. Spillmann and J. S. Werner, eds., *Visual*

Perception: The Neurophysiological Foundations (San Diego: Academic Press, 1990).

8. B. J. Scholl, "Objects and Attention: The State of the Art," *Cognition* 80, nos. 1–2 (2001): 1–46.

9. D. H. Hubel, *Eye, Brain, & Vision* (New York: W. H. Freeman, 1988). For modern examples of eye movements and their dependence on task, see: J. D. Nelson, "Task-Directed Eye Movement Trials" (2008); http://mplab.ucsd.edu/~jnelson/foveation.html.

10. Wikipedia contributors, "Gestalt Psychology," *Wikipedia, The Free Encyclopedia*, http://en.wikipedia.org/w/index.php?title=Gestalt_psychology&oldid=293476942.

11. K. Boff, L. Kaufman, and J. Thomas, *Handbook of Perception and Performance*, 2 vols. (New York: John Wiley & Sons, 1986).

12. W. L. Braje, B. S. Tjan, and G. E. Legge, "Human Efficiency for Recognizing and Detecting Low-Pass Filtered Objects," *Vision Research* 35, no. 21 (1995): 2955–2966.

13. Boff, Kaufman, and Thomas, *Handbook of Perception and Performance.*

14. G. E. Legge, *Psychophysics of Reading in Normal and Low Vision* (Mahwah, NJ: Lawrence Erlbaum Associates, 2007).

15. M. M. Amick, J. Grace, and B. R. Ott, "Visual and Cognitive Predictors of Driving Safety in Parkinson's Disease Patients," *Archives of Clinical Neuropsychology* 22, no. 8 (2007): 957–967.

16. G. E. Legge, G. S. Rubin, D. G. Pelli, and M. M. Schleske, "Psychophysics of Reading. II. Low Vision," *Vision Research* 25 (1985): 253–266.

17. *It's a Kid's World, PBS Scientific American Frontiers,* Season 5 (1994–1995).

18. Wikipedia contributors, "Swastika," *Wikipedia, The Free Encyclopedia*, http://en.wikipedia.org/w/index.php?title=Swastika&oldid=293881535.

19. Paul Ekman, "Facial Expression of Emotion," *American Psychologist* 48, no. 4 (1993): 384–392.

Chapter 3: Seeking Truth in Marketing

1. Raphael Bemporad and Mitch Baranowski, BBMG Five Principles of Sustainable Branding White Paper, www.bbmg.com/enewsletter/b4s_whitepaper.html. Triple Value Proposition™ is a registered trademark of BBMG.

2. Dominique Conseil, president, Aveda Web site, http://aveda.aveda.com/aboutaveda/mission.asp.

3. *The Economist*, "Saving the Rainforest," July 22, 2004.

4. Jim Carlton, "Retailer Leans on Suppliers to Protect Forests Abroad; Playing Mediator in Chile Indonesian Loggers Resist," *Wall Street Journal*, August 6, 2004.

5. Nike press release, April 13, 2005, www.nikebiz.com/media/pr/2005/04/13_FY04_CRReport.html.

6. United Nations Educational, Scientific and Cultural Organization. (2006) *Understanding Creative Industries: Cultural Statistics for Public Policy-Making.* UNESCO, Paris; United Nations Educational, Scientific and Cultural Organization. (2005) *International Flows of Selected Cultural Goods and Services, 1994–2003.* UNESCO, Paris.

7. I. Robertson, ed. *Understanding International Art Markets and Management.* Routledge, London. (2005, p. 19).

8. In 2005, the value of world trade in: coffee and coffee substitutes (SITC 071) was $14.0 billion; cotton (SITC 263), $8.4 billion; manufactured tobacco (SITC 122), $16.9 billion; and road motor vehicles (SITC 783), $30.1 billion.

9. For example, art exports from Switzerland are 0.25 percent of its total economic activity; art imports, 0.41 percent.

10. The exceptions are Singapore and Cyprus, which are identified as high-income countries by the World Bank.

11. Center for Biodiversity and Conservation, "Biodiversity in Crisis? Losses of Species and Habitats: An Introduction to the Issues and Comparison of Opinions from Scientists and the Public," American Museum of Natural History, http://cbc.amnh.org/crisis/resconpercap.html.

12. Rich Pirog, "Food, Fuel, and Freeways: An Iowa Perspective on How Far Food Travels, Fuel Usage, and Greenhouse Gas Emissions," Leopold Center for Sustainable Agriculture (June 2001), www.leopold.iastate.edu/pubs/staff/ppp.

13. www.guardian.co.uk/environment/2007/may/31/greenpolitics.retail/print. www.greenbiz.com/news/news_third.cfm?NewsID=36271.

14. Heather Green, "How Green Is That Gizmo?" *Business Week*, December 20, 2007; www.businessweek.com/magazine/content/07_53/b4065036215848.htm?chan=innovation_innovation+%2B+design_green+design.

15. "FTC Announces Workshop on 'Green Guides' and Packaging," February 25, 2008, www.ftc.gov/opa/2008/02/greenguides.shtm.

16. Cone LLC press release, "Cone Releases 2008 Green Gap Survey," Boston, April 15, 2008. www.coneinc.com/content1136.

17. Ibid.

18. Actual comments made to author in innumerable meetings.

19. GreenBiz.com, "Most Green Marketing Claims Aren't True, Says New Report," www.greenbiz.com/news/news_third.cfm?NewsID=36271.

20. Green Seal Standards and Certification, *International Standards for Eco-Labeling*, www.greenseal.org/certification/international.cfm.

21.	Britt Bravo, *Online Storytelling & Cause Marketing: An Interview with Jonah Sachs of Free Range Studios*, September 29, 2006, www.netsquared.org/blog/britt-bravo/online-storytelling-cause-marketing-an-interview-with-jonah-sachs-of-free-range-studios.

22.	Free Range Studios, "Giving Back," www.freerangestudios.com/giving-back.html/.

23.	Wikipedia contributors, "The Story of Stuff," *Wikipedia, The Free Encyclopedia*, http://en.wikipedia.org/w/index.php?title=The_Story_of_Stuff&oldid=29376104.

24.	Laura Everage, "Understanding the LOHAS Lifestyle," *The Gourmet Retailer*, October 1, 2002, www.gourmetretailer.com/gourmetretailer/magazine/article_display.jsp?vnu_content_id=1738479.

25.	Paul H. Ray and Sherry Ruth Anderson, *The Cultural Creatives: How 50 Million People Are Changing the World* (New York: Harmony Books, 2000); www.culturalcreatives.org.

26.	"Are You a Cultural Creative?" www.culturalcreatives.org/questionnaire.html.

Chapter 4: Systems Thinking

Notes on Chapter Material

This section includes more detail and references on information in this chapter.

DESIGNERS INFLUENCED BY FULLER'S IDEAS

Jay Baldwin, *Buckyworks* (New York: John Wiley, 1996) Thanks to Jay for review comments.

Paul MacCready: August 2007, May 2008, www.achievement.org/autodoc/page/mac0pro-1.

John Todd, *From Eco-Cities to Living Machines* (Berkeley: North Atlantic, 1994), May 2008, www.toddecological.com/ecomachineprincipals.html.

Stewart Brand: Sept. 2006, May 2008, http://sb.longnow.org/Home.html.

Medard Gabel: 2008, May 2008, www.bigpicturesmallworld.com/index.shtml.

Harold Brown: 2007, May 2008, www.osearth.com.

Lovins and Lovins: 2008, May 2008, www.rmi.org.

William McDonough: April 2008, May 2008, http://en.wikipedia.org/wiki/William_McDonough.

EXPLORING BUCKMINSTER FULLER'S IDEAS

Many resources are available at the Buckminster Fuller Institute, www.bfi.org.

The World of Buckminster Fuller, dir. Robert Snyder, DVD, Mystic Fire Video, 1995.

Amy Edmondson, *A Fuller Explanation* (Boston: Birkhauser, 1985) Online at: May 2008, www.angelfire.com/mt/marksomers/40.html.

R. Buckminster Fuller, *Synergetics* and *Synergetics II* (New York: MacMillan, 1975, 1979) Online at: Summer 1997, May 2008, DATES www.rwgrayprojects.com/synergetics/toc/toc.html.

DESIGN DECISIONS

For more information on Nine Boxes and other Triz approaches, *see* Darrell Mann *Hands On Systematic Innovation*. www.systematic-innovation.com/.

The Triz Journal, www.triz-journal.com.

Many of the ideas on linking designs into larger systems come from John Moes: http://themightyodo.com/.

PATTERN LANGUAGES

See the references on Christopher Alexander, and look at resources in the links here: http://en.wikipedia.org/wiki/Pattern_language.

UNDERSTANDING SYSTEMS PROPERTIES

Christopher Alexander, *The Timeless Way of Building and A Pattern Language* (New York: Oxford, 1979, 1977). These teach the basics of building multilayer systems in a way which connects the user and designer. In addition, the pattern language form allows design information to be shared as open source.

Mark Buchanan, *Nexus* (New York: Norton, 2002). This book summarizes the latest topics on network theory and emergence.

These next books are at a higher systems level, yet the principles are clear:

Sim Van Der Ryn, *Ecological Design* (Washington: Island Press, 2007).

Edward Goldsmith, *The Way* (Athens: University of Georgia Press, 1998).

John Todd, *From Eco-Cities to Living Machines* (Berkeley, CA: North Atlantic, 1994), May 2008, www.toddecological.com/ecomachineprincipals.html.

LIFE CYCLE ASSESSMENT

Dr Heinz Stichnothe of The University of Manchester School of Chemical Engineering and Analytical Science for review comments,

COMMERCIAL LCA SOFTWARE

Simapro, May 2008, www.pre.nl/simapro.

Gabi, May 2008,www.gabi-software.com.

NONCOMMERCIAL LCA

Eco-Indicator 99 and Eco-Indicator 95. May 2008, www.pre.nl/eco-indicator99/default.htm.

EXAMPLES ON HOW TO CONDUCT LCA

Design for Sustainability at Delft: May 2008 www.io.tudelft.nl/research/dfs.

Jensen et al., *Overview of Life Cycle Assessment (LCA): A guide to approaches, experiences and information sources*, 2008, http://reports.eea.europa.eu/GH-07-97-595-EN-C/en.

CRADLE TO CRADLE

W. McDonough and M. Braungart, *Cradle to Cradle: Remaking The Way We Make Things* (New York: North Point Press, 2002), May 2008, www.mcdonough.com/cradle_to_cradle.htm.

Design examples: 2007, May 2008, www.mbdc.com/c2c.

BIOMIMICRY CONSULTING

The Biomimicry Guild: May 2008, www.biomimicryguild.com/indexguild.html.

BIOMIMICRY EDUCATION

The Biomimicry Institute 2008, May 2008, www.biomimicryinstitute.org.

PERMACULTURE

Ross Mars, *The Basics of Permaculture Design* (White River Junction, VT: Chelsea Green, 2005).

CHANGE MANAGEMENT

Manns and Rising, *Fearless Change* (Indianapolis, IN: Addison Wesley, 2004) May 2008, www.cs.unca.edu/~manns/intropatterns.html.

ENDNOTES

1. R. C. Baker, "Deep Time, Short Sight: Bracing for Yucca Mountain's Nuclear Forever," *Village Voice*, May 28, 2002; www.villagevoice.com/2002-05-28/news/deep-time-short-sight/1.
2. Daniel H. Pink, *A Whole New Mind: Why Right-Brainers Will Rule the Future* (New York: Riverhead Books, 2005).
3. Wikipedia contributors, "Dymaxion Map," *Wikipedia, The Free Encyclopedia*, http://en.wikipedia.org/w/index.php?title=Dymaxion_map&oldid=213706482 (accessed May 2008).
4. Neenah Paper, "Stochastic Printing vs. Conventional Printing," www.neenahpaper.com/Articles/articles.asp?ft=OHH&articleType=printing&article=7. Note on stochastic printing: The disadvantage is that this printing process can reproduce too much detail and is more difficult to proof and control dot gain on press.
5. Mahlon Hoagland and Bert Dodson, *The Way Life Works: The Science Lover's Illustrated Guide to How Life Grows, Develops, Reproduces, and Gets Along* (New York: Three Rivers Press, 1998).
6. "United Nations Environment Programme Division of Technology, Industry and Economics" (May 2008), www.unep.fr/pc/sustain/design/pss.htm.
7. The term "cradle to cradle" comes from the book of the same name: William McDonough and Michael Braungart, *Cradle to Cradle: Remaking the Way We Make Things* (New York: North Point Press, 2002).
8. Spencer Johnson, *Who Moved My Cheese* (New York: Putnam, 1998).
9. "3M-inent thinking" *The Engineer*, Centaur Media PLC, May 31, 2005; www.theengineer.co.uk/Articles/290942/3M-inent+thinking.htm.
10. The term "technical nutrients" comes from McDonough and Braungart's book, *Cradle to Cradle*.
11. Tyler Volk, *Metapatterns* (New York: Columbia University Press, 1996).
12. Wikipedia contributors, "Competitive Exclusion Principle," *Wikipedia, The Free Encyclopedia*, http://en.wikipedia.org/w/index.php?title=Competitive_exclusion_principle&oldid=205650952 (accessed April 2008).
13. Edward de Bono, *Surpetition* (New York: HarperCollins, 1992).
14. David G. Ullman, *Making Robust Decisions* (Victoria, BC: Trafford, 2006).
15. Karl A. Smith, *Teamwork and Project Management*, 3rd ed. (New York: McGraw-Hill, 2005).
16. Ken Thompson, *Bioteams: High Performance Teams Based on Nature's Most Successful Designs* (Tampa, FL: Meghan-Kiffer Press, 2008); www.bioteams.com.
17. J. Lagerstedt, "Functional and Environmental Factors in Early Phases of Product Development—Eco Functional Matrix", *The International Journal of Life Cycle Assessment*, Volume 8, Number 3 / May, 2003, Pages 160-166, Springer Berlin / Heidelberg.
18. CTQ Media LLC, *Triz Journal* 2006, May 2008; www.triz-journal.com.
19. Darrell Mann, "Hands-On Systematic Innovation," Presentation, 2003; www.systematic-innovation.com.

20. Alan Van Pelt and Jonathan Hey, *Using Triz and Human-Centered Design for Consumer Product Development*, http://best.berkeley.edu/~jhey03/files/Publications/TRIZ%20and%20Human-Centered%20design%20TF2006%20Van%20Pelt%20Hey.pdf.

21. ENERGY STAR is a joint program of the U.S. Environmental Protection Agency and the U.S. Department of Energy, www.energystar.gov.

22. Christopher Alexander, *The Timeless Way of Building* (Oxford: Oxford University Press, 1979).

23. David Holmgren, *The Essence of Permaculture*, 2002, ww.holmgren.com.au/html/Writings/essence.html (accessed May 2008).

24. Bill Mollison, "Permaculture: Design for Living." *In Context*, no. 28 (Spring 1991): 50; www.context.org/ICLIB/IC28/Mollison.htm (accessed May 2008).

25. David Holmgren, *Permaculture: Principles and Pathways beyond Sustainability* (Hepburn, Victoria, Australia: Holmgren Design Services, 2002).

26. Ray Jardine, *Beyond Backpacking, A Guide to Lightweight Hiking* (LaPine, OR: Adventurelore Press, 1999).

27. Bill Mollison, *Permaculture: A Designers' Manual* (Tasmania, NSW: Tagari, 1997).

28. Wikipedia contributors, "Change Management (People)," *Wikipedia, The Free Encyclopedia*, http://en.wikipedia.org/w/index.php?title=Change_management_(people)&oldid=293672059 (accessed June 2008).

29. Wikipedia contributors, "Everett Rogers," *Wikipedia, The Free Encyclopedia*, http://en.wikipedia.org/w/index.php?title=Everett_Rogers&oldid=257810421 (accessed June 2008).

30. Wikipedia contributors, "Change Management (People)."

31. Fred Nickols, "Change Management 101: A Primer," http://home.att.net/~nickols/change.htm (accessed May 2008).

32. Wikipedia contributors, "Twelve leverage points," *Wikipedia, The Free Encyclopedia*, http://en.wikipedia.org/w/index.php?title=Twelve_leverage_points&oldid=206754218 (accessed May 2008).

33. Such as the *Journal of Industrial Ecology*, www.mitpressjournals.org/jie.

34. Wikipedia contributors, "Industrial ecology," *Wikipedia, The Free Encyclopedia*, "External Links for Industrial Ecology Academic depart ments, http://en.wikipedia.org/w/index.php?title=Industrial_ecology#External_links (accessed May 2008).

35. Paraphrased from G. A. Keoleian et al., *Life Cycle Design Framework and Demonstration Projects* (Washington, DC: Risk Reduction Engineering Laboratory, Office of Research and Development, U.S. Environmental Protection Agency, July 1995), EPA 600/R-95/107. See also G. A. Keoleian and D. Menerey: "Sustainable Development by Design: Review of Life Cycle Design and Related Approaches," *Journal of the Air and Waste Management Association* 44 (1994): 644–668.

36. Mary Lynn Manns and Linda Rising, *Fearless Change* (Indianapolis: Addison-Wesley 2004); www.cs.unca.edu/~manns/intropatterns.html (accessed May 2008).

37. Wikipedia contributors, "Analytic Hierarchy Process," *Wikipedia, The Free Encyclopedia*, http://en.wikipedia.org/w/index.php?title=Analytic_Hierarchy_Process&oldid=211638724 (accessed May 2008).

38. Wendy Jedlicka, "The Times They Are a-Changin,'" *Package Design Magazine*, www.packagedesignmag.com/issues/2006.06/sustainable.shtml (accessed May 2008).

39. European Food Transport System, www.europoolsystem.com (accessed May 2008).

40. *Wikipedia*, "Environmental impact assessment," May 2008, May 2008, http://en.wikipedia.org/wiki/Environmental_impact_assessment.

41. The EcoCost approach, www.ecocostsvalue.com (accessed May 2008).

42. "World Business Council for Sustainable Development," www.wbcsd.org/templates/TemplateWBCSD5/layout.asp?MenuID=1 (accessed 2008).

43. Joost G. Vogtländer, "The Model of the Eco-costs/Value Ratio (EVR)," TUDelft, Delft University of Technology, www.ecocostsvalue .com (accessed May 2008).

44. GreenBlue, "Sustainable Packaging Coalition," www.sustainablepackaging.org.

45. Sustainable Packaging Coalition, "Definition of Sustainable Packaging," www.sustainablepackaging.org/about_sustainable_packaging.asp (accessed October 2005).

46. Ibid.

47. GreenBlue, "The Design Guidelines for Sustainable Packaging" www.greenblue.org/resources_documents.html (accessed May 2008).

48. Ibid.

49. Sustainable Packaging Coalition, "What Is Sustainable Packaging?" www.sustainablepack aging.org/about_sustainable_packaging.asp (accessed May 2008).

50. Remigijus Ciegis and Rokas Grunda, "Sustainable Business: The Natural Step Framework," www1.apini.lt/includes/getfile.php?id=115 (accessed May 2008).

51. Architecture for Humanity, May 2008, www.architectureforhumanity.org. (accessed May 2008).

52. Ciegis and Grunda, "Sustainable Business."

53. Architecture for Humanity.

54. Universal Design, www.design.ncsu.edu/cud/about_ud/udprincipleshtmlformat.html#top (accessed May 2008).

55. McDonough and Braungart, *Cradle to Cradle*.

56. Ron Romanik, "The Wal-Mart Sustainability Scorecard Becomes Interactive, Competitive Reality," *Package Design Magazine* (November/December 2006); www

.packagedesignmag.com/issues/2006.11/special
.walmart.shtml.

57. Design for Environment (February 2008), www.pca.state
.mn.us/oea/p2/design.cfm (accessed May 2008).

58. McDonough and Braungart, *Cradle to Cradle*.

59. Designtex, cti.itc.virginia.edu/~meg3c/ethics/cases/
dtex/dtex_1.html (accessed May 2008).

60. Andrew C. Revkin and Matthew L. Wald, "Solar Power"
(July 16, 2007), www.nytimes.com/2007/07/16/
business/16solar.html?_r=1&oref=slogin (accessed May
2008).

61. *Wikipedia*, "Process Flow Diagram," Feb. 2008, May 2008,
en.wikipedia.org/wiki/Process_Diagram. (accessed May
2008).

62. Shaw Contract Group, Processes Web page, www
.shawcontractgroup.com.

63. Carbohydrate Economy, www.carbohydrateeconomy.org.
(accessed May 2008).

64. Cradle to Cradle Design Protocol, www.mbdc.com/
c2c_mbdp.htm (accessed May 2008).

65. Mariann Zanardo, "ISO 14001: An Environmental David
for Tackling Sustainability's Goliath," *Package Design
Magazine* (December 2008). www.packagedesignmag
.com/issues/2009.12/index.shtml.

66. International Organization for Standardization,
"ISO—ISO 9000/ISO 14000—ISO 14000 Essentials" www
.iso.org/iso/iso_catalogue/management_standards/
iso_9000_iso_14000/iso_14000_essentials.htm (accessed
May 2008).

67. Hannover Principles, 1992, www.mcdonough.com/
principles.pdf (accessed May 2008).

68. Sim van der Ryn, *Ecological Design Principles* (Washington, DC: Island Press, 1996).

69. Nancy Todd and John Todd, *From Eco-Cities to Living
Machines* (Berkeley, CA: North Atlantic 1993).

70. Eric Von Hipple, *Democratizing Innovation* (Cambridge,
MA: MIT Press, 2006).

71. Wikipedia contributors, "Innovation," *Wikipedia, The
Free Encyclopedia,* http://en.wikipedia.org/w/index.php
?title=Innovation&oldid=294116643 (accessed May 2008).

72. John Thackara, *In the Bubble* (Cambridge, MA: MIT Press,
2005).

73. "What Is Triz?" www.triz-journal.com/archiveswhat_is
_triz/ (accessed May 2008).

74. Universals of Culture. 2005, May 2008, http://
everything2.com/index.pl?node_id=1744457.

Chapter 5: Materials and Processes

1. Facts and figures regarding the true cost of plastic bags,
http://reusablebags.com/facts.php.

2. FRIDGE: Socio-economic impact assessment of the
proposed plastic bag regulations, life cycle assessment of
paper and plastic checkout carrier bags, www.nedlac.org
.za/research/fridge/plastics/life.pdf.

3. Environmental Protection Agency, "Municipal Solid
Waste in the United States: 2007 Facts and Figures"
(November 2008), www.epa.gov/waste/nonhaz/
municipal/pubs/msw07-rpt.pdf, p. 7.

4. Purina Pet Centric, RecycleBank, April 2009. http://
petcentric.com/article.aspx?C=1&OID=302.

5. Six-Month Report of Beverage Container Recycling &
Significant Carbon Reductions, California Department of
Conservation, 2008 www.conservation.ca.gov/dor/
Notices/Documents/6MonthReport.pdf.

6. Jacob Sørensen, "Ecological Rucksack for Materials Used
in Everyday Products, NOAH—Friends of the Earth
Denmark," www.noah.dk/baeredygtig/rucksack/
rucksack.pdf.

7. "Rice University's Chemical 'Scissors' Yield
Short Carbon Nanotubes; New Process Yields Nanotubes
Small Enough to Migrate Through Cells," *ScienceDaily*,
July 23, 2003, www.sciencedaily.com/releases/2003/07/
030723083644.htm.

8. Lorie A. Wagner, "Materials in the Economy—Material
Flows, Scarcity, and the Environment," U.S. Geological
Survey Circular 1221, http://pubs.usgs.gov/circ/2002/
c1221.

9. "How Long Does Litter Last?" www.donttrash nevada
.org/facts_figures.htm.

10. Ugo Bardi, "The Oil Drum: Europe," http://europe
.theoildrum.com/node/3086.

11. David Cohen, "Earth's Natural Wealth: An Audit,"
NewScientist.com, May 23, 2007.

12. Frank T. Manheim, "A New Look at Mining and the
Environment: Finding Common Ground," *Geotimes* (April
2006), www.agiweb.org/geotimes/apr06/feature
_MiningCommonGround.html.

13. 2000 TRI Data Release, www.epa.gov/tri/tridata/tri00/
index.htm.

14. *Encyclopedia of Earth*, www.eoearth.org/article/
Computer_recycling.

15. "A Brief History of Paper," Conservatree Web site
(accessed January 29, 2009), www.conservatree
.com/learn/Essential%20Issues/EIPaperCon tent.shtml.

16. Green America's WoodWise™ Consumer Program
involves consumers by educating them about sustainable
forest practices. Quote sourced by Envirofacts.com
(accessed January 26, 2009, on the WoodWise Web site):
www.coopamerica.org/programs/woodwise.

17. Environmental Protection Agency, "Municipal Solid
Waste in the United States: 2007 Facts and Figures"
(November 2008), www.epa.gov/waste/nonhaz/
municipal/pubs/msw07-rpt.pdf, p. 7.

18. As clients, AIGA members alone specify or purchase $9.1 billion in printing and paper, as sourced from "Partnering with AIGA" Webpage (accessed January 29, 2009): www .aiga.org/content.cfm/sponsorship-why-partner.

19. Forest Products Industry Analysis Briefs: Energy Use, January 28 2004, www.eia.doe.gov/emeu/mecs/iab98/ forest/energy_use.html.

20. Claudia G. Thompson, *Recycled Papers: The Essential Guide* (Cambridge, MA: MIT Press, 1992).

21. Ibid. Patented by Nicholas-Louis Robert, and adapted and financed by the Fourdrinier brothers, stationers in London. Today most papermaking machines operate in the same way and many bear the Fourdrinier name.

22. Ibid.

23. "A Brief History of Paper."

24. Quoted on Envirofacts.com (accessed on the WoodWise Web site, January 26, 2009). Current project Web site: www.greenamericatoday.org/programs/woodwise.

25. "Facts on the Boreal," ForestEthics Web site (accessed January 26, 2009): www.forestethics.org/article.php ?id=1067.

26. "Ontario's Boreal Forest," ForestEthics Web site (accessed January 26, 2009): www.forestethics.org/article.php ?id=2032;.Dogwood Alliance Press Release, "Dogwood Alliance Launches No Free Refills in Louisville," March 31, 2008, http://pressroomda.greenmediatoolshed.org/ node/19359.

27. Design Can Change is an effort to bring together the world's graphic design community to address the issues surrounding climate. Design Can Change Web site (accessed January 29, 2009): www.designcanchange. org/?#home.

28. Environmental Protection Agency, "Municipal Solid Waste Generation, Recycling, and Disposal in the United States."

29. "Fast Food Packaging and the Forests of the Southern United States," Dogwood Alliance Fact Sheet, www .dogwoodalliance.org/content/view/37/94/.

30. As quoted in "Banks, Pulp and People: A Primer on Upcoming International Pulp Projects," published by urgewald e.V. (a German nonprofit organization whose mission is to address the underlying causes of global environmental destruction and poverty (June 2007) (accessed January 27, 2009): www.greenpressinitiative .org/documents/BPP_A_FIN_2.pdf.

31. "Why Packaging?" "Genetically Engineered Trees," Genetic Engineering Web page on the Sierra Club Web site (accessed January 26, 2009): www.sierraclub.org/ biotech/trees.asp.

32. "A Brief History of Paper," Conservatree Web site (accessed January 29, 2009), www.conservatree.com/ learn/Essential%20Issues/EIPaperCon tent.shtml.

33. M. Anielski and S. J. Wilson, "Counting Canada's Natural Capital: Assessing the Real Value of Canada's Boreal Ecosystems," Ottawa, ON, Pembina Institute and Canadian Boreal Initiative (2005), p. 4, www .borealcanada.ca/docu ments/Boreal_Wealth_Report _Nov_2005.pdf.

34. Forest Stewardship Council, "History," FSC Web site (accessed January 19, 2009): www.fsc.org/history.html.

35. Forest Stewardship Council, "About the Forest Steward- ship Council," FSC Web site (accessed January 19, 2009): www.fsc.org/about-fsc.html.

36. Forest Stewardship Council, "FSC Certified Paper," FCS Web site (accessed January 19, 2009): www.fscus.org/ paper.

37. "What Is Forest Stewardship Council (FSC) Chain-of-Custody (CoC) Certification?" Rainforest Alliance Web site (accessed January 19, 2009): www .rainforest-alliance.org/forestry/faq_fsc_coc.html.

38. Ibid.

39. Forest Stewardship Council, "Forest Stewardship Council Product Labeling Guide" (December 2004) (accessed on the Scientific Certification Systems Web site, January 21, 2009): www.scscertified.com/forestry/fsclabels.html.

40. "What Is Controlled Wood?" Rainforest Alliance Web site (accessed January 21, 2009): www.rainforest-alliance.org/ forestry/faq_cw.html.

41. To learn more about FSC-Certified paper and for listings of certified papers, paper merchants, paper manufactur- ers, printers, and pulp suppliers, visit the Forest Stewardship Web site via this link: www.fscus.org/paper.

42. "Ancient Forest Friendly™ Usage Guidelines, Marketing Advantages, and the Science Behind the Brand," Markets Initiative, 2007, www.marketsinitiative.org, (now Canopy at www.canopyplanet.org) www.canopyplanet.org/index .php?page=your-guide-to-the-ancient-forest-friendly -designation.

43. Ibid.

44. Ibid.

45. "About Us," Markets Initiative Web site, visited January 21, 2009, (now Canopy at www.canopy planet.org) www .canopyplanet.org/?page=55.

46. "Sustainable Forestry: Who We Are," Rainforest Alliance Web site (accessed January 19, 2009): www.rainforest -alliance.org/forestry.cfm?id=who.

47. Courtesy of Rainforest Alliance, via e-mail conversation with Abby Ray, Communications Associate, Media Outreach, with Dion Zuess, on January 26, 2009.

48. "ISO 14000 Essentials," ISO Web site (accessed January 19, 2009): www.iso.org/iso/iso_14000_essentials.

49. Jason Metnick, Director, Market Access and Product Labeling, Sustainable Forestry Initiative, Inc., via e-mail correspondence on June 9, 2009.

50. "About PEFC," PEFC Web site, www.pefc.org/internet/html/about_pefc.htm.

51. "Environmental Paper Procurement: Review of Forest Certification Schemes in Canada," Ibid.

52. World Wildlife Fund, National Wildlife Federation, Natural Resources Defense Council, Sierra Club, and Fifty-Eight Other Conservation Groups, "Why the PEFC, SFI, and CSA Are Not Credible Forest Certification Systems," May 21, 2001, http://credibleforestcertification.org/fileadmin/materials/old_growth/dont_buy_sfi/sfi_facts/factsheets/Why_SFI_CSA_PEFC_not_Credible.pdf; "What is Credible Certification," World Wildlife Forest and Trade Network Web Site, http://gftn.panda.org/practical_info/basics/sound_forest/certification/credible_certification/ and "Forest Certification Assessment Guide (FCAG), A Framework for Assessing Credible Forest Certification Systems/Schemes," A Publication of the WWF/World Bank Global Forest Alliance, July 2006, www.worldwildlife.org/what/globalmarkets/forests/WWFBinary item7372.pdf.

53. "A Paper Buyer's Guide to Forest Certification Schemes: Finding the Certification System to Fit Your Needs," Canopy Planet Web Site: www.canopyplanet.org/index.php?page=paper-buyers-guide-certification-schemes, (three page summary PDF available: www.canopyplanet.org/uploads/EEM%20cert%20comp%20overview-1.pdf) and "Environmental Paper Procurement: Review of Forest Certification Schemes in Canada," ÉEM Inc., February 2007, with information current to December 31, 2006. Revised January 2008. Project Number: 07A033, www.canopyplanet.org/uploads/MI-EEMcert-3.pdf.

54. "On the Ground, Forest Certification: Green Stamp of Approval or Rubber Stamp of Destruction?" Case study comparisons of the FSC, CSA, and SFI systems, report commissioned by ForestEthics, Greenpeace, and Sierra Club Canada, 2003, http://credibleforestcertification.org/sfi_facts/factsheets_and_reports/.

55. "A Common Vision for Transforming the Paper Industry: Striving for Environmental and Social Sustainability," Drafted by the Center for a New American Dream, Conservatree, Co-op America, Dogwood Alliance, Environmental Defense, ForestEthics, the Green Press Initiative, the Markets Initiative, Natural Resources Defense Council, the Recycled Products Purchasing Cooperative, Ratified at The Environmental Paper Summit Sonoma County, California. November 20, 2002, www.environmentalpaper.org/documents/CommonVision-guidance.pdf, and via email correspondence with Joshua Martin, Director, Environmental Paper Network, on June 12, 2009.

56. Ibid., "Environmental Paper Procurement: Review of Forest Certification Schemes in Canada."

57. "Paper Products Recovered Materials Advisory Notice II," EPA *Federal Register,* June 8, 1998 (accessed on EPA Web site): www.epa.gov/EPA-WASTE/1998/June/Day-08/f15175.htm.

58. Presidential Documents, "Executive Order 13423 of January 24, 2007 Strengthening Federal Environmental, Energy, and Transportation Management," *Federal Register,* Vol. 72, No. 17, January 26, 2007, accessed on the Center for a New American Dream's Responsible Purchasing Network Web site, www.responsiblepurchasing.org/UserFiles/File/Paper/policies/EO%2013423.pdf.

59. Thompson, *Recycled Papers.*

60. Ibid.

61. California Public Contract Code, Division 2, Part 2, Chapter 4, Public Contract Code Section 12160–12169, http://yosemite1.epa.gov/oppt/eppstand2.nsf/ef1431c4615697008525676100775eca/ebb39b60b8ad54298525696c0068c2f4/$FILE/cacode1.PDF.

62. EcoLogo Program: Third-Party Certification of Environmentally-Preferable Products, www.ecologo.org/en/; EcoLogo[CM] Program Certification Criteria Document, CCD-077, Printing and Writing Paper, www.ecologo.org/en/seeourcri teria/details.asp?ccd_id=302.

63. Ibid. Green Seal's "Choose Green Report" (April 2006): www.greenseal.org/resources/reports/CGR=P&W2.pdf.

64. "Green Seal Environmental Standards," Green Seal Web site (accessed January 30, 2009): www.greenseal.org/certification/environmental.cfm.

65. American Forest and Paper Association, "Paper Recycling Symbol Guidelines and Environmental Marketing Claims" (June 2001): www.stopwaste.org/docs/recycling.pdf.

66. Electronic Code of Federal Regulations: Title 16—Commercial Practices, Chapter I—Federal Trade Commission, Subchapter B, Guides and Trade Practice Rules; Part 260 Guides for the Use of Environmental Marketing Claims (accessed January 26, 2009): http://ecfr.gpoaccess.gov/cgi/t/text/textidx?c=ecfr&sid=b2333ddf96abf25788ef3037ffcfb40a&tpl=/ecfrbrowse/Title16/16cfr260_main_02.tpl; "Facts for Business: Complying with the Environmental Marketing Guides" (accessed January 26, 2009): www.ftc.gov/bcp/edu/pubs/business/energy/bus42.shtm.

67. Green America's WoodWise, "Glossary of Terms" (accessed January 27, 2009): www.coopamerica.org/programs/woodwise/about/glossary.cfm.

68. World Business Council for Sustainable Development and World Resources Institute, "Sustainable Procurement of Wood and Paper-based Products Forest Products: Guide and Resource Kit" (March 2008): www

.sustainableforestprods.org/files/pdfs/Forest%
20Procurement%20full%20_web_links.pdf.

69. Ibid. As quoted in "Banks, Pulp and People."

70. Ibid. Also see Robert McCormack, "Safety and Occupational Health in Forestry Operations in Australia—Changes in Approach through Time," Forest Technology Program, CSIRO Forestry and Forest Products (accessed on January 17, 2008, on the FAO Corporate Document Repository Web site): www.fao.org/docrep/005/ac805e/ac805e0m.htm.

71. "Paper Related Definitions," Environmental Paper Network Web site (accessed January 17, 2009): www.environmentalpaper.org/PAPER-DEFINITIONS.html.

72. Ibid.

73. Green Seal's "Choose Green Report."

74. Ibid; Wendy Jedlička, Packaging Sustainability: Tools, Systems and Strategies for Innovative Package Design (Hoboken, NJ: John Wiley & Sons, 2009).

75. Green Living: Green Living Guides, "Avoiding Chlorine in the Paper Bleaching Process," September 20, 2006, www.nrdc.org/cities/living/chlorine.asp.

76. Pew Center for Climate Change, "Coal and Climate Change Facts," (Accessed, June 11, 2009) www.pewclimate.org/global-warming-basics/coalfacts.cfm.

77. Sierra Club, "Clean Air: Dirty Coal Power." (Accessed, June 11, 2009) www.sierraclub.org/cleanair/factsheets/power.asp.

78. "Neenah Paper Looks 'Marvel'ous on History Channel's 'Modern Marvels' Program; Scores Big for the Paper Industry," January 11, 2007, www.neenahpaper.com/neenahgreen/pressrelease_historychannel.asp.

79. Monadnock Paper Mills Environmental Commitment brochure, published by Monadnock Paper Mills, 2007.

80. New Leaf Paper Press Release, "All New Leaf Paper Inventory Items Manufactured with Green-E® Certified Renewable Energy," San Francisco, February 20, 2007.

81. "Biogas Energy," Environment statement of the Environmental by Choice Web site (accessed January 28, 2009): www.environmentalbychoice.com/biogas_environment.php.

82. Green-e and Center for Resource Solutions Web sites (accessed January 28, 2009): www.green-e.org/gogreene.shtml and www.resource-solutions.org/index.php.

83. "Organizations Using Renewable Energy," Green-e Web site (accessed January 26, 2009): www.green-e.org/base/pl_products.

84. "No Recession for Biogas Industry 2009," NewsBlaze.com, December 2, 2008: http://news blaze.com/story/20081202105203zzzz.nb/topstory.html.

85. Chicago Climate Exchange, "Overview" Web page (accessed January 28, 2009): www.chicago climatex.com/content.jsf?id=821.

86. EPA Climate Leaders Web site, January 23, 2009, www.epa.gov/climateleaders.

87. "Designers make strides in sustainability," quote courtesy of Dion Zuess and ecoLingo, www.ecolingo.com.

88. Neenah ECO calculator (accessed January 23, 2009): www.neenahpaper.com/sustainability/ENVIRONMENTALCalculator/default.aspx; EPA eGrid (accessed on EPA Web site): www.epa.gov/cleanenergy/energy-resources/egrid/index.html.

89. Colin Berry, "Fiber Optimistic," Print Magazine (July/August 2005).

90. "Calculators" available on Mohawk's Web site: www.mohawkpaper.com/resources/resources-calcs.

91. International Institute for Environment and Development, "Toward a Sustainable Paper Cycle Executive Summary" (November 2000).

92. As reported in "Markets Initiative: The Science behind the Brand," New URL: www.canopy planet.org/index.php?page=science-behind-the-brand.

93. Dan Imhoff, The Guide to Tree-free Recycled and Certified Paper Page 13 (Healdsburg, CA : Watershed Media, 1999).

94. "The Wheat Sheet: A New Era of Papermaking in Canada." Publication with trial results of these partners: Markets Initiative, Alberta Research Council, New Page, Canadian Geographic Magazine, and Dollco (June 2008): http://marketsinitiative.org/uploads/MI-wheatsheet 3-screen.pdf. Also available at: www.arc.ab.ca/documents/WS%20backgrounder.pdf.

95. The paper contains 20 percent wheat straw, 40 percent recycled fiber, and 40 percent wood pulp; see Times Colonist, Magazine Printed on Wheat Sheet," May 23, 2008: www2.canada.com/victoriatimescolonist/news/business/story.html?id=ce18d24a-08d0-4d47-b563-20389a7f5bc2.

96. Ibid. "The Wheat Sheet: A New Era of Papermaking in Canada.

97. Aaron G. Lehmer, "Bamboo Paper Is Not Forest-Friendly," Earth Island Journal (Summer 1998). Joe Zammit-Lucia, in collaboration with The Nature Conservancy, "Green-in-Print™: A Guide to Environmentally Friendly Choices in Photographic Paper" (2008); (accessed on January 28, 2009): www.conservatree.com/paper/Choose/GreenInPrintApril08.pdf.

98. Zammit-Lucia, "Green-in-Print™."

99. Lehmer, "Bamboo Paper Is Not Forest-Friendly."

100. Laura Johannes, "Green Battles: Mine Pits Two Green Goals Against Each Other in Town," Wall Street Journal, October 7, 2002 (accessed online): www.vtce.org/omyaminepits.html.

101. William McDonough and Michael Braungart, Cradle to Cradle (New York: North Point Press, 2002).

102. Chiang Mai, "Panda Poop Paper Yields Big Profits," CBS

News, Thailand, November 23, 2006; www.cbsnews.com/
stories/2006/11/23/ap/strange/mainD8LIIBN02.shtml.

103. "Why Sri Lanka," Web page from the Mr. Ellie Pooh Web
     site (accessed February 3, 2009): www.mrelliepooh.com/
     aboutus.html.

104. Green Seal's Choose GREEN Report, "Alternative Fiber
     Papers" (April/May 1998): www
     .greenseal.org/resources/reports/CGR
     =TreeFree.pdf.

105. Susan S. Szenasy, speech delivered to the Power of
     Design: AIGA National Design Conference entitled
     "Ethics and Sustainability: Graphic Designers' Role," in
     Vancouver, October 23–26, 2003, and posted on http://
     powerofdesign.aiga.org/content.cfm/szenasy.

106. "Neenah Paper Looks 'Marvel'ous." Full quote: "'Neenah
     Paper recognizes that our industry is one of the most
     resource-intensive in the world. The manufacturing of
     paper consumes more water per ton of product than
     any other manufacturing process,' says Meredith
     Christiansen, Product Manager for Neenah Paper.
     'Therefore, it's important as a leading fine paper mill to
     promote the technological advancements that allow us
     to recycle the water used in making recycled papers,
     return the water to the Fox River cleaner than when
     it left and decrease our dependence on fossil fuels.'"

107. "Toolkit for Responsible Paper Use," Green Press
     Initiative Web site (accessed January 19, 2009): www
     .greenpressinitiative.org/documents/BookPublisher
     Toolkit.pdf.

108. Ibid.; "P2 Tips for You," EPA Pollution Prevention (P2) Web
     page (accessed January 19, 2009): www.epa.gov/p2/
     pubs/tips.htm#paper.

109. NAPIM, "Formulating Printing Inks to Minimize
     Environmental Impact," www.napim.org/PublicArea/
     Printers/Enviro.aspx.

110. Gary Jones, director of environmental health and safety
     affairs for Printing Industries of America/Graphic Arts
     Technical Foundation (PIA/GATF), e-mail conversations
     and phone interview with coauthor Dion Zuess,
     September 26, 2007.

111. Rainforest Action Network, "Rainforest Agribusiness"
     (accessed November 2008): http://ran.org/what_we_do/
     rainforest_agribusiness/about_the_campaign.

112. Michael Maiello, "Food vs. Fuel," Forbes.com (November
     2007): www.forbes.com/2007/11/11/
     funds-food-corn-forbeslife-food07-cz_mm
     _1113foodfunds.html?partner=yahootix; "Food versus
     Fuel: Is a Happy Ending Possible?," *Food Quality News*
     (February 2007): www.foodqualitynews.com/Innovation/
     Food-versus-fuel-is-a-happy-ending-possible.

113. David Savastano, "Waxes, Solvents and Additives,"
     InkWorld (December 2007): www.inkworldmagazine.

com/articles/2007/12/waxes-solvents-and-additives
.php.

114. Ibid.

115. Sean Milmo, "Energy Efficiency, Sustainability Are Key
     Topics at drupa 2008," *Ink World* www
     .inkworldmagazine.com/articles/2008/07/energy
     -efficiency-sustainability-are-key-topics-at.php.

116. Michelle Hearn, director of marketing, North America
     Packaging, Sun Chemical. Phone interview with coauthor
     Dion Zuess, January 18, 2008.

117. "A Realistic Appraisal of Soy Oil Printing Inks—2007," an
     updated version of the NAPIM document previously
     issued in 1991, NAPIM Bulletin No. 07–15, November 8,
     2007.

118. Various sources, including "Nazdar Health and Safety
     FAQs" (accessed December 2007): www.nazdar.com/
     health_safety_faqs.asp#UVINKS. Printers' National
     Environmental Assistance Center Fact Sheet, "What Is
     Hazardous Waste?" (accessed December 2007): www
     .pneac.org/sheets/all/whatisahazwaste.cfm.

119. Various sources, including "Guidelines for Printers on the
     Safe Use of Energy Curing Printing Inks and Varnishes,"
     European Council of the Paint, Printing Ink and Artists'
     Colours Manufacturers' Industry Guideline Paper
     (October 2001): http://cepe-myeteam.eudata
     .be/EPUB//easnet.dll/GetDoc?APPL=1&DAT
     _IM=10175A&DWNLD=Guidelinesforprinterssafeuse
     energycuringpiandvarnishes.pdf.

120. "Anderson Lithograph's Sustainability Policies and
     Practices," Science and Sustainability Documents (2007);
     accessed on www.andlitho.com/downloads/Enviro
     _Story.pdf.

121. A fountain solution is a chemical solution applied to a
     lithographic printing plate before ink is applied in order
     to desensitize a plate's nonimage areas.

122. Michelle Carstensen, "Biochemicals for the Printing
     Industry," report published by The Institute for Local
     Self-Reliance, as posted on The Carbon Economy
     Clearinghouse Web site (1997): www.carbohydrate
     economy.org/library/admin/uploadedfiles/
     Biochemicals_for_the_Printing_Industry.pdf.

123. Office of Technical Assistance Executive Office of
     Environmental Affairs Commonwealth of
     Massachusetts," Toxics Use Reduction Case Study: Water
     and Ink Waste Reduction at F.C. Meyer Company,"
     Printers' National Environmental Assistance Center Fact
     Sheet (accessed December 2007): www.pneac.org/
     sheets/Flexo/fcmeyer.cfm.

124. Environmental Protection Agency, "Municipal Solid
     Waste in the United States: 2007 Facts and Figures"
     (November 2008), www.epa.gov/waste/nonhaz/
     municipal/pubs/msw07-rpt.pdf.

125. "What Are VOCs and Do Printing Related Materials Contain Them?" Printers' National Environmental Assistance Center (PNEAC) Fact Sheet (accessed December 2007): www.pneac.org/sheets/all/vocs.cfm.

126. United States Environmental Protection Agency, Region 5 Air and Radiation Division, "Ozone" (accessed October 2008): www.epa.gov/reg5oair/naaqs/ozone.html.

127. "What Are VOCs and Do Printing Related Materials Contain Them?"

128. U.S. EPA, "Ozone."

129. Green California, "Best Practices Manual: Printing—Inks," California Government Web site (accessed December 2008): www.green.ca.gov/EPP/Printing/Inks.htm.

130. U.S. EPA, "Clean Air Act": www.epa.gov/air/caa/.

131. U.S. EPA, "Method 24—Surface Coatings," Technology Transfer Network Emission Measurement Center (accessed December 2007): www.epa.gov/ttn/emc/methods/method24.html.

132. CP Adhesives, Inc., "Determining VOC Content," (accessed December 2007): http://cpadhesives.com/ArticleVocContent.php.

133. David Lunati, "5 Steps to Green," posted on PFFC-online.com, September 1, 2007; .http://pffc-online.com/mag/paper_steps_green/.

134. Ibid.

135. John Adkin, product director, Europe, Sun Chemical, via phone interview with coauthor Dion Zuess, January 18, 2008.

136. "Profile of the Printing Industry, EPA Office of Compliance Sector Notebook Project," September 1995, EPA 310-R-95-014, www.epa.gov/Compliance/resources/publications/assistance/sectors/notebooks/print.pdf.

137. John Holusha, "Technology; Farewell to Those Old Printing Ink Blues, and a Few Reds and Yellows, *New York Times,* May 13, 1990, http://query.nytimes.com/gst/fullpage.html?res=9C0CE7D71E39F930A25756C0A966958260.

138. Coalition of Northeastern Governors, www.coneg.org, and "Toxics in Packaging Clearinghouse Fact Sheet" (January 2005): www.toxicsinpackaging.org/adobe/TPCH-fact-sheet.PDF or www.toxicsinpackaging.org.

139. "Emergency Planning and Community Right-to-Know Act Section 313 Reporting Guidance for the Printing, Publishing, and Packaging Industry" (May 2000): www.epa.gov/tri/guide_docs/pdf/2000/00printing.pdf.

140. Various sources, including EPA's "Green Chemistry 2004 Designing Greener Chemicals Award" (accessed November 2007): www.epa.gov/gcc/pubs/pgcc/winners/dgca04.html.

141. Poppy Evans, *The Complete Guide to Eco-Friendly Graphic Design* (Cincinnati, OH: North Light Books, 1997).

142. John Adkin, via phone interview with Dion Zuess, January 18, 2008.

143. Roger Telschow, "Reducing Heavy Metals in Offset Printing Inks" in *Innovative Clean Technology Case Studies, Second Year Project Report* (Document No. EPA 600/R-94/169), pp. 117–125 (April 1994). Available at http://nepis.epa.gov.

144. Ecoprint, "Metal-free Eco-ink," www.ecoprint.com/inks.shtml.

145. George Fuchs, environmental affairs and information systems manager for the National Association of Printing Ink Manufacturers, via e-mail correspondence with coauthor Dion Zuess, October 4, 2007.

146. Oregon Department of Human Services, Lead Poisoning Prevention Program, "2007 Consumer Product and FDA Recalls: Lead Hazards," with numerous 2007 index dates on Web site: www.oregon.gov/DHS/ph/lead/recalls2007.shtml.

147. Toxics in Packaging Clearinghouse, "An Assessment of Heavy Metals in Packaging: Screening Results Using a Portable X-Ray Fluorescence Analyzer—Final Report, June 20, 2007," submitted to the U.S. Environmental Protection Agency under Assistance Agreement No. X9-83252201 to the Northeast Recycling Council, Inc. © 2007 Northeast Recycling Council, Inc.: www.toxicsinpackaging.org/adobe/TPCH_Final_Report_June_2007.pdf.

148. Ibid.

149. Lisa Wade McCormick, "Toxic Toy Tests Show High Chemical Contamination," Consumer Affairs.com (December 2008): www.consumeraffairs.com/news04/2008/12/toxic_toy_tests.html.

150. Marijah McCain, "Chemtrails and Barium Toxicity" (October 1997): www.rense.com/general21/tox.htm.

151. Aqua MD, "Barium: The Poison in Water No One Talks About": (accessed June 12, 2009). www.aquamd.com/water_health/barium.cfm.

152. Michael Belliveau and Stephen Lester, "PVC: Bad News Comes in 3's. The Poison Plastic, Health Hazards and the Looming Waste Crisis" (December 2004): www.besafenet.com/pvc/documents/bad_news_comes_in_threes.pdf.

153. "NAPIM Bio-Derived Renewable Content Labeling Program Guidelines." NAPIM Web Site: www.napim.org/PublicArea/BRC/BRC.aspx.

154. John Daugherty and George Fuchs of the NAPIM in an audio conversation with Gail Nickel-Kailing posted on "What They Think—A Resource for Today's Green Business" Blog archive, January 11, 2009, http://sections.whattheythink.com/environment/2009/01/napim-talk-inks-audio.

155. NAPIM, "Formulating Printing Inks to Minimize Environmental Impact."

156. Dan Weisenbach, "Switching to Soy Inks for Commercial Offset Printing," *QPP Magazine* (February 2000): www.recycledproducts.com/index.php?cid=25.

157. Kate Scholz, Hemlock Printers, Ltd., "White Paper: Environmental Attributes of Lithographic Inks and Coatings" (November 2007): www.hemlock.com/resources/White_Paper_-_Inks_and_Coatings.pdf.

158. Mark Beach and Eric Kenly, *Getting It Printed*, 3rd ed. (Cincinnati, OH: North Lights Books, 1999).

159. "After 20 Years, Soy Ink Continues to Make an Impression on Users," *United Soybean Board*, vol. 7, no. 4 (July 2006): www.unitedsoybean.org/FileDownload.aspx?File=LIB_BBS_TOCJULY2006.HTM.

160. National Soy Ink Information Center, "Soy Ink Historical Summary," fact sheet provided to coauthor Dion Zuess (February 2003).

161. Ibid.

162. Ibid.

163. Linda Cooke, "Soy Ink's Superior Degradability," Agricultural Research Magazine, January 1995, Vol 43, No.1, page 19. According to this report, researchers at the Agriculture Research Service (ARS) National Center for Agricultural Utilization Research in Peoria, Illinois found that soy ink was five times as degradable as petroleum-based commercial inks. United States Department of Agriculture, ARS Web site (Accessed December 18, 2007): www.ars.usda.gov/is/AR/archive/jan95/ink0195.htm and www.ars.usda.gov/is/ARarchive/jan95/.

164. John Adkin, phone interview with Dion Zuess, January 18, 2008.

165. "GreenerPrinter's Inks and the Environment," Greener Printer Web page (accessed October 2007): www.greenerprinter.com/grp/jsp/inks.jsp.

166. National Soy Ink Information Center, "The Soy Seal Trademark," fact sheet provided to coauthor Dion Zuess (February 2003) and verified with Julie P. Hawkins, executive assistant/meeting planner, American Soybean Association, via phone and e-mail, December 18, 2007. To download the application form for SoySeal use, go to: www.soygrowers.com/resources/soyinkagreement.pdf.

167. Ibid.

168. Ibid.

169. Mike Ukena, "UV Curable Inks: Will They Work for Everyone?" PNEAC Fact Sheet (accessed November 2007): www.pneac.org/sheets/screen/UVCurableInk.pdf.

170. Rick Sanders, "Electron Beam: One Way to Mitigate Rising Energy Costs," *Radtech Report* (March/April 2006): www.radtech.org/Industry/pdf_articles/ebcosts.pdf.

171. Campaign for Safe, Consumer Health Products, Center for Health, Environment and Justice, "PVC—the Poison Plastic" (accessed December 2008): www.besafenet.com/pvc/factsheet_on_pvc.htm.

172. Dry-back refers to when density and/or gloss of newly printed ink film decreases more than expected after drying, often due to overly absorbent paper surface or poor ink-paper match.

173. Dave Anderson, Shapco Printing, Inc., via e-mail conversation with coauthor Dion Zuess, December 19, 2007.

174. Various sources, including David Lanska, "Stork Sheds Light on UV Inks," Stork Cellramic (June 1997): www.flexoexchange.com/gorilla/uvink1.html.

175. Sean Milmo, "UV Ink Sales Continue to Expand, Although Challenges Remain," *Ink World* October 2006): www.inkworldmagazine.com/articles/2006/10/uv-ink-sales-continue-to-expand-although-challenge.php.

176. "Nazdar—Health and Safety FAQs" (accessed December 2007).

177. " Ink Control" in *Packaging & Converting Intelligence* (Spring 2009), pp. 17–20. Available at www.pci-mag.com/editorial/025_spring09/PCI025_ink.pdf.

178. Fuji Hunt Photographic Chemicals, *Aqueous Coatings Guide* (2004).

179. "MSDS Translation: Material Safety Data Sheets in any language," Translink.net Web site (accessed November 2007): www.translinknet.be/msds_translation_en.html.

180. U.S. EPA, "Emergency Planning and Community Right-to-Know Act Section 313 Reporting Guidance for the Printing, Publishing, and Packaging Industry," May 2000, www.epa.gov/tri/guide_docs/pdf/2000/00printing.pdf.

181. Environment, Health, and Safety Online, "The Free Guide to the Emergency Planning and Community Right-to-Know Act Environment," available at www.ehso.com/EPCRA_Guide.htm (accessed February 2008).

182. MSDS On File Web site: www.msdsonfile.com.

183. Printers' National Environmental Assistance Center Fact Sheet, "How to Read and Use an MSDS for Environmental Purposes" (accessed December 2007): www.pneac.org/sheets/all/msds.cfm.

184. ENERGY STAR is a joint program of the U.S. Environmental Protection Agency and the U.S. Department of Energy, "Frequently Asked Questions"(December 2008): www.energystar.gov; www.energystar.gov/index.cfm?c=power_mgt.pr_power_mgt_faq.

185. Jack Neff, "How Cutting Down on Colors May Save Unilever $26 Million," *Financial Week*, December 7, 2008, www.financialweek.com/apps/pbcs.dllarticle?AID=/20081207/REG/812049948.

186. "Communicating with the Printer—BRC Index," *Ink World* (December 2008, accessed June 12, 2009). Available at www.entrepreneur.com/tradejournals/article/191212870.html.

187. The ISO14000 Environmental Management Group, "ISO14000 Series Environmental Management Systems,"

ISO 14000/ISO 14001 Environmental Management Guide (accessed December 2008), www.iso14000-iso14001 -environmental-management.com/iso14000.htm.

188. "What Is RoHS," RoHS home page (accessed December 2008): www.rohs.gov.uk.

189. Ibid.

190. John Folkers, "Inks Can Spearhead a 'Green' Strategy," *Packaging Digest*, November 1, 2008, (accessed June 12, 2009). www.packagingdigest.com/index.asp?layout= articlePrint&articleID=CA6610058&article_prefix= CA&article_id=6610058.

191. Ibid.

192. Ibid.

193. Intertek, "The Impact of RoHS—Now and in the Future" (July 1, 2008), www.hktdc.com/info/mi/a/psls/ en/1X0014H7/1/Product-Safety-Laws-and-Standards/ The-impact-of-RoHS—now-and-in-the-future.htm.

194. William McDonough and Michael Braungart, "Regulation and Re-Design/Tapping Innovation and Creativity to Preserve the Commons," *green@work Magazine* (September/October 2004); posted on www.Mcdonough .com, www.mcdonough.com/writings/regulation _redesign.htm

195. Bay Area Working Group on the Precautionary Principle, "What Is the Precautionary Principle?" (2004): www .takingprecaution.org; Center for Health, Environment & Justice's BE SAFE CAMPAIGN: "The precautionary approach looks at how we can prevent harm from environmental hazards. It is a 'better safe than sorry' practice motivated by caution and prevention. Why ask 'what level of harm is acceptable?' when we can prevent pollution and environmental destruction before it happens. The Center for Health, Environment & Justice's BE SAFE campaign is a nationwide initiative to build support for the precautionary approach." Accessed Web site on January 11, 2009: www.besafenet.com.

196. "PIA/GATF, SGIA, and FTA Join Together to Create the 'Sustainable Green Printing Partnership,'" *Printing Impressions*, September 19, 2007: www.piworld.com/ article/76000–76999/76747_1.html.

197. Nan Faessler, "Paper Tips: Confused over Brightness and Whiteness?" (December 2008): www.creativepro.com/ article/paper-tips-confused-over-brightness-and- whiteness-.

198. Sabine Lenz, "10 Steps to the Right Paper" (December 2008): www.paperspecspro.com/blog/?p=34#more-34.

199. John Holusha, "Greens Pick an Enemy: Chlorine, the Everywhere Element," *New York Times*, December 20, 1992.

200. Allan Finney, Mainstream Water Solutions, "Alternatives to Chlorine for Swimming Pools," http://swimming. about.com/od/allergyandasthma/a/cl_pool_problem_3 .htm.

201. Natural Resources Council of Maine, "Maine's Dioxin Problem: The Paper Mill Connection" (December 2008): www.nrcm.org/dioxin_facts.asp; Robert Weinhold, "A New Pulp Fact?" *Environmental Science and Technology*, American Chemical Society, 10.1021/es803564j, January 14, 2009.

202. Jedlička, *Packaging Sustainability*.

203. Green Living: Green Living Guides, "Avoiding Chlorine in the Paper Bleaching Process," September 20, 2006, www .nrdc.org/cities/living/chlorine.asp.

204. United States-Asia Environmental Partnership, "*Clean Technologies in U.S. Industries: Focus on the Pulp and Paper Industry,*"Washington, DC (September 1997).

205. United Nations General Assembly, *Water Year 2003: International Year Aims to Galvanize Action on Critical Water Problems,* New York (December 2002): www.un. org/events/water/pressrelease.pdf.

206. William J. Cosgrove and Frank R. Rijsberman, *World Water Vision* (London: Earthscan Publications, 2000); www.worldwatercouncil.org/fileadmin/wwc/Library/ WWVision/TableOf Contents.pdf.

207. L. F. Konikow and E. Kendy, "Groundwater Depletion: A Global Problem," *Hydrogeology Journal* (2005): http:// water.usgs.gov/nrp/proj.bib/Publications/konikow. kendy.2005intro.html.

208. Chicago Green Drinks, "Every Drop Matters: The Lake and the City," May 16, 2007, panel discussion); John G. Mitchell, "Down the Drain," *National Geographic Online Extra*, (September 2002): http://ngm.nationalgeographic. com/ngm/0209/feature2/fulltext.html.

209. Waterless Printing Association, "What Is Waterless?" (accessed December 2007): www.water less.org/NwhatIs/ whatIs.htm.

210. Warren's Waterless Printing, "Go Waterless. Achieve More" (accessed December 2007): www.warrenswaterless.com/ waterless_process.html.

211. ODO Project Work Sheet 2006, www.themighty odo.com.

212. Rich Pirog, "Checking the Food Odometer: Comparing Food Miles for Local versus Conventional Produce Sales to Iowa Institutions," Leopold Center for Sustainable Agriculture (July 2003), www.leopold.iastate.edu/pubs/ staff/files/food_travel072103.pdf.

213. John G. Mitchell, "When Mountains Move," *National Geographic* (March 2006): http://science.nationalgeo graphic.com/science/earth/surface-of-the-earth/ when-mountains-move.html.

214. "Can the Spam." *The Economist*, Jun 15,2009.

215. Corporate GHG Accounting and Reporting Standard (Corporate Module), www.wbcsd.org/templates/ TemplateWBCSD1/layout.asp?type=p&MenuId=Mjc3.

216. Stern Review on the Economics of Climate Change, Report to UK Chancellor of the Exchequer (2006), Executive Summary, vii.

217. Jeremy Wheatland, *The L.E.K. Consulting Carbon*

Footprint Report 2007: Carbon Footprints and the Evolution of Brand-Consumer Relationships, L.E.K. London. Available at http://www.lek.com/UserFiles/File/Carbon_Footprint.pdf.

218. Team Treehugger, "How to Green Your Carbon Offsets," July 13, 2007, www.treehugger.com/files/2007/07/how-to-green-your-carbon-offsets.php.

219. "A Consumer's Guide to Retail Carbon Offset Providers. A Report from Clean Air—Cool Planet" (December 2006, accessed June 12, 2009). Available at www.cleanair-coolplanet.org/ConsumersGuidetoCarbonOffsets.pdf.

220. U.S. EPA, *Life Cycle of Waste Image and Description* (December 2007): www.epa.gov/climatechange/wycd/waste/lifecycle.html.

221. U.S. EPA, Landfill Methane Outreach Program (August 2007): www.epa.gov/lmop/overview.htm.

222. "'New Car Smell' Includes Toxins," CNNMoney.com, January 31, 2006, www.cnn.com/2006/AUTOS/01/31/toxic_cars.

223. *2008 Promotional Products Fact Sheet*, www.ppai.org/NR/rdonlyres/D3C6895B-34E7–49D2-A75D-768C246BDABE/0/2008PPAIFactSheet.pdf.

Chapter 6: Working Smarter

1. According to ENERGY STAR, system standby or hibernate features can provide savings of $75 or more per computer. ENERGY STAR is a joint program of the U.S. Environmental Protection Agency and the U.S. Department of Energy. "Frequently Asked Questions" (December 2008): www.energystar.gov. www.energystar.gov/index.cfm?c=power_mgt.pr_power_mgt_faq.

2. As reported in LOHAS Online, "Computers Left on at Night Cost U.S. Businesses $1.7 Billion, Says Study" (June 2007): www.lohas.com/articles/100422.html.

3. Various sources, including Michigan Department of Environmental Quality, "Recycling Office Paper Waste" (May 2004): www.deq.state.mi.us/documents/deq-ead-recycle-redofcpw.pdf.

4. Environmental Protection Agency, "Municipal Solid Waste in the United States: 2005 Facts and Figures" (October 2006): www.epa.gov/epawaste/nonhaz/municipal/pubs/mswchar05.pdf, p. 45.

5. Paper Task Force, "White Paper No. 3—Lifecycle Environmental Comparison: Virgin Paper and Recycled Paper-Based Systems." Duke University, Environmental Defense Fund, Johnson & Johnson, McDonald's, The Prudential Insurance Company of America, Time Inc., originally published in 1995 and updated in February 2002–2004, www.edf.org/documents/1618_WP3.pdf. Environmental Defense and the Alliance for Environmental Innovation, "Q & A on the Environmental Benefits of Recycled Paper," fact sheet (accessed December 18, 2008): www.edf.org/documents/2602_QArecycledpaper.pdf.

6. Environmental Paper Network, "Social Aspects of the Paper Industry" (July 2007): www.greenpressinitiative.org/documents/socialimpactsfactsheet.pdf.

7. *GCP Annual Review 2007: Demonstrating that Forests Are Worth More Alive than Dead*, www.globalcanopy.org/files/annualreview2007.pdf, p. 5.

8. "A Brief History of Paper," part of Conservatree's "Environmentally Sound Paper Overview: Essential Issues, Part III—Making Paper: Content" (accessed December 18, 2008); www.conservatree.org/learn/Essential%20Issues/EIPaperContent.shtml.

9. Ibid.

10. As cited on WoodWise's™ "Paper Production and Consumption Facts, Green America" Web site (formerly Co-op America) site (accessed December 19, 2008): www.coopamerica.org/programs/woodwise/consumers/stats/index.cfm.

11. FilmLoc, Pressure-Sensitive Tutorial, www.filmloc.com/pstutorial.html.

12. Trey Granger, "Five Common Paper Contaminants," Earth 911.com, September 1, 2008: earth911.com/blog/2008/09/01/five-common-paper-contaminants.

13. Town of Orono, Maine, Web page, "Public Works Recycling" (accessed December 23, 2008): www.orono.org/recycle.html.

14. Campaign for Safe, Consumer Health Products, Center for Health, Environment and Justice, "PVC—the Poison Plastic" (accessed December 2008): www.besafenet.com/pvc/factsheet_on_pvc.htm.

15. Printers' National Environmental Assistance Center Fact Sheet, "How to Read and Use an MSDS for Environmental Purposes" (accessed December 2007): www.pneac.org/sheets/all/msds.cfm.

16. *National Geographic*'s Green Guide "Tip of the Day," January 6, 2009: www.thegreenguide.com/greenguide/fastfact.

17. As cited on WoodWise's™ "What You Can Do: WoodWise™ Magazines, Green America" Web site (accessed December 19, 2008): www.coopamerica.org/programs/woodwise/consumers/whatyoucando/wwmags.cfm.

18. Richard Black, "Shun Meat, Says UN Climate Chief," September 7, 2008, BBC Web site, news.bbc.co.uk/2/hi/science/nature/7600005.stm Food and Agriculture Organization of the United Nations, Agriculture and Consumer Protection Department, "Spotlight/2006" (November 2006): www.fao.org/ag/magazine/0612sp1.htm.

19. As reported in Rainforest Action Network's "Rainforest Agribusiness" article (accessed January 13, 2009): ran.

org/campaigns/rainforest_agribusiness/resources/fact
_sheets/growing_disaster_how_agribusiness_expansion
_into_rainforests_is_threatening_the_climate.

20. Urbanist, "More Creative Furniture for Cramped Urban
Living: 20 Pieces of Ingenious 'Flat
Pack' Furniture," January 13, 2008: weburbanist.
com/2008/01/13/more-creative-furniture-for-cramped
-urban-living-20-pieces-of-ingenious-flat-pack-urban
-furniture. Also see Collin Dunn, "Embrace Flat-Pack as
Part of Your Green Lifestyle," Planet Green (May 2008):
planetgreen.discovery.com/home-garden/flat-pack
-furniture-design.html.

21. Melinda Stoker, "Green Intervention: How the Right
Content Management System Can Help You Meet Your
Sustainability Goals while Saving Time and Money,"
December 19, 2008, www.dmreview.com/
dmdirect/2008_102/10002310-1.html.

22. Courtesy of ecoLingo: earth friendly graphic design. A
certified green business, ecoLingo collaborates with
people or businesses who share a caring commitment to
the environ-ment, good causes, and the community;
www.ecoLingo.com.

23. As reported by RecycleWorks, a program of San Mateo
County, California, in "Why Buy Recycled" and sourced
by the Department of Conservation (accessed January 8,
2009): www.recycleworks.org/paper/paper_wbr.html.

24. Town of Townsend, Middlesex County, Massachusetts,
"Why Recycle" fact sheet (June 2006): www.townsend
.ma.us/towngov/landuse/recycling/whyrecy.htm.

25. As reported on ForestEthics, "Do Not Mail" Web site "The
Facts about Junk Mail" (accessed December 24, 2008):
www.donotmail.org/article.php?list=type&type=3.

26. Ibid.

27. Anne-Marie "Her Geekness" Concepcion, "Her Geekness
Says: Screen-Share with Your Clients," March 2, 2008:
www.creativepro.com/article/hergeekness-says-screen
-share-with-your-clients.

28. PDF/X 1-a Whitepaper available at adobe.com/products/
acrobat/pdfs/pdfx.pdf.

29. "Global Warming Basics," Natural Resources Defense
Council Web page, October 18, 2005, www.nrdc.org/
globalWarming/f101.asp.

30. Chris Robertson and Joseph Romm, "Data Centers,
Power, and Pollution Prevention Design for Business and
Environmental Advantage," Center for Energy and
Climate Solutions (www.cool-companies.org), A Division
of The Global Environment and Technology Foundation
(www.getf.org) (June 2002): files.harc.edu/Sites/
GulfCoastCHP/Publications/DataCentersBusinessEnvi
ronmentalAdvantage.pdf.

31. EPA, EPA Report to Congress on Server and Data Center
Energy Efficiency, August 2, 2007: www.energystar.gov/ia/

partners/prod_development/downloads/EPA_Report
_Exec_Summary_Final.pdf.

32. Thomas L. Friedman, "Go Green and Save Money,"
New York Times, August 22, 2007, select.nytimes.
com/2007/08/22/opinion/22friedman.html?
_r=1&hp=&adxnnl=1&adxnnlx=1187798919-u55zkEo
Nbz047vcxvSdsXA.

33. "How Utilities and REPs Use Monitor Power Management," ENERGY STAR Web page (accessed December
2008): www.energystar.gov/index.cfm?c=power_mgt
.pr_power_manage_reps.

34. U.S. Department of Energy, Energy Efficiency and
Renewable Energy, Commercial Buildings "Appliances
and Equipment," June 4, 2008, www1.eere.energy.gov/
buildings/commercial/appliances.html; "Office
Equipment and Small Power Loads," Carbon Trust Web
page (accessed January 1, 2009): www.carbontrust.co.uk/
energy/startsaving/tech_office_equipment_
introduction.htm.

35. Ibid.

36. U.S. Department of Energy, "Appliances and Electronics"
(accessed December 15, 2008): www.energy.gov/
applianceselectronics.htm.

37. Thomas Catan, "Switching Off Standby Mode," Smart
Money's Small Business Site, November 28, 2008, www
.smsmallbiz.com/technology/Switching_Off_Standby_
Mode.html; "Spook the Phantom—Plugging Electricity
Leaks in Your Home," GREENWorks: Ideas for a Cleaner
Environment (September 2006), des.nh.gov/organiza-
tion/commissioner/pip/newsletters/greenworks/06sept
.htm; "'Vampire' Appliances–They Suck Electricity Even
when Switched Off—Cost Consumers $3 Billion a Year,
Says Cornell Energy Expert," Cornell News, September 17,
2002, www.news.cornell.edu/releases/Sept02/vampire
.appliances.ssl.html.

38. Natural Resources Defense Council, Battery Chargers and
Energy Efficiency: Summary of Findings and Recommendations (August 2003): www.efficientproducts.org/
reports/bchargers/NRDC_Battery_Charger_Final.pdf.

39. City of Portland Office of Sustainable Development,
Green Office Guide: A Guide to Greening Your Bottom Line
through a Resource-Efficient Office Environment
(November 2001): www.oregon.gov/ENERGY/CONS/
BUS/docs/Green_Office_Guide.pdf, p. 8.

40. Richard Martin, "Want to Save the Planet? Turn Off that
PC," Intelligent Enterprise, November 5, 2007, www
.intelligententerprise.com/showArticle.jhtml?articleID=
202802459.

41. U.S. Department of Energy, Energy Efficiency and
Renewable Energy, Commercial Buildings, "Appliances
and Equipment."

42. Megan Bray, "Review of Computer Energy Consumption

and Potential Savings" White Paper, Sponsored by Dragon Systems Software Limited (December 2006): www.dssw.co.uk/research/computer_energy _consumption.html.

43. Climate Savers Computing Initiative, "Power Management: Recommended Settings" (October 2007): www .climatesaverscomputing.org/docs/Power_manage ment_instructions.pdf.

44. U.S. Department of Energy, Energy Efficiency and Renewable Energy, "When to Turn Off Personal Computers," December 30, 2008, apps1.eere.energy.gov/consumer/ your_home/appliances/index.cfm/mytopic=10070.

45. U.S. Environmental Protection Agency and the U.S. Department of Energy, "Computers for Consumers" (accessed January 13, 2009): www.energystar.gov/index .cfm?fuseaction=find_a_product. ShowProductGroup&pgw_code=CO.

46. U.S. Department of Energy—Energy Efficiency and Renewable Energy, Federal Energy Management Program—Energy-Efficient Products, "How to Buy an Energy-Efficient Computer Monitor," February 5, 2007, www1.eere.energy.gov/femp/procurement/printable _versions/eep_vmonitor.html.

47. Blackle, created by Heap Media, www.blackle .com. Kedar Soman, "Saving Energy—One Monitor at a Time," WordPress Blog, November 21, 2006, savingenergy .wordpress.com/2006/11/21/saving-energy-one -monitor-at-a-time.

48. Robert McMillan, "Could Your Web Surfing Be Greener?" IDG News Service, December 1, 2008, www.pcworld .com/article/154748/.html?tk=rss_news.

49. Carl Bialik, "Does a Darkened Google Really Save Electricity?" *Wall Street Journal*, May 11, 2007, blogs.wsj .com/numbersguy/does-a-darkened-google-really -save-electricity-104.

50. Lloyd Alter, "Green Your Home for Winter: Get a Programmable Thermostat" (March 2003):, http://planetgreen. discovery.com/home-garden/energy-efficiency -get-a-progra.html.

51. Greenpeace USA, "What Is E-Waste?" (accessed December 1, 2008): www.greenpeace.org/usa/campaigns/ toxics/hi-tech-highly-toxic/e-waste.

52. Scott Pelley, "The Electronic Wasteland," November 10, 2008, www.cbsnews.com/video/watch/?id=4586903n. Also see: CBS, *60 Minutes*, "Following the Trail of Toxic E-Waste," November 9, 2008: www.cbsnews.com/stories/ 2008/11/06/60minutes/main4579229.shtml.

53. Tam Harbert, "The World Confronts Its E-waste Nightmare," NRDC OnEarth (Fall 2006); www.nrdc.org/ onearth/06fal/frontlines.asp.

54. "Global Toxic E-Waste Dumping," Take Back My TV Web site (accessed December 1, 2008), http://takebackmytv .com/pages/global_toxic_e_waste_dumping.

55. Indian e-Waste Guide, "Hazardous Processes" (accessed November 25, 2008), http://india.ewasteguide.info/ hazardous_processes.

56. Jon Mooallem, "The Afterlife of Cellphones, *New York Times*, January 13, 2008; reported on the e-Stewards Web site, www.e-stewards.org/news/080113_the_afterlife_of _cellphones.html.

57. Earth 911.org, "Facts about Inkjet Cartridges" (accessed December 1, 2008), http://earth911.com/electronics/ inkjet-cartridge/facts-about-inkjet-cartridges.

58. Alameda County Waste Management Authority, and Alameda County Source Reduction and Recycling Board, "Remanufactured Toner Cartridges in Alameda County," Fact sheet, updated May 2004; available at www .stopwaste.org/docs/toner.pdf.

59. Electronic Product Environmental Assessment Tool: "EPEAT is a system to help purchasers in the public and private sectors evaluate, compare and select desktop computers, notebooks and monitors based on their environmental attributes." www.epeat.net.

60. Town of Beloit Recycling Program, Beloit, Wisconsin: www.townofbeloit.org/recycling/recycling.html#2.

61. Clean Air Council, "Waste Reduction and Recycling: Waste Facts and Figures" (accessed December 24, 2008): www.cleanair.org/Waste/wasteFacts.html.

62. Mission Recycling Committee, "Facts," posted on Web site (accessed January 2008): mrcsf.org/facts. Also note that this site has information about plastic recycling numbers.

63. 3M™ Transparency Film Recycling program, 3M Web site (accessed January 28, 2008), http://solutions.3m.com/ wps/portal/3M/en_US/Meetings/Home/ProductsAnd Services/Product_Catalog/Transparency_Film/RecProg.

64. U.S. Department of Labor, Bureau of Labor Statistics, *American Time Use Survey*, November 12, 2008: www.bls. gov/tus.

65. Environmental Protection Agency, *Indoor Air Facts No. 4 (revised): Sick Building Syndrome* (February 1991): www .epa.gov/iaq/pdfs/sick_building_factsheet.pdf.

66. Consumer Product Safety Commission and Environmental Protection Agency, *The Inside Story: A Guide to Indoor Air Quality*, CPSC Document #450, www.cpsc.gov/ cpscpub/pubs/450.html.

67. *Consumer Reports* Greener Choices, "Dry Cleaning Alternatives" (October 2006): www.greenerchoices.org/ products.cfm?product=drycleaning.

68. Various sources, including: Co-op America, "Living Green: Green Alternatives to Toxic Interior Paints" (accessed December 19, 2008): www.coopamerica.org/ programs/livinggreen/articles/GreenAlternativestoToxic InteriorPaints.cfm.

69. "*LEED® for New Construction & Major Renovations*, Version 2.2, for Public Use and Display," (October 2005): www.usgbc.org/ShowFile.aspx?DocumentID=1095.

70. David Malin Roodman and Nicholas Lenssen, *World-watch Paper #124: A Building Revolution: How Ecology and Health Concerns Are Transforming Construction*, Worldwatch Institute, March 1, 1995: www.worldwatch.org/node/866.

71. Ibid., p. 5. Also reported in "Green Building Basics," California Integrated Waste Management Board (January 15, 2008), www.ciwmb.ca.gov/GREENBUILDING/Basics.htm.

72. "The First Step to Improving Building Water Efficiency," ENERGY STAR Web page (accessed December 15, 2008): www.energystar.gov/index.cfm?c=business.bus_water.

73. Environmental Protection Agency, "Frequent Questions—Green Buildings," April 16, 2008, www.epa.gov/greenbuilding/pubs/faqs.htm.

74. "LEED Rating Systems—What is LEED®?" U.S. Green Building Council Web site (accessed December 15, 2008): www.usgbc.org/Display Page.aspx?CMSPageID=222.

75. "LEED® for Existing Buildings: Operations and Maintenance, for Public Use and Display" (September 2008): www.usgbc.org/ShowFile.aspx?DocumentID=3617.

76. Anne Bertino via e-mail correspondence with author Dion Zuess, December 22, 2008.

77. Ibid.

78. "LEED® for Existing Buildings: Operations and Maintenance Rating System," p. 78.

79. "Guidelines for Energy Management Overview," ENERGY STAR Web site (accessed December 2008): www.energystar.gov/index.cfm?c=guidelines.guidelines_index.

80. "LEED® for Existing Buildings: Operations and Maintenance Rating System."

81. Environmental Protection Agency "Integrated Pest Management (IPM) Principles," March 13, 2008: www.epa.gov/pesticides/factsheets/ipm.htm.

82. Also see the Center for Health, Environment & Justice's BE SAFE CAMPAIGN, "a nationwide initiative to build support for the precautionary approach." "The precautionary approach looks at how we can prevent harm from environmental hazards. It is a 'better safe than sorry' practice motivated by caution and prevention. Why ask 'what level of harm is acceptable?' when we can prevent pollution and environmental destruction before it happens" (accessed January 11, 2009): www.besafenet.com.

83. Various sources, including David L. Greene and Andreas Schafer, *Reducing Greenhouse Gas Emissions from U.S. Transportation*, Prepared for the PEW Center on Global Climate Change (May 2003): www.pewclimate.org/docUploads/ustransp.pdf.

84. "Miles Outlandish: How to Green Your Commute," GRIST, May 27, 2008: www.grist.org/advice/how/2008/05/27.

85. David Schrank and Tim Lomax, *2007 Urban Mobility Report*, Texas Transportation Institute (September 2007), http://mobility.tamu.edu/ums.

86. California Green Solutions, "Tire Air Pressure Maintenance Saves Money," July 17, 2007: www.californiagreensolutions.com/cgi-bin/gtt/pl.h,content=647.

87. David Rizzo, "Save the Environment, One Commute at a Time," MSNBC, Technology and Money column, April 26, 2008: www.msnbc.msn.com/id/24312866. David Rizzo is also author of *Survive the Drive! How to Beat Freeway Traffic in Southern California* (Fullerton, CA: Lorikeet Express Publications, 2006).

88. Telework Coalition, "Telework Facts" (accessed January 6, 2008): www.telcoa.org/id33.htm.

89. As quoted in Steven Heller and Veronique Vienne, eds., *Citizen Designer: Perspectives on Design Responsibility* (New York: Allworth Press, 2003).

Chapter 7: Innovation Toolkit

1. GreenBlue, "The Design Guidelines for Sustainable Packaging" www.greenblue.org/resources_documents.html (accessed May 2008).

2. Wendy Jedlička, "Consumers: The Best Force for Change," Twin Cities Green Guide, 2000. www.thegreenguide.org/article/goods/environmental.

3. *The Hannover Principles: Design for Sustainability*. Prepared for EXPO 2000, 1992 (accessed May 2008): www.mcdonough.com/principles.pdf.

4. Sim van der Ryn, *Ecological Design Principles* (Washington, DC: Island Press, 1996).

5. Nancy Todd and John Todd, *From Eco-Cities to Living Machines* (Berkeley, CA: North Atlantic Books, 1993).

6. Eric Von Hipple, *Democratizing Innovation* (Cambridge, MA: MIT Press, 2006).

7. *Wikipedia*, "Innovation" May 2008, May 2008 http://en.wikipedia.org/wiki/Innovation#Technological_concepts_of_innovation.

8. John Thackara, *In The Bubble*, (Cambridge, MA: MIT, 2005).

9. "What is Triz?" May 2008, www.triz-journal.com/archives/what_is_triz/.

10. TerraChoice Environmental Marketing "Seven Sins of Greenwashing," www.terrachoice.com.

11. Green Living: Green Living Guides, "Avoiding Chlorine in the Paper Bleaching Process," September 20, 2006, www.nrdc.org/cities/living/chlorine.asp.

12. Green Seal's Choose GREEN Report, "Alternative Fiber Papers" (April/May 1998): www.greenseal.org/resources/reports/CGR=TreeFree.pdf.

Index